Racial Domination

Race is arguably the single most troublesome and volatile concept of the social sciences in the early twenty-first century. It is invoked to explain all manner of historical phenomena and current issues, from slavery to police brutality to acute poverty, and it is also used as a term of civic denunciation and moral condemnation. In this erudite and incisive book based on a panoramic mining of comparative and historical research from around the globe, Loïc Wacquant pours cold analytical water on this hot topic and infuses it with epistemological clarity, conceptual precision, and empirical breadth.

Drawing on Gaston Bachelard, Max Weber, and Pierre Bourdieu, Wacquant first articulates a series of reframings, starting with dislodging the United States from its Archimedean position, needed to capture race-making as a form of symbolic violence. He then forges a set of novel concepts to rethink the nexus of racial classification and stratification: the continuum of ethnicity and race as disguised ethnicity, the diagonal of racialization and the pentad of ethnoracial domination, the checkerboard of violence and the dialectic of salience and consequentiality. This enables him to elaborate a meticulous critique of such fashionable notions as "structural racism" and "racial capitalism" that promise much but deliver little due to their semantic ambiguity and rhetorical malleability – notions that may even hamper the urgent fight against racial inequality.

Wacquant turns to deploying this conceptual framework to dissect two formidable institutions of ethnoracial rule in America: Jim Crow and the prison. He draws on ethnographies and historiographies of white domination in the postbellum South to construct a robust analytical concept of Jim Crow as caste terrorism erected in the late nineteenth century. He unravels the deadly symbiosis between the black hyperghetto and the carceral archipelago that has coproduced and entrenched the material and symbolic marginality of the African-American precariat in the metropolis of the late twentieth century. Wacquant concludes with reflections on the politics of knowledge and pointers on the vexed question of the relationship between social epistemology and racial justice.

Both sharply focused and wide ranging, *Racial Domination* will be of interest to students and scholars of race and ethnicity, power and inequality, and epistemology and theory across the social sciences and humanities.

Loïc Wacquant is Professor of Sociology at the University of California, Berkeley, and Research associate at the Centre européen de sociologie et de science politique, Paris. His books have been translated into 20 languages and include *Urban Outcasts* (2008), *The Invention of the "Underclass"* (2022), and *Pierre Bourdieu in the City* (2023), all published by Polity Press.

Racial Domination

Loïc Wacquant

polity

Copyright © Loïc Wacquant 2024

The right of Loïc Wacquant to be identified as Author of this Work has been asserted in accordance with the UK Copyright, Designs and Patents Act 1988.

First published in 2024 by Polity Press

Excerpt from *The Way of White Folks* by Langston Hughes © 1934. Used by Permission of the Estate of Langston Hughes, Harold Ober Associates, and International Literary Properties LLC.

Polity Press
65 Bridge Street
Cambridge CB2 1UR, UK

Polity Press
111 River Street
Hoboken, NJ 07030, USA

All rights reserved. Except for the quotation of short passages for the purpose of criticism and review, no part of this publication may be reproduced, stored in a retrieval system or transmitted, in any form or by any means, electronic, mechanical, photocopying, recording or otherwise, without the prior permission of the publisher.

ISBN-13: 978-1-5095-6301-2
ISBN-13: 978-1-5095-6302-9(pb)

A catalogue record for this book is available from the British Library.

Library of Congress Control Number: 2023946994

Typeset in 10.5 on 12pt Plantin MT Pro
by Cheshire Typesetting Ltd, Cuddington, Cheshire
Printed and bound in Great Britain by TJ Books Ltd, Padstow, Cornwall

Cover image: Winfred Rembert *Overseers in the Field #1*, 2007
32 × 32.5 inches
Acrylic paint on carved and tooled leather © 2023 Winfred Rembert Estate / ARS NY
Photo: John Bigelow Taylor

The publisher has used its best endeavours to ensure that the URLs for external websites referred to in this book are correct and active at the time of going to press. However, the publisher has no responsibility for the websites and can make no guarantee that a site will remain live or that the content is or will remain appropriate.

Every effort has been made to trace all copyright holders, but if any have been overlooked the publisher will be pleased to include any necessary credits in any subsequent reprint or edition.

For further information on Polity, visit our website:
politybooks.com

Pour Megan, vie de ma vie

Contents

Figures ix
Preface: Bachelard, Weber, Bourdieu xi

***Problemstellung*: When the Politics and Analytics of Race Collide** 1
   Sociological reset: epistemology, methodology, theory 2
      1. Bachelard's historical epistemology 5
      2. Weber's concept of ethnicity and method of the ideal type 8
      3. Bourdieu's theory of social space and symbolic power 12
   Specifying domination 16
   Caveats and preview 29

1. Reframing Racial Domination 46
   1. Historicize 48
   2. Spatialize 56
   3. Dislodge the United States 61
   4. Forsake the logic of the trial 72
   5. Race as denegated ethnicity 78
   Diagonal of racialization 86
   Excursus: the radical abdication of Afropessimism 91
   Dialectic of salience and consequentiality 99
   Race-making through classification struggles 106

2. Elementary Forms of Ethnoracial Rule 112
   1. Categorization 113
   2. Discrimination 123

Contents

3. Segregation	130
4. Seclusion	137
5. Violence	144
Architecture and articulations	154
The lure of "racial capitalism"	161
Classification, stratification, and the state	168
The mystification of "structural racism"	174
"Structural racism" redux: a penal illustration	188
Race-making as group-making	197
Group hysteresis, denigration, and disgrace	205

3. Jim Crow as Caste Terrorism — 210
- From song and dance to doxic notion to analytic concept — 212
- The rise and reign of the one-drop rule — 223
- Economic infrastructure: sharecropping and peonage — 232
- Social core: bifurcation and deference — 238
- Superstructural lock: political and judicial exclusion — 248
- The omnipresent specter of "white death" — 257
- Jim Crow as caste terrorism: virtues of conceptual clarity — 268

4. Deadly Symbiosis: When Ghetto and Prison Meet and Mesh — 278
- Reframing black hyperincarceration — 281
- Four peculiar institutions — 290
- How the ghetto became more like a prison — 311
- How the prison became more like a ghetto — 320
- How prison is remaking "race" and reshaping citizenship — 338
- History, penality, and place — 350

Coda: From Racial Domination to Racial Justice — 355
- Varieties of racial domination — 357
- Three paths to racial justice — 363
- Historicity of racial domination — 370

Acknowledgments — 377
References — 379
Index of names — 446
Index of notions — 451

Figures

1. The conceptual relationship between ethnicity and race. 82
2. The continuum of ethnicity from ordinary to racialized. 85
3. The diagonal of racialization. 87
4. The dialectic of ethnoracial salience and consequentiality. 100
5. The checkerboard of ethnoracial violence. 149
6. The conceptual architecture of racial domination. 155
7. The social fabrication of groups. 200
8. The economy of deference and violence. 241
9. The building blocks of Jim Crow as caste terrorism. 268
10. Black prisoners guarded by white correctional officers. 334
11. The symbiosis between hyperghetto and warehouse prison. 338
12. The analytic space of commodification and racialization. 360
13. Three paths to racial justice. 365

"With race theories, you can prove and disprove anything you want."
Max Weber, second meetings of the
Deutsche Gesellschaft für Soziologie (1912)

Preface

Bachelard, Weber, Bourdieu

This book has two distant roots, the one personal and the other scholastic. The first is the existential and intellectual shock of landing in Chicago in 1985 and residing on the edge of the hyperghetto of Woodlawn for six years. Having to "learn race" *à l'américaine* to navigate its shoals day-to-day was a heart-rending and mind-bending experience.[1] The second is the lecture course entitled "Elementary Forms of Racial Domination" that I have taught regularly at Berkeley since I moved there in 1994. To design this course, I had to educate myself because, although I had worked closely with William Julius Wilson, the leading sociologist of race and class in the country, I had never taken a course on "race" myself and, following a series of absurd circumstances, I had been hired at Berkeley to cover the topic. So I read widely and voraciously across epochs and continents, since it was obvious to me, given my French, universalist categories of perception and appreciation – which functioned at once as *lenses and blinders*, as do all cognitive constructs – that the United States was the wrong place to use as sociological template.

At the outset, I thought the question to start with was: why is it *so hard to (re)think "race"*? Why is the topic enwrapped in mental confusion, moral emotion – Du Bois speaks of "passion and distress" – and political vituperation, more so than any other on the anthropological horizon? Does the fact that racial inequality offends our democratic sensibility and violates our civic commitment to universal dignity, combined with the unspeakable horrors committed in its

---

[1] I retrace this intellectual peregrination and its prehistory in colonial New Caledonia in "Carnal Concepts in Action" (2023d).

name, suffice to account for the scalding heat generated by the topic? This made me turn to the philosopher of science Gaston Bachelard and his signal concept of "epistemological obstacle": notions, beliefs, and turns of thinking that stand in the way of the production of rigorous knowledge.[2] The reframings proposed in chapter 1 of the present book are so many attempts to push these obstacles out of the way and to set the parameters of a new landscape of inquiry.

The next question was: *what is "race" a case of?* The answer is what Pierre Bourdieu calls "symbolic violence," the imposition of "a social principle of vision and division,"[3] that is, a basis for classification, in the symbolic order, that becomes realized as stratification, in the material order, and validated by that very correspondence which makes ethnoracial difference and hierarchy seem founded in the order of things. This means that we must grasp race-making as a particular case of group-making, with both generic and specific properties, derived from the fact that race is a cultural construct fashioned by history that presents itself as a natural construct stamped by biology.

This raised the issue of how to study race as symbolic violence and material encasement across epochs and continents without falsely universalizing and unthinkingly transporting everywhere the particular folk constructs and ethnoracial doxa of one society, the United States, France, Brazil, Indonesia, etc., posturing as scientific concepts. This called for taking a decidedly *analytic stance* which recommends breaking down a social form into its constituent elements and specifying their articulations. The methodological device tailor-made to actualize that stance is Max Weber's ideal type. And so I turned to the latter's essays in *Wissenschaftslehre* for guidance to erect my conceptual scaffoldings, to which chapter 2 is devoted.[4] I also found in Weber's theory of "status groups," that is, collectivities marked out by public claims to honor, a solid peg on which to hang my conception of race as a denegated subtype of ethnicity.

A final query that has guided and goaded me to write this book is this: can we *reconcile the analytics and the politics* of the "race ques-

---

[2] Gaston Bachelard, *La Formation de l'esprit scientifique. Contribution à une psychanalyse de la connaissance objective* (1938).
[3] Pierre Bourdieu, "Espace social et pouvoir symbolique", in *Choses dites* (1987).
[4] Max Weber, *The Methodology of the Social Sciences* (1949 [1920]). See also the book-length introduction by Julien Freund to Max Weber, *Essais sur la théorie de la science* (1992 [1965]).

Preface

tion"?[5] This is a particularly thorny matter writing in the turmoil of black mobilization in the United States and beyond in the 2020s, but that question has haunted students of ethnoracial domination for over a century, ever since W. E. B. Du Bois's prophetic 1903 pronouncement that "the problem of the twentieth century is the problem of the color line." How do we strike a balance between these two standpoints without the one disregarding or overwhelming the other? The path I have taken is guided by the view, decidedly unpopular in the current moment, that defends and draws on the relative autonomy of science from current affairs. It postulates that scholarship needs to be sheltered enough from the heat of battle to secure its epistemic footing, build its models, and articulate the mechanisms that produce, reproduce, or transform the realities of ethnoracial rule, and *only then* engage that knowledge in the civic debates and battles aimed to topple it.

This means being clear-eyed and resolute about the need to meet criteria of analytic integrity and empirical validity before worrying about the political popularity and policy repercussions of the research conducted. I take heart in the fact that it is the same Du Bois who wrote, in the conclusion to a summation of "The Study of the Negro Problems" published in 1898:

> We live in a day when in spite of the brilliant accomplishments of a remarkable century, there is current much flippant criticism of scientific work; when the truth-seeker is too often pictured as devoid of human sympathy, and careless of human ideals. We are still prone in spite of all our culture to sneer at the heroism of the laboratory while we cheer the swagger of the street broil. At such a time true lovers of humanity can only hold higher the pure ideals of science, and continue to insist that *if we would solve a problem we must study it*, and that there is but one coward on earth, and that is the coward that dare not know.[6]

---

[5] I raised that question way back then in Loïc Wacquant, "For an Analytic of Racial Domination" (1997), which is manner of abbreviated ancestor to this book.
[6] William E. B. Du Bois, "The Study of the Negro Problems" (1898), p. 23, my emphasis.

Problemstellung

When the Politics and Analytics of Race Collide

The scientific mind forbids us to have an opinion on questions that we do not understand, on questions that we do not know how to formulate clearly. Above all, one must know how to pose problems. And, whatever one might say, in scientific life, problems do not pose themselves. It is precisely this *sense of the problem* that is the hallmark of the true scientific mind. For a scientific mind, all knowledge is a response to a question. If there was no question, there cannot be scientific knowledge. Nothing is taken for granted. Nothing is given. Everything is constructed.
    Gaston Bachelard, *La Formation de l'esprit scientifique*, 1938

Race everywhere, race all the time, race *über alles*. Accelerating since the turn of the century, a seemingly epochal shift in academic and public debate has taken place devaluing class and valorizing race, gender, and sexuality as principles of social vision and division, analytic categories, and foundations for civic claims-making.[1] Battles

---

[1] Four controversial books signal this shift in the French social sciences, an intellectual province that has long resisted the topic: Éric Fassin and Didier Fassin (eds.), *De la question sociale à la question raciale. Représenter la société française* (2006); Elsa Dorlin, *La Matrice de la race. Généalogie sexuelle et coloniale de la nation française* (2006); Pap N'Diaye, *La Condition noire. Essai sur une minorité française* (2009); and Stéphane Beaud and Gérard Noiriel, *Race et sciences sociales. Essai sur les usages publics d'une catégorie* (2021). See also the rediscovery and republication of Colette Guillaumin's prescient *L'Idéologie du racisme. Genèse et langage actuel* (2017 [1972]). Another indicator is the translation into French of W. E. B. Du Bois's *The Souls of Black Folk* and *The Philadelphia Negro*; his intellectual biography by Magali Bessone and Matthieu Renault, *W. E. B. Du Bois. Double conscience et condition raciale* (2021); and the selection of key English texts in translation by Magali Bessone and Daniel Sabbagh (eds.),

over the social organization of production and economic redistribution have been overshadowed, if not entirely displaced, by struggles for the recognition and promotion of embodied identities, ascribed by nature or fashioned by culture. The (re)discovery of the historical horrors and contemporary ramifications of Western colonialism, the excavation of the branching consequences of transatlantic slavery in the *longue durée* and the acceleration of non-Western immigration in countries of the global North have solidified this shift. The diligent denunciation of racism, deemed "institutional" or "structural," and of its insidious effects has become de rigueur and "diversity" is now celebrated and promoted, not only by universities, but also by the media, corporations, governments, transnational organizations, politicians, and citizens' associations, creating a vibrant market for a new cadre of diversity consultants.[2] The proliferation of legislation, conventions, and administrative apparatuses entrusted with detecting and fighting ethnoracial discrimination in the European Union and, *a contrario*, the growing electoral appeal of racialized populism across the continent all attest to the burning urgency of the question.[3] But how are we to make sense of the protean, slippery, yet seemingly self-evident reality of "race" that claims such priority in academic attention and civic energy?

Sociological reset: epistemology, methodology, theory

The present book takes heed of these trends and troubles and seeks to assemble the building blocks of a neo-Bourdieusian theory of racial domination as a *relation of symbolic violence and material encasement*.

Race, racisme, discriminations. Anthologie de textes fondamentaux (2015). Even Thomas Piketty has recently felt obliged to address the issue in his booklet *Mesurer le racisme, vaincre la discrimination* (2022), noting that "in Europe as in the United States, India or Brazil, the political debate turns more and more often around identity hysteria and the obsession of origins" (p. 7). A new academic journal devoted to the topic has just been launched: *Marronnages. Les questions raciales au crible des sciences sociales.*

[2] Réjane Sénac, *L'Invention de la diversité* (2012); Olivier Masclet, *Sociologie de la diversité et des discriminations* (2017); Natasha Warikoo, *The Diversity Bargain and Other Dilemmas of Race, Admissions, and Meritocracy at Elite Universities* (2019); Frank Dobbin and Alexandra Kalev, *Getting to Diversity: What Works and What Doesn't* (2022); Laure Bereni, *Le Management de la vertu. La diversité en entreprise à New York et à Paris* (2023). The British publisher Policy Press has a book series devoted specifically to the "Sociology of Diversity."

[3] Rosita Fibbi et al., *Migration and Discrimination* (2021), pp. 80–2.

Problemstellung

It draws on Pierre Bourdieu's genetic structuralism and its derivative, the agonistic theory of group-making, to develop an *analytic of race-making*, that is, a parsimonious set of interlinked categories designed to help us parse the "race question." In a nutshell, it pours cold analytical water onto a hot topic in the hope that we can thus reformulate it on paper so as to better advance toward its resolution in historical reality.[4]

This approach stems from the observation that, to a degree unmatched in other domains of social inquiry, *the politics of race gravely skew the analytics of race*. Consider the mandate to denounce the phenomenon under scrutiny in the terms of the current political debate (and the more vitriolic the denunciation, the better);[5] the propensity to drown it in an endless flow of moral emotions; the near-exclusive focus on groups mobilized in the national political and academic fields (to the neglect of other categories that remain invisible); the exportation of US-based categories and problematics around the globe regardless of the configuration of racial division in the receiving country; the race to discover race where others failed to detect it, leading to endless historical regress (from the modern era to feudalism to antiquity) and relentless geographical annexation (of countries where ethnoracial divides are blurred or faint); the urge to celebrate subordinate categories (their agency, creativity, and resistance), or the common presumption that members of racialized populations are endowed with a special sociological perspicuity and even unique insights into the foundations of racial inequality (as opposed to its phenomenology).[6] To be sure, some of these postulations, turns of thinking, and civic commitments can energize research and serve the requirements of creative social inquiry as well as public

---

[4] A model of "cold" inquiry into a "hot" topic is Wolfgang Sofsky's study of Nazi concentration camps, *Die Ordnung des Terrors* (1993), in which the German sociologist deploys the tools of organizational theory to deepen Hannah Arendt's concept of "absolute power" and thence stretch the moral parameters of the Holocaust.

[5] Solène Brun and Claire Cosquer go so far as to call it a "traumatic object" in *Sociologie de la race* (2022), p. 4.

[6] For illustrations, see France Winddance Twine and Jonathan Warren (eds.), *Racing Research, Researching Race: Methodological Dilemmas in Critical Race Studies* (2003); Leith Mullings, "Interrogating Racism: Toward an Antiracist Anthropology" (2005); José Medina, *The Epistemology of Resistance: Gender and Racial Oppression, Epistemic Injustice, and Resistant Imaginations* (2012); and Alf Gunvald Nilsen and Srila Roy (eds.), *New Subaltern Politics: Reconceptualizing Hegemony and Resistance in Contemporary India* (2015).

engagement.⁷ But, all too often, they adulterate "this *sense of the problem*" that Gaston Bachelard saw as "the hallmark of the true scientific mind," and by crimping social inquiry they risk curtailing the historical possibilities for transforming the realities of "race" on the ground.

This book rests on the conviction that, to parse ethnoracial domination, we need an infusion of epistemological clarity, conceptual precision, historical depth, and geographical breadth more than we need yet more excited expressions of moral fervor and chaste vows to pursue racial justice, a topic to which I return in the conclusion to this volume. We need a fundamental analytical reset – a new *Problemstellung* that derails accepted ways of studying "race and racism" or "race and ethnicity" (in the most common designation), dissolves long-standing issues, and generates fresh questions and novel empirical insights.

To articulate this agenda, I draw on three thinkers: the French philosopher of science Gaston Bachelard, the German legal scholar and political economist Max Weber, and the sociologist and anthropologist Pierre Bourdieu. In Bachelard's tow, I follow the precepts of *historical rationalism*, which holds that scientific knowledge proceeds through rupture with common sense and involves, not the discovery of ready-made "facts" waiting to be "collected" in reality, but their construction by the controlled deployment of theoretical and technical instruments.⁸ From Max Weber, I borrow the characterization of *ethnic and status groups* as collectivities rooted in "positive or negative estimations of honor," the concept of *closure* referring to strategies aimed at restricting the life chances of subordinate categories, and the methodological device of the *ideal type* as means for "univocal communication."⁹ Lastly, I draw on Bourdieu's theory of *social space and symbolic power* as the institutionalized capacity to impose cognitive categories of construction of the social world and his genetic sociology of *classification struggles* through which agents strive to impose

---

⁷ Three examples on three continents are Robin D. G. Kelley, *Hammer and Hoe: Alabama Communists during the Great Depression* (2015 [1990]); Richard M. Siddle, *Race, Resistance and the Ainu of Japan* (2012); and Michel Naepels, *Conjurer la guerre. Violence et pouvoir à Houaïlou (Nouvelle-Calédonie)* (2013). It is not by happenstance that the most cautious authors use the historical approach, which buffers them from the immediate demands of current politics.
⁸ Gaston Bachelard, *Épistémologie* (1980), and *La Philosophie du non* (1940).
⁹ Max Weber, *Economy and Society: An Outline of Interpretive Sociology* (1978 [1918–1922]), and *The Methodology of the Social Sciences* (1949 [1920]).

Problemstellung

those categories and shape the social world accordingly.[10] Let me then provide the rudiments of the epistemology, methodology, and theory that undergird my analytical endeavor.

1. Bachelard's historical epistemology

This book is grounded in the "historical epistemology" of Gaston Bachelard, Alexandre Koyré, and Georges Canguilhem, elaborated during the period 1928–68, based on studies in the history of the physical, astronomical, and life sciences respectively, and imported into the social sciences by Michel Foucault and Pierre Bourdieu.[11] This philosophy of science diverges sharply from the two epistemological traditions that have historically dominated Anglo-American social science and the continental *Geisteswissenschaften*, namely, positivism and hermeneutics. It asserts an unshakeable faith in the creative powers of reason and in scientific progress through rupture and discontinuity, what Bachelard calls *surrationalisme*.[12]

Bachelard's revolutionary approach to knowledge formation starts from the premise that epistemology must be grounded in the history of scientific practices and not in a priori principles. It must familiarize itself with work in the laboratory to grasp science as the concrete mating of thought and experiment, reason and reality, concept and percept, which varies with each discipline. This work is collective; it is the task of a community of inquirers and it requires what Bachelard

---

[10] Pierre Bourdieu, "Sur le pouvoir symbolique" (1977), *Langage et pouvoir symbolique* (2000 [1982, 1991]), and *Sociologie générale*, vol. 1, *Cours au Collège de France, 1981–1983* (2015).
[11] The term was coined by Dominique Lecourt, *L'Épistémologie historique de Gaston Bachelard* (1969). Other names given to this school of thought are "applied rationalism" and "philosophy of the concept" (by opposition to the "philosophy of the subject" driven by phenomenology). For a compact presentation and situation in the stream of twentieth-century philosophy of science, see Hans-Jörg Rheinberger, *On Historicizing Epistemology: An Essay* (2010). Bachelard was Canguilhem's intellectual mentor and Canguilhem was the personal mentor of both Foucault and Bourdieu. For an overview of Bachelard's thought, see Mary Tiles, *Bachelard: Science and Objectivity* (1984) in English, and Vincent Bontems, *Bachelard* (2010) in French. This covers the epistemological side of Bachelard's work only; there is also a prolific side on the poetics of imagination.
[12] Bachelard means the term by analogy with the artistic movement of surrealism, which broke with aesthetic conventions, to designate the avant-guarde of rationalism intent on breaking with the conservatism of reason frozen into normal science. Bachelard, *La Philosophie du non*.

calls "the union of the laborers of proof." Anticipating many of the ideas later popularized by Thomas Kuhn's theory of scientific paradigms,[13] historical epistemology conceives truth as "error rectified" in an endless effort to dissolve the prenotions born of ordinary and scholarly common sense. It proposes that science advances, not through the encyclopedic accumulation of facts, but through discontinuities by constantly questioning its own foundations to foster *the emancipation of the mind from previous scientific conceptions*. Equally distant from theoretical formalism and from empiricist operationalism, idealism and realism, it teaches that facts are necessarily suffused with theory, that laws are but "momentarily stabilized hypotheses" (in the words of Canguilhem), and that rational knowledge progresses through a polemical process of collective argumentation and reciprocal control. Moreover, epistemology takes sides: it is the judge which "passes judgment on the past of knowledge and the knowledge of the past."[14]

Canguilhem singles out three axioms at the center of Bachelard's thought: "the theoretical primacy of error," which records the fact that science never starts *tabula rasa* but always by pushing aside knowledge already there and gives error a positive role in the process of discovery; "the speculative depreciation of intuition" captured in Bachelard's pithy expression, "intuitions are very serviceable: they serve to be destroyed";[15] and "the positioning of the object as the perspective of ideas," by which Bachelard means that the vector of knowledge formation goes from the mind to the world, from the rational to the real, and not the other way around as empiricism would have it. From the first axiom the French philosopher derives his key concept of *epistemological obstacle*, which designates, not just the external knowledges circulating in the world, but the internal and necessary moves of the mind that stand in the way of scientific production.[16] Applied to the sociology of racial domination, the notion points, first, to the ordinary racial doxa that every researcher encounters in the society she studies; second, to the racial expertise the sociologist believes she holds as an investigator of the phenomenon; and, third, to the tendency to think the social world in substantialist terms – epitomized by the duo of "race and racism" (as if race was a thing independent of racism, however defined) and by the group-

---

[13] Thomas S. Kuhn, *The Structure of Scientific Revolutions* (1970 [1962]). The expression "scientific revolution" was coined by Koyré, who was a major influence on Kuhn.
[14] Georges Canguilhem, *Études d'histoire et de philosophie des sciences* (1968), p. 13.
[15] Bachelard, *La Philosophie du non*, p. 139.
[16] Gaston Bachelard, *La Formation de l'esprit scientifique. Contribution à une psychanalyse de la connaissance objective* (1938), p. 15.

Problemstellung

oriented approach that dominates scholarship on the topic. A fourth obstacle consists in the temptation to derive the sociology of race from its politics, which negates the relative autonomy of scientific production.[17]

To circumvent epistemological obstacles, Bachelard recommends that we effect an *epistemological rupture* by breaking with commonsense notions and ready-made scholarly problematics.[18] Importantly, rupture is an activity, not an inaugural act carried out once and for all at the start of research; its implementation must be embedded and continually reiterated in scientific practice itself. It follows that there is a fundamental and necessary distinction between *folk notions* and *analytic concepts* – and this applies most urgently to "race."[19] Issued out of the social world, folk notions are practical recipes that help us navigate in that world, resolve mundane issues, and satisfy ordinary needs. Not so the analytic constructs that the scientist forges for the express purpose of empirical description, hermeneutic interpretation, and causal explanation. Elaborated in and for the scientific field, tested by the community of scholars, they must obey minimal standards of semantic stability and neutrality, display logical consistency and type specificity, and prove heuristic in the formulation of theory and the conduct of research.[20] So much to say that, insofar as it necessarily carries the historical unconscious of a particular society and time, the notion of "race" cannot be included in the analytical tool box of the sociology of racial domination. It enters in the latter as an object and not as an instrument of analysis.

The notion of epistemological rupture, in turn, leads to the imperative of *epistemological vigilance*: "The scientific mind forbids us to have

---

[17] This temptation is embraced by some theorists of race steeped in substantialism: "*Racial theory derives from racial politics*; it lags behind the self-activity of both individuals and groups (*yes, there are groups*), trying as always, in Hegel's 'owl-of-Minerva' fashion, to make sense of what is already happening." Howard Winant, "Is there a Racial Order? Comments on Emirbayer and Desmond" (2016: 2290, my italics).

[18] Bachelard, *La Formation de l'esprit scientifique*, pp. 23–4. "Opinion is, on principle, always wrong. It *thinks* badly. It does not *think*; it translates needs into knowledges . . . One cannot found anything on opinion. We must first destroy it. It is the first obstacle to be overcome" (p. 16).

[19] For a contrary argument, see Michael Banton, "Analytical and Folk Concepts of Race and Ethnicity" (1979), who contends that it is both undesirable and impossible to distinguish ordinary and scientific constructs of race.

[20] For an elaboration of this epistemological position, see Loïc Wacquant, *The Invention of the "Underclass": A Study in the Politics of Knowledge* (2022), pp. 150–3. The reflection of social scientists on concept formation is woefully sparse and thin, but see Gary Goertz, *Social Science Concepts and Measurements* (2020).

an opinion on questions that we do not understand, on questions that we do not know how to formulate clearly."[21] We must constantly beware of the notions, half-conceptual, half-descriptive, that we come across in our scientific investigations; query our own concepts as to their origins, structure, and meaning; step back and question our own questions, the terms in which we formulate them, and the blind spots they imply. In short, we must be reflexive when we articulate our scientific *problématique* – another term introduced by Bachelard to stress the fact that scientific problems do not pose themselves but must be articulated by the scientists, plural, over and against conventional ways of thinking.[22] The French philosopher thus speaks directly to the agenda of a sociology of racial domination when he writes: "All scientific culture must begin with an intellectual and emotional catharsis. Then remains the most difficult task: to put scientific culture in a state of permanent mobilization, to replace closed and static knowledge with an open and dynamic knowledge."[23]

If Bachelard is right that scientific knowledge grows discontinuously, by rupture with "knowledge already there," this requires periodically resetting the epistemic parameters of scholarly production so that new concepts, original theories, and a novel landscape of empirical objects may emerge.[24] This is what I try to do in the first chapter by proposing five reframings of ethnoracial domination that, together, seek to clear the path for a conceptualization of race-making, not as an object *sui generis*, but as a particular case of the dynamics and dilemmas of group-making.

2. Weber's concept of ethnicity and method of the ideal type

In an oft-mentioned but rarely dissected section of *Wirtschaft und Gesellschaft*, Weber fashions a provisional definition of ethnic groups as "those human groups that entertain a subjective belief in their common descent because of similarities of physical type or customs, or both, or because of memories of colonization and migration."[25] The symbolic element is the lynchpin of the construct and group-

---

[21] Bachelard, *La Formation de l'esprit scientifique*, p. 16.
[22] Pierre Bourdieu extends this imperative in *Science de la science et réflexivité* (2001a).
[23] Bachelard, *La Formation de l'esprit scientifique*, p. 21.
[24] Bachelard, *Épistémologie*.
[25] Weber, *Economy and Society*, p. 389.

Problemstellung

ness varies accordingly: "This belief must be important for the propagation of group formation. Conversely, it does not matter whether or not an objective blood relationship exists." It follows that ethnic membership (or "common ground," *Gemeinsamkeit*) is "a presumed identity" that "*does not constitute a group; it only facilitates group formation* of any kind, particularly in the political sphere."[26]

Earlier in the same chapter, Weber defines "race identity" as "common inherited and inheritable traits that actually derive from common descent. Of course, race creates a 'group' only when it is subjectively perceived as a common trait," which happens when physical proximity between groups is "the basis for joint (mostly political) action" or "when some common experiences of members of the same race are linked to some antagonism against members of an *obviously different group*."Weber presses on: "The resulting social action is *usually merely negative*: those who are obviously different are avoided and despised or, conversely, viewed with superstitious awe."[27] Remarkably, then, Weberian "race" is made via the same process as ethnicity, through collective belief born from historical experience and fastened on a culturally salient trait, here a physical feature.[28] This means that *race is a subtype of ethnicity* and that ethnicity flows from identification (by members) whereas race flows from categorization (by outsiders).

This clarification of Weber's conception of ethnicity and race further implies that ethnicity itself may be grasped as a *subtype of status group*, which Weber defines as a category based on "an effective claim to social esteem in terms of positive or negative privileges."[29] The German sociologist suggests as much in this passage: "The belief in common ethnicity often delimits 'social circles'" made up of persons brought together by "the belief in a specific 'honor' of their members, not shared by the outsiders, that is, the sense of 'ethnic honor' (a phenomenon *closely related to status honor*)."[30] Reconceptualizing ethnicity

---

[26] Ibid., my italics.

[27] Ibid., p. 385.

[28] "Similarity and contrast of physical type and custom, regardless of whether they are biologically inherited or culturally transmitted, are subject to the same conditions of group life, in origin as well as in effectiveness, and identical in their potential for group formation" (ibid., p. 388).

[29] Ibid., p. 305.

[30] Ibid., p. 390, my italics. Elsewhere we read: "All differences of customs can sustain a specific sense of honor or dignity in their practitioners" (p. 387); and "the conviction of the excellence of one's customs and the inferiority of alien ones, a conviction which sustains the sense of ethnic honor, is actually quite analogous to the sense of honor of distinctive status group" (p. 391).

as a particular kind of status group is fruitful because it leads us to the concepts of class and closure.

Regarding *class*, Weber notes that "class distinctions are linked in the most varied ways with status distinction," but that they may be understood as the material (production, objective) and symbolic (consumption, subjective) side of group-making, respectively.[31] Regarding closure (*Schließung*), that is, the varied strategies whereby a group effects "the monopolization of cultural and material goods and opportunities,"[32] it is key to group formation. The creation of "closed relations" is pivotal to the formation of ethnoracial groups, amorphous or instituted. Notably for our model-building, it admits of gradations situated on a continuum: "Both the extent and the methods of regulation and exclusion in relation to outsiders may vary widely, so that the transition from a state of openness to one of regulation and closure is gradual."[33] We will indeed see in chapter 2 that discrimination, segregation, seclusion, and violence are so many instruments for effecting closure, extracting economic value, and tracing as well as enforcing boundaries between ethnoracial categories.

On the methodological level, I draw on Weber to deploy the notion and mode of reasoning of the ideal type (*Idealtypus*), the abstract mental construct that the social scientist necessarily elaborates to approach and order analytically the empirical manifold. Weber explains: "An ideal type is formed by the one-sided *accentuation* of one or more points of view and by the synthesis of a great many diffuse, discreet, more or less present and occasionally absent *concrete individual* phenomena, which are arranged according to those one-sidedly emphasized viewpoints into a unified mental construct (*Gedankenbild*). In its conceptual purity, this mental construct cannot be found empirically anywhere in reality . . . Historical research faces the task of determining in each individual case, the extent to which this ideal construct approximates to or diverges from reality."[34] Weber gives as illustration

---

[31] Ibid., pp. 932 and 303–7.

[32] Ibid., p. 935. Weber's extended discussion of "open and closed relationships" is on pp. 43–6. He notes that "there is a wide range of different degrees of closure and of conditions of participation. Thus regulation and closure are relative concepts" (p. 45). Moreover, one of "the principal motives for closure of a relationship is "the maintenance of quality, which is often combined with the interest in *prestige* and the consequent opportunities *to enjoy honor*, and even profit" (p. 46, my italics).

[33] Ibid., p. 45.

[34] Weber, *The Methodology of the Social Sciences*, p. 90. For a lucid and engaging discussion of the ideal type and its role in Weber's attempt to marry interpretation and

Problemstellung

the concepts of neoclassical economic theory that presume a rational actor and a free market; these do not describe actual economic conduct and institutions – they are not an anthropology – but they offer a benchmark to map and understand the deviations of reality from the pure model. They are "limiting concepts" that serve to delineate and dissect social reality, and thus provide a basis for the imputation of meaning and of adequate causation, including the formulation of counterfactuals.

The ideal type thereby fosters the wedding of theory and history. It can be modified as the research unfolds, as some properties are subtracted and others added for heuristic power, and it is a multiscalar tool: one can ascend or descend in level of abstraction and elaborate an ideal type of a component of an ideal type (as I do in chapter 4 in my analysis of the relations between the black hyperghetto and the prison archipelago in the United States). Critics of the approach have complained that the ideal type is artificial, simplifying, if not simplistic, and thus cannot capture the profuseness and multisidedness (*Vielseitigkeit*) of historical reality. But these are the very strengths of methodological perspectivism: "The more sharply and precisely the ideal type has been constructed, thus the more abstract and unrealistic in this sense it is, the better it is able to perform its functions in formulating terminology, classifications, and hypotheses."[35]

Another common critique is that the ideal type is arbitrary relative to the essence of the phenomenon. Again, it is a strength of the method that it does not make strong ontological claims – as do many theoretical approaches, such as Marxism. For Marx, the essential truth of capitalism resides in the extraction of surplus value via wage labor for structure and the class struggle for dynamics. Weber would retort that this is nothing but an ideal type, and a very fruitful one at that. Like Monsieur Jourdain speaking in prose, social scientists who endeavor to theorize build ideal types all the time without realizing it and the latter "serve as harbor until one has learned to navigate safely in the vast sea of empirical facts."[36] We will see in chapter 3 that,

---

explanation, see Fritz Ringer, *Max Weber's Methodology: The Unification of the Cultural and Social Sciences* (1997).

[35] Weber, *Economy and Society*, p. 21. Indeed, ideal-typical construction is especially recommended when empirical reality is complex and shifting: "Sharp differentiation in concrete fact is often impossible, but this makes clarity in the analytical distinction all the more important" (p. 214).

[36] Weber, *The Methodology of the Social Sciences*, p. 104. For an elaborate treatment, see Thomas Burger, *Max Weber's Theory of Concept Formation* (1976).

because they disregard the need for methodical abstraction, historians of "Jim Crow" (a folk concept) have amassed quantities of facts without the means to capture and compare the many variants of that regime of racial domination across time and space.

3. Bourdieu's theory of social space and symbolic power

Bourdieu's theory of social space and symbolic power may be characterized as *genetic structuralism* insofar as it fastens on the twofold process whereby history becomes sedimented in socialized organisms as *cognitive structures* (systems of dispositions) and objectified in the form of *social structures* (systems of positions). Retracing this double genesis allows the sociologist to illumine the resulting dialectic between dispositions and positions, habitus and social space (or fields), from which practice springs. This dialectic spans the gamut from full agreement – leading to social acquiescence and reproduction – to complete discordance – leading to social contestation and transformation.[37] Bourdieu's theory, in turn, rests on a social ontology that is radically historicist in the sense that there is no ultimate foundation to this dialectic, no overriding causal factor and directionality to history, no invariant other than the unremitting struggles for social recognition and thence position characteristic of the human condition.[38]

This applies to groups in particular, which are not given readymade in reality but are the product of a symbolic work whereby mental constructs are turned into historical realities. The core of Bourdieu's sociology thus resides in the *social alchemy of the realization of categories in things and bodies*: "Nation, 'race' or 'identity', in the current phrase, are inscribed in things – in the form of objective structures, de facto segregation, economic, spatial, etc. – and in bodies, in the form of tastes and distaste, sympathies and antipathies, attraction and repulsion that are often said to be visceral."[39] Resolving

---

[37] Pierre Bourdieu, "Espace social et pouvoir symbolique," in *Choses dites* (1987), and idem, *Le Sens pratique* (1980a), chapter 3 ("Structures, habitus, pratiques").
[38] Pierre Bourdieu, *Méditations pascaliennes* (1997), chapter 6. If there is one engine that drives humans "in the final analysis" (as the Marxists like to say), it is access to symbolic capital, that is, existence in the eyes of others: "A human is a being without *raison d'être*, inhabited by the need for justification, legitimation, recognition. Now, as Pascal suggests, in this quest for justifications for one's existence, what he calls 'the world' or 'society' is the only agency capable of competing with the recourse to God" (p. 282).
[39] Ibid., p. 216.

Problemstellung

the mystery of group-making entails two analytical moves. First, we must situate agents in *social space*, that is, the multidimensional distribution of capitals (economic, cultural, social, and symbolic, for the main species) that anchor objective positions and constraints bearing on actions and representations. Second, we must heed what Bourdieu calls the "semantic elasticity of the social world," the fact that it is the object of rival perceptions and thus "can be uttered and constructed in different ways, according to different principles of vision and division – for instance, economic divisions or ethnic divisions."[40]

This paves the way for struggles to capture and deploy *symbolic power* defined as the power to conserve or to transform the social world by conserving or transforming the categories of perception of that world. These struggles can be waged individually (as with gossip and insult in everyday life) or collectively by symbolic entrepreneurs (such as unions, parties, and social movements) vying to make their vision of the world come true. At stake in these battles is "the monopoly over the legitimate representation of the social world, this classification struggle that is a dimension of all manner of struggles between classes, age classes, sexual classes, or social classes."[41] Following this approach, race can be construed as a *naturalizing principle of social vision and division* that shapes subjectivity, society, and history *to the degree* that it has affirmed itself over and against rival principles and thus, to a minimal degree, succeeded in shaping social reality in its image.

What I call the *agonistic theory of group-making* is an account of the process whereby competing mental categories are "realized," in the sense of turned into entities endowed with facticity. It tackles "the question with which all sociology should begin: that of the existence and of the mode of existence of collectives."[42] The analytic of racial

---

[40] Bourdieu, "Espace social et pouvoir symbolique," p. 137.
[41] Pierre Bourdieu, *Leçon sur la leçon* (1982a), p. 14. "Properly political action is possible because agents, who are part of the social world, have a (more or less adequate) knowledge of this world and because one can act upon the social world by acting upon their knowledge of that world. This action aims to produce and impose representations (mental, verbal, visual or theatrical) of the social world which are capable of acting upon the world by acting upon the representations that agents have of it. Or, more precisely, it aims to make or unmake groups ... by producing, reproducing or destroying the representations that make these groups visible to themselves and to others." Pierre Bourdieu, "Décrire et prescrire" (1981), p. 187.
[42] Pierre Bourdieu, "Espace social et genèse des 'classes'" (1984a), p. B321. Bourdieu goes on to characterize a social class as "a veritable mystical body, created at the cost of an immense historical labor of theoretical and practical invention" (p. B322), a contention that applies to any group, including ethnoracial.

domination I will develop in chapter 2 is a particular derivation of that general theory spawned by Bourdieu's genetic structuralism as follows:

genetic structuralism
↓
agonistic theory of group-making
↓
analytic of racial domination

One last implication of Bourdieu's theory concerns the *special role of the state as paramount symbolic agency*. For the French sociologist, the state is "the locus par excellence of the concentration and the exercise of symbolic power," "the central bank of symbolic capital that guarantees all acts of authority."[43] It shapes the creation and conformation of social collectives insofar as it *inculcates* categories of perception (through the school system and the law in particular); *arbitrates* conflicts between rival symbolic agencies and entrepreneurs which advocate for competing principles of classification; and it *validates* identities through bureaucratic procedures, rites and ceremonials. A racial state is a state that does all three of these things based on ethnoracial grounds.

classification ⟶ **stratification**
(symbolic)   **(material)**
↑_____|

I rework Bourdieu's dyad of social space and symbolic power – which constitutes the irreducible conceptual core of his thought, and not the usual triad of habitus, capital, and field[44] – into the *duet of classification and stratification*. As a concrete manifestation of symbolic power, classification operates in the symbolic order; it organizes perception

---

[43] Pierre Bourdieu, "Esprits d'État. Genèse et structure du champ bureaucratique" (1993a), reprinted in *Raisons pratiques. Sur la théorie de l'action* (1996), pp. 122 and 117. See also idem, *Sur l'État. Cours au Collège de France, 1989–1992* (2012), pp. 24–9, 53–4, 61–2, 110–12, 163–6, 196–9, 259–78, 302–5, 337–9, 351–4, and 359–66. Among the many characterizations that Bourdieu gives of the state, these are pertinent to race-making: "the point of view on points of view" (p. 53); the agency that "theatricalizes the official and the universal" (p. 54); "the *fictio juris* that grounds all acts of juridical creation" (p. 99); "the locus of the management of the universal" (p. 155); "the producer of the principles of classification" (p. 262); "the principle constitutive of the categories universally diffused throughout its jurisdiction" (p. 276); the "theoretical unifier" (p. 337); and the agency that "integrates" through domination (p. 359).

[44] Loïc Wacquant, "Four Transversal Principles for Putting Bourdieu to Work" (2018).

Problemstellung

and directs patterns of thought, feeling, and action. This results in the differential accrual and accumulation of forms of capital across the different categories composing the operant classification and thus a distinctive stratification in the material order, as a slice of social space. The differential distribution of efficient resources to the classified agents, in turn, impacts their ability to preserve or overturn the existing classification, creating a *recursive relationship between classification and stratification* as the two central pegs of the agonistic theory of race-making as indicated above. It follows that ethnoracial classification and ethnoracial stratification are the *two modalities of existence of race*.[45]

The challenge of the sociology of racial domination is to hold together these two modalities and to identify the concrete institutions that embody and enforce each of them. Analysis of the logics of categorization must imperatively be accompanied by an analysis of the material grounding of these categories and in the correlative potency of paramount agencies of symbolic power. This is implied by Bourdieu when he writes: "If the notion of ethnicity or race – which is the most ordinary expression of the thing – exists through the perception that agents have of it, this does not mean that it is a subjective creation that could be transformed by a wave of a magic wand, by an ethical conversion determined by moral preaching of any kind."[46]

This schema allows us to make two much-needed correctives to the conventional constructivist approach as applied to ethnoracial inequality which I call the fluidity thesis and the suffusion thesis. The *fluidity thesis* refers to the commonly expressed view that, because it is "socially constructed" and can therefore be contested, race is endowed with a "fluidity," "inherent instability," and even "volatility" that would make it almost evanescent and allow it to be reconfigured anew at any moment.[47] In fact, as we shall see throughout this book,

---

[45] This is not just "dynamic nominalism" à la Hacking. Hacking suggests that people classified are altered by classification and may cause classificatory systems to change in turn – what he calls "the looping effects of human kinds" or "interactive kinds." My claim is that, in addition to the "interaction of ideas and people," stratification serves as the material springboard for symbolic struggles, individual and collective aiming to bolster or alter classifications, a sort of "looping effect" of the modalities of race. Ian Hacking, *The Social Construction of What?* (1999), pp. 34, 59, 104 and 105–6.
[46] Pierre Bourdieu, *Sociologie générale*, vol. 2, p. 941.
[47] This is an argument popular among historians who wish to stress the "agency" of racialized agents, for instance Ira Berlin, *Many Thousands Gone: The First Two Centuries of Slavery in North America* (1998), pp. 1–3. But it is also common among sociologists, as when Matthew Desmond and Mustafa Emirbayer stress "the incredibly unstable and fluid nature of racial categories" ("What Is Racial Domination?" [2009a], p. 342). The thesis of the cognitive and contingent makeup of ethnicity is brought to its log-

fluidity is historically variable, running from evanescent to hard-wired. The more racialized forms of ethnic domination are deeply entrenched by dint of the *inertia* of material structures embedded in social and physical space (think segregated neighborhoods) and by the *hysteresis* of habitus (think ethnically inflected taste and moral emotions).[48] The *suffusion thesis* refers to the widely held presumption that if race is operative in a given social formation, it necessarily pervades all of its institutions and impacts all patterns of action, cognition, and relations. I propose to drop this presumption so that we can make the sectoral pertinence of race an empirical question. Drawing on Weber's critique of Marx's suffusionist view of economic causation, I suggest that we distinguish between racial *phenomena*, racially *relevant* phenomena, and racially *conditioned* phenomena,[49] to which I would add racially *indifferent* phenomena.

Specifying domination

Having provided a liminary definition of "race," the next step in a theory of ethnoracial domination is to specify what the term domination means. The notion is commonly thrown around in the social sciences but just as rarely defined. It is remarkable that, in their lucid article "What Is Racial Domination?" published under the "State of the Art" rubric of the *Du Bois Review* in 2009, Desmond and Emirbayer delineate race with precision but forget to explicate domination, other than to say it assumes two forms, "interpersonal and institutional racism" (with the term "racism" itself left undefined).[50] To specify domination, I will draw on the work of Weber,

---

ical pinnacle by Rogers Brubaker's discussion of "groupness as event" in "Ethnicity Without Groups" (2002), especially pp. 168–9.

[48] Loïc Wacquant, *Bourdieu in the City: Challenging Urban Theory* (2023a), chapter 3, especially pp. 128–30. Andreas Wimmer puts it best: "*Hélas*, not everything is possible, not all ethnic boundaries are fluid and in motion, not all are cognitively and emotionally unstable, contextually shifting, and continuously contested" (*Ethnic Boundary Making: Institutions, Network, Power* [1913], p. 204).

[49] Weber draws a distinction between "economic phenomena" (a firm), "economically relevant phenomena" (the gendered division of labor), and "economically conditioned phenomena" (the voting tendencies of social classes). Weber, *The Methodology of the Social Sciences*, pp. 64–5.

[50] Desmond and Emirbayer, "What Is Racial Domination?," pp. 344–5 and 348–9. The same occurs in their bold book *The Racial Order* (2015), in which they endeavor to "gain analytic leverage on the deeper meanings and significance of the commin-

Problemstellung

Foucault, and Bourdieu to craft a compact analytical definition of the same.

Domination is at the core of Max Weber's foundational tome, *Wirtschaft und Gesellschaft* (1920). It anchors his sociology of politics, charisma, bureaucracy, and democracy in capitalist society. It captures his vision of the social world as organized by intersecting modes of rulership and traversed by the eternal clash of antagonistic interests and values.[51] The German sociologist defines domination (*Herrschaft*) as "the probability that certain specific commands (or all commands) will be obeyed by a given group of persons." It does not encompass all manners of exercising power or influence insofar as it always "implies a minimum of voluntary compliance."[52] Compliance may be obtained by habit, expediency, or as a result of the belief that the dominated have in the validity of the command. This belief, in turn, undergirds three types of legitimate domination: traditional (appealing to the sanctity of custom), charismatic (flowing from faith in the special powers of a leader), and legal-rational (rooted in the impersonal formalities of law and bureaucracy).[53] In historical reality, any existing regime of domination will be a dynamic combination of these three pure types. Moreover, domination fosters consociation and tends to transform amorphous action into persistent association and thus stimulate the formation of social groups.[54]

It is useful, to better delineate Weber's concept of domination, to compare it to his definition of "power" or might (*Macht*) as "the probability that one actor within a social relationship will be in a posi-

---

gling of racial domination and racial progress," with domination left unspecified (p. 6). It is revealing also that the book's extremely detailed index contains no entry for the concept.

[51] See the introduction by Yves Sintomer to the French selection of key texts, Max Weber, *La Domination* (2020).

[52] Weber, *Economy and Society*, p. 53. Weber elaborates: "The situation in which the manifested will (*command*) of the *ruler* or rulers is meant to influence the conduct of one or more others (*the ruled*), and actually does influence it in such a way that their conduct, to a socially relevant degree, occurs as if the ruled had made the content of the command the maxim of their conduct for its very own sake. Looked upon from the other end, this situation will be called *obedience*" (p. 946).

[53] There is, in addition, an institution that embodies "non-legitimate domination," the Western medieval city, in which citizens broke with traditional authority to rule themselves. Max Weber, *The City* (1950 [1920]).

[54] "Without exception every sphere of social action is profoundly influenced by structures of dominancy. In a great number of cases the emergence of rational association from amorphous social action has been due to domination and the way in which it has been exercised." Weber, *Economy and Society*, p. 941.

tion to carry out his own will despite resistance, regardless of the basis on which this probability rests."[55] Domination generates obedience while power overcomes defiance. This categorical differentiation on paper gets blurred in social reality where the two phenomena overlap or morph into each. On the one side, the subordinate may obey because her resistance has been defeated, in which case the successful exercise of power leads to the establishment of domination, legitimate or not. Conversely, to resist, the agent has to withdraw obedience, if it was hitherto granted, in which case the failure of domination leads to the exercise of power. Moreover, logically, domination obviates the exercise of power – which contradicts Weber's contention that "domination constitutes a special case of power"[56] – but power may rely on domination to achieve its end with a lower expenditure of social energy. The upshot of this disquisition is that it is difficult to maintain a clear distinction between the two concepts and the two phenomena, and that domination works by entering into the subjectivity of the dominated to bend their will, leading Weber to speak of "psychic coercion."[57]

The Weberian conception of domination finds its expression in the subsequent works of Michel Foucault and Pierre Bourdieu, whose inquiries divulge the varied mechanisms, modalities, and outcomes of domination – even though neither provides a stable definition of the notion as they use it. Foucault, for one, never quotes Max Weber, which suggests he did not read him in depth, which is a mystery and a pity considering the overlap between their intellectual concerns: the culture–power nexus, the metamorphoses of reason, and the uniqueness of Western modernity.[58] But his conception is strikingly germane to that of the German sociologist, although he consistently equivocates between domination and power. Foucault rarely stops to define his major concepts or gives multiple definitions in the course of specific historical analyses that do not always cohere. This is particularly the case with the notion of domination, which remains polygonal and

---

[55] Ibid., p. 53. A third germane concept specified by Weber is that of "discipline" defined as "the probability that by virtue of habituation a command will receive prompt and automatic obedience in stereotyped forms, on the part of a given group of persons" (Ibid., p. 53).
[56] Ibid., p. 941.
[57] Ibid., p. 324.
[58] Weber does not appear once in Didier Éribon's definitive biography of Foucault, *Michel Foucault* (1986). He rates a mere dozen passing mentions in the 3,000 pages of the compendium of Foucault's dispersed articles, essays, and interviews, *Dits et écrits* (4 vols., 1994a).

Problemstellung

elusive throughout his corpus. Let me nonetheless essay a compact characterization anchored by the concepts of discipline, biopower, and governmentality.

In his classic study of the birth of the prison, *Surveiller et punir* (1975), Foucault portrays disciplines as "general formulas for domination" targeting the body, noting that they imply "the formation of a relation that, in the mechanism itself, makes [the body] more obedient as it becomes more useful, and conversely."[59] Disciplines partake of the multiplication of apparatuses of judgment and normalization; they are "methods of domination" whereby subjectivity is formed, subjection effected, and value extracted. Their net-like spread manifests the crystallization of a new constellation Foucault calls "power-knowledge" (*pouvoir-savoir*), whereby the workings of power implicate the formation of a corpus of information about its targets and where that knowledge, in turn, oils the wheels of domination. According to Foucault, after the mid-eighteenth century, disciplines proliferated across institutions that each generated new domains of inquiry: schools begat pedagogy, hospitals birthed medicine, asylums fostered psychiatry, barracks fomented military strategy, workshops spawned industrial engineering, and, last but not least, the prison gave birth to criminology.[60] Whereas sovereign power centers on the state and works from the top down, disciplinary power works from the bottom out as it "descends deeply into the thickness of society" and diffuses capillary-style: "The political technology of the body" partakes of a "sort of microphysics of power" that generates obedience by shaping the subject through what Foucault calls *dressage* – which can be translated indifferently as training or taming – and obviates the need for force.[61]

In the first volume of *Histoire de la sexualité* (1976), Foucault differentiates power from "a general system of domination exerted by one group over another, a system whose effects, through successive der-

---

[59] Michel Foucault, *Surveiller et punir. Naissance de la prison* (1975), pp. 137, 138, 191. "Many disciplinary procedures had existed for a long time – in convents, armies, factories. But, in the 17th and 18th century, the disciplines became general formulas for domination" (p. 162). It is a pity that Foucault did not know Weber's short but stimulative analysis of discipline.

[60] Foucault, *Surveiller et punir*, p. 162. Note that, for Weber, "bureaucratic administration," the apparatus of legal-rational domination, "means fundamentally domination through knowledge" (*Economy and Society*, p. 225).

[61] Foucault, *Surveiller et punir*, pp. 35–6f. "It is not necessary to resort to means of force to constrain the convict to behave, the madman to calm down, the worker to labor, the pupil to apply himself, the sick to take his medication" (p. 237). In *Power/Knowledge* (1980, p. 96), Foucault talks of "polymorphous techniques of subjugation."

ivations, pervade the entire social body."[62] He elaborates the notion of "biopower" as a technique for the "subjugation of bodies and the control of populations" essential to the growth of capitalism through the "accumulation of people." In his later writings, the French philosopher crafts the concept of "governmentality" as a vehicle for domination. Governmentality is "the conduct of conduct" or "the meeting between techniques of domination and techniques of the self."[63] In the modern West, "the techniques and procedures for directing human behavior" admit many derivations that effect "the government of children, the government of souls and consciences, the government of a household, of a state, or of oneself."[64] An implication of these analyses is that domination is *productive of new subjects and objects*; it is also multi-institutional, insinuating, and suffusive, a view that converges with Weber's position that "without exception every sphere of social action is profoundly influenced by structures of domination."[65]

Pierre Bourdieu was an early and avid reader of Max Weber, and he refers to the German sociologist profusely in his lecture courses at the Collège de France from 1983 to 1997. In the early 1960s, he mined Weber's economic sociology to parse the cataclysmic social transformation of colonial Algeria. He then absorbed Weber's theory of science and wedded it to the French tradition of historical rationalism to elaborate his sociological epistemology in *Le Métier de sociologue* (1968). In the 1970s, Bourdieu drew on Weber's sociology of religion to develop his signal concept of field. He also showed in *La Distinction* (1979) that Weber's opposition between class and status could be collapsed into the material and the symbolic dimensions of class. Indeed, in his lifelong efforts to develop a theory of symbolic domination, Bourdieu comes back time and again to Weber, whom he credits with suggesting the very possibility of "a materialist theory of the 'symbolic'."[66]

Bourdieu uses the term domination in a broad Weberian sense when he proposes that the phenomenon is suffusive and multifaceted; but he is chiefly concerned with one variant, namely, *symbolic* domination.[67] Tersely put, symbolic domination arises when the dominated

---

[62] Michel Foucault, *Histoire de la sexualité* (1976), p. 92.
[63] Foucault, "Technologies du soi" (1994a [1982]), p. 785.
[64] Michel Foucault, *Ethics: Subjectivity and Truth. Essential Works of Michel Foucault, 1954–1984*, Vol. 1 (1997), p. 82.
[65] Weber, *Economy and Society*, p. 941.
[66] Pierre Bourdieu, "With Weber, Against Weber" (2011 [2000]), p. 116.
[67] Bourdieu is rather lax in his prolific use of the term. Under his pen, domination

Problemstellung

sees herself through the eyes of the dominant. It operates invisibly via knowledge, a process captured by the triad cognition–recognition–misrecognition. It consists in the inculcation of categories of perception and appreciation (mental structures, taxonomies, but also desires and aspirations) that lead the dominated to collaborate in her subjection because, being issued from the world, these taxonomies mirror its objective divisions and thereby make that world appear as the only possible world.[68] For example, if I perceive a society objectively organized around the Malay/Chinese opposition (with institutions, networks, and neighborhoods segregated accordingly) through mental categories grounded in a series of homologous dichotomies, Malay/Chinese, high/low, inside/outside, straight/crooked, culture/nature, honor/dishonor, etc., I am inclined to agree with the social order. I take it for granted: it becomes *doxic*. I cannot envision a world beyond this ethnoracial division and I spontaneously act in manifold and banal ways that reproduce it – for instance, by patronizing stores run by my co-ethnics and ostracizing members of my community who marry outside of it.[69]

For Bourdieu, symbolic violence is this "soft, gentle coercion," this "censored and euphemized violence, that is misrecognizable and recognized" through which the dominated comes to act in compliance with the social order by anticipating its dictates.[70] It allows the dominant to economize energy by diminishing the amount of material force needed to impose their commands and thus secure the social order. So much to say that there exists an *inverse relationship between physical and symbolic violence*. We will see indeed in chapter 3 how

covers subordination, preeminence, authority, supremacy, superiority, rule, command, and control. See his *Sociologie générale*, vol. 2, *Cours au Collège de France, 1983–1986* (2016), passim. Sometimes he tacitly equates domination with *legitimate* domination; at other times he adds the adjective *symbolic*, suggesting that not all domination is legitimate. In his entry on "Domination" in the *Dictionnaire International Pierre Bourdieu* (2020), François Denord mentions the influences of Marx, Weber, and Durkheim but does not cite a definition from Bourdieu's corpus.

[68] "Symbolic violence is that coercion which is instituted only by the intermediary of the consent that the dominated cannot fail to give to the dominator (and therefore to domination) when, in order to think him and to think herself or, better, to think her relation to the dominator, she only has instruments of knowledge that they have in common and which, being nothing but the embodied form of the structure of the relation of domination, make that relation appear as natural." Bourdieu, *Méditations pascaliennes*, p. 204.

[69] Eugene K. B. Tan, "From Sojourners to Citizens: Managing the Ethnic Chinese Minority in Indonesia and Malaysia" (2001).

[70] Bourdieu, *Le Sens pratique*, p. 217.

that dialectic plays out in the brutal regime of racial domination colloquially known as Jim Crow in the postbellum South of the United States.

Three further conceptual points need stressing here to grasp how Bourdieu construes the office of knowledge in domination. Against the tradition of Kantian idealism, the author of *Distinction* proposes, first, that cognitive categories are not a priori but *historical constructs issued out of classification struggles*. Indeed, social taxonomies are at once products, weapons, and stakes in the battles, waged in fields of cultural production (science, law, journalism, politics) as well as in the state, to impose symbolic templates through which people will see the social order and organize their conduct.[71] Second, the French sociologist insists, again against the spiritualist bias of the Kantian tradition, that categories are not just mental constructs but, rather, that they are wired *deep into the socialized organism* in the form of moral emotions, visceral likes and dislikes that are beyond the grasp of consciousness,[72] such that agreement with the world "transcends the alternative between constraint by *forces* and consent to *reasons*, between mechanical coercion and willful, free, deliberate submission." Bourdieu explains: "The effect of symbolic domination (gender, ethnic, cultural, linguistic, etc.) is exerted, not according to the pure logic of a knowing consciousness, but in the obscurity of the dispositions of habitus." Through symbolic violence, submission to domination is at once "spontaneous and extorted";[73] it eludes the Weberian distinction between obedience and resistance; it springs from the *structural complicity* born of the correspondence between social structures and mental structures, position and disposition, social world and socialized body.

The third point is the distinction Bourdieu establishes between two modes of domination: the personal and the structural.[74] The *personal*

---

[71] "As soon as there is a social space, there is a struggle, there is a struggle of domination, there is a dominant pole, there is a dominated pole, and from this moment there are antagonistic truths. No matter what, truth is antagonistic. If there is a truth, it is that truth is a stake of struggles" (*Questions de sociologie* [1980b], pp. 93–4). On this point, see Franck Poupeau, "Lutte(s)," in *Dictionnaire International Pierre Bourdieu* (2020).

[72] "The moral passions of all racisms (of ethnicity, gender, or class) perpetuate themselves because they are pegged to the body in the form of dispositions and also because the relation of domination of which they are the product perpetuates itself in objectivity" (Bourdieu, *Méditations pascaliennes*, p. 216).

[73] Ibid., p. 204.

[74] Pierre Bourdieu, "Les Modes de domination" (1976). This article is revised as

Problemstellung

mode of domination, characteristic of precapitalist formations, relies on the direct, face-to-face, relationship between two persons, say, the planter and his sharecropper or the small shopkeeper and his employees. It is stamped by "the coexistence of overt, physical and economic violence, and of the most refined symbolic violence,"[75] as when paternalism overlays relations of brute exploitation. The *structural mode* of domination, by contrast, relies on such faceless mechanisms as the labor market, bureaucracy, the law, and the state to secure the social order. "Objectification in institutions guarantees the permanence and the cumulativity of acquisitions, material as well as symbolic, which can subsist without the agents having to recreate them continually and integrally by deliberate action."[76] In *La Noblesse d'État* (1989b), Bourdieu illustrates this notion by showing how the distribution of prestigious credentials by elite universities effects a social selection under the guise of an academic selection, allowing the children of the dominant class to return to positions of eminence, but with the symbolic benefit of seeming to owe their eminence to their superior valor and merit, in their own eyes as well as in the eyes of those denied these credentials.[77]

Pierre Bourdieu on racism(s)

In his first book *Sociologie de l'Algérie* published 1958, the young Bourdieu tackles *colonial racism*. He presents the French capture and rule of Algeria as a "social vivisection" deliberately and methodically effected by the imperial power, and not a mere "cultural encounter" between civilizations (1). The growing social distance between Algerian natives and French settlers is fictively bridged by "paternalism and racism." Bourdieu writes: "Considered synchronically, the colonial society makes one think of a caste system," complete with the juxtaposition of two unequal and endogamous communities marked out by birth, physical type, dress, and patronym. The two communities are "separated by a host of invisible barriers," resulting in "de facto racial segregation. The function of racism is nothing other than to furnish a rationalization of this factual order by making

---

chapter 5 of *Le Sens pratique* (1980a), which I am citing here.
[75] Bourdieu, *Le Sens pratique*, p. 218.
[76] Ibid., p. 225.
[77] Pierre Bourdieu, *La Noblesse d'État. Grandes écoles et esprits de corps* (1989b).

it appear as a legitimate order." Each caste is internally hierarchized into classes but "the caste mindset smothers class consciousness," leading poor whites to defend colonial rule (2).

Jump to France in the 1980s: drawing on his extensive research on higher education, taste, and class, especially *La Reproduction* and *La Distinction*, Bourdieu coins and deploys the notion of *class racism*, which comes in two variants. The elitist variant consists in attributing the eminent properties of the bourgeoisie to their innate virtues and capacities when they are due to their inheritance of capital in its different form and, *a contrario*, to portray the cultural practices of the working class as inherently vulgar, base and lacking, forgetting to link them to the position of that class in social space and the constraints it entails (3). The populist variant of class racism resides in the principled celebration of the good sense, spontaneity, authenticity and creativity of "the folk" (*le peuple*). The self-mystifying praise of the culture of "the people" has "the effect of effacing the effects of domination" (4). Moreover, "the fact of being or feeling authorized to speak *for* the people (in the twofold sense)," as in the approving invocation of folk art, folk religion, folk medicine, etc., is "an asset in the struggles" internal to the political, religious, and artistic fields. The concern to "rehabilitate" popular practices is but an inverted form of class scorn that similarly essentializes "the folk."

Essentialization is at the root of the most euphemized expression of class racism which Bourdieu calls the *racism of intelligence*: "Every racism is an essentialism and the racism of intelligence is the form of sociodicy characteristic of a dominant class whose power rests in part upon the possession of titles, which like school credentials, are supposed to be warrants of intelligence" and which function in the manner of titles of property and nobility. Bourdieu invokes here Weber's analysis of religion as producing a "theodicy of their privilege" for the dominant. He adds: "There is not one racism but *racisms*: there are as many racisms as there are groups that need to justify themselves to exist as they exist, which constitutes the invariant function of racisms" (5). The routine operation of the school system transmutes social properties into academic properties that seem founded in gifted intelligence. "Religions were never so successful. Educational classification is a socially legitimated discrimination that receives the sanction of science" (6).

Lastly, Bourdieu tackled the concrete manifestations of *state racism* in France in his public interventions and writings in civic sociology, especially in the late 1990s as the press of neoliberal policy and right-wing turn of the political field (including the Socialist Party) brought the question of postcolonial immigration to the fore. Thus, in a sortie of August 1996 run by the Agence-France Presse, he inveighs against the "state xenophobia" manifested by the tenacious refusal of the French government to regularize the paperless migrants then mobilized in a nationwide hunger strike (7). In November 1997, in an intervention published by the cultural monthly *Les Inrockuptibles* entitled "We have had enough of state racism," Bourdieu pinpoints how the immigration policy of the government legitimizes discriminatory practices by street-level bureaucrats in their everyday dealings with people "with black faces or Arab-sounding names" (as when they ask them for their passports for routine administrative procedures that do not require one). "I say that a law is racist which authorizes a street-level bureaucrat to question the citizenship of a citizen on the sole basis of her visage or her family name, as happens a thousand times every day" (8).

So much to indicate that Bourdieu viewed race as a social principle of social vision and division that essentializes domination, legitimating the social order by dressing the arbitrary of culture and power in the garb of the necessity of nature, and that he assigned to the state a preeminent responsibility in fostering its diffusion and invocation in action.

1. Pierre Bourdieu, *Sociologie de l'Algérie* (2000 [1958]), p. 106.
2. Ibid., pp. 115–16. "The fact of being born in the superior caste automatically confers privileges, and this tends to develop in those who enjoy them the sentiment of a superiority of nature."
3. Pierre Bourdieu, *La Distinction. Critique sociale du jugement* (1979), pp. 173, 175, 338.
4. Pierre Bourdieu, "Les Usages du 'peuple'," in *Choses dites* (1987), p. 181.
5. Pierre Bourdieu, "Le Racisme de l'intelligence," in *Questions de sociologie* (1980b), pp. 264–5.
6. Ibid., p. 266.
7. Pierre Bourdieu, "Combattre la xénophobie d'État," in *Interventions, 1961–2001. Science sociale et action politique* (2002), pp. 345–6.
8. Pierre Bourdieu, "Nous en avons assez du racisme d'État," in *Interventions, 1961–2001. Science sociale et action politique* (2002), pp. 347–8.

What are the take-aways from this summary and selective recapitulation of the meaning of domination in Weber, Foucault, and Bourdieu?[78] First, the phenomenon is diffuse and protean, and so is the concept; this suggests the need to *decompose and articulate* their elements. Next, multiple types for Weber, multiple techniques for Foucault, and multiple modes for Bourdieu secure domination: it is an *architectured* phenomenon. Finally, for all three authors, the analysis of domination requires prying into the *meaning* given by agents to the relation that binds them. These three points foreshadow the conception of racial domination I will develop in this book: it assumes manifold forms – the five elementary forms – modulated and maintained by various mechanisms; it is at its core a symbolic relation; and it is productive of subjectivities, apparatuses, and material realities.

Building on this exegesis, I deploy a concept of domination that is at once broader and more specific than the neo-Weberian conception. I define *domination as the extraction of compliance to the social order by material or symbolic means* whereby the dominant achieve, secure, and eventually reproduce their position. It manifests itself in three processes I will call the three faces of domination: *exploitation* (the extraction of economic value), *subordination* (relegation to an inferior social position), and *exclusion* (the denial of access to institutions, opportunities, and resources).[79] *Domination is ethnoracial* inasmuch as it opposes and binds social categories defined along racialized lines, that is, when it secretes and crosses *naturalized boundaries of difference and hierarchy*. The important word here is "inasmuch" because racialization – or, more precisely, ethnic (dis)honor – is a matter of degree and not kind.

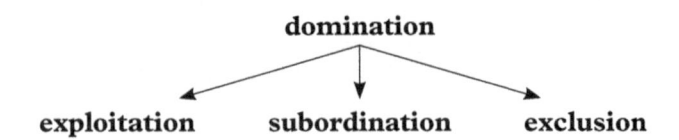

domination

exploitation   **subordination**   **exclusion**

---

[78] Béatrice Hibou's *Anatomie politique de la domination* (2011) offers a different deployment of the Weberian legacy, drawing on the work of Foucault, Antonio Gramsci, and Michel de Certeau to highlight how the subaltern shake their way through the net of domination.

[79] This conception is more compact and coherent than Young's typology of the "five faces of oppression": exploitation, marginalization, powerlessness, cultural imperialism, and violence. Iris Marion Young, *Justice and the Politics of Difference* (1990), chapter 2.

Problemstellung

This means that, whereas our concepts can isolate pure types of domination on paper, actually existing regimes always interlace multiple bases of classification and stratification, not least among them class, gender, age, and place. Put differently, racial domination takes the form of the exploitation, subordination, and/or exclusion of racialized populations. We will see in chapter 3 how the institutional architecture of the Jim Crow regime of caste terrorism in the postbellum South of the United States rested on exploitation via sharecropping extending into debt peonage, subordination through institutional bifurcation and the forcible extraction of deference, and exclusion from the ballot box and the criminal court.

Following Weber, I propose that one of the signal effects of domination is to boost "groupness" by transforming amorphous populations into practical groups and practical groups into instituted groups (I elaborate that distinction, adapted from Bourdieu, *infra*, pp. 198–201) existing both in the subjective order of classification and in the objective order of stratification. Put differently, *domination is constitutive of race as a social principle of vision and division*. Race has no existence outside of the extraction of compliance inscribing it in historical reality. It starts with cognition but it is never cognition *tout court*;[80] it always comprises the *realization of naturalized categories* in material forms, embodied dispositions, uneven distributions of economic assets and credentials, segregated networks and neighborhoods, bifurcated political pull, a skewed bureaucratic field, etc. This implies that, instead of treating them as ontological foundations, we must join the symbolic and material as two *moments* of analysis. Against discursivist theories of race, we must assert that mental categories matter only to the extent that they enter reality by stamping action and institutions. Against materialist and especially economistic theories of race, we must stress that ethnoracial inequalities do not arise *unless agents cognize the world through a naturalizing ethnic grid*. Racial domination blossoms through the mating of symbolic violence and material encasement.

The analytical approach adopted in this book entails two simple steps. The first consists in breaking down the putatively racial *phenomenon* into the combination of *elementary forms* of domination that compose it, namely, categorization, discrimination, segregation, seclusion, and violence. The second step is to excavate the multiple

---

[80] Rogers Brubaker et al., "Ethnicity as Cognition" (2004); Karen E. Fields and Barbara J. Fields, *Racecraft: The Soul of Inequality in American Life* (2014).

mechanisms of production, reproduction, and transformation of these five forms as well as to disclose their structural and functional linkages across history and geography, as indicated by the generic formula:

phenomenon ⟶ elementary forms ⟶ mechanisms

The expression "elementary form" is, of course, inspired by Émile Durkheim's bold quest in *Les Formes élémentaires de la vie religieuse* (1995a [1912]), in which the founder of modern sociology combines history and ethnography into "an explicative analysis" of the essential character of religion. What I take from Durkheim is the intellectual posture "to resolve an institution into its constituent elements."[81] No strong ontological claim need be made here that the five forms of domination capture the essence and totality of the phenomenon – that would be incompatible with the Weberian perspectivism I adopt as methodological foundation. My more modest claim is that it is scientifically fruitful to break ethnoracial phenomena down into their "constituent elements," and then to trace the mechanisms that subtend these forms and link them together.

As basic as it is, this schema – which can be deployed to study the gamut of durable social constellations – is rarely implemented. The analysis of ethnoracial constellations too often remains enshrouded in a mist of shifting conceptual arguments, empirical particulars, and rhetorical moves. Many an author fails even prior to the first step, which entails establishing the phenomenon before rushing to interpret or explain it.[82] Others transport the notion of "race" across societies and epochs without first giving it a clear meaning, so that it is difficult to detect whether it keeps the same referent, or give it a meaning so broad that virtually any difference made in social life qualifies as racial (if not racist).[83]

---

[81] "Because all religions are comparable, because they are all species from the same genus, there is necessarily essential elements common to them." Émile Durkheim, *Les Formes élémentaires de la vie religieuse* (1995a [1912], p. 6). Here Weber would argue that Durkheim constructs a fruitful ideal type.

[82] This is a common flaw in scientific research, natural and social, as indicated long ago by Robert K. Merton, "Three Fragments from a Sociologist's Notebooks: Establishing the Phenomenon, Specified Ignorance and Strategic Research Materials" (1987), pp. 2–5.

[83] This is the case with Cedric Robinson in his revisionist reading of the history of capitalism leading to the birth of "racial capitalism" (*Black Marxism: The Making of the Black Radical Tradition* [2000 (1983)]). I discuss this drift *infra*, pp. 161–8.

Problemstellung

The pentad of elementary forms provides a clear analytical language to specify what dimensions of ethnoracial domination we are dealing with. Without such a language, even the most careful investigators find themselves equivocating. Thus, in his stimulating book *Pour une histoire politique de la race*, the historian Jean-Frédéric Schaub vacillates between different terms, themselves left undefined: discrimination, segregation, and antipathy (p. 155); persecution and exclusion (p. 246); rejection, phobia, scorn (p. 250); and reprobation and revulsion (p. 257).[84] Another common misstep is to reduce the multiplicity of forms of ethnoracial domination at work to a single one of them, as does the subaltern historian Gyanendra Pandey for whom American race and Indian caste both come down to the simple work of "prejudice," and the political scientist Michael Hanchard, who sees "discrimination" as the singular force that "haunts Western democracy."[85] Finally, many authors identify the relevant form of domination but fail to specify the mechanisms at work, as when segregation is tacitly attributed to discrimination and discrimination to prejudice, when they each are the product of multiple recurrent processes and might in actuality be decoupled.[86]

Caveats and preview

First caveat: some readers will no doubt be disappointed that I do not discuss and cross swords with the theories of race that vie for supremacy over that specialized subfield of social inquiry in the Anglophone world. It would take a whole other book to address them in their full complexity and richness.[87] But this evasion is deliberate and an

---

[84] Jean-Frédéric Schaub, *Pour une histoire politique de la race* (2015).
[85] Gyanendra Pandey, *A History of Prejudice: Race, Caste, and Difference in India and the United States* (2013), especially pp. 192–7 and 217–20; Michael G. Hanchard, *The Spectre of Race: How Discrimination Haunts Western Democracy* (2018), especially pp. 12–18.
[86] On the importance of specifying mechanisms in social scientific argumentation, see Peter Hedström and Peter Bearman (eds.), *The Oxford Handbook of Analytical Sociology* (2009), chapter 1.
[87] For foundational statements and recent updates of US theories, see for racial formation theory, Michael Omi and Howard Winant, *Racial Formation in the United States* (2015), and Aliya Saperstein et al. "Racial Formation in Perspective: Connecting Individuals, Institutions, and Power Relations" (2013); for systemic racism, Eduardo Bonilla-Silva, *Racism without Racists: Color-Blind Racism and the Persistence of Racial Inequality in the United States* (2021 [2008]), and Joe R. Feagin, *The White Racial Frame:*

integral part of my foundational argument: to grasp race-making, we need to approach it with a *generic* theory of group-making grounded in the dialectic of classification and stratification, rather than with theories *specific* to that particular object. And we need to escape the US centrism that threatens to universalize the racial unconscious of America by inscribing it in the presuppositions, topics, and tropes of its sociology.[88] One manifestation of this tropism is the continuing ignorance of the ballooning body of research on "race" conducted in other parts of the world, and in Western Europe and Latin America in particular, even when this work is published in English.[89] I would also retort that mainstream students of "race and racism," for their part, often do not take the trouble to clarify their epistemological tenets and to engage the broader social theories most directly germane to their endeavors (with the exception of the recent burst of Du Boisian

Centuries of Racial Framing and Counter-Framing (2020 [2009]); for intersectionality, Patricia Hill Collins and Silma Bilge, *Intersectionality* (2020), and Patricia Hill Collins, "Intersectionality's Definitional Dilemmas" (2015); for critical race theory, Richard Delgado and Jean Stefancic, *Critical Race Theory: An Introduction* (2023), and Ali Meghji, *The Racialized Social System: Critical Race Theory as Social Theory* (2021); for Du Boisian sociology, José Itzigsohn and Karida L. Brown, *The Sociology of W. E. B. Du Bois* (2020), and Katrina Quisumbing King, "The Global Color Line and White Supremacy: W. E. B. Du Bois as a Grand Theorist of Race" (2022); and, for the critical philosophy of race, Charles W. Mills, *The Racial Contract* (2014 [1997]), and Naomi Zack (ed.), *The Oxford Handbook of Philosophy and Race* (2016). Surprisingly, colonial, postcolonial, and decolonial theories have yet to produce a major theoretical statement on race in English, but one finds elements for such a theory in Julian Go, "Postcolonial Possibilities for the Sociology of Race" (2018), and Leela Gandhi, *Postcolonial Theory: A Critical Introduction* (2019). Across the Atlantic, see Hourya Bentouhami, *Races, cultures, identités. Une approche féministe et postcoloniale* (2015), and Norman Ajari, *La Dignité ou la mort. Éthique et politique de la race* (2019).

[88] Pierre Bourdieu and Loïc Wacquant, "The Cunning of Imperialist Reason" (1998 [1997]), and Pierre Bourdieu, *Impérialismes. Circulation internationale des idées et luttes pour l'universel* (2023).

[89] See, for France alone, the references in foonote 1 *supra* and the comprehensive overview by Daniel Sabbagh, "De la race en sciences sociales (France, XXIe siècle). Éléments pour une synthèse comparative" (2023), comprising a 30-page bibliography. Special mention should be made of the works of Norman Ajari, Magali Bessone, Jean-Luc Bonniol, Gwénaële Calvès, Claude-Olivier Doron, Stéphane Dubois, Juliette Galonnier, Abdellalli Hajjat, Emmanuelle Saada, Jean-Frédéric Schaub, and Patrick Simon. See also the works of Manuela Boatca, Christy Kulz, Martina Löw, and Anja Weiß in Germany; Peter Ervik, Lars Jensen, Suvi Keskinen, and Kathrine Vitus in Scandinavia; Anna Curcio, Valeria Deplano, Gaia Giuliani, Cristina Lombardi-Dio, Miguel Mellino, and Tatiana Petrovich-Njegosh in Italy; Ainhoa Nadia Douhaibi, Nicolás Jiménez, and Manuel Angel Río Ruiz in Spain; and Fernando Luís Machado, Maria Manuela Mendes, and Jorge Vala in Portugal.

Problemstellung

theory), relying instead on a tacit agreement with their readers which papers over vexing issues of epistemology, methodology, and theory such as I have tried to clarify in this introduction.

Second caveat: the blueprint of the architecture of racial domination I sketch leaves out important topics that have been and can be best developed by others. In particular, I do not treat the intersectional dynamics of gender and race (two germane embodied forms of division), the formation of ethnoracial subjectivities (of the dominated as well as the dominant), horizontal forms of ethnoracial subordination (internal to and between subordinate categories), and the question of resistance to domination (for reasons discussed in chapter 3, *infra*, pp. 220–2). I center the role of the state as the authority that validates classification and consecrates identities. This means that I give short shrift to other paramount symbolic agencies such as religion, science, and the law, which are diversely embroiled in the constitution of "race" as an operative principle of social vision and division.[90]

Third caveat: as a theoretical work of comparative and historical synthesis, this book relies mostly on single-country case studies. This leaves me open to the fashionable charge of "methodological nationalism" and to the criticism that I do not pay sufficient attention to the circulation of racial constructs, discourses, and technologies of rule across the borders of societies and world regions – especially between metropole and colony.[91] My response is fourfold. First, news of the death of the national society and state are wildly exaggerated and one must beware of not falling into the trap of "methodological globalism," which leads one to ignore the rooted specificities of ethnoracial formations in a given country. Second, save for the minuscule proportion of the world population that has migrated across its native borders (under 4 percent by the most generous estimates), people experience racial domination in the society in which they were born; they are not globe-trotters – unlike scholars who like to think that, like them, everyone spends half of their life in international airports. Third, deep knowledge of national cases is a logical prerequisite for "global studies," lest the latter devolves into platitudes about the interconnectedness of the modern world. Lastly, nothing prevents

---

[90] On the constitutive power of the law, see the fascinating study by Alejandro de la Fuente and Ariela J. Gross, *Becoming Free, Becoming Black: Race, Freedom, and Law in Cuba, Virginia, and Louisiana* (2020); for the same on religion, Kathryn Gin Lum, *Heathen: Religion and Race in American History* (2022).
[91] Andreas Wimmer and Nina Glick Schiller, "Methodological Nationalism and Beyond: Nation-State Building, Migration and the Social Sciences" (2002).

Racial Domination

the agonistic sociology of racial domination from scaling up from the national to the transnational level. Indeed, the conceptual tools it proposes, in particular the pentad of categorization, discrimination, segregation, seclusion, and violence, can serve well to organize just such a move.[92]

Another acknowledgment is in order here: the attentive and knowing reader will not be surprised that the theory I develop bears a "family resemblance" with the varied works of Rogers Brubaker, Kimberly DaCosta, Mara Loveman, Andreas Wimmer, Matt Desmond and Mustafa Emirbayer, and Ellis Monk. The reason is simple: they all draw creatively, among other sources, on the theory of practice and power of Pierre Bourdieu and therefore share the historicist ontology and the cognitivist perspective that anchor his work.[93] They are alert to the merits but also the limits of social constructivism, and they all focus on the fabrication and deployment of social categories instead of taking them for granted. As will become clear throughout the book, I both crosscut and amplify their arguments in a number of places even as I deviate in my analytic strategy. I also depart from them in that I emphasize the special dynamics of symbolic power as the *imposition of classification*, focus on the *embodiment* of social constructs, and give *the state* a larger role in the constitution of collectives. Crucially, I differ in stressing the logical and historical *subsidiarity of race to ethnicity* rather than granting race continued analytical independence *alongside* ethnicity and nation.

The approach adopted in this volume also has affinities with that of John Lie in his bold and brilliant book *Modern Peoplehood* (2004),

---

[92] For model studies of the struggles driving the international circulation of the building blocks of ethnoracial rule, see the journey of categorization and discrimination from the United States to Nazi Germany charted by James Q. Whitman in *Hitler's American Model: The United States and the Making of Nazi Race Law* (2017); the global diffusion of techniques and patterns of segregation traced by Carl Nightingale in *Segregation: A Global History of Divided Cities* (2012); the travels and travails of the "ghetto" as racial trope and imaginary recapitulated by Loïc Wacquant in *The Two Faces of the Ghetto* (2025); and the connections between imperial and metropolitan law enforcement excavated by Julian Go in *Policing Empires: Militarization, Race, and the Imperial Boomerang in Britain and the US* (2023).

[93] Rogers Brubaker, *Ethnicity Without Groups* (2004); Kimberly McClain DaCosta, *Making Multiracials: State, Family, and Market in the Redrawing of the Color Line* (2007); Andreas Wimmer, *Ethnic Boundary Making: Institutions, Power, Networks* (2013); Mara Loveman, *National Colors: Racial Classification and the State in Latin America* (2014); Mustafa Emirbayer and Matthew Desmond, *The Racial Order* (2015); Ellis P. Monk Jr., "Inequality without Groups: Contemporary Theories of Categories, Intersectional Typicality, and the Disaggregation of Difference" (2022).

Problemstellung

which seeks to provide a general account of group-making encompassing race, ethnicity, and nationality, which he sees as fabrications of the modern state. I differ from Lie on three points. First, one needs to move beyond this hallowed triad, and shed the restrictive parameter of "common descent," real or imagined, to incorporate other forms of ethnicity as well as class, gender, region, religion, etc., in the family of collectivities covered by our account. Second, the state is the paramount but not the only symbolic agency involved in the inculcation and enforcement of social vision and division; think of the role of religion in drawing social boundaries and shaping identity even in the post-Enlightenment era.[94] Third, one should incorporate premodern constructs of peoples even at the cost of flirting with conceptual anachronism because they are "good to think with"; they force us out of our analytic comfort zone and make vivid the specificities of group-making in post-imperial liberal-democratic societies.[95]

Relatedly, Ludwig Wittgenstein once remarked that "language is a network of immensely accessible wrong turnings," so we have to exert special care and discipline when it comes to the terms we employ in the course of social analysis. Analytically, I will use the expression *ethnoracial* as a way of constantly reminding the reader – and myself – that what is commonsensically referred to as "race" is but a subtype of ethnicity, albeit a well-disguised one. For stylistic relief, however, I will employ the terms race and racial as shorthand, but always with the silent prefix "ethno." Likewise, I will use the terms discrimination, segregation, ghettoization, etc., strictly in the distinct *technical* senses specified in chapter 2, not in their everyday meanings, which tend to confuse and amalgamate them.

Finally, just to be certain, this book is not intended as a treatise, even in size mini, but as a *provocation by an interloper*. I do not expect to convince the true professionals of "race and racism." But I hope that I will encourage them to boost the analytical clarity, specificity, and coherence of their work – if only by way of defensive reaction.

---

[94] John Lie, *Modern Peoplehood* (2004). Even in aggressively secular societies, such as contemporary France with its notion of *laïcité*, religion continues to play a distinctive role in group-making, if only as a foil at the top and basis for an "anti-politics" at the bottom. Its potency cannot be restricted to premodern societies. See Naomi Davidson, *Only Muslim: Embodying Islam in Twentieth-Century France* (2017); and Z. Fareen Parvez, *Politicizing Islam: The Islamic Revival in France and India* (2017).

[95] Rogers Smith demonstrates the fruitfulness of travelling across a wide geographical and temporal span in *Stories of Peoplehood: The Politics and Morals of Political Membership* (2003).

I hope also that different readers will be stimulated by the different tenets and components that make up the agonistic analytic of race-making and pilfer this or that principle, concept, or argument contained in the book, epistemological, theoretical, or empirical. This is why the four chapters, though conceptually linked and thematically articulated, can be read and evaluated separately. In short, it is not necessary to buy into the neo-Bourdieusian theory of racial domination lock, stock, and barrel to appreciate that it can chart new pathways across an all-too familiar landscape.

Let me close with a preview of the book. My goal is to develop a theory that is problem-centered and not group-centered; articulates the material and the symbolic dimensions of domination; eschews master narratives of irrevocable progress, eternal stagnation, or surreptitious regress alike;[96] and defends and strengthens the *analytic posture* relative to *activist posing*. It leads to an unfashionable political position one may characterize as *radical reformism*, rooted in expanding and exploiting historical possibilities, rather than spinning imaginative improbabilities, and thus equally distant from quietist abdication as from the chic rhetoric of "abolition" – which pertains, at best, to the realm of political uchronia.[97]

In the first chapter, I implement Bachelard's imperatives of rupture and vigilance to effect a series of *epistemic displacements* needed to clear and reset the table for the sociology of ethnoracial domination. The first step is to historicize race-making, which leads to three "origin stories" I call the religious, the colonial, and the scientific. The

---

[96] The critique of the racial "progress paradigm" by self-professed racial radicals discards one telos to adopt another, the narrative of the impossibility of progress, as articulated by Afropessimism (about which see *supra*, pp. 91–9), along with the theoretical promotion of racism to the rank of "fundamental cause" by mere postulation. Victor Erik Ray et al., "Critical Race Theory, Afro-Pessimism, and Racial Progress Narratives" (2107); Louise Seamster and Victor Ray, "Against Teleology in the Study of Race: Toward the Abolition of the Progress Paradigm" (2018).

[97] The paradigm here is Ruth Wilson Gilmore, *Abolition Geography: Essays towards Liberation* (2022). A more tempered position is Tommie Shelby, *The Idea of Prison Abolition* (2022). Both fail to connect with the prosaic realities of the court and the prison. The utter fiasco of "defund the police" in Minneapolis, the city where it was first advocated and best placed to succeed, and elsewhere across the US speaks volume about the lack of social support for, and purchase of, the radical toppling of penal government. The hyperpolicing of poor black districts in the city by a brutal force acting like an army of occupation is a grave and urgent civic issue: tackling it requires more than slogans. See Eamon Whalen, "The Police are Defunding Minneapolis: Two Years since George Floyd was Murdered, the Minneapolis Police Department is a Fiscal Disaster" (2022); Ernesto Londoño, "How 'Defund the Police' Failed" (2023).

Problemstellung

scientific variant emerging in the eighteenth century is unique for coalescing against the backdrop of the doctrine of natural rights and civic equality. This makes racial oppression an incipient institutional anomaly and a political quandary needing to be resolved by elaborating a counter-doctrine of congenital difference justifying inherent inequality and exclusion, the creation of "racial subpersons"[98] – which is not needed in a caste- or estate-based society where social position is ascribed, hierarchical, and static, and the notion of equality absent. The second step involves redrawing the geography of racial rule to join the study of West and East as well as the colonial and the metropolitan domains. This entails building a bridge between the Euro-Atlantic sphere and the Asian-Pacific sphere, in which forms of racialization are at once common, rigid, and suffusive.

A third related move is to provincialize the United States by revoking its status as de facto benchmark for the global sociology of race. The corollary of these geographical moves is to question the exclusive equation of racial domination with the dominion of "whites" or Europeans over "people of color."[99] This, in turn, makes it possible to retrieve and investigate homegrown lineages of ethnoracial classification and stratification in the so-called global South, historical and contemporary lineages that cannot be reduced to mere derivations from the Western traditions. This brings me to the fourth move, whereby I spotlight the epistemological chasm between the righteous logic of the trial and the analytical logic of social science and argue in favor of their watertight separation, notwithstanding the moral magnetism of the former. Indeed, it is the will to indict the West that has precluded Western scholars from investigating ethnoracial domination beyond the West, because they *felt* – I use this verb advisedly – that it would seem to minimize the stranglehold of Western racial rule. But documenting the workings of racial domination in one civilization in no way "exonerates" another, if one is indeed intent on establishing historical culpability.

The fifth imperative is theoretical: it involves the double move of demarcation and repatriation to capture what Pierre Bourdieu calls the

---

[98] Mills, *The Racial Contract*, pp. 16–17. This antinomic creation of natural equality and racial inferiority is what Siep Stuurman calls "the Janus-faced character" of the Enlightenment in *The Invention of Humanity: Equality and Cultural Difference in World History* (2017).

[99] Frank Dikötter illustrates this point with examples from the contemporary US to colonial Rwanda to modern China in "The Racialization of the Globe: An Interactive Interpretation" (2008).

two "orders of objectivity."[100] Demarcation involves breaking with the representations of agents, including racial common sense, to construct an objective model of domination (first order); repatriation consists in bringing back into that model the very subjective representations that had to be swept aside to build it because those representations are an integral part of social reality (second order). This double move is crucial because, unlike other paramount principles of social vision and division, class, gender, age, and nationality, at its root, race is uniquely predicated on cognition: it has *no stable, self-standing, transhistorical material basis*. I develop this argument in the course of disentangling the vexed conceptual relationship between "ethnicity" and "race" to demonstrate that the former encompasses the latter both historically and logically.[101] Race is best construed as a *denegated subtype of ethnicity*, that is, a classificatory principle that claims to be based in the necessity of nature when it is predicated on the arbitrary of culture.

Building on this conceptual foundation, I delineate the *continuum of ethnicity*, based on the quantum of honor, running from "ordinary ethnicity," openly situated on the side of history, to "racialized ethnicity," ostensibly or covertly positioned on the side of biology. I then trace the *diagonal of racialization*, that is, the process whereby malleable and inconsequential ethnicity stamped by aura is turned into rigid and consequential ethnicity stained by stigma. Position and movement along this diagonal are determined by struggles that inscribe race into the flesh (habitus, classification) and into institutions (social space, stratification). The point here is that racialized ethnicity results from the deployment of *symbolic violence in history*, a position that provides a launching pad for my critique of the race primordialism and radical abdication of Afropessimism in the face of racial domination. This brings up the relationship between the salience and the consequentiality of race, two properties pertaining to classification and stratification, respectively, that are often conflated in social analysis. I show that they can vary independently from each other and

---

[100] Bourdieu, *Le Sens pratique*.

[101] The historical sequence runs roughly from ethnolinguistic, ethnoregional, and ethnoreligious to ethnoracial proper and ethnonational. The point is that ethnic modalities of grouping existed well before their racial cousin showed up on the scene. Stuart Hall argues for the opposite historical sequence: race as color distinction emerges first, between the Renaissance and the Enlightenment, and ethnicity arises second, during the twentieth century. But was "race" not a cultural reading of skin tone, that is, an ethnicity based on phenotype? See Stuart Hall, *The Fateful Triangle: Race, Ethnicity, Nation* (2017).

Problemstellung

then return to the question of the foundations and principles of variation of "groupness" with a framework that balances the structuralist and the constructivist moment of race-making.

The second chapter dissects and deploys the *five elementary forms of racial domination*: categorization (comprising classification, prejudice, bias, and stigma), discrimination (unwarranted differential treatment and disparate impact), segregation (differential allocation in social and physical space), seclusion (entailing institutional parallelism and covering the ghetto, the camp and the reservation), and violence (of both the expressive and instrumental varieties). I introduce conceptual distinctions that allow us to examine the internal intricacy and layering of each form, such as the plural bases of ethnoracial classification, the vexed relationship between disparity and discrimination, the fivefold dimensions of segregation, the Janus-faced character of ghettoization, and the varied paths of escalation of violence. I disclose the array of mechanisms that sustain each of these forms and link them together, loosely or tightly, into a given regime of racial domination. This schema can be used to trace the trajectory of a group over time or across space, and thus to draw its historical *profile* of domination; to compare two groups in the same or different societies; or to dissect one form, say stigma or expressive violence, across groups, time periods, and societies. All told, racial domination emerges as a *multi-layered and architectured phenomenon* calling for meticulous unpacking made difficult by such lumpy notions as "structural racism."

Having laid bare the structural complexity, functional variability, and causal multiplicity of ethnoracial domination, I turn to the articulation of race, economy, and state. I stress the role of the state as *paramount race-making institution*: as the fount of public honor and dishonor, it stamps habitus, shapes social space, and organizes physical space, as well as ensures their correspondence which grants race its doxicity and facticity. Put differently, the state sanctifies racial classification and molds racial stratification, thus contributing decisively to group-making along ethnoracial lines. Turning to the economy, I scrutinize the fabulously fashionable notion of "racial capitalism" and find it in serious need of conceptual elaboration and historical specification. One of the flaws of that concept is indeed that it masks the diversity of regimes of racial domination behind the seemingly obvious and falsely universal adjective "racial."[102]

---

[102] This is typically achieved by tacitly treating as universal the US categorical framework of racial classification and by failing to articulate different forms of stratification,

I also inspect, and express reservations about, the notion of "structural racism," not because racial domination is not entrenched and ramifying – I would obviously not be writing this book if I believed so – but because that notion is too mushy and malleable and typically invoked rhetorically without being put to work analytically, so that it creates more trouble than it resolves. I flesh out my misgivings by considering the application of "structural racism" to the workings of the criminal justice system and the real-life possibilities of reforming a system that is not one. I close with an extended consideration of race-making as a poisonous form of group-making, the process whereby a mental category is turned into a "practical group" and thence into an "instituted group." I propose that we use Bourdieu's agonistic theory of collectivity formation to articulate the analytic of racial domination and, conversely, that we draw on the sociology of race to throw light on the formation of social collectives generically.[103]

Having laid out my framework, I turn to case studies that deploy the principles and concepts of the agonistic sociology of race-making to fashion novel interpretations of two key periods and institutions of ethnoracial domination in the United States: "Jim Crow" in the agrarian South and hyperincarceration in the postindustrial metropolis.[104] In chapter 3, I break down the virulent regime of white supremacy colloquially known as Jim Crow into its constituent elements: an inflexible, dichotomous, descent-based classification system, projected onto three orders of stratification, economic (exploitation), social (subordination), and civic (exclusion), and upheld by the constant threat and suffusive delivery of multifaceted violence.

If there ever was a regime of ethnoracial domination that deserves the tag of "structural racism," Jim Crow in the US South after the Civil War is definitely it. Historian George Fredrickson counts it among what he calls "overtly racist regimes," along with Nazi Germany and South African apartheid.[105] I prefer to eschew moralizing labels

---

as illustrated by Prentiss Dantzler et al., "Introduction: What Does Racial Capitalism Have to Do with Cities and Communities?" (2022).

[103] I formulated that agenda, starting from class-making, in "Symbolic Power and Group-Making: On Pierre Bourdieu's Reframing of Class" (2013).

[104] Scholars and activists generally refer to the accelerating rise and extraordinary rates of incarceration in the United States after the mid-1970s as "mass incarceration" (see David Garland, *Mass Imprisonment: Social Causes and Consequences* [2001]). I find the notion obfuscating and prefer the concept of "hyperincarceration" for reasons discussed in chapter 4, pp. 284–5.

[105] George Fredrickson, *Racism* (2002), pp. 2–3.

Problemstellung

and will speak instead of a regime of *extreme ethnoracial domination*: extreme for the salience, pervasiveness, and consequentiality of naturalized ethnicity as social principle of social vision and division. The Jim Crow South is nearly always included in comparative-historical studies of racial inequality, most often alongside South Africa and Brazil, and typically to spotlight its unparalleled brutality. It is not by happenstance that the state ideologues and legal experts of the Third Reich studied closely and borrowed heavily from Jim Crow rules concerning citizenship and racial mixing to devise the anti-Jewish legislation of Nazi Germany. Indeed, the Nazis rejected some American racial practices because they found them excessively harsh.[106]

But to assert that Jim Crow is a case of "structural racism" tells us just about nothing. It stops the inquiry dead in its tracks in that it posits peremptorily that we already grasp the nature of the social constellation at hand, which we do not except in the inchoate and incoherent form of scholarly or ordinary common sense. It does not disclose what racial categorization this regime deploys, what modalities of racial domination it articulates, and what social mechanisms of production, reproduction, and transformation governed its rise, bloom, and eventual demise. And, crucially, "structural racism," which can refer to any ingrained system of racial domination, from mild to severe, does not begin to convey the *ramifying violence* that sustained a regime that never was legitimate in the eyes of the dominated. Violence under Jim Crow was not just Weberian but also Foucauldian: it spread through the social body as through capillaries and irrigated the depths of subaltern subjectivity.

Following Bachelard, the task of chapter 3 is to fill these gaps by replacing the folk notion with a robust analytic concept of Jim Crow as *caste terrorism* that specifies its constituent parts, their structural articulation, their functional linkages, and the social experiences they spawned. For this I rely on a close inductive reading of monographs on Jim Crow, so-called, by leading historians of the American South

---

[106] On the American South as legal blueprint for Nazi racial rule, read the astonishing study by James Q. Whitman, *Hitler's American Model: The United States and the Making of Nazi Race Law* (2017). On the comparison of Jim Crow with other regimes of racial domination, see Carl Degler, *Neither Black Nor White: Slavery and Race Relations in Brazil and the United States* (1971); Marvin Harris, *Patterns of Race in the Americas* (1980); George M. Fredrickson, *White Supremacy: A Comparative Study of American and South African History* (1982); John Cell, *The Origins of Segregation in South Africa and the American South* (1982); and Antony W. Marx, *Making Race and Nation: A Comparison of the United States, South Africa, and Brazil* (1998).

along with the field studies conducted by the anthropologists of the "caste and class school" led by W. Lloyd Warner in the interwar years. This reading is informed by the diagonal of racialization, the pentad of ethnoracial domination, and the duo of classification and stratification. It gets us started on the way to constructing our scientific object instead of accepting it ready-made from social reality. It focuses on the *what* that historians overlook, or assume known, when they rush to study the when, where, and how of Jim Crow.[107]

Jim Crow customs, laws, and violence ensured the *total domination* of a dishonored descent-based category and (re)produced a steep and rigid stratification order disallowing all ethnic promotion under the principle I call "less racial eligibility," according to which the lowest white was statutorily and irrevocably higher than the highest black. I articulate an ideal type of Jim Crow as composed of three building blocks corresponding to the three faces of domination. First, *exploitation*: sharecropping tied blacks to the land, wrung economic value out of family labor, and prevented African Americans from gaining the minimal geographical and occupational mobility needed to escape debt peonage, effectively consigning them to "neo-slavery."[108] Next, *subordination*: the "racial etiquette" descended from the days of slavery and institutional bifurcation into "colored" and "white" tracks combined to extract deference, repudiate reciprocity, and demand the universal subservience of blacks to whites in everyday interactions. Finally, *exclusion*: denial of access to the ballot box and to the criminal court entrenched black economic exploitation, social subordination, and vulnerability to white abuse by depriving them of the means of collective voice and legal redress; it ensured their utter powerlessness in the face of stringent domination.[109]

But African Americans did not spontaneously acquiesce to the dictates of Jim Crow and so these three structural components had to be glued together and safeguarded by *terroristic violence*. By terror-

[107] C. Vann Woodward, "*Strange Career* Critics: Long May They Persevere" (1988), p. 857, and Jennifer Ritterhouse, "The Etiquette of Race Relations in the Jim Crow South" (2007), p. 32.

[108] This economic regime is summed up by the two formulas, "Cheap cotton depends on cheap niggers" and "I will murder you if you don't do that work," as told by Douglas A. Blackmon in his Pulitzer-prize winning book, *Slavery by Another Name: The Re-Enslavement of Black Americans from the Civil War to World War II* (2008).

[109] According to Orlando Patterson (*Slavery and Social Death: A Comparative Study* 2018 [1982], pp. 2–13), the three constituent elements of slavery are total powerlessness, generalized dishonor, and natal alienation. Jim Crow reestablished and enforced the first two.

Problemstellung

istic I mean violence looming over every social exchange and that may strike at any moment; violence that instills fear into members of its target category by mere virtue of membership; violence that communicates a political message – in this case, the imperiousness of white rule. There thus exists an intelligible relationship between the categorical nature of the racial boundary patrolled and the instruments used to enforce it: white obsession with purity explains the relentless press for social bifurcation and feeds the brutality needed to maintain it.

In the fourth chapter, I turn to the stupendous overrepresentation of African Americans behind bars that fueled the drive to hyperincarceration in the United States over the half-century following the "race riots" of the 1960s.[110] Here again, analytical progress is contingent on epistemological rupture and conceptual construction. I break out of the "crime-and-punishment" paradigm to reckon the extrapenological function of the criminal legal apparatus as instrument for the marking and management of dispossessed and dishonored categories. I place the prison of the postindustrial era in the multisecular *historical sequence of "peculiar institutions"* that have shouldered the task of defining and confining African Americans since colonial days, including slavery, Jim Crow terrorism, and the ghetto of the industrial metropolis.

The term "peculiar institution" was coined by Southern politician John C. Calhoun and used by Southern advocates of slavery starting in the 1830s in response to the abolitionists led by William Lloyd Garrison, Frederick Douglass, and Angelina Grimké. It intimated that human bondage in America was a benign form of paternalism that benefited the slaves and formed the bedrock of an organic civilization superior to the individualistic and competitive society of the North. The historian Kenneth Stampp made the expression famous with his landmark monograph, *The Peculiar Institution: Slavery in the Ante-Bellum South* (1956), in which he inverted its meaning to imply strange, abnormal, deviant.[111] I *pluralize* the expression to capture

---

[110] The basic facts of the fantastical rise and racial slant of incarceration after the mid-1970s are recounted by Bruce Western, *Punishment and Inequality in America* (2006). The backdrop of the *longue durée* is set by Elizabeth Hinton and DeAnza Cook, "The Mass Criminalization of Black Americans: A Historical Overview" (2012).

[111] Kenneth C. Stampp, *The Peculiar Institution: Slavery in the Ante-Bellum South* (1989 [1956]). For an assessment of the book's boldness and continuing pertinence, read William Fitzhugh Brundage, "American Slavery: A Look Back at *The Peculiar Institution*" (1997).

the full lineage of institutions that have shaped blackness as the foundation of ethnoracial vision and division in America over four centuries.

Against the facile thesis, popularized by civil-rights attorney Michelle Alexander in her cultic book *The New Jim Crow*, that "mass incarceration" was a revival of the regime of caste domination established in the postbellum South,[112] I show that the chief engine propelling the rise of the penal state was the *collapse of the ghetto* as an organizational device for the joint economic exploitation and social ostracization of a reviled population in the city.[113] I build on the characterization of urban seclusion developed in chapter 2 to show how the ghetto imploded once it lost its role as a reservoir of unskilled labor power with the onset of deindustrialization. This implosion spawned a dual sociospatial formation: on the one hand, flourishing black middle-class districts reverted to segregation as the chief modality of racial domination; on the other, a new contraption I call the *hyperghetto* combined subordination and exclusion but forsook exploitation. Doubly segregated by race and class, devoid of an economic function and stripped of the communal institutions that acted as a protective buffer during the heyday of the ghetto, the hyperghetto entrapped the precarious fractions of the black proletariat – the precariat – rendered redundant and tagged as deviant, devious, and dangerous by the demonic discourse of the urban "underclass."[114]

The hyperghetto served as staging ground for the dramaturgy and as target for the policy of penalization of poverty launched in the stream of the backlash against black civic incorporation and the urban uprisings of the tumultuous 1960s. The rolling out of bellicose policing and aggressive prosecution bypassed the new black middle-class districts to concentrate on the dilapidated vestiges of the historic Black Belt. This spatial selectivity explains why the drivers of hyper-incarceration are class first, race second, and class inside of race, making the penal state of the fin de siècle both a *race-making and a*

---

[112] Michelle Alexander, *The New Jim Crow: Mass Incarceration in the Age of Colorblindness* (2010).

[113] Remarkably, the term "ghetto" does not appear *once* in the 465 pages of the thorough report on the roots and implications of carceral expansion commissioned by the National Research Council and written by two dozen of the country's leading students of imprisonment. See Jeremy Travis et al. (eds.), *The Growth of Incarceration in the United States: Exploring Causes and Consequences* (2014).

[114] Wacquant, *The Invention of the "Underclass."* The notion of "precariat" is developed on pp. 162–8.

class-splitting institution. The penalization of the black precariat was further accelerated by a series of changes that "prisonized" the ghetto and "ghettoized" the prison, creating a carceral continuum anchored by the functional convergence, structural continuity, and cultural syncretism between the barren hyperghetto and the booming carceral archipelago. Thus, in every major postindustrial city, prisoners churn in and out from the same dilapidated and despoiled neighborhoods in an endless circulus that entrenches their material and symbolic marginality. Crucially then, the fourth "peculiar institution" is not the prison but the organizational contraption born of its enmeshment with the hyperghetto.

The hyper-penalization of the vestiges of the dark ghetto did not just revivify the association of African-American masculinity with violent criminality first established a century earlier. It extended "the condemnation of blackness" in the lower regions of social and physical space.[115] It extruded convicts and former convicts from the civic compact by excluding them from college education subsidies, social redistribution via welfare and public housing, and the voting booth. The penal state thus recast American citizenship around a series of homologous oppositions, middle class/"underclass," righteous/criminal, deserving/undeserving, pure/polluted, suburbs/"inner city" roughly aligned with the white/black binary. Punishment and place thus converge to bolster race as dishonor, in America as in all advanced societies where dispossessed and defamed neighborhoods are the priority targets of the police, courts, and prison.

I hope that the theoretical framework I bring to bear upon two eras of racial domination in the United States, the half-century following Reconstruction in the South and the half-century following the peaking of the Civil Rights Movement in the North, provokes sufficient *analytic estrangement* from the conventional ways of approaching Jim Crow and racialized hyperincarceration to make novel facets of these phenomena come into full view and thus to stimulate new research on the nexus of naturalized ethnicity and violence, social and state. I hope also that, upon sifting through these two case studies in two ages of ethnoracial exploitation, subordination, and exclusion, the reader will see the benefits of historicizing and forsaking the logic of trial; disaggregating forms of racial domination and specifying their mechanisms; and focusing on the institutions that secrete and

---

[115] The expression is that of Khalil Gibran Muhammad, *The Condemnation of Blackness: Race, Crime, and the Making of Modern Urban America* (2010).

enforce "race" as a distinct social principle of vision and division, rather than taking it as a given. If there is one epistemological lesson to gain, it is that the urge to denunciate must be superseded by the wish to explicate to create an analytical synergy between theoretical model-building and empirical casing.

In the conclusion to the book, I bring the neo-Bourdieusian theory of racial domination to bear on the question of racial justice. Autonomizing and prioritizing the scientific over the civic moment in knowledge production does not imply indifference or irrelevance to the ongoing struggles to reduce or erase ethnoracial denigration and disparity. If I argue for the strict separation of the analytics from the politics of race, it is not to deny the latter but to *reengage it* with an improved model of social reality and of its mechanisms of reproduction that can facilitate derailing them. Here I make mine these words of Émile Durkheim: "We would not deem our research worth an hour's labor if it were only of speculative interest. If we carefully separate the theoretical problems from the practical problems, it is not to neglect the latter: on the contrary, it is to put us in a position to better resolve them."[116]

To facilitate the rejoining of the sociological and the political, I argue that we must recognize the *varieties of regimes of racial domination* instead of lumping them together under a single label like "structural racism," which, precisely, hides structural heterogeneity. To organize this variety, I craft an ideal-typical opposition between "genuine race-divided societies," in which ethnoracial splitting is axial to the social order, and "societies with race," where it is present but ancillary to the formation of social space, the state, and civic subjectivity. We can then deploy the pentad of ethnoracial domination to chart five targets for policies and movements in favor of racial justice: reduce the negative valence of classification, fight discrimination, undermine segregation, prevent seclusion, and deter violence.

Approached through the dialectic of classification (symbolic salience or recognition) and stratification (material consequence or distribution), there emerge three paths to racial justice: the equalization of life chances by reducing ethnic disparities and penalties; destigmatization, which turns negative into positive symbolic capital; and deracialization proper, which combines equalization and destigmatization to erode and possibly efface the symbolic and material foundations of

---

[116] Émile Durkheim, *De la division du travail social* (1995b [1893]), p. xxxix.

Problemstellung

ethnicity itself. The neo-Bourdieusian sociology of racial domination ultimately gives us tools with which to build a bridge between the positive and the normative, social science and the civic good, inquiry and action.

1
Reframing Racial Domination

> Nothing is more important than the formation of fictional concepts, which teach us at last to understand our own.
> Ludwig Wittgenstein, *Vermischte Bemerkungen*, 1944

Race is arguably the single most troublesome and volatile category of the social sciences in the early twenty-first century – as Zora Neale Hurston put it, it is "like fire on the tongues of men." Do you put it in scare quotes or not? Do you pair it with ethnicity to specify its scope or extend its reach? Do you use it as a substantive (as if it were a "thing" out there in the world) or as an adjective (racial, racialized, racialist, or the accusatory racist) attached to a perception, belief, action, or institution? Is race premised on descent, skin tone, or other phenotypical markers? But what of such varied social properties as legal status, region, language, migration, and religion that have also long served as vectors of racialization?[1]

---

[1] The luminous but little-known essay by Charles Wagley, "On the Concept of Social Race in the Americas" (1965 [1958]), suffices to demonstrate the variability of ethnoracial foundations. For empirical support from diverse countries, see Nadia Y. Kim, *Imperial Citizens: Koreans and Race from Seoul to LA* (2008); John Lie, *Multiethnic Japan* (2009); Kristen Ghodsee, *Muslim Lives in Eastern Europe: Gender, Ethnicity, and the Transformation of Islam in Postsocialist Bulgaria* (2009); Lahra Smith, *Making Citizens in Africa: Ethnicity, Gender, and National Identity in Ethiopia* (2013); Edward Telles, *Pigmentocracies: Ethnicity, Race, and Color in Latin America* (2014); Patrick Wolfe, *Traces of History: Elementary Structures of Race* (2016); Rhiannon Noel Welch, *Vital Subjects: Race and Biopolitics in Italy* (2016); Giovanni Picker, *Racial Cities: Governance and the Segregation of Romani People in Urban Europe* (2017); Peter Hervik,

Reframing Racial Domination

What is the relationship between the social understanding of race and its putative genetic and medical designations, which are making a major comeback in the tow of the genomic revolution and its technological offshoots?[2] Is race a self-propelled social force or does it derive from other causal powers (for instance, class or nationality)? A recent notion coeval with modernity or one that has been lurking around for millennia? A historical construct of utility in certain societies, such as imperial powers and their colonies, or an abstract construct of universal reach? Most urgently still, is it a "sin of the West" (linked to transatlantic slavery), as proclaimed by many race scholars and activists, or does it operate across civilizations and within subordinate populations themselves? The principles enunciated in the prologue and guiding the conceptual autopsy of the "underclass" as racialized category elaborated in my book *The Invention of the "Underclass"* may help us gain some clarity and traction on these issues.[3] They mandate epistemological clarification, conceptual control, and analytic specification – elaborating the most articulate, parsimonious, and fruitful constructs for sociohistorical inquiry, ones that can claim semantic clarity, logical coherence, and heuristic power.

These principles goad me to sketch a theoretical framework anchored by four notions: the continuum of ethnicity, the diagonal of racialization, the dialectic of ethnoracial classification (in the symbolic realm) and stratification (in the material realm), and the pentad of elementary forms of racial domination: categorization, discrimination, segregation, seclusion, and violence. This framework proposes that racial domination is a *multilayered and architectured phenomenon* that calls for analytical disaggregation and then reassembly. It further reveals how notions that have recently gained wide scholarly currency and political popularity, such as "structural racism" and "racial capitalism," may create more trouble than they resolve. But, before we get there, we must first effect a series of *reframings* and reset the analytical

---

Racialization, Racism, and Anti-Racism in the Nordic Countries (2019); Yasmeen Abu-Laban and Abigail B. Bakan, *Israel, Palestine and the Politics of Race: Exploring Identity and Power in a Global Context* (2019); and Sylvia Zamora, *Racial Baggage: Mexican Immigrants and Race Across the Border* (2022).

[2] Dorothy Roberts, *Fatal Invention: How Science, Politics, and Big Business Re-Create Race in the Twenty-First Century* (2011); Rogers Brubaker, *Grounds for Difference* (2015), chapter 2.

[3] Loïc Wacquant, *The Invention of the "Underclass": A Study in the Politics of Knowledge* (2022), especially pp. 122–31 and 150–67, where I propose a set of criteria to assess the validity of concepts pertaining to semantics, logics, and heuristics.

parameters of race-making as a particular form of group-making. This is the agenda of this chapter.

1. Historicize

First principle, *historicize*. The trouble with race in the West did not start this or the previous century. It is coextensive with the life of the modern notion, which, from its coalescence in the mid-eighteenth century, has constantly trafficked in the *complicity between common sense and science*.[4] The naturalists of that era, who concocted the idea that humanity could be divided into biophysical categories – Carolus Linnaeus's four races, white, black, yellow, red, corresponding to the four humors of the body, phlegm, black bile, yellow bile and blood, to the four natural elements of air, earth, fire, and water, and to the four continents of the earth, which survive under various guises to this day – that would later be decreed inherently unequal by Joseph-Arthur de Gobineau and his followers, were both codifying an extensive array of ordinary premodern perceptions and participating in a scientific revolution that, for the first time, was posing the question of how to fit together human diversity and hierarchy.[5]

That originary confusion between common sense and scholarship has continued into the present and is embedded in the conventional coupling of "race and ethnicity." Whenever social scientists deploy this doxic duet, *they endorse and amplify the defining symbolic effect of race*, which is, precisely, the mystified and mystifying belief that it is fundamentally different from ethnicity (about which more *infra*, pp. 81–5).

---

[4] In *Corps noirs et médecins blancs. La fabrique du préjugé racial, XIXe–XXe siècles* (2022), Delphine Peiretti-Courtis shows how, starting in the late eighteenth century, medical research elevated to the rank of scientific truth common prejudice about black bodies, including "intellectual inferiority, physical resistance, the predominance of the emotions and hypersexuality."

[5] Ivan Hannaford, *Race: The History of an Idea in the West* (1996); Anthony Pagden, *The Burdens of Empire: 1539 to the Present* (2015), especially chapter 3. A precursor of the modern notion of race as dividing practice, East and West, is found in religion, Shinto and Christian, respectively: Frank Dikötter, *The Discourse of Race in Modern China* (1992); George M. Fredrickson, *Racism: A Short History* (2002). Religion, not race (i.e., the belief in the innate inferiority of black people), was the criterion that initially codified the enslavement of Africans for the transatlantic trade: they belonged to "pagan nations." On the question of diversity versus hierarchy in this period, read Justin E. H. Smith, *Nature, Human Nature, and Human Difference: Race in Early Modern Philosophy* (2015).

Reframing Racial Domination

The same applies to the pairing of "race and racism": what is race if not a figment of the collective belief in its autonomous existence, that is, racism, so why the duplication? And the pluralization of the category as with the seemingly self-evident and endlessly multiplying "racisms" only compounds the trouble. This dubious commerce between common sense and science has gone on uninterrupted for three centuries, so that countless presociological tenets about "race" survive, indeed thrive, in contemporary social science. One example is the commonly propounded notion that race everywhere pervades every nook and cranny of society and subjectivity, leaving no social relation and existential domain untouched. Inside too many racial constructivists, there is a racial essentialist struggling to get out.[6]

To historicize means recognizing the multiple roots of the phenomenon. Roughly put, there are three schools on the origins of "race" as a category of mental and social organization in the West, which, for convenience, I will call the religious, the colonial, and the scientific, each with a different chronology (fifteenth, sixteenth and mid-eighteenth century, respectively).[7] The difference between them turns on how authors define the term and when they decide that the phenomenon has crystallized.

The *religious thesis*, grounded in the history of the relations between Christianity, Judaism, and Islam, contends that racialization emerged

---

[6] A vivid illustration is Howard Winant, *The World is a Ghetto: Race and Democracy since World War II* (2001), for whom race is "a flexible dimension of human variety that is valuable and permanent"; "race is present everywhere ... Race has shaped the modern economy and nation-state. It has permeated all available social identities, cultural forms, and systems of signification"; it is "infinitely incarnated in institution and personality"; "it is the foundation of every dream of liberation ... It is a fundamental social fact! To say that race endures is to say that the modern world endures" (pp. xiv, 1, 6). But being everywhere means that race is nowhere in particular, which makes it difficult to attack politically. Also, the notion that "the world is a ghetto" not only denies the specificity of the ghetto as a sociospatial mechanism of ethnoracial domination (distinct from discrimination and segregation, as we shall see *infra*, pp. 137–9, 305–10); it implies, curiously, that the ghetto has no exterior and therefore that the dominant reside within it.

[7] Banton proposes a different typology and chronology in *Racial Theories* (1987), in which race refers to lineage from the sixteenth to the eighteenth century; physical type during the nineteenth century; and minority status in the twentieth. The claim that race was an operative category in European antiquity does not have many followers but it has been forcefully formulated by Benjamin Isaac, *The Invention of Racism in Classical Antiquity* (2013). A stimulative discussion of the temporalization of race is Jean-Frédéric Schaub, "Temps et race" (2018), who discusses five possible chronologies and settles for what I call the religious thesis.

in the fifteenth century, with roots extending back to the Crusades of the eleventh century when Christian kingdoms sent military missions to free the Holy Land from Islamic control.[8] In the late medieval period, as part of a societal drift toward intolerance against marginal categories, Christian attitudes toward Jews hardened and became more hostile.[9] Jews were castigated as a deicide people, associated with the devil and witchcraft as well as perceived as a spiritual threat. They were made the scapegoat for a range of social ills and disruptions, such as the Black Death in the middle of the fourteenth century, and they were targeted for confiscation, persecution, and massacres. They were expelled from England in 1290, France in 1394, and Spain, Sicily, and Portugal in the 1490s unless they converted to Christianity. Muslims and Jews could convert but then the Spanish doctrine of *"limpieza de sangre,"* first enacted in 1449, held that their blood was malefically impure. It followed that the *moriscos* (converts from Islam) and *conversos* (converts from Judaism) were always suspected of secretly holding on to their religion, thus endangering the Church from within.[10] That became the basis for official discrimination and exclusion. The essentialist notion that one was Jewish or Moorish by ancestry rather than faith marks the onset of racialization as representation and practice. Medieval antisemitism is the crucible of the racial gaze that would later be directed toward Africans and Amerindians.

The provocative book by Jean-Frédéric Schaub and Silvia Sebastiani, *Race et histoire dans les sociétés occidentales (XVe–XVIIIe siècle)*, adds a twist to the thesis of the religious roots of race.[11] It argues that the naturalization of social difference that informed the Iberian concern for "blood purity" was itself based on an obsession with the intergenerational transmission of social properties through lineal descent marking social eminence (following the medieval

---

[8] Francisco Bethencourt, *Racisms: From the Crusades to the Twentieth Century* (2013), pp. 11–62. Geraldine Heng also dates religious racism from the twelfth century in *The Invention of Race in the European Middle Ages* (2018).

[9] Robert I. Moore, *The Formation of a Persecuting Society: Authority and Deviance in Western Europe 950–1250* (1987). Moore brings under the same historical canopy the Holy Inquisition, the expropriation and mass murder of Jews, and the quarantining of lepers.

[10] Gregory B. Kaplan tracks the antecedents and promulgation of the statutes on blood purity in "The Inception of *limpieza de sangre* (Purity of Blood) and its Impact in Medieval and Golden Age Spain" (2012).

[11] Jean-Frédéric Schaub and Silvia Sebastiani, *Race et histoire dans les sociétés occidentales (XVe–XVIIIe siècle)* (2021).

invention of the genealogical tree). Belief in the hereditary character of the qualities said to distinguish noble lineages from commoners justified the privilege granted to certain families, even when their social position was acquired rather than inherited, as with the berobed nobility (resulting from the purchase of an office) and the anomaly of adoption. In other words, the institution of the nobility was one of the matrices of racialization, albeit of the social superior rather than inferior.

The second thesis associates the birth of "race" with the dawn of Western *colonialism* and transatlantic *slavery* and often chooses Christopher Columbus's discovery of a sea route to the Americas in 1492 as its inaugural date – a few years later, Vasco de Gama would sail to India. The conquest of the ocean spawned the conquest of new territories and thus new peoples.[12] At first, the European view of these strange populations was polarized between primal innocence and subhumanity. It pictured "the Indian as either a noble savage who could be civilized or a wild beast who could at best be tamed and at worst should be exterminated."[13] But they were not seen as fundamentally different biologically and psychologically from Europeans. The great Valladolid *disputatio* between Juan Gínes de Sepúlveda and Bartolomé de la Casas in 1550 as to whether Amerindians were endowed with reason was decided in the positive. The cleavage that mattered most then was still that between pagans and infidels and it was believed that Indians could be brought to Christ.

This changed dramatically with the mass deportation of African slaves to the Americas, which swiftly reconfigured the totality of economic, political, and cultural relations across the Atlantic sphere. According to Winthrop Jordan's influential tome, *White Over Black*, in the North American colonies, enslavement was motivated by the preexisting notion, informed by early English views, that Africans were constitutively different, defective, savage, and libidinous. William Cohen makes a similar argument in *The French Encounter with Africans*: negative stereotypes shaped the relations of the French with blacks in Africa, in the slave colonies of the West Indies, and

---

[12] Anthony Pagden, *Peoples and Empires: A Short History of European Migration, Exploration, and Conquest, from Greece to the Present* (2001), chapter 4. Mahmood Mamdani chooses 1492 as the birthdate of the nation-state and political modernity, a birth marked not by tolerance but by violent conquest, in *Neither Settler nor Native: The Making and Unmaking of Permanent Minorities* (2020), pp. 2–4.
[13] Frederickson, *A Short History of Racism*, p. 36.

in the metropole.¹⁴ Race and transatlantic slavery were thus coeval, with the former shaping the latter. More recently, this argument has been taken up and expanded by scholars who make the colonization of the Americas the historical inauguration of Western modernity as characterized, not by freedom and tolerance, but by racial bondage and violence.¹⁵

There are three problems with this thesis. First, slavery is not itself a racial institution; it is an institution of extreme domination and most slave systems in history have featured masters and slaves from the same ethnicity.¹⁶ Second, slavery served, among many functions, as a mode of forced labor recruitment in the Americas that needed no justification in an age where bonded labor was the norm. Third, slaves were purchased in West Africa because that was the only large-scale pool of bonded people commercially available and African slaves gradually became cheaper than English indentured servants, their only plausible alternative, as the transatlantic trade developed and attempts to enslave Amerindians en masse failed. Race as the belief in the inborn closure and inferiority of a human grouping was not the cause but the *consequence* of the association of blackness with the degraded status of the slave.¹⁷

There is yet another historical twist to the thesis of the colonial origins of "race": Europe's first settler colony was not in the exterior but in the interior of the continent, in the form of the English conquest of Ireland and its policy of "plantation" from 1540 to 1660.¹⁸ Under that policy, inspired by the Roman model in antiquity, English, Scottish, and Welsh protestants were sent to take over and farm the land of the Gaelic Irish – colony comes from the Latin *colonum*, which means

---

[14] Winthrop D. Jordan, *White over Black: American Attitudes toward the Negro, 1550–1812* (1968); William B. Cohen, *The French Encounter with Africans: White Response to Blacks, 1530–1880* (1980).

[15] Mamdani's *Neither Settler nor Native* is the strongest case made so far. Aníbal Quijano insists on what he calls "the coloniality of power" in "Coloniality and Modernity/Rationality" (2007). See the germane argument of Sylvia Wynter in "1492: A New Worldview" (1996).

[16] Orlando Patterson, *Slavery and Social Death: A Comparative Study* (2018 [1982]), pp. 176–7.

[17] Edmund Morgan, *American Slavery, American Freedom: The Ordeal of Colonial Virginia* (1975); Barbara Fields, "Slavery, Race and Ideology in the United States of America" (1990); Schaub and Sebastiani, *Race et histoire dans les sociétés occidentales (XVe–XVIIIe siècle)*.

[18] Jane Ohlmeyer, "Conquest, Civilization, Colonization: Ireland, 1540–1660" (2016).

farmer. Calls to civilize and Anglicize the island go back to the twelfth century and the first English settlers established themselves on its west coast in the thirteenth century. But it took until the sixteenth century for colonization to effect the wholesale transfer of land from catholic to protestant hands and to impose English legal, administrative, and economic structures as well as English language and culture. Over time, English occupation grew harsher through the prism of racialist thinking that portrayed the Irish as incorrigible "beasts in the shape of men," and so it was punctuated by genocidal massacres that anticipated those committed later on the African and American continents.[19]

The *scientific* origin story focuses on the development and diffusion of scholarly knowledge about the different races said to compose humanity in the eighteenth century as "the great age of classification" during which natural historians strove to "lay the grid of reason over the unwieldy stuff of nature."[20] At first, the term "race" was used in reference to noble lineages and to animal husbandry. Now it came to drive the distribution of humans into categories grounded not in religion but in biology. The taxonomist Carolus Linnaeus, the cosmologist Georges-Louis Buffon, the naturalist Johann Friedrich Blumenbach, the botanist Jean-Baptiste Lamarck, and the comparative anatomist Georges Cuvier all elaborated racial taxonomies variously based on complexion, body type, aesthetics, lushness of the male beard, geography, etc.[21] These did not necessarily entail an explicit rank-order (although Bernier described the non-European races as "*vilains animaux*").

---

[19] Ben Kiernan, *Blood and Soil: A World History of Genocide and Extermination from Sparta to Darfur* (2007), chapter 5, p. 210.

[20] Londa Shiebinger, *Nature's Body: Gender in the Making of Modern Science* (1993), p. 117. A precursor was physician François Bernier, who produced the first systematic racial taxonomy in his "New Divisions of the Earth by the Different Species or Races of Humans who Inhabit Them" (1684). His classification separated humans not by color but by facial features, especially hair and lips. He also did not single out a specific European race; rather he lumped Europeans with North Africans and West and South Asians as well as Mongols, Chinese, and Japanese. Siep Stuurman, "François Bernier and the Invention of Racial Classification" (2000). The leading historian of European expansion Anthony Pagden puts the birth of racism even later, in the mid-nineteenth century in the tow of positivism. Pagden, *The Burdens of Empire: 1539 to the Present*, pp. 97–8.

[21] For a thorough discussion of these and other theories of race as nobility and husbandry, read Claude-Olivier Doron, *L'Homme altéré. Races et dégénérescence (XVIIe–XIXe siècles)* (2016).

It would fall to nineteenth-century scholars to articulate a clear hierarchy. Although Arthur de Gobineau's 1853 *Essai sur l'inégalité des races humaines* did not bother to define the notion of race, it clearly asserted the primacy of the white over the black and yellow races. The American "school of ethnology," which flourished in the mid-nineteenth century in defense of Southern slavery, added to hierarchy the idea of the natural "repugnance of some human races to mix with others" and asserted, rather conveniently, that mulattoes born of the union of white and black were infertile and fated to die young so that mixing the two races would lead to their joint extinction.[22] Racial anthropology spread and bloomed across Western nations, creating a veritable "scientific international" legitimating ethnoracial inequality and joining with biological evolutionism to feed Social Darwinism and eugenics.[23]

Scientific racism matters, not just because it diffused among political and cultural elites and thus informed state policies, domestic and colonial, and then percolated among the general population through colonial exhibitions, human zoos, and popular illustrations,[24] but because of its timing: it was *synchronous with the four world-historical revolutions*, the American Revolution (1765–91), the French Revolution (1789–99), the Haitian Revolution (1791–1804), and the Bolivarian Revolution of 1811. These revolutions all trumpeted the doctrine of natural rights and established the ideal, if not the reality, of democratic citizenship for males. In this regard, the Western conception and institution of racial division differ fundamentally from its non-Western counterparts in that they were developed and deployed against the *backdrop of secular equality*, which made them a constitutively contentious if not contradictory historical practice. It is because it violates their civic and moral sensibilities as members of formally democratic societies premised on universal personhood and the rejection of ascriptive hierarchies that scholars are inclined to write "against" race and to see their work as partaking of a struggle

---

[22] Physician George Morton, author of *Crania Aegyptica* (1844), which purported to demonstrate that blacks in Egypt had been servants and slaves as justification for their current enslavement, quoted by Banton, *Racial Theories*, p. 38. The American strand of racial pseudo-science is mercilessly dissected by Stephen Jay Gould in *The Mismeasure of Man* (1981), chapter 2.

[23] Mike Hawkins, *Social Darwinism in European and American Thought, 1860–1945* (1997).

[24] Nicolas Bancel et al., *L'Invention de la race. Des représentations scientifiques aux exhibitions populaires* (2014).

Reframing Racial Domination

to erode and end its interference with human equality and dignity. When they do so, they enter into the *history* of the very phenomenon of which they are supposed to provide an *anatomy*.[25]

Retracing these three origins stories of "race" is not intended to adjudicate between them since they are each valid, to a degree, in their own terms, with the qualifications entered in the foregoing. Moreover, they are not mutually incompatible, with early antisemitic proto-racism morphing into Negrophobia as a result of transatlantic slavery before being rearticulated by naturalists in the eighteenth century and exponents of "scientific racism" in the nineteenth, to spawn the hardened doctrines that propelled colonial conquest, eugenics, and the genocidal policies of the Third Reich. We must heed Ann Laura Stoler's advice to forsake "the scholarly quest" for "the 'original' moment in which the dye of race was cast" and the "original sin" of the West committed.[26] Instead, we must embrace the task of constructing a robust analytic of racial domination that does not logically hinge on this or that genealogical accounting but is capacious enough to embrace all of their historical particulars.

This implies that, armed with a minimalist definition of race as a *naturalizing and hierarchizing social principle of vision and division*, we must range beyond Europe and bring into our analytic purview other continents, other empires, and other lineages of racialization. Fredrickson makes the case that we should prioritize the study of racism in the West because "it had greater impact on world history than any functional equivalent that we might detect in another era or part of the world," and because "it was fully worked out, elaborately implemented, and carried out to its ultimate extremes in the West."[27] This is fact but it should not preclude us challenging the Occidentalism of contemporary studies of "race and ethnicity" in the Western academy, including the insurgent decolonial strands of research which perpetuate the tunnel vision of the colonialists when they put the West at the epicenter of the historical universe.

---

[25] They also act as foot soldiers in the centuries-long battle to shape and diffuse the idea of human unicity and equality, as shown by Siep Stuurman in *The Invention of Humanity: Equality and Cultural Difference in World History* (2017).
[26] Ann Laura Stoler, "Racial Histories and their Regimes of Truth" (1997), p. 185.
[27] Fredrickson, *A Short History of Racism*, p. 11.

2. Spatialize

The second principle for forging a capacious analytic of racial domination, then, is: expand the *geographic scope to decenter* the discussion. This entails three moves. The first is to *bring West and East together* to escape continental parochialism. It is a curiously Eurocentric vision of history to believe that race as an essentialist principle of classification and stratification is a monopoly of Western nations and empires. The Japanese, to take but one example, did not wait for Commodore Perry's arrival in 1853 to racialize the medieval caste of the *eta* (meaning "filth abundant") and the criminal class of the *hinin* ("non-human") into the "invisible race" of the *burakumin* ("hamlet people"), believed to be innately different, inferior, and defiling, and to treat them as such across the centuries, including after their emancipation in 1871, even as no phenotypical property marked them out. Similarly, the Japanese penetration of Korea in the early twentieth century was a colonial project steeped in racial thinking and action, even as the Japanese cloaked this capture in the language of amalgamation and assimilation grounded in the paradox of common ancestry.[28]

Last, but not least, to stay in East Asia, the Pacific War, opening with the Pearl Harbor attack in December 1941 and closing with the atomic bombing of Hiroshima and Nagasaki in August 1945, which cost Japan the lives of some 2.5 million soldiers and over one million civilians, was through and through a *racial war* of extermination waged to establish the global supremacy of the "Yamato race" (*yamato minzoku*). The Japanese claimed to be the sole race endowed with pure blood owing to its divine descent and thus destined to superiority. They saw themselves as tasked with the mission to free their country, then Asia, and ultimately the world from the racial oppression of the English and the Americans, whom they perceived as beastly, inferior, and polluted by transposition to Europeans of the domestic mental

---

[28] See, respectively, Hiroshi Wagatsuma and George DeVos (eds.), *Japan's Invisible Race: Caste in Culture and Personality* (2021 [1968]), and Peter Duus, *The Abacus and the Sword: The Japanese Penetration of Korea, 1895–1910* (1998). For accounts of the Eastern, Middle-Eastern, and African histories and realities of ethnoracial division in these regions, see Bernard Lewis, *Race and Slavery in the Middle East: An Historical Enquiry* (1990); Frank Dikötter (ed.), *The Construction of Racial Identities in China and Japan: Historical and Contemporary Perspectives* (1997); Bruce S. Hall, *A History of Race in Muslim West Africa, 1600–1960* (2011); and Gyanendra Pandey, *A History of Prejudice: Race, Caste, and Difference in India and the United States* (2013).

structures issued from their caste order.[29] Racial categories informed military strategy and racial emotions intensified hostilities on both the American and the Japanese sides, escalating hostilities and casualties to disastrous proportions even after it was clear that the Allied Forces were headed toward victory.[30] This Japanese excursus suggests that a theory of racial domination cannot be based narrowly on the specifics of the Western experience and must make room for accounts of *hyperracialization*, the process whereby the dominant elevate themselves symbolically, elaborate their grandeur, and secure their monopoly over honor, virtue, and purity – by opposition to *hyporacialization*, the denigration and inferiorization of the dominated.

The second move consists in *linking the colonial and the metropolitan domains* to track down the similarities and differences in the treatment of the subaltern of the interior (peasants, working class, ethnic minorities on grounds of descent, region, and religion) and the subaltern of the exterior (colonial subjects), as well as the two-way transfers of racialized representations, techniques of government, and subjectivities between the imperial center and its periphery. This move is essential because, as the historian Patrick Wolfe put it, "leaving colonialism out of race is like leaving the prince out of Hamlet."[31] This is the task of a new generation of scholars promising to produce a colonial and postcolonial sociology whose work bears directly on theories of race (and group-making) in the global North of the contemporary era.[32]

The precursor study on the symbolic commerce between colony and metropole is Anna Julia Cooper's (2006 [1925]) astonishing but little known *L'Attitude de la France envers l'esclavage pendant*

---

[29] John Dower, *War without Mercy: Race and Power in the Pacific War* (1987), pp. 235–6.

[30] "The depiction of the enemy as demons, devils, and ogres permitted the rise of an exterminationist rhetoric in Japan comparable to the metaphors of the hunt or of exterminating vermin in the West." Ibid., p. 255.

[31] Patrick Wolfe, "Race and Racialisation: Some Thoughts" (2002), p. 54.

[32] The broad parameters of this research program are set out by George Steinmetz, "The Sociology of Empires, Colonies, and Postcolonialism" (2014), and in the case studies contained in George Steinmetz (ed.), *Sociology and Empire: The Imperial Entanglements of a Discipline* (2013), part 3. On ethnoracial division specifically, see the literature scanned by Julian Go, "Postcolonial Possibilities for the Sociology of Race" (2018), most of which is still programmatic or declamatory. Three provocative studies linking metropole and colony are Zine Magubane, *Bringing the Empire Home: Race, Class, and Gender in Britain and Colonial South Africa* (2004); Todd Shepard, *The Invention of Decolonization: The Algerian War and the Remaking of France* (2006); and Frederick Cooper, *Citizenship between Empire and Nation: Remaking France and French Africa, 1945–1960* (2014).

la Révolution, defended as a doctoral dissertation in history at the Sorbonne in Paris in 1925 (and yet unpublished in the French language), linking the French and the Haitian revolutions and contending that racial division played a role in the promulgation of the Rights of Man. That problematic was taken up in C. L. R. James's eloquent *The Black Jacobins* which traces the boomerang effect of Toussaint L'Ouverture's insurrection on French politics.[33] An important restatement of that problematic is Frederick Cooper and Ann Laura Stoler's edited volume on *Tensions of Empire*, which shows how bourgeois culture and social relations were projected onto, and in turn inflected by, the colonial experience.[34] The "new imperial history" has likewise posed the question of the "counterflows to colonialism" that impacted the metropole in myriad ways, from state-building and the city to the economy and everyday culture, leading to the crafting of the concept of "imperial social formation" to rethink the trajectory of Western societies.[35] The boldest expression yet of this relationship between colony and metropole is Mahmoud Mamdani's thesis that the modern nation-state and the colonial enterprise were co-constituted the Western world over.[36] This thesis invites us to rethink the origins and tenor of political modernity by putting violence at its epicenter, a violence that was made possible by the consistent racialization of imperial subjects. Western citizenship and colonial subjecthood, then, are the two sides of the same material and symbolic coin.

Another agenda is to extend the analytic of racialized ethnicity initially built on and for Western domestic cases to attend to patterns of naturalized inequality in past colonies and present postcolonies. This entails studying the construction by the colonizer of the racial (or caste) order of the colony as well as excavating native strands of racialization and their hybridization with imports from the West – or from the East, Middle East, and Africa, as the case may be. Reviewing recent historical work on ethnic ordering and politics among the

---

[33] The original French text by Cooper is published as an appendix and translated into English as *Slavery and the French and Haitian Revolutionists*, edited by Frances R. Keller (2006 [1925]). On the founding of Haiti, see C. L. R. James, *The Black Jacobins: Toussaint L'Ouverture and the San Domingo Revolution* (1963).

[34] Frederick Cooper and Ann Laura Stoler (eds.), *Tensions of Empire: Colonial Cultures in a Bourgeois World* (1997).

[35] Kathleen Wilson (ed.), *A New Imperial History: Culture, Identity, and Modernity in Britain and the Empire, 1660–1840* (2004), and Harald Fischer-Tiné and Susanne Gehrmann (eds.), *Empires and Boundaries: Race, Class, and Gender in Colonial Settings* (2008).

[36] Mamdani, *Neither Settler nor Native*.

Reframing Racial Domination

peoples of the Sahel region, historian Bruce Hall observes: "Whatever role European colonial rule played in transforming this region of the world, and whatever racial ideas flowed to Sahelian intellectuals from western sources, the core contents of the racialized ideas in these conflicts are local, drawn from a long (and continuing) history of inequality and exploitation within this region." And elsewhere he urges social scientists to "resist the search for origins and instead try to think about how race works in the particular contexts where we find it."[37]

Two topics need to be brought front and center in this regard. The first is slavery, its multiple forms, native and imperial, its multi-sided impact on ethnoracial classification and stratification, and its aftermaths, historical and contemporary, in the wake of Patterson's majestic study of *Slavery and Social Death*.[38] The second is war, inasmuch as organized military conquest, suppression and occupation were central to the creation and control of colonies. Who says empire says warfare, better yet "total warfare," aimed at "pacification" entailing the subdual and sometimes the destruction of peoples considered "backward," an equation that the social sciences need to elucidate if they are to fully grasp the role of violence in the creation and maintenance of ethnoracial domination.[39]

Tackling the diptych of race and empire also implies capturing the haphazard character of settler colonialism and destabilizing the simple binary of colonizer and colonized to detect racialized subdivisions within the latter.[40] An exemplary case is the long-standing antagonism

---

[37] Bruce Hall, "Race" (2019), p. 194, and idem, "Reading Race in Africa and the Middle East" (2020), p. 42. Here, "we must abandon the cliché of the colonial encounter. It is just as misleading to speak of two discrete spheres of discourse – one colonial, the other indigenous – as it is to speak of the colonial state domination of its subjects' consciousness." Jonathon Glassman, *War of Words, War of Stones: Racial Thought and Violence in Colonial Zanzibar* (2011), pp. 17–18.

[38] Patterson, *Slavery and Social Death*. See also idem, "The Denial of Slavery in Contemporary American Sociology" (2019). The Pattersonian approach is amplified by Alain Testart, *L'Institution de l'esclavage. Une approche mondiale* (2018), and by the stunning *summa* gathered by Paulin Ismard (ed.), *Les Mondes de l'esclavage. Une histoire comparée* (2021).

[39] The innovative and canonical text on the topic is Jacques Frémeaux, *De Quoi fut fait l'empire. Les guerres coloniales au XIXe siècle* (2010).

[40] A further complication is "subcolonialism," as when Egypt treated Sudan as a colonial other (conquered in 1820, well before the British invasion in 1882) and racialized its population long after the withdrawal of Western imperialists and the ending of the slave trade. Eve Troutt Powell, *A Different Shade of Colonialism: Egypt, Great Britain, and the Mastery of the Sudan* (2003).

between Berbers and Arabs in Algeria, which French imperial power reworked into the "Kabyle myth." Supported by racial representations prevailing then in Europe, the Kabyle myth held that Berbers were assimilable due to being sedentary, monogamous, industrious, and democratic, whereas Arabs could only be suppressed and contained due to being nomadic, polygamous, lazy, deceitful, and fanatically religious.[41] This ethnoracial bifurcation resulted in the denigration of Arabs and the castigation of Islam which continues to resonate in France to this day.

The metropolis is an especially fertile ground for documenting and theorizing the stamping of the racialized symbolic structures of colonialism onto social and physical space. The topography and architecture of settler colonial cities were the legible material concretization of imperial power relations, and struggles over the built environment were epicentral to the dialectic of colonial domination and resistance – cities were crucibles of incubation and diffusion of nationalist ideology and insurrection. The hybrid urbanism that resulted shows the need to attend to the racial projects of both colonizer and colonized.[42] A historical-analytical extension is to show how empire continues to shape the city of the metropole after independence and, through battles over housing, urban citizenship itself, reworking racialized identities and cleavages in the process.[43] This provides an opening for a second agenda: recovering colonial racialization in the metropoles in the form of the formation of subjectivities among the "second generation" of immigrants; the interweaving of race, space, and religion in the form of Islam in the urban periphery; the resurgence of the collective memory of slavery and colonization and their recognition in the political sphere; and the rising mobilization of postcolonial populations, including in countries with a long-standing tradition of universalist citizenship such as France.[44]

---

[41] Patricia M. E. Lorcin, *Imperial Identities: Stereotyping, Prejudice and Race in Colonial Algeria* (1995), chapter 7.

[42] Loïc Wacquant, *Bourdieu in the City: Challenging Urban Theory* (2023a), pp. 25–6, 57–8. The precursor study of Anthony D. King, *Colonial Urban Development: Culture, Social Power and Environment* (1976) is essential reading. Another landmark tome is Janet Abu-Lughod, *Rabat: Urban Apartheid in Morocco* (1980). For further illustrations from the French empire, see Gwendolyn Wright, *The Politics of Design in French Colonial Urbanism* (1991); Zeynep Çelik, *Urban Forms and Colonial Confrontation: Algiers under French Rule* (1997); and Catherine Herbelin, *Architectures du Vietnam colonial* (2016).

[43] Minayo Nasiali, *Native to the Republic: Empire, Social Citizenship, and Everyday Life in Marseille since 1945* (2016).

[44] Jean-Loup Amselle, *L'Ethnicisation de la France* (2011); Crystal Marie Fleming,

Reframing Racial Domination

Yet an urgent amendment to coming studies of the racialization of symbolic, social, and physical space in former colonial powers is to *bring class back in* and carry out the joint elucidation of the material and symbolic forces at play in their articulation. The confluence of the polarization of the class structure and the effacement of class in party politics and public culture have gravely skewed studies of the continuing ramifications of empire in the urban metropole, where many of the ethnic disparities and frictions are *also* the by-product of nonracial mechanisms, chief among them class (de)composition and trajectory.

3. Dislodge the United States

The final spatial move to develop the analytic of racial domination is to *dislodge the United States from its Archimedean position*. Just as the tripartite tale of the "underclass" was a uniquely American story nourished by virulent anti-urbanism and suffusive racial fear activated by the black revolt of the 1960s, academic and civic debates on race globally are dominated by American categories, assumptions, and claims – as illustrated recently by the international diffusion of intersectionality in the academy and Black Lives Matter among justice activists. But the American definition of race as civic felony and of blackness as public dishonor transmitted through strict hypodescent are historical outliers.[45] No other ethnic group in the United States is bounded on that basis and no other society on the planet defines blackness thus. The limitations of the best theorizing on race in American social science can be traced directly to the reliance of its progenitors upon the *oddities* of the national historical experience.[46]

To stick with the descendants of the African diaspora displaced by slavery, it suffices to compare the trajectories of blacks in the United

Resurrecting Slavery: Racial Legacies and White Supremacy in France (2017); and Paul A. Silverstein, *Postcolonial France: Race, Islam, and the Future of the Republic* (2018). See also Abdelmalek Sayad, *Femmes en rupture de ban. Entretiens inédits avec deux Algériennes* (2021).

[45] Loïc Wacquant, "Race as Civic Felony" (2005b), and F. James Davis, *Who Is Black? One Nation's Definition* (1991). A masterful geographic decentering of the race question is Mara Loveman, *National Colors: Racial Classification and the State in Latin America* (2014).

[46] Glenn Loury, *The Anatomy of Racial Inequality* (2021 [2002]); Karen E. Fields and Barbara J. Fields, *Racecraft: The Soul of Inequality in American Life* (2014); Mustafa Emirbayer and Matthew Desmond, *The Racial Order* (2015).

States and blacks settled on other shores of the Atlantic to realize the great variety of "modes of ethnosomatic stratification" through which they have become incorporated and the varied historical possibilities each harbors.[47] The brute fact of transatlantic slavery itself does not mechanically dictate the meaning of blackness because the latter gets reworked through local histories of classification and stratification. Thus, the black Peruvians of the northern coast of Peru do not construe themselves as Afro-Peruvians but as Peruvians, *criollos* or agricultural workers first and foremost. They are not color blind; they recognize full well the discrimination they suffer; but "they do not see themselves as part of a broader community of people descended from African slaves."[48] For them, blackness is just a phenotypical trait devoid of cultural and historical resonance because their collective identity was forged in the *hacienda* system based on debt peonage that first coexisted with and then outlasted slavery for over a century.

Return to the United States and its fixation on the idea that race equals "color," meaning skin tone. This conception leaves out cases of ethnoracial domination where other phenotypical markers are used (such as hair, height, or eye color as in China, East and Central Africa, and the Andes); situations where no phenotypical difference exists (cagots in medieval Southwestern France, Jews and Slavs in Nazi-era Europe, the Burakumin in Japan) or only faint and unreliable ones (the Sámi of Norway, the Roma of Eastern Europe, the Dalits of India and Nepal, the Kurds of Turkey and Syria); instances where the racializer is a "colored" population (the empires of precolonial Africa and Asia, mulattoes in Haiti, the Tuareg in Mauritania, the Yamato Japanese, Cambodians with regard to Vietnamese ethnics, Africans with regard to Asians in post-independence Kenya and Uganda). What is more, phenotypical properties are never read singly and in isolation from other embodied markers. Explaining the visual signage of caste hierarchy among the Tamil of India, anthropologist André Béteille notes that "carriage, bearing, and facial expression often contribute as much to the physical identity of an individual or a group as do measurable somatic traits" such as height, skeletal build, thinness of the nose, and skin tone.[49]

---

[47] Orlando Patterson, "Four Modes of Ethno-Somatic Stratification: The Experience of Blacks in Europe and the Americas" (2005).
[48] Tanya Maria Golash-Boza, *Yo Soy Negro: Blackness in Peru* (2011), p. 115.
[49] André Béteille, *Caste, Class and Power: Changing Patterns of Stratification in a Tanjore Village* (1965), p. 49.

Reframing Racial Domination

Assimilating racial domination to color oppression crucially omits cases where the racialized category is "white," as in the case of the Irish in the eyes of the English from the twelfth to the twentieth century (or Jews, Poles and Slavs in the eyes of Nazis). Thus the nineteenth-century scientific and political discourse portraying the Irish as racially separate from, and inferior to, their Anglo-Saxon neighbors underwent a spectacular revival in Britain in the interwar years even as scientific racism was being discredited. Hibernophobia portrayed the population of Ireland as of low-grade Mediterranean stock whereas Britons were of high-grade Nordic ancestry, a difference said to explain the congenital backwardness of the former. Yet, in contrast with the American obsession with ethnoracial purity, the English believed that they could resolve the Irish question through ethnic melting. As one ardent advocate of miscegenation characteristically put it in 1916, "the Irish race is, when undiluted with Anglo-Saxon blood, a weak, ignorant, lazy, emotional race, quite incapable of loyalty even to its own chiefs or leaders, and it has been so for centuries. Though the untravelled and pure-blooded Irishman is about the most unsatisfactory citizen of this great Empire, yet if he is half English, Scotch, or Canadian, or Australian, he becomes one of the finest people in the world ... Mix the races, import Irish into England, and *vice versa*."[50]

Nazi racial colonies at the heart of Europe

A historical case of racial subjugation of "white people," unparalleled for its scope and destructiveness, is the imperial war of occupation waged by the Nazi regime to capture and subdue the whole of Eastern Europe – quenching its *Ostrausch*, the intoxication of the East (1). The goal of the war was to lift the country to rival the United States and England on the geopolitical stage and to realize its all-embracing vision of racial supremacy over the Eurasian landmass. Nazi Germany does not fit the conventional definition of a colonial power including overseas expansion, but historian Mark Mazower shows, in his master-book *Hitler's Empire*, that this is the framework needed to capture the geographical and ethnoracial dynamics of its rule. Heirs to the modern European tradition of conquest and

---

[50] Cited in Raymond M. Douglas, "Anglo-Saxons and Attacotti: The Racialization of Irishness in Britain between the World Wars" (2002), p. 42.

control of external peoples deemed inferior and uncivilized, "the Nazis shared that imperial desire but did something with it that was unprecedented and shocking to the European mind of the early twentieth century: they tried to build their empire in Europe itself and, what is more, to do it at a breakneck speed in only a few years" (2).

German empire-building at the heart of the continent effectively *fused race and space* by capturing territory and imposing on its populations an extreme regime of racial rule giving force and materiality to the Aryan fantasy of blood purity and innate human superiority. It was not just *inspired* by the "colonial spirit" expressed in overseas dominions (3); it was a colonial project in its own right, an engine to turn the Eastern part of Europe into both a "colony of exploitation," whereby the captive labor, food, and natural resources were extracted to enrich the Reich, and a "colony of settlement," as when Germans were invited to migrate and populate the Polish cities and towns emptied of their residents, the paradigm being the plan to turn Łódź into Litzmannstadt, a clean, cultured, Germanized city for ethnic Germans from across Central Europe, requiring the sequestration, exploitation, starvation, and mass murder of Jews as well as the marginalization and racial subordination of the Poles (4). The racial obsession of the regime was such that new colonists were carefully selected to ensure that they would be of "only the best, the soundest German blood" (in Hitler's own words). The criteria included racial type, body type, intellectual capacity, moral character, political beliefs, and ancestral background (5), in short, racial criteria par excellence.

The occupation and subjugation of Poland served as a laboratory for what German empire-building in Europe would entail. It started with the targeted annihilation of the country's political, social, and cultural elite and the closing down of their organizations while the mass of the Polish people would be "turned into a minimally educated slave labor force for the Germans" (6). Humiliation and discrimination, compulsory labor service and deportation to work in German factories, removal from cities and internment within so-called "ghettos" (about which see *infra*, p. 138, n. 81), executions and casual shootings, and collective punishment were some of the manifestations of ethnoracial domination, characteristic of colonial practice but wielded upon Europeans.

The barrage of prohibitions that turned Poles into "subpersons" à la Charles Mills is worth enumerating because it reveals the intent to deny honor and enforce inferiority, and it is virtually identical with the racial interdictions imposed on African Americans in the Jim Crow South: "They were forbidden to use public beaches, swimming pool or public gardens ... Forbidden from wearing military decorations or even school uniforms, they were obliged to occupy the rear portions of platforms in stations, trains, and buses, and to stand if necessary to allow Germans to sit down. Adults had to salute Germans in uniform and were beaten if they omitted to do so. They had to bare their heads in the presence of German officials and to stand aside when they passed. Shopkeepers were told to serve German customers first, and Poles were allowed to shop only at certain times. They were granted much lower rations (though they were higher than those set for Jews) on grounds that "a lower race needs less food" (to quote a high-ranking Nazi official) (7). Much like the enforcement of the "racial etiquette" of Jim Crow varied across localities, the behavioral dictates imposed upon Poles were sometimes contradictory, as when the "Hitler salute" was mandatory in some areas when a German official walked by but forbidden in other areas because "it was a privilege of the Germans and of recognized Germanic fellow-racials like the Flemish, the Dutch, the Norwegians, etc., but not of those of unequal blood like Poles, Czechs, Ukrainians and so on" (8).

To impose their rigid regime of racial domination, the Nazis had to resolve a conundrum specific to *intra*-European colonialism: how to tell a German from a Pole in the absence of visible physical differences. One way was to instruct Germans to wear distinguishing marks; another was to force Poles to pin a violet letter P on their garment. As with Jim Crow, all relationships implying equality and reciprocity were banned. Fraternizing with Poles could lead to prosecution ("There are no decent Poles just like there are no decent Jews"), and sexual congress with a Pole could cost the latter their life. The principle was what a senior Nazi administrator called "the ruthless separation" of Germans from Poles, and Germans who violated this principle could be arrested and sent away to a concentration camp (9).

The Nazis thus captured and ruled their Eastern European satellites much the way European imperial powers captured and ruled their colonies in Africa and Asia. They imposed upon them a system of racial domination manifested in ruthless exploitation, punctilious subordination, and systematic exclusion drenched in violence on a scale unmatched in history. This is because this domination was not tempered by a *mission civilisatrice* as Poles, Slavs, and Jews were considered irredeemably inferior and utterly unfit as candidates for assimilation. The lack of phenotypical and cultural distance between the Nazis and the peoples they subjugated did not restrain them from exerting murderous violence ultimately resulting in tens of millions of dead. The creation of the Nazi colonies at the heart of Europe is thus a standing invitation to rethink colonialism itself as a racial enterprise by questioning the equation of colony with overseas and allowing that, in arguably its most extreme case, its perpetrators and victims were of the same "color" (10).

1. Christian Ingrao, *La Promesse de l'Est. Espérance nazie et génocide, 1939–1943* (2016).
2. Mark Mazower, *Hitler's Empire: How the Nazis Ruled Europe* (2009), p. xxxix. See also Shelley Baranowski, *Nazi Empire: German Colonialism and Imperialism from Bismarck to Hitler* (2011), which traces the arc of what she calls "the tension of empire" from 1871 to 1945, inclusive of European capture.
3. Jürgen Zimmerer, "The Birth of the Ostland Out of the Spirit of Colonialism: A Postcolonial Perspective on the Nazi Policy of Conquest and Extermination" (2005); Benjamin Madley, "From Africa to Auschwitz: How German South West Africa Incubated Ideas and Methods Adopted and Developed by the Nazis in Eastern Europe" (2005); Casper Erichsen and David Olusoga, *The Kaiser's Holocaust: Germany's Forgotten Genocide and the Colonial Roots of Nazism* (2010).
4. Gordon Horwitz, *Ghettostadt: Łódź and the Making of a Nazi City* (2008).
5. Mazower, *Hitler's Empire*, pp. 191–3.
6. Ibid., p. 74.
7. Ibid., p. 92.
8. Diemut Majer, *"Non-Germans" Under the Third Reich: The Nazi Judicial and Administrative System in Germany and Occupied Eastern Europe, 1939–1945* (2003), p. 208, cited by Mazower, p. 93.
9. Mazower, *Hitler's Empire*, p. 94.
10. "Perverted by Nazism's abandonment of liberalism, and distorted by the cultural proximity of Poland to Germany, the Nazi occupation of Poland was colonialism nonetheless." David Furber, "Near as Far in the Colonies: The Nazi Occupation of Poland" (2004), p. 579.

The equation of race with color has a further limitation: it cannot explicate how a gradational continuum is turned into discrete categories nor into how many, especially as skin tone is generally read together with other phenotypical features, as documented by the profusion of flexible color categories (*côr*) used in everyday life by Brazilians, ranging from five to five dozen depending on the studies.[51]

[51] Harry William Hutchinson found that peasants commonly used ten terms with

The latter consider three bodily properties to slot individuals along an ethnoracial ladder running from light (or white, *branco*) down to dark (or black, *preto*) with a plethora of categories in-between (in the masculine: *pardo, moreno, sarara, mulatto, escuro, cabo verde, cabra, claro*, etc.): complexion, shape of the nose and mouth, and texture of the hair. But, secondarily, these properties are inflected by taking into account such class variables as education, income, residence, and social network, in keeping with the popular saying, "money whitens" – an expression that is nonsensical for blackness in the US context. Full siblings thus can be slotted into different ethnoracial boxes, which again is impossible in a strict descent-based classification system, and an individual can change ethnoracial category during her lifetime. Because the boundaries between categories are blurred and ambiguous, ethnoracial placement is also fluid and inconsistent across classifier and context, as well as across regions in the country. This explains why gradational color categories are a better predictor of stratification outcomes than the racial triad of black–brown–white.[52] The degree and span of mobility along the gradational system of ethnoracial ranking is a matter of dispute among students of Brazil, but there is agreement that some mobility is possible both intra- and intergenerationally, in particular by "marrying light," via what historian Carl Degler famously called the "mulatto escape hatch."[53]

There is an irony in the doxic notion that race and color are synonyms: it excludes the "canonical race," African Americans, who historically have been defined by strict hypodescent *regardless* of physical appearance and other ancestry[54] – what we might call the *Walter White*

---

wooly and porous boundaries in his classic study *Village and Plantation Life in Northeastern Brazil* (1957). A national survey in 1995 found that, put in the artificial situation of an interview, 97 percent of the Brazilian population used seven terms, even though the national census uses only three categories (white, brown, black). Edward E. Telles, *Race in Another America: The Significance of Skin Color in Brazil* (2004), p. 82.

[52] Ellis P. Monk Jr., "The Consequences of 'Race and Color' in Brazil" (2016).
[53] Carl N. Degler, *Neither Black nor White: Slavery and Race Relations in Brazil and the United States* (1971). For a systematic analysis of the architecture and determinants of ethnoracial classification in four Latin American countries, see Edward Telles and Tianna Paschel, "Who is Black, White, or Mixed Race? How Skin Color, Status, and Nation Shape Racial Classification in Latin America" (2014). Read also the caution of Peter Wade, "Images of Latin American *Mestizaje* and the Politics of Comparison" (2004).
[54] I provide a compressed account of the rise and spread of the "one-drop rule" in chapter 3, *infra*, pp. 223–32.

paradox. Walter F. White (1893–1955) was the leader of the National Association for the Advancement of Colored People (NAACP) from 1931 to 1955, and the architect of its strategy of legal challenge to racial segregation leading to the victorious *Brown v. Board of Education* Supreme Court decision in 1954 overturning legal separation. He was phenotypically white, with European facial features, thin blond hair, and blue eyes, and he could "pass" effortlessly – as could his father before him. He did so to go underground as a "white" journalist to investigate racial lynchings and pogroms first-hand, leading to his stunning 1929 book, *Rope and Faggot*. He was "a Negro by choice," as he himself put it, and no one seriously questioned his identity and his legitimacy to lead black people despite his mismatched phenotype.[55]

One last trouble created by the equivalence of race and color is that it obfuscates the pervasiveness and persistence of *color differentiation and discrimination among people of color*. A long line of black sociologists from W. E. B. Du Bois to E. Franklin Frazier to Oliver Cox to St. Clair Drake and Horace Cayton tackled the issue among African Americans. Thus, in their portrait of Chicago's ghetto at the mid-twentieth-century point, Drake and Cayton document how the city's Negroes were "partial to color" and even "color struck," preferring to socialize with, to employ, and to marry light-skin blacks, to the point of strongly "favoring 'brownness' in contradistinction to 'blackness'."[56] Then the topic disappeared from the sociological radar and became socially taboo as the Civil Rights Movement took off and the Black Power movement burst on the scene: the imperative of black political unity made it unacceptable to acknowledge internal divisions, especially divisions based on the very principle African Americans were fighting against. But color distinctions among blacks have endured so much so that, remarkably, the disparities between light-skinned and dark-skinned blacks on a range of social outcomes (income, education, health, incarceration, etc.) are more pronounced today than the disparities between blacks and whites, suggesting that both blacks and whites establish strong distinctions by color in how they treat "persons of color."[57]

---

[55] Kenneth Robert Janken, *White: The Biography of Walter White, Mr. NAACP* (2003); Walter White, *Rope and Faggot: A Biography of Judge Lynch* (2002 [1929]).

[56] St. Clair Drake and Horace R. Cayton, *Black Metropolis: A Study of Negro Life in a Northern City* (1993 [1945]), p. 503. Indeed, black Americans during this era thought of themselves as a "brown people." Heavyweight world champion Joe Louis, arguably the leading race hero at the time, was nicknamed "The Brown Bomber."

[57] Ellis Monk, "The Unceasing Significance of Colorism: Skin Tone Stratification in

Traveling around the world, preference for lighter skin *within* subordinate ethnic categories is well documented, if little studied, in Latin America, the Caribbean, and East Asia, and this partly independently of the black–white racial dichotomy.[58] In the Tamil society of India, "the Brahmins are extremely conscious of their fair appearance and often contrast it with the 'black' skin color of the Kallas, or the [low caste] Adi-Dravidas. A dark-skinned Brahmin girl is often a burden to the family because it is difficult to get a husband for her."[59] As for the Japanese, persons of color no doubt in the eyes of Westerners, they have traditionally valued pale skin "long before any sustained contact with either Caucasoid Europeans or dark-skinned Africans or Indians."[60] Indeed, the word "white" (*shiroi*) is the one they use to describe lighter shades of their own skin as well as white paper and snow. As early as the eighth century, Japanese aristocrats viewed lighter skin as evidence of honor and distinction; men at the court powdered their faces just as the ladies did: "The whiteness of untanned skin was the symbol of this privileged class which was spared any form of outdoor labor."[61] Correspondingly, persons with lighter skin tone were viewed as superior to compatriots of darker complexion.

Lastly, there is the case of the many black ethnicities that are scorned and discriminated against by other black ethnicities in Africa according to divisions predating the colonial era. A paradigmatic instance is the indigenous Twa (also known as Batwa, Pygmies, or "people of the forest"), whom both Tutsis and Hutus in Rwanda openly disparage, vigorously ostracize, and routinely subject to maltreatment.[62] This racialized hostility and denigration preexisted the

---

the United States" (2021). The pervasive anti-indigenous denigration and discrimination among Latino populations in the United States is documented by Cecilia Menjívar, "The Racialization of 'Illegality'" (2021).

[58] Evelyn Nakano Glenn (ed.), *Shades of Difference: Why Skin Color Matters* (2009), and Angela R. Dixon and Edward E. Telles, "Skin Color and Colorism: Global Research, Concepts, and Measurement" (2017).

[59] Béteille, *Caste, Class and Power*, p. 48.

[60] Hiroshi Wagatsuma, "The Social Perception of Skin Color in Japan" (1967), p. 407.

[61] Ibid., p. 408.

[62] This paragraph draws on José Kagabo and Vincent Mudandagizi, "Complainte des gens de l'argile. Les Twa du Rwanda" (1974); Serge Bahuchet, "Les Pygmées d'aujourd'hui en Afrique centrale" (1991); Séverin Cécile Abega and Patrice Bigombe Logo (eds.), *La Marginalisation des Pygmées d'Afrique Centrale* (2006); Christopher C. Taylor, "Molders of Mud: Ethnogenesis and Rwanda's Twa" (2011); and Bennett Collins et al., "Becoming 'Historically Marginalized Peoples': Examining Twa

intrusion of Europeans and finds its root in the negative symbolic associations that Rwandans make with the forest as a place of danger and malevolent spirits. Traditionally, Rwandans have viewed Twas as lazy, voracious, thieving, sexually immodest, smelly and unintelligent, congenitally polluted and polluting, people with whom one should avoid commensality and intimate contact – in short, an inferior "race" – even though they shared ancestors, spoke the same language, and enjoyed the same oral lore. To this day, marriage with a Twa is unthinkable and children born of such unions are considered Twa and disdained in their turn, reproducing the dishonor attached to the group. A Rwandan proverb says, "If you shelter from the rain in a Twa hut, then remain there."[63] Twas are always missing from national historical accounts and public policy and, in 2008, the Rwandan government refused to recognize their rights as an indigenous minority under international law.

Ethnosomatic differences have also been seized upon and accentuated to draw rigid internal boundaries after the crumbling of colonial rule, and this with deadly consequences. Thus, black South Africans use a combination of skin tone and language to distinguish themselves sharply from African migrants and refugees, whom they believe to be darker skinned and congenitally inferior, irrespective of their varied hues. This is especially the case with Zimbabweans, whom they treat as "the archtypical Other, often viewed as dirty, smelly criminals – the untouchables of South Africa."[64] African foreigners generically are defined and despised as *makwerekwere*, "the bogeyman who stains the nation with excessive blackness" and, despite their internal heterogeneity based on bodily, economic, ethnolinguistic, and social capital (they sport the range of phenotypes, many speak South African languages, and they have extensive social ties in the country), they were the target of rolling waves of ethnoracial violence that resulted in the killing of thousands (including South Africans, by mistake) and the displacement of tens of thousands in the two decades following the

---

Perceptions of Boundary Shifting and Re-Categorization in Post-Genocide Rwanda" (2021). The Twa people are also present in Burundi, Uganda, and Zaïre, where they are equally scorned and marginalized to the point where some analysts refer to them as an outcaste.

[63] Susan M. Thomson, "Ethnic Twa and Rwandan National Unity and Reconciliation Policy" (2009), p. 315.

[64] Godwin Dube, "Levels of Othering: The Case of Zimbabwean Migrants in South Africa" (2017), p. 392.

ending of apartheid.⁶⁵ So much to show that processes of racialization are operative outside of the black–white binary as well as beyond the Euro-American sphere.

We are well advised to include in the universe of cases on which we build and refine our analytic of racial domination constellations in which the perpetrator and the target belong to the same ethnosomatic category (white/white and black/black, Brahmin/Dalit, Yamato/Burakumin, etc.). The point here is emphatically not to minimize the subjugation of "people of color" on a global scale, as a hasty reader might claim through prosecutorial lenses, but to learn from varied and even *outlier cases*, much like students of gender domination benefit from including in their purview the treatment of transgender, intersexed, and nonbinary people, even as these compose a very small percentage of the population.⁶⁶ Indeed, avoiding Western-centrism will put us in a stronger position to grasp the logics of categorization that underpins the distinctively expansionary dynamics of white racial rule.

To be clear: the point of provincializing the United States is not to pin the "sin of race" on that country and then absolve others, thereby denying, for instance, that ethnoracial domination festers in Western Europe, including France in particular (given the nationality of the author), as is sometimes claimed in public debate and by some academics enamored with speed-reading. Quite the contrary: it is to create the epistemic conditions, first, for rethinking race in the US in light of its own and other histories and, second, for avoiding the imposition of the ethnoracial unconscious of any one society on all the others. It is to open the diptych of classification and stratification to full inquiry without presuming its contents and freezing its dynamics a priori. No one society should serve as explicit or implicit yardstick for comparative analysis, for *each society has developed the symbolic conception and material encasement of racialized ethnicity suited to its historical trajectory,* allowing for cross-pollination across continents and oceans. This is why we need an analytic – a parsimonious set of abstract categories – that is neutral and capacious enough to characterize the phenomenon, capture its facets, and encompass the

---

⁶⁵ David M. Matsinhe, *Apartheid Vertigo: The Rise in Discrimination against Africans in South Africa* (2011a), p. 133, and idem, "Africa's Fear of Itself: The Ideology of *Makwerekwere* in South Africa" (2011b).
⁶⁶ Kristen Schilt and Danya Lagos, "The Development of Transgender Studies in Sociology" (2017).

full diversity of cases without enshrining one as prototype, positive or negative.⁶⁷

4. Forsake the logic of the trial

The fourth principle to develop this analytic is to *avoid the logic of the trial*, which truncates inquiry by seeking to prove culpability and assign blame, in favor of a relentless commitment to the cold-blooded logic of theoretical construction and empirical validation, no matter where these take you. The logic of the trial impels investigators to seek out victims and vituperate culprits rather than identify mechanisms. Here is an illustration of how the urge to denounce can cloud analytic judgment of even the most perceptive sociologists: "The contours and complexities of race and racism continue to confound the social sciences. This problem originates in the historical *complicity* of the social science disciplines with the establishment and maintenance of the systems of racial predation, injustice and indeed genocide upon which the modern world was built. All the social sciences originate in raciology and race management, a fact that is rarely acknowledged."⁶⁸ In the ensuing paper, Howard Winant offers not a shred of evidence backing up this damning accusation thrown at "all the social sciences," because he knows that this *argumentum ad populum* will please readers who read his article through the same accusatory lens.

Indeed, Winant continues: "Because of this complicity, which is *not only historic but ongoing*, there can be no such thing as a social science of REN [race, ethnicity, nationality], no elision of race into ethnicity or nation." In five words, Winant obliterates the "peculiar history of scientific reason" which has, over some four centuries, endowed scientific procedures of knowledge formation and adjudication with a

---

⁶⁷ The best means of sidestepping the trap of scholarly ethnocentrism is to enroll the collaboration of researchers from different nationalities and countries, as Morning and Maneri do in their meticulous study of how Americans and Italians think and talk about descent-based difference. Ann Morning and Marcello Maneri, *An Ugly Word: Rethinking Race in Italy and the United States* (2022). See, in particular, their candid reflections of how their national and personal identities angled their view of racial identity, pp. 22–5, and their lucid epistemological reflections on the question, pp. 43–51.

⁶⁸ Howard Winant, "Race, Ethnicity and Social Science" (2015), p. 2176. The term "complicity" is italicized in the original. Compare this tar-brush claim with Johan Heilbron's finely textured excavation of *The Rise of Social Theory* (1995) a *full century before* the development of "raciology."

relative independence from their historical conditions of genesis and operation.⁶⁹ Surely, Winant would agree that his own social scientific assertion is not complicit with "racial predation," which effectively makes his argument self-refuting.⁷⁰

It is W. E. B. Du Bois who admonished that, when carrying out a social study, "the utmost that the world can demand is, not lack of human interest and moral conviction, but rather the heart-quality of fairness, and an earnest desire for the truth despite its possible unpleasantness."⁷¹ This implies a strict, if provisional, ban on moral judgment and a permanent rejection of appeals to emotions which too often drive inquiry into ethnoracial inequality – as when the white author of a book on the topic feels obligated to flaunt their racial *bona fides* in a preface confessing their "privilege" and asserting their ethnic solidarity (in a way that a male or upper-class colleague writing on gender or class would not think of doing). Expressions of personal contrition are signals of virtue that make the author and their readers feel good, but they get in the way of elucidating the logics of ethnoracial domination insofar as they skew the scientific gaze. Another source of skewing of sociological vision is explicitly or implicitly reckoning the ethnoracial identity of the researcher: the present book would be read differently if its author were African American (some readers will be doubly suspicious of its argument because it is penned by a Frenchman).

A sociologist of class, the family, the state, modernity does not mechanically and unthinkingly write *against* class, the family, the state, modernity, to denounce the phenomenon in question. And when they do, the result can be rather questionable: *vide* Marx's unfortunate prediction that the mechanical polarization of the class

---

⁶⁹ Pierre Bourdieu, "The Peculiar History of Scientific Reason" (1991).
⁷⁰ Another example among many: for an oral presentation of her forthcoming book *Predatory Cities: Replenishing the Public Purse* at Berkeley's Center for the Study of Law and Society (April 11, 2022, my italics), legal scholar Bernadette Atuahene supplied the following abstract: "Writing in first person, the author describes how she discovered the problem of illegally inflated property tax assessments in Detroit … How does a majority Black city run primarily by Black politicians and administrators perpetrate a racialized housing crime? While many want to attribute the rampant illegality to corruption or incompetent politicians and administrators, these are not the primary drivers here. The *chief culprit is structural racism, otherwise known as racist policy*. That is, the *true villain is an invisible structure* and not a visible individual, but the dominant culture rejects this, instead demanding an easily digestible good/bad, black/white narrative."
⁷¹ W. E. B. Du Bois, *The Philadelphia Negro: A Social Study* (2010 [1899]), p. 3.

structure of capitalism would inevitably lead to the communist revolution and the abolition of class that he so fervently wished for. Why do sociologists of race feel obligated to write *against* race instead of *about* race – or, better, why do they so easily let the first impulse overwhelm the second, and vituperation crimp elucidation? A typical expression of the compulsory fusion of the analytics and politics of race is this fiery moral tirade by Golash-Boza: "Race is not a topic that one should study only for its intellectual interest. *It should be studied to the end of eradicating racial oppression.* Knowledge is most useful when it is produced *in community and through struggle*. An understanding of racial oppression *cannot be an armchair exercise*. Instead, race scholars have to start with empirical questions about why things are the way they are and push forward theoretical understandings that help us to explicate and *end racial oppression*. Working toward dismantling racism both helps us to understand it better and moves us toward its demise."[72]

This is not to say that social scientists should remain indifferent to ethnoracial struggles for equality and justice; far from it. It is to assert, with Max Weber, that they should participate in these struggles as citizens, while making sure to dispatch their scientific duties according to specifically scientific criteria.[73] Indeed, it is when they stringently *sublimate* their social passions into rigorous theory-building, robust methodological designs, and scrupulous empirical observation that sociologists best serve the historical interests of the dominated by producing cogent explications of the complex and shifting structures that keep them down. In Pierre Bourdieu's crisp expression of *scholarship with commitment*, the word scholarship comes first and researchers must imperatively safeguard their intellectual autonomy in order to maximize the civic value of their engagement.[74]

Because it obeys the logic of the trial, much of the sociology of "race and ethnicity" is *group-oriented rather than problem-oriented*. It concentrates on documenting the trajectory, condition, and experiences of one or several ethnic groups, as defined by bureaucratic and everyday common sense, in keeping with the urge to show how this or that category was/is oppressed, suppressed, and/or actively engaged

---

[72] Tanya Golash-Boza, "A Critical and Comprehensive Sociological Theory of Race and Racism" (2016), p. 139, my italics.
[73] Max Weber, "Science as a Vocation" (1958 [1919]). Scientific criteria include egological, textual, and epistemic reflexivity (as discussed in Wacquant, *The Invention of the "Underclass,"* pp. 4–6), and thus encompass effects of "positionality."
[74] Pierre Bourdieu, "Pour un savoir engagé" (2001b).

Reframing Racial Domination

in valiant resistance. In so doing, this grievance-driven sociology typically takes for granted the existence of these coherent groups, falling into what Rogers Brubaker aptly calls the trap of "groupism,"[75] and misses the dynamic process whereby these were fabricated (or disbanded) at the cost of a complex work of group-making that has inscribed ethnoracial boundaries in the objectivity of social space and in the subjectivity of habitus (as will be argued *infra*, pp. 198–201).

This same proclivity restricts attention to *inter-racial* relations at the expense of *intra-racial* differentiations, to the near-total exclusion of the study of racial(ized) practices, beliefs, and institutions *among* subordinate categories.[76] This thwarts an adequate understanding of the differential impact of racial rule upon the collective psychology of the dominated and of the suffusive *sociological ambivalence* characteristic of the position and dispositions of intermediate groupings, such as the Coloured of South Africans or the *métis* of the French Caribbean. It is as if revealing that subjugated categories also have their own ethnoracial distinctions would tarnish them and blunt the critique of racial domination. This tendency is particularly pronounced today due to the reviviscence of populist epistemologies that accord on principle a privileged cognitive status to the putative concerns and viewpoints of the subordinate and treat the latter as a homogeneous bloc as a matter of course.[77]

The logic of the trial is premised on the accepted wisdom that "racism" is *in toto* the product of Western colonial expansion manufactured by "whites" to inferiorize "people of color." But we have seen earlier that this oddly Eurocentric view does not withstand historical and comparative scrutiny. To take one more example: a rich syncretic tradition of racial thinking played an integral role in the formation of national consciousness and society in modern China.[78] Mixing homegrown Confucian categories (rooted in the dualism between a "civilized" center and a "barbarian" periphery) with Western concepts of physical type, this tradition portrayed the Han Chinese as a distinct

---

[75] "Groupism" is the "tendency to take discrete, sharply differentiated, internally homogeneous and externally bounded groups as basic constituents of social life, chief protagonists of social conflicts, and fundamental units of social analysis." Rogers Brubaker, "Ethnicity Without Groups" (2002), p. 164.

[76] A demonstration of the fruitfulness of this approach is R. Douglas Cope, *The Limits of Racial Domination: Plebeian Society in Colonial Mexico City, 1660–1772* (1994).

[77] For a germane critique, see Olúfẹ́mi O. Táíwò, *Elite Capture: How the Powerful Took over Identity Politics (and Everything Else)* (2022).

[78] Frank Dikötter, *The Discourse of Race in Modern China* (1992).

biological grouping descended from the mythical Yellow Emperor. It anchored a rigid vision of a planetary racial hierarchy featuring "yellow" and "white" at the top and "black, red, and brown" at the bottom and it made eugenics into a preeminent instrument of national revival from the overthrow of the Manchu dynasty in 1911 until racial discourse was officially banned in 1949 by the new communist regime intent on promoting class as the preeminent principle of social vision and division.

Chinese beliefs about human physical discontinuity and inequality are particularly interesting because the Chinese considered skin tone an impermanent characteristic, self-evidently liable to change with exposure to cold and heat, with the result that "whiteness as a factor in racial differentiation was dismissed as a myth."[79] Under the impetus of the New Culture movement, the ideal of Occidentalism, and the spread of the press during the first Republic, Chinese racial thinking came to base its taxonomies first on blood purity (in an effort to salvage Sinocentrism), then on hair (hairiness being associated with bestiality), odor (each "race" with its own distinctive smell), and brain size (conveniently recomputed as "relative cranial capacity" so as to put the Chinese on top). Last and least reliable came skin color, admitting of ten shades, with pure yellow reserved for the Chinese.

An offshoot of the logic of the trial is what one might call *principled racial pessimism*: the automatic negation of any sort of positive change or trend, favorable fact, or encouraging development in the study of ethnoracial inequality. It is a point of honor of the true "radical" on the question: they are not deceived by the cunning of racial (racist) reason.[80] Evidence of the softening of stigmatization, reduction of disparities, amelioration of the social condition, or expansion of civic participation of the subordinate are treated as illusory, inconsequential or, worse, as deceitful backsliding. Thus the de-rigueur wholesale denunciations, by leading US scholars of "race and ethnicity," of the presidency of Barack Obama as, not just disappointing, but downright regressive. For Michael Omi and Howard Winant, "though modernized and 'moderated', structural racism has been fortified, not under-

---

[79] Ibid., p. 136.

[80] This principled pessimism finds a hyperbolic expression in "Afropessimism," for which the domination of blacks specifically is eternal, universal, and unyielding, the spawn of an ontological abjection constitutive of the white-dominated world regardless of time, place, and institution. I dissect this *radicalisme de papier* later in this chapter, *infra*, pp. 91–9.

mined, by civil rights reform."[81] For Eduardo Bonilla-Silva, during the period 2008–16, "racism has remained firmly in place and, even worse, is becoming a more daunting obstacle. The apparent blessing of having a black man in the White House is likely to become a curse for black and brown folks."[82] What is problematic is not the negative score given Obama so much as the fact that it is theoretically prefigured, that is, dictated by an *a priori* catastrophism spawned by the moral condemnation of "racism." One needs to ask here, in passing, what is the counterfactual, that racial trends in America would have improved under President McCain or that racial inequalities built over four hundred years would vanish in eight?

This is what Pierre Bourdieu excoriates as "the functionalism of the worst case": everything and all things always work to reproduce a nefarious social system, "as if they were the spawn of a Machiavellian intention."[83] This kind of reasoning – or mood – is fundamentally antithetical to social science in that it arbitrarily *freezes history* and invites moral-political over empirical-analytical judgment. In racial matters, as in other questions of durable inequality, we must beware of not willfully or inadvertently validating the "perpetual stasis" paradigm when we rightfully jettison the "progress paradigm."[84] Racial domination is a dynamic, multilayered, and complex phenomenon that requires *disaggregated parsing* and calls for *nuanced inquiry* rather than academic sloganeering and wholesale castigation,[85] which may be morally pleasing in the short term but is politically counterproductive in the long run since it masks possible levers for unhinging ethnoracial rule.

All these reasons make it urgent to reassert that to conduct *sociological analysis is not to conduct a trial*. The purpose of sociohistorical investigation is not to establish guilt and to affix blame for unpalatable social facts but to break those down into their constituent

---

[81] Michael Omi and Howard Winant, *Racial Formation in the United States* (2015), pp. 229–30.

[82] Eduardo Bonilla-Silva, *Racism without Racists: Color-Blind Racism and the Persistence of Racial Inequality in the United States* (2021 [2008]), p. 118.

[83] Pierre Bourdieu, *Questions de sociologie* (1980b), p. 111.

[84] This is the trap into which Louise Seamster and Victor Ray fall in their provocative article, "Against Teleology in the Study of Race: Toward the Abolition of the Progress Paradigm" (2018).

[85] The disaggregative approach is exemplified by Matthew Desmond and Mustafa Emirbayer's nuanced and deep dissection of *Racial Domination, Racial Progress: The Sociology of Race in America* (2009b), in which they break ethnoracial inequality down into eight separate yet interlinked domains.

Racial Domination

components so as to uncover the social and symbolic mechanisms that produce, reproduce, or transform them over time and across space. Its end-purpose is to *describe, explain and understand*, not to inculpate or exculpate, denigrate or celebrate. In his well-known 1904 essay on "Objectivity in Social Science and Social Policy," Max Weber writes: "There is, and always will be, an unbridgeable distinction among (1) those arguments which appeal to our capacity to become enthusiastic and our feeling for concrete practical aims or cultural forms and values, (2) those arguments in which, once it is a question of the validity of ethical norms, the appeal is directed to our conscience, and finally (3) those arguments that appeal to our capacity and need for *analytically ordering* empirical reality in a manner which lays claim to *validity* as empirical truth."[86] In this historical moment marked by the pull of epistemological populism and the push for rhetorical radicalism, it is particularly important to reaffirm the analytical imperative.

5. Race as denegated ethnicity

A fifth imperative to develop a robust framework for the sociology of ethnoracial domination is *to demarcate and repatriate*. To demarcate means *breaking with common sense*, ordinary and scholarly, and elaborating an analytic capacious enough to encompass the varied forms of racial rule deployed across time and space. The notion that science advances by breaking with opinion and prior knowledge already there, treated as "epistemological obstacles," to engage in an endless process of "rectification" producing "approximations" of reality as well as historical discontinuities in knowledge formation, is the core teaching of historical epistemology, the philosophy of science elaborated by Gaston Bachelard, Alexandre Koyré, and Georges Canguilhem, and put to work in social science by Michel Foucault and Pierre Bourdieu.[87] It is also the first commandment of the sociological method on which Marx, Durkheim, and Weber agree: folk and analytic concepts pertain to different knowledge registers; the former respond to social needs, express or veil conflictive interests, and

---

[86] Max Weber, *The Methodology of the Social Sciences* (1949 [1920]), p. 58.
[87] For an overview, see Dominique Lecourt, *Marxism and Epistemology: Bachelard, Canguilhem, Foucault* (2018 [1975]); Hans-Jörg Rheinberger, *On Historicizing Epistemology* (2010); and the discussion *supra*, pp. 5–8.

constitute practical cognitive recipes for action; the latter are forged specifically for purposes of scientific description, interpretation, and explanation.

Enter Bourdieu, who builds on this epistemological foundation to spotlight the fact that Marx's "ideologies," Durkheim's "prenotions," and Weber's "complexes of meaning," far from being mere illusions, are part and parcel of the objective reality of the social world – they form what he calls the "objectivity of the second order."[88] This means that we must effect a *double break*: in a first move, sweep aside ordinary racial beliefs to construct the material and symbolic political economy subtending ethnoracial stratification (that is, demarcate); then, in a second move, reincorporate in the objectivist model of racial domination those very perceptions and beliefs (that is, repatriate classification). This, Bourdieu stresses, is because "the 'social reality' of which the objectivists speak is also an object of perception. And social science must take as its object both this reality and the perception of this reality, the perspectives, the points of view that, depending on their position in objective social space, the agents form of this reality."[89] Racial subjectivity, emotions, discourses, and interpellation are part and parcel of the objective reality of racial rule and so they must figure fully in its science.

To effect repatriation, the second move of the double break, is essential because ethnicity is ultimately predicated upon *perception and discernment*, unlike other canonical principles of social vision and division which all have a stable and self-standing material foundation independent of cognition, class (the mode of production), gender (the mode of reproduction), age (the unfolding of biological life), and citizenship and nationhood (affiliation with a state). Racial phenomenology is integral to racial reality in a way that is not true of other bases of stratification – that is, classes exist absent class consciousness; not so ethnoracial groups in the absence of ethnically inflected cognition, if only by the dominant. Sartre put it best when he remarked that it is not history, religion, or territory that makes a person Jewish: "It is the anti-semite who makes the Jew."[90]

---

[88] Pierre Bourdieu, *Le Sens pratique* (1980a), chapter 9, "The Objectivity of the Subjective."

[89] Pierre Bourdieu, *Choses dites*, p. 154. No historical case demonstrates this proposition better than Nazism: Edouard Conte and Cornelia Essner, *La Quête de la race. Une anthropologie du nazisme* (1995), and Johann Chapoutot, *La Loi du sang. Penser et agir en nazi* (2014).

[90] Jean-Paul Sartre, *Réflexions sur la question juive* (1946), p. 84.

This specificity of race as basis for classification and stratification is also acknowledged by the African-American philosopher Charles Mills in these terms: "The mere existence of races, R1s and R2s, as phenotypically demarcated populations in a society would not on its own (*unlike class and gender*) delimit social possibilities. *What is required is the intersubjective recognition of race*, and the (possible) concomitant development of racial views, attitudes and dispositions."[91] In other words, *race is a pure modality of symbolic violence*, the bending of social reality to fit an asymmetric mental map of reality or, to put it more tersely still, a limiting case of the *realization of categories*, the conundrum at the heart of Pierre Bourdieu's sociology.[92]

A perfect illustration of the mapping of symbolic space onto social and physical space from above is the violent restructuring of a class-based into a race-based society by the Nazis in the momentous 12 years during which they held state power. Another is the reorganization along racial lines of the mental, social, and physical geography of South Africa under apartheid, seeking to align officially designated ethnoracial categories with social networks and neighborhoods. A third is provided by episodes of ethnic cleansing throughout history, especially those that seek both to remove the undesirable population and to erase all traces of the process of ethnic erasure itself, as with the violent ejection of 800,000 Palestinians and the destruction of over 570 Palestinian villages and towns at the founding of Israel, carefully omitted from the country's official history. A fourth is the mobilization by indigenous people in Bolivia seeking to realign state categories with social space from below in reaction to the neoliberal and multicultural reforms of the turn of the century.[93]

---

[91] Charles W. Mills, "Racial Justice" (2018), p. 75, my emphasis.

[92] The template for this analytic move is Pierre Bourdieu, "À propos de la famille comme catégorie réalisée" (1993b). An explication is Loïc Wacquant, "Symbolic Power and Group-Making: Bourdieu's Reframing of Class" (2013), pp. 276–7 and 281. I develop this argument in the next chapter, *infra*, pp. 197–205. When he obliquely touches on the question of the foundations of racial domination, Bourdieu stresses collective perception, positive or negative: "I am thinking, for instance, of the notion of ethnicity. It is a serious problem: why, in most societies, are some ethnicities devalorized, why are certain social groups stigmatized? On the contrary, why is there a sort of capital in being a member of certain groups, in having a certain skin color, a certain bodily hexis?" (Pierre Bourdieu, *Sociologie générale*, vol. 2 (2016), p. 867).

[93] See, respectively, Michael Burleigh and Wolfgang Wipperman, *The Racial State: Germany 1933–1945* (1991); A. J. Christopher, *The Atlas of Changing South Africa* (2001); Ilan Pappe, *The Ethnic Cleansing of Palestine* (2006); and Nancy Grey Postero, *Now We Are Citizens: Indigenous Politics in Postmulticultural Bolivia* (2007).

Reframing Racial Domination

But how do we capture the specificity of race as realized basis of classification and stratification? In what follows I lay down the lineaments of a framework that treats race as a *paradoxical subtype of ethnicity*, paradoxical in that it denies being ethnic, that is, founded on the accidents of history, and yet reveals that it is by this very denial (in the Freudian sense of *Verneinung*). By way of prelude, a clarification of the vexed conceptual relationship between ethnicity and race is in order. Stuart Hall famously noted that these two notions "play hide and seek with one another,"[94] but there are three commonly accepted manners of conceiving their relationship: disjunction, intersection, and subsumption or nesting (see figure 1).

It is conventional in Anglophone social science to represent these two principles of social vision and division as *different and disjoint*, the former being based on cultural characteristics (language, religion, mores, etc.) and the latter on physical characteristics (phenotype and ancestry).[95] This is the position exemplified by Michael Omi and Howard Winant in their influential book *Racial Formation in the United States*, which strives hard to prevent the "reduction" of race to ethnicity, class, and nationality and in which we read: "Race is a concept which signifies and symbolizes social conflicts and interests by reference to different types of human bodies."[96] This definition is nothing more than the inscription, onto the mental structures of US social scientists, of the folk notions born of the peculiarities of American history as a settler colony and land of immigration. Race as descent was invoked and legally codified in the seventeenth century to bolster the exploitation of African slaves while ethnicity was coined in the early twentieth century to express and tame the fear that non-Anglo-Saxon migrants from South and Eastern Europe would not "assimilate" into the national pattern. What is more, as Desmond King has shown in *Making Americans*, ethnicity was formulated by and for whites to distinguish themselves from blacks. That is, the

The implications of the misalignment of official classification systems are explored by Cecilia Menjívar, "State Categories, Bureaucracies of Displacement, and Possibilities from the Margins" (2023).
[94] Stuart Hall, *The Fateful Triangle: Race, Ethnicity, Nation* (2017), p. 26.
[95] For a deft genealogy of the two terms, see Werner Sollors, "Ethnicity and Race" (2001). Different national intellectual traditions are more or less welcoming to the race–ethnicity dualism. In Francophone social research, it is considered confusing if not invalid, and the term "ethnoracial" is commonly used instead. Solène Brun and Claire Cosquer, *Sociologie de la race* (2022), p. 67.
[96] Michael Omi and Howard Winant, *Racial Formation in the United States* (2015), p. 55. Loury adopts a similar definition in *Anatomy of Racial Inequality*, pp. 20–1.

Racial Domination

1. DISJOINT
(Omi and Winant)

2. OVERLAPPING
(Cornell and Hartmann)

3. NESTED
(Wimmer)

E = ethnicity
R = race

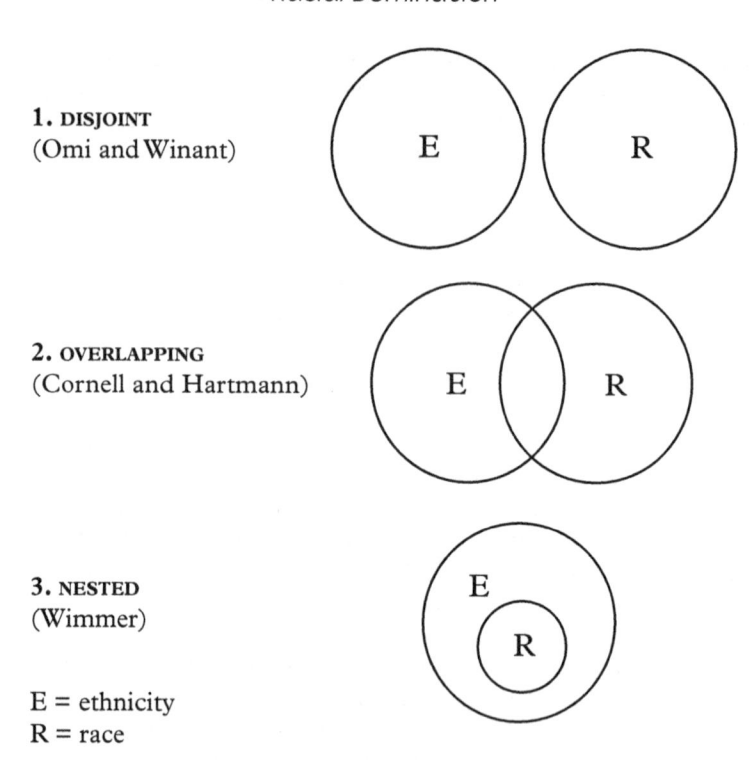

Figure 1 The conceptual relationship between ethnicity and race.

opposition between the two concepts is *historical and political, not logical*.[97]

Racial formation theory is thus not a general theory of racial domination so much as a stylized redescription of the folk understanding of the ethnoracial trajectory of two populations in one country during roughly one century. What is more, Omi and Winant's definition of race surprisingly excludes hegemonic and doxic racial regimes which by definition preclude conflict.[98] It is also inapplicable in a host of cases, starting with Japan, China, India, Nazi Germany, and even

---

[97] Fields, "Slavery, Race and Ideology in the United States of America"; Kathleen Conzen et al., "The Invention of Ethnicity in the United States" (1998); Desmond S. King, *Making Americans: Immigration, Race, and the Origins of the Diverse Democracy* (2002). See also Victoria Hattam, *In the Shadow of Race: Jews, Latinos, and Immigration Politics in the United States* (2007).

[98] For a forceful critique of the notion that ethnicity always entails "ethnic groups in conflict," see Rogers Brubaker, *Ethnicity Without Groups* (2004), chapter 1.

Brazil and South Africa where body type is not the sole foundation of ethnoracial classification (as we shall see *infra*, pp. 172–4). It confounds race with other classifications based on "different types of human bodies" such as gender, height, and looks which are all deeply consequential in contemporary societies.[99] Finally, the disjunctive conception is incoherent in that "signification" is a quintessentially symbolic activity, which makes race a cultural construct formally indistinguishable from ethnicity.

The second position, defended by Stephen Cornell and Douglas Hartmann, agrees that ethnicity and race differ but proposes that they *overlap*.[100] Some groups are defined by reference to culture, other groups by reference to nature, and yet others by reference to both. This creates an area of intersection in which two processes converge: on the one side, ethnicity is racialized when it entails beliefs about the phenotypical characteristics of the group formed; on the other side, race is ethnicized when it fosters a sense of peoplehood. In addition, some groups migrate from one category to the next over time – the classic example being the deracialization of Eastern and Southern European immigrants within a few decades of landing in the United States in the early twentieth century.[101] This position attenuates but does not quite resolve the logical inconsistency of the distinction between race and ethnicity born of the American experience, which is this: it is not the brute fact of bodily difference (e.g., skin tone) that determines membership in a race but the significance that people accord (or not) to such and such phenotypical property, that is, a *particular cultural reading of the body*. A racial marker is always the product of an ethnic fabrication.

Mustafa Emirbayer and Matthew Desmond also adopt the view that ethnicity and race are different but that they are both needed for sociological analysis, a variant of the intersectional position that one might characterize as analytic-historicist. On the one hand, they recognize that ethnicity encompasses race conceptually; on the other, they wish to retain race to capture the brute fact that "white privilege

---

[99] Ellis P. Monk Jr. et al., "Beholding Inequality: Race, Gender, and Returns to Physical Attractiveness in the United States" (2021).

[100] Stephen Cornell and Douglas Hartmann, *Ethnicity and Race: Making Identities in a Changing World* (2006), pp. 26–36. See also idem, "Conceptual Confusion and Divides: Race, Ethnicity, and the Study of Immigration" (2004).

[101] Matthew Frye Jacobson, *Whiteness of a Different Color: European Immigrants and the Alchemy of Race* (1998).

is the essential defining feature of the global racial order."[102] The problem with this position is that it is inherently unstable, always liable to capsize into the primacy of one or the other notion and, given the pressure of public expectations, to swim with the political tide of the moment. After all, why does the fact that Euro-Americans dominate the world necessitate its own concept? The fact that men dominate the world does not necessitate a special concept of masculinity that cannot be rolled under that of gender domination.

The third position, best explicated by Andreas Wimmer in his landmark book *Ethnic Boundary Making*, draws the logical consequence of this historical fact and *nests race squarely inside ethnicity* as indicated in figure 1.[103] This approach is analytically coherent and historically capacious. It allows us to travel across epochs and regions without unconsciously using the ethnoracial trajectory of one society, the United States, as yardstick by which to measure the trajectories of other societies.[104] But concentric circles is not the best way to represent visually the relationship between race and ethnicity. This much is suggested by going a couple of steps further than Wimmer. First, race results from *paradoxical subsumption* in that it defines itself through the very negation of its symbolic rooting. Race is a form of cultural membership that loudly proclaims "I am not cultural" (meaning historical and arbitrary) and this has real effects – one of which is the reification of this claim in the disjunctive conception and another that domination is facilitated to the degree that it is naturalized. In short, *race is denegated ethnicity*, a form of ethnicity that cloaks itself in the garment of nature and yet reveals its historical rooting by this very dissimulation.

Second step: the relation between ethnicity and race is not well captured by a concentric diagram in which race has clear boundaries; rather, the distinction between the two categories is labile and

---

[102] Emirbayer and Desmond, *The Racial Order*, p. 61. This is a different position than that put forth a few years earlier in "What Is Racial Domination?" (2009, p. 339) in which they assert that "race, ethnicity, and nationality are overlapping symbolic categories" that are "mutually reinforcing insofar as each category educates, upholds, and is informed by the others."

[103] Andreas Wimmer, *Ethnic Boundary Making: Institutions, Power, Networks* (2013). Two other clear-eyed articulations of the subsumption position are Orlando Patterson, *The Ordeal of Integration: Progress and Resentment in America's "Racial" Crisis* (1997), and Joane Nagel, *Race, Ethnicity, and Sexuality: Intimate Intersections, Forbidden Frontiers* (2003).

[104] Pierre Bourdieu and Loïc Wacquant, "The Cunning of Imperialist Reason" (1999 [1998]).

porous because *racialization is a symbolic process and therefore a matter of degree.*[105] This is why I prefer to the figure of subsumption the *continuum of ethnicity* along which the latter gradually acquires more and more properties pertaining to race (imposition, stigma, rigidity, consequentiality, etc.) as indicated in figure 2 and further elaborated in the next section. This is consistent with the usage by Max Weber, who writes: "If we ignore cases of clear-cut linguistic boundaries and sharply demarcated political or religious communities as a basis of differences of customs ... then there are *only gradual transitions of custom and no immutable ethnic frontiers* except those due to gross geographical differences."[106]

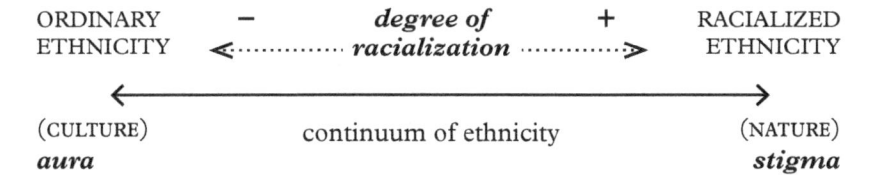

```
ORDINARY        −      degree of       +      RACIALIZED
ETHNICITY     <········ racialization ········>  ETHNICITY
<─────────────────────────────────────────────>
(CULTURE)           continuum of ethnicity        (NATURE)
aura                                              stigma
```

Figure 2 The continuum of ethnicity from ordinary to racialized.

This conception of racialization as naturalizing ethnicization allows us to encompass all the cases that the disjunctive and intersectional conceptions cover and more, and it enables us to unload the baggage of the historical ethnoracial unconscious of America that "weighs like a nightmare on the brains" of Anglophone and increasingly global social scientists, to quote one of Marx's celebrated formulas.

---

[105] To be fair, Wimmer stresses that ethnicity itself entails boundaries that are more or less diffuse and passable: "Ethnic distinctions may be fuzzy and boundaries soft, with unclear demarcation and few consequences ... The concept of boundary does not imply closure and clarity, which vary in degree from one society, social situation, or institutional context to another. It represents one of the foremost tasks of the comparative study of ethnicity to account for such *varying degrees of boundedness*." Wimmer, *Ethnic Boundary Making*, pp. 9–10, my italics.
[106] Max Weber, *Economy and Society: An Outline of Interpretive Sociology* (1978 [1918–22]), vol. 1, p. 392.

Diagonal of racialization

But the continuum of ethnicity does not tell the whole story. The process of racialization unfolds, not only in the order of *difference*, which stipulates gradations of recognition, but also that of *inequality*, based on increments of distribution.[107] So the *horizontal axis of classification*, running from the aura of ethnic self-identification to the stigma of imposed racial categorization must be supplemented by the *vertical axis of stratification*, which records the unequal allocation of capital in all of its forms, as well as living conditions and life chances across categories.

Figure 3 offers a synoptic view of the analytic of ethnoracial vision and division bringing together these two dimensions. It combines Gaston Bachelard's mandate to effect a clean "epistemological rupture" with common sense (lay and scholarly), considering the "illusory character of [the] primary experience" of race in any given society; Max Weber's theory of "status group" as a collective based on an "effective claim to social esteem in terms of positive or negative privileges"; and Pierre Bourdieu's theory of "symbolic power" as "the power to constitute the given by enunciating it," that is, "to impose the legitimate definition of the divisions of the social world, and thence to make and unmake groups."[108] It offers an *ideal-typical blueprint* with which to investigate the causes, forms, and consequences of ethnoracial domination.

This framework posits that ethnicity as basis for social identity, strategy, and structure runs along a *continuum* rooted in what Weber calls "the social estimation of honor," whatever its basis. It may indeed be granted or denied on a wide range of grounds, for "any cultural trait, no matter how superficial, can serve as a starting point for the familiar tendency to monopolistic closure."[109] Honor is another name for

---

[107] A stimulative discussion of the dissimilarity and dialectic between difference and inequality is Rogers Brubaker, *Grounds for Difference* (2015), chapter 1.

[108] Gaston Bachelard, *La Formation de l'esprit scientifique. Contribution à une psychanalyse de la connaissance objective* (1938), p. 26; Weber, *Economy and Society*, p. 305; Pierre Bourdieu, *Langage et pouvoir symbolique* (2000 [1982, 1991]), p. 283.

[109] Weber, *Economy and Society*, vol. 1, pp. 388. "The more or less easy emergence of social circles in the broadest sense (*soziale Verkehrsgemeinschaft*) may be linked to the most superficial features of historically accidental habits just as much as to inherited racial [i.e., physical] characteristics ... Differences in the styles of beard and hairdo, clothes, food and eating habits, division of labor between the sexes, and all kinds of other visible differences can, in a given case, give rise to repulsion and contempt, but the actual extent of these differences is irrelevant for the emotional impact ... All

Reframing Racial Domination

what Bourdieu calls *symbolic capital*, which is the form that any capital assumes when it is misrecognized as such. It resides thus, not in a specific attribute, but in the collective gaze that valorizes this attribute and in the collective belief in the dignity, glory, gallantry and repute of its possessors (in Middle English, the word honor also means splendor, beauty, excellence, and for women it connotes chastity).[110]

```
IDENTIFICATION – choice              constraint – CATEGORIZATION
thin – inconsequential                    consequential – thick
malleable           [CLASSIFICATION]              rigid
                 "social estimation of honor"
 –  ←─────────────────────────────────────────→  +
                    horizontality

                       racialization
                                              verticality   [STRATIFICATION]

                                          caste
```

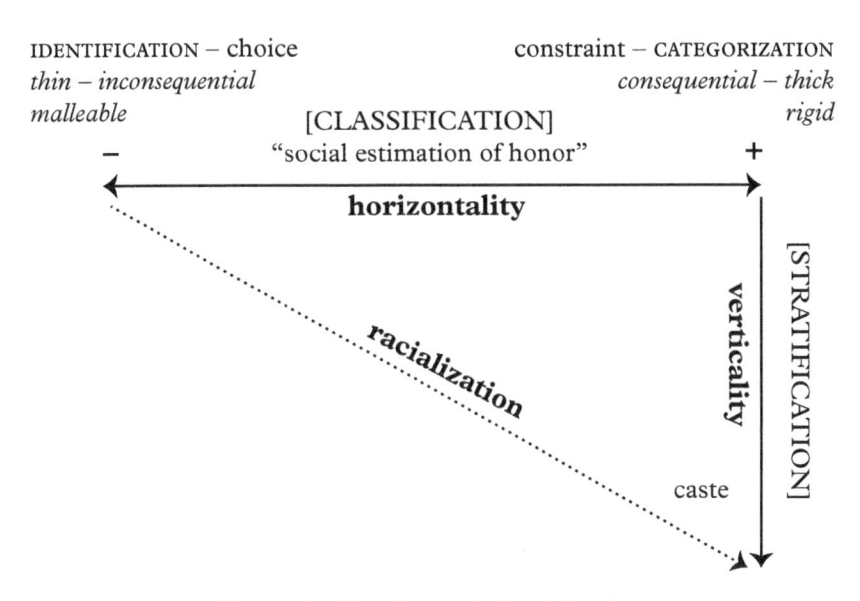

Figure 3 The diagonal of racialization.

Grasped along the axis of heterogeneity, ethnicity runs the gamut from pure identification (a self-attributed identity), based on choice, stamped by aura and tending toward *horizontality* (meaning that ethnicized populations are on a plane of symbolic equality, each endowed with dignity), to pure categorization (an other-attributed identity, where dignity is graded and can be denied), imposed by constraint, stamped by stigma or collective dishonor, and tending toward *verticality*, that is, increasingly steep and durable inequality. At one end of the continuum, "thin" ethnicity fully admits its arbitrariness:

differences of customs can sustain a specific sense of honor or dignity in their practitioners" (ibid., p. 387).
[110] Bourdieu, *Le Sens pratique*, pp. 200–1. A remarkable interdisciplinary collection on the topic is John G. Peristiany and Julian Pitt-Rivers (eds.), *Honor and Grace in Anthropology* (1992).

it is overtly "ethnic" in the sense that it is self-evidently grounded in the vagaries of *culture and history*, as with variants of ethnoreligious, ethnonational, and ethnoregional categories – Jews in contemporary France, Uzbeks in the former Soviet Union, Okinawans in modern Japan, Toltecs in present-day Mexico, for instance.[111]

This pole of the spectrum is often labeled "symbolic ethnicity," following Herbert Gans and students of "white ethnicity" in the US after him.[112] This is confusing because all ethnic forms, thin or thick, malleable or rigid, racialized or not, are fundamentally symbolic: absent an act of cognitive classification based on (dis)honor, there is no ethnicity, however flimsy (e.g., claiming one's Mexican-American identity only on Cinco de Mayo). Also, we must imperatively avoid the trap of treating symbolic power as "merely symbolic" in the common sense of decorative, efflorescent, secondary to material reality, and devoid of consequentiality. For *ethnoracial domination is rooted in symbolic violence*, the capacity to preserve or transform the world by imposing categories of perception, appreciation, and action (habitus) and making the world as it is seem like the only possible world.[113] So much so that any theoretical approach that does not foreground, let alone acknowledge, the constitutive dimension of symbolic power, its "world-making" efficacy, is fated to miss the specificity of racial rule.

At the other end of the continuum, "thick" ethnicity denies its own historicity (which thus becomes covert) and claims to be rooted in the necessities of *nature and biology* – or its logical analogue, culture understood as hard-wired and virtually unchanging – materialized in its most extreme form by caste and caste-like arrangements. Thin or ordinary ethnicity is malleable, often temporary or episodic, and it applies differently in different sectors of social life (indeed, it can be present and consequential in some and absent in others); thick or racialized ethnicity is rigid, seemingly permanent, it impregnates all zones of social structure and subjectivity, and it impacts the gamut of social outcomes resulting in multiform closure and thus strong group formation.[114] Max Weber put it lucidly in *Wirtschaft und Gesellschaft*:

---

[111] This expansive conception resolves the definitional dilemmas pointed out by Kanchan Chandra, "What Is Ethnic Identity and Does It Matter?" (2006).

[112] Herbert Gans, "Symbolic Ethnicity: The Future of Ethnic Groups and Cultures in America" (1979); Richard D. Alba, *Ethnic Identity: The Transformation of White America* (1990); Mary C. Waters, *Ethnic Options: Choosing Identities in America* (1990).

[113] Pierre Bourdieu, *Méditations pascaliennes* (1997), pp. 206–14.

[114] An illustration of the former is what Brubaker et al. call "everyday ethnicity"

"A status segregation grown into a caste differs in its structure from a mere 'ethnic' segregation: the caste structure transforms the horizontal and unconnected coexistences of ethnically segregated groups into a vertical social system of super- and subordination."[115]

It bears stressing here that a Weberian ideal type, such as figure 3 captures, is *not* a description of social phenomena but a "mental construct" (*Gedankenbild*) obtained through "one-sided accentuation," which provides an analytic benchmark against which to dissect social formations and formulate hypotheses.[116] Thus, in historical reality, the various oppositions featured in the diagram are not so neatly aligned but often collapsed, combined, enmeshed, or nested one inside the other. For instance, identification and categorization are always both present in ethnic formation; choice and constraint are also intermingled in different proportions and in different institutions; identification is seemingly permanent until it dissolves under the press of social change, as when ethnoregional identities get swamped, nay erased, by ethnonational ones, or vice versa, with the collapse of national states devolving into ethnoreligious splinters. As for attributions of stigma, they can be challenged and even inverted, as when a category develops internal forms of collective pride under the hard crust of symbolic denigration by the dominant.[117] Nonetheless, this ideal type has the virtue of providing "unambiguous means" – to quote Weber again – for traveling across the span of historical cases and fostering rigorous comparison liable to nourish further theorizing. Particular historical cases can be gauged by their *empirical distance* from the "pure" model so that we may ask what social conditions and mechanisms account for this divergence.

In particular, this framework helps us to focalize and to problematize what I call the *diagonal of racialization*, the historical process whereby a population or category is pushed or pulled from the top-left side of the horizontal axis of the diagram down toward the bottom-right side of the vertical axis where ethnicity turns ethnoracial, that is, thick, rigid, all-encompassing, and consequential across

---

(*Nationalist Politics and Everyday Ethnicity in a Transylvanian Town* [2006]); a case of the latter is ethnoracial categorization under apartheid as dissected by John Western in *Outcast Cape Town* (1997 [1981]).

[115] Weber, *Economy and Society*, p. 934.

[116] Weber, "'Objectivity' in Social Science and Social Policy" (1947 [1904]), p. 90.

[117] For examples of these two configurations, see, respectively, Eugen Weber, *Peasants into Frenchmen: The Modernization of Rural France, 1870–1914* (1976), and Drake and Cayton, *Black Metropolis*, chapters 14 and 23.

all sectors of social reality, as in a caste regime.[118] An illustration is the racialization of Kurds after the Turkish state abandoned its official policy of assimilation at the end of the 1980s.[119] Kurdish identity, which had hitherto been perceived as a matter of malleable culture and self-assertion, became a question of external assignation as well as perceived as inherently different, inferior, and threatening. Phenotypical characteristics such as complexion and facial hair came to the fore as did the belief that Kurds were born criminals and morally corrupt.[120]

This model of ethnoracial domination can also be used to study cases of *deracialization*, as when Irish-Americans and Jews in the US lose their status as a separate "race" to merge into the "white" ethnic designation as well as cases of failed ethnoracial submersion, such as the Zainichi in Japan after World War II, or ethnic absorption as experienced by Portuguese immigrants in France.[121] It can also be deployed to illumine the vexed question of resistance and the two major forms it can assume: under what material and symbolic conditions do the subordinate come to challenge ethnoracial classification (e.g., asking for the recognition or erasure of categories as well as for the reduction of stigma attached to them) and to contest ethnoracial stratification (i.e., asking for an equal or equitable distribution of resources across categories).

In this perspective, to racialize means (i) to *naturalize*, to turn history into biology, cultural differences into dissimilarities of essence;

---

[118] Gerald D. Berreman, "Race, Caste, and Other Invidious Distinctions in Social Stratification" (1972); John Dollard, *Caste and Class in a Southern Town* (1937); Susan Bayly, *Caste, Society and Politics in India from the Eighteenth Century to the Modern Age* (2001). Briefly put, a caste regime is a hierarchical system of fixed categories that are ascribed at birth, culturally distinct, endogamous, and sustained by a doctrine of purity or inherent superiority (validated by religion, science, or folk belief). See *infra*, pp. 269–72 for an elaboration.

[119] Murat Ergin, "The Racialization of Kurdish Identity in Turkey" (2014).

[120] This finds an expression in "exclusive recognition," that is, categorization leading to the rejection of Kurds in face-to-face interaction, as shown by Cenk Saraçoğlu, *Kurds of Modern Turkey: Migration, Neoliberalism and Exclusion in Turkish Society* (2011).

[121] Noel Ignatiev, *How the Irish Became White* (1994), but see Thomas Angelo Guglielmo, *White on Arrival: Italians, Race, Color, and Power in Chicago, 1890–1945* (2000); Karen Brodkin, *How Jews Became White Folks and What That Says about Race in America* (1998); John Lie, *Zainichi (Koreans in Japan): Diasporic Nationalism and Postcolonial Identity* (2008); Marie-Christine Volovitch-Tavares, *Cent ans d'histoire des Portugais en France, 1916–2016* (2016), but see Margot Delon, "Des 'Blancs honoraires'? Les trajectoires sociales des Portugais et de leurs descendants en France" (2019).

(ii) to *eternalize*, to stipulate that those differences are enduring if not unchanging across time, past, present, and future; (iii) to *hierarchize* by setting up a rank-ordering of population groups; and (iv) to *homogenize*, to perceive and picture all members of the racialized category as fundamentally alike, as sharing an essential quality that warrants differential treatment of its members in symbolic, social, and physical space. Like racialization itself, naturalization, eternalization, hierarchization, and homogenization are not things or states but symbolic activities, involving a real and imagined relation between the racializer and the racialized, and a matter of degree; but they tend to proceed apace and closely implicate one another. One paradoxical form of racialization is the belief by the subordinate, or their self-appointed spokespersons, that they possess some shared essence, unchanging and uniform, as in variants of Afropessimism for which all blacks everywhere face the same forces of anti-blackness forever, no matter their social position and the institutional constellations they face, as if they, and they alone, had the ontological burden of existing outside of history.[122]

Excursus: The radical abdication of Afropessimism

The term Afropessimism was first used in print in 1987 by the French minister of Cooperation (that is, African affairs) Michel Aurillac in an editorial published in *Le Monde* cautioning against the view that economic development and political democratization in sub-Saharan Africa were forever stalled.[123] It was used and abused in the two ensuing decades by African economists and Africanist commentators who refused to see colonialism as the root cause of the continent's predicament and stressed instead postcolonial corruption, ethnic dissension, and the patrimonialization of the state as sources of societal stasis. It was later evoked in discussion of the prospects and pitfalls of foreign investment in Africa.[124]

---

[122] Frank B. Wilderson, III, *Afropessimism* (2020).
[123] The notion is developed by Aurillac in *L'Afrique à coeur* (1987).
[124] David Rieff, "In Defense of Afro-pessimism" (1998); Gareth Austin, "Markets, Democracy and African Economic Growth: Liberalism and Afro-Pessimism Reconsidered" (2000). The term continues to be used in this sense by economists. It sparked a counteroffensive, led by the Nigerian political scientist Ebere Onwudiwe, under the banner of "Afro-optimism": Ebere Onwudiwe and Minabere Ibelema (eds.), *Afro-Optimism: Perspectives on Africa's Advances* (2003).

The term Afropessimism, but not its early referent, was then appropriated in the 2010s by a new generation of black academics in American departments of ethnic studies and humanities to refer to the anti-humanist notion that "blackness is coterminous with slaveness" and that *"Blacks are not Human subjects, but are instead structurally inert props, implements for the execution of White and non-Black fantasies and sadomasochistic pleasures."*[125] To the narrative of racial progress, Afropessimism opposes a counter-narrative in which the perpetual denial of black humanity is everywhere built into the very makeup of civil society: "Afropessimism gives us the freedom to say out loud what we would otherwise whisper or deny: that no Blacks are in the world, but, by the same token, there is no world without Blacks . . . The violence perpetrated against us is not a form of discrimination; it is a necessary violence; a health tonic for everyone who is not Black."[126] It is, moreover, perpetual and without recourse: workers can oppose and yearn to overthrow capitalism, women patriarchy, LGBT people heterosexism, colonial subjects imperialism. For blacks, there is no politics of liberation; they are excluded forever from "a narrative of redemption" because the world "find[s] its nourishment in Black flesh."[127] As for other "people of color," their plight cannot be compared or merged with the predicament of blacks: "Analogy *mystifies*, rather than clarifies, Black suffering. Analogy mystifies Black peoples' relationship to other people of color."[128]

What are we to make of this claim? Frank Wilderson's book *Afropessimism* is a disconcerting memoir and a provocative travelogue about being black in America from the vantage point of the cultural bourgeoisie. Wilderson, a Dartmouth-, Columbia- and Berkeley-educated author and professor of drama and African-American studies with varied life experiences as activist, stock-broker, and academic, is the son of a university dean father and a school administrator

---

[125] Frank Wilderson, III, *Afropessimism*, p. 15, original italics. The other leading thinkers of Afropessimism include the literary scholar Saidiya Hartman, the poet and critic David Marriott, and the film and media study scholar Jared Sexton. The same ontological mood is captured by the varied contributions to Moon-Kie Jung and João H. Costa Vargas (eds.), *Antiblackness* (2021).

[126] Wilderson, *Afropessimism*, p. 40. This is a universalization of the claim made 30 years ago by the black legal scholar Derrick Bell, that racism is an "integral, permanent, and indestructible component" of American society. Derrick Bell, *Faces at the Bottom of the Well: The Permanence of Racism* (1992), p. ix. Bell's book was republished in 2018 to ride the wave of black protest and pessimism.

[127] Wilderson, *Afropessimism*, pp. 16–17.

[128] Ibid., p. 228.

mother who also had a private practice as psychologists. His childhood growing up in an upscale district of Minneapolis was stamped by the cultural capital and racial bridging endeavors of his parents on and off campus. Wilderson presents his book as "storytelling" whose "narrator is a slave."[129] It is perhaps best read as an exercise in "auto-theory," the "commingling of theory and philosophy with autobiography," a "critical artistic practice indebted to feminist writing activism."[130]

Afropessimism is difficult to gauge and critique because, when it takes leave from its memoirist voice, it situates itself at an abstract "meta-theoretical" level so high that no historical reality can possibly reach it and, when the time comes for conceptual explication, it escapes back into narration.[131] It then proceeds by postulation rather than demonstration, by allegory rather than argument. It weaves a rich and vibrant tapestry of childhood memories, family anecdotes, work and love experiences, political sorties, academic encounters, novels, movies, philosophical texts, conceptual disquisitions, and historical accounts, which it places on a plane of epistemic equality. How can we assess this intellectual position from the standpoint of the agonistic sociology of ethnoracial domination? Note that a principled defense might be that Afropessimism is a (or the) *poetics* of blackness, written by a dramatist; and so that it should not be taken literally and appraised by social scientific standards. But Wilderson claims this approach is an analytic, one that "labors as a corrective to Humanist assumptive logic," and this analytic is being used by sociologists to develop and reorient empirical arguments or to deny their very possibility.[132]

---

[129] Ibid., p. xiv.
[130] Lauren Fournier, *Autotheory as Feminist Practice in Art, Writing, and Criticism* (2021).
[131] "Afropessimism, then, is less of a theory and more of a *metatheory*: a critical project that, by deploying Blackness as a lens of interpretation, interrogates the unspoken, assumptive logic of Marxism, postcolonialism, psychoanalysis, and feminism." Wilderson, *Afropessimism*, p. 14. A missed opportunity here: to engage the long strand of pessimistic social theorizing running from Hobbes's state of nature to Weber's iron cage to Freud's death wish.
[132] See, for instance, Victor Erik Ray et al., "Critical Race Theory, Afro-Pessimism, and Racial Progress Narratives" (2017); George Weddington, "Political Ontology and Race Research: A Response to 'Critical Race Theory, Afro-Pessimism, and Racial Progress Narratives'" (2019); Sirma Bilge, "The Fungibility of Intersectionality: An Afropessimist Reading" (2020); Anthony Ryan Hatch, "The Data will not Save Us: Afropessimism and Racial Antimatter in the COVID-19 Pandemic" (2022).

Afropessimism is an exclusivist brand of race primordialism. It is *primordialist* in that it sees race – or, rather, blackness, as uniquely institutionalized in the United States and then universalized by a stroke of the pen – as foundational to being, knowledge, and power; as permanent, pervasive, and impossible to dislodge from its role as structural mooring and existential pivot.[133] It is *exclusivist* in that it reserves this ontological burden for blacks and for blacks alone: "Afro-pessimism is a lens of interpretation that accounts for civil society's dependence on antiblack violence – a regime of violence that positions black people as internal enemies of civil society, and cannot be analogized with the regimes of violence that disciplines the Marxist subaltern, the postcolonial subaltern, the colored but non-black Western immigrant, the nonblack queer, or the nonblack woman."[134] The uniqueness of the black plight is asserted, not through methodical genealogy and comparison, but on the authority of the author's own identity, experience, and meta-theoretical prowess.

The epicentral notion of Afropessimism is that of *slaveness*: "Afropessimism is premised on a comprehensive and iconoclastic claim: that Blackness is coterminous with Slaveness: Blackness *is* social death: which is to say that there was never a prior meta-moment of plenitude, never equilibrium: never a moment of social life."[135] Afropessimists claim that their use of slavery is not metaphorical but tautegorical, grounded in Orlando Patterson's sociology of slavery: "The black is positioned, a priori, as slave. The definition of slave is taken from Orlando Patterson who theorizes slavery as a relational dynamic between 'social death' (the slave) and 'social life' (the human)."[136]

However, for Patterson, slavery is *not* a racial institution but an organization of extreme domination that may or may not be racialized. It is, moreover, an institution that, not only varies immensely

---

[133] "What is essential is neither the interpersonal nor institutional orientation toward blackness, but the fact that blackness is the essence of that which orients. Put differently, the coherence of reality (be it institutional or interpersonal coherence) is secured by anxiety over both the idea and the presence of blacks." Patrice Douglass et al., "Afro-Pessimism" (2018).

[134] Ibid. "Black suffering is of a different order than the suffering of other people" and "Black suffering is the life force of the world" (Wilderson, *Afropessimism*, p. 200).

[135] Wilderson, *Afropessimism*, p. 102; that passage is repeated word for word on page 226.

[136] Douglass et al., "Afro-Pessimism." Note that the notion of "social death" was coined by French anthropologist Michel Izard, as duly noted by Patterson, *Slavery and Social Death*, p. 38.

across the span of human history, from the familial to the genocidal, but also everywhere fails to quash the slave's humanity. Indeed, it is *haunted* by the slave's refusal of the denial of their humanity. This is why it needs brute force to sustain itself. This is why the analysis of the internal relations of slavery must be articulated with the analysis of enslavement (entry) and manumission (exit): "Enslavement, slavery, and manumission are not merely related events: they are one and the same process in different phases."[137] Thus the master dangles the possibility of manumission before the eyes of the slaves *precisely because they remain human under bondage*: "The slave desires nothing more passionately than dignity, belonging, and release. By holding out the promise of redemption, the master provides himself with a motivating force more powerful than any whip. Slavery in this way was a self-correcting institution: what it denied the slave it utilized as the major means of motivating him."

In sum, slavery contains its own negation: for Patterson, *slave marks a liminal state, not an ontological one*. Again, this is because human bondage curtails but fails to annihilate the humanity of the slave: "Everywhere the slave's zest for life and fellowship confounded the slaveholder class; and in all slaveholding societies the *existential dignity* of the slave belied the slaveholder's denial of its existence."[138] To conceive of "the Black" as "the Slave," in the singular, also belies the fact that slaves are not alone; they live in a *community of slaves* which is the crucible sustaining their humanness, as Patterson demonstrates in his ground-breaking 1967 book on the distinctive social relations and communal values of slaves on the plantations of Jamaica in the eighteenth and nineteenth centuries.[139]

It follows that the violence of slavery is not "gratuitous," indiscriminate, and Pavlovian, as Wilderson and his followers would have it.[140] Patterson is clear that "it was necessary continually to repeat the original, violent act of transforming free man into slave" because

---

[137] Patterson, *Slavery and Social Death*, p. 296.

[138] Ibid., pp. 337–8, my italics.

[139] Orlando Patterson, *The Sociology of Slavery: Black Society in Jamaica 1655–1838* (2022 [1967]). This bold thesis was validated a decade later by the classic studies of Eugene D. Genovese, *Roll, Jordan, Roll: The World the Slaves Made* (1976), and John W. Blassingame, *The Slave Community: Plantation Life in the Ante-Bellum South* (1979).

[140] "The Slave's relationship to violence is open-ended, gratuitous, without reason or constraint, triggered by prelogical catalysts that are unmoored from her transgressions and unaccountable to historical shifts" (Wilderson, *Afropessimism*, pp. 216–17, also pp. 93–4 and 248–9). This claim is repeated by Ray et al., "Critical Race Theory, Afro-Pessimism, and Racial Progress Narratives," p. 150.

enslavement was never accepted. "The continuous violence in the slave order was also made necessary by the low motivation of the slave to work."[141] Far from being needless and wanton, then, the brute force of the master was *strategic and calibrated*, and thus highly variable in both form and frequency across societies and epochs. It was needed to reduce a human to a living thing (*res*) which existed only as an extension of the master, but remained human all the same.

So much for slavery and violence, but what of blackness? In his critique of *Afropessimism* in *The New Yorker*, Vincent Cunningham notes wryly that "Wilderson's book is the story of an American who thinks of his Blackness as normative and therefore as characteristic of Blackness around the world."[142] Indeed, mired in the racial doxa of his home country, Wilderson takes blackness as a self-evident, fixed, and homogeneous category. He never stops to ponder the question posed by the sociologist F. James Davis in his classic book *Who Is Black?*, which establishes that the US definition of blackness through strict hypodescent (the "one-drop rule"), disregarding phenotype, social status, and non-African ancestry, is a global outlier.[143] Even within the United States, a rival system of ethnoracial classification built on gradations of color and recognizing intermediate categories between blacks and whites (mulatto, quadroon, octoroon, sambo, mango, etc.) was operative in southern states such as South Carolina and Louisiana until the mid-nineteenth century under the influence of Caribbean migration and imports from Catholic French and Spanish culture.[144] So the clear-cut black–white or black–other dichotomy is neither universal nor necessary. The racial classification of "blacks" varies across societies and times and so does their racial stratification. This historical variation in modes of racial domination is just what the rhetoric of Afropessimism unknowingly denies and magically disappears.

But there is more when it comes to blackness in the United States specifically. The notion that it is a compact construct is a social fiction and thus a literary facility that ignores the long history and continued

---

[141] Patterson, *Slavery and Social Death*, pp. 2–3.
[142] Vincent Cunningham, "The Argument of 'Afropessimism'" (2020).
[143] F. James Davis, *Who Is Black? One Nation's Definition* (1991).
[144] Joel Williamson, *New People: Miscegenation and Mulattoes in the United States* (1980); Arnold R. Hirsch and Joseph Logsdon (eds.), *Creole New Orleans: Race and Americanization* (1992); Cécile Vidal, *Caribbean New Orleans: Empire, Race, and the Making of a Slave Society* (2019). I return to this point in chapter 3, *infra*, pp. 223–31.

reality of skin tone differentiation and discrimination among both blacks and nonblacks. It is well established that, since the days of Emancipation, African Americans have been "color struck," establishing invidious distinctions among themselves based on complexion along a gradient nested inside descent-based categorization that has operated to diffract life chances and inflect social strategies such as marriage, social club membership, and political support.[145] Whites also distinguish African Americans, native and immigrant, by phenotype, including complexion, facial features, body size and corpulence. In a string of innovative papers, the Harvard sociologist Ellis Monk has, moreover, revealed that the disparity between light-skin and dark-skin blacks is greater than the white–black disparity for a range of critical life outcomes, including education, household income, health and aging, police contact and incarceration.[146] This suggests that, at minimum, the proposition that "Blackness is a locus of abjection to be instrumentalized on a whim" needs to be qualified to connect with historical reality.[147]

Where does this time-stamped Americanocentric ontologization of blackness based on the "structural antagonism between humans and blacks" lead us on the political front? It is hard to see light at the end of an intellectual tunnel dug on the principled negation of black agency, individual and collective. Indeed, the only goal one can meaningfully pursue in this perspective is nothing less than "the end of the world" – real or metaphorical, it is hard to say.[148] The Afropessimistic diagnosis of the black predicament yields the futility,

---

[145] Williamson, *New People*; Drake and Cayton, *Black Metropolis*; and Kimberly Jade Norwood (ed.), *Color Matters: Skin Tone Bias and the Myth of a Postracial America* (2013).

[146] Ellis P. Monk Jr., "Skin Tone Stratification among Black Americans, 2001–2003" (2014); idem, "The Cost of Color: Skin Color, Discrimination, and Health among African-Americans" (2015); and idem, "The Color of Punishment: African Americans, Skin Tone, and the Criminal Justice System" (2019).

[147] Wilderson, *Afropessimism*, p. 12.

[148] "We should use the space opened up by political organizing which is geared toward reformist objectives – like stopping police brutality and ending racist immigration policies – as an opportunity to explore problems for which there are no coherent solutions. Anti-Black violence is a paradigm of oppression for which there is no coherent form of redress, other than Frantz Fanon's 'the end of the world'" (Wilderson, *Afropessimism*, p. 171). For an inadvertent illustration of the *necessary paralysis* generated by Afropessimism in the realm of politics, read Jared Sexton, "Afro-Pessimism: The Unclear Word" (2016). See also Wilderson's evasion on the question of Afropessimistic praxis in Linette Park, "Afropessimism and Futures of . . . A Conversation with Frank Wilderson" (2020), p. 35.

worse the utter impossibility, of a politics of freedom. At most, its paradoxical quietism yields an ethic, one sustained by those "in the know" of the necessary eternity of black enslavement. For Wilderson, "Blackness is a positionality of 'absolute dereliction', abandonment, in the face of civil society and therefore cannot be liberated or be made legible through counter-hegemonic interventions."[149] Instead of seeking to liberate blackness, Wilderson urges us to "embrace its disorder, its incoherence."[150] This is a comfortable position to take for a tenured university professor and kindred specialists in cultural production who trade in symbolic representations, the more captivating the better, but for a black janitor, a black fast-food worker, a black accountant, or a black physician in their day to day?

Which raises a conundrum: what is the status of Wilderson's own discourse as the "narrative" of a "slave"? Does its author not believe that Afropessimism offers a sober and true assessment of the quandary of blackness? Does this not mean, then, that there is an "outside" to the condition of "slaveness" from which a black author can speak – and eventually speak truth to power? An erudite slave writing for an attentive audience of educated readers, black and nonblack, is surely more than a generic Slave capital-S. His very existence points, if not to an outside of slaveness, at least to gradations within. Does the ability of Wilderson to reflect on his own social position and existential injuries suffered on the sole account of being black in American society, share his insights, broadcast his view in and out academia, and enlighten his readers not invalidate his account of blackness as *paralyzing* slaveness?[151]

Afropessimism is not a theory so much as a *mood* coalescing out of the post-Obama hangover and a paradoxical expression of the *yearning* of the African-American cultural bourgeoisie for black solidarity, be it negative, made more tenuous by their upward class mobility or inheritance. It offers a rhetorical radicalization of racial nihilism in the face of shifting yet enduring white oppression that leads straight to political abdication. It is ironic and revealing that it would thrive in the academy and seduce college-educated black millennials at the very moment when the most significant movement of black mobilization since the Civil Rights Movement surges in the street and

---

[149] Wilderson, *Afropessimism*, p. 222.
[150] Ibid., p. 250.
[151] For a perceptive account of the micro-dynamics of African-American racial injury in contemporary American society, see Elijah Anderson, *Black in White Space: The Enduring Impact of Color in Everyday Life* (2022).

Reframing Racial Domination

challenges the premises of white rule across the gamut of American institutions, starting with the university.[152] Ultimately, Afropessimism flounders because *it denies the varieties of blackness and the historicity of racial domination* that has been demonstrated time and again, first and foremost, by the long string of hard-fought victories of black struggles for dignity in America, Africa, and beyond.[153]

Dialectic of salience and consequentiality

Two key properties of ethnoracial categorization that are often confounded in both academic and public debate but must be clearly distinguished are salience and consequentiality. *Salience* is a property of classification and pertains to the symbolic order: it refers to (i) noticeability and protrusiveness on the phenomenological horizon of everyday life and to (ii) currency in fields of cultural production, including the political and the journalistic fields, and (iii) in the bureaucratic field (in the form of administrative taxonomies and legal codification by the state).[154] *Consequentiality* is a property of stratification and pertains to the material order: it captures the degree to which ethnoracial categorization impacts life chances in a variety of realms (education, income, wealth, morbidity, life expectancy, incarceration, etc.),

---

[152] Keeanga-Yamahtta Taylor, *From #BlackLivesMatter to Black Liberation* (2016), and Christopher J. Lebron, *The Making of Black Lives Matter: A Brief History of an Idea* (2017). A less sanguine assessment is Cedric Johnson, *After Black Lives Matter* (2023).

[153] Nan Elizabeth Woodruff, *American Congo: The African American Freedom Struggle in the Delta* (2009); David Taft Terry, *The Struggle and the Urban South: Confronting Jim Crow in Baltimore before the Movement* (2019); Aldon D. Morris, *The Origins of the Civil Rights Movement: Black Communities Organizing for Change* (1986); Zebulon Vance Miletsky, *Before Busing: A History of Boston's Long Black Freedom Struggle* (2022); Taylor, *From #BlackLivesMatter to Black Liberation*; George Reid Andrews, *Afro-Latin America: Black Lives, 1600–2000* (2016); Tianna S. Paschel, *Becoming Black Political Subjects: Movements and Ethno-Racial Rights in Colombia and Brazil* (2016); George M. Fredrickson, *Black Liberation: A Comparative History of Black Ideologies in the United States and South Africa* (1996); Julian Brown, *The Road to Soweto: Resistance and the Uprising of 16 June 1976* (2016); Marcel Paret, *Fractured Militancy: Precarious Resistance in South Africa after Racial Inclusion* (2022); John Munro, *The Anticolonial Front: The African American Freedom Struggle and Global Decolonisation, 1945–1960* (2017); Hakim Adi, *Many Struggles: New Histories of African and Caribbean People in Britain* (2023).

[154] On the state as the agency constructing common sense by fabricating and diffusing categories of perception, see Pierre Bourdieu, *Sur l'État. Cours au Collège de France, 1989–1992* (2012), pp. 266–8.

SALIENCE
[classification]

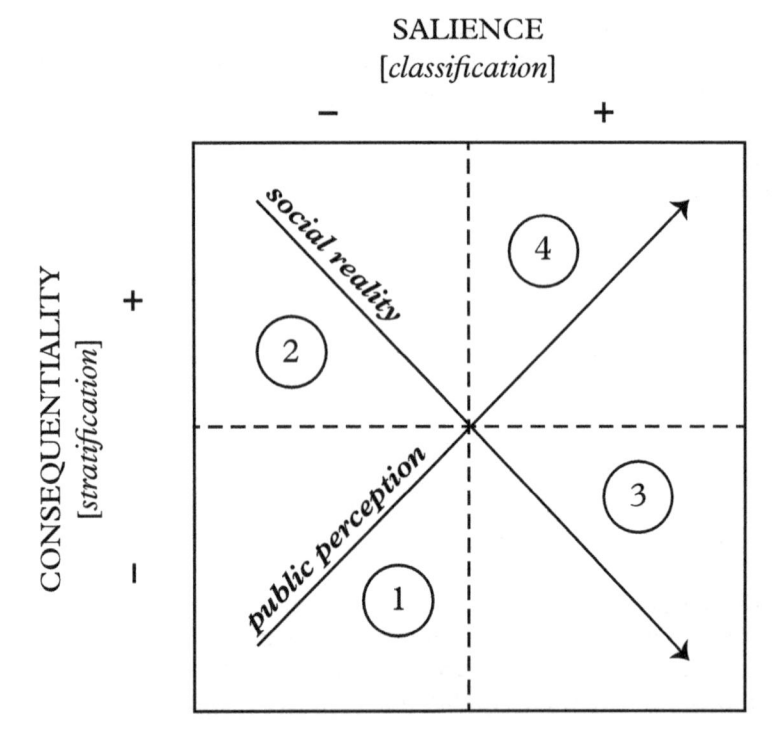

Figure 4 The dialectic of ethnoracial salience and consequentiality.

creating disparities between categories and fueling inequality more generally. These two properties vary independently of each other as indicated in figure 4, so that we may encounter historical situations where ethnicity is both muted and relatively inconsequential (quadrant no. 1), muted and consequential (quadrant no. 2), increasingly salient but of diminishing consequentiality (quadrant no. 3) and increasingly salient and consequential at the same time (quadrant no. 4).

These two dimensions commonly get conflated so that analysts and commentators on all things racial assume that, if "race" (and its derivatives: ethnicity, diversity, discrimination, segregation, etc.) becomes more visible and contentious as a principle of classification, it must be because its weight is increasing as a principle of stratification.[155]

---

[155] Rosita Fibbi and her colleagues thus assert as a matter of fact that "the magnitude of discrimination, at least to a certain extent, defines its salience as a practical issue." Rosita Fibbi et al., *Migration and Discrimination* (2021), p. 43.

Reframing Racial Domination

In common parlance, people, politicians, and the media, but also scholars, talk and worry more about, say, discrimination because discrimination is rising on the labor or housing market and growing more common in everyday life.[156] Take the example of French society over the past half-century. Public perception has it that "racism" has become more pronounced in both salience and consequentiality over that period, a move indicated by the arrow going from quadrant no. 1 to quadrant no. 4.

There is indeed abundant evidence of the *increased salience of "race" in France*, which includes, pell-mell, the eruption of public controversies around ethnicized issues (the alleged formation of "ghettos" and threat of "communitarianism," periodic rioting triggered by clashes between the police and youths from the urban periphery, the supposed link between non-Western immigration and terrorism, intolerance toward Muslims, the bogeyman of the "great replacement," etc.), the deployment by the state of new measures and agencies tasked with enforcing civic equality, the burgeoning of organizations devoted to fighting discrimination (SOS Racisme, Conseil Représentatif des Associations Noires, Indigènes de la République, Brigade Anti-Négrophobie, Union des démocrates musulmans français), the recognition of the country's role in the Atlantic slave trade (including the official designation of slavery as a "crime against humanity" in 2001), the diffusion of the imperative of diversity and of the language of multiculturalism, and, last but not least, the electoral success of the Front National (now Rassemblement National) and the profusion of academic research on the topic as well as a vitriolic running controversy over whether the French state should allow the collection of "ethnic statistics" (which are forbidden by law and deemed unconstitutional).[157] This is taken to validate the thesis of the increasing press

---

[156] On the ascension of the category "discrimination" in public discourse and state policy in France in the 1990s, see Didier Fassin, "L'invention française de la discrimination" (2002). Its operationalization and documentation in social research is the path-setting study by Cris Beauchemin et al., *Trajectoires et origines. Enquête sur la diversité des populations en France* (2016).

[157] Amidst the ocean of publications mounting over the past two decades, one may single out five books by leading social scientists: Didier Fassin and Eric Fassin (eds.), *De la question sociale à la question raciale? Représenter la société française* (2006); Robert Castel, *La Discrimination négative. Citoyens ou indigènes?* (2007); Amselle, *L'Ethnicisation de la France*; Marco Oberti and Edmond Préteceille, *La Ségrégation urbaine* (2016); and Stéphane Beaud and Gérard Noiriel, *Race et sciences sociales. Essai sur les usages publics d'une catégorie* (2021), which created a furore among academics

of racial domination in the self-professed country of the universal "Rights of man."

The trouble is, *public perception and social reality have evolved in diametrically opposed directions* over the past half-century as material inequalities visited upon postcolonial migrants and their children have systematically decreased, steadily closing the gap between nationals and foreigners, as indicated by the arrow going from quadrant 2 (muted salience and extreme consequentiality) to quadrant 3 (increased salience and diminishing consequentiality) in figure 4. First of all, if ethnicity was hushed in the public sphere in the 1970s, it is because the marginalization of Maghrebine immigrants in particular was total and totally *taken for granted*. Vituperative prejudice against them was overtly expressed privately and publicly – as recorded, for instance, by the popular expression *travail d'arabe* ("Arab work") to refer to shoddy work and the routine use of ethnic slurs, *bougnoule, raton, crouille, bicot, melon*, to designate North African migrants – none of which can be publicly uttered today without universal condemnation and even criminal charges for "incitement to racial hatred."[158] Foreign workers were openly discriminated against on the labor market, in hiring, pay, and work assignments, concentrated in the most difficult and dirty occupations, and routinely mocked, insulted, and mistreated on the job.[159] Their housing situation was beyond dire: they were legally barred from public housing, corralled in transit camps, and isolated in insalubrious barracks reserved for migrant workers under despotic surveillance.[160] Police brutality and random acts of racist violence, including hate killings, were common. Premeditated collective assaults on Maghrebines even had a special name: *ratonnade*, meaning rat-hunting. In the 1970s, a wave of anti-Arab attacks shook up the South of France. In 1973 alone, some 50 Maghrebine

and activists by daring to assert the continued preeminence of class. See also the two textbooks aimed at the undergraduate market: Olivier Masclet, *Sociologie de la diversité et des discriminations* (2017); Brun and Cosquer, *Sociologie de la race*; and a study of neighborhood-based affirmative action deployed by the French state since the 1990s: Milena Doytcheva, *Une Discrimination positive à la française? Ethnicité et territoire dans les politiques de la ville* (2007). One book has sought to establish an agenda for "black studies" à la French: Pap Ndiaye, *La Condition noire. Essai sur une minorité française* (2008). See also the virulent collective manifesto against the use of ethnic statistics by Hervé Le Bras et al. (ed.), *Retour de la race. Contre les statistiques ethniques* (2009).

[158] Anne Cammillieri-Subrenat, "L'incitation à la haine et la Constitution" (2002).
[159] Maryse Tripier, *L'Immigration dans la classe ouvrière en France* (1991).
[160] Marc Bernardot, *Loger les immigrés. La SONACOTRA 1956–2006* (2008).

men were killed in a string of assaults that culminated with an attack on the Algerian consulate in Marseille in which four Algerians were murdered. Yet the reaction of the authorities was restrained and the courts consistently showed shocking leniency toward the murderers, police or civilian. In many cases, prosecutors simply declined to file charges.[161]

All these forms of ethnoracial domination have decreased steadily in intensity over the past several decades while public intolerance toward them has shot up, resulting in the *collective illusion of a worsening of ethnoracial disparities*. Consider segregation: for the past three decades, the French policy and scholarly discussion has turned on the fear of "ghettoization," assuming that the segregation of immigrants and their children was increasing, becoming more encompassing, and creating mono-ethnic areas in which a "counter-society" was coalescing.[162] In reality, with the exception of Turks in the recent period, ethnic segregation in France has slowly and steadily decreased from 1968 to the 2010s for all ethnonational categories, with indices of dissimilarity reaching the thirties, which American demographers would consider indicative of "integration." Postcolonial migrants have diffused broadly through physical and social space, even as areas of high ethnic density solidified; and households living in the urban periphery have proved more mobile residentially than the average native-born household, and the majority of movers migrated into better neighborhoods.[163] Far from constituting ghettos, these

---

[161] Rachida Brahim, *La Race tue deux fois. Une histoire des crimes racistes en France, 1970–2000* (2021). The level of overt violence, including state violence, against immigrants of a half-century ago is hard to fathom today. In October of 1961, a peaceful demonstration against the curfew promulgated in France in reaction to the Algerian war by Algerians, men, women, and children, in Paris city center was savagely repressed. The police attacked the demonstrators, beat them, shot them, and threw them to drown in the Seine river, resulting in between 200 to 300 dead. None of the officers responsible for this colonial massacre in the heart of Paris were charged with crimes and no politician was castigated for it. The general reaction of the citizenry bordered on indifference. The fact of this massacre was officially recognized by President Hollande only in 2012. Jean-Luc Einaudi, "Octobre 1961, un massacre au coeur de Paris" (1994).

[162] This moral panic spread throughout Western Europe at the *fin de siècle*, fueling the symbolic denigration and punitive containment of neighborhoods of dispossession, as shown in Wacquant, *Bourdieu in the City*, chapter 2.

[163] Jean-Louis Pan Ké Shon and Gregory Verdugo, "Ségrégation et incorporation des immigrés en France. Ampleur et intensité entre 1968 et 2007" (2014); Jean-Louis Pan Ké Shon, "Ségrégation ethnique et ségrégation sociale en quartiers sensibles. L'apport des mobilités résidentielles" (2009).

stigmatized and pauperized districts of the urban periphery have moved steadily away from the pattern of rigid segregation, ethnic homogeneity, class heterogeneity, institutional duplication, and geographical containment that define a ghetto: they are better characterized as *anti-ghettos*.[164]

This is congruent with the fact that the sociodemographic profile of immigrants and their families has become more similar to that of the native-born population, as a result of the gradual reduction of disparities in education, occupation, income, housing, household composition, fertility, and mortality – in spite of persistent prejudice and discrimination. It is also reinforced by the steady merging of the immigrant and native populations due to high rates of mixed unions (cohabitation and marriage): 66 percent of second-generation descendants of immigrants in France form a couple with a nonimmigrant; by the third generation, nine out of ten grandchildren of immigrants have only one or two immigrant grandparents.[165]

The same *scissor-like movement of divergence* between the public perception and the social reality of ethnoracial inequality is observed in other European countries as well as in the United States. In recent years, activist and academic discourse in America has turned to *catastrophism as a trope* to garner attention and press for policies of reduction of ethnoracial inequality.[166] This trope has fostered a disconnect from social reality which cannot but hamper the struggle for social and racial justice inasmuch as it misrepresents the woes to be overcome. For instance, the black–white disparity in incarceration has decreased spectacularly from 1 to 8 in 1995 to 1 to 3 in 2015 while class disparity for both blacks and whites has shot up (from 1 to 10 in 1995 to 1 to 28 comparing men with no college versus some

---

[164] The structural and functional differences between ghetto, hyperghetto, and anti-ghetto are elaborated in Loïc Wacquant, "Designing Urban Seclusion in the Twenty-First Century" (2010a), and idem, *The Two Faces of the Ghetto* (2025), chapters 6–9.

[165] Jérôme Lê et al., "La diversité des origines et la mixité des unions progressent au fil des générations" (2022).

[166] An example of this racial catastrophism, conveniently devoid of any empirical indicators that would contradict personal impressions, is Cameron D. Lippard et al. (eds.), *Protecting Whiteness: Whitelash and the Rejection of Racial Equality* (2020), which bemoans "the resurgence of white supremacy and overt racism in the United States," with chapters on topics such as the standoff at Clive Bundy's ranch (a cattle rancher who refused to pay grazing fees to the federal government), white supremacists' flyers on campus and videos on YouTube, "the whitening of South Asian women," and how art museums maintain elite "white space."

college education),[167] suggesting that mobilization for criminal justice reform needs to focus on class bias built into judicial procedures to reduce the racial impact of penal policy. And yet the class variable is strikingly absent from activist mobilization around criminal justice.[168]

This is emphatically not to say that prejudice, discrimination, segregation, seclusion, and violence – the five elementary forms of ethnoracial domination I will dissect in the next chapter – do not represent an urgent political and policy problem today on both sides of the Atlantic. They unquestionably do. It is to warn against the conflation between ethnic salience and ethnic consequentiality when probing the dynamics of racial domination, because real racial domination is hard enough to fight that we do not need to waste energy on battling a fictive and distorted image of it.

But there is more: the salience of "race" increased precisely *because* consequentiality decreased on both sides of the Atlantic.[169] The steady improvement of the social condition of subordinate ethnoracial categories such as French people of North African descent, visible in the elevation of their educational level and the ascent of a (petty) bourgeoisie of cultural intermediaries (teachers, social workers, community activists, artists, journalists, researchers, professionals, local politicians, etc.), fuels at once the sense of structural *frustration* at being treated as a second-class citizen, the *ability* to translate personal experiences into collective claims, and the *organizational capacity* to press these claims in the public sphere.[170] The cultural assimilation and rising educational level of the immigrant-descended population translate into a heightened expectation of fairness in treatment that feeds an increased intolerance for discrimination, even as the latter decreases. Degrading or discriminatory behavior that used to be accepted as a matter of course is requalified as unfair and becomes intolerable in the literal sense of the term.

---

[167] Christopher Muller and Alexander Roehrkasse, "Racial and Class Inequality in US Incarceration in the Early Twenty-First Century" (2022).

[168] Cathy Hu, *The Struggle to Define Justice: Community Organizing in the Criminal Courts* (2022).

[169] This is what John Lie calls the "paradox of oppression," the counterintuitive fact that "precisely when structural racism is waning, the claim of racism and the action of counter-racism proliferate" (*Modern Peoplehood*, 2003, p. 256).

[170] On the formation of a cultural petty bourgeoisie of Maghrebine origin, see Catherine Wihtol de Wenden and Rémy Leveau, *La Beurgeoisie. Les trois âges de la vie associative issue de l'immigration* (2001).

This same causal mechanism explains the apparent paradox that the Black Lives Matter movement has risen and spread in a period during which the social and educational achievements of African Americans improved rapidly (even as their economic condition stagnated): the number of blacks over 25 who have completed four years of college or more increased from 8 percent in 1980 to 17 percent in 2000 to 29 percent in 2020. It is this growing cadre of young highly educated African Americans which constitutes the primary recruitment pool and public of Black Lives Matter, Color of Change, and related racial justice organizations. They are living proof that the increased symbolic salience of race can walk hand in hand with its diminished material consequentiality.

Race-making through classification struggles

The neo-Bourdieusian model proposed here makes "race," as acknowledged and practiced in a given society at a given time, a disguised variant of ethnic classification and stratification that must be explained (*explanandum*) rather than taken for granted and treated as a self-propelled cause (*explanans*) of the gamut of social outcomes; and, for that purpose, duly located on the analytic map of possible forms of ethnicities, racialized or not. Position and movement along the diagonal of racialization is, moreover, explained by *material and symbolic struggles* over the partitioning of social space and the naming of populations in which paramount symbolic powers, chief among them the state, law, science, religion, and party politics, compete for the "monopoly over the legitimate means of symbolic violence."[171]

So much to say that race is at once the *product, the instrument, and the stake of classification struggles* aiming to bolster or subvert its use as preeminent "social principle of vision and division," over and

---

[171] Here I diverge from Bourdieu (whose striking formulation it is) in proposing that religion, politics, science, and the law can effectively contest the status of the state as "central bank of symbolic capital" (Pierre Bourdieu, *Sur l'État* [2012]) by challenging and even overturning its verdicts. In other words, the status of the bureaucratic state as monopolist of symbolic legitimacy cannot be assumed and is always disputed, with various degrees of success. For illustrations, see Ali Banuazizi and Myron Weiner (eds.), *The State, Religion, and Ethnic Politics: Afghanistan, Iran, and Pakistan* (1988); Joane Nagel, *American Indian Ethnic Renewal: Red Power and Resurgence of Identity and Culture* (1996); and Birol Başkan, *From Religious Empires to Secular States: State Secularization in Turkey, Iran, and Russia* (2014).

against other possible bases of clustering and claims-making, class, gender, age, sexuality, religion, region, nation, etc. Writes Bourdieu: "Struggles over ethnic or regional identity, that is, over properties (stigmata or emblems) linked to *origin* through the *place* of origin and to the durable marks associated with it, such as an accent, are a particular case of classification struggles, that is, struggles over the monopoly of the power to make people see and believe, to make people cognize and recognize, to impose the legitimate definition of the divisions of the social world and, thereby, to *make and unmake groups*."[172]

> "Symbolic struggle has for stake to change the groups, the relations between the groups, the division in groups, the hierarchy of the groups, by changing the vision of the groups, that is to say, the vision that the groups have of the groups, the vision that the people being part of the groups have of the groups of which they are part, and also their vision of the other groups. The stake is to change the principle of vision or di-vision, and there is no vision that is not also division: as soon as I lay down a class, I lay down a complementary class; if I lay down a form, I lay down a backdrop."
>
> Pierre Bourdieu, *Sociologie générale*, Vol. 1 (2015), p. 132.

One can unravel the logics of classification struggles by tracking down the course through which a mental category is turned into an objective reality, deposited in bodies (habitus) and in institutions (social space and fields) that agree with each other because they are patterned after one and the same symbolic form.[173] This entails: (i) the symbolic production and social ordering of ethnoracial categories as cognitive constructs, "ethnicities on paper"; (ii) their dissemination and inculcation to the pertinent populations, especially through the school system, the law, and the media, yielding "ethnicities embodied"; (iii) the reactions and strategies of agents differently positioned in the sociopolitical structure and in fields of cultural production

---

[172] Bourdieu, *Langage et pouvoir symbolique*, pp. 282–3, italics in the original.
[173] On this agreement, see Pierre Bourdieu, "Le mort saisit le vif. Les relations entre l'histoire incorporée et l'histoire réifiée" (1980c). I am concerned here with the stages in the creation of ethnoracial categories, which is different than the pathways through which their boundaries can be altered once they exist, as laid out by Andreas Wimmer, "Elementary Strategies of Ethnic Boundary Making" (2008).

(academia, journalism, politics, state managers, religious leaders, etc.), that is, "ethnicities objectified" in social space and the bureaucratic field, leading to (iv) the eventual acceptance or rejection, active or passive, by those whom the ethnoracial taxonomy designates and the corresponding diffusion of ethnoracial thoughts, emotions, and actions. The impetus to alter or preserve an existing categorization system can come from below through the private actions of ordinary people, the mobilization of social movements, and the machinations of symbolic entrepreneurs, or from above through the dictates of the state and other paramount symbolic agencies (science, religion, law, political parties).[174]

An example of successful mobilization from below is the campaign waged by small clusters of American college graduates of mixed black–white and white–Asian descent to get the Census Bureau to add the category "multiracial" to its official nomenclature in 2000. The bureau did not insert that exact label but it allowed census respondents to tick more than one racial category. This was something of an ironic victory: by striving to get public bureaucracy to recognize their mixed descent, these ethnoracial entrepreneurs reinforced the notion that "there is race, it is carried in the body, and it is mixed through sexual reproduction" and so they "reaffirmed the right of the state to label individuals in racial terms," in effect reinforcing the racial state.[175]

A case featuring the cooperation between activists, commercial operators, and the state is the invention of the "Hispanic" in the US of the 1970s.[176] The coining and diffusion of this panethnic category grew out of the alignment of the interests of Mexican, Puerto-Rican, and Cuban organizations wanting to go national in a bid to increase their lobbying influence in Washington; Spanish-language media seeking to increase publicity revenues by fusing hispanophone populations into a single market; and government officials eager to under-

---

[174] For a compact account of the struggles over the public naming, administrative recognition and thereby social constitution of the "Untouchables," "Scheduled Classes," "Scheduled Tribes," and "Backward Classes" in colonial and postcolonial India migrating across these different moments, see Roland Lardinois, "Les luttes de classement en Inde" (1985).
[175] Kimberly McClain DaCosta, *Making Multiracials: State, Family, and Market in the Redrawing of the Color Line* (2007), pp. 183–4, and idem, "Multiracial Categorization, Identity, and Policy in (Mixed) Racial Formations" (2020).
[176] G. Cristina Mora, *Making Hispanics: How Activists, Bureaucrats, and Media Constructed a New American* (2014).

mine regional ethnic militancy and to legitimize their categorization procedures after a bungled census. These three actors then collaborated in disseminating and explicating the category (e.g., Univision TV broadcast special programs tutoring its viewers on how to check the box "Hispanic" on the census form), and two generations later a paper ethnicity had morphed into a doxic category of academic and public debate and, to a degree, a genuinely felt identity. Tianna Paschel adds an international flavor to this story by showing how, against all odds, black militants in Colombia and Brazil pushed their respective states from color-blindness to ethnoracial legislation fostering recognition and redistribution by aligning their domestic interests with those of international organizations promoting multiculturalism and indigenous rights as markers of societal advancement and global status.[177] The converse case is the continuing refusal by European countries – *primus inter pares* France – to introduce ethnicity in official categorization procedures in the face of mounting pressure from domestic activists, scholars, and (rare) politicians.[178]

Categorical change can come from above and yet fail, as with the Rwandan government's National Unity and Reconciliation (NURC) campaign aiming to submerge the Hutu/Tutsi cleavage along which the 1994 genocide was perpetrated. The NURC sought to promote "Rwandan-ness" as a national category supposedly in line with the class comity of the precolonial era. In 2001, the Tutsi-led government instituted thousands of communal justice commissions known as *gacaca*, also supposedly in line with precolonial structures, to establish guilt for local massacres, mete out sanctions, and impose national reconciliation. Furthermore, the NURC erased official markers of ethnicity and made public references to ethnicity a crime punishable by up to seven years in prison and a million Rwandan Francs ($1,800). But the state's nationalizing project crumbled for three reasons: ordinary Rwandans resented the mandate to "forge national unity on the basis of a false binary" between Hutu killers and Tutsi victims that did not accord with their lived experience of the genocide; *gacaca* revived trauma and "exacerbate[d] ethnicity's salience by forever placing the past in the present"; and mandatory participation in these commissions interfered with the pressing concerns of economic survival day to day. In the end, the policy to "unmake 'race'

---

[177] Paschel, *Becoming Black Political Subjects*.
[178] Patrick Simon et al., *Social Statistics and Ethnic Diversity: Cross-National Perspectives in Classifications and Identity Politics* (2015).

in favor of the 'nation'" failed: Rwandan-ness was seen by the population as "a government ruse they [were] forced to enact, even while privately they resist[ed] it."[179] The general logic of classification struggles is illuminated by such negative cases in which powerful symbolic agencies fail to institutionalize categories, showing how ethnoracial constructs already inscribed in bodies in the form of habitus can derail paper categories.

But the most decisive of all classification struggles, which too often goes unexamined because history has resolved it, is the struggle waged in the first place to establish the primacy of this or that principle of social vision and division, class, ethnicity, gender, age, region, nationality, etc., as *paramount basis for classification and stratification*, and thereby to shape subjectivities, social space, and the state accordingly. This is because, being multisided, the social world can be "practically perceived, uttered, and constructed after different manners – for example, economic divisions or ethnic divisions."[180] This means, to put it crudely, that there is a *battle over race* before there can be a *battle between races*.

The site par excellence of this battle is the political field, where operators vie to impose, say, nationality over class or race over class as the basis for garnering votes and delivering civic dignity and public goods. Thus, in the South of the United States, the People's Party waged an epic if brief crusade at the end of the nineteenth century to unite black and white farmers against their landlords and thereby establish class as the foundation of collective clustering and claims-making over and against white planters and politicians who campaigned just as fiercely to make race the dominant cleavage of the Southern social order both subjectively (habitus, classification) and objectively (social space, stratification). This piece of oratory addressed to black and white farmers by the populist leader Tom Watson captures that struggle well: "You are made to hate each other because on that hatred is rested the keystone of the arch of financial despotism which enslaves you both. You are deceived and blinded because you do not see how this race antagonism perpetuates a monetary system that beggars you both. The colored tenant is in the same boat as the white tenant, the colored laborer with the white laborer and that the accident of color can make no difference in the interests

---

[179] Aliza Luft and Susan Thomson, "Race, Nation, and Resistance to State Symbolic Power in Rwanda Since the 1994 Genocide" (2021), p. 125.
[180] Pierre Bourdieu, "Espace social et genèse des 'classes'" (1984a), p. 298.

of farmers, croppers and laborers."[181] Advocates of a racialist vision of society and politics triumphed over the partisans of class and erected the Jim Crow regime of caste terrorism that is commonly presented as the inevitable sequel to slavery, but was in truth only one of several forks on the road to social change. History thus erases the traces of the lateral historical possibles foreclosed by past struggles.

---

[181] Cited in George B. Tindall (ed.), *A Populist Reader: Selections from the Works of American Populist Leaders* (1966), pp. 125–6.

2

Elementary Forms of Ethnoracial Rule

An institution is not an indivisible unit, distinct from the facts that manifest it; it is only their system.
           Marcel Mauss, "La prière" (1909)

Historicize, spatialize, provincialize the United States, forsake incrimination, demarcate, and repatriate. A sixth recommendation to develop the sociology of ethnoracial domination on solid conceptual footing is to *disaggregate*.[1] The scholarly-cum-policy myth of the "underclass" emerged from, and traded on, the conflation of disparate social relations rooted in ethnicity, geography, the labor market, the family, and the state. It was a lumpy category that, for this reason, created empirical confusion and theoretical trouble – not to mention policy misdirection and political regression.[2]

The lesson to draw from this episode in scholarly demonology is to break ethnoracial phenomena into their constituent elements, what I call the *five elementary forms of ethnoracial domination*: categorization (assignation to a hierarchical and naturalizing classification system,

---

[1] To disaggregate ethnoracial domination is not the same as differentiating the possible meanings of race in an effort to salvage one of them, as does philosopher Michael Hardimon, *Rethinking Race: A Case for Deflationary Realism* (2017), when he distinguishes "racialist," "populationist," "minimalist," and "socialrace" conceptions of race and recommends retaining the latter three in keeping with the American folk concept. A different path to disassembling racial domination is forged by Andreas Wimmer, "Elementary Strategies of Ethnic Boundary Making" (2008).
[2] Loïc Wacquant, *The Invention of the "Underclass": A Study in the Politics of Knowledge* (2022), pp. 110–21, 123–32.

Elementary Forms of Ethnoracial Rule

encompassing prejudice, bias, and stigma), discrimination (differential treatment and disparate impact based on real or putative categorical membership), segregation (differential allocation in social and physical space), seclusion (institutional enclosure and parallelism, comprising the ghetto, the camp, and the reservation), and violence, deployed to signal and enforce racial boundaries, ranging from intimidation and assault to pogroms and ethnic cleansing to war and extermination – the ultimate form of ethnoracial domination. Let me expound on what each elementary form entails with an eye toward semantic clarification and analytic specification. I will also try to formulate fresh questions as I go along.

Having explicated the pentad of ethnoracial rule, I will pose the question of the articulation of the five elementary forms and query their relationship to the economy and the state. This will lead me to sketch a friendly critique of two notions that have become fashionable if not irresistible in the academic and civic debate alike: racial capitalism and structural racism. I will then close by arguing that race-making is best understood as a *particular case of group-making*, rather than as a phenomenon requiring its own separate theory, as generally posited by scholars of "race and ethnicity."

1. Categorization

Categorization pertains to the realm of cognition. It encompasses the act of differential perception, the frame through and in which persons are sorted, and the contents of the different slots in that frame.[3] It is crucial to realize that *social* classification differs fundamentally from *natural* classification – say, classifying rocks or lizards – in five ways: (i) the entities classified also classify themselves; (ii) the classifier is comprised in the classification; (iii) classification is hierarchical and judgmental as well as (iv) consequential inasmuch as we attach profits, perils, and penalties to the different categories. It follows that (v) people can and do contest their placement, the meaning, order, and basis of the categories, as well as their material and symbolic attributions, all of which are stakes in the *classification struggles* waged in

---

[3] The founding text of cognitive sociology is Durkheim and Mauss's *De quelques formes primitives de classification* (2017 [1903]). Its theory runs sinuously through Lévi-Straussian structuralism, Aaron Cicourel's ethnomethodology, Bourdieu's theory of practice, and such American proponents as Eviatar Zerubavel, Karen Cerrulo, Paul DiMaggio, Stephen Vaisey, and Omar Lizardo.

Racial Domination

everyday life, in fields of cultural production, and inside the bureaucratic field.[4] People can even contest the very fact of classification, as when a subject population denies the colonial state the authority or the ability to enumerate and sort it.

The first step in the sociology of ethnoracial domination is therefore to study the genesis, foundation, shape, nomenclature, and rules of functioning of the classification system at work because that system shapes the stratification order as well as the subjectivity and social strategies of agents.[5] One illustration: in French Martinique, a historically plantocratic society characterized by a "colorist obsession," ethnoracial classification descends from the days of slavery. It is premised on a dialectic between descent and phenotype yielding three major categories: *blanc* (divided into *béké*, the descendants of settler whites, and *z'oreilles*, whites from the metropole), *mûlatre*, and *noir* or *nègre* allowing for mobility between the bottom two categories.[6] For the latter, education, money, and social status "whiten," as recorded

---

[4] On classification struggles, see especially Pierre Bourdieu, *La Distinction. Critique sociale du jugement* (1979), pp. 559–64, and idem, *Sociologie générale*, vol. 1. *Cours au Collège de France, 1981–1983* (2015), pp. 81–2, 97, 112–14, 129–30, 138–40, where we read: "Classification struggles are part and parcel of the objective truth of classifications, even though they have a relative autonomy from classifications" (p. 112).

[5] For illustrations, read Siep Stuurman, "François Bernier and the Invention of Racial Classification" (2000); Nicholas Hudson, "From 'Nation' to 'Race': The Origin of Racial Classification in Eighteenth-Century Thought" (1996); John Clammer, "Ethnicity and the Classification of Social Differences in Plural Societies: A Perspective from Singapore" (1985); John McCorquodale, "The Legal Classification of Race in Australia" (1986); Ann Stoler, "Sexual Affronts and Racial Frontiers: European Identities and the Cultural Politics of Exclusions in Colonial Southeast Asia" (1992); Cees Fasseur, "Cornerstone and Stumbling Block: Racial Classification and the Late Colonial State in Indonesia" (1994); Deborah Posel, "Race as Common Sense: Racial Classification in Twentieth-Century South Africa" (2001); Bonita Lawrence, "Gender, Race, and the Regulation of Native Identity in Canada and the United States: An Overview" (2003); Kenneth Prewitt, "Racial Classification in America: Where Do We Go from Here?" (2005); Stanley R. Bailey, "Unmixing for Race Making in Brazil" (2008); and Edward Telles and Tianna Paschel, "Who is Black, White, or Mixed Race? How Skin Color, Status, and Nation Shape Racial Classification in Latin America" (2014). A selective survey of recent work centered on the US and Latin America is Lauren Davenport, "The Fluidity of Racial Classifications" (2020).

[6] This paragraph draws on Michel Giraud "Races, classes et colonialisme à la Martinique" (1980), and idem, "Dialectique de la descendance et du phénotype dans la classification raciale martiniquaise" (1989); Isabelle Michelot, "Du Neg nwe au Beke Goyave, le langage de la couleur de la peau en Martinique" (2007); and Ulrike Zander, "La hiérarchie 'socio-raciale' en Martinique. Entre persistances postcoloniales et évolution vers un désir de vivre ensemble" (2013).

Elementary Forms of Ethnoracial Rule

in the local saying, "a rich negro is a mulatto." Two subcategories of mulattoes are *chabin* (light-skin persons from very dark-skinned parents, described as *bleus*) and *câpre* (mulatto with thin hair). Another black category is *congo*, which designates the descendants of African indentured servants of the colonial era, as opposed to slaves.

The *békés* themselves are divided along class and blood lines into *grands békés* (the rich descendants of planters), *békés moyens*, and *petits blancs* (poor whites). Mulattoes who have grown rich are symbolically elevated by being called *békés goyave* (literally whites colored like a guava) but are kept at the doorstep of the white category.[7] Gradations of skin tone are popularly associated with distinctions of intelligence, character, and manners, and this among both whites and blacks. This triadic symbolic structure is stamped onto the structure of social space and informs social strategies of preservation or penetration of existing ethnoracial boundaries as manifested by opposite matrimonial strategies: creole whites maintain strict endogamy (a marriage with a person of color is considered an inexcusable moral fault and can lead to social and family exclusion) whereas blacks seek to move up – a light-skinned child is always predicted to succeed socially.

A cursory survey of the extant taxonomies of racialized ethnicities across continents and epochs reveals that they can rest on three foundations and their combinations.[8] The first is *descent*: tell me what your ancestors were and I will know what you are. Note that defining race by blood implies that there must be a rule to allocate persons of mixed descent: hypodescent (black Americans), hyperdescent (the offspring of Dutch colonials in Indonesia), creation of an intermediate category (the Métis of colonial Canada, the Mestizos in Spanish Mexico), rejection into an outcaste category placed below all others (the offspring of American soldiers with local women in Korea and Vietnam), or placement varying according to physical appearance and class (ancien régime France, Hawaii).[9] Some societies are permissive and even appraisive of mixing, while others are restrictive and obsessed with ethnoracial purity; this divergence is

---

[7] In the early twentieth century, the distinction between *béké* and *mulâtre* was porous, as documented by Frédéric Régent, *La France et ses esclaves* (2007), pp. 62–3, 193.

[8] This triadic schema is suggested by Charles Wagley in his survey of the Americas ("On the Concept of Social Race in the Americas" [1965 (1958)]). I adapt and expand it to cover the globe by allowing for combinations of the three bases of ethnoracial classification.

[9] See the examples compiled by F. James Davis, *Who Is Black? One Nation's Definition* (1991), chapter 5, "Other Places, Other Definitions."

typically rooted in long-standing differences in economics, religion, and gender power balance.[10]

The second basis for ethnoracial enumeration and ranking is *phenotype*: let me see you and I will tell you what you are. Skin tone comes to mind but, as we saw earlier, many other physical traits can be the basis for ethnoracial sorting and they typically tend to come in clusters. The canonical case here is Brazil, with its hierarchy based on complexion, facial features, texture and color of the hair, modulated by class and region. The third foundation for racialized classification is the range of *sociocultural variables* that can be naturalized and hierarchized: language, region, religion, occupation, customs, etc. Many racial sorting schemas combine these three foundations in different proportion. The Martinique case discussed above is particularly rich because it clearly displays the workings of a classification system *combining* descent, phenotype, and sociocultural criteria, with the latter two criteria nested under the first. Similarly, the Roma are categorized as such by Bulgarians based on poverty status, neighborhood of residence, language, and physical attributes. Even a regime of racial domination as rigid and virulent as Nazi Germany mixed blood, religion, and phenotypical features while apartheid South Africa used physical appearance, social acceptability, and lifestyle.[11]

Ethnoracial classification systems, like all social classifications, vary along three critical dimensions. The first is their *degree of institutionalization*: in some societies, racial categories are official categories instituted by the state and anchored by multiple "classification machines," such as the law, public bureaucracies (civil registries, schools, hospitals, the military, courts and prisons, etc.), private firms, and assorted organizations involved in cultural production. In others, they circulate only in everyday life in a more or less inchoate form. A solid indicator of officialization is the national census, which is a manner of Rorschach test of the elite understanding of race and nation, resulting from struggles, at the intersection of the academic, political, and bureaucratic fields, aiming to impose the

---

[10] George M. Fredrickson, "Mulattoes and Métis. Attitudes Toward Miscegenation in the United States and France since the Seventeenth Century" (2005). See also the classic discussion of the two patterns of ethnoracial classification across the Caribbean by Harry Hoetink, "'Race' and Color in the Caribbean" (1985).

[11] Cornelia Essner, "Qui sera 'juif'? La classification 'raciale' nazie des 'lois de Nuremberg' à la conférence de Wannsee'" (1995); Posel, "Race as Common Sense: Racial Classification in Twentieth-Century South Africa." I discuss the South African case at length later in this chapter, see *infra*, pp. 172–4.

dominant nomenclature of groups promoted to public existence.[12] Census bureaus are deeply involved in the politics of race-making and state-building: they make categories visible, to themselves and to others; they teach the official nomenclature to the citizenry; and they transform the idea of race itself, helping to produce the very realities they claim only to record.[13]

The second dimension is the *degree of congruence* between different conceptions distributed across social and physical space and especially between lower-class and elite variants – this is a geographical variable – as well as between official and everyday categories. In Brazil, ethnoracial categorization varies considerably across regions and across levels in the class structure. It admits many more fine-grained categories in the northeast, where the black population is demographically dominant, than in the southwest, where the white population prevails. In the former Soviet Union, every citizen had an official ethnonational identity assigned at birth (*natsional' nost'*) but "personal ethnic identification [could] diverge from 'passport nationality', which for its part [could] diverge from the nationality registered by the official census taker."[14] In France, the everyday ethnic nomenclature used by youths from the stigmatized *banlieues* (*céfran* for whites, *rebeu* or *gris* for Maghrebines, *black*, and *feuj* for Jews)[15] is very different from

---

[12] The best demonstration, building on a comparison between the US and Brazil, is Melissa Nobles, *Shades of Citizenship: Race and the Census in Modern Politics* (2000). See also the meticulous social and political history of the US census by Paul Schor, *Compter et classer. Histoire des recensements américains* (2009). A world survey of census forms reveals that the designation "race" is used in only 17 percent of 141 countries (as against 61 percent for "ethnicity"), the three major ones being the United States, Brazil, and Jamaica. Ann Morning, "Ethnic Classification in Global Perspective: A Cross-National Survey of the 2000 Census Round" (2008).

[13] A panoramic study of ethnoracial counting and state-building across Latin America is Mara Loveman, *National Colors: Racial Classification and the State in Latin America* (2014). A stimulative collection of national and comparative studies is David Kertzer and Dominique Arel (eds.), *Census and Identity: The Politics of Race, Ethnicity, and Language in National Censuses* (2002). An update with a broader sample of cases in a changed political and intellectual landscape is Patrick Simon et al., *Social Statistics and Ethnic Diversity: Cross-National Perspectives in Classifications and Identity Politics* (2015).

[14] Rasma Karklins, *Ethnic Relations in the USSR: The Perspective from Below* (1986), p. 23.

[15] These terms are obtained by reversing the syllables in the French word, a street slang known as *verlan*. For a subtle portrait of these youths and a dissection of their categories of perception, read Fabien Truong, *Des Capuches et des hommes. Trajectoires de "jeunes de banlieue"* (2013).

the one used by journalists or essayed by public officials as they cautiously attempt to promote "diversity" – indeed the naming of ethnicities is taboo and avoided in favor of the generic euphemism "issued from diversity." When the state endorses and enforces a particular ethnoracial taxonomy, it unifies the cognitive schemata that its population uses to distribute persons and social properties into ethnic categories, thus promoting congruence within the territory under its rule.[16] *A contrario*, when the state rejects the use of ethnoracial constructs, it fosters by default the proliferation of potentially discordant taxonomies circulating in social space. Institutionalization fosters group formation by making groups visible to its putative members and to other groups.

The third dimension is the degree to which ethnoracial classifications are *contested versus doxic* – this is a historical variable. There are periods during which taxonomies solidify and are broadly accepted as a matter of course, like the period 1920–90 in the United States, and other periods when naming and recording ethnicities are disputed, as they have been in France over the past decade with the push by some scholars to insert ethnoracial categories in national surveys and the pressure on government to accommodate "diversity" in the state apparatus.[17] In such a conjuncture, parameters of "racial appraisal" – "the way that people classify the race of others, both particular individuals and larger groups" – are dislodged and literally up for grabs.[18] Social scientists can then find themselves caught squarely in classification struggles, as when a team of American sociologists deploys their scientific capital to argue in favor of the official recognition of the MENA (persons of Middle Eastern and North African origin) by the state on grounds that lumping them into the "white category," as currently happens in the Census, hides the fact that people do not see them as whites and the corresponding inequalities of treatment they

---

[16] See Bourdieu's demonstration in the case of the creation of an official national language as the result of political unification in *Langage et pouvoir symbolique* (2000 [1982, 1991]), pp. 69–80.

[17] Michèle Tribalat, *Statistiques ethniques, une querelle bien française* (2016). For the broader sociolegal context, see Angéline Escafré-Dublet et al., "Fighting Discrimination in a Hostile Political Environment: The Case of 'Colour-Blind' France" (2023). The dispute at the European level is broached by Patrick Simon, "The Failure of the Importation of Ethno-Racial Statistics in Europe: Debates and Controversies" (2017).

[18] Wendy D. Roth, "Unsettled Identities amid Settled Classifications? Toward a Sociology of Racial Appraisals" (2018).

Elementary Forms of Ethnoracial Rule

suffer, not to mention that the MENA do not consider themselves white.[19]

Knowledge of the ethnoracial categorization system current in a given place and time is crucial because *classification at the symbolic level informs stratification at the material level* by cutting up the social world into categories differentially valorized and denigrated, rewarded and penalized. Due to what Bourdieu calls "the semantic elasticity of the social world,"[20] the type of classification, continuous or discrete, and its malleability do not mechanically determine the structure of social space via the distribution of persons into positions. But it makes certain configurations more or less (im)possible and (im)probable, perceivable, defensible, and actionable by shaping the individual and collective cognition of agents.

Classification fosters or hinders group-making along definite symbolic lines. *Ceteris paribus*, a gradational classification system based on multiple criteria resulting in a plethora of fuzzy categories makes it more difficult for members of the subordinate categories to identify with the collective and to take joint action because such classifications tend to encourage Goffmanian "out-group alignment" and exit via strategies of individual ethnic mobility as we saw in the case of Afro-Brazilians.[21] Classification can induce mass "passing" and group disidentification when ethnic markers are ambiguous or invisible, as with the Roma in Eastern Europe and the Burakumin in Japan. The Burakumin are visually undetectable while stigma attached to membership is pungent and suffusive and discrimination pronounced and diffuse. This stimulates strategies of *ethnic desertion and submersion* into the broader society that weaken the putative group by depriving it of its social and cultural elite. So much so that Buraku political leaders, and scholars after them, have deplored the dissipation of community culture and institutions (such as the Buraku Liberation League) caused, paradoxically, by the success of the public policy of upgrading of Dōwa districts in big cities.[22]

---

[19] Neda Maghbouleh et al., "Middle Eastern and North African Americans May not be Perceived, nor Perceive Themselves, to be White" (2022). The MENAs comprise 19 different nationalities and include a range of phenotypes, so it is unclear whether to institute them as an official category will create an aggregate endowed with more than a paper coherence.

[20] Pierre Bourdieu, "Social Space and Symbolic Power" (1989a [1987]), p. 20.

[21] Erving Goffman, *Stigma: Notes on the Management of Spoiled Identity* (1963), pp. 114–15.

[22] Noah McCormack, "Affirmative Action Policies under the Postwar Japanese Constitution: On the Effects of the Dōwa Special Measures Policy" (2018).

This Burakumin example confirms that the *relationship between classification and stratification is recursive* as changes in the latter alternately solidify, destabilize, undermine, or otherwise reshuffle the former by providing resources and incentives to various protagonists in classification struggles and by altering both the salience and the consequentiality of group membership. The decrease in occupational segregation that has long associated the Burakumin with polluted and polluting tasks, the diffusion in physical space that has loosened the association with residence in Dōwa districts, higher educational achievement made possible by increased resources allocated to schools in these districts: all these factors have rendered the categorical boundary enclosing the Burakumin more blurred and porous.[23] In short, the present model of racial domination allows us to *endogenize classification* by grounding it firmly in the materiality of social space and its transformation, through the mediation of symbolic strategies of group-making.

As for contents, categorization comprises prejudice, implicit bias, and stigma. Prejudice, from the Latin *praejudicium* meaning judgment before the fact, was famously defined in the 1950s by psychologist Gordon Allport as "an aversive or hostile attitude toward a person who belongs to a group, simply because she belongs to that group and is therefore presumed to have the objectionable qualities ascribed to the group."[24] Group antipathy has three components: cognitive (beliefs, stereotypes), emotive (feelings of dislike, scorn, fear, etc.), and conative (the inclination to act on one's beliefs and emotions), but prejudice is not itself an action. An individual may or may not act on their prejudicial belief depending on prevalent cultural views, social position, network ties, and power relations. A decisive property in this regard is whether public expressions of prejudice are authorized, sponsored, or prohibited by social norms, organizations, and the state via bureaucratic practice and the law, which prompts or prevents the passage from cognition and emotion to conduct.[25]

Implicit bias extends the notion of prejudice to the realm of the unconscious by proposing that we make flash categorical judgments

---

[23] John H. Davis, Jr, "Blurring the Boundaries of the Buraku(min)" (2000).

[24] Gordon Allport, *The Nature of Prejudice* (1954), p. 9. A reconsideration and update of Allport's conceptualization is John F. Dovidio et al. (eds.), *On the Nature of Prejudice: Fifty Years after Allport* (2008).

[25] All liberal democracies, with the notable exception of the US, subject violent ethnic speech to legal penalty, criminal or civil. French law sanctions "incitement to hatred, violence, or discrimination" based on "skin color, origin, religion, sex or sexual orientation, or disability" with up to a year of prison and a fine of €45,000.

about people when primed by certain cues based on "traces of past experience" that are not accessible to introspection or self-report.[26] Over the past decade, the notion has spread like wildfire across the scholarly and professional disciplines, public policy, and the gamut of organizations from businesses to criminal courts to third-sector associations, and bias consultants, audits, and trainings have proliferated apace. Millions of people have taken the Harvard Implicit Association Test (at https://implicit.harvard.edu/implicit/takeatest.html). But "the implicit revolution" in cognition is still in the process of establishing itself scientifically: the validity of the construct is in question, the term "implicit" is itself a matter of dispute (does it mean unconscious, automatic, or indirectly measured?) and, for many psychologists, implicit bias remains a method in search of a distinctive phenomenon.[27] Moreover, four thorny questions remain in suspense: does the test measure bias in the individual or bias in the surrounding cultural milieu? Is the null hypothesis of unbiased cognition in real life plausible? Under what conditions does biased cognition lead to biased action? How would rooting out individual bias change institutions, if at all?[28] And what does it matter if a person is biased so long as they act in a nondiscriminatory manner? Implicit bias fits well with the national American culture of moral individualism and fascination for technical solutions to social problems and it takes the focus away from institutions and relations of power. Still, it alerts us to the work of the unconscious in routine ethnoracial categorization.

Stigma is an indispensable concept to grasp the nature and workings of racial domination, for subordinate ethnic groups are invariably carriers of "discrediting differentness" à la Goffman. The Canadian sociologist distinguishes three such differences: those rooted in "abominations of the body," those born of "blemishes of moral character," and "the tribal stigma of race, nation, and religion,

---

[26] Anthony G. Greenwald and Mahzarin R. Banaji, "The Implicit Revolution: Reconceiving the Relation between Conscious and Unconscious" (2017). The popular version of this approach is Mahzarin R. Banaji and Anthony G. Greenwald, *Blindspot: Hidden Biases of Good People* (2013).
[27] Ulrich Schimmack, "The Implicit Association Test: A Method in Search of a Construct" (2021).
[28] Jonathan Kahn, *Race on the Brain: What Implicit Bias Gets Wrong about the Struggle for Racial Justice* (2017). For an earlier critique of a germane notion, see Hart Blanton and James Jaccard, "Unconscious Racism: A Concept in Pursuit of a Measure" (2008).

these being stigma that can be transmitted through lineages and equally contaminate all members of a family."²⁹ The conceptual affinity between stigma and race is evident once we insert between them the overlapping notion of *dishonor* as the public denial or diminishment of dignity.³⁰ Indeed, racialization and stigmatization advance in lock-step as indicated by figure 2 (*supra*, p. 85). It should be stressed that a "spoiled identity" does not reside in this or that bodily, moral, or genealogical property: rather, it is the gaze of the dominant which turns a given attribute into *negative symbolic capital* and "a whole and usual person into a tainted, discounted one." In a crucial but overlooked passage of *Stigma*, Goffman notes that "the normal and the stigmatized are not persons, but rather perspectives" and that stigmatization "can function as a means of social control."³¹

At the other end of the continuum of ethnicity are the dominant categories who possess and accrue positive symbolic capital, that is, marks of dignity, esteem, prestige, and who extract from others acts of deference and reverence that feed their *aura*. The contrapuntal interplay of aura and stigma, the one rooted in culture and the other treated as a nature, is pivotal in the symbolic struggles of ethnoracial domination (as we shall see in the next chapter about Jim Crow rule in the postbellum United States). So much so that, "in history, many groups have been formed without any other basis than the stigmatizing effects of an earlier symbolic struggle."³² Stigmata vary along two orthogonal dimensions, visibility and detachability, whose combination creates four categories: visible and detachable (Afro-Brazilians at the edge), visible and undetachable (African Americans except at the

---

²⁹ Goffman, *Stigma*, p. 4. In the polarized metropolis, ethnicized lower-class populations also commonly suffer from the *territorial stigma* attached to their neighborhood of residence. See Loïc Wacquant, *Bourdieu in the City: Challenging Urban Theory* (2023a), pp. 81–97, and the discussion *infra*, pp. 125–6, 353–4.

³⁰ See the pellucid theoretical elaboration of Glenn Loury in *The Anatomy of Racial Inequality* (2021 [2002]), especially p. 70, where he writes: "By racial dishonor I mean something specific: an entrenched if inchoate presumption of inferiority, of moral inadequacy, of unfitness for intimacy, of intellectual incapacity, harbored by observing agents when they regard the race-marked subjects." I agree with Loury that, in the case of African Americans, this dishonor issues from the historical experience of enslavement, but I disagree when he avers that "chattel slavery was an institution grounded in America's primordial racial classification – the 'social otherness' of blacks" (p. 68). I will argue in chapter 4 (see *infra*, pp. 259–300) that the causal arrow runs in the opposite direction: slavery spawned race as indictive blackness.

³¹ Goffman, *Stigma*, pp. 26, 138 and 139. This point is expanded by Bruce Link and Jo Phelan in their influential article "Conceptualizing Stigma" (2001).

³² Bourdieu, *Sociologie générale*, vol. 1, p. 130.

Elementary Forms of Ethnoracial Rule

edge), invisible and detachable (nationality, religion), and invisible and undetachable (Burakumin). Strategies of management of ethnoracial taint vary accordingly and group formation is most likely and most sturdy when this taint cannot be hidden and shed.

2. Discrimination

Goffman indicates why stigma as sulfurous cognition matters: "We believe the person with a stigma is not quite human. On this assumption, we exercise varieties of discrimination, through which we effectively, if often unwittingly, reduce his life chances."[33] This takes us *from the realm of cognition into the realm of conduct*, grasped as both flowing in interaction and enmeshed in structural relations, with our second elementary form of racial domination. *Discrimination* refers to the differential treatment of persons or populations based on their assignment in a classification system (ethnoracial or other) and to an institutional regime that systematically produces disparate impacts along some categorical line without plausible warrant.

This is not the place to produce a full genealogy of the notion other than to note, first, that it took until 1949 for sociologists to realize that prejudice and discrimination could vary independently of each other, as captured by Robert Merton in his famous typology of active and timid bigots versus fair-weather and all-weather liberals.[34] To this day, however, some scholars continue to conflate the two forms as if they were a single phenomenon or seamlessly morphed one into the other. Second, more than a half-century later, the concept of discrimination remains uneasily suspended between the social sciences, the law, and common sense and often mixes positive and normative considerations. As currently used, it suffers from four serious limitations.

First, there is the problematic equation of discrimination with *negative* discrimination, overlooking the fact that discrimination may also be at once moral, legal, and legitimate.[35] In Latin, *discrimen* means establishing a distinction, which is integral to social life at large and is typically taken for granted and accepted, as indicated for instance by discrimination by age for driving, voting, and retirement and by

---

[33] Goffman, *Stigma*, p. 5.
[34] Robert K. Merton, "Discrimination and the American Creed" (1948).
[35] On the (im)morality of discrimination as treatment that demeans, see Deborah Hellman, *When Is Discrimination Wrong?* (2008).

nationality for citizenship, residence, and social rights. This conflation obviates formulating this crucial question: under what social conditions does discrimination turn negative, that is, not just invidious and prejudicial but *unfair* in regards of social, moral, and legal norms; and, conversely, what propels negative discrimination into neutral and then possibly positive discrimination? For instance, how and why did discrimination against gays go from legally mandated to legally prohibited in advanced societies (California treated homosexual relations as a crime until 1975 and was the first US state to legalize same-sex marriage in 2013)? How does French *laïcité* generate a disparate impact on persons of the Muslim faith in public space, and this in full legality but with increasingly disputed legitimacy?[36] A robust sociology of discrimination ought to include the struggles over the legitimacy, morality, and legality of differential treatment based on the full spectrum of categories and include *negative cases* in which members of a discriminated category fail to mobilize or to achieve public recognition of their predicament, as with short men.[37] It takes a specific symbolic labor of categorization and a social labor of mobilization, including agencies within the bureaucratic field, for discrimination to be constituted as a social, and thence state, problem and this collective labor implies a "juridification" of the struggle against unfair treatment that shifts the civic focus from social causes to individual consequences.[38]

A second limitation of conventional approaches to discrimination is the common and unquestioned equation in Anglophone research of negative discrimination with *racial* discrimination, overlooking other bases of invidious treatment (with the recent exception of gender),[39]

---

[36] Gwénaële Calvès, *La Laïcité* (2022), chapter 5. On the political genesis of the racialized vision of Islam by the French state in the interwar decades, read Naomi Davidson, *Only Muslim: Embodying Islam in Twentieth-Century France* (2017).

[37] Short men have failed to mobilize as a group even as they suffer steep penalties in occupation, income, marriage, and family formation (as shown by Nicolas Herpin, *Le Pouvoir des grands. De l'influence de la taille des hommes sur leur statut social* [2006]). The inability of the National Association of Short-Statured Persons (NOSSA, launched in 2006 and disbanded in 2013) to attract members suffices to demonstrate that objective discrimination does not always lead to public acknowledgment and successful recruitment of the aggrieved category.

[38] Didier Fassin, "L'invention française de la discrimination" (2002).

[39] This routine conceptual slippage is prevalent to the point of going unnoticed. Even the best sociologists fall into it: *vide* Lincoln Quillian, "New Approaches to Understanding Racial Prejudice and Discrimination" (2006), and Devah Pager and Hana Shepperd, "The Sociology of Discrimination: Racial Discrimination in

Elementary Forms of Ethnoracial Rule

in particular *discrimination by class* (based on accent, educational credentials, income and property, and even physique) at both the interactional and the structural levels, which has the effect of naturalizing class domination and legitimating the doxic view that market mechanisms are by nature fair.[40] Moreover, the conventional study of racial discrimination in the US using the black/white categorical opposition routinely overlooks, and indeed *hides*, gradational distinctions of color between darker-skinned and lighter-skinned African Americans even as research has consistently revealed that dark–light disparities are deeper than black–white disparities for such key life outcomes as employment, income, health, and incarceration.[41]

A related form of differential treatment intertwined with race has recently crystallized in the labor market that further muddies the waters: *discrimination by place* in response to territorial stigmatization. In the dual metropolis of advanced societies, marginalized neighborhoods harboring high densities of populations trapped at the bottom of the orders of class and honor are hypervisible in public culture and commonly perceived as urban hellholes, nests of vice and violence that threaten the safety and morality of the urban citizenry. Employers have responded by selecting out job applicants coming from notorious towns and districts. Which raises the thorny question: stigmatized ethnicity and stigmatized territory, which is the proxy for which?[42] Is the job applicant denied because she comes from a neighborhood that is viewed through racialized lenses or because she is viewed as

---

Employment, Housing, Credit, and Consumer Markets" (2008). In recent years, research on discrimination by age, ability, and neighborhood has appeared, but it remains comparatively small in terms of volume and impact.

[40] French law timidly acknowledges discrimination by class (since 2016) in the form of "special vulnerability resulting from economic situation." The trouble is, enforcement is nonexistent. Gwénaële Calvès and Diane Roman, "La discrimination à raison de la précarité sociale: progrès ou confusion?" (2016).

[41] Ellis P. Monk Jr., "Skin Tone Stratification Among Black Americans, 2001–2003" (2014); idem, "The Cost of Color: Skin Color, Discrimination, and Health among African-Americans" (2015); idem, "The Color of Punishment: African Americans, Skin Tone, and the Criminal Justice System" (2019). For an intriguing explanation as to why darker-skinned African Americans do not mobilize to make public and fight color discrimination, see Jennifer L. Hochschild and Vesla Weaver, "The Skin Color Paradox and the American Racial Order" (2007b).

[42] Loïc Wacquant et al., "Territorial Stigmatization in Action" (2014); Paul Kirkness and Andreas Tijé-Dra (eds.), *Negative Neighbourhood Reputation and Place Attachment: The Production and Contestation of Territorial Stigma* (2017); Pascale Petit et al., "Effets de quartier, effet de département. Discrimination liée au lieu de résidence et accès à l'emploi" (2016).

a member of an ethnic category concentrated in a reviled place? I return to the vexed dialectic of race and place in the last chapter of the book when dealing with the penal state (see *infra*, pp. 311–20, 353–4). Suffice it to note here that racialization always operates by marking the cityscape but that the projection of symbolic space onto physical space endows the latter with a relative autonomy and causal power that feeds back into racialization.

A third limitation of conventional approaches to discrimination is the routine conflation of racial disparity and discrimination and the related error that consists in assuming that an ethnic disparity, say, in school performance, is necessarily produced by an *ethnic* mechanism when it can be the spawn of a *nonethnic* mechanism, such as the lower class composition or the geographical distribution of students (which may themselves be produced by an ethnic or a nonethnic mechanism, say, discrimination in the housing market or income distribution). This is the case for pupils of Maghrebine descent in France who lag behind French-descended pupils in academic achievement overall but perform just as well or *even better* when one controls for family type and social class of the parents.[43] In this regard, is the null hypothesis of no gap that guides quantitative studies using the method of unexplained residuals to detect discrimination sociologically plausible? Because of the myriad variables embroiled in dynamic relationships, there is virtually no process in the social world that does not generate disparities of some sort. So it is not tenable to expect that selection on the labor or housing markets, for instance, would yield perfect equality between categories in the absence of discrimination.[44] Furthermore, does it makes sense for sociologists to separate out through statistical manipulation and fictively treat as independent variables that are constitutively entwined in social life, rather than *study this entwinement itself?*

Last, there is the presumption that ethnoracial discrimination is committed only by members of the dominant group against the dominated. Yet, in addition to vertical discrimination, *horizontal* discrimination among and between subordinate categories is a phenomenon

---

[43] Yaël Brinbaum and Annick Kieffer, "Les scolarités des enfants d'immigrés de la sixième au baccalauréat. Différenciation et polarisation des parcours" (2009); Mathieu Ichou, *Les Enfants d'immigrés à l'école. Inégalités scolaires du primaire à l'enseignement supérieur* (2018).

[44] Fibbi and her colleagues concede as much in their review of studies of residual gaps, which they conclude by noting that "ethnic penalties are not equivalent to discrimination." Rosita Fibbi et al., *Migration and Discrimination* (2021), p. 49.

Elementary Forms of Ethnoracial Rule

that a sociology of racial rule cannot ignore. It tends to undermine group formation and thwart political mobilization as it creates both objective disparities and collective sentiments of antipathy, jealousy, and resentment among the subcategories of the subordinate, as with the ethnic tensions between native Indonesians and Chinese in the colonial Dutch East Indies and between blacks and coloureds in post-apartheid South Africa.[45] Likewise, black French people from France's overseas territories respond to racial discrimination by stressing their citizenship and deep roots in the country to create social and symbolic distance from black immigrants from Africa. "By refusing conflation with other groups categorized as 'black' or 'Arab', the people from the French overseas living in mainland France reject the reductive mechanism of racism. They assert an intermediate position without denying the injustices they have witnessed or suffered."[46]

But the thorniest question yet in the study of discrimination is the move from the individual to the structural level and the linkages between discrimination and other forms of ethnoracial domination. Two sophisticated efforts to make that jump are those of Samuel Lucas and Barbara Reskin. Lucas boldly proposes that discrimination consists in a "damaged social relation," resulting not from an act but from a context, a "matrix of norms, values, and public support mechanisms," and that it generally makes *both* the discriminator and the discriminated worse off.[47] Reskin avers that "*über* (or meta) discrimination" is at work whenever a system of interlinked disparities in various domains (employment, schooling, housing, access to credit, etc.) sustains unequal outcomes between whites and blacks in the US.[48] But she equates racial domination *in toto* with racial discrimination and

---

[45] Fasseur, "Cornerstone and Stumbling Block"; Kogila Moodley and Heribert Adam, "Race and Nation in Post-Apartheid South Africa" (2000).

[46] Marine Haddad, "Des minorités pas comme les autres? Le vécu des discriminations et du racisme des ultramarins en métropole" (2018).

[47] Samuel R. Lucas, *Just Who Loses? Discrimination in the United States* (2013), pp. 6–9, 132–3 and 175.

[48] Barbara Reskin, "The Race Discrimination System" (2012). As always in American research, Reskin focuses solely on the United States, ignoring studies conducted in other countries, and only on African Americans, whose historical trajectory and position in symbolic, social, and physical space is unique. Is it not risky to construct a theory of a given phenomenon based on an outlier case? Compare with the French study which measures discrimination for eight national categories of immigrants and also includes perceived discrimination: Beauchemin et al., *Trajectoires et origines*, translated into English as *Trajectories and Origins: Survey on the Diversity of the French Population* (2018).

racial discrimination with racial disparity (albeit in multiple "subsystems"); she conflates the *production* with the *reproduction* of disparities once they are established; and she fails to consider nonracial bases of discrimination and disparity. For instance, intense racial segregation in residence can cause a range of negative outcomes in schooling, social networks, occupation, and exposure to crime or police brutality in the *absence* of racial discrimination *stricto sensu*. Labeling a system of self-sustaining disparities discrimination only confuses the issue.

This diagnostic difference has practical implications. The policy recommendation that flows from an analysis in terms of discrimination is to correct biased procedures and to *widen access* to desired positions or resources, whereas the recommendation flowing from disparity analysis is more radical: it is to *reduce inequality*, regardless of its source. Moreover, there is nothing specifically racial about the dynamic interlinkage of multiple disparities: any subordinate category, for instance lower-class people, suffers the same adverse systemic effects. Indeed, such cascades of cumulative disadvantage rooted in position in the mode of production (for Marxists) or in the job market (for Weberians) are central to class formation, structure, and identity.

To end on a positive note, sociology is well placed to spotlight two dimensions of what one might call *micro-discrimination* that call for more research as well as more public discussion. The first is the social dynamics and effects of the relatively minor but routine and repeated unfair treatments faced in everyday interaction.[49] This includes, for instance, being followed by a security guard in a store, served with abruptness in a restaurant, denied access to a night club, handled with condescension by a bureaucrat, seeing women suddenly clutch their purse as one gets on the bus, being ogled on the street because

---

[49] Mario Luis Small and Devah Pager, "Sociological Perspectives on Racial Discrimination" (2020), pp. 61–2. This is close to what psychologists call "microaggression" after the work of the African-American psychiatrist Chester Middlebrook Pierce (who coined the concept in 1970) and the elaboration of Derald Wing Sue and his colleagues, who establish a typology differentiating microassault, microinsult, and microinvalidation. See Derald Wing Sue and Lisa Spanierman, *Microaggressions in Everyday Life* (2020). The term aggression is not useful because it suggests clear-eyed hostility, negative emotions, and the intention to harm, denotations not carried by the term discrimination, which may entail withdrawal from interaction rather than assault. Also, I diverge from Sue and Spanierman in that I hold that differential social treatment is inherent to social life and, much like crime according to Émile Durkheim, cannot be eradicated. For an empirical panorama of the phenomenon and its differential incidence, see Kiara Wyndham Douds and Michael Hout, "Microaggressions in the United States" (2020).

one wears a hijab or a turban, etc. The cumulative impact of these *petty racial indignities* and *symbolic encroachments* upon the sanctity of the self, suffered again and again over time and across the life course, can turn out to be as damaging for the ego and quality of life as the economic impact of the macro forms of unfair treatment in the labor, housing, or financial markets.[50]

Another, seemingly anodyne, form of racial belittlement in everyday life is denigrating ethnic humor. Such humor stands at the interface of prejudice and discrimination, representation and action, and, when occurring in ordinary conversation, is fruitfully construed as racialized verbal conduct. It broadcasts stereotypical representations that inferiorize the target category with little recourse short of derailing the interaction and triggering embarrassment and hostility. In a comparative study of Mexico and Peru, Christina Sue and Tanya Golash-Boza show how black and indigenous people in both countries are routinely subjected to offensive jokes and generally react by going along with them or recasting them as benign, thus absorbing the injuries to the self they cause and inadvertently reproducing ethnoracial boundaries and hierarchies.[51] But ethnic jokes can also be deployed by the dominated in their reserved spaces to talk about taboo topics and to express their sense of hurt and discontent with ethnoracial subordination, as documented by Donna Goldstein in her ethnography of race, class, and humor in everyday life among the poor women of a Brazilian favela.[52] So we must stay alert to the "underlife" of discriminatory forms and capture their two-sidedness: they put and keep the subordinate in their inferior position but they can also generate solidarity and nourish recalcitrance if not resistance among them.

A second, related, aspect of the micro-sociology of racial domination is *the phenomenology of discrimination*, captured from both ends of the relation. From the perpetrator's standpoint, what are the "vocabularies of motives" they deploy to minimize or justify to themselves

---

[50] Anderson gives myriad examples of sanctions for "being while Black" in ordinary interaction in *Black in White Space: The Enduring Impact of Color in Everyday Life* (2022). There is a voluminous body of American research on the impact of discriminatory slights on physical and mental health. See, for instance, Brian D. Smedley, "The Lived Experience of Race and its Health Consequences" (2012).

[51] Christina Sue and Tanya Golash-Boza, "'It Was Only a Joke': How Racial Humor Fuels Race-Blind Ideologies in Mexico and Peru" (2013). Raúl Pérez refers to such humor as "amused racial contempt" in *The Souls of White Jokes: How Racist Humor Fuels White Supremacy* (2022).

[52] Donna Goldstein, *Laughter Out of Place: Race, Class, Violence, and Sexuality in a Rio Shantytown* (2003).

and to others the unfair treatment they mete out?[53] From the target's standpoint, what are the cues, idioms, and effects of perceived discrimination, regardless of whether it happened? Capturing the sense of biased action that subordinate categories develop matters because this perception shapes their cognition and affect, including feelings of self-doubt, humiliation, resentment, and rage.[54] It also shapes their conduct in the form of strategies of avoidance or confrontation, resignation or resistance, and eventually retreat. For instance, it leads some young Maghrebi men from France's urban periphery to pass on applying for open jobs to avoid the anticipated disgrace of being ignored, mistreated, or turned down.[55] It can cause diffident or aggressive behavior in interaction in an effort to ward off symbolic slights (for instance, being over-assertive in job interviews), which behavior may then trigger the unfair treatment feared in the first place, a textbook case of self-fulfilling prophecy. Misplaced perception can also turn into ethnoracial paranoia which, even as it rests on an imaginary basis, is itself a real psychosocial condition that creates suffering and warps interethnic relations in everyday life.

3. Segregation

This takes us to the third form of ethnoracial domination: *segregation*, which consists in distributing people differentially based on categorical membership, actual or perceived, across two spaces: *social space* as the system of positions defined by the distribution of forms of capital (economic, cultural, social, and symbolic) and *physical space* (the geographical location and expanse wherein social action and institutions "take place," literally).[56] Four major manifestations

---

[53] Charles W. Mills, "Situated Actions and Vocabularies of Motive" (1940). Employers can prove very candid about their rationale for discriminating among job candidates, as reported by Joleen Kirschenman and Kathryn M. Neckerman, "'We'd Love to Hire Them, but . . .': The Meaning of Race for Employers" (1991).

[54] François Dubet et al., *"Pourquoi moi?" L'expérience des discriminations* (2013). But see the critique of Gwénaële Calvès, "La discrimination, une expérience impossible" (2013).

[55] Roxane Silberman and Irène Fournier, "Les secondes générations sur le marché du travail en France: une pénalité ethnique ancrée dans le temps. Contribution à la théorie de l'assimilation segmentée" (2006).

[56] On social space, see Pierre Bourdieu, "Espace social et genèse des 'classes'" (1984a). The trialectic of symbolic space, social space, and physical space is unpacked in Wacquant, *Bourdieu in the City*, pp. 3–10.

of segregation in social space are the occupational structure, student composition in schools, the categorical distribution of networks (kin, friends, coworkers), and intermarriage patterns. Three key zones of physical space are residential neighborhoods, workplaces, and public spaces (including places of travel, commerce, and entertainment).[57] Again, one must be careful not to automatically equate segregation with *ethnoracial* segregation:[58] not only can the process be based on other major social principles of social vision and division, such as religion in many major cities around the world (Beirut, Belfast, Baghdad, Jerusalem, Delhi); ethnoracial and other kinds of segregation are often deeply intertwined, as with the high correlation between color and class segregation in the Brazilian, French, and Belgian metropolis. In Chinese cities, once distinctive for their egalitarianism, it is housing tenure, school credentials, and *hukou* (household registration status) that drive accelerating rates of residential segregation.[59]

For the Chicago School of urban sociology launched by Robert Park and Ernest Burgess in the 1920s, residential segregation was the blind product of ecological processes, similar to those found among plants and animals, and ultimately driven by population movements, economic activity, the environment, and technology.[60] For decades, the ecological paradigm ruled unchallenged and segregation was portrayed by American researchers as an inevitable and mostly benign corollary of urban modernity – except when it was threatened: the entry of blacks into white neighborhoods was labeled "invasion." Then came the Civil Rights Movement which contested

---

[57] In the interest of brevity and given data availability, I focus my discussion on residential segregation, but I note that intermarriage rates provide a better indicator of the social incorporation or isolation of ethnicized populations in national social space.
[58] This is the *raccourci* taken by Carl Nightingale in *Segregation: A Global History of Divided Cities* (2012), which equates segregation around the world with "a new technique of racial control" applied by "white people almost everywhere" to create a "coerced residential color line," leading to the current "apocalypse of segregation" (pp. 1, 5, 386). This overlooks the fact that "the design of colonial cities was never wholly imposed from above by colonial rulers" but was instead the result of the "'joint enterprise' of rulers and colonial elites" (Thomas R. Metcalf, "Colonial Cities" [2013], p. 758). It also ignores other potent bases of spatial division, such as class, gender, and religion.
[59] Zhigang Li and Fulong Wu, "Tenure-Based Residential Segregation in Post-Reform Chinese Cities: A Case Study of Shanghai" (2008).
[60] Robert Park and Ernest Burgess, *The City* (1925); Amos A. Hawley, *Human Ecology: A Theory of Community Structure* (1950).

racial separation in space on the streets and in the courts. In the academy, the successive surge of Marxist, political-economic, and feminist theory in the three decades following the urban upheavals of the 1960s changed the social science of the city. For the Marxists, the shape of the metropolis was determined by the needs of capital; for the advocates of political economy, by the wishes of urban elites controlling the local state; and for feminist scholars, by the requirements of the gender division of labor.[61] None of these theoretical strands tackled segregation frontally, but they made it possible to rethink the latter as the means and result of closure strategies in Weber's sense of *Schließung*. For this approach, ethnoracial segregation in the city is determined by struggles, waged in social space and the field of power, over the distribution of people, activities, and material and symbolic goods across physical space, struggles in which state structures and policies play a predominant role – even in countries that think of themselves as having a "weak state," such as the United States.[62]

Segregation seems on first look to be a straightforward phenomenon readily explained by discrimination in occupation, schooling, or housing. But it is in reality a multilayered phenomenon that admits of a multiplicity of sources, many of which are not discriminatory. First, residential segregation may be willful, based on choice and affinity, or imposed, based on constraint and hostility – this is the major difference between the ethnic cluster and the ghetto. The ethnic cluster results from the voluntary concentration of co-ethnics in a neighborhood which serves as acclimation chamber and springboard into the broader expanse of the city and beyond; it is best represented architecturally by a bridge. The ghetto, as we shall soon see, is the spawn of compulsion and aims to durably quarantine an undesirable but needed population in a reserved territory; its architectural figure is the wall.[63] In addition, "segregation is by no means a universal corollary of racial differentiation" and its antithesis is not "integration" but dispersion, since a social system may gain its coherence precisely through spatial separation, as demonstrated by traditional Indian

---

[61] See, respectively, David Harvey, *Social Justice and the City* (1973); John R. Logan and Harvey L. Molotch, *Urban Fortunes: The Political Economy of Place* (2007 [1987]); and Daphne Spain, *Gendered Spaces* (1992).
[62] Wacquant, *Bourdieu in the City*, pp. 8–9, 33–4, 164–9.
[63] Loïc Wacquant, "A Janus-Faced Institution of Ethnoracial Control: A Sociological Specification of the Ghetto" (2012), pp. 3–4 and 20–2.

Elementary Forms of Ethnoracial Rule

caste society or by the creation of a mosaic of racially exclusive districts in the cities of apartheid South Africa.[64]

Second, following Douglas Massey, one can differentiate between four independent dimensions of residential segregation, namely, dissimilarity (the unevenness of ethnic population distribution across neighborhoods), isolation (the degree of exposure of the subordinate category to other ethnic categories in their vicinity), clustering (the formation of contiguous areas of ethnic density), and centrality (location in or near the urban core), each of which contributes to the spatial enclosure of the population considered and reinforces the others.[65] This makes it possible to construct the *four-dimensional segregative profile* presented by different ethnicized populations in the city and to counter moral panics around the formation of "ghettos" of the kind that has gripped Europe over the past quarter-century as postcolonial migrants settled in the metropolis.[66]

One example: Dutch city managers and media have grown alarmed at the alleged formation of Surinamese ("black") enclaves closed unto themselves and threatening civic inclusion. While the Surinamese have indeed clustered in some areas in Amsterdam such as the Bijlmermeer, only one-third of all Surinamese reside in districts one-third Surinamese or more and a paltry 3 per cent of all Surinamese live in districts that are majority Surinamese.[67] Similarly, in France, ethnic density, measuring the proportion of the local population issued from postcolonial migration, has increased continuously in many stigmatized neighborhoods of the urban periphery over the past three decades, turning them into *hypnotic points* monopolizing public and political attention, while at the same time foreign-origin populations were slowly but steadily growing more dispersed throughout the national territory. Thus, the dissimilarity index for residents of Algerian origins declined from 49 percent in 1968 to 38 percent in 2007; from 53 percent to 38 percent for Moroccans; and from 48 percent to 27 percent for the Portuguese. Only the Turks saw

---

[64] Leo Kuper, "Segregation" (1968), pp. 147 and 144, and Paul Maylam, "Explaining the Apartheid City: 20 Years of South African Urban Historiography" (1995).
[65] Douglas S. Massey, "Reflections on the Dimensions of Segregation" (2012). See also the illustrations in the canonical study by Douglas Massey and Nancy Denton, *American Apartheid: Segregation and the Making of the Underclass* (1993).
[66] Loïc Wacquant, *The Two Faces of the Ghetto* (2025), prologue.
[67] Sako Musterd, "Social and Ethnic Segregation in Europe: Levels, Causes, and Effects" (2005), p. 335.

their dissimilarity score stay constant around 50 percent.[68] As a result, the index of neighborhood ethnic diversity for the native population increased from 14.9 in 1968 to 19.4 in 2007, meaning that natives and immigrants have become more mixed in space – the exact opposite of public and policy perception.

Moreover, as noted earlier, there is considerable population *turnover* in the French urban periphery: nearly 70 percent of all residents of the officially designated "sensitive urban zones" move out of their neighborhood over the course of a decade and the majority of movers migrate to a better neighborhood. This is in sharp contrast with black Americans residing in the hyperghetto, who tend to be residentially immobile or to *churn* in similarly dispossessed and segregated neighborhood both intra- and inter-generationally.[69] This suggests adding two dimensions to the four-sided makeup of segregation according to Massey: the fifth is diachronic and captures the degree to which the population of the neighborhood gets renewed over time; the sixth is longitudinal and covers the trajectories of resident households across the ranked spatial order of neighborhoods.

This suggests also the need to pay special attention to the scale at which segregation is measured: the smaller the unit, the higher the index of dissimilarity for the same distribution. Indeed, macro-segregation can be declining at the level of the city district and hide the persistence of *micro-segregation* at the block, street, or even building level, while segregation can migrate from residence to social networks and collective activities. *Ceteris paribus*, physical distance fosters social distance but physical propinquity does not automatically translate into social proximity, as shown by Javier Ruiz-Tagle in a comparison of two defamed low-income neighborhoods of Chicago and Santiago de Chile targeted by urban policies of social and ethnic mixing.[70] Worse: spatial diffusion can inflame prejudice and harden

---

[68] Jean-Louis Pan Ké Shon and Gregory Verdugo, "Ségrégation et incorporation des immigrés en France. Ampleur et intensité entre 1968 et 2007" (2014), p. 254.

[69] On residential turnover in the French urban periphery, see Jean-Louis Pan Ké Shon, "Ségrégation ethnique et ségrégation sociale en quartiers sensibles. L'apport des mobilités résidentielles" (2009); on churning without exit inside the American hyperghetto, Patrick Sharkey, "The Intergenerational Transmission of Context" (2008). A similar pattern of "hypnotic points" hiding growing dispersion has emerged in England and Sweden, as shown by Ceri Peach, "Does Britain Have Ghettos?" (1996), and Bo Malmberg et al., "Residential Segregation of European and Non-European Migrants in Sweden: 1990–2012" (2018).

[70] Javier Ruiz-Tagle, "Bringing Inequality Closer: A Comparative Look at Socially Diverse Neighbourhoods in Chicago and Santiago de Chile" (2018).

Elementary Forms of Ethnoracial Rule

discrimination by making the stigmatized ethnoracial category more visible in the public space of the dominant, as was the case with the Roma in Budapest in the 1980s.[71]

Lastly, mechanisms of ethnic segregation vary widely across cities, countries, and epochs. Spatial constellations can result from top-down and intentional processes with clear centers of command, as with the rigid partitioning of the colonial city based on the colonists' fear that the native population was the carrier of infectious disease and moral turpitude; the rebuilding of the black American ghetto by the state in the postwar period through public programs of "urban renewal" launched to stem urban decline and corral a new wave of African-American migrants; and the planned concentration of public housing harboring working-class families in the "Red Belt" of Paris initially thought to facilitate Communist Party control of its municipalities.[72] Segregated neighborhoods can also arise from the bottom up as a product of multiple micro-mechanisms, as illustrated again by the enforcement of the boundaries of the black American ghetto: hostility and assault on the streets by established residents, the firebombing of abodes when blacks moved in, pressure by white homeowners' associations and restrictive covenants preventing the rental or sale of housing to African Americans (and Jews). These micro-mechanisms were reinforced at the meso level by racial steering and panic peddling by realtors and by biased lending by banks, and further bolstered and legitimated at the macro level by "red-lining" by the government.[73]

Ethnic segregation can also result from impersonal and blind forces such as the differential class composition of the various population groups: a lower socioeconomic distribution mechanically translates into ethnic concentration in low-income neighborhoods, all the more so when class inequality is steep (as is the case in the US relative to Western Europe). This explains most of the color segregation in the large cities of Brazil, which is, moreover, low to moderate by US standards partly because ethnoracial categories are not

---

[71] János Ladányi, "Patterns of Residential Segregation and the Gypsy Minority in Budapest" (1993).
[72] Metcalf, "Colonial Cities," p. 758; Arnold R. Hirsch, *Making the Second Ghetto: Race and Housing in Chicago 1940–1960* (2009 [1984]); Annie Fourcaut, *Bobigny, banlieue rouge* (1986).
[73] Richard Rothstein, *The Color of Law: A Forgotten History of How Our Government Segregated America* (2017).

clearly bounded.[74] Welfare states also play a major role in curbing if not reversing segregative tendencies through the widespread provision and dispersion of social housing and the development of public transport systems that widen the spectrum of neighborhoods accessible to low-income households.[75] And they largely determine the degree of spatial inequality in the distribution of public and private goods, as with the quality of schools or the diligence of policing across neighborhoods. Another feeder of segregation in the putative absence of discrimination is family size among the lower class.[76] In France, multi-bedroom apartments in public housing are found in the least desirable clusters of buildings in the urban periphery. By virtue of their poverty and larger number of children, households of West and Sub-Saharan African immigrants end up concentrated in these projects, from which native-born French households have moved out due to the shrinking of their family, the deterioration of the housing stock as well as to the class lowering and ethnic turnover of the tenant population.

Other non-discriminatory processes sustaining residential segregation once it is established include such "social structural sorting" as the propensity of prospective home buyers to search for housing near family and in neighborhoods that feel familiar, and to garner housing information from networks of kin, friends, and coworkers that tend to be of the same ethnicity and are therefore likely to steer buyers toward an area of ethnic concentration.[77]

All in all, segregation emerges as a complex, dynamic, and resilient form of ethnoracial domination that can perpetuate itself absent prejudice and discrimination and is therefore irreducible to other forms. It results from multiple mechanisms operating conjointly and its consequentiality varies depending on the political articulation of symbolic, social, and physical space. This articulation hinges on the degree to which segregation, both ethnic and class, is decried, accepted, or ignored by central and local authorities, which is in turn

---

[74] Edward E. Telles, "Residential Segregation by Skin Color in Brazil" (1992). Segregation in Brazil has decreased significantly over the past 30 years while continuing to be closely correlated with class, according to Rubia da Rocha Valente and Brian J. L. Berry "Residential Segregation by Skin Color: Brazil Revisited" (2020).
[75] Musterd, "Social and Ethnic Segregation in Europe," p. 340.
[76] Gregory Verdugo, "Logement social et ségrégation résidentielle des immigrés en France, 1968–1999" (2011).
[77] Maria Krysan and Kyle Crowder, *Cycle of Segregation: Social Processes and Residential Stratification* (2017).

Elementary Forms of Ethnoracial Rule

shaped by the makeup of the state, urban history and geography, as well as national conceptions of citizenship.[78]

4. Seclusion

Seclusion is a capacious category encompassing such racialized constellations as ghettos, camps, and reservations on the side of the subaltern, and upper-class districts and gated communities, born of elective self-encompassment, on the side of the dominant.[79] Focusing on the former, it refers to the forcible confinement of a population to a particular sector of social and physical space assigned uniquely to that population, such that the latter develops its own *parallel institutions* there. Ghettos are urban constellations, reservations rural contraptions, and the variety of camps (transit, labor, refugee) covers the whole spectrum between city and country.

The fullest materialization of ethnoracial seclusion is the urban *ghetto*. I have elaborated elsewhere a sociological specification of the ghetto as a Janus-faced institution of ethnic control and succor by applying analytic induction to three historical cases: Jews in Renaissance Europe, African Americans in the Fordist city, and the Burakumin in the Japanese metropolis of the post-Tokugawa era.[80] Let me draw out the main lineaments of my argument and, in so doing, flesh out the nature and workings of the fourth elementary form of ethnoracial domination whose specificity resides in its two-sided character, at once an apparatus of control and an instrument of protection thanks to organizational duplication.

Ghettoization entails the concatenation of four structural elements: stigma, constraint, spatial encasement, and institutional duplication. Put differently, a ghetto arises in the city when a population deemed defiled and defiling, whom the dominant wants to exploit but also to exclude from spaces of intimacy, is forced to reside in a special district. In this district, typically a compact, dense, and sharply bounded

---

[78] See the contrast among six cities, two each in the Netherlands, Belgium, and Germany, drawn by Patrick Ireland, "Comparing Responses to Ethnic Segregation in Urban Europe" (2008).
[79] Loïc Wacquant, "Designing Urban Seclusion: The 2009 Roth-Symonds Lecture" (2010a), pp. 165–7. The verb to seclude, originating in 1451 from the Latin *secludere*, means to shut off, to isolate, to confine.
[80] Wacquant, "A Janus-Faced Institution of Ethnoracial Control" (2011), and *The Two Faces of the Ghetto*, chapters 1 and 2.

settlement, that population gains the room to grow a network of communal organizations run by the group and for the group. The ghetto thus serves two conflictive functions: social ostracization and economic extraction (of financial services, medical knowledge, and long distance trade in the case of Jews in sixteenth-century Venice, of unskilled labor in the case of blacks in twentieth-century Chicago).[81] Suffusive stigma begets systematic discrimination which aggregates into forcible segregation, but a distinctive kind of segregation born of the *mutual assignation of category and territory*, which feeds limited but real institutional autonomy. Accordingly, the ghetto develops along two axes of structuration: the vertical axis of inequality and denigration tying the dominant and the dominated categories – the ghetto as sword – and the horizontal axis of reciprocity, dignity and solidarity among the dominated – the ghetto as shield.[82]

This two-sidedness explains why, contrary to conventional wisdom, both ordinary and scholarly, ghettos have historically been not foils but magnets attracting their designated ethnic population. It reveals how they have served as instruments of collective economic betterment even in the face of exclusion, poverty, and dilapidation, as well as vibrant centers of cultural production leading to the creation of a shared collective identity fueling a frontal attack on group stigma.[83] This is a dimension of ghettoization that, with few exceptions, has been missed by sociologists of race and poverty in the metropolis for two reasons. The first is that they have imported from everyday and journalistic discourse the current folk concept that mistakenly

---

[81] By that specification, the so-called Nazi ghettos of World War II were not ghettos. They were conceived and run as *provisional sociospatial devices* to extirpate, concentrate, and eventually eliminate Jews. They were never intended to serve an economic function as Nazi labor camps were. On this point, read the stunning study by Gordon J. Horwitz, *Ghettostadt: Łódź and the Making of a Nazi City* (2008), and Mitchell Duneier, *Ghetto: The Invention of a Place, the History of an Idea* (2016), chapter 1.

[82] This theme implicitly traverses St. Clair Drake and Horace R. Cayton, *Black Metropolis: A Study of Negro Life in a Northern City* (1993 [1945]), especially chapters 14–18, which document the flourishing of Chicago's Bronzeville in the shadow of white rule. See also Emily Gottreich, *The Mellah of Marrakesh: Jewish and Muslim Space in Morocco's Red City* (2007), pp. 3–5 and passim.

[83] On the Jewish case, see Cecil Roth, *History of the Jews in Venice* (1930), especially chapters 5 and 7. On the African American experience, read Davarian L. Baldwin, *Chicago's New Negroes: Modernity, the Great Migration. and Black Urban Life* (2007), and Adam Green, *Selling the Race: Culture, Community, and Black Chicago, 1940–1955* (2007), which capture the extraordinary prolixity of the African-American ghetto as cultural cauldron fashioning a unified black identity out of the myriad color and geographic divisions brought into the city by migrants from the South.

Elementary Forms of Ethnoracial Rule

equates the ghetto with a space of social disintegration, dread, and despair – confusing the ghetto and its successor, the *hyperghetto*, shorn of an economic function, doubly segregated by race and class, and stripped of communal institutions.[84] Second, they have adopted a prosecutorial posture aimed at denouncing ghettos as violations of basic standards of individual dignity, civic equality, and group inclusion. Here we see concretely how submission to sentiment and the logic of the trial can lead to serious scientific errors.

This robust conceptual construction of the ghetto has an added advantage: it applies not only to the experience of stigmatized diasporas in the Western city but to urban configurations around the world. Thus it enables us to detect the major reason why Latin American countries have failed to develop ghettos as shown by geographer Alan Gilbert: on my reading, their gradational systems of ethnoracial classification comprised of flexible and porous categories sustained by *mestizaje* made it difficult to create rigid segregation in the city, a structural precondition for ghettoization.[85] Similarly, politologist Charlotte Thomas deploys the institutionalist concept of the ghetto to dissect the sociospatial seclusion of Muslims in the Indian city of Ahmedabad, the country's most segregated metropolis. She reveals how the district of Juhapura turned from an ethnically mixed shantytown into an exclusive Muslim ghetto between 1973 and 2002 under the press of pogroms by Hindu nationalists. Repeated eruptions of collective violence pushed Hindus to move out and upper-class Muslims to move back in to seek physical safety, and the confinement of the group led to the bolstering of cross-class institutions as well as to the differential treatment of the district by the state of Gujarat. The result is that Muslims in that city are distributed across three different spatial contraptions of ethnoreligious domination: the ethnic cluster, the enclave, and the ghetto.[86]

---

[84] Loïc Wacquant, "Revisiting Territories of Relegation: Class, Ethnicity and State in the Making of Advanced Marginality" (2015), and idem, *The Two Faces of the Ghetto*, chapters 5–7. The Palestinian neighborhoods of Israeli "mixed cities" come close to this type, characterized as they are by vertical control without horizontal solidarity, as shown by Silvia Pasquetti, "Experiences of Urban Militarism: Spatial Stigma, Ruins and Everyday Life" (2019).

[85] Alan Gilbert, "On the Absence of Ghettos in Latin American Cities" (2012), pp. 192–8.

[86] For a discussion of these three sociospatial constellations, see Wacquant, *The Two Faces of the Ghetto*, chapter 9. On Juhapura, see Charlotte Thomas, *Pogroms et ghetto. Les musulmans dans l'Inde contemporaine* (2018). Further studies of ghettoization in the Indian city deploying variants of the analytic concept elaborated here include

How does the *camp* fit under the conceptual canopy of seclusion? Seclusion implies that the subordinate ethnoracial category is corralled within an exclusive, bounded, and tainted territory. That sociospatial constellation, whether labor camp, transit camp (including internment and concentration camps), or refugee camp, differs from the ghetto in that it is a *liminal space* where workers, displaced persons, and exiles are forced to reside and wherein they seek to construct a life under conditions of social, spatial, and political *uprooting and precarity*.[87] By definition, the camp is not supposed to be there, not expected to last, not recognized or accepted as part of the city, and its residents are not to make any demands on the state and citizenry. Indeed, they are vulnerable to the capricious intrusion and the arbitrary dictates of the forces of order, guards, police, or military. The result is that they yearn to escape this accursed space to which they have no attachment, other than forced. The camp is the concrete materialization of ethnic marginality, and not structural integration as with the ghetto. It typically allows its inhabitants to absorb but not to challenge their subjugation. So it endures, becomes part of the landscape, straddling the urban and the rural, and morphs into an integral cog in the machinery of ethnoracial domination in the form of exclusion.[88]

Christophe Jaffrelot and Laurent Gayer (eds.), *Muslims in Indian Cities: Trajectories of Marginalisation* (2012); Juliette Galonnier, "The Enclave, the Citadel and the Ghetto: The Threefold Segregation of Upper-Class Muslims in India" (2015); Raphael Susewind, "Muslims in Indian Cities: Degrees of Segregation and the Elusive Ghetto" (2017); Anasua Chatterjee, *Margins of Citizenship: Muslim Experiences in Urban India* (2017); and Christophe Jaffrelot et al., "Les paradoxes de la ghettoïsation en Inde. Le cas de Juhapura" (2020).

[87] The literature on camps is sprawling and uneven. Much of it is purely theoretical, engaging the likes of Carl Schmitt, Michel Foucault, and Giorgio Agamben, rather than studying actually existing camps. See, for instance, Claudio Minca, "The Return of the Camp" (2005) and Bülent Diken and Carsten B. Laustsen, *The Culture of Exception: Sociology Facing the Camp* (2005). My working definition is constructed from empirical studies, including those gathered by Michel Agier (ed.), *Un Monde de camps* (2014). I exclude concentration camps which arise in situations of crisis or war to gather and extirpate populations deemed threatening, treasonous, or diseased, as shown by Dan Stone, *Concentration Camps: A Very Short Introduction* (2019).

[88] A particularly fruitful case for theoretical elaboration is Palestinian seclusion in Israel/Palestine insofar as it combines attributes of the ghetto, camp, reservation, and prison. See Alina Korn, "The Ghettoization of the Palestinians" (2008); Julie Peteet, *Landscape of Hope and Despair: Palestinian Refugee Camps* (2005); Jean-Pierre Filiu, *Histoire de Gaza* (2012); Andy Clarno, *Neoliberal Apartheid: Palestine/Israel and South Africa after 1994* (2017); and Silvia Pasquetti, *Refugees Together and Citizens Apart: Control, Emotions, and Politics at the Palestinian Margins* (2023).

Elementary Forms of Ethnoracial Rule

An example is the Algerian shantytown of Nanterre, west of Paris, during the 1950s, deftly analyzed by sociologist extraordinaire Abdelmalek Sayad.[89] A hybrid between labor and transit camp, the *bidonville* was a continuous "creation by the immigrants for the immigrants" and it reflected their vulnerable condition on the labor market and in the city. North African laborers were presumed to be birds of passage; their abodes were to be transitory, in-between residence and hostel. In reality, the slum's emergence marked the conversion of a labor migration into a settlement migration. For wives and children soon joined as the Algerian War of Liberation supplied the pretext for relocating families. But where to put them? The penury of vacant housing, colonial prejudice and hostility, the pull of ethnic solidarity, and the lure of profit turned the owners of immigrant taverns and hostels into "*marchands de sommeil*" (literally, "sellers of sleep"): basements, run-down buildings, garages, and cellars were converted into dwelling places in which families piled up and beds were shared in shifts. Small shacks and stores sprouted along roughly drawn alleyways in vacant land around the hostels. The camp was born. By the mid-1950s, 60 percent of the Algerian and Moroccan population of the city was concentrated in the "Petit Nanterre." Men were mortified at the wretched quarters they imposed on their own kind ("Before coming to France, I didn't know that this could exist somewhere, and even less that I could live in it").[90] But there was nothing they could do about it.

Life in Nanterre's Algerian camp was dominated by the daily negotiation with the problematic triad of "water, mud, and shame," as well as by the fear of rats and fires. City administrators preferred to turn a blind eye: officially the *bidonville* did not exist, it did not need public services, and therefore its inhabitants had no claim on anything. To deflect public indignation, a convenient syllogism was devised: the *bidonville* is the Arab city; Arabs are dirty; therefore the slum is dirty.[91] In truth, no one wanted to confront the latter's grimy reality. Not even the immigrants themselves, who partook of the collective work of denial by taking refuge in "fantasizing and scheming." Only the young vehemently denounced it: "We are like rats, we hide away in holes."[92]

---

[89] Abdelmalek Sayad, *Un Nanterre algérien, terre de bidonvilles* (1995).
[90] Ibid., p. 26.
[91] A similar syllogism was deployed to legitimize the segregation of Mexicans across Texas in the interwar period, as shown by David Montejano, *Anglos and Mexicans in the Making of Texas, 1836–1986* (1987).
[92] Sayad, *Un Nanterre algérien, terre de bidonvilles*, p. 56.

But this is not the whole story, for there is another side to seclusion: due to the press of ethnic prejudice, discrimination, and segregation, the residents of the camp evolved a parallel micro-city of their own. Underneath the dirt, despite the daily dangers and grinding poverty, the *bidonville* evolved a complex social structure and rich collective existence. The rough regrouping of families by *douar* (native village) at the heart of clusters of shacks reproduced the "architectural logic of the Arab town" and allowed residents to reconstitute "the familiar universe of traditional mutual acquaintanceship."[93] A space of cultural refuge, the camp supported an autarkic "economy of misery" mixing solidarity and exploitation, centered on the dyad of *cafés-baraques* and *cafés-comptoirs*, each with its form of sociability. In 1954, the 3,000 Algerians and Moroccans populating the slum of La Garenne Street enjoyed the services of 40 commercial establishments, most of them unregistered, including 11 taverns, 12 grocery shops, and two barbers. The "Algerian Nanterre" not only mimicked the spatial order of the *casbah*: it was tightly controlled by expatriate representatives of the National Liberation Front (FLN) who subjected residents and visitors to punctilious political surveillance. So much to verify that seclusion goes beyond mere segregation to generate institutional parallelism.

A few notations on the reservation as the third materialization of ethnoracial seclusion. First, shockingly given its distinctive role as a tool of racial rule, the social science literature on the reservation *qua* reservation is thin and shallow – with the exception of chapters in two major books: Patrick Wolfe's *Traces of History* and Mahmoud Mamdani's *Neither Settler nor Native*. The available body of empirical research is dispersed, group-oriented as opposed to problem-oriented, and siloed in separate specialist areas such as colonial history distributed by country and Native American studies in the United States.[94] Historians have not even drawn up a full legal genealogy of the notion in the colonies where it has been used.[95] Now, a reservation arises in

---

[93] Ibid., p. 113.

[94] Patrick Wolfe, *Traces of History: Elementary Structures of Race* (2016), and Mahmoud Mamdani, *Neither Settler nor Native: The Making and Unmaking of Permanent Minorities* (2020). The brunt of research on contemporary American Indians centers narrowly on settlement, demography, health, linguistics and economic development, and does not reflect theoretically and comparatively on the institutional peculiarity of the reservation. For a different take, see Pauline Turner Strong, "Recent Ethnographic Research on North American Indigenous Peoples" (2005).

[95] Klaus Frantz gets us started in *Indian Reservations in the United States: Territory, Sovereignty, and Socioeconomic Change* (1999 [1993]), chapter 3.

Elementary Forms of Ethnoracial Rule

a settler colonial territory where the colonists seek to appropriate, not the labor of the natives, but their land. It entails removing that population and stacking it into bounded and reserved tracts, typically located in remote and economically fallow areas. These areas will be governed through special legal and customary rules designed to forcibly regroup and immobilize their assigned populations, which are sometimes granted supervised sovereignty.

The canonical case is the capture, displacement, and near-annihilation of Native Americans in what is now the United States. For a variety of reasons, American Indians were not a suitable supply of labor and they could not be exterminated – they knew the land better; they maneuvered adroitly between England, France, and Spain; and they played a key role in early trading networks.[96] So sociospatial seclusion was wielded to remove and relocate them to restricted areas so as to neutralize the threats that they presented for the settlers of the "frontier" and to release the land they inhabited to fund the government and attract settlers as they moved westward.[97] After they were officially designated by the Supreme Court as "domestic dependent nations" and characterized as "an inferior race of people" fated to disappear or assimilate into "civilization," the territorial claims of Native Americans were extinguished by the Indian Removal Act of 1830. They were systematically evicted from land east of the Mississippi and marched at the point of a bayonet into zones of exclusion created by the Indian Appropriations Act of 1851 which instituted the reservation system.[98]

This was the fate also of the Kanaks, the Melanesian natives of New Caledonia, a French colony island in the South Pacific which is unique in France's former empire in that it developed a dual system of law and property materialized by native reservations that endure to this day.[99] In the half-century after France seized the island in 1853, the Kanaks were displaced by force or ruse to turn the arable land they occupied over to French settlers. This land was allotted, first, to ex-convicts deported to the island from the metropole and other colonies, then to cattle ranchers and, later, to the state-run company

---

[96] Jane Burbank and Frederick Cooper, *Empires in World History: Power and the Politics of Difference* (2011), p. 253.
[97] Stephen Cornell, *The Return of the Native: American Indian Political Resurgence* (1990).
[98] Patrick Wolfe, "Settler Colonialism and the Elimination of the Native" (2006).
[99] Claude Liauzu, *Colonisation. Droit d'inventaire* (2004); Isabelle Merle, *Expériences coloniales. La Nouvelle-Calédonie, 1853–1920* (2020).

entrusted with the open-sky mining of nickel ore. The native population was gradually pushed back against the ridges of the central mountain chain to be eventually corralled into ever-smaller rural districts assigned to the colonial fiction of "tribes" put under the tutelage of "chieftains" nominated by the colonial administration, making the land question the Gordian knot of the colonial society to this day.[100]

The reservation had two contradictory effects. On the one side, it provided a measure of protection that enabled the Kanaks to avoid physical extinction through disease and despair as well as to partially preserve their languages, kinship and political forms, and customs. On the other side, it scrambled customary rights to the land and fostered social isolation and a cultural schism that strengthened colonial prejudice and discrimination, including the European belief that the Kanaks were hopelessly backward and fundamentally inassimilable.[101] This is another example of how stratification in physical and social space helps bolster and justify classification in symbolic space by validating the stigmatizing and inferiorizing representations of the subordinate category.

5. Violence

Violence, defined summarily as the deliberate threat or use of force to inflict injury, is a hybrid form of ethnoracial domination.[102] In its consumptive or *expressive modality*, it is an end unto itself; it aims to cause harm and damage to the targeted ethnic group seemingly for its own sake. But, in so doing, it communicates a triple message, to the perpetrator group, which it unifies; to the violated group, which it singles out and impairs; and to bystanders who need to be educated

---

[100] Alain Saussol, *L'Héritage. Essai sur le problème foncier mélanésien en Nouvelle-Calédonie* (1981). Until 1946, the Kanaks were obligated to reside in their assigned reservation and they had to supply a set number of days of labor to the local colonial authority as well as to pay a head tax.

[101] Alban Bensa, "Colonialisme, racisme et ethnologie en Nouvelle-Calédonie" (1988).

[102] A compact account of theory and research on violence is Philip Dwyer, *Violence: A Very Short Introduction* (2022), and idem, "Violence and Its Histories: Meanings, Methods, Problems" (2017). A provocative selection of social science texts is Nancy Scheper-Hughes and Philippe Bourgois (eds.), *Violence in War and Peace: An Anthology* (2004), in which the authors distinguish between structural, interpersonal, everyday, and symbolic violence. An effort to organize its ethnic variant analytically is Rogers Brubaker and David D. Laitin, "Ethnic and Nationalist Violence" (1998).

Elementary Forms of Ethnoracial Rule

about the parameters of racial rule. A paradigmatic instance is the funneling of the Sinti and Roma into death camps near the close of the Nazi era, which, unlike that of Jews, served no putative material function.[103] Its sole goal was to "cleanse" the national body of a population deemed polluting, a core symbolic function at play in the definition of all identity, as demonstrated by Mary Douglas in *Purity and Danger*.[104] In its *instrumental modality*, ethnic violence is deployed as a means to the ends of protecting and enforcing one or more of the other four forms of ethnoracial domination – categorization, discrimination, segregation, and seclusion – as when a Venetian Jew is attacked for being outside of the *gietto nuovo* at night, a Burakumin entering a Shinto temple in Tokugawa Japan is expelled and beaten, an African-American sharecropper is menaced with murder by his white landlord as he contests the value of his cotton harvest, or the Herreros and Namas are exterminated as part of the establishment of German colonial rule in South West Africa. In each case, ethnoracial violence bolsters domination as exclusion, subordination, and exploitation, eventually escalating into elimination.

I will treat the deployment of intimidation and violence as tools of racial control in considerable detail in the next chapter in the case of the erection and defense of Jim Crow in the postbellum South of the United States. Here I want to flag some analytic distinctions and achieve minimal conceptual clarity while suggesting that ethnoracial violence is a complex, dynamic, and multilayered phenomenon – so that denunciations of "racial violence" without further specification do not advance an explanatory agenda and also muddle political responses.[105] Here again, one should take pains to eschew the logic of the trial, which seeks to establish guilt and activate emotions to extract moral condemnation. Social scientists are not in the business of denunciation; their agenda is to ruthlessly describe, interpret, and explain, and let the political chips fall where they may.

By way of preliminary, let me dispose of the prevalent idea that violence is atavistic, rooted in "human nature," and somehow integral

---

[103] Michael Burleigh and Wolfgang Wipperman, *The Racial State: Germany 1933–1945* (1991); Rose Romani (ed.), *The Nazi Genocide of the Sinti and Roma* (1995).
[104] Mary Douglas, *Purity and Danger: An Analysis of Concept of Pollution and Taboo* (1956).
[105] I converge with Kalyvas in seeking to introduce analytical clarity in ambiguous and shifting processes involving multiple actors, but without making strong claims as to the deep essence of violence as he does. Stathis N. Kalyvas, "The Ontology of 'Political Violence': Action and Identity in Civil Wars" (2003).

to ethnicity.[106] We commonsensically see violence as easy to carry out and its urge in need of restraint, especially when it comes to relations between ethnoracial categories. But, in fact, violence is *hard* to commit and relatively *rare* – although there are situations (such as civil war) and extreme social systems in which it is suffusive: we shall examine one in the next chapter. In his astute micro-sociological theory of violence as situational achievement, Randall Collins shows that to act in a violent manner is very difficult and necessitates overcoming many obstacles to chart a "pathway around confrontational tension and fear."[107] The same is true at the macrosociological level, where violence absorbs energy and organizational resources, creates disruption, and generates friction and opposition: an efficient regime of racial rule would rather do without.

First question, when is violence *specifically ethnic*? There is no agreement on this elementary problem among scholars who study the phenomenon broadly conceived. This is an academic dispute with significant theoretical, empirical, and policy ramifications. But, more crucially, there is a *struggle, within reality itself,* to determine and label the nature of violent acts – as when targets of an assault seek to be recognized as victims of a "hate crime" or prosecutors and politicians grapple to weigh whether an attack is terroristic, for instance. Thus, to this day, Turkish authorities adamantly dispute the reality of the Armenian genocide perpetrated by the waning Ottoman empire by means of massacres, deportation, organized famine, and death marches resulting in between 600,000 and 1.5 million dead between 1915 and 1923.[108] The designation of ethnoracial violence is a stake

---

[106] A critique of this notion, long-standing in Western social thought, from Hobbes and Machiavelli to Sigmund Freud and William James, is John Keane, *Reflections on Violence* (1996). In its specifically ethnoracial variant, "ethnic groups lie in wait for one another, nourishing age-old hatreds and restrained only by powerful states. Remove the lid, and the cauldron boils over. Analysts who advance this idea differ in their predictions for the future: some see the fragmentation of the world into small tribal groups; others, a face-off among several vast civilizational coalitions. They all share, however, the idea that the world's current conflicts are fueled by age-old ethnic loyalties and cultural differences. This notion misrepresents the genesis of conflict and ignores the ability of diverse people to coexist. The very phrase 'ethnic conflict' misguides us." John Richard Bowen, "The Myth of Global Ethnic Conflict" (1996), p. 3.
[107] Randall Collins, *Violence: A Micro-Sociological Theory* (2008), p. 9.
[108] Ben Kiernan, *Blood and Soil: A World History of Genocide and Extermination from Sparta to Darfur* (2007), chapter 10. On the sociology and psychology of collective violence denial, see the luminous study by Stanley Cohen, *States of Denial: Knowing about Atrocities and Suffering* (2001). For an illustration in the works of a canoni-

Elementary Forms of Ethnoracial Rule

not just for academics but also for the parties involved in it, the authorities that govern them, and outside observers and audiences.

Conservatively, violence may be said to be ethnic if it is *delivered or suffered based on real or perceived ethnic membership*, that is, if it purposefully crosses ethnic boundaries or is motivated by the production or reproduction of relations of ethnoracial domination – as with, for example, the firebombing of the houses of African Americans who dared seek residence in a white neighborhood in Chicago from the 1910s to the 1960s.[109] In other words, ethnoracial violence is best characterized by its actors rather than by its stakes since many ethnic conflicts are also about class outcomes or political power, not just access, social position, and group honor. Violence then flows in multiple directions: *vertically* downward from the dominant to the subaltern and upwards from the dominated toward their superordinate (in defense, retaliation, or challenge), but also *horizontally* between different sectors of the dominated population, a pattern of internecine violence mediated by the strategies of the dominant or inherited from historical structures of racialized domination as in the case of postcolonial India.[110]

Two historical instances of ethnic violence pitting subordinate categories among themselves are the violent discourses and clashes between Muslims and Jews, replicating those of Christians toward them, in fifteenth-century Spain, and the Durban riot of 1949 during which black South Africans attacked Indians as the white police looked on, resulting in 142 deaths and over a thousand injured, a riot that has scarred the collective memory of Indians to this day.[111] A third illustration is the astronomical levels of interpersonal aggression in territories bounded and shaped by inflexible ethnoracial domination, such as the American hyperghetto at century's turn,[112] where homicidal rates among blacks cannot be fully accounted for without

---

cal thinker, see Cheryl B. Welch, "Colonial Violence and the Rhetoric of Evasion: Tocqueville on Algeria" (2003).

[109] The suffusive use of violence to bolster the boundaries of the coalescing black ghetto in industrial America via intimidation, assault, firebombing, and raids is well documented. See Drake and Cayton, *Black Metropolis*, pp. 178–9, and Hirsch, *Making the Second Ghetto*, pp. 40–67.

[110] Ajay Verghese, *The Colonial Origins of Ethnic Violence in India* (2016).

[111] David Nirenberg, *Communities of Violence: Persecution of Minorities in the Middle Ages* (2015), chapter 6; Ravi K. Thiara, "The African-Indian Antithesis? The 1949 Durban 'Riots' in South Africa" (1999).

[112] David Eitle, "Dimensions of Racial Segregation, Hypersegregation, and Black Homicide Rates" (2009).

reckoning the century-long historical formation of racialized spaces of dispossession and dishonor in the city under the press of white domination (as we shall see in the fourth chapter of this book).

Ethnic violence among the dominated can also be deployed to effect in-group policing, as with intimidating "snitches" who would cooperate with law enforcement in the black hyperghetto, "kneecapping" among the IRA and "necklacing" in South African townships, to outbid rival factions, to recruit members, and to demonstrate commitment to a collective ideal.[113] Finally, intra-ethnic violence can mutate into family violence and suicide, seemingly untouched by ethnoracial domination but fostered by conditions of extreme racialized marginality, as with people living on Native American reservations in the United States and Canada.[114]

A second key property of ethnoracial violence is its *scale* on both the committer and the victim side – leaving aside the role of bystanders for the moment. Here the key analytical distinction is between individual, group (including posses, gangs, crowds, and local communities), and state violence. Cross-tabulating these three actors on both the perpetrator and the target side yields a set of nine configurations I call the *checkerboard of ethnoracial violence* whose diagonal marks the gradual escalation from assault to pogrom to racial war (see figure 5). Admittedly, some forms of violence, such as ethnic cleansing, straddle different cells as scale is a continuous and not a discrete variable, but the figure serves well as an orienting device to map out the different intensities and pathways of ethnic violence and to focus on how one form morphs (or not) into another. On the perpetrator side, the extent of coordination increases with scale, leading to the organized delivery of violence, as when the Soviet Union removed an estimated 12 million Germans from Eastern Europe immediately after the end of World War II, nearly two million of whom died from hunger, cold, and disease.[115]

---

[113] Brubaker and Laitin, "Ethnic and Nationalist Violence," pp. 433–5.

[114] Ronet Bachman, *Death and Violence on the Reservation: Homicide, Family Violence, and Suicide in American Indian Populations* (1992); Laurence J. Kirmayer, "Suicide among Canadian Aboriginal Peoples" (1994); Joseph P. Gone et al., "The Impact of Historical Trauma on Health Outcomes for Indigenous Populations in the USA and Canada: A Systematic Review" (2019).

[115] Andrew Bell-Fialkoff, "A Brief History of Ethnic Cleansing" (1993), p. 115. But see the critique of the "umbrella concept" of "forced migration" for obscuring the heterogeneity of mechanisms and motives of mass relocation even in situations of overt ethnonational violence by Rogers Brubaker in "Aftermaths of Empire and the Unmixing of Peoples: Historical and Comparative Perspectives" (1995).

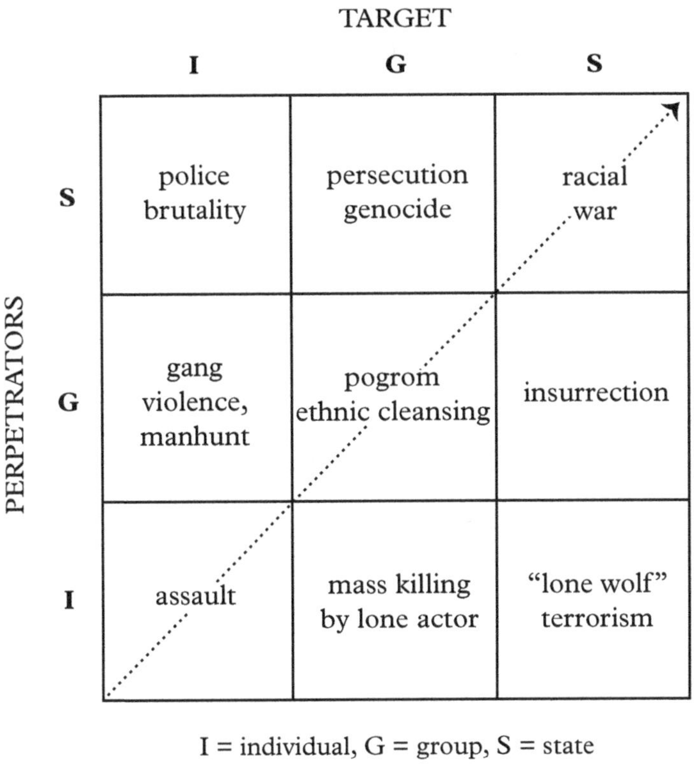

Elementary Forms of Ethnoracial Rule

	TARGET		
PERPETRATORS	**I**	**G**	**S**
S	police brutality	persecution genocide	racial war
G	gang violence, manhunt	pogrom ethnic cleansing	insurrection
I	assault	mass killing by lone actor	"lone wolf" terrorism

I = individual, G = group, S = state

Figure 5 The checkerboard of ethnoracial violence.

The two-dimensional space of perpetrator and target can be extended by adding a *third dimension: the public*, actual or virtual, unified or stratified, which "consumes" the violence. In his classic discussion of the nature of crime, Émile Durkheim suggests that punishment is aimed, not so much at the offender, as at the third parties who witness and hear about it.[116] It serves, not to correct or deter deviant behavior, but to dramatize the values held sacred by the community and thus to unify it symbolically and emotionally. This applies to many forms of ethnoracial violence, especially those that are deliberately turned into spectacles (in the etymological sense of

---

[116] "Punishment is mainly destined to act upon the honest people, not upon the criminal, and we reprove of an act not because it is criminal, but it is criminal because we reprove of it." Émile Durkheim, *De la division du travail social* (1995b [1893]), p. 43.

spectaculum, meaning a public show). As will be shown in the next chapter, in the Jim Crow South, lynching, and especially public torture lynching entailing advance publicity, crowds, racial pageantry, and sadistic cruelty, is best understood as ritualized caste murder aiming to unify whites as well as to terrorize blacks by effecting their literal abjection.

The checkerboard is also an invitation to combine micro-interactionist and macro-structural approaches to the delivery of ethnoracial violence in the mold of Aliza Luft's work on the Rwandan genocide. Luft shows that categorical membership obscures behavioral variations in the perpetrator group ranging from killing to desistance to saving potential victims. Decoupling practice from category enables her to include negative cases and to excavate the transactional, relational, social-psychological, and cognitive mechanisms that combine to determine genocidal behavior.[117] An important addendum: the forms of violence filling the cells of the checkerboard are themselves multilayered and can be further disaggregated. Types of ethnic cleansing, for instance, include those that do not use coercion ("induced assimilation, induced immigration, and induced emigration") and those that do, including coerced assimilation (cultural or biological), coerced emigration, deportation, murderous cleansing, and genocide.[118]

The entry of the state on the scene marks a dramatic development as it augments the means, intensity, scope, and degree of organization of violence. It also lends legitimacy to ethnic brutality, which is an invitation to increase and systematize it, as demonstrated by the Hutu government's frenetic encouragement via the media to kill Tutsis leading to the Rwanda genocide of 1994.[119] It also lends symbolic force to the activation of collective emotions fueling ethnoracial violence, fear, scorn, hatred, resentment, and aversion, as demonstrated by the World War II propaganda campaigns of the US government to justify its "race war" on the Japanese pictured as vermin, apes, rep-

---

[117] Aliza Luft, "Toward a Dynamic Theory of Action at the Micro Level of Genocide: Killing, Desistance, and Saving in 1994 Rwanda" (2015). Robert Braun adds an ecological mechanism in *Protectors of Pluralism: Religious Minorities and the Protection of Jews in the Low Countries during the Holocaust* (2019).

[118] Michael Mann, *The Dark Side of Democracy: Explaining Ethnic Cleansing* (2005), p. 22.

[119] Elizabeth Baisley, "Genocide and Constructions of Hutu and Tutsi in Radio Propaganda" (2014).

Elementary Forms of Ethnoracial Rule

tiles, rodents, insects, and vipers.[120] On a global scale over the past two centuries, ethnic exclusion as vehicle for, or by-product of, nation-building has consistently increased the chances for insurrection, civil war, wars of secession, and international war.[121] Accordingly, the formation of racial states, that is, states whose history, structure, and policies spring from and are wired to diffuse and defend ethnoracial vision and division, must be brought to the epicenter of the sociology of ethnoracial domination. For not only has race informed the formation of the modern nation-state, as argued by David Theo Goldberg;[122] *the state is a paramount race-making institution* in its own right. This much is suggested by Michael Mann's argument about the "modernity" of ethnic cleansing: when a state incarnates an "organic community," as opposed to a "stratified" one, it is wont to engage in ethnic cleansing in the name of this clearly bounded ethnonational collective.[123]

A number of overlapping continua or dual oppositions can help us further organize inquiry into the different forms and dynamics of ethnoracial violence as it scales up: improvised versus planned, diffuse versus targeted, routinized versus eruptive, dissimulated versus spectacularized, and prohibited to tolerated to sponsored to carried out by the authorities. But a third and more critical question is whether there is a *specifically ethnoracial logic to the escalation of violence*, from intimidation and assault/rape to lynching and pogrom to ethnic cleansing, genocide, and all-out racial war. Here is

---

[120] Michael Dower, *War Without Mercy: Race and Power in the Pacific War* (1987), chapter 4. Academic studies produced – at a safe distance – by American proponents of the "culture and personality" school, including such luminaries as Margaret Mead, Gregory Bateson, Ruth Benedict, and Talcott Parsons, portrayed the Japanese as primitive and tribal, childish and immature, and psychologically deranged. The Japanese drive to conquer the world was said to stem from their drastic toilet training, with forced control of the sphincter muscle in early childhood explaining their aggression (pp. 118–36). For their part, Japanese intellectuals and propagandists represented Americans as brutes and beasts (drawn in popular illustrations with claws, fangs, animal hindquarters, and small horns), demons, and degenerates. A provocative comparative analysis of the role of collective emotions in ethnoracial violence is Roger Dale Petersen, *Understanding Ethnic Violence: Fear, Hatred, and Resentment in Twentieth-Century Eastern Europe* (2002).

[121] Andreas Wimmer, *Waves of War: Nationalism, State Formation, and Ethnic Exclusion in the Modern World* (2012).

[122] David Theo Goldberg, *The Racial State* (2002); Mamdani, *Neither Settler nor Native*. I endeavor to demonstrate that the penal state secretes and supports race as civic felony in chapter 4.

[123] Mann, *The Dark Side of Democracy*, pp. 21–2.

a hypothesis: racialized ethnicity readily lends itself to the "cumulative radicalization" of violence – a concept elaborated by historians of the Holocaust[124] – *to the degree* that (i) it is recognized and institutionalized by the state, which makes ethnoracial division salient, pervasive, and consequential, and (ii) it creates clear-cut identities with impermeable boundaries charged with a collective sense of *superiority, purity, and even sacrality* threatened or diminished by the target group.[125]

This suggests that categorical classification systems based on descent or membership in exclusive imagined communities (such as ethnoreligious sects or ethnopolitical associations), especially dual systems anchored by a paramount "us" versus "them" opposition, are more likely to produce high volumes and wide diffusion of violence than gradational classification systems with multiple fuzzy categories. The escalation of the genocidal policy of the Khmer Rouge and its shift from a political to a racial definition of the populations to be eliminated is a case in point.[126] *A contrario*, this helps explain, for instance, the absence of ceremonial caste murders such as lynching and urban race riots in Brazil and South Africa in contrast with the United States: blackness is defined by hypodescent in the latter country, skin tone in Brazil, and phenotype plus social acceptability in South Africa. This also provides a theoretical hunch for mining the rich trove of comparative research on genocide that has not paid sufficient attention to the *kind* of racialization at work, gradational or categorical.[127]

To finish, one recommendation: the imperial domain offers an especially fruitful terrain for the comparative study and theoretical elaboration of the intersection of racialization, violence, and the state insofar as *both race and violence were integral to the establishment*

---

[124] Hans Mommsen, "Cumulative Radicalisation and Progressive Self-Destruction as Structural Determinants of the Nazi Dictatorship" (1997). An illustration is Donald Bloxham, "The Armenian Genocide of 1915–1916: Cumulative Radicalization and the Development of a Destruction Policy" (2003).

[125] Lieberman and Singh highlight the role of the state in "The Institutional Origins of Ethnic Violence" (2012). They find that the officialization of ethnic categories deepens ethnic differentiation, which in turn "irrespective of power configurations, creates a competitive dynamics that increases the likelihood of spiraling aggression" (p. 2).

[126] Kiernan, *Blood and Soil*, pp. 540–54.

[127] To get a flavor of the field, consult Susanne Karstedt, "Contextualizing Mass Atrocity Crimes: Moving Toward a Relational Approach" (2013); Jens Meierhenrich (ed.), *Genocide: A Reader* (2014); and Kiernan, *Blood and Soil*, for a historical panorama of cases.

Elementary Forms of Ethnoracial Rule

of colonies, especially settler as opposed to exploitation colonies. In his analytic history of Western colonial conquest, Dierk Walter documents that imperialism presents coherent structural features and spawned a specific logic of warfare as asymmetrical, low-intensity, and open-ended.[128] The organized violence of imperialism was fueled by the colonizer's vision of the natives as recalcitrant children in need of a lesson and the corresponding notion that violence had a pedagogical virtue. But colonial brutality was not limited to conquest: guided by the "ethnological science" produced both locally and in the metropole, it was a crucial instrument in extracting labor and riches, appropriating land and controlling space, managing cities, enforcing colonial hierarchy, and putting down rebellions.[129]

The endings of colonies were marked by tsunamis of ethnoracial violence as well. Across France's empire, from Algeria to Madagascar to Indochina, the proclamation of the end of World War II was punctuated by the ruthless repression of native subjects demonstrating for their right to national self-determination. This repression caused tens of thousands of deaths that have yet to be properly counted and recounted by historians, let alone acknowledged by the French authorities to this day.[130] And it resulted in two bloody wars in Indochina from 1945 to 1954 and Algeria from 1954 to 1962, marked by organized

---

[128] Dierk Walter, *Colonial Violence: European Empires and the Use of Force* ([2014] 2017).

[129] Settler colonial societies are the epitome of what Christian Gerlach calls *Extremely Violent Societies* (2010), a concept he proposes in lieu of genocide, which he deems too narrow and contentious. On colonial violence, read Adam Hochschild, *King Leopold's Ghost: A Story of Greed, Terror, and Heroism in Colonial Africa* (1998); Olivier Le Cour Grandmaison, *Coloniser, exterminer. Sur la guerre et l'État colonial* (2005); Ned Blackhawk, *Violence over the Land: Indians and Empires in the Early American West* (2006); Toyin Falola, *Colonialism and Violence in Nigeria* (2009); Jonathon Glassman, *War of Words, War of Stones: Racial Thought and Violence in Colonial Zanzibar* (2011); Martin Thomas, *Violence and Colonial Order: Police, Workers and Protest in the European Colonial Empires, 1918–1940* (2012); Nancy Rose Hunt, *A Nervous State: Violence, Remedies, and Rêverie in Colonial Congo* (2015); Durba Ghosh, *Gentlemanly Terrorists: Political Violence and the Colonial State in India, 1919–1947* (2017); Philip Dwyer and Amanda Nettelbeck (eds.), *Violence, Colonialism and Empire in the Modern World* (2017); Bart Luttikhuis and A. Dirk Moses (eds.), *Colonial Counterinsurgency and Mass Violence: The Dutch Empire in Indonesia* (2018); and Caroline Elkins, *Legacy of Violence: A History of the British Empire* (2022).

[130] Yves Benot, *Massacres coloniaux, 1944–1950. La IVe République et la mise au pas des colonies françaises* (1994); Fabian Klose, *Human Rights in the Shadow of Colonial Violence: The Wars of Independence in Kenya and Algeria* (2013). On the similar erasure from the Dutch public mind of the murderous making and ending of colonial rule in the Dutch East Indies, see Paul Bijl, "Colonial Memory and Forgetting in the Netherlands and Indonesia" (2012).

mass displacement, collective punishment, torture, extra-judicial killings, and massacres on both sides. After independence, a great many new nations experienced war, civil, secessionist or inter-state, as well as the normalization of high levels of interethnic violence, ethnoregional and ethnoreligious in particular.[131] Indeed, worldwide, 48 out of 140 pre-independence or pre-nation-state territories passed through a war of national liberation. After their founding, 38 of 155 newly independent countries experienced non-secessionist civil wars and 31 had secessionist civil wars.[132]

Architecture and articulations

In the preceding discussion, I have sought to show that the different forms of racial domination are *multilayered and articulated phenomena* and that each requires unpacking to be made useful in historical analysis and comparative theorizing. For each, I have suggested *varied mechanisms* that produce, reproduce, or transforms the ethnic constellation at hand. Now comes the time to reassemble those five elementary forms to get a synoptic view of the *analytical architecture of ethnoracial domination* (see figure 6). In its simplest expression, each modality of ethnoracial domination from one to four begets the next. Racialized categorization, that is, the deployment of an ethnoracial classification system filled with naturalizing prejudice, bias, and stigma, drives discrimination as differential treatment and disparate impact across categories. Discrimination in access to social position and physical place produces segregation, which can then reproduce itself in the absence of discrimination. Segregation, in turn, is the necessary but not sufficient condition for seclusion, which entails the added attribute of forced institutional parallelism. Individual, collective and state violence are mobilized to patrol ethnoracial boundaries and perpetuate domination in its different forms.

---

[131] On postcolonial violence, see Vigdis Broch-Due, *Violence and Belonging: The Quest for Identity in Post-Colonial Africa* (2004); Assis Malaquias, *Rebels and Robbers: Violence in Post-Colonial Angola* (2007); and Verghese, *The Colonial Origins of Ethnic Violence in India*.

[132] Wimmer, *Waves of War*. Some countries experienced both a civil war and a war of secession. The vast majority of these conflicts happened in what was later christened the global South.

Elementary Forms of Ethnoracial Rule

```
5. VIOLENCE (individual, collective, state)
         ↑
4. SECLUSION (ghetto, reservation, camp)
         ↑
3. SEGREGATION (social space, physical space)
         ↑
2. DISCRIMINATION (treatment, disparate impact)
         ↑
1. CATEGORIZATION (classification, prejudice, bias, stigma)
```

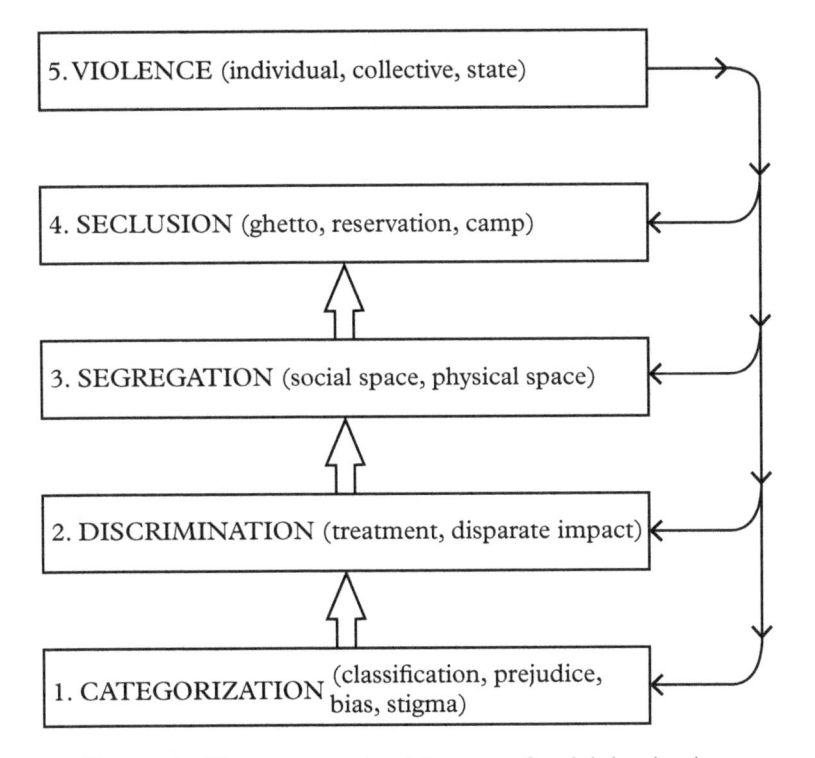

Figure 6 The conceptual architecture of racial domination.

Now, remove the qualifier *ethnoracial* in "ethnoracial categorization" and substitute another social principle of vision and division, class, gender, age, nationality, and you obtain class/gender/age/national discrimination, segregation, seclusion, and violence. The framework is *analytically agnostic as to the basis of domination*, but it captures the specificity of racial domination by illuminating the full concatenation of material and symbolic relations that constitute it. This "generalism" facilitates the integration of ethnoracial domination into a *generic* theory of group-making as the meeting of classification (habitus and symbolic power) and stratification (social space and fields, including the bureaucratic field), as opposed to seeking to produce a *specific* theory that isolates ethnoracial from other collectives, as is characteristic of the dominant approaches to "race and ethnicity" today.[133]

[133] In a slim tome that richly repays a close reading a half-century after its publication, Van den Berghe argues that we should develop theories of race, not as a self-standing

These five elementary forms of ethnoracial domination get enmeshed together and articulated differently in different societies, for different populations, and at different epochs in the same society.[134] They can vary in unison (tight coupling) or, on the contrary, evolve independently of each other (loose coupling). Accordingly, different groups present different *profiles of ethnoracial domination* across time and space, as shown vividly by the experience of African Americans as they navigated from slavery to the caste terrorism of Jim Crow to the urban ghetto to the triadic contraption of hyperghetto, penal system, and segregated black middle-class district after the racial uprising of the 1960s. In the past half-century, the iron hold of ethnoracial domination over blacks has relaxed and shifted: overt public prejudice has virtually disappeared (to be unanimously excoriated when its vestiges resurge); discrimination has diffracted across institutions (persisted in the labor market, increased in schools, diminished in the courts); hypersegregation has endured (fed by both racial and nonracial mechanisms), ghettoization collapsed (depriving the group of the paradoxical profits of institutional parallelism), and homicidal violence turned internecine. But the fulcrum of ethnoracial oppression in America, namely, the one-drop rule that uniquely corrals blacks inside a "blood fence" (rather than behind a "color line") has withstood the onslaught of the multisided social changes, immigration, the spread of genomics and multiculturalism, and cohort replacement, which influential analysts of the black question in America confidently predicted would usher in a new democratic racial order.[135]

domain, but as a "special case of differentiation and stratification." Pierre L. Van den Berghe, *Race and Racism: A Comparative Perspective* (1967), pp. 21–5.

[134] Iris Marion Young follows a similar approach when she distinguishes five forms of oppression which enter into different combinations for different groups, which "makes it possible to compare oppressions without reducing them to a common essence or claiming that one is more fundamental than another" (*Justice and the Politics of Difference* [1990], p. 64).

[135] Jennifer L. Hochschild et al., *Creating a New Racial Order: How Immigration, Multiracialism, Genomics, and the Young Can Remake Race in America* (2012). But see the partial dissent of Ariela Schachter et al., "Ancestry, Color, or Culture? How Whites Racially Classify Others in the US" (2021). A middle position is staked out by Wendy Roth in "The End of the One-Drop Rule? Labeling of Multiracial Children in Black Intermarriages" (2005, p. 64): "The one-drop rule may have weakened, so that people with any amount of Black blood are no longer necessarily considered Black, but children with Black and White parents still face unique racial barriers. Embracing *interracial identities* is simply a new way around the barriers, rather than a sign that they have been dismantled."

Elementary Forms of Ethnoracial Rule

Crucially, the profile of ethnoracial domination imposed upon blacks has sharply *bifurcated by class over* the past half-century in ways that current thinking and mobilization about racial inequality fail to take fully into account. One brutal illustration: in 2015, African Americans with no college education were 22 times more likely to serve prison time than blacks with some college, whereas the black–white differential was less than 3 to 1.[136] This means that the penal state is both a *race-making institution and a class-splitting institution*, which belies emotive denunciations of criminal justice as a "New Jim Crow" that have served as the rallying cry of militants for penal reform.[137] Such reforms are unlikely to succeed in disconnecting race from penality inasmuch as they proceed from a wrong specification of their relationship.

A further illustration: there is a plethora of studies of the black–white wealth gap but virtually none simultaneously takes into account the class distribution of wealth inside each ethnic category. It turns out that 75 percent of black wealth today is owned by the richest 10 percent of blacks, the same proportion as for white households. Because rich whites are much richer than rich black, whites as a whole are immensely richer than blacks as a whole. But three-quarters of the racial wealth gap is caused by black–white disparities among the wealthiest decile of families in each group.[138] So much to suggest that racial disparities must always be cross-tabulated by class (and place) to arrive as a sober diagnostic of their extent, sources, and evolution.

Now travel across the Atlantic to contrast with the Roma spread out across Eastern Europe – a group often referred to derogatorily

---

[136] Christopher Muller and Alexander F. Roehrkasse, "Racial and Class Inequality in US Incarceration in the Early Twenty-First Century" (2022).
[137] Loïc Wacquant, "Class, Race and Hyperincarceration in Revanchist America" (2010b). I return to this issue in chapter 4, *infra*, pp. 281–6.
[138] Matt Bruenig, "The Racial Wealth Gap Is about the Upper Classes" (2020). This skew is a more general problem in the study of inequality by ascriptive categories: "Earnings inequality within racial and gender groups is getting worse. From the standpoint of developing more comprehensive studies of inequality, there is not much to be gained by studying differences between groups" as opposed to disaggregating them into class categories. "Our inability to explain differences between groups is probably tied to our shrinking ability to explain inequality within groups." Kevin T. Leicht, "Broken Down by Race and Gender? Sociological Explanations of New Sources of Earnings Inequality" (2008), pp. 242 and 250. A powerful theoretical argument in favor of subcategorical analysis is Ellis P. Monk Jr., "Inequality without Groups: Contemporary Theories of Categories, Intersectional Typicality, and the Disaggregation of Difference" (2022).

as Gypsies, *gitanos* in Spain, *gitans* in France, and *tsingani* in Eastern Europe. The pentad of racial rule gives us a template to ascertain their predicament. Overall, their contemporary profile combines pervasive prejudice openly expressed and stinging stigma (they are commonly viewed as lazy, cunning, dirty, aggressive, and natural thieves, regardless of social position), moderate and fluctuating discrimination, high segregation in both physical space (residence) and social space (schooling, occupation, and marriage, partly based on strong affinity), incipient ghettoization (which helps reproduce the other forms of domination but also offers a platform for collective mobilization and resistance), and dispersed incidents of violence, an articulation that is complicated by widespread "passing" inflected by class, and that varies sharply across countries as well as along the urban–rural divide.[139]

One can deploy the pentad of racial domination to map out variations across countries for the same ethnic category. In the case of the Roma, they are notably more segregated both residentially and maritally in Bulgaria than in Romania and Hungary.[140] Now consider the layering of residential segregation again: it is produced by *multiple mechanisms* which include the lower class composition of the Roma, *both* ethnic *and class* discrimination by realtors and landlords, the uneven distribution by the state of low-income housing in the city, the avoidance of known Roma districts by non-Romas (both to avoid Romas and to eschew areas with a bad reputation, decrepit housing, and poor infrastructure), and clustering based on ethnic affinity and extended family ties.

This uneven profile results in large part from the ambiguity and porosity of the categorical boundary enclosing the Roma as an ancestry-based grouping with fuzzy phenotypical features (sometimes darker skin and dark thin hair, sometimes not) and more or less pronounced distinctive cultural traits that may or may not be

---

[139] This is my reading of János Ladányi and Iván Szelényi, *Patterns of Exclusion: Constructing Gypsy Ethnicity and the Making of an Underclass in Transitional Societies of Europe* (2006); Roni Stauber and Raphael Vago (eds.), *The Roma, a Minority in Europe: Historical, Political and Social Perspectives* (2007); Michael Stewart, "Roma and Gypsy 'Ethnicity' as a Subject of Anthropological Inquiry" (2013); Ryan Powell and John Lever, "Europe's Perennial 'Outsiders': A Processual Approach to Roma Stigmatization and Ghettoization" (2017); Giovanni Picker, *Racial Cities: Governance and the Segregation of Romani People in Urban Europe* (2017).
[140] János Ladányi and Iván Szelényi, "The Social Construction of Roma Ethnicity in Bulgaria, Romania, and Hungary during Market Transition" (2001).

detected in social interaction (language, patronym, and toponym). Oftentimes, Roma ethnicity is inferred from neighborhood of residence, and the stigmata of category and territory then reinforce each other, fostering denigration, hostility, and strategies of avoidance and denunciation among outsiders. Roma who move up in the class structure are openly suspected of drawing their wealth from begging and theft, when they are not accused of being part of a mafia.[141] Dishonor follows them wherever they go in social and physical space. The same authorities that actively participate in the marginalization of the Roma bemoan their alleged unwillingness to "integrate" and ignore their class diversity, social adaptability, and cultural vitality. All four processes of racialization are at work here: naturalization, eternalization, inferiorization, and homogenization.

To say that African Americans and Europe's Roma are targets or victims of "racism" does not tell us anything and gets us nowhere. It gives us no purchase on either profile and it undermines a rigorous comparison of their evolution over time. These brief illustrations demonstrate the *structural complexity, functional variability, and causal multiplicity* of ethnoracial domination. The latter is built up from diverse elements, each of which is further layered, and produced by diverse mechanisms, racial and nonracial, embedded in a plethora of institutions. The pentad guides us to identify these institutions and probe these mechanisms, and thereby to reconstruct the *bi-directional traffic* between classification and stratification. The task of the sociology of ethnoracial domination is to disassemble such articulations of ethnoracial domination on paper, thereby helping us to forge better tools for possibly dismantling them in reality.

Two crucial pivots here are the *intersections between ethnoracial rule, political economy, and the state*. The economic foundations and implications of racial rule are an immense topic of daunting breadth and complexity, which cannot be even adumbrated within the confines of this chapter. Suffice it to note here that economic interests both *motivate and moderate* different articulations of ethnoracial domination; that ethnoracial and class divisions can be intertwined or orthogonal; and that racial division is not always functional for the economy. Thus the ethnic partitioning of the workforce, flowing from categorization and discrimination, has everywhere facilitated exploitation, but it has also crimped economic development (the US South) and triggered

---

[141] Remus Crețan et al., "Everyday Roma Stigmatization: Racialized Urban Encounters, Collective Histories and Fragmented Habitus" (2022).

ethnonational fusion and rebellion (South Africa).[142] Ghettoization has served to extract economic value out of a stigmatized population – Jews in Renaissance Europe, blacks in the Fordist US, Muslims in contemporary India – while limiting social intercourse with its members; but in so doing it has given that population a separate *Lebensraum* in which to experience dignity and accumulate the social and symbolic capital needed to challenge ethnoracial denigration and subordination.[143] Economic imperatives have both driven and contained ethnoracial violence, as when the need for labor thwarts ethnic cleansing and checks genocidal projects, and they also fail to explain expressive violence serving to mark caste superiority or national exclusivity *absent economic interests.*[144]

Here we must resist the reflex to limit the sociology of race and the economy, first, to slavery and wage labor, second to capitalism, and third to the US experience. For racialization has also worked to oil the wheels of bonded labor such as late serfdom, indentured servitude, and convict labor, which have all played a central role in capital accumulation and colonialism; it has operated in imperial, communist, and despotic regimes; and the continental American experiment with race is a poor guide to the diversity of configurations assumed by racialized economies, rolled under the catchy and catch-all category of "racial capitalism."[145]

---

[142] See, for instance, Philippe Bourgois, *Ethnicity at Work: Divided Labor on a Central American Banana Plantation* (1989); Gavin Wright, *Slavery and American Economic Development* (2006); and George M. Fredrickson, *Black Liberation: A Comparative History of Black Ideologies in the United States and South Africa* (1996).

[143] Roth, *History of the Jews in Venice*; Drake and Cayton, *Black Metropolis*; Thomas, *Pogroms et ghetto*.

[144] Mann, *The Dark Side of Democracy*; Guy Lancaster, *Racial Cleansing in Arkansas, 1883–1924: Politics, Land, Labor, and Criminality* (2014); Stanley J. Tambiah, *Levelling Crowds: Ethnonationalist Conflicts and Collective Violence in South Asia* (1996).

[145] See, for instance, Peter Kolchin, *Unfree Labor: American Slavery and Russian Serfdom* (1990); Anand A. Yang, *Empire of Convicts: Penal Labor in Colonial Southeast Asia* (2021); Thomas, *Violence and Colonial Order*; Eiichiro Azuma, *In Search of Our Frontier: Japanese America and Settler Colonialism in the Construction of Japan's Borderless Empire* (2019); Evelyn Nakano Glenn, *Unequal Freedom: How Race and Gender Shaped American Citizenship and Labor* (2004); Stanley Greenberg, *Race and Class in Capitalist Development: Comparative Perspectives* (1980); Justin Leroy and Destin Jenkins (eds.), *Histories of Racial Capitalism* (2021).

The lure of "racial capitalism"

Is racial capitalism a conceptual solution or a conceptual problem? Let me briefly weigh the meaning, potential, and pitfalls of the construct for studying the nexus of race and the economy. The expression first appears in print in 1976 under the pen of the South African historian Martin Legassick and union organizer David Hemson in a 16-page technical report in reference to the *specific* interweaving of international capital and white rule during the three decades of apartheid.[146] It was picked up on American shores and *generalized* to the entire West across a millennium by the African-American political scientist Cedric Robinson in his 1983 book *Black Marxism*.[147] At first the book went unnoticed, but its 2000 republication gradually garnered readers and its expanded 2020 edition, motivated by the spread of the thematics of "racial capitalism" in the tow of black street protests, has become the object of a mantric cult among factions of Left intellectuals, scholars, and activists.[148]

For Robinson, Marxism got its history, ontology, and politics wrong and a focus on race as advocated by the "black radical tradition" can set them right all at once. Western capitalism was born, not through the negation of feudalism, as Marx would have it, but by extending its social relations and harnessing the racialism Robinson argues was already woven deep into the fabric of medieval Europe.[149] Going against the whole body of Marxist theory but also against a

---

[146] Martin Legassick and David Hemson, *Foreign Investment and Reproduction of Racial Capitalism in South Africa* (1976). The report was commissioned by the Anti-Apartheid Movement based in London. It uses the term "racial capitalism" 16 times but does not define it, suggesting its meaning was transparent to South African readers. For a fascinating account of the prehistory of the term and of the South African debates within which the concept emerged as a "strategic critique" at the crossroads of scholarship and activism, see Zachary Levenson and Marcel Paret, "The Three Dialectics of Racial Capitalism: From South Africa to the US and Back Again" (2022). Levenson and Paret are the editors of a forthcoming thematic issue of *Racial and Ethnic Studies* on "The South African Tradition of Racial Capitalism: From Margins to Center."

[147] Cedric J. Robinson, *Black Marxism: The Making of the Black Radical Tradition* (2000 [1983]). To situate Robinson in the long stream of black radical thought, read the lucid "Preface" by Robin D. G. Kelly to the 2000 reedition of the book.

[148] William I. Robinson et al. "The Cult of Cedric Robinson's *Black Marxism*: A Proletarian Critique" (2022).

[149] For a meticulous critique of Robinson's wholesale repudiation of Marx's account of the genesis of capitalism, see Michael Ralph and Maya Singhal, "Racial Capitalism" (2019), pp. 860–5.

hundred years of plain academic economic history, Robinson boldly asserts that "the tendency of European civilization through capitalism was thus not to homogenize but to differentiate – to exaggerate regional, subcultural, and dialectical differences into 'racial' ones."[150] Thus England's industrial working class was not the "universal proletariat" of Marxist theory but formed *ab initio* on the basis of the racialization of the Irish. Bourgeois society did not "rationalize social relations and demystify social consciousness," quite the contrary. "The development, organization, and expansion of capitalist society pursued essentially racial directions, so too did social ideology. As a material force, then, it could be expected that racialism would inevitably permeate the social structures emergent from capitalism. I have used the term 'racial capitalism' to refer to this development and to the subsequent structure as a historical agency."[151]

Robinson does not elaborate on what he means by "racialism": he also uses the adjectives ethnic, national, regional, tribal, linguistic, and immigrant to characterize the subalterns of Europe's interior.[152] Moreover, in the new preface to the 2000 edition of the book, he makes Aristotle's "inferiorization" of women, non-Greeks, and all laborers (not just slaves but also artisans, wage-workers, and farmers) in the *Nicomachean Ethics* the root of "an uncompromising racial construct" and asserts that, "from the twelfth century on, one European ruling order after another, one cohort of clerical or secular propagandists following another, reiterated and embellished this racial calculus."[153] It is not clear what is "racial" about this ancient construct and what makes it specifically Western: did other civilizations *not* inferiorize women, laborers, and assorted ethnic outsiders? It is also unclear what exactly Robinson means by "permeate" and what makes such permeation "inevitable." It does not help that he invokes the expression "racial capitalism" only three times in the rest of the book (it rates a single mention in the index). Similarly, Robinson does not employ the expression *even once* in his rich posthumous collection of essays spanning four decades of scholarship published in 2019 under the somewhat misleading title *On Racial Capitalism*,

---

[150] Robinson, *Black Marxism*, p. 26.

[151] Ibid., p. 2. Note the puzzling formulation making the structure an agent.

[152] "From its very beginnings, this European civilization, containing racial, tribal, linguistic, and regional particularities, was constructed on antagonistic differences." Ibid., p. 10.

[153] Ibid., preface to the 2000 edition, p. xxxi.

Elementary Forms of Ethnoracial Rule

Black Internationalism, and Cultures of Resistance.[154] In any case, is it not theoretically risky to infer the objective workings of the capitalist economy from the subjective visions of it among state rulers and cultural elites?

No matter. The tag "racial capitalism" caught on and spread like wildfire in the late 2010s among American scholars, mostly in the humanities, eager "to understand the mutually constitutive nature of racialization and capitalist exploitation"[155] in the wake of the financial crisis of 2008 and to respond to the current insurgent movement for racial justice on America's streets. Workshops, reading groups, research networks, multi-institution projects, special journal issues and symposia have boomed and spilled over into public debate, as with the 2017 issue of the *Boston Review* on "Race, Capitalism, Justice" featuring leading historians of the African-American experience.[156] One would think that this extraordinary outpouring of intellectual energy would spawn a crisply enunciated concept informing a set of clear claims about the nature of race, the logics of capitalism, and the dynamics of their causal, structural, and functional interweaving. But one searches in vain for this clarification. Instead, one finds the mere *stipulation of their "articulation,"* as in the introduction to a leading volume of essays on *Histories of Racial Capitalism* (2021), where we read: "Racial capitalism is the process by which the key dynamics of capitalism – accumulation/dispossession, credit/debt, production/surplus, capitalist/worker, developed/underdeveloped,

---

[154] Cedric J. Robinson, *On Racial Capitalism, Black Internationalism, and Cultures of Resistance* (2019). All 13 mentions of "racial capitalism" are in the foreword and introduction by the volume's editors. Only one of the 26 chapters deals *obliquely* with race and capitalism in the course of an analysis of the Rodney King uprising in Los Angeles in 1992. It makes one wonder: was "racial capitalism" in *Black Marxism* more than a throwaway line for Robinson?

[155] Charisse Burden-Stelly, "Modern US Racial Capitalism" (2020). A provocative analysis of how the Black Lives Matter movement has appropriated the term (if not the concept) is Siddhant Issar, "Listening to Black Lives Matter: Racial Capitalism and the Critique of Neoliberalism" (2021).

[156] Walter Johnson with Robin D. G. Kelley (eds.), *Race, Capitalism, Justice* (2018). A widely cited piece from that feature is Robin D. G. Kelley's short essay, "What Did Cedric Robinson Mean by Racial Capitalism?" (2017). See the dialogue between philosopher Nancy Fraser and Barnaby Raine, Jordan T. Camp, Christina Heatherton, Manu Karuka, and Bruce Robbins in *Politics Letters*, May 15, 2019; also the exchange between Michael Waltzer and Olúfẹ́mi O. Táíwò and Liam Kofi Bright in *Dissent* in summer of 2020. Most stimulative are the running contributions to the "Race and Capitalism" online project diffused by the Social Science Research Council under the editorship of the political scientist Michael Dawson.

contract/coercion, and others – become articulated through race."[157] But, precisely, it is the nature of this "articulation" that needs explication.

The editors of that collection, the historians Justin Leroy and Destin Jenkins, deserve credit for striving to derive from this spongy definition three defensible scholias, but, upon examination, each makes the central concept, not more firm, but more brittle: (1) "Capital has not historically accumulated without previously existing relations of racial inequality." But, aside from the contestable historical accuracy of the claim as applied to all historical variants of capitalism (think of the South Korean or Norwegian variants, for instance), the same is true of, say, state formation, wars, and urbanization:[158] does that *eo ipso* produce *state* capitalism, *military* capitalism, and *urban* capitalism? Historical precedence is not social causation or structural linkage. (2) "The violent dispossession inherent to capital accumulation operates by leveraging, intensifying, and creating racial distinctions." But, again, capitalism has used and generated a variety of distinctions, one of which was racial in certain geographic zones and historical periods: does the use of national distinctions, prominent in twentieth-century Europe as attested by two world wars, produce *national* capitalism? Does the gendered division of labor spawn *gender* capitalism? And what of the erosion, if not erasure, of ethnonational, ethnoreligious, and ethnolinguistic differences widely attested in the formation of European working classes in the period of Fordist industrialism, the United States aside?[159] (3) "Race serves as a tool for naturalizing the inequalities produced by capitalism": this minimalist definition of the ideological function of race applies to any and all forms of inequality, capitalist or not, whose beneficiaries always try to cloak them in the mantle of legitimacy. And another institution provides for a more implacable sociodicy of the

---

[157] Leroy and Jenkins (eds.), *Histories of Racial Capitalism*, p. 3. Note that the first three of these processes are not specific to capitalism, as shown by David Graeber, *Debt: The First Five Thousand Years* (2011). Julian Go notes that advocates of racial capitalism have not supplied a rigorous characterization of capitalism in "Three Tensions in the Theory of Racial Capitalism" (2020), p. 5.

[158] On the central role of war and cities in the birth of capitalism, see Charles Tilly, *Coercion, Capital, and European States, AD 990–1992* (1992).

[159] A single example suffices here: Gérard Noiriel, *Le Creuset français. Histoire de l'immigration, XIX–XX siècles* (1988, English translation: *The French Melting Pot: Immigration, Citizenship, and National Identity*, Minnesota, MN: University of Minnesota Press, 1996).

Elementary Forms of Ethnoracial Rule

established order, the higher education system: do we for that live under *credential* capitalism?[160]

Then Jenkins and Leroy flag "the devastating effects of the subprime crisis for communities of color" and the growth of "the prison industrial complex" as two tangible expressions of racial capitalism – those are the usual suspects in numerous invocations of the notion.[161] But the racial skew of the subprime debacle was an American peculiarity linked to the unique combination of high levels of racial and class segregation in the American metropolis with the specially lax federal regulation of the country's financial industry.[162] As for the capitalistic nature of hyperincarceration, it is a non-starter: the notion that prisons serve to extract labor and generate private profits (beyond the firms supplying the services needed for the maintenance of the inmate population) pertains to political demonology, not to the sociology of the penal state, which remains a doggedly public institution. The myth of the Prison Industrial Complex is hardly the salvation of racial capitalism. One figure: fewer than 2,000 inmates out of 2.1 million were working for private employers at the peak of private prison employment in 2002; all correctional expenditures in the United States came to less than one-half of one percent of its GDP that same year. The construction of a gargantuan prison archipelago pertains to state-building, not to economic accumulation; it is a drain on the public coffers and ultimately deeply dysfunctional to neoliberal capitalism, aside from temporarily disappearing a vilified surplus population that will cycle back into the underbelly of cities in any case.[163] Hyperincarceration is another American extremity that cannot be explained in terms of a universal logic of capitalism, racialized or not.

Racial capitalism, we are told, is "a highly malleable structure," *so malleable* indeed that it encompasses exploitation and expropriation that draw populations into capitalist production ("slavery,

---

[160] Randall Collins crafted a close conceptual cognate more than 40 years ago in *The Credential Society: A Historical Sociology of Education and Stratification* (1979).

[161] See, for instance, Donna Murch, *Assata Taught Me: State Violence, Racial Capitalism, and the Movement for Black Lives* (2022), especially pp. 41–52, 73–86, and 105–19.

[162] Jessica Trounstine, *Segregation by Design: Local Politics and Inequality in American Cities* (2018), and Neil Fligstein, *The Banks Did It: An Anatomy of the Financial Crisis* (2021).

[163] Loïc Wacquant, *Punishing the Poor: The Neoliberal Government of Social Insecurity* (2009), pp. 181–5, and idem, "Prison Reentry as Myth and Ceremony" (2010c), for a methodical dismantling of the demonic myth of the "Prison Industrial Complex."

colonialism, and enclosure") as well as their opposite, exclusion ("containment, incarceration, abandonment").[164] But what remains racial about capitalist exploitation after it has expelled racialized populations from the economy? On the other hand, is racial capitalism *malleable enough* to encompass the varieties of capitalisms well documented by comparative political economists, not only in the West, but also in East and Southeast Asia,[165] or is it irredeemably mired in unrepentant Occidentalism or, more narrowly still, in Atlantico-centrism?

It is good that the expression "racial capitalism" has energized research on the intersection of ethnoracial division and economic inequality and supplied historians, geographers, sociologists, and other scholars with a language to make their work relevant to the contemporary American politics of race. If it encourages activists for racial justice to take class seriously, this is all to the good. Trouble is, if we start from the *premise* of the "inextricability of race and capitalism" and the *postulation* that "the temporality of racial capitalism is one of ongoingness,"[166] we foreclose the question of the social conditions under which capitalism takes (or not) racial division on board *differentially* and eventually throws it overboard.[167] Then we cannot construe the racialization of capitalism as a *historical variable* that ranges from coevalness and synergy to parasitism and disconnection, and changes as capitalism moves from its competitive to monopoly to neoliberal incarnations.

I note with some worry five parallels between today's vogue of "racial capitalism" and the academic craze of the "underclass" in the 1980s that sidetracked and neutralized an entire generation of scholars of race and poverty in the metropolis: (i) the mistaken belief that the concept is *novel* and should reign supreme over its ever-expanding research province; (ii) the notion that racial capitalism is essentially a *black issue*; (iii) its resonance and currency emerge out of *traumatic racial events* piercing the screen of US public attention (the ghetto revolts of the 1960s, the spate of police killings of black men in the 2010s); (iv) the prime role that the Social Science Research Council has taken in supporting work animated by the category; (v) the doggedly and doxically *Americano-centric cast* of the debate. Which leads

---

[164] Jenkins and Leroy, "Introduction" to *Histories of Racial Capitalism*, p. 3.
[165] Magnus Feldmann, "Global Varieties of Capitalism" (2019).
[166] Jenkins and Leroy, "Introduction," pp. 15 and 12.
[167] Racial capitalism does not resolve "whether the interconnectedness of racial difference and capitalism is a logical or a contingent necessity." Go, "Three Tensions in the Theory of Racial Capitalism," pp. 6–7.

Elementary Forms of Ethnoracial Rule

one to wonder whether we are not witnessing a typical *lemming effect* caused by the ardent and commendable wish to reconnect academic debate with the burning racial issues of the day, but a wish that leads to burning up a lot of intellectual fuel for very limited scientific mileage.[168]

Finally, there is the claim that, because (Western-Atlantic) capitalism and slavery were *historically* linked, capitalism and race are *necessarily* linked, and this forever more. But, as we saw earlier, *slavery is not a racial institution*. It does have an internal affinity with race in that both inflict generalized dishonor on the people they strike. But, as Patterson points out, among the 55 slave societies for which the requisite data is available, "75 percent had populations in which both slaves and masters were of the same mutually perceived racial group."[169] Moreover, for centuries, enslavement was a doxic practice that did not need legitimation and, when it did, it could turn to religion. Even in the United States, the racial defense of slavery was not fully articulated and broadly diffused until the 1840s by the works of the School of "American ethnology."[170] Besides, in many civilizations, slaves played a marginal economic role. They were captured, bought, and held for ritual purposes, sexual or marital congress, administrative tasks, military impressment, or for attesting to the grandeur of a ruler, chief, prince, sultan, or emperor.[171] Here is a crucial triple question that racial capitalism eludes because it presupposes it resolved: when, how, and why did the *economic variant of slavery become racialized* in the Atlantic world? To say that capitalism and racism are "co-constituted," to cite a common vocable, or that their relationship is one of "historical intimacy" is an analytical cop-out. We must find a way to disentangle their relationships and specify the constituent components of "racial capitalism" or else the notion will remain a mere oratorical gesture to echo the American racial politics of the day.

It is fine for activists to use a nebulous notion to provide a *diagnostic vision* of the task at hand and a *rhetorical tool* for mobilization.[172] It is

---

[168] "The *lemming effect* denotes a bandwagon of enthusiastic scholars rushing en masse to invoke a notion because everyone around them is invoking it, only to fall into a scientific precipice because the notion was flawed or impertinent to the phenomenon at hand." Wacquant, *The Invention of the "Underclass,"* p. 172.
[169] Patterson, *Slavery and Social Death*, p. 176.
[170] Peter Kolchin, *American Slavery, 1619–1877* (2003), pp. 192–3.
[171] Patterson, *Slavery and Social Death*, p. 173.
[172] The notion then serves as vehicle for ever more encompassing, totalizing, if not

an altogether different matter for scholars who are *ex officio* expected to deploy rigorous concepts with a clear meaning and controlled uses subjected to the constructive critique of peers. The nexus of racial rule and capitalism is of paramount importance to a theory of both historical capitalism and ethnoracial domination. Therefore, we should collectively beware to not let the momentary political allure of racial capitalism turn into an enduring analytic lure. Ultimately, a construct that has attained minimal semantic clarity and logical consistency must prove scientifically heuristic to justify its further use and extension by social scientists. At this writing, it is unclear what, if anything, the use of "racial capitalism" has revealed that we would not otherwise know – indeed that we already knew from the masterworks on the topic of W. E. B. Du Bois, Eric Williams, Oliver Cromwell Cox, Walter Rodney, and Manning Marable.[173] It behooves the advocates of "racial capitalism" to pause, then, and put in the hard work of epistemological elucidation, logical clarification, and historical elaboration needed to make the label more than another *conceptual speculative bubble*.[174]

Classification, stratification, and the state

A second analytic pivot for the pentad of ethnoracial forms is the degree to which categorization and the correlative distribution of capitals (economic, cultural, social, and symbolic) are recognized, codified, and sponsored by the state, or supported by other para-

apocalyptic, visions, as illustrated by geographer Ruth Wilson Gilmore's characterization of "racial capitalism" as a "catastrophe on a world scale" manifested by "austerity, neoliberalism, and permanent war" with no end in sight: "Racial capitalism is all of capitalism" because "capitalism is racial since its beginning and it will continue to depend on racial practice and racial hierarchy no matter what" (Ruth Gilmore, "Racial Capitalism" [2021]). But, then, what is the point of mobilizing when faced with such a resistant, all-encompassing, and seemingly eternal structure?

[173] Retro-projecting the term "racial capitalism" onto the work of these scholars, as Jenkins and Leroy do in *Histories of Racial Capitalism* (pp. 7–10), does not clarify and validate its currents uses. A similar move seeking to annex to the notion a long string of "Black anticapitalist thinkers" going back a full century is made by Burden-Stelly, "Modern US Racial Capitalism," p. 11.

[174] "A *conceptual speculative bubble* develops when an inchoate, unbounded, or unfinished notion, often borrowed from political discourse and action, is invoked to capture an ever wider range of historical realities before its semantics have solidified." Wacquant, *The Invention of the "Underclass,"* p. 173.

Elementary Forms of Ethnoracial Rule

mount symbolic agencies such as the law, religion, and science, as distinct from the common sense of everyday life. As we saw earlier, the dynamics of racialization take on a whole different tenor when the state, as the *fount of public honor and dishonor*, validates ethnic classification and solidifies, nay aggravates, the corresponding disparities of stratification. Accordingly, the study of ethnoracial domination must imperatively include a systematic comparative sociology of racial states, their genesis, structure, and functioning in history.[175]

This study has to resolve three vexing complications. First, the state is not a monolith but a space of forces and struggles over its very boundaries, architecture, and missions, such that some administrative units may act as racializing forces while others are racially neutral or even deracializing. This was the case with the US military after World War II, when it desegregated the armed forces even as the federal government refused to intervene in the South to dismantle Jim Crow, and with the public provision of water and sewer systems which drastically reduced black–white inequality in deaths from typhoid and waterborne infectious diseases even in the segregationist South.[176]

The unity of racial thinking and action by state managers must be established and not assumed. For instance, Tudor officials who drove the imperial capture of Ireland in the sixteenth century were of two minds when it came to its purpose and method: some "favored the annihilation of the native people followed by the wholesale colonization of the island" while others wished to "promote the assimilation of the resident population to the culture and religion of the metropole" by the gradual implantation of English political, legal, and economic structures.[177] Similarly, the battles raging inside the German state in the late nineteenth century spawned the radical divergence between the policies pursued in different colonies: extermination of

---

[175] Studies of colonial formations are the prime ground for advancing the sociology of the racial state: George Steinmetz, "Social Fields, Subfields and Social Spaces at the Scale of Empires: Explaining the Colonial State and Colonial Sociology" (2016), and idem, *The Devil's Handwriting: Precoloniality and the German Colonial State in Qingdao, Samoa, and Southwest Africa* (2008a); Crawford Young, *The African Colonial State in Comparative Perspective* (1994); Peter B. Zinoman, *The Colonial Bastille: A Social History of Imprisonment in Colonial Viet Nam, 1862–1940* (1996); and Marie Muschalek, *Violence as Usual: Policing and the Colonial State in German Southwest Africa* (2019).

[176] Werner Troesken, *Water, Race, and Disease* (2004).

[177] Jane Ohlmeyer, "Conquest, Civilization, Colonization: Ireland, 1540–1660" (2016), p. 22.

the natives in South West Africa, cultural conservation in the Samoa Islands, and respectful civilizational exchange in Qingdao, China (after a brief period during which Chinese subjects were treated as inferior beings with an incommensurable culture). The key resource deployed in these battles was the "ethnographic capital" garnered by protagonists in different sectors of the colonial state, that is, their authoritative claim to know the mores of the colonized and therefore to steer policy toward them.[178]

Next, there is always a gap between the blueprints of state policy intended to institute and enforce ethnoracial boundaries from above and the reality of their implementation by extant bureaucracies at ground level, which have to make do with varying degrees of recalcitrance and resistance. This is why the historian of Nazism Devin Pendas prefers – controversially – to characterize even the Third Reich as "a racializing regime, not a racial state."[179] Part of the incoherence of the Nazi state when it came to realizing its murderous ethnoracial fantasy was that it was traversed by two antinomic representations of race: the one was a contagionist conception obsessed by the "prepotence" and "eternity" of "Jewish blood"; the other was a genetic conception which drew on "racial biology" to assert that "German blood" could, through "demendelization," suppress "Jewish genes."[180] The struggles to decide who was and who was not a Jew by frontline bureaucracies had tragic consequences for their target population since they could literally mean the difference between life and death.

Lastly, even in the most coherent of cases, ethnoracial taxonomies promulgated by the state are jumbled, multilayered, riven by contradictions, and weakened by exceptions. This is because, being historical products of past classification struggles, they incorporate multiple criteria born from, and geared toward, everyday life and political action, not scholarly knowledge or strict bureaucratic conformity. Often, they are no more than ethnic nomenclatures, listings of names of groups devoid of formal rationality. And they commonly diverge from the richer folk designations invoked by people in everyday life.[181]

---

[178] George Steinmetz, "The Colonial State as a Social Field: Ethnographic Capital and Native Policy in the German Overseas Empire before 1914" (2008b).

[179] Devin O. Pendas, "Racial States in Comparative Perspective" (2017), p. 135. For a contrary case and argument, see Ivan Evans, *Bureaucracy and Race: Native Administration in South Africa* (1997).

[180] Essner, "Qui sera 'juif'? La classification 'raciale' nazie des 'lois de Nuremberg' à la conférence de Wannsee'," pp. 3–9 and 28.

[181] On the "misalignment" between official and ordinary categories, read the fruitful

Elementary Forms of Ethnoracial Rule

Ordinary ethnic categories are also always to some degree fuzzy because they admit of multiple readings and they can be manipulated and contested, even in the seemingly most rigid of regimes of domination, not to mention more flexible ones. For illustration of the hiatus between identification and categorization, two-thirds of persons classified as Roma by the interviewers in a cross-national survey of poverty and ethnicity in Hungary and Romania did not regard themselves as Roma, whereas two-thirds of those identified as Roma by interviewers self-identified as such in Bulgaria, reflecting the different levels of Roma residential segregation and use of the Romani language in these three countries. Another case is the ethnoracial labeling and treatment of Eurasians in the city-state of Singapore, where race is both salient and consequential: "They are positioned as simultaneously mixed and pure, old and new." They do not fit in the official schema of Chinese, Malay, and Indian, yet constitute a growing segment of the population due to rising interethnic marriages that is singled out and recognized as such in everyday life both individually and collectively.[182]

Such are the inescapable *illogics of ethnoracial classification* that sociology must be careful not to erase from its accounts.[183] The combination of these three factors – the horizontal struggles between protagonists inside the bureaucratic field, the vertical struggles between policy-makers and policy implementers at ground level, and the

---

elaboration of Cecilia Menjívar, "State Categories, Bureaucracies of Displacement, and Possibilities from the Margins" (2023), especially what she calls "anticategories," that is, populations that are underestimated, omitted, neglected, or otherwise made invisible.

[182] Zarine L. Rocha and Brenda S. A. Yeoh, "Managing the Complexities of Race: Eurasians, Classification and Mixed Racial Identities in Singapore" (2021).

[183] The study of the Roma is the gem by Ladányi and Szelényi, "The Social Construction of Roma Ethnicity in Bulgaria, Romania, and Hungary during Market Transition" (2001). The illogics of racial classification are fully documented and dissected in Loveman's *National Colors*, covering 19 countries over two centuries, which reclaims the hidden history of ethnoracial categorization as instrument of state-making and nation-building. See also Emmanuelle Saada, *Les Enfants de la colonie. Les métis de l'Empire français entre sujétion et citoyenneté* (2007); Ilona Katzew and Susan Deans-Smith (eds.), *Race and Classification: The Case of Mexican America* (2009); and Thomas Mullaney, *Coming to Terms with the Nation: Ethnic Classification in Modern China* (2011). Two model studies of the socially flexible and semantically fluid deployment of ethnic categories in everyday life are Virginia R. Domínguez, *White by Definition: Social Classification in Creole Louisiana* (1993), especially part III, and Rogers Brubaker et al., *Nationalist Politics and Everyday Ethnicity in a Transylvanian Town* (2006), especially "Categories," pp. 207–38.

built-in incoherencies of racial taxonomies – make the comparative sociology of the *ethnoracial state as classifying and stratifying machine* both difficult and indispensable.

Consider the workings of ethnoracial classification under South African apartheid (1948–91). Apartheid is always rightfully presented as a uniquely oppressive regime of ethnoracial domination, to the point where the expression is used metaphorically as a term of accusation of other regimes – as when American historians castigate Jim Crow as "American apartheid."[184] The term has great rhetorical resonance and suggests all-around rigidity and coherence. But, when it came to classification and its implementation as stratification, the South African state was surprisingly lax.

Apartheid was methodically erected by partitioning symbolic, social, and physical space via legal edicts designed to bolster the control of the white minority.[185] The Population registration Act of 1950 required all South African citizens to officially register their race according to a four-fold schema: White (English and Afrikaans speakers), Coloured, Indian, and Africans or "pure-blooded individuals of the Bantu race" (themselves split into eight main ethnicities). The Group Areas Act of 1950 assigned to each ethnoracial category its exclusive neighborhoods in the city while the Native Resettlement Act of 1954 called for the removal of blacks from central-city areas. The Immorality Amendment Act of 1950 bolstered the Mixed Marriage Act of 1949 prohibiting interracial unions involving whites. The 1953 Reservation and Separate Amenities Act instituted racial segregation in public services and facilities as well as commercial establishments. Blacks were required to carry passbooks restricting where and how long they were allowed to travel, stay, and work; these books were the instrument of stringent police surveillance and violence. More legislation set up and administered the Bantustans, the puppet states created to fictively grant Africans their political rights "outside" of South Africa. By one estimate, the compiled racial regulations of the country topped 3,000 pages.[186]

This legal edifice was intended to order state and society so as to protect them from "*die swart gevaar*" (the black danger) threatening to swamp cities and thereby topple white rule. But, when it came to

---

[184] James Beeby and Donald G. Nieman, "The Rise of Jim Crow, 1880–1920" (2002).
[185] A. J. Christopher, *The Atlas of Changing South Africa* (2001), chapters 2–5.
[186] Joseph Lelyveld, *Move Your Shadow: South Africa, Black and White* (1985), p. 82.

Elementary Forms of Ethnoracial Rule

defining and deploying race, the architects of apartheid were far less rigid and organized. They eschewed strict biology, rejecting descent, and mixed phenotypical features with class, social ties, and public opinion.[187] This created a welter of symbolic incoherencies with an array of jumbled material consequences as judgments about physical appearance and social acceptability evolved. Moreover, different laws and state agencies invoked racial categories in varied and inconsistent manners. Thus the Population Registration Act categorized the children of mixed unions in the lower of the two categories whereas the Group Areas Act assigned them to the ethnicity of the father. For instance, the child of an Indian father and an African mother would live in an Indian area until receiving his personal identity card at age 16, at which time he would be recategorized as Bantu and forced to leave his parents, neighbors, and friends to move into an African district. An individual could change symbolic classification, and by the same token location in social and physical space, multiple times during their lifetime.[188]

The result of this jumble of rules is that people at the margins of categories were allowed to move up and down the racial hierarchy and found themselves caught amidst contradictory edicts. A special Race Classification Board handled legal requests for recategorization, with most applicants seeking to become Coloured instead of Bantu and White instead of Coloured.[189] To adjudicate cases, the board first examined *physical appearance*: skin tone, eyes, hair, facial profile, body size, and skeletal structure were all visually inspected. Combs and the infamous "pencil test" were used to assess the texture of the hair; sometimes a barber would be called to testify on this critical matter. "There was no pretence at formal, scientific rationality" when it came to phenotype: "the law gave free rein to the miscellanei of biological myths about racial appearances that inhabited the realm of common sense."[190] Some officials claimed they could tell a Coloured person by the softness of their ear lobes, the feel of their cheekbones, and the way they spat – even the degree of pigmentation of the genitalia could be checked as an indicator of race. Others

---

[187] This is so in spite of the advanced development of national raciology, as recounted by Saul Dubow, *Scientific Racism in Modern South Africa* (1995).
[188] See the examples given by Geoffrey C. Bowker and Susan Leigh Star, "The Case of Race Classification and Reclassification Under Apartheid" (1999), pp. 203–5.
[189] Christopher, *The Atlas of Changing South Africa*, p. 102.
[190] Posel, "Race as Common Sense," p. 58.

inquired whether the complainant ate porridge or slept on the floor as opposed to in a bed.[191]

Next the racial reclassification tribunal considered what it called "*general acceptance*" by ascertaining the appellant's location in social and physical space: where were they born and raised, what schools they attended (or their own children attended), what neighborhoods they had resided in; what race were their spouse, friends, and the friends of their children; where did they work and what wages they earned (presuming that the employer was a reliable source of racial assignment). Some classifiers weighed heavily patronym and place of provenance; others took into consideration dress and deportment, types of leisure activities (a soccer player was easily considered Bantu, a rugby player Coloured), and alimentary consumption (drinking "kaffir beer" was a sure sign of being "Native").[192] The burden of proof rested on the person seeking reclassification; they were the ones expected to produce documents, witnesses, and any material proof of their "real" racial membership as manifested by their body and social properties. The vast majority of cases concerned requests to be categorized up. But in some cases appellants sought to be categorized down in a bid to reunify a family split apart in space by state racial assignments.

Many families played on the incoherencies and ambiguities of official classification to "pass": they resided and worked in neighborhoods outside of their official category. But then they restricted their social relations and the options of their children for fear of being detected.[193] Indeed, it was not rare for "snitches" to inform government officials that a Bantu in their district was passing for Coloured and a Coloured for White. These incoherent categorization practices by one of the most deliberate racial states in history provide a *demonstratio a fortiori* of the social illogics of ethnoracial classification as realized category.

The mystification of "structural racism"

A notion frequently used to refer to societies where ethnoracial division traverses the economy, social space, and the state, as well

---

[191] Bowker and Star, "The Case of Race Classification and Reclassification Under Apartheid," p. 210.
[192] Posel, "Race as Common Sense," pp. 60–1.
[193] John Western, *Outcast Cape Town* (1997 [1981]), pp. vi–vii.

as infects everyday life and subjectivity, is *structural racism*. Reviving the concept of "institutional racism" coined over 50 years ago by the Black Power intellectuals Stokely Carmichael and Charles V. Hamilton,[194] the term and its close cousin "systemic racism" have resurged in scholarly discussion and diffused beyond the academy at blinding speed over the past decade. They have been eagerly adopted by think tanks, philanthropic foundations, and professional associations wishing to conform to the new Racespeak of the moment and signal their moral virtue in the tow of social movements for racial justice.[195] My concern is that they may work well as political mottos to mobilize people and to give them a personal sense of civic benevolence; they are nonetheless poor guides for dissecting, and thence disrupting, the racial order. Let me elaborate on my epistemic qualms with the intent, not to undermine the scientific thrust and political yearning of the notion, but to put them on more solid footing with the pentad of racial domination.

There are three cumulative problems with the notion of "structural racism" as commonly used and abused: the first is with the noun racism, the second concerns the adjective structural, and the third arises from their pairing. *Racism*: the word was coined in 1903 but came into broad use in the 1930s to refer to a *doctrine of innate superiority* of a biologically defined human grouping as propounded by the Nazis in Germany.[196] It was then clearly bounded and semantically coherent. It has since undergone exponential conceptual inflation such that it now refers pell-mell to beliefs, attitudes, affects, behaviors, institutions, state policies, discourses, frames, worldviews, and more. In addition, it has become politically, emotionally, and ethically charged, and this charge has increased over time to the point where the adjectival form "racist" is a term of universal reprobation. Should sociology use a word that is so protean, slippery, and suffers from what philosopher Lawrence Blum calls "moral overload"[197]?

---

[194] Stokely Carmichael and Charles V. Hamilton, *Black Power: The Politics of Liberation* (1967); Louis L. Knowles and Kenneth Prewitt (eds.), *Institutional Racism in America* (1969).

[195] See, for instance, the "Glossary for Understanding the Dismantling [of] Structural Racism/Promoting Racial Equity Analysis" formulated and diffused by the Aspen Institute via its 15 locations around the world, and the rubric "Structural Racism in America" on the website of the Urban Institute (accessed May 15, 2022) which, interestingly, was a leading proponent of the racially regressive myth of the "underclass" at century's turn. Wacquant, *Invention of the "Underclass,"* pp. 48–9, 82–9.

[196] Robert Miles, *Racism* (2003), pp. 43–4.

[197] Lawrence Blum, *"I'm Not a Racist, But . . .": The Moral Quandary of Race* (2002).

Structural: the noun "structure" derives from the Latin *structura*, meaning building, arrangement, or a fitting together (the root verb is *struere*, to construct). In the social sciences, its adjectival form is used to refer to any number of features such as institutional (as opposed to individual), embedded (as opposed to superficial), perennial (as opposed to conjunctural), functional (as opposed to intentional), blind (as opposed to guided), and crescive (as opposed to enacted). In short, the adjective makes reference to an entity that is *supra-individual, objective, and architectured*. Additional adjectives closely associated with structural are relational, positional, and macrosocial. The conceptual antonyms of structure are all "big words" of social theory: agency, event, culture, and history.[198] There is nothing problematic about the term itself – indeed, structure is an indispensable keyword of the social sciences[199] – so long as one points to the edifice in question and gives a minimal account of the arrangement of elements that constitute it and of its mode of functioning.

Mais voilà, when paired with racism, all too often, "structural" is used as a rhetorical device to evade just such a specification. It is invoked as a self-evident qualifier or morphs into a laundry list that potentially extends to just about any imaginable organizational entity, as when structural racism is defined as "the interrelated network of a society's institutions, with their policies and practices, that favor one or more racial groups over others and operate without the need on the part of their actors to intend harm or hold dislike of certain racial groups."[200] Where does the phenomenon stop and start? Which institutions and policies exactly are part of this machinery, and which not, if any? Is racial harm the cause or the consequence? What does "favor" mean, on what temporal horizon, who defines these "groups," and are they coherent and bounded entities? Scanning current usages, the *coupling* of "structural" and "racism" only compounds the problems besetting each word. It trebles the confusion; it encourages oratorial

---

For an energetic argument in favor of saving the concept of racism as social injustice, read Tommie Shelby, "Racism, Moralism, and Social Criticism" (2014).

[198] William H. Sewell, Jr., *Logics of History: Social Theory and Social Transformation* (2005); Dave Elder-Vass, *The Causal Power of Social Structures: Emergence, Structure and Agency* (2010).

[199] Pierre Bourdieu, "Structuralism and the Theory of Knowledge" (1968b).

[200] Margaret T. Hicken et al., "Linking History to Contemporary State-Sanctioned Slow Violence through Cultural and Structural Racism" (2021), p. 50. A similar definition, almost word for word, opens the panoramic article by Hedwig Lee, "How Does Structural Racism Operate (in) the Contemporary US Criminal Justice System" (2024), introducing the concept to the readers of the *Annual Review of Criminology*.

obfuscation, lazy thinking, and empirical circumvention. By doing so, it amputates our collective capacity to specify the *social mechanisms* that produce, reproduce, and could potentially transform ethnoracial constellations.

Structural racism is typically *invoked without being defined* – taking it as self-evident is indeed putative proof that one has opened their racial eyes wide open and taken full measure of the gravity of the evil and its consequences.[201] Or it is explicated by the variable enumeration of heterogeneous elements which are then dropped in the subsequent analysis. Or by invocation of metaphors, such as those of the "iceberg," the "epidemic," and the "spider's web."[202] Or defined in such broad and all-encompassing terms that it provides no analytic or policy guidance.[203] Such is the stipulation offered by the Aspen Institute, routinely invoked by scholars in practical disciplines such as psychiatry, medicine, nursing, and public policy who rightly bemoan the fact that there exists no accepted definition of the concept in the social sciences: "Structural Racism: A system in which public policies, institutional practices, cultural representations, and other norms work in various,

---

[201] Thus the Urban Institute writes in a post on its "Urban Wire" entitled "Reckoning with Structural Racism in Research" (accessed June 20, 2022): "Until recently, we have failed to recognize the role of structural racism and white supremacy in our research writ large ... Our work does not routinely reflect a deep analysis of structural racism. When we highlight racial disparities or deficits without examining the structural causes or explicitly denouncing common racist myths, we end up pathologizing communities and families of color and ignoring those who face intersectional oppression ... Urban Institute has been examining research's role in structural racism – and research's role in ending it. We cannot ignore centuries of subjugation, discrimination, exclusion, and injustice by excluding ourselves from our analyses. Bringing communities into our research is challenging, but we can 'bridge the gulf' and connect seekers of truth, progress, and equity."

[202] "The metaphor of an iceberg is useful for describing the levels at which racism operates. The tip of the iceberg represents acts of racism, such as crossburnings, that are easily seen and individually mediated. The portion of the iceberg that lies below the water represents structural racism; it is more dangerous and harder to eliminate." Gilbert C. Gee and Chandra L. Ford, "Structural Racism and Health Inequities: Old Issues, New Directions" (2011), p. 116. The notion that "racism is endemic in American society," with fluctuations from "hypoendemic" to "hyperendemic" to pandemic is proposed by Lee, "How Does Structural Racism Operate (in) the Contemporary US Criminal Justice System." The image of the "spider-like web of societal racism" is drawn by Eduardo Bonilla-Silva, "What Makes Systemic Racism Systemic?" (2021), p. 524.

[203] Julian M. Rucker and Jennifer A. Richeson. "Toward an Understanding of Structural Racism: Implications for Criminal Justice" (2021). I return to this exemplary article in the next section, *infra*, p. 189.

often reinforcing ways to perpetuate racial group inequity. It identifies dimensions of our history and culture that have allowed privileges associated with 'whiteness' and disadvantages associated with 'color' to endure and adapt over time. Structural racism is not something that a few people or institutions choose to practice. Instead, it has been a feature of the social, economic and political systems in which we all exist."[204] Note in passing that the moral term "inequity" has been surreptitiously substituted for the sociological term inequality.[205]

The tourists of "structural racism" in health research

Pointing to the boom of funding for, and publications on, "structural racism and health" in medical research (the number of citations in PubMed exploded from five in 2015 to nearly 400 in 2021), two noted epidemiologists complain that "across these publications and funding opportunities, there is much heterogeneity in the definition and measurement of structural racism in health studies. Few offer explicit definitions, which leads to conceptual inconsistencies and, consequently, varying measurements. Some academics have observed that 'health equity tourists' have infiltrated work on structural racism, contributing to greater confusion by untrained scholars who mischaracterize health equity concepts" (1).

1. Lorraine T. Dean and Roland J. Thorpe, Jr., "What Structural Racism Is (or Is Not) and How to Measure It: Clarity for Public Health and Medical Researchers" (2021), p. 1521.

---

[204] See, for instance, Ruth S. Shim, "Dismantling Structural Racism in Psychiatry: A Path to Mental Health Equity" (2021), and Saleem Razack and Thirusha Naidu, "Honouring the Multitudes: Removing Structural Racism in Medical Education" (2022). A variant displaying the same logical fuzziness and semantic indeterminacy is the one proposed by the National Academies of Science (2022): "Structural racism refers to the public and private policies, institutional practices, norms, and cultural representations that inherently create unequal freedom, opportunity, value, resources, advantage, restrictions, constraints, or disadvantage for individuals and populations according to their race and ethnicity both across the life course and between generations."

[205] Legal scholar Martha Minow tries to clarify the meaning of "equity" but inadvertently demonstrates its obdurate semantic incoherence in "Equality v. Equity" (2022). Stripped to its essentials, the word is another name for fairness and its diffusion amounts to little more than the moral rediscovery of the banal opposition between formal and actual equality of opportunity or access.

Elementary Forms of Ethnoracial Rule

Note also that structural racism knocks down a senescent straw man: what social scientist seriously believes that racism, however defined, is an "interpersonal matter" or the result of the behavior of "a few bad apples"?[206] The differentiation between "individual racism," rooted in personal animus, and "systemic racism" was a conceptual advance *back in 1956* when Frantz Fanon first introduced it. In his essay "Racisme et culture," Fanon proposed to revoke "the habit of considering racism like a disposition of a mind, as a psychological defect" of individuals and to replace it with the notion of "a disposition embedded in a determinate system" spanning politics, the economy, and culture, namely the colonial system.[207] Today, this elementary differentiation is a conceptual step backward when we can develop a more nuanced and richer analytic such as the pentad of ethnoracial domination that allows us to disaggregate forms, specify mechanisms, and recombine constituents into historical regimes of racial domination.

The paradigm of this discursive distraction and analytical short-circuiting is found in Michael Omi and Howard Winant's *Racial Formation in the United States*, arguably the most influential theoretical text in the subfield, in which "structural racism" is repeatedly invoked without ever being defined (see box below).[208] These criticisms apply *mutatis mutandis* to Critical Race Theory (CRT): the latter *postulate*s the centrality of race to the law, and thence to all institutions, instead of engaging in the hard work of demonstrating it; it substitutes rhetorical invocation for theoretical articulation and storytelling for empirical inquiry; it universalizes the American experience, thereby obscuring its specificities. Worse, leading advocates of Critical Race Theory insists that CRT should invoke social science only when it reinforces its pet propositions but reject it when it undermines them to preserve its self-professed status as an oppositional discourse.[209] Even the sociological variant of CRT promoted by a brave new generation of scholars focused on the dissection of white supremacy cherry-picks topics specially suited to demonstrating the latter's enduring power; prioritizes narrative accounts taking "race" as a given – even as "racism" shifts – over more robust empirical

---

[206] The fictitious puppet of the overtly racist actor who openly discriminates is periodically trotted out by Bonilla-Silva to justify his "systemic racism" approach. See his "More than Prejudice: Restatement, Reflections, and New Directions in Critical Race Theory" (2015), and "What Makes Systemic Racism Systemic?," pp. 514–16.
[207] Frantz Fanon, "Racisme et culture" (2011 [1956]), pp. 721, 724.
[208] Michael Omi and Howard Winant, *Racial Formation in the United States* (2015).
[209] Devon W. Carbado and Daria Roithmayr, "Critical Race Theory Meets Social Science" (2014).

designs questioning its referential stability; and remains locked inside the narrow perimeter of contemporary US issues approached from a perspective that turns out to be just the inverted mirror image of the conventional sociology of "race and ethnicity."[210]

> ### The elusiveness of "structural racism" in *Racial Formation in the United States* (1986, 1994, 2015)
>
> In the third edition of their landmark tome, *Racial Formation in the United States* (2015), the single most cited book on race stateside, Michael Omi and Howard Winant use the term "structural racism" a total of 19 times but never define it, riding on the tacit agreement that the reader will know what they are talking about. Early on, they suggest that the notion is distinct from "institutional racism" (p. 17) but without defining the latter notion either. In the first chapter, in a passage placed *in parentheses*, they write: "We discuss structural racism later in this book, but for now think red-lining, racial steering and residential segregation, school segregation, hiring patterns, imprisonment" (p. 38), a laundry list that has nothing specifically racial about it (with the exception of red-lining, an American peculiarity). It is not clear whether this list is comprehensive or how these different institutions relate to each other to form a distinct structure. Later Omi and Winant evoke the "unbroken history of structural racism" (p. 81), the "ongoing realities of structural racism" (p. 95), "underlying structural racism" (p. 149), and "everyday and structural racism" (p. 190) but, again, never stop to specify what they mean by either racism or by structural: the notion is impeccably doxic. And it would seem to contradict the view, expressed in the book's introduction, that "race is unstable, flexible, and subject to constant conflict and reinvention" (p. viii), an anti-structuralist view if there ever was one. (A similar incongruity arises when they "define racial formation as the sociohistorical process by which racial identities are created, lived out, transformed, and *destroyed*," p. 109, my italics.)

---

[210] Michelle Christian et al., "New Directions in Critical Race Theory and Sociology: Racism, White Supremacy, and Resistance" (2019). Does one need CRT to discover that Donald Trump is a rabid white supremacist; that campus free speech rules provide a platform for right-wing groups; that university policies of "diversity" are decorative moves designed to assuage white liberal guilt; and that racist humor among police officers contributes to dehumanizing and mistreating people of color?

Elementary Forms of Ethnoracial Rule

> In their account of the Obama period, Omi and Winant assert that, "though modernized and 'moderated', structural racism has been fortified, not undermined, by civil rights reform" (pp. 229–30), but they do not explicate how and point to no empirical indicators supporting this strong assertion. Instead, they contend that "structural racism still steers the ship of state" (p. 260): is this not reifying and making the structure an agent? This is followed by another shopping list that includes "ongoing racial inequality, racial violence, racial disenfranchisement, racial profiling, quasi-official resegregation of schools and neighborhoods, and anti-immigrant racism" (p. 258). But adding the adjective racial to a string of social patterns is a rhetorical, not an analytical, move. And what about the institutions *not* listed under the umbrella of "structural racism": the medical care system, social welfare, the police, the courts, higher education, the media, the entertainment industry, cultural amenities, the financial industry, urban infrastructure, and the physical environment? One can seemingly shorten or lengthen the list at will since no underlying principle of selection is put forth.
>
> One last confusion: is structural racism the network of racially inflected institutions or the root cause of that network, as suggested by the contention that "structural racism *determines* that a comprehensive system of advantages and disadvantages – economic, political, cultural, and psychological – suffuses U.S. society" (p. 266, my italics). Is this statement not circular? All in all, structural racism appears as a *deus ex machina* that ensures that "racism" rules the roost everywhere and forever – without consideration, for instance, of whether "structural classism" or "structural statism" might account for its apparent outcomes to some degree, and without specifying in what domains it is or it is not operative. It is an *oratorical gesture* to suggest that "racism" is entrenched, pervasive, multi-sited, and enduring (nay, perpetual), but it offers no guidance to investigate and link those sites, no clue as to the mechanisms of this endurance, and it presumes suffuseness when the task is precisely to demonstrate it.

Eduardo Bonilla-Silva is arguably the American social scientist who has shown the most perseverance in elaborating the notion of structural or "systemic racism" under the label "Racialized Social System" (RSS). But his efforts consistently elude what one can call the *problem of specification*: what, precisely, constitutes "race," "racism," "raceness," and "the system," *in intension rather than extension*? This lack of specification is covered up by rhetorical circularities, logical tautologies (or fallacies) and stock-in-trade images of American society. Thus, in *Racism Without Racists*, Bonilla-Silva writes: "Racialized social systems, or white supremacy for short, became global and affected all societies where Europeans extended their reach. I therefore conceive a society's racial structure as the *totality of the social relations and practices that reinforce white privilege*."[211] The logical structure of this proposition is: System S comprises all the elements ($s_1, s_2, \ldots s_n$) that make up System S: it is a definitional tautology. It gives us no hint as to what relations and practices fall under or escape that canopy. In addition, it ignores cases of domination that do not involve whites, wiping out in passing native patterns of ethnoracial classification and stratification in Africa, the Middle East and the Indo-Pacific domain as well as myriad ethnoracial patterns inside the United States and Europe. It notably omits situations where "whites" are the racialized target of domination, as in Nazi Germany and with anti-Semitism in its varied historical instantiations.[212]

The definition of the RSS also does not tell us how to determine that a given conduct or institution "reinforces white privilege" or not. Does reinforcement count when it arises immediately, in the midterm or in the long term? What about social practices and institutions that are racially ambiguous or contradictory in their effects, working at the same time to bolster and undermine racial rule, or have contrary effects on the black proletariat and the black bourgeoisie, or on white workers as opposed to white managers?[213] What about actors that engage in racially bifurcated strategies? Take the case of an American county that is reducing the racial disparity in infant mortality while having historically fueled black hyperincarceration – this

---

[211] Eduardo Bonilla-Silva, *Racism Without Racists* (2021 [2008]), p. 9. In a section of his introductory chapter entitled "Key Terms: Race, Racial Structure, and Racial Ideology," Bonilla-Silva is content to note that race is socially constructed yet real and structural, but does not define the term.

[212] A contemporary example is the "gray racialization" of low-wage Polish workers in Norway who, though "white," are perceived as inherently different from Nordic people and treated accordingly: they are seen as born workers, respectful of authority, and naturally suited to manual labor, and especially "dirty" work which makes them "polluted." Mette Andersson and Johan Fredrik Rye, "Gray Racialization of White Immigrants: The Polish Worker in Norway" (2023).

[213] This latter scenario does not arise for Bonilla-Silva because, in his vision, whites are "a team" and "historically cracks on the White team have sealed rather quickly" (Bonilla-Silva, "What Makes Systemic Racism Systemic?," p. 515).

is the case of Alameda County, wherein sits Berkeley. Is this county reproducing "white privilege" or reducing it? The black/white disparity in prison admissions has declined dramatically in the past quarter-century, dropping from nearly 9 to 1 in 1993 down to less than 3 to 1 in 2015 while class disparity contrasting men with no college versus some college has exploded in the same period from 7 to 1 to 27 to 1, meaning that the fastest growing segment of the male carceral population in the twenty-first century is poor whites:[214] does this mean that the criminal justice apparatus is no longer part of the RSS since it now works to reduce "white privilege"?

In a recent article recapitulating his perspective, entitled "What Makes Systemic Racism Systemic?," Bonilla-Silva asserts that "we all participate in Systemic Racism (SR)" and "all express our *raceness*." Moreover, "racism is systemic because it incorporates *all* actors into the game" and "all actors are racially preconditioned" because "no one can be outside SR." In other words, racism is systemic because it is systemic.[215] Bonilla-Silva then proceeds by a series of stipulations upheld by the sociological common sense shared by his American readers cognizant about "the heavy weight of racism" or the "spider-like web of societal racism."[216] The "theory" boils down to adding the adjective "racialized" to a string of common sociological predicates, system, interaction, interests, emotions, ideologies, grammar. The adjective itself is left conveniently undefined.

In lieu of conceptual specification, Bonilla-Silva unspools folksy metaphors: some white actors are "rotten apples" in the proverbial basket (p. 521) while others are "nice Whites" (p. 521); there are "cracks on the White team" (p. 518); "SR is like playing Whack-a-mole except that to win the game the player should try to *simultaneously* seal all the holes from which the mole can come through" (p. 524); whites contribute to systemic racism by "leading a '(White)

---

[214] I thank Chris Muller and Alex Roerkhasse for computing these figures especially for me based on the data in their article, Christopher Muller and Alexander F. Roehrkasse, "Racial and Class Inequality in US Incarceration in the Early Twenty-First Century" (2022).
[215] Bonilla-Silva, "What Makes Systemic Racism Systemic?," pp. 514, 520. For a quixotic attempt to marry Bonilla-Silva's race primordialism and Bourdieu's historicist ontology, which is to say, mix sociological water and oil, read Ali Meghji, "Just What Is Critical Race Theory, and What Is It Doing in British Sociology? From 'Britcrit' to the Racialized Social System Approach" (2021). But see the fuller attempt in idem, *The Racialized Social System: Critical Race Theory as Social Theory*, especially chapter 1.
[216] Bonilla-Silva, "What Makes Systemic Racism Systemic?," pp. 514 and 524. The pagination of the quotes in this paragraph are given in parentheses in the text.

Leave it to beaver' life" (p. 524) and by "oil[ing] the wheels of the racial regime" (p. 524); "the conscious, unconscious, and semi-conscious on race affairs merge like chunky monkey ice cream in Whites' minds" (p. 525); whites "are the main cog that maintain the Racial System running smoothly" (p. 525). As for those who would want to fight Systemic Racism, Bonilla-Silva advises them to follow "the sage words of Spike Lee, 'Do the right thing'" (p. 526). Have these allegories moved us closer to grasping the distinctive logics of racial domination? Not to mention the final, most daunting difficulty, that the "raceness" of the reader directly determines their ability to see the truth of the RSS perspective: "Mainstream and some progressive social analysts cannot accept the argument that racism is structural because they are white and whites form a social collectivity bonded by the fact that they receive benefits from the way the racial regime is organized."[217] This is a classic case of the fallacy of affirming the consequent.

Finally, a half-century after its coinage, "structural racism" has *failed to produce a single major study demonstrating the distinctive scientific benefits* of the construct. Indeed, the best works on the historical production of structures of racial rule in America (and beyond) advance smoothly without the notion. The signal social history of the multi-sited institutional roots of African-American exclusion from urban home-ownership, Keeanga-Yamahtta Taylor's *Race for Profit*, does not invoke it a single time.[218] Other areas of inquiry into domination have done just fine without such a notion – a Google Scholar search on "structural sexism" yields 1,540 hits and on "structural classism" a paltry 111, compared to 52,900 hits for "structural racism." Why can't students of ethnoracial rule do the same? Indeed, since *all forms of durable inequality are "structural"* in the basic sociological sense of resulting from complex and dynamic institutional interlocks, the distinctive conceptual value of "structural racism" must stand or fall on the analytical value of "racism" and therefore it flounders.

---

[217] Eduardo Bonilla-Silva, "More than Prejudice" (2015b), p. 76. For the Duke sociologist, "race scholars [must] decolonize their imagination, unlearn received truths on race, and conduct a 'For-Us science on racial affairs'" by embracing "an epistemology of racial liberation to challenge 'white logic' and 'white methods'" (ibid., p. 79).

[218] Keeanga-Yamahtta Taylor, *Race for Profit: How Banks and the Real Estate Industry Undermined Black Homeownership* (2019).

Elementary Forms of Ethnoracial Rule

Still, in *The Blue and Brown Books*, Ludwig Wittgenstein teaches us that "the meaning of a word is its use in the language." This suggests that "structural racism" *could* be put to good use to produce conceptually clear, empirically defensible, and politically cogent arguments *provided* that the user specifies the "structures" involved and identifies the mechanisms linking and activating them – that is, reaches beyond the confines of the concept as commonly construed. This is exactly what Zinzi Bailey and her colleagues do in a widely cited article published in the *New England Journal of Medicine* which explicates "How Structural Racism Works – Racist Policies as a Root Cause of US Racial Health Inequities."[219] The telling irony is that their invocation of "structural racism" is effective *precisely because they reach beyond the structure to flag specific policies and actors set in a temporal frame*. They relate health outcomes to red-lining and racialized residential segregation, police violence and carceral expansion, and the unequal provision of health, three institutional anchors of racial domination in the American metropolis. But "structural racism" per se plays no analytic role; it is merely an umbrella term deployed for rhetorical convenience and political signaling.

Moreover, this engagement is the exception and not the rule. As commonly used, structural racism *essentializes* racial domination by presenting it as an unchanging and monolithic bloc traversing time and space. It *reifies and anthropomorphizes it*, turning it into a cold and calculating shadow-actor.[220] Consider this *cri du coeur* from historian and anti-racist activist Ibram Kendi commenting on the latest mass killing in an American city in May of 2022: "Structural racism killed Black people in East Buffalo, and then a gunman killed the survivors."[221] Here is a claim that, typically, makes structural racism the *cause* of the very inequalities presented as proof of its existence – a textbook case of begging the question or the fallacy of circularity.[222] It

---

[219] Zinzi D. Bailey et al., "How Structural Racism Works – Racist Policies as a Root Cause of US Racial Health Inequities" (2021).

[220] For a forceful critique of the personalization of social collectives and institutions, and how it vitiates social scientific thought, see Bourdieu, *Sociologie générale*, vol. 1, pp. 365–8.

[221] Ibram Kendi, "The Double Terror of Being Black in America" (2022). Kendi's statement can be generously interpreted as invoking the notion of "structural violence" dear to radical anthropologists. But that notion itself is vague, incoherent, and circular: structural violence resides in steep inequalities that produce harmful effects *and* it is the cause of these inequalities.

[222] "The proponents of the notion of 'structural racism' are generally content with speculations that tend to tautologies on the 'racial frame' (Feagin) or 'the white

is good sloganeering for political action but poor sociology, yet sociologists seduced by the logic of the trial are wont to echo this kind of condemnation.

Structural racism transfers the logic of the trial from the individual to organizations to the "system" they are said to form. It works with a crudely simplified map of symbolic and social space built on a rigid dual opposition between privileged "whites" and victimized "people of color," (mis)taken as homogeneous, unified, and petrified collectives ("communities") endowed, not only with shared interests, but also with the same sentiments and experience of existential injury.[223] Being nowhere in particular, the "structure" is everywhere, like *a specter and a poison* diffusing throughout the social body; it is omnipresent, omniscient, and omnipotent; there is no outside to its ambit. Thus, in her 2023 panoramic article on structural racism in criminal punishment, Hedwig Lee asserts that, due to the ignoble origins of the country in Indian genocide and African-American slavery, "it is insufficient to describe racism as operating within the criminal justice system. Rather, racism operates this system," a disconcerting combination of the *post hoc ergo propter hoc* and *petitio principii* fallacies. This, moreover, follows from the "grounding premise that racism in the United States is ubiquitous" and from the fact that "structural racism is systemic,"[224] a patent definitional tautology.

Paradoxically, *by dehistoricizing ethnoracial domination, "structural racism" risks reinforcing it* – much like Afropessimism does by ontologizing the injurious experience of blackness in the United States. It makes it seem eternal, uniform, untouched by social discontinuity, and impervious to human action short of wholesale social destruction – among the favorite terms of the proponents of structural racism is "to dismantle" and "abolition." But, again, who seriously believes that abolishing the police or prisons is more than a figment of the political imagination suited for moral philosophizing and campus disquisition?[225] Why not abolish also schools, public hospitals, job train-

---

habitus' (Bonilla-Silva) supposed to suffice to account for the behavioral regularities observed." Daniel Sabbagh, "Le 'racisme systémique': un conglomérat problématique" (2022), p. 62.

[223] For a cogent critique of this presumption of a unified dominant category, see Andreas Wimmer, "Race-Centrism: A Critique and Research Agenda" (2015), pp. 2194–7.

[224] Lee, "How Does Structural Racism Operate (in) the Contemporary US Criminal Justice System?"

[225] Or what philosopher Shelby kindly calls "utopian imagination": "If the opposi-

ing and welfare programs, and public defender offices: are they not *complicit* with the established racial order given that they are integral parts of the "structure"? And when they do take the trouble to specify realistic measures needed to "dismantle systemic racism," advocates of the notion enumerate conventional reforms consisting in bolstering the social state, shrinking the penal state, and enlarging institutional access for African Americans, proof that the concept has no special added value when it comes to practical remedies.[226]

These incantations fail to provide purchase on the *institutional layering and complexity* that the notion of "structural racism" paradoxically erases while purporting to highlight them.[227] It makes it more difficult to identify points of realistic intervention. Like "racial capitalism" and "intersectionality," structural racism thrives on *semantic opacity, ambiguity, and malleability*.[228] Its condemnation is premised on *sociological fictions* and is therefore fated to disappoint those engaged in the struggle to unsettle or upend it. The conceptual liability of the notion is even more glaring when one travels around the world to probe and compare regimes and profiles of ethnoracial domination. Do we learn anything when we lump together under that umbrella term constellations as diverse as South African apartheid, the castigation of the Roma in Bulgaria, hiring discrimination in the French urban periphery, immigrant segregation in Sweden, and the ostracization of the Dalits within the Indian diaspora around the world? My response is negative and I will endeavor to demonstrate it in the

---

tion has so far proved so powerful that it could successfully thwart all attempts at fundamental reform, why should history give us hope that an abolitionist movement, which involves contending with the same reactionary forces, would prevail?" Tommie Shelby, *The Idea of Prison Abolition* (2022), p. 189.

[226] See Shantel Gabrieal Buggs et al., "Systemic Anti-Black Racism Must Be Dismantled: Statement by the American Sociological Association Section on Racial and Ethnic Minorities" (2020).

[227] The call to "dismantle" structural racism in American society has recently been sounded in areas as diverse as medicine and psychiatry, education and philanthropy, corporate governance and public employment, scientific research and publishing, drug policy and criminal punishment, the environment, psychology, the entertainment industry, and gender relations, to mention a few. It has created a thriving market for "diversity and equity" consultants and managers who have professionalized the art of ethnoracial quietism masquerading as alarm. Even the White House (2023) has promulgated the goal of "equity and racial justice."

[228] See Kathy Davis, "Intersectionality as Buzzword: A Sociology of Science Perspective on What Makes a Feminist Theory Successful" (2008); Go, "Three Tensions in the Theory of Racial Capitalism;" and my discussion of "racial capitalism" in this chapter, *supra*, pp. 161–8.

case of the Jim Crow regime of caste terrorism and of the interlock between hyperghettoization and hyperincarceration in the postindustrial metropolis in the next two chapters.

In conclusion, the notion of "structural racism" suffers from underspecification and overstretch at the same time. It is a *rhetorical and metaphorical, not an analytical, construct*.[229] It is deficient in terms of semantics, logics, and heuristics, the three criteria by which to judge a robust social science concept. *Semantics*: its meaning is unclear, indistinct and unstable. *Logics*: it is not coherent, type-specific, and parsimonious. *Heuristics*: 57 years in, it has failed to facilitate theoretical advance and empirical discovery. This suggests that, whereas it may be useful to drum up practical support for institutional change in public and private bureaucracies that need to be educated about the ingrained, multi-sited, and resistant nature of racial domination, it is scientifically fruitless and the genetic sociology of ethnoracial rule is better off doing without it.

"Structural racism" redux: A penal illustration

To assert that race is a subtype of ethnicity, logically as well as historically, is not to deny the brute and brutal reality of racial domination, as feared by activists and scholars who cling to the distinction between race and ethnicity as if their life depended on it. On the contrary: it is to give ourselves the analytic means to discover under what conditions and due to what social forces *ordinary ethnicity gets turned into racialized (denegated) ethnicity*, and the difference that naturalization makes in different arenas of social action – say, friendship, marriage, schooling, the labor market, policing or civic membership. Far from helping us capture this dynamic and disclosing its mechanisms, clumpy terms such as "structural racism" constitute an *epistemological obstacle* that needs to be removed.[230]

Indeed, aside from its progressive valence and virtue-signaling function, the resurrection of "institutional racism" under the guise of "structural racism" could turn out to be to the 2020s what the invention of the "underclass" was for the 1980s: a lumpy notion that

---

[229] For an extended discussion of these three modalities of argumentation in social science, read the prologue to Loïc Wacquant, *The Two Faces of the Ghetto* (2025).

[230] On the notion of "epistemological obstacle," see Gaston Bachelard, *La Formation de l'esprit scientifique. Contribution à une psychanalyse de la connaissance objective* (1934), and *supra*, pp. 6–8.

stops analytic work just where it should begin, confuses forms and conflates mechanisms of ethnoracial domination (themselves racial and nonracial), and thus presents a practical obstacle to the surgical removal of operative sources of racial inequality. This is the case, for instance, with broad-brush rhetorical attacks on "structural racism in criminal justice" that confuse the different scales of the American penal state (federal, state, county, and city), overlook the hyperlocalism and administrative fragmentation of a criminal justice system that is not a system, and amalgamate the different practices of legislating, policing, pretrial detention, prosecution, public defense, plea negotiation and litigation, sentencing, supervision via probation and parole, court-mandated programming, incarceration, and sentence administration, each of which has layers of internal complexity, entail variable degrees of operational discretion, and may or may not produce looping ethnoracial disparities.[231]

The mist of "structural racism" enshrouds the prison

A paradigmatic illustration of the theoretical short-circuiting, analytical conflation, and empirical obfuscation commonly produced by trotting out the notion of "structural racism" is the article by Julian M. Rucker and Jennifer A. Richeson, "Toward an Understanding of Structural Racism: Implications for Criminal Justice," published in the October 2021 issue of *Science* devoted to "mass incarceration," the premier scholarly journal in the land (1).

Rucker and Richeson purport to show that Americans "tolerate a racially inequitable criminal justice system" because they are "willfully ignorant of structural racism" (p. 286). Drawing on "social dominance theory," they define the latter as a "pattern of allocation [of positive societal goods], codified by law, reinforced by cultural norms and practices, and enforced by both official police as well as extralegal vigilante groups" (ibid.). Is pattern the equivalent of structure? What makes this pattern specifically racial? Is vigilantism

---

[231] A brilliant exploration of the crevasse between the slogan and the counterintuitive realities of "court reform" spotlighting this organizational intricacy is Malcolm M. Feeley, *Court Reform on Trial: Why Simple Solutions Fail* (1983). It is striking and worrisome that the current generation of criminal justice activists blissfully ignore the sobering lessons of the failure, 50 years ago, of exactly those changes they are now seeking: bail reform, pretrial diversion, sentencing reform, and speedy trial rules.

a feature of structural racism? Is the black–white gap in unemployment or wealth, for instance, "codified by law"? What criminal statutes specify sentences differentiated by race? If you remove police and vigilantes, what you obtain is an anodyne definition of social inequality writ large. Is structural racism, then, simply racial inequality with "ism" added for the sake of sounding theoretical or truly committed to racial justice?

For documentation of "structural racism" at work in penal institutions, our authors offer all of two graphs, the one showing the evolution of the prison admission rate for blacks and whites and the other their imprisonment rates between 1930 and 2000, with not a word of explication, contextualization, and qualification. For one, they forget to mention that 80 percent of the black–white disparity in incarceration in the 1990s was fully explained by the different serious crime rates of the two groups (2). They also do not elucidate how structural racism explains *both* a low rate of black incarceration of 80 per 100,000 coupled with a low black–white disparity of 2 to 1 in 1930 (when racial domination was direct and brutal) *and* a catastrophic rate of 250 coupled with a booming disparity of 5 to 1 by 1990 (when racial domination was indirect and comparatively mollified). The notion does not do any theoretical work here; worse, it gets in the way of serious theoretical engagement and historical grounding (such as I will essay in chapter 4 of this book).

Again and again, Rucker and Richeson *posit* that structural racism explains "inequities" in criminal justice, without a single sentence suggesting how, and then bemoan the fact that "white Americans largely fail" to establish that linkage through "miseducation on the topic," whereas "racial minority Americans" make the link due to their "direct and vicarious experience" with penal discrimination (p. 386). But does discrimination in structural racism not consist of a blind process that can only be captured statistically by scoping out impersonal linkages, rather than individual acts available to the immediate perception of those it strikes? Altogether, this article is an exercise in logomachy that obscures the phenomenon it purports to explain, collapses its dimensions, and fails to specify its underlying mechanisms – as is characteristic of the uses of "structural racism" in the study of penality (3).

1. Julian M. Rucker and Jennifer A. Richeson, "Toward an Understanding of Structural Racism: Implications for Criminal Justice" (2021).

Elementary Forms of Ethnoracial Rule

> 2. Michael Tonry, *Malign Neglect: Race, Crime, and Punishment in America* (1995), pp. 66–74. Tonry concludes his meticulous review of the best studies on the topic thus: "The main reason that black incarceration rates are substantially higher than those for whites is that black crime rates for imprisonable crimes are substantially higher than those for whites" (p. 79). The only exception to this pattern is the enforcement of drug laws, for which most offenses are not imprisonable.
> 3. The same applies to Hedwig Lee's article "How Does Structural Racism Operate (in) the Contemporary US Criminal Justice System," which is long on rhetoric (it uses the word racism no fewer than 107 times, discounting the bibliography) but short on sound empirical facts; strident in denunciation but silent about social mechanisms; vibrant with moral fervor but inattentive to organizational complexity, historical variation, and analytical nuance.

Disaggregating these steps and following the flow of criminal cases at ground level reveals this counterintuitive fact: some justice processes are *structurally advantageous* to lower-class African-American defendants from the hyperghetto relative to other defendants.[232] Consider the court as an input-output machine. The fact that most black defendants, victims, and witnesses are closely overlapping and largely interchangeable populations in neighborhoods with a high incidence of street crime and high rates of mutual acquaintance creates strong disincentives to resort to the authorities in response to offenses. Hostility to the police, distrust of the District Attorney, and fear of retaliation against self or family (according to the street adage "snitches get stitches") make it unlikely that victims or witnesses will cooperate and testify in court hearings, which translates into a high rate of charge reduction or dismissal, even in cases of homicide.[233] Thus the murder clearance rate for the city of Oakland,

---

[232] The arguments in this section are informed by two-and-a-half years of ethnographic observation of the everyday work of criminal courts in two counties of northern California and over 200 in-depth interviews with prosecutors, public defenders, defense attorneys, and judges at both the misdemeanor and felony levels. Observation covered the full sequence of judicial steps, from charging and arraignment to preliminary hearing and plea negotiation to trial and sentencing. It was anchored, not in the public side of the courtroom and its gallery, to which the bureaucratic ceremonial is addressed, but on the private side of the District Attorney's and Public Defender's offices, court corridors and witness rooms, and judges' chambers where the actual judicial work is done. I also draw on the analysis of geo-coded criminal justice data for the 58 counties of the state, including an analysis of the relative "purchase" of prison cells from the state's correctional administration by the different counties revealing that poor rural counties effectively subsidize cells for criminals in rich urban counties.
[233] This is painstakingly demonstrated by the remarkable reporting in South Central Los Angeles of Jill Leovy, *Ghettoside: A True Story of Murder in America* (2015).

where most murders are committed in the two black hyperghettos of West Oakland and East Oakland, was 33 percent in 2022 compared to a statewide rate of 64 percent over the past decade. Perversely, this "advantage" for the criminal defendant translates into further disadvantage for the neighborhood from which they issue and helps explain the paradoxical demand of its residents for both less police (exerting surveillance) and more police (responding to crime).[234] What use is "structural racism" to detect and explain this counterintuitive pattern?

Another advantageous structural factor is the geographical distribution of poor black populations: they are concentrated in large urban centers whose police and prosecutors have to prioritize serious crimes due to the sheer volume of felony offenses; judges must also reserve limited courtroom space for "heavier" cases; this translates mechanically into greater leniency at the misdemeanor level, which tends to be used mostly as training ground for young attorneys anyway.[235] Controlling for criminal justice background, poor urban defendants are thus more likely to be put on probation; but, because city probation departments are also overwhelmed by caseloads, these defendants are likely to be put on "court probation," which entails no supervision, rather than on "formal probation," which does.[236] Even for more serious felonies, the scarcity of space and staff in overworked and underfinanced urban courts makes it more likely that defendants will receive and accept more favorable plea offers than comparable defendants in suburban and rural areas for the same crimes.

For mutually reinforcing cultural and institutional reasons, prosecutors and judges in peri-urban and rural counties are considerably more punitive than their urban colleagues. Moreover, indigent criminal defense in remote locations typically relies on low-skill, underpaid, indifferent, and itinerant "contract attorneys" compared to the high-skilled, well-resourced, and more motivated public defenders

---

[234] Gwen Prowse et al., "The State from Below: Distorted Responsiveness in Policed Communities" (2020).

[235] This is why most low-level offenders suffer administrative penalties rather than properly penal punishment, as shown by Issa Kohler-Hausmann, *Misdemeanorland: Criminal Courts and Social Control in an Age of Broken Windows Policing* (2018).

[236] On the transformation of probation in the age of hyperincarceration, see Michelle S. Phelps, "Mass Probation from Micro to Macro: Tracing the Expansion and Consequences of Community Supervision" (2020). For a demonstration of the centrality of infractions, violations, and misdemeanors in the work and impact of criminal courts, see Issa Kohler-Hausmann, "Don't Call It a Comeback: The Criminological and Sociological Study of Subfelonies" (2022).

benefiting from the support and collective experience of a defender's office in the city.[237] These structural features of criminal justice in the polarized metropolis are counterintuitive facts that must be taken into account in both the scholarly and policy debate. Militants for criminal justice reform ignore them at the cost of limiting their purchase on reality.[238]

Finally, prosecutors in large urban counties are not "Pavlovian dogs" oblivious to racial disparities seeking to "rack up" the maximum penalty for each case (to use their own florid language). Rather, their priority is to "move stuff" and resolve matters in an efficient manner lest they be submerged by the relentless wave of cases coming their way – a judge describes the onslaught as "trying to drink water out of a firehose." To start with, the discretion of prosecutors is far from absolute.[239] It is bounded, not only by legal statutes, but also by their experience, seniority, embeddedness in a team, office policy and culture, and by what the local criminal court (and even the specific courthouse) considers the "going rate" for each type of offense.[240] If deputy district attorneys make an offer outside of the expected range at the pretrial stage, the judge handling the sentencing calendar will refuse to validate their "deal" with the defense. Also, many District Attorney's offices use a set arithmetic formula to make prison offers pegged at one-third the maximum exposure for the crimes charged, give or take a few years to adjust to the circumstances of the offense and the judicial profile of the accused, a standard discount which works to minimize possible racial bias in bargaining.

Prosecutors are also not blind to the role of race in criminal processing and pride themselves on doing their best to uphold standards

---

[237] Laurence A. Benner, "The California Public Defender: Its Origins, Evolution and Decline" (2010).
[238] The focus of justice activists on the evils of the prison overlooks the fact that most defendants are sentenced to probation (even in the case of felonies). Their mobilization would have a greater impact if they targeted their energies on the submerged body of the penal iceberg instead of on its visible tip.
[239] This is a misconception prevalent in the scholarly literature on the courts, as in the canonical book written by the former public defender Angela J. Davis, *Arbitrary Justice: The Power of the American Prosecutor* (2007).
[240] James Eisenstein et al., *The Contours of Justice: Communities and their Courts* (1988). On the impact of the social structure and culture of the office on the day-to-day work and professional persona of prosecutors, see Kay L. Levine and Ronald F. Wright, "Prosecution in 3-D" (2012). On the deep organizational embeddedness of judicial processing, see Jeffery T. Ulmer, "Criminal Courts as Inhabited Institutions: Making Sense of Difference and Similarity in Sentencing" (2019).

of substantive, as opposed to formal, justice, to satisfy the sense of fairness that sustains their work day to day. Some of them use their discretion to modulate the quantum of punishment offered in plea bargaining to black and white defendants for the same offense in ways that close racial gaps whenever they consider the adverse social background of the former relative to the latter. The reasoning here is that black defendants "never had a chance" in life and so deserve some measure of leniency, whereas white defendants with more favorable upbringings "have no excuse" for committing the crimes with which they are charged. This suggests that prosecutors may well use their discretion to *reduce rather than increase racial disparities*, particularly for first-time offenders.[241] This is another unexpected judicial process that requires getting into the guts of the system rather than presuming that its functioning is inherently and irreversibly detrimental to the subordinate ethnoracial category at all stages of the penal chain.

Paying attention to the workings of the courts at ground level and in particular to the mechanics of plea bargaining and sentencing as they happen in real time further reveals that there is a *systematic gap between the sentencing offense and the underlying offense* with which defendants who plead guilty were initially charged as criminal counts are routinely dropped or downgraded as part of the bargaining process to speed up matters. For instance, a person charged with murder may plead to the "lesser-included offense" of manslaughter; burglary may be reduced to trespassing, robbery to larceny, and manufacturing a controlled substance to simple possession of narcotics (while the associated charge of felon in possession of a weapon is dropped due to "proof problems"). It is also not uncommon for a serious felony charge to be bargained down to an offense far removed from the alleged criminal conduct, as when robbery, grand theft or drug trafficking are replaced by a mere public order offense (such as disturbing the peace or loitering to commit a crime). So the sentencing offense is

---

[241] My field observations in the country of San Pedrito in northern California are supported by the statistical study of Shaffer in North Carolina using a full decade of court data to track the impact of prior convictions on felony sentencing by race. See Hannah Shaffer, "Prosecutors, Race, and the Criminal Pipeline" (2023). A similar mechanism is detected in a study of racial disparities in criminal sentencing in Australia, where the wide output gap between whites and Aboriginals disappears when measured legal factors are taken into account, suggesting that sentencing courts "place less weight on the prior criminal record of an Indigenous offender than on the prior criminal record of a non-Indigenous offender." Lucy Snowball and Don Weatherburn, "Does Racial Bias in Sentencing Contribute to Indigenous Overrepresentation in Prison?" (2007).

Elementary Forms of Ethnoracial Rule

often only loosely related to the underlying charge. Moreover, felony offenders pleading to a misdemeanor, sentenced to felony probation, or who have their case dismissed are by definition excluded from investigations focusing on sentencing based on the judicial profile of the prison population.

Now, with precious few exceptions, quantitative studies of racial disparities use the "method of residuals" to document presumed racially discriminatory treatment in criminal processing, but they use the sentencing offense as their dependent variable and do not control for the underlying offense.[242] But part of the white–black disparity may well be accounted for by racial differences in charges at preliminary hearing themselves related to differential charging, differential policing, or differential criminal conduct instead of differential sentencing – *we just do not know*. Moreover, what we do know about offense of conviction invites further caution, especially since, with rare exceptions, *existing studies do not control for class*.[243] Thus, Spohn and Cederblum report that race has a significant effect on incarceration decisions but only in less serious cases. Synthesizing 71 studies, Mitchell shows that "the race effect is statistically significant but small and highly variable." King and Light find that unwarranted racial disparities are small and decreasing over time, and that the two main theories supposed to account for them, racial threat and focal concern, are not supported by the data while evidence on the role of implicit bias and social distance is mixed. Finally, in a model investigation of Georgia prisoners allowing for multiple social controls, including – a rarity – employment, education, social class, and marital status, Burch ascertains that, for every 100 days of prison imposed on the average white convict, the average black convict is sentenced to 105 days – a disparity of 1 to 1.05 suggesting that the *racial impact of sentencing net of class is close to nil*. Furthermore, Burch detects that light-skin blacks receive the same sentences as whites,

---

[242] For a thorough and rigorous synthesis of existing studies, see Cassia Spohn, "Thirty Years of Sentencing Reform: The Quest for a Racially Neutral Sentencing Process" (2000), and idem, "Race and Sentencing Disparity" (2017). A rare study that captures the downgrading of initial into conviction charge and its impact on gender and racial (but, as always, not class) disparities is Brian D. Johnson and Pilar Larroulet, "The 'Distance Traveled': Investigating the Downstream Consequences of Charge Reductions for Disparities in Incarceration" (2019).

[243] The four controls commonly introduced in quantitative studies of sentencing are the offender's sex, age, criminal history, and the sentencing guidelines of the relevant juridiction. Due to the limitations of administrative data, these studies omit occupation, income, education, and housing status as four critical indicators of class position.

indicating that gradational color, rather than categorical race, is the operative cause.[244]

In other words, while evidence of *systematic disparities* by race in sentencing *output* is strong, claims of *systemic discrimination* are weak and largely based on a priori postulations or beliefs about an imagined judicial machinery, not systematic study of the *throughput* of actually existing courts. The problem with "structural racism" here is that it posits that which needs to be discovered and demonstrated. It stops the search for mechanisms and their articulation. It obfuscates the primacy of class disparity in penal treatment and its *cascading effects* through processes of "cumulative disadvantage" at the successive stages of criminal processing as well as through the entire life course.[245] Even "controlling" for class as a unitary variable would not fully capture its multidimensional effects.[246] Poor blacks caught in the judicial apparatus are typically much poorer than corresponding poor whites so they are less likely to proffer the evidence of "community attachment" (employment, residence, family ties) needed to be released "on their own recognizance" or on low bail at arraignment. This will result in a detectable racial disparity in release entirely accounted for by class. This disparity, in turn, will impact conviction and sentencing at the other end of the judicial chain.

Similarly, the past criminal record of black and white defendants may look identical on the face of it but, again, because of their abiding poverty across the life span, the record of African Americans will often be longer (extending into juvenile years, which record the prosecutor may access and take into account in serious cases even when the law formally forbids it) and comprise subtle subcriminal signals to the court (such as repeated "FTAs," failure to appear at a hearing) that the judicial leash needs to be tighter. Finally, the offenses to which black and white defendants plead guilty (or *nolo contendere*) may read the same on paper at sentencing but what court attorneys call "the

---

[244] Cassia Spohn and Jerry Cederblom, "Race and Disparities in Sentencing: A Test of the Liberation Hypothesis" (1991); Ojmarrh Mitchell, "A Meta-Analysis of Race and Sentencing Research: Explaining the Inconsistencies" (2005); Ryan D. King and Michael T. Light, "Have Racial and Ethnic Disparities in Sentencing Declined?" (2019); Traci Burch, "Skin Color and the Criminal Justice System: Beyond Black-White Disparities in Sentencing" (2015).

[245] Megan C. Kurlychek and Brian D. Johnson, "Cumulative Disadvantage in the American Criminal Justice System" (2019).

[246] The great virtue of Burch's study of "Skin Color and the Criminal Justice System" is to treat class as multidimensional but, like other students of penality, she is so obsessed with race that she underplays her class findings.

equities of the case" may differ and the initial or underlying charge(s) may also differ to the detriment of African-American defendants, insofar as they tend to be more deeply involved in criminal street activity (due to racial and class exclusion), resulting in higher punishment for what is statistically mischaracterized as the "same crime." These are some of the mechanisms based on class that will produce a racial gap even in the absence of discriminatory processes.

"Structural racism" does not give us the *conceptual flexibility* needed to capture these social, legal, and organizational complexities. It overlooks structurally favorable mechanisms in the interest of wholesale castigation. It conflates class and racial mechanisms of production of judicial disparity, ignoring the former as a matter of course. It replaces meticulous study with facile sloganeering, and pinpoints remedial action with vague calls for systemic changes that are unlikely to come about or to produce their expected results. In so doing, this *vogue word* betrays its ostensive purpose: to excavate the social conditions of possibility of ethnoracial justice.

Race-making as group-making

The stipulation of the concept of "race" sketched in this chapter meets the criteria that make for a solid analytic construct: it is semantically discrete, clear, and neutral; it is logically coherent, specific, and parsimonious; and it is heuristic in that it allows us to dissect empirically and bring within a single theoretical framework the varied forms assumed by ethnic ordering in history and across continents – ethnolinguistic, ethnoregional, ethnoreligious, ethnonational, and ethnoracial proper, in rough order of historical appearance. A similar vigorous conceptual effort to unify these categories "as a single integrated family of forms" on a comparative and historical basis is Rogers Brubaker's *Grounds for Difference*. It does not go far enough: instead of subsuming race and nationalism *under ethnicity*, as biologized ethnicity and state-affiliated ethnicity, respectively, Brubaker retains them as three coequal cognitive and conative perspectives on the social world (to which he later adds religion as both a "component" and an "analogue" of ethnicity).[247] Andreas Wimmer goes further in that direction in *Ethnic Boundary Making* by developing

---

[247] Rogers Brubaker, *Grounds for Difference* (2015), p. 162, and idem, "Ethnicity, Race, and Nationalism" (2009).

an analytic of ethnic formation in global perspective which encompasses race within ethnicity. But neither Brubaker nor Wimmer takes the next step of rolling the categories of ethnicity, race, and nationalism under a *general neo-Bourdieusian theory of symbolic power and group-making* – encompassing class, gender, age, sexuality, religion, citizenship, locality, etc. – whose very possibility and necessity they demonstrate.[248]

Let me offer a sketch of that theory anchored by three nodes and sources of social action that play but a minor role in Brubaker's and Wimmer's approach: the *body* as socialized seat of cognitive, cathectic, and conative categories that guide agents (which cannot be reduced to the cognitive alone); *social space* as the multidimensional distribution of forms of capital (which cannot be reduced to networks, even as it contains them); and the *state* as paramount symbolic power that shapes both social space and habitus and that sets the terms and impacts the outcome of classification struggles (which require an authority to settle disputes in the last instance).[249]

In three pivotal articles on ethnoregional identity, class formation, and the family, Bourdieu provides the conceptual instruments and theoretical pointers needed for developing a sociology of racial domination as the realization of naturalizing categories.[250] Put together, these texts sketch a model of the *sociosymbolic alchemy* whereby a mental construct (that is, a group on paper) is turned into a minimally cohesive social collective – what Bourdieu calls "a practical group" – and thence into a historical agent, a mobilized group capable of concerted action on the political stage – "an instituted group."

---

[248] Wimmer suggests this move in his recommendation for future research, but he does not make it: "The theoretical model of the making and unmaking of social boundaries introduced here could easily be applied to other social cleavages as well, to class, gender, professions, subcultures, age groups, and the like." *Ethnic Boundary Making*, p. 213.

[249] Here I hew closer to Emirbayer and Desmond who make room for embodied cognition and emotions in their rich model of race-making (pp. 245–9). But we differ in that they give analytic priority to field over social space (to focus on what they call the "field of blackness"), and they scatter rather than center the role of the state (which, revealingly, has no entry in their remarkably detailed index). *The Racial Order*, pp. 92–3, 103, 171–3, 212–13, 335–6.

[250] These articles are "Identity and Representation," first published with the subtitle, "Elements for a Critical Reflexion on the Notion of Region" (1980d); "Social Space and the Genesis of 'Classes'" (1984), translated into English a year later under the broader title, "Social Space and the Genesis of Groups"; and "The Family as Realized Category" (1993). The arguments in these articles are amplified in *Méditations pascaliennes*, especially chapter 5, "Symbolic Violence and Political Struggles."

This model applies to any principle of social vision and division: one can readily substitute "race" for "region," "classes," and "family" to obtain an agonistic theory of race-making.[251]

Figure 7 condenses my interpretation of these three texts (and other relevant writings of Bourdieu where needed). The transmutation starts with (i) a labor of symbolic and material construction that (ii) *sediments* cognitive categories into the socialized body in the form of habitus (classification) and (iii) *inscribes* them into social space or fields, in the form of a corresponding distribution of capital (stratification). The gestation of the group hinges (iv) on the degree of agreement between body and world, dispositions and positions, habitus and social space. When these *two modalities of historical action concord*,[252] (v) a social aggregate coalesces, which can be transformed via classification struggles into a collective recognized by the state, officially or not, endowed with shared interests, animated by similar sentiments, and guided by a unifying world vision. In its most accomplished form, this collective acquires a publicly recognized name (better yet, births an endonym: working class, LGBTQ, Sardus, Kanak); it selects emblems of membership (flag, insignia, dress, hairdo); and it develops organizations that strive to gain material goods (in the order of distribution) and symbolic credit (in the order of recognition). These organizations, parties, leagues, trade unions, associations, lodges, etc., claim to represent the group through a process of delegation whereby the delegate makes the group exist publicly by speaking in its name and, to a degree, in its stead (according to the built-in antinomy of delegation between representation and usurpation).[253]

In this fashion, "an arbitrary social construction seems to belong on the side of the natural and the universal."[254] The collective appears to insiders as well as outsiders as rooted in the order of things, *cum fundamento in rei*. Bourdieu elaborates: "Such is the specific ontology

---

[251] Indeed, Bourdieu himself repeatedly pairs region and ethnicity in "Identité et représentation." In this essay, Bourdieu is evidently inspired by his own outsider ethnic status, as a son of rural Béarn in the mountains of Southwestern France who had to battle to lose his heavy regional accent and surmount the initial Parisian scorn of his mates at the École normale supérieure.

[252] On the dynamics of this correspondence wherethrough "history speaks with itself" and produces fluid action, see Pierre Bourdieu, "Le mort saisit le vif. Les relations entre l'histoire incorporée et l'histoire réifiée" (1980c); and idem, *Le Sens pratique*, chapter 3, and *Méditations pascaliennes*, pp. 162–4, 175–93.

[253] Pierre Bourdieu, "La délégation et le fétichisme politique" (1984b).

[254] Bourdieu, "La famille comme catégorie réalisée," p. 139.

HABITUS
(dispositions)

SOCIAL SPACE
(positions)

STATE

group as historical actor

} name
emblems
organization

classification struggles

agreement

sedimentation

inscription

labor of symbolic construction

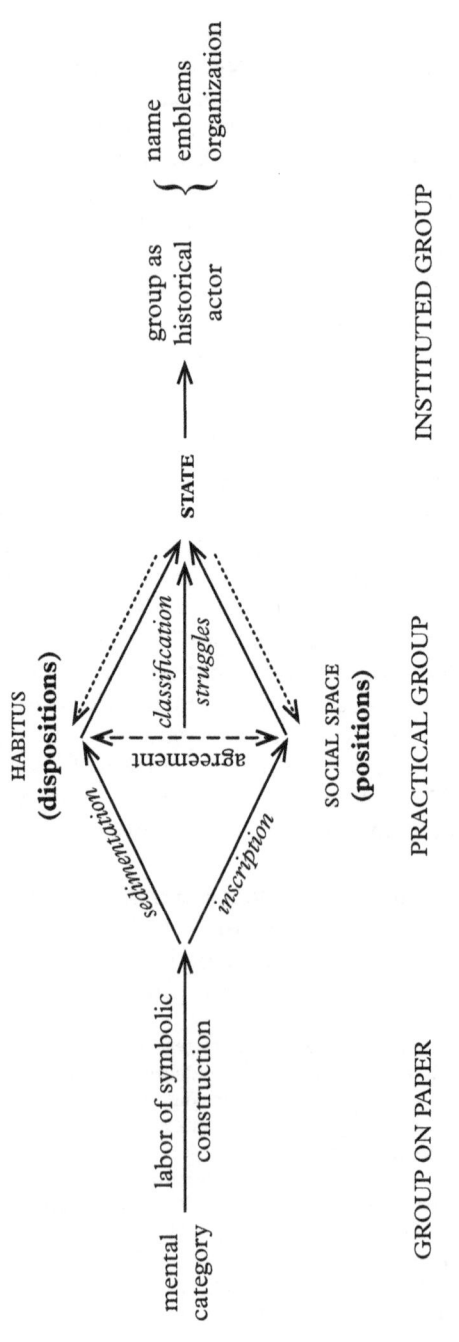

mental category

GROUP ON PAPER   PRACTICAL GROUP   INSTITUTED GROUP

Figure 7 The social fabrication of groups.

of social groups (families, ethnicities or nations): inscribed at once in the objectivity of social structures and in the subjectivity of objectively orchestrated mental structures, they present themselves to experience with the opacity and resistance of things, although they are the product of acts of construction which, as certain ethnomethodological critique suggests, seemingly relegates them to the inexistence of pure figments of thought."[255] When habitus, social space, and classification struggles converge, *groups happen*.

So much to say that *groupness varies in degree as well as fluctuates in time* depending on the success and durability of this work of fabrication.[256] A category can lay dormant and become activated by conjunctural factors or by the actions of symbolic entrepreneurs: think of defensive class mobilization to fight a factory closure, reactive ethnicity in response to ethnoreligious restrictions, or the constitution of a hardened ethnonational bloc as a result of the electoral campaign of a xenophobic party.[257] It can erupt into existence by surprise, roil the political and journalistic fields, and vanish almost as quickly, as with the evanescent fate of France's "Yellow Vests," who were in turn energized and undermined by their defiance of official institutions.[258] It can expand its scope demographically and increase its weight politically even as it becomes more amorphous by attracting would-be members eager to cash in on the new profits of affiliation, as with the stupendous growth of the officially recorded American Indian population in the wake of the rise of Red Power in the 1970s and the correlative

---

[255] Ibid., p. 138. This is my translation of the version of "Family as Realized Category" reprinted in revised form in Bourdieu's *Practical Reason* (1994), which, crucially for our purpose here, adds "(families, ethnicities or nations)" to this passage.

[256] Rogers Brubaker puts it well when he argues, from a germane neo-Bourdieusian position, that "'groupness' is a variable, not a constant; it cannot be presupposed. It varies not only across putative groups, but within them. It may wax and wane over time, peaking during exceptional – but unsustainable – moments of collective effervescence" (*Ethnicity Without Groups* [2004], p. 4). See the parallel discussion of the differences and transitions between "collections," "nominal groups," and "collective entities" by Magali Bessone and Philippe Uirfalino, "Entités collectives et groupes nominaux" (2017), and the articles in the same issue of *Raisons pratiques* (no. 66).

[257] Rick Fantasia, *Cultures of Solidarity: Consciousness, Action, and Contemporary American Workers* (1989); Jan Doering and Efe Peker, "How Muslims Respond to Secularist Restrictions: Reactive Ethnicity, Adjustment, and Acceptance" (2022); John E. Roemer et al., *Racism, Xenophobia, and Distribution: Multi-issue Politics in Advanced Democracies* (2007).

[258] Christian Le Bart, *Petite sociologie des Gilets jaunes. La contestation en mode post-institutionnel* (2020).

increase in the material and symbolic rewards of membership.[259] An established collective may go into a involutive phase due to changes in stratification (as when deindustrialization and the generalization of secondary schooling undermine the unity of the Fordist working class and its capacity for collective action)[260] or changes in classification (as when a new symbolic frame devalorizes class, preempts ethnicity, or alters the existing ethnic grid): the demotion of Canada's *métis* from hybrid middle-minority located between white and Indian to lower caste at the bottom of the ethnoracial order is a case in point.[261]

One institution plays a central role in group-making insofar as its input enters at multiple stages in the process (but to make the figure legible I have plugged it in only as the site and target of classification struggles): the *state as the "central bank of symbolic capital,"* in Bourdieu's compact expression.[262] The state is the agency that inculcates categories (through education and the law), officializes identities (with its nomenclatures, credentials, and ceremonies), validates collective claims (by distributing or denying public goods such as prebends, jobs, educational access, and fiscal privileges), and sets the broader parameters of classification struggles aiming to conserve or subvert the symbolic order. It also shapes the makeup and facilitates the mapping of social space onto physical space, thus hard-wiring categorical divisions into the built environment (as with ethnically segregated neighborhoods, camps, and reservations).[263] Indeed the projection of symbolic space onto physical space is an underestimated source of the formation, endurance, and naturalization of groups.

The state as holder of "the power of official naming" lends its authority to certain constructions as against others and thus decisively orients the process of group-making and unmaking.[264] This was the case in

---

[259] Joane Nagel, *American Indian Ethnic Renewal: Red Power and the Resurgence of Identity and Culture* (1996).

[260] Stéphane Beaud and Michel Pialoux, *Retour sur la classe ouvrière. Enquête aux usines Peugeot de Sochaux-Montbéliard* (1999).

[261] Chris Andersen, *Métis: Race, Recognition, and the Struggle for Indigenous Peoplehood* (2014). The erasure of the mulattoes from the social and symbolic scene of the United States via their merging with Negroes in the early twentieth century is another example of dissolution, as shown by Joel Williamson, *New People: Miscegenation and Mulattoes in the United States* (1980).

[262] Pierre Bourdieu, "Esprit d'État," p. 122, and idem, *Sur l'État*, pp. 196 and 342.

[263] Wacquant, *Bourdieu in the City*, pp. 6–11.

[264] "All the symbolic strategies through which agents aim to impose their vision of the divisions of the social world and of their position within it, may be located between two extremes: the insult, an *idios logos* with which a single individual tries to impose his

Elementary Forms of Ethnoracial Rule

China in 1949 when the new communist regime banished reference to race, denounced as a tool of Western imperialism, and implemented policies fostering class as the paramount principle of social and political organization, even as it officially recognized 41 so-called "minority nationalities" targeted for merging into the Han majority.[265] The state may also inadvertently foster or undermine group-making due to the unintended consequences of its group-specific policies. This was the case in the Netherlands in the 2000s when redistributive measures toward ethnic migrants intended to foster their civic integration ended up promoting ethnic fragmentation instead because of a hiatus in the logics of categorization between policy-making at the national level and policy implementation at the city level.[266] The Soviet institutionalization of national minorities during the interwar period is a textbook example of the rich ironies of state-led ethnic formation. The Soviet state deployed extensive measures of "affirmative action" toward the myriad nationalities of the former Russian empire, sponsoring their languages, cultures, and elites, in an effort to secure its territorial integrity. But the ensuing proliferation of ethnic groups led to a powerful backlash from the Russians and internal dissension within the party that eventually pushed it to pivot toward a policy of intensive "Russification" backed by terror reestablishing Russian supremacy over the union – the very result the Soviet leaders had sought to obviate.[267]

The synoptic diagram of the fabrication of social groups, articulated by the triptych category–practical group–instituted group, presents another limitation that should be spotlighted and corrected textually: it artificially "freezes" a set of *ongoing dynamic* activities into a synchronic snapshot and it presents as linear a process that is *circular and iterative*.[268] Thus emergent social collectives continually engage in the

point of view while taking the risk of reciprocity, and *official nomination*, an act of symbolic imposition which has behind it all the strength of the collective, the consensus, the common sense, because it is performed by a delegated agent of the state as holder of the *monopoly of legitimate symbolic violence*" (Bourdieu, "Espace social et genèse des 'classes'," p. 307, original italics).

[265] Frank Dikötter, "Race in China" (2001), p. 504. See also Xiaowei Zang, *Ethnicity in China: A Critical Introduction* (2015), pp. 11–18.

[266] Frank De Zwart and Caelesta Poppelaars, "Redistribution and Ethnic Diversity in the Netherlands: Accommodation, Denial and Replacement" (2007).

[267] Terry Martin, *The Affirmative Action Empire: Nations and Nationalism in the Soviet Union, 1923–1939* (2001).

[268] In that regard, it is compatible with Hacking's "dynamic nominalism," to which it adds a structural mooring by means of the concept of social space. Ian Hacking, "Making Up People" (1985), pp. 228–9.

labor of symbolic construction, to maintain or increase their groupness, and fully formed groups deploy their power of mobilization to shape both social space and habitus and to press the state (through demonstrations, elections, lobbying, and other means of influence) to their advantage. The stake of classification struggles waged by social collectives and their representatives could not be higher: they are life and death symbolic battles for acceding to public existence and reap the attendant material perks and symbolic proceeds. A good example is the fight by the Indisch, Eurasians "repatriated" from Indonesia to the Netherlands, to be recognized by the Dutch authorities and citizenry as a distinct collective one half-century after the ending of the colony in 1949. It took the form of the publication of press articles and popular books broadcasting and valorizing Indisch identity (as expressed in food, music, family forms, religion, and attitudes toward elders and authority); lobbying for an official history of the group commissioned by the government; and a push by a union of Indisch organizations to be incorporated into minority politics and policy. This success fostered the "coming out" of hitherto assimilated Indisch people which in turn reinforced group coalescence.[269]

Negative cases, where putative leaders fail to mobilize the collective in whose name they claim to speak, are particularly valuable for theorizing group-making, as shown by Brubaker in his analysis of the disconnect between the invocation of Hungarian ethnicity in the political field in the Romanian city of Cluj and the indifference of ethnic Hungarians to this brand of politics and to the nationalist claims made in their name. The result is low levels of groupness with minor fluctuations around specific events such that "groups fail to happen and to crystallize."[270] Another negative case is the inability of the Conseil Représentatif des Associations Noires (CRAN, created in 2005 with the support of a network of established French intellectuals and politicians) to generate identification and support from the black French people it is supposed to represent. Despite its proven aptitude to push its agenda in the journalistic field, it has failed to foster a unified "black consciousness" (it is opposed by associations of French blacks issued from the country's overseas dominions, who reacted by founding a rival council, the CREFOM) and so

---

[269] Vincent J. H. Houben, "Boundaries of Race: Representations of Indisch in Colonial Indonesia Revisited" (2008).
[270] Brubaker, "Ethnicity Without Groups," p. 182, and *Nationalist Politics and Everyday Ethnicity in a Transylvanian Town*, passim.

the thorny question of its representativity continues to sap its credibility.[271] As a result, the council has been riven by internal conflict and personal squabbles that have eroded its capacity to foster "groupness from above." French blacks thus remain caught in that liminal zone between a group on paper and a practical group.

Group hysteresis, denigration, and disgrace

So much to say that *groups wax and wane*, so to speak, but not just as they please, not overnight, and not without the expenditure of considerable material and symbolic capital, by their members, the delegates who represent them (in the triple sense of psychology, dramaturgy, and politics), and other protagonists in the battles over group-making taking place simultaneously in the political field, the bureaucratic field, and the field of power as well as in everyday life.[272] It is essential here to *balance the constructivist with the structuralist moment*: groups are an ongoing social performance, granted, *but* these performances are heavily scripted, the roles preestablished (by social positions) and the talent hard-wired (by dispositions), and take place on a stage where the props and the audience (including the state) are very real, their appreciation continual and consequential, and their support critical to the success of the show.

We must be careful, then, not to exaggerate the fluidity and evanescence of groups: once they are embodied and institutionalized, existential and organizational interests become attached to their actuality. *Group hysteresis* sets in and fosters the tendency of minimally cohesive or symbolically attractive collectives to endure.[273] The institution of social collectives creates a social and symbolic demand for groupness that wires these collectives, not only into the collective psychology of their members, but also in the objectivity of social space (the distribution of capital in its different forms) and physical space (the built environment). This explains why state projects of top-down "degrouping," for instance, often fail unless they resort to the physical displacement or outright elimination of the target category,

---

[271] Yoann Lopez, *Les Questions noires en France. Revendications collectives contre perceptions individuelles* (2010); Samuel Ghiles-Meilhac, "Qui parle pour les Noirs de France?" (2016).

[272] Loïc Wacquant (ed.), *Pierre Bourdieu and Democratic Politics* (2005a), chapter 1.

[273] Here I diverge from Brubaker who stresses the "agentic" side of "groupness as event." Brubaker, "Ethnicity Without Groups," p. 168.

as with the Kulaks in the interwar Soviet Union, Palestinians at the founding of Israel, and the Bosnian Muslims and Croats at the hands of the Serbs in the Balkans circa 1990. It also explains the passive resistance that existing groups, practical or instituted, oppose to projects of revolutionary transformation by their very existence.[274]

In keeping with this radically historicist social ontology, the analytic framework sketched in this chapter sets for the agonistic sociology of racial domination the central task of uncovering how a system of ethnoracial *classification* – a taxonomy trading on the overt or covert correspondence between social and natural orderings – is created and inculcated, deposited in the socialized body in the form of an ethnically inflected habitus, and mapped onto a system of ethnoracial *stratification* through the differential distribution of material and symbolic goods, privileges and penalties, profits and perils, across social and physical space, and how stratification, in return, shapes the symbolic struggles that historically produce, reproduce, or transform the operative classification system.

Classification comprises the politically informed and bureaucratically inscribed taxonomies of the state and the everyday modes of sorting people deployed by ordinary people in the course of their daily round and during moments of collective action and emotion, both of which are multilayered, variably incongruent, and differentially malleable and manipulable.[275] Stratification refers to the macro-allocations of resources and rewards underlying the structure of social space as well as to the micro-allocations shaping face-to-face interactions, including acknowledgment, respect, and deference, or the denial thereof. At the analytic intersection of classification and stratification, we find the state as paramount symbolic agency that inculcates categories, validates identities, and distributes essential public goods, chief among them public recognition and dignity – which is another name for honor.

The *creation, crystallization, and recursive conversion of classification into stratification and vice versa* constitute the core problematic suited for reformulating the sociology of race-making as a particular modality of group-making without falling into the twin traps of

---

[274] "Because what has been, history, is inscribed in both things and bodies, each day that a power endures brings about a rise in the proportion of the irreversible encountered by those who want to overturn it." Bourdieu, "Le mort saisit le vif," p. 14.

[275] On the historical manipulation, rationalizations, and consequences of legal and ordinary ethnoracial labels, and the social dissensus they generate and thrive on, read Domínguez, *White by Definition*, esp. pp. 262–77.

Elementary Forms of Ethnoracial Rule

"groupism" and "race-centrism." This approach avoids Brubakerian *groupism* by shunning the tacit postulation that ethnoracial categories are already preconstituted, clearly bounded, internally homogeneous and necessarily cohesive,[276] and so it remains alert to categorical heterogeneity, porosity, and contestation as well as to horizontal forms of racialization. This approach avoids Wimmerian *race-centrism* by dropping the principled presumption, constitutive of a separate field of "ethnic and racial studies," that race trumps other principles of social vision and division,[277] making the relative priority, salience, and consequentiality of race and other bases of identity, strategy, and structure a matter of historical investigation and sectoral variation, rather than axiomatic affirmation and presumed suffusion. It amplifies these two decisive analytic moves by mating them with the distinctively Bourdieusian principle of *agonism*, the notion that "struggle is thus at the very basis of the construction of the class (social, ethnic, sexual, etc.): every group is the site of a struggle for the imposition of the legitimate principle of construction of groups."[278]

Now that I have recapitulated the steps and disclosed the mechanisms involved in the formation of groups in general, I can attend to the specificities of the creation of *properly racial* groups. Max Weber stresses that "the sense of ethnic honor is a specific honor of the masses (*Massenehre*), for it is accessible to anybody who belongs to the subjectively believed community of descent."[279] Racialization entails the diminishment, denial or stripping of such honor and the wholesale denigration and inferiorizing of the target population. It follows that it spawns a *negative category*, a poisoned and poisonous group which, in its most aggravated form, generates scorn, resentment, and fear among the dominant (and other subaltern populations), and commands distancing in symbolic, social, and physical space, especially spaces of intimacy that entail bodily contact or

---

[276] See Brubaker, "Ethnicity Without Groups," for an implacable critique of groupism.

[277] The definitive dismantling of US-based race-centric approaches is Andreas Wimmer, "Race-Centrism: A Critique and a Research Agenda" (2015).

[278] Pierre Bourdieu, "Décrire et prescrire. Note sur les conditions de possibilité et les limites de l'efficacité politique" (1981), p. 191.

[279] Max Weber, *Economy and Society: An Outline of Interpretive Sociology* (1978 [1818–1922]), p. 391. Weber gives as illustration the case of the "poor whites" in the postbellum South of the United States whose "social honor was dependent upon the social *déclassement* of the Negroes."

sexual congress guaranteed to cause *group pollution*.[280] The ethnic dishonor of race strikes and devalues all of the members of the category – this is why the subordinate racialized group is perceived by the dominant as homogeneous. This is why its own members often perceive it as devalued and devaluing, as evidenced by the widespread practice of intra- and inter-generational passing in the case of ethnoracial categories with porous boundaries or symbolic distancing from within in the case of rigid group membranes.[281] This is also why, *a contrario*, stigmatized ethnicities valorize cultural production – music, dance, literature, theater – aimed at showcasing the group's dignity and achievements.[282]

This takes us to the thorny question, raised frontally by the political philosopher Magali Bessone, of the special ontological status of "races." Bessone first shows convincingly that the latter can be construed as "real kinds" rather than "nominal kinds" (in the language of John Stuart Mill), but *socially constructed real kinds* as opposed to natural real kinds. She then contends that "racialized groups are *social groups* in a robust and dynamic sense" – again, not just nominal entities – because their members "share specific negative experiences" of oppression.[283] She seeks to demonstrate this by opposing the cohesiveness of the putative racial group to the dispersed figure of the Sartrian "series" (an inert gathering of people devoid of joint life experiences and purposes, such as passengers waiting in line at a bus stop). There is a definite theoretical romanticism in assuming that shared treatment automatically begets shared aspirations, social amalgamation, and a capacity for collective action animated by "a political project of emancipation."[284]

First of all, common position and treatment based on other principles of social vision and division, say class or gender, have hardly

---

[280] Douglas, *Purity and Danger*. For Hacking, pollution rules are at the foundation of racial categorization, along with empire. Ian Hacking, "Why Race Still Matters" (2005).

[281] A profusion of examples of rules for climbing up the "chromatic ladder" from the Spanish, Portuguese, and English slave colonies is Jean-Frédéric Schaub and Silvia Sebastiani, *Race et histoire dans les sociétés occidentales (XVe–XVIIIe siècles)* (2021), pp. 285–97.

[282] See Wacquant, *The Two Faces of the Ghetto*, chapter 2, on the cases of Jews in Renaissance Europe and African Americans in the Fordist United States.

[283] Magali Bessone, "Quel genre de groupe sont les races? Naturalisme, constructivisme et justice sociale" (2017), p. 135. See also idem, *Sans distinction de race? Une analyse critique du concept de race et de ses effets pratiques* (2013).

[284] Bessone, "Quel genre de groupe sont les races?," p. 141.

Elementary Forms of Ethnoracial Rule

sufficed historically to yield robust groups – think of Marx's famous quip about the French peasantry being akin to a "sack of potatoes" or the serial dispersion and political isolation of women prior to the feminist revolution. Next, race is a stigmatic category and we know from Erving Goffman that categories burdened with a spoiled identity do not necessarily engage in "in-group alignment"; they also frequently seek individual accommodation with the world of the "normals," whether by concealment, passing, or the segregation of social circles.[285] Lastly, members of an incipient social group that is negatively typed can seize on secondary properties (class, color, region, migration, language, etc.) to distinguish themselves from that very group, rather than merge within it, as shown by the deadly cleavage between Hutus and Tutsis in postcolonial Rwanda and by the strategies of ethnic distancing of Caribbean blacks from African Americans in the United States.[286]

Bessone commits the scholastic fallacy which consists in presupposing that one can resolve in theory what can only be resolved in historical reality: that race will have existential, structural, and symbolic potency and even primacy over other principles of group-making. Comparative history is replete with instances showing that racialized populations can plainly remain *stuck in ontological liminality*, mired somewhere between the mere mental category on paper of the social scientist and the full-fledged, instituted group mobilized as such in the political field. This is indeed the distinct historical burden that these populations have to lift in order to open up pathways toward public recognition and social justice.

---

[285] Erving Goffman, *Stigma: Notes on the Management of Spoiled Identity* (1963).
[286] Mahmood Mamdani, *When Victims Become Killers: Colonialism, Nativism, and the Genocide in Rwanda* (2001); Mary C. Waters, *Black Identities: West Indian Immigrant Dreams and American Realities* (2009).

3

Jim Crow as Caste Terrorism

> The little Negro . . . began to choke on the blood in his mouth. And the roar of their voices and the scuff of their feet were split by the moonlight into a thousand notes like a Beethoven sonata. And when the white folks left his brown body, stark naked, strung from a tree at the edge of town, it hung there all night, like a violin for the wind to play.
>
> Langston Hughes, *The Ways of White Folks*, 1934

The expression Jim Crow comes from the title of a 1832 song and dance, "Jump Jim Crow," performed by the "blackface" artist Thomas Dartmouth "Daddy" Rice (1808–60), who for two decades was the most acclaimed actor of his era in both the United States and England.[1] Along with Jim Dandy and Zip Coon, the farcical Jim Crow became a stock character of minstrel shows mocking the supposed traits of plantation blacks that were widely popular in the nineteenth century. Dressed in patched-up clothes, weaving his hat, he would assume convoluted postures intended to provoke laughter and sing the tale of a slave contented with his condition. Indeed, the term appears for the first time in the *Dictionary of American English* in 1904 as a derogatory synonym for blacks, similar to the epithets "coon" and "darkie".[2] By then it also referred to the separate cars ("Jim-Crow cars") and waiting rooms reserved for colored people

---

[1] W. T. Lahmon, Jr., *Jump Jim Crow: Lost Plays, Lyrics, and Street Prose of the First Atlantic Popular Culture* (2003).

[2] Catherine Lewis and J. Richard Lewis (eds.), *Jim Crow America: A Documentary History* (2009), p. xi.

that southern railroad companies started to run in the 1880s and, by extension, to the series of legal and social devices intended to exploit, subordinate, and exclude blacks hardening across the former confederate states in reaction to African-American claims to citizenship a quarter-century after abolition.

In 1955, the historian C. Vann Woodward published his classic study, *The Strange Career of Jim Crow*, that cemented the term as academic short-hand for the virulent vertical patterning of race relations in the US South between the 1890s and the 1950s based on legally prescribed "racial ostracism" extending across the gamut of public conveyances and private institutions.[3] What became known as "the Woodward thesis" states that this regime was not a direct extension of slavery but, rather, that it had arisen only in the late nineteenth century after a fluid racial interregnum, an "era of experimentation and variety in race relations" during which African Americans had enjoyed a range of economic, social, and even political opportunities. This thesis has been debated ever since by historians.[4] Nowadays, the expression Jim Crow is commonly invoked in both scholarly and public debate as an elastic eponym for racial segregation, oppression, and injustice more generally. And it has become increasingly popular of late: Google Books NGram viewer records a stupendous twentyfold jump in the frequency of the term since 2000 after flatlining during the previous two decades. One of the most widely read activist books of the past decade in the United States features it for dramatic effect in its title: *The New Jim Crow: Mass Incarceration in the Age of Colorblindness*.[5]

---

[3] C. Vann Woodward, *The Strange Career of Jim Crow* (2001 [1957]).
[4] Howard N. Rabinowitz, "More than the Woodward Thesis: Assessing the Strange Career of Jim Crow" (1988). On the waves of scholarship responding to Woodward, see James Beeby and Donald G. Nieman, "The Rise of Jim Crow, 1880–1920" (2002), and Raymond Gavins, "Literature on Jim Crow" (2004). For the broader picture, consult Blair Kelley and Claudrena Harold, "The Historiography of the Black South from Reconstruction to Jim Crow" (2020). An engrossing account of the development and impact of Woodward's work in biographical and social perspective is James Cobb, *C. Vann Woodward: America's Historian* (2022).
[5] Michelle Alexander, *The New Jim Crow: Mass Incarceration in the Age of Colorblindness* (2010). I return to this book and the reasons for its success in chapter 4, *infra*, pp. 281–6.

> ### Lyrics of "Jump Jim Crow" by
> ### Thomas Dartmouth Rice (c. 1830s)*
>
> Come listen all you galls and boys I's jist from Tuckyhoe,
> I'm going to sing a little song, my name's Jim Crow,
> Weel about and turn about and do jis so,
> Eb'ry time I weel about and jump Jim Crow.
>
> Oh I'm a roarer on de fiddle, and down in old Virginny,
> They say I play de skyentific like Massa Pagannini.
> Weel about and turn about and do jis so,
> Eb'ry time I weel about and jump Jim Crow.
>
> I went down to de riber, I didn't mean to stay,
> But dere I see so many galls, I couldn't get away.
> Weel about and turn about and do jis so,
> Eb'ry time I weel about and jump Jim Crow.
>
> I git upon a flat boat, I cotch de uncle Sam,
> But I went to see de place where de kill'd Packenham.
> Weel about and turn about and do jis so,
> Eb'ry time I weel about and jump Jim Crow.
>
> And den I do to Orleans and feel so full of fight,
> Dey put me in de Calaboose and keep me dare all night.
> Weel about and turn about and do jis so,
> Eb'ry time I weel about and jump Jim Crow.
>
> * Cited in Nikki Brown and Barry M. Stentiford, *The Jim Crow Encyclopedia* (2008), p. 418.

From song and dance to doxic notion to analytic concept

Jim Crow is a *folk concept issued from the very phenomenon it is supposed to capture*. Historians have used it widely as a descriptive designator of an era (the "era of segregation," bound by two US Supreme Court decisions endorsing and then invalidating legal separation, *Plessy v. Ferguson* in 1896 and *Brown v. Board of Education* in 1954), a political region and its distinctive culture, a historical mentality supportive of rigid racial rule, and a nexus of institutions enforcing white supremacy. But this use has been equally vague, loose, and shifting to the

Jim Crow as Caste Terrorism

point of bordering on incoherence. Thus, in a long introduction to her excellent selection of texts and documents on *The Age of Jim Crow*, Jane Dailey characterizes the phenomenon in turn narrowly as "a body of law that enforced inequality and discrimination" and expansively as "the interwoven legal and economic system, political regimen, and variegated social and political worlds" that were "anchored in the antebellum period but continue to structure American society," and then again at ground level as "a way of life, a culture, a code of everyday behavior, a mode of experience, a set of mind for whites as well as blacks."[6]

In a rich and thorough survey of the recent historiographic literature on "Daily Life in the Jim Crow South, 1900–1945," Jennifer Ritterhouse stresses that "separation, whether by law or custom, was one of multiple tools whites used to subordinate and exclude blacks and to maintain notions of white racial purity" in a "complex multiracial world." She reviews the racial patterning of face-to-face interaction, space, work, consumption, and institution-building characteristic of the region during that half-century, but she never stops to analytically delineate the core constituents of Jim Crow, noting instead that it "was an inconsistent and uneven system of racial distinction and separation."[7] But distinction and separation are overly vague terms, and even the most rigid regimes of ethnoracial domination – one thinks here of Nazi Germany and South African apartheid – are inconsistent and uneven due to the internal differentiation of racial states, the strategies of evasion and resistance of target categories, and the complexities of group-making in social, physical, and geographical space.[8]

Similarly, none of the new-generation historians contributing to a state-of-the-art volume on *The Folly of Jim Crow* takes the trouble to articulate what they mean by the term and what institutions carried out the work of race-making during that period. The notion is glossed as legal segregation, "state-mandated constraints on the private and public lives of its citizenry, including even intimate matters such as marriage," and as "the most intrusive and pervasive social engineering ever undertaken on American soil" to maintain "the systematic

---

[6] Jane Dailey (ed.), *The Age of Jim Crow: A Norton Casebook in History* (2009), pp. xi–xiii.
[7] Jennifer Ritterhouse, "Daily Life in the Jim Crow South, 1900–1945" (2018).
[8] Devin Owen Pendas et al. (eds.), *Beyond the Racial State: Rethinking Nazi Germany* (2017); Nigel Worden, *The Making of Modern South Africa: Conquest, Apartheid, Democracy* (2011).

subordination of blacks." Then follows a list comprising "political chicanery, economic coercion, and outright violence," a list which none of the authors in the book quite follows, and by default the core meaning of the term emerges as *de jure* segregation designed by whites to avoid contamination and retardation by an inferior race.[9]

A quick survey of recent noted monographs similarly reveals that disagreements persist as to whether white supremacy à la Jim Crow is a structure rooted in custom or in law; residing primarily in formal institutions of bureaucratic rule or in informal patterns of everyday intercourse; specific to the South or national in scope; applying uniquely to black Americans or bearing onto other dishonored categories; coterminous with "racism" after slavery or designating a narrower epoch; and dead and gone as opposed to surviving in modified form into the present.[10] More troubling still, the roster of institutions or concatenation of social mechanisms that constitutes the *differentia specifica* of this regime of racial rule is generally left unspecified: the enumeration varies not only across authors but very often inside the same text.

So much to say that, while they have written entire libraries of remarkable books on "Jim Crow," American historians have not produced a stable and *robust analytic concept* of the same – which is not surprising, for to do so would expose them to being criticized by colleagues for being sociologists.[11] As for sociologists, they have borrowed the term from historians without elaboration in spite of its fuzziness and lability. The only frontal call to articulate a clear-cut notion is a short and completely unknown 1948 article by the NAACP soci-

---

[9] W. Fitzhugh Brundage, "Introduction," in Stefanie Cole and Natalie J. Ring (eds.), *The Folly of Jim Crow: Rethinking the Segregated South* (2012), p. 2. A similar conceptual confusion mars Anders Walker's "New Takes on Jim Crow: A Review of Recent Scholarship" (2018).

[10] The literature and documentation on Jim Crow are immense and immensely variegated, cutting across history, law, ethnic studies, memoirs, and film documentary, and spilling over from the academic to the popular and the activist register. I limit my references to select key scholarly monographs in the interest of brevity and clarity. I especially mine the classic field studies carried out by anthropologists (Dollard, Powdermaker, and Davis and the Gardners) in the interwar years. A popular rendering is the widely viewed and praised PBS television series produced by Richard Wormser, *The Rise and Fall of Jim Crow* (2003), which is available on YouTube.

[11] The empirical confusion and historical conflation caused by the analytic underspecification of "Jim Crow" is in full evidence in the stimulative collection assembled by Matthew D. Lassiter and Joseph Crespino (eds.), *The Myth of Southern Exceptionalism* (2009).

ologist and lawyer Hugh Smythe, arguing for incorporating "The Concept 'Jim Crow'" into the sociological canon.[12] Smythe reports that Jim Crow is "accepted as part of standard American English" in the sociology of ethnic groups and stratification, in scholarship across the social sciences and humanities, legal debates, and national newspapers. But he, too, does not tell us what it is and his call has gone unheeded. More recently, sociologists who have invoked Jim Crow to characterize patterns of racial inequality have taken its meaning for granted and tacitly equated it narrowly with legal discrimination and segregation.[13]

Can one forge a clear and coherent yet flexible model of "Jim Crow" that bounds and sets out a *distinctive regime of racial domination*, and can then serve as baseline for historical comparison and theoretical elaboration? This chapter follows the principle of *analytical disaggregation* proposed in chapter 2 (see *supra*, pp. 112–13, 154–6) to formulate just such an ideal-typical characterization, based on three preliminary points. First, with Max Weber, we must recall that an *Idealtypus* is not an empirical picture claiming correspondence with reality but an abstract mental image (*Gedankenbild*) "formed by the one-sided *accentuation* of one or more points of view" according to which "*concrete individual phenomena*" are "arranged into a unified analytical construct." An ideal type is a deliberately crafted methodological "utopia [that] cannot be found empirically anywhere in reality" but helps us in ordering and parsing that reality based on "unambiguous meaning."[14] It serves to guide inquiry, formulate hypotheses and develop theory.

Second, although it is often pictured as monolithic, the phenomenon of interest displays wide variations across time and space, and so the concept should help us grasp these variations. Jim Crow is not identical in the period of its initial establishment (the turn into the twentieth century) as during its hegemonic bloom (the interwar

---

[12] Hugh H. Smythe, "The Concept 'Jim Crow'" (1948). Remarkably, this article has never been cited, except once in passing by a Canadian jurist writing on "driving while black." David M. Tanovich, "Moving Beyond Driving While Black: Race, Suspect Description and Selection" (2004).

[13] Among many instances, see William Julius Wilson, "Class Conflict and Jim Crow Segregation in the Postbellum South" (1976); Steven J. Gold, "From Jim Crow to Racial Hegemony: Evolving Explanations of Racial Hierarchy" (2004); Lawrence D. Bobo, "Somewhere between Jim Crow and Post-Racialism: Reflections on the Racial Divide in America Today" (2011); and Eduardo Bonilla-Silva, "The Structure of Racism in Color-Blind, 'Post-Racial' America" (2015a).

[14] Max Weber, *The Methodology of the Social Sciences* (1949 [1904]), p. 90.

years) and in its phase of open contestation and gradual dissolution (the two decades after World War II).[15] It also presented diverse functional inflections across the dozen former confederate states, with the pole of "civility" represented by Virginia and North Carolina, at one end, and the pole of "brutality" incarnated by Mississippi at the other end, with states such as Florida, Georgia, and Arkansas falling somewhere in the middle of the spectrum; and it did not operate in quite the same ways in the border states as in the Deep South, and especially in cities as in rural areas.[16] Thus, "white elites in Virginia embraced a concept of managed race relations that emphasized a particularly genteel brand of paternalism," under which baseline services were provided to African Americans and a modicum of ethnic uplift was allowed in return for black submission, deference, and the channeling of protests through venues deemed acceptable by whites.[17] That was anathema to white Mississippians, who devoted massive public and private efforts to closing all avenues of black advancement and to maximizing racial marginalization and humiliation on every front while convicting more African Americans for racial transgressions through the courts as well as staging more lynchings than any other state.[18]

Third, the model sketched in this chapter uses the "base-superstructure" imagery only as a convenient expository device and not to make strong claims as to the causal primacy of this or that component of the special system of racial rule developed by the postbellum South of the United States. Indeed, if pressed to make such a claim, I would argue that the epicenter of Jim Crow resides in its *sociosymbolic structure*, that is, the strict and suffusive socioracial

---

[15] Two remarkable studies dissect this dissolution: Jason Sokol, *There Goes My Everything: White Southerners in the Age of Civil Rights, 1945–1975* (2008), and Stephen A. Berrey, *The Jim Crow Routine: Everyday Performances of Race, Civil Rights, and Segregation in Mississippi* (2015). A deft analysis of the post-1960s impact of the unmaking of Jim Crow rule is Joseph Crespino, *In Search of Another Country: Mississippi and the Conservative Counterrevolution* (2009).

[16] Compare George C. Wright, *Life Behind a Veil: Blacks in Louisville, Kentucky, 1865–1930* (2004), with Hortense Powdermaker, *After Freedom: A Cultural Study of the Deep South* (1993 [1939]); and for variation across the rural spectrum, Mark Schultz, *The Rural Face of White Supremacy: Beyond Jim Crow* (2005). Jennifer Ritterhouse stresses the distinction between urban and rural areas in "Daily Life in the Jim Crow South, 1900–1945."

[17] J. Douglas Smith, *Managing White Supremacy: Race, Politics, and Citizenship in Jim Crow Virginia* (2002), p. 4.

[18] Neil R. McMillen, *Dark Journey: Black Mississippians in the Age of Jim Crow* (1990).

asymmetry between whites and blacks that proclaims the inferiority and infamy of the latter. For whites, the imperative of maintaining their monopoly over ethnic honor took precedence over the naked pursuit of material interest, as demonstrated by the historical defeat of the Southern Populists at the end of the nineteenth century. W. E. B. Du Bois was right, in *Black Reconstruction*, to highlight the "public and psychological wage" of whiteness for, during the bloom of Jim Crow, the logic of the accumulation of symbolic capital trumped and twisted the valorization of economic capital.[19] At the very least, one must hold together these two dimensions of capital and carry out a materialist analysis of the symbolic economy of ethnoracial division in the spirit of Bourdieu's genetic theory of symbolic power sketched in the book's prolegomena.[20]

The symbolic capital of deference granted*

It must be remembered that the white group of laborers, while they received a low wage, were compensated in part by a sort of public and psychological wage. They were given public deference and titles of courtesy because they were white. They were admitted freely with all classes of white people to public functions, public parks, and the best schools. The police were drawn from their ranks, and the courts, dependent on their votes, treated them with such leniency as to encourage lawlessness. Their vote selected public officials, and while this had small effect upon the economic situation, it had great effect upon their personal treatment and the deference shown them. White schoolhouses were the best in the community, and conspicuously placed, and they cost anywhere from twice to ten times as much per capita as the colored schools. The newspapers specialized on news that flattered the poor whites and almost utterly ignored the Negro except in crime and ridicule.

* W. E. B. Du Bois, *Black Reconstruction, 1860–1880* (2017 [1935]), pp. 700–1.

Based on these analytical principles, I submit that Jim Crow is the ordinary name for an *extraordinary regime of extreme racial rule*, that

---

[19] W. E. B. Du Bois, *Black Reconstruction, 1860–1880* (2017 [1935]). A provocative reinterpretation of this notion is Ella Myers, "Beyond the Psychological Wage: Du Bois on White Dominion" (2019).
[20] Pierre Bourdieu, *Raisons pratiques. Sur la théorie de l'action* (1994), chapters 4 and 5.

is, a coherent, interlocking, and self-reproducing set of institutions designed to effect the *total domination* of a uniformly dishonored descent-based category, namely, African Americans as defined by variants of the "one-drop rule" and tarnished by the historical stigma of slavery.[21] It is composed of four elements: (1) an economic infrastructure of *deep economic dependency via sharecropping morphing into debt peonage*, supporting (2) a core structure of *systematic social bifurcation, extraction of deference, and denial of equality and dignity*; and locked in by (3) a superstructure of *joint political and judicial exclusion* preventing African Americans from resorting to elections and appealing to the courts as means of protection, redress, and institutional change.

But the most distinctive and indispensable constituent of the system was (4) the deployment of the *specter and suffusive reality of private and public violence*, the ever-present possibility of racially motivated assault and assassination for defying the dictates of the three previously mentioned components (exploitation, subordination, and exclusion, the three faces of domination). After retracing the genesis and consolidation of the system of racial classification operative in the postbellum South, I consider each of these four constellations in turn, starting with the economy and moving up through social structure to government to conclude with the special place of terror as an instrument of caste rule.

A final note of caution: this chapter is an exercise in concept formation and clarification based on an inductive reading of ethnographies and historiographies and guided by the theory of racial domination outlined in chapter 2. It is emphatically not a comprehensive account of all the facets of Jim Crow, so-called, nor of its many varieties and variations. In particular, it does not cover three major topics. The first is the role of gender, which runs through the body of Jim Crow domination like a capillary and powers its symbolic core, namely, the intimate *association between race and sex*.[22] It is not happenstance if black men were portrayed as beastly and hypersexual, which mandated segregation, lynching, and disenfranchisement. Also, sharecropping, the economic foundation of Jim Crow, was as much a patriarchal as it was a racial institution; the same is true of the motivations of white terrorist groups such as the Klu Klux Klan. But to tackle the

---

[21] F. James Davis, *Who Is Black? One Nation's Definition* (1991). On the role of stigma in ethnoracial formation more broadly, Glenn C. Loury, *The Anatomy of Racial Inequality* (2021 [2002]), pp. 67–88.

[22] The best demonstration of this association is Ann Laura Stoler, *Carnal Knowledge and Imperial Power: Race and the Intimate in Colonial Rule* (2002).

Jim Crow as Caste Terrorism

gendered dimension of racial rule is simply beyond the scope of this chapter and of my current analytic abilities. I refer the reader to the remarkable body of work produced by historians on the topic and hope that this omission is read as a standing invitation to students of masculine domination to enter the fray.[23]

The second omission is the evolving social structure, strategies, and sensibilities of whites, especially lower-class whites in rural areas who toiled and lived under conditions not unlike those imposed on black tenants, croppers, and laborers, yet profited symbolically from the regime. There is a rich and expansive historical literature on the white South, but it is heavily focused on family, class, labor, culture, and politics, and gives short shrift to *ordinary whites as racial dominators*, aside from their participation in violence and political exclusion.[24] The historiography of Jim Crow *stricto sensu* is thus dangerously

---

[23] See the landmark books by Evelyn Brooks Higginbotham, *Righteous Discontent: The Women's Movement in the Black Baptist Church, 1880–1920* (1994); Glenda Elizabeth Gilmore, *Gender and Jim Crow: Women and the Politics of White Supremacy in North Carolina, 1896–1920* (1996); and Deborah Gray White, *Too Heavy a Load: Black Women in Defense of Themselves, 1894–1994* (1999). Also notable are Jacqueline Jones, *Labor of Love, Labor of Sorrow: Black Women, Work, and the Family, from Slavery to the Present* (1985); Nancy MacLean, *Behind the Mask of Chivalry: The Making of the Second Ku Klux Klan* (1994); Tera W. Hunter, *To "Joy My Freedom": Southern Black Women's Lives and Labors After the Civil War* (1997); Marlon Bryan Ross, *Manning the Race: Reforming Black Men in the Jim Crow Era* (2004); Crystal N. Feimster, *Southern Horrors: Women and the Politics of Rape and Lynching* (2009); Danielle McGuire, *At the Dark End of the Street: Black Women, Rape, and Resistance* (2010); LaKisha Michelle Simmons, *Crescent City Girls: The Lives of Young Black Women in Segregated New Orleans* (2015); Sarah Haley, *No Mercy Here: Gender, Punishment, and the Making of Jim Crow Modernity* (2016); and Elizabeth Gillespie McRae, *Mothers of Massive Resistance: White Women and the Politics of White Supremacy* (2018).

[24] A signal exception is Kirby Moss, *The Color of Class: Poor Whites and the Paradox of Privilege* (2010). See also, obliquely, Jason Morgan Ward, *Defending White Democracy: The Making of a Segregationist Movement and the Remaking of Racial Politics, 1936–1965* (2011); McRae, *Mothers of Massive Resistance* and Jason Sokol's *There Goes My Everything*. Dispersed materials can be found in David Goldfield, *Black, White, and Southern: Race Relations and Southern Culture, 1940 to the Present* (1991); Neil Foley, *The White Scourge: Mexicans, Blacks, and Poor Whites in Texas Cotton Culture* (1998); Charles L. Flynn Jr., *White Land, Black Labor: Caste and Class in Late Nineteenth-century Georgia* (1999); Donald Wayne Walden, *The Southern Peasant: Poor Whites and the Yeoman Ideal* (2000); Wayne Flynt, *Dixie's Forgotten People: The South's Poor Whites* (2004); and Kristina DuRocher, *Raising Racists: The Socialization of White Children in the Jim Crow South* (2011). This relative ignorance partakes of the generalized invisibility of poor whites in American academic, political, and cultural life, with the notable exception of Southern fiction (e.g., Erskine Caldwell, William Faulkner, James Autry), as demonstrated by Nancy Isenberg, *White Trash: The 400-Year Untold History*

unbalanced, tilted toward the experience of African Americans – and toward urban and elite blacks, for that matter. Yet racial domination is a relationship and, to probe its architecture, it is just as crucial to investigate it from the standpoint of the superordinate category.[25] Historians of Jim Crow highlight and commend the "agency" and endurance of African Americans but, with precious few exceptions, ignore the same about poor whites, except under the vague and denigrating term of "mob." This singular focus on the "black side" of ethnoracial oppression due to academic convention, namely, the existence of a distinct specialty in African-American history in the university, represents a methodological regression from the anthropological studies of the caste and class school of the interwar decades, expressly designed to capture that relation from both ends.[26]

The third omission is the variegated strategies and rich phenomenology of black resistance to racial rule in the US South during the period considered, on which there is also a considerable body of rich research.[27] This omission is, first, a question of logical priority:

---

of *Class in America* (2016). For the postwar period, there is, moreover, a distinct tradition in studies of the South which focuses on the folkways of whites as a "quasi-minority" that puts geography above race and minimizes or elides entirely their role as ethnoracial oppressors. See, for instance, John Sheldon Reed, *The Enduring South: Subcultural Persistence in Mass Society* (1986).

[25] Gavins's broad survey of "Literature on Jim Crow" contains not a single reference to a monograph on white Southerners. Beeby and Nieman close their panorama of research on "The Rise of Jim Crow, 1890–1920" (2004) by calling for more studies of white women and middle-class whites (p. 344), typically overlooking lower-class whites.

[26] At the outset of their classic study, Davis et al. stress that "the methodological aim from the beginning was to see every Negro–white relationship from both sides of the society" (Allison Davis et al., *Deep South: A Social Anthropological Study of Caste and Class* (1992 [1941]). A demonstration of the fruitfulness of taking this two-sided, "biracial" perspective is Jennifer Lynn Ritterhouse, *Growing Up Jim Crow: How Black and White Southern Children Learned Race* (2006), and William Sturkey, *Hattiesburg: An American City in Black and White* (2019).

[27] The classic statement on the question remains Robin D. G. Kelley, *Race Rebels: Culture, Politics, and the Black Working Class* (1994). See also Steven Hahn, *A Nation Under Our Feet: Black Political Struggles in the Rural South from Slavery to the Great Migration* (2005); Nan Elizabeth Woodruff, *American Congo: The African American Freedom Struggle in the Delta* (2009); Eric S. Gellman, *Death Blow to Jim Crow: The National Negro Congress and the Rise of Militant Civil Rights* (2012); David Taft Terry, *The Struggle and the Urban South: Confronting Jim Crow in Baltimore before the Movement* (2019); and Mia Bay, *Traveling Black: A Story of Race and Resistance* (2021). A moving account that skillfully melts together biography, memory, and history to capture the vision of Jim Crow percolating down African-American generations is

Jim Crow as Caste Terrorism

we must characterize a regime before we can study active or passive opposition to it. But it is also based on my assessment of the historical record: caste terrorism leaves little institutional room and precious few social options to those it targets, outside of *exit via migration*. And the Great Black Migration eclipsed all other movements of protest against caste rule by its sheer scale and impact until the blossoming of the Civil Rights Movement after the mid-twentieth-century point.[28] There is ample evidence that, despite the extreme (but variable) oppressiveness of Jim Crow, African Americans created a rich life for themselves "behind the veil" (to evoke Du Bois's resonant expression). They remained as fiercely committed to the ideal of equality as Southern whites were to the principle of white supremacy.[29] It remains nonetheless that, under Jim Crow, the symbolic violence of denigration and humiliation joined with the material violence of intimidation and physical assault to *fragilize black social space* and *fashion a precarious habitus*, that is, a set of durable and transposable dispositions stamped by insecurity, anxiety, and a sense of vulnerability that flooded black subjectivity.[30]

Next, the institutions that African Americans built to cope with, and lessen the hold of, Jim Crow arose mostly in cities, whereas the vast majority of blacks resided in dispersed and isolated rural settlements well into the twentieth century. Negro businesses, professionals, fraternal lodges, the black press, colleges, women's clubs, and civic and political organizations were all urban creatures whose activities did not reach far into the hinterland – the church was the major exception as it spanned city, town, and country. They partook of the early formation of the *ghetto, a different vehicle for ethnoracial domination* that developed most fully in the Northern metropolis but

---

Jonathan Scott Holloway, *Jim Crow Wisdom: Memory and Identity in Black America since 1940* (2013).

[28] Carole Marks, *Farewell, We're Good and Gone: The Great Black Migration* (1989); James R. Grossman, *Land of Hope: Chicago, Black Southerners, and the Great Migration* (1989); Kimberley Louise Phillips, *AlabamaNorth: African-American Migrants, Community, and Working-Class Activism in Cleveland, 1915–45* (1999); and Eric Arnesen (ed.), *Black Protest and the Great Migration: A Brief History with Documents* (2003).

[29] Jane Dailey et al. (eds.), *Jumpin' Jim Crow: Southern Politics from Civil War to Civil Rights* (2000); Jason Morgan Ward, *Defending White Democracy: The Making of a Segregationist Movement and the Remaking of Racial Politics, 1936–1965* (2011); Elizabeth Gillespie McRae, *Mothers of Massive Resistance: White Women and the Politics of White Supremacy* (2018).

[30] This is beautifully captured by Richard Wright in his autobiography *Black Boy: A Record of Childhood and Youth* (2020 [1945]).

Racial Domination

hybridized with Jim Crow in the Southern city in the early twentieth century.[31] Moreover, until World War II and the shock, inseparably cognitive and social, it provoked, black institution-building consisted mainly in "improving segregated facilities, trying to make them the equal of their white counterparts"; it was an adaptation and not a challenge to Jim Crow.[32]

This is for a simple reason: in its most accomplished form, say in Mississippi in the 1920s, Jim Crow was a suffocating regime that delivered disaster and death onto those who dared oppose it openly.[33] We must be careful not to let the *academic romance of resistance* get in the way of a cold-blooded assessment of its functioning and ferocity. The celebration of the "agency" of the dominated is morally pleasing, and it has been de rigueur in the historiography of Jim Crow for the past half-century, but it can lead to grievous errors both scientific and political when it results in the gross under-evaluation of the power grip of the dominant.[34]

A final caveat is in order about the analytic concept of "caste terrorism" I forge at the conclusion of this chapter. In activating the notion of caste, I revive a long tradition of use of the term running

---

[31] Loïc Wacquant, *The Two Faces of the Ghetto* (2025).
[32] Leon F. Litwack, "Jim Crow Blues" (2004), p. 10. For a more sanguine assessment, see James R. Grossman, "A Chance to Make Good, 1900–1929" (2000), pp. 365–74.
[33] This is strikingly and inadvertently demonstrated by Neil McMillen's magnificent *Dark Journey*, the single most comprehensive and meticulous case study of Jim Crow from below. McMillen sets out to focus on "the world [former slaves] made in the aftermath of Emancipation"; his explicit "purpose at the outset was to make the black Mississippians the subjects rather than the objects of their own story." But then he ran up against brute historical reality and reports apologetically: "It became increasingly difficult to ignore the obvious fact that African Americans were indeed both objects and subjects; that while they were always actors in their own right, the range of their actions was nevertheless profoundly influenced by white supremacy." ("Influence" is a stunningly mild way to put it.) Thus the need to explore the "exterior forces that operated on the black community" to develop "an adequate history of the interior life of the people within the community" (p. xiii). The entire book demonstrates how locked in black Mississippians were and how little room for self-determination they enjoyed, both individually and collectively, until the floodgates of migration opened. The principled celebration of the subaltern can turn into the absurd as when black female inmates in Southern prisons are portrayed as potent agents of resistance destabilizing racial authority through such practices as "running away," "feigning obsequity," and composing blues music to commit "sonic sabotage" (Sarah Haley, *No Mercy Here: Gender, Punishment, and the Making of Jim Crow Modernity* [2016]).
[34] The opposite perspective is defended and illustrated by Dailey et al., for whom white supremacy is "not an overwhelming force" but "a precarious balancing act." Dailey et al., *Jumpin' Jim Crow: Southern Politics from Civil War to Civil Rights*, p. 4.

from early abolitionists to W. E. B. Du Bois to W. Lloyd Warner and his students to contemporary anthropologists of rigid regimes of ethnic stratification in the East Asian domain. Caste was employed in the interwar years to characterize race relations in the United States; but, in the postwar period, it evaporated from social inquiry into the African-American experience and the "caste and class" school was soon forgotten. An intellectual history of this disappearance remains to be written. But it is likely that caste fell out of favor because it suggests the permanence of subordination, with connotations of structural stasis, cultural immobility, and political acquiescence, and this clashed with the stunning ethnoracial transformation ushered in by the Civil Rights Movement. Whatever the reason, it is clear that caste has become *vocabulum non gratum* in the social sciences while the mystical notion of race has achieved doxic status, thanks to the converging support of such paramount symbolic agencies as the bureaucratic state, the law, social science, journalism, and politics.[35] I retrieve the notion and machine it into a robust ideal-typical construct by identifying its constituents and their articulation.

Similarly, I am not the first to use the term "terrorism" to describe Jim Crow. It was famously invoked by Ida B. Wells in the 1890s in her characterization of lynching as "racial terror" (note: without the -ism) as well as by a long if neglected strand of activist discourse for racial justice.[36] And it is sprinkled throughout the work of historians of the postbellum South. But these diffuse uses are conceptually undeveloped and inchoate. They appeal to the reader's folk notion of terrorism to evoke negative emotions and moral condemnation whereas I propose a compact analytic concept of terrorism by specifying its semantic constituents and boundaries.

The rise and reign of the one-drop rule

As argued in chapter 2, the first step in the sociology of ethnoracial domination, no matter when and where, is always to establish the nomenclature and foundation of the socially pertinent categories: the

---

[35] The anthropologist of India André Béteille noted in 1990 that "any attempt today to bring together race and caste for comparison and contrast is likely to meet with a cold reception" and even invite intellectual "opprobrium" ("Race, Caste and Gender" [1990], p. 489).

[36] Philosopher Verena Erlenbusch-Anderson recovers and dissects these uses in "Historicizing White Supremacist Terrorism with Ida B. Wells" (2022).

classification system that anchors the stratification system and provides a cognitive frame for social action and institutions. The classification system operative in the Southern United States after abolition was a descent-based schema that recognized only two discrete categories, whites and Negroes, homologous to the opposition between free and enslaved, in spite of widespread sexual mixing under bondage as evidenced by the range of hues and phenotypes exhibited by the population deemed black. This system was based on the *strict application of hypodescent* to the descendants of African and creole slaves, and to them alone, meaning that the offspring of mixed parentage are automatically assigned to the lower category, here blacks, regardless of appearance, status, or other ancestry.[37] The "one-drop rule" emerged in the early American colonies of the Upper South to bolster slavery by refraining liaisons and marriages between white indentured women and black slaves or freedmen. In 1662, Virginia passed the first anti-miscegenation law, prohibiting sexual intercourse between the "races" and consigning mulattoes born of such union to bondage as lineage would now pass through the mother (reversing the English tradition). By the early 1700s, the rule had become dominant throughout the Upper South, but other Black Belt states took longer to embrace it.[38]

The reason is that there was a *rival ethnoracial classification schema* in the Lower South, prevalent for instance in South Carolina and Louisiana under the cultural influence of immigrant islanders from the Caribbean, which allowed for fluidity along a gradational ladder based on phenotype. Thus, as late as 1850, the mulattoes of South Carolina were considered a third class between blacks and whites and, as the elite of freeperson communities around Charlestown, received fair treatment. Many of them, artisans and planters in particular, even owned slaves and they aligned with the white gentry in defense

---

[37] David A. Hollinger, "Amalgamation and Hypodescent: The Question of Ethnoracial Mixture in the History of the United States" (2003). As Max Weber notes, "in the United States, the smallest admixture of Negro blood disqualifies a person unconditionally, whereas very considerable admixtures of Indian blood do not. Doubtlessly, it is important that Negroes appear esthetically even more alien than Indians, but it remains very significant that Negroes were slaves and hence disqualified in the status hierarchy. The conventional *connubium* is far less impeded by anthropological differences than by status differences." Max Weber, *Economy and Society: An Outline of Interpretive Sociology* (1978 [1918–1922]), p. 387.

[38] For a fascinating account of the efforts of people of blended descent to escape this rigid classification, see Aaron B. Wilkinson, *Blurring the Lines of Race and Freedom: Mulattoes and Mixed Bloods in English Colonial America* (2020).

of human bondage.[39] Restrictions on sexual congress between whites and slaves were comparatively lax and "known and visible mulattoes could by behavior and reputation be 'white', and people of mixed blood could and did marry into white families" as well as worship in white churches.[40] Correspondingly, South Carolina mulattoes developed a veritable phobia of dark-skinned people, avoided marrying with them, and excluded them from their social circles.

Likewise, in Louisiana, the status of mulattoes derived from Spanish and French Catholic culture and followed the Haitian pattern in which they constituted a separate, intermediate category with fuzzy boundaries. Even though it was legally prohibited since the eighteenth century, miscegenation was both tolerated and facilitated by such institutions as "fancy girls" sold on internal slave markets, the custom of *plaçage*, and "quadroon balls" patronized by wealthy whites.[41] This was reflected by the profusion of ethnoracial categories used to distinguish persons of color of visible mixed descent, "quadroon" and "octoroon" (one-fourth and one-eighth black, respectively), "sambo" and "mango" (three-quarters and seven-eighth black), *sang mêlé* (one sixty-fourth black) as well as "mustee" (mixed black and Native American).[42]

The flexible phenotypical continuum of ethnoracial classification was particularly pronounced in Louisiana and South Carolina, but some racial ambiguity was present in other Southern states as the categorical black–mulatto distinction was salient throughout the nation in both everyday and official representations. Using national census data from 1870 to 1920, sociologists Saperstein and Gullickson

---

[39] Michael P. Johnson and James L. Roark, *Black Masters: A Free Family of Color in the Old South* (1984); Larry Kroger, *Black Slaveowners: Free Black Slave Masters in South Carolina, 1790–1860* (1985).
[40] Joel Williamson, *New People: Miscegenation and Mulattoes in the United States* (1980), p. 19.
[41] Monique Guillory, *Some Enchanted Evening on the Auction Block: The Cultural Legacy of the New Orleans Quadroon Balls* (1999). *Plaçage* refers to a type of socially but not legally sanctioned concubinage, imported from French and Spanish colonial culture, involving a woman of color, enslaved or free, who used her beauty, deportment, and conversational skills to save herself and her progeny from her condition. The laxity of interracial relations in the nineteenth century gave way to intense white anxiety about purity in the twentieth, as shown by Michelle Brattain, "Miscegenation and Competing Definitions of Race in Twentieth-Century Louisiana" (2005). See also Cécile Vidal, *Caribbean New Orleans, Empire, Race, and the Making of a Slave Society* (2019), which documents the blurring of mainland and Caribbean racial cultures.
[42] Williamson, *New People*, p. 24.

document "substantial fluidity" in the categorization of Negroes and mulattoes across time by census takers, with black individuals moving both upward and downward along a color gradient in keeping with their changing occupational status across the decades.[43]

Soon the *classification battle* between the British, Protestant-inspired, dichotomous descent-based system elaborated in the Upper South (and adopted by the North) and the French-Spanish inflected, Catholic, triadic phenotypical system imported from the Caribbean into the Lower South was joined and it was won decisively by the former.[44] Exceptions to the one-drop rule and the buffer status of mulattoes in some areas quickly eroded in the years leading to the Civil War. The specter of abolition and the fear of slave insurrection resulted in growing hostility toward miscegenation, "passing" by blacks, and manumission. Whites turned against mulattoes even in South Carolina and Louisiana where vigilante groups formed to enforce an impassable caste line with the eager backing of Southern white women now openly opposed to mulatto concubinage. Agitation to expel all non-property-holding *métis* led to the spread of the one-drop rule and to the generalization of a twofold racial schema supported by the notions, popular in those days, that persons of mixed racial background were against nature and fated to physical extinction. Mulattoes had little choice but to accept the new principle of ethnoracial division and they began to pull away from whites and to identify with their colored brethren.

The one-drop rule further hardened during the Jim Crow era when animus against miscegenation took on the tenor of collective hysteria. Fueled by white guilt about the visible presence of mixed individuals, vigilante committees and anti-miscegenation leagues organized throughout the South.[45] Fourteen of fifteen Southern states promptly adopted rigid legal statutes that formally defined the racial

---

[43] Aliya Saperstein and Aaron Gullickson, "A 'Mulatto Escape Hatch' in the United States? Examining Evidence of Racial and Social Mobility during the Jim Crow Era" (2013).

[44] Williamson, *New People*, chapter 2; Davis, *Who Is Black?*, pp. 47–50; Arnold R. Hirsch and Joseph Logsdon (eds.), *Creole New Orleans: Race and Americanization* (1992).

[45] On the dynamics of inner guilt and prejudice, see Joel Kovel, *White Racism: A Psychohistory* (1984), pp. 57–9 and 74–5. As Weber noted circa 1917 (*Economy and Society*, p. 386), "sexual relations between the two races are now abhorred by both sides, but this development began only with the Emancipation and resulted from the Negroes' demand for equal civil rights. Hence this abhorrence on the part of the Whites is socially determined by the previously sketched tendency toward the monopolization of social power and honor."

Jim Crow as Caste Terrorism

status of "Negro" on the basis of some variant of the one-drop rule. In Florida, the state constitution set the quotient of black blood at one-sixteenth; in Maryland and Mississippi, it was one-eighth; in Kentucky, any "appreciable amount" of black blood rendered one black; in Arkansas, Negro was made to apply to "any person who has in his or her veins any Negro blood whatever," while in Alabama, the law specified that mulattoes were categorized under Negro.[46] In court testimony, physical appearance was used as a visual proxy for descent, with a focus on complexion, hair texture, and shape of the nose and mouth. Along with phenotype, acceptable proofs of whiteness included being reputed to be white, associating with whites, enjoying high social status, and exercising the prerogatives of whites (in access to transportation, public buildings, and parks, etc.).[47]

But that did not resolve the mulatto question and whites insecure about their own racial identity grew paranoid about "invisible blackness" (as expressed in William Faulkner's novels such as *Light in August* and *Absalom Absalom*). Concern about "passing" became so intense that associating with descendants of slaves of any hue sufficed to be classified as black (or as "white nigger") even in the absence of proof of African ancestry. Simultaneously, as Southern white elites shed their paternalistic concerns for blacks and joined with working-class whites in support of segregation statutes, mulattoes turned hostile toward their white ancestors and bitterly opposed further mixing with Caucasians. By the 1920s, the symbolic and social erasure of the mulattoes (as well as quadroons, octoroons, etc.) was complete,[48] leaving whites and blacks as *doxic dichotomous racial categories*, at once fictive and real, separated by an impassable blood fence, nowhere more so than in the Southern states. From the 1920s to the 1990s, the black–white division thus formed the anchor of the American racial order, until the multiracial movement reopened a phase of conflict and contention over ethnoracial classification by frontally questioning the public effacement of persons of mixed descent.[49]

---

[46] Information on blood quotient and phenotype is taken from Stetson Kennedy, *Jim Crow Guide: The Way It Was* (1910 [1959]), pp. 48–50.

[47] On the legal adjudication of racial identity, Ariela Gross, *What Blood Won't Tell: A History of Race on Trial in America* (2008), especially chapters 2 and 3. For a fruitful comparison, read Jan Hoffman French, *Legalizing Identities: Becoming Black or Indian in Brazil's Northeast* (2009).

[48] Jennifer L. Hochschild and Vesla Weaver, "Policies of Racial Classification and the Politics of Racial Inequality" (2007a).

[49] Kimberly McClain DaCosta, *Making Multiracials: State, Family, and Market in the*

> ### "Race" and "miscegenation" according to Georgia law under Jim Crow*
>
> "The term 'white person' shall include only persons of the white or Caucasian race, who have no ascertainable trace of either Negro, African, West Indian, Asiatic Indian, Mongolian, Japanese, or Chinese blood in their veins. No person, any of whose ancestors has been duly registered with the State Bureau of Vital Statistics as a colored person or person of color, shall be deemed a white person . . . It shall be unlawful for a white person to marry anyone except a white person." . . .
>
> "Applications for marriage licenses must state the race of both applicants and their parents. False statements may be punished by imprisonment from two to five years. Anyone issuing a forbidden marriage license shall be fined 500 dollars and sentenced to 10 years. Parties to an interracial marriage are subject to imprisonment from one to two years. . . ."
>
> Special prohibition: "Ordained colored ministers of the Gospel may celebrate marriages between persons of African descent only."
>
> Sexual intercourse: "Any charge or intimation against a white female of having intercourse with a person of color is slanderous, without proof of special damage."
>
> * Stetson Kennedy, *Jim Crow Guide: The Way It Was* (1990 [1959]), pp. 49 and 65.

Mississippi circa 1900, where 10 percent of the black population was recorded as mulattoes by the US Census, offers a capsule of the sudden *subsumption of color gradations among blacks under the caste divide between whites and Negroes.* The black elite was composed mostly of persons of mixed parentage among whom the notion that "white is better" prevailed. European physical appearance and light skin (showing "blue veins") was a condition of membership in ladies' clubs and campus organizations, and successful darker-skinned men

Redrawing of the Color Line (2007). Of course, there were other ethnically marked populations throughout the Jim Crow era, such as Native Americans and Mexicans. Their marking complicated but never unsettled the binary opposition between white and Negro in both classification and stratification. Two model studies are Malinda Maynor Lowery, *Lumbee Indians in the Jim Crow South: Race, Identity, and the Making of a Nation* (2010), and Julie M. Weise, *Corazón de Dixie: Mexicanos in the US South since 1910* (2015).

preferred to "marry light." But mulatto exclusiveness retreated steadily over time as "their claims to a tenuous racial middle ground were discounted by both whites and blacks." African Americans came to oppose "passing" not just as personal betrayal but also as "treason to the race."[50]

The result is that black–white mixing decreased sharply and black–mulatto mixing increased rapidly, leading to the merging of the latter with Negroes, making the whole black population physically browner but symbolically unified under a single caste category. The gradational classification based on phenotype had been effaced by the categorical descent-based classification, making the United States the only country on the planet to define blackness by the one-drop rule.[51] *Nested within the black–white dualism*, however, color gradations continued to be salient and consequential among the black population. Thus, in small-town Mississippi in the 1940s, light skin was an asset on the economic, social, and sexual front. Standards of beauty were white; successful black men strove to marry "light"; and, when broached, the topic caused slight embarrassment among Negroes.[52]

The one-drop rule was evolved socially and instituted legally to bolster slavery but it survived the latter's death. By then, the imperative of blood purity was grounded in the doxic white belief in the degraded and degrading nature of the black body, its impulses, its substance, and its fluids, a belief that was the *product* – and not the cause – of the association of slavery with blackness. After the Civil War, the prevalent view among white elites was that, with the removal of the supposedly beneficial strictures of bondage, the "child race" of the Negro was reverting to savagery and bestiality, and thus that mixing with it presented a mortal threat to civilization.

---

[50] McMillen, *Dark Journey*, p. 22. On the social, cultural, and existential complexities of "passing" while black, read Allyson Hobbs, *A Chosen Exile: A History of Racial Passing in American Life* (2014). For a different account stressing the pragmatic, instrumental, and even frivolous tenor of *passant blanc* in the "phenotypic gumbo" of Louisiana in the 1960s, see Adolph L. Reed, Jr., *The South: Jim Crow and Its Afterlives* (2022), pp. 92–8.
[51] For historical alternatives to the principle of hypodescent, see Davis, *Who Is Black?*, chapter 4, and, for a broader panorama, Edward E. Telles and Christina A. Sue, "Race Mixture: Boundary Crossing in Comparative Perspective" (2009).
[52] Powdermaker, *After Freedom*, pp. 175–80; Davis et al., *Deep South*, p. 21. Color classification and stratification continue to be pronounced within the African-American population to this day. Ellis P. Monk Jr., "Skin Tone Stratification among Black Americans, 2001–2003" (2014).

The image of the Negro as a brutish and lustful fiend "had its origins in the proslavery imagination, which had conceived of the black man as having a dual nature – he was docile and amiable when enslaved, ferocious and murderous when free."[53] By the turn of the century, this view was amplified by the thesis, promulgated by some religious intellectuals, that the mixing of blood was the greatest of sins and that the criminals and rapists who terrorized white women were nearly all mulattoes.[54] But there was more: Negroes were found to be uniquely susceptible to diseases and omnipresent yet invisible carriers of infections such that intimate congress with them would effectively lead to "race suicide" among whites. Thus the predicament of the postbellum South was not just economic – how to keep and extract Negro labor – and symbolic – how to exclude the Negro from ethnic honor. It was also medical: how to protect whites from insidious black contamination. To contain this health threat necessitated the strict control of descent lines and segregative measures such as those instituted under Jim Crow.

By the end of the nineteenth century, medical scientists stressed what they saw as the contrast in morbidity and mortality, not just between whites and blacks, but also, and more crucially still, between blacks before and after abolition.[55] First, the black race was said to be highly prone to disease due to what specialists called "its high sensuality and intemperance" as well as its "total disregard for the laws of sanitation and hygiene." This implied that interracial sex should be strictly proscribed on private and public health grounds alone.[56] Next, the "diseased race" – an expression commonly used then by scientists and politicians alike – was believed to be congenitally inapt to developing once released from bondage. According to J. Willington Byers, the foremost authority in "ethnological medicine" of the 1880s, "the Negro is particularly unfortunate. He has not only the inherent frailties of his nature to war against – instincts, passions, and

---

[53] George M. Fredrickson, *The Black Image in the White Mind: The Debate on Afro-American Character and Destiny, 1817–1914* (1971), p. 276.

[54] This is because, to cite a newspaper editorial of 1899, the mulatto has "enough white blood in him to replace native humility and cowardice with Caucasian audacity." Cited by Fredrickson, *The Black Image in the White Mind*, p. 277.

[55] Melissa Stein, "'Nature is the Author of Such Restrictions': Science, Ethnological Medicine, and Jim Crow" (2012).

[56] Early American sociology contributed to the elaboration of this race–disease nexus and thus to the pathologizing vision of African Americans. Vernon J. Williams, *The Social Sciences and Theories of Race* (2006).

appetites; but also those seductive, destroying influences that emanate from free institutions in a country of civil liberty."[57] It follows that the imposition of segregation and the curtailing of contact was nothing more than the establishment of a cordon sanitaire needed to protect whites from contamination and degradation. The isolation of African Americans and their descendants in symbolic space (classification) thus found its extension and support in the rigid dual division of social space (stratification).

Denigrating representations of African Americans endured and kept a doxic character in Southern states – and much of the nation – right into the mid-twentieth century. Thus, whites in Mississippi held the view that "the Negro is a lower form of organism, biologically more primitive, mentally inferior, and emotionally undeveloped. He is insensitive to pain, incapable of learning, and animal-like in his behavior."[58] It was the will of God to separate the races and the behavior of blacks was read as proof of their innate inferiority: they are naturally indolent so that the compulsion of force is needed to make them work; they are childlike, comical, and carefree, with no sense of time and thus incapable of deferred gratification or planning for the future; they obey the herd instinct and do not wish to improve their lot. This is why they prefer to be led and ordered by whites ("Not one in a thousand wants to be independent").[59] But whites must beware because Negroes are also natural liars and thieves, unstable and unreliable, and gullible, so that they may be seduced by the calls of "outside agitators" for "social equality."[60] Left to their own devices and inclinations, African Americans prefer "the Southern way" as they recognize that they need and benefit from the benevolent guidance of whites. These deprecating representations of the Negro character directly informed economic relations, especially in the mainstay sector of agricultural production, to which I now turn.

---

[57] Cited by Stein, "'Nature is the Author of Such Restrictions'," p. 130.
[58] Davis et al., *Deep South*, p. 16. The following portrait draws also on Dollard, *Caste and Class in a Southern Town*, pp. 369–89, and Powdermaker, *After Freedom*, pp. 23–42.
[59] Davis et al., *Deep South*, pp. 17–18.
[60] A favorite defense of the racial status quo by Southern whites in the 1950s was that blacks supporting civil rights reform were manipulated by the Communist Party and wanted to set up "an independent Negro Soviet Republic." Sokol, *There Goes My Everything*, pp. 37–42, citation p. 39. See also Berry, *The Jim Crow Routine*, pp. 157–9.

Economic infrastructure: sharecropping and peonage

After the close of Reconstruction in 1877, rulers of the South had to solve two pressing problems: to extract Negro labor and to uphold the monopolistic claim of whites over ethnic honor by locking blacks in a menial position. The economic basis of Jim Crow resided in superexploitative sharecropping arrangements morphing into debt peonage and crop liens that fixed African Americans on the land, maintaining the hegemony of the region's agrarian upper class and the work discipline of the antebellum plantation – the lash remained in use in Mississippi well into the interwar years.[61]

After abolition, the hope and aim of the former slaves had been to secure economic independence by acquiring plots to farm on their own account. But the promise of "forty acres and a mule" did not materialize and white landowners ensured the occupational immobility of their Negro workforce, whom they regarded as naturally suited to agricultural toil, by barring them from owning the soil.[62] In some states the Black Codes promulgated right after the Civil War prohibited Negro ownership of arable land. In others, the violent raids of the Ku Klux Klan (from 1866 till 1872 and then again after 1915) and the "Whitecappers" (around the turn of the century) terrorized black homesteaders and farm renters. And everywhere most descendants of slaves lacked the means to lease or purchase arable tracts and encountered "the active solidarity among white people to prevent Negroes from acquiring land."[63] So the vast majority of them became sharecroppers working "on halves," cash renters, or hired field hands on the former plantations where they had previously been slaves: a landless peasantry devoid of economic stake and political pull.

Now, like slavery, sharecropping is not in itself a racial institution; it is an organizational device for labor supervision and land management in agricultural production that has shown surprising

---

[61] Roger L. Ransom and Richard Sutch, *One Kind of Freedom: The Economic Consequences of Emancipation* (2001).

[62] An instructive exception to this denial was the case of the freedpeople of Indian Territory (present-day Oklahoma), who received land from the Cherokee who had enslaved them, as documented by Alaina Roberts in *I've Been Here All the While: Black Freedom on Native Land* (2023), an experiment that blurs the neat categorical distinction between perpetrators and victims of settler colonialism.

[63] Gunnar Myrdal, *An American Dilemma: The Negro Problem and Modern Democracy* (1944, reprint 1962), p. 242.

Jim Crow as Caste Terrorism

adaptability and resilience on several continents.[64] In the former confederate states, it was imposed on Southern whites as well as blacks, with deleterious consequences for both.[65] But, coupled with the dichotomous racial division inherited from the era of bondage, the opposition between white landlords and Negro croppers functioned inseparably as the mainspring of economic extraction and as the hinge of symbolic domination perpetuating the dishonor of African Americans by perpetrating their dispossession and dependency. What is more, for whites, farming tenancy was a temporary status whereas for African Americans it was typically a terminal status.[66]

Under sharecropping as an economic arrangement, the tenant or cropper and his family provided the labor and the owner supplied the soil, seed, tools, work animals, and a bare, windowless cabin to dwell in. The landlord also advanced minimal cash funds (around ten dollars a month in the interwar decades for a tenant household of five) or coupon books usable only at the plantation store and he provided minimal medical coverage during the six months until the crop was made. The patriarchal family, supported by extended kin networks, was the basic farming unit in the cultivation of cotton, and economic viability depended chiefly on family size, with children as young as seven tasked with hoeing and picking while boys of 12 and over ran the plough.[67]

After harvest, the cotton was ginned and sold with the cropper entitled to one-third to one-half of the receipts. But his share was typically deemed by the landlord (who controlled both the sale and the accounting) to be worth less than sum of the "furnish" received and of the debt accrued over the previous year at the plantation commissary or the local merchant at astronomical interest rates ranging from 40 to 70 percent – no wonder those stores were nicknamed "robbersaries."[68] The result is that, at season's close, sharecroppers barely broke even or, worse, found themselves further in arrears. They were thus forced to move to another nearby farm in hopes of better conditions or compelled to continue to work for their landlord under whatever new terms he imposed. For instance, around 1930, over

---

[64] Susan Archer Mann, *Agrarian Capitalism in Theory and Practice* (1990).
[65] James Agee, *Cotton Tenants: Three Families* (2013 [1936]); Margaret Jarman Hagood, *Mothers of the South: Portraiture of the White Tenant Farm Woman* (1939).
[66] Stewart E. Tolnay, *The Bottom Rung: African American Family Life on Southern Farms* (1999).
[67] Davis et al., *Deep South*, pp. 409–13.
[68] Kennedy, *Jim Crow Guide*, p. 135.

80 percent of sharecroppers in Indianola, Mississippi, failed to turn a profit while 91 percent were stuck in the red in Macon County, Georgia.[69] Many sharecroppers were too poor to survive on the farm during the winter months and had to move in with kin or to migrate to nearby towns in search of menial work until the next planting season. Negro tenants fared no better, living in semi-starvation during winter and summer when they had neither money, nor credit or stored victuals. They ate milk and bread, which they begged from their landlord, and endured on food rations lower than those enjoyed by slaves.[70]

This is where race enters into the equation: black croppers were uniquely vulnerable to such structural deception insofar as challenging the "settlement" invited the instant wrath of the white planter, who resorted indifferently to private violence or to the law to uphold this asymmetric arrangement. "The boss man sits at the desk, a forty-five revolver beside him.... The tenant cannot dispute or the boss will grasp the gun and ask him if he's going to argue. If he does, 'boom-boom'."[71] African Americans who balked at being defrauded and had the impudence to ask for an itemized statement of their advances or a sale receipt for their cotton were flogged, run out of the county, or murdered with no judicial consequences since being called a liar or a thief by a Negro was customarily considered ground for "justifiable homicide." In isolated rural counties, black life was dirt cheap, cheaper than it had been under slavery, as captured by the Southern expression, "Kill a mule, buy another. Kill a nigger, hire another."[72]

Racial violence was integral to the workings of the postbellum plantation economy. Intimidation against black tenants was rampant to prevent them from getting "impudent" or "too smart," that is, from claiming their economic due. The threat of being beaten, whipped, shot, or hung served well to control farm hands, extract their labor, prevent theft and the maltreatment of stock, and dissuade them from challenging the landlord's reckoning of accounts pertaining to credit and crop sale. "A Negro tenant who questions a white landlord's reckoning is always regarded as a 'bad Negro' and a danger to the operation of the plantation system itself. He is usually driven off the plantation

---

[69] Powdermaker, *After Freedom*, pp. 86–7.
[70] Davis et al., *Deep South*, p. 383. For a fuller portrait of the functioning of the rural economy in Alabama in the 1920s, read Charles S. Johnson, *Shadow of the Plantation* (1934), chapter 3.
[71] John Dollard, *Caste and Class in a Southern Town* (1988 [1937]), pp. 122–3. See also Ransom and Sutch, *One Kind of Freedom*.
[72] Litwack, "Jim Crow Blues," p. 10.

before he can 'spoil' the other tenants."[73] It was even customary in one Mississippi county for a landlord to invite other planters to join in "whipping-parties" and discipline wayward tenants in front of their comrades.

Violence escalated steeply whenever field hands and croppers tried to organize to improve their lot, as they "aroused the most intense white anxieties, evoking ancient fantasies of Negro 'risings', threatening white social and economic control, provoking unreasoning white violence." Companies of state militia were called in to suppress organizing; suspected leaders of unions were beaten, castrated, and assassinated. "The union's message of hope and solidarity was no match for white terror."[74] In most states, moreover, the sharecropping contract had this peculiarity that it was enforceable by the planter in criminal rather than civil court: "A sharecropper who skipped out after planting a crop would not be sued (he was not likely to have any assets anyway) but arraigned on criminal charges" and jailed,[75] before being turned over to toil for his landlord (in exchange for erasing his debt) or leased out to a private operator as convict labor. Either way labor would be wrung from him, with the stiff assistance of criminal justice.[76]

Indeed, law enforcement officials were prompt to inflict heavy fines and fees on blacks (for flimsy or trumped-up charges such as disorderly conduct, loitering, and vagrancy) to raise funds for the budget of the local police and court, making "legal punishment a paying business operating against the Negroes": "When white employers are short of workers, they inform the sheriff who will suddenly enforce vague laws such as that against vagrancy"[77] and thereby forcibly recruit the hands needed to till the land. Once behind bars, inmates were pressed to sign contracts that allowed planters to use such private force as they deemed necessary to extract service, to lock them up, and even to deduct the expense of capturing and bringing back

---

[73] Davis et al., *Deep South*, p. 398.
[74] McMillen, *Dark Journey*, pp. 134 and 137. And yet, black agricultural laborers and sharecroppers joined with workers in unionization efforts in parts of the Deep South, as shown by Robin D. G. Kelley, *Hammer and Hoe: Alabama Communists during the Great Depression* (2015 [1990]).
[75] Grossman, "A Chance to Make Good, 1900–1929," p. 352, and McMillen, *Dark Journey*, p. 126.
[76] Christopher Muller and Daniel Schrage. "The Political Economy of Incarceration in the Cotton South, 1910–1925" (2021). I elaborate on the role of criminal justice in solidifying Jim Crow later in this chapter, see *infra*, pp. 251–7.
[77] Myrdal, *An American Dilemma*, p. 551.

fugitives from their wages. "Once a prisoner became indebted, he was sucked into the swirl of peonage" as court costs escalated faster than whatever earnings he could make while captive.[78]

The 1867 federal law prohibiting peonage was not activated until the 1900s and only in rare and egregious cases. Even then, wide public support for the customs, legalities, and pseudo-legalities subtending the practice of peonage effectively nullified federal protection, on grounds that "the Negro is congenitally lazy and must be kept in debt in order to be made to work."[79] Together with statutes making "tenant stealing" a capital offense and ordinances severely restricting the activities of labor agents in search of recruits for urban wage work, this combination of economic dependency and legal suasion amounted to establishing what W. E. B. Du Bois called a "slavery of debt" in lieu of slavery *tout court* that was in many ways worse than its predecessor.[80] From the standpoint of white planters, it was indeed economically superior to bondage in that they no longer needed to feed and tend to their laborers in sickness and old age even as they continued to look upon them in a proprietary way as "their niggers."[81]

The minority of blacks who escaped from the long shadow of the plantation by seeking employment in turpentine camps and sawmills or in emerging mining and industrial towns found that their economic opportunities were similarly limited to the most dirty and dangerous "nigger work." They got such jobs because they could be worked harder, for lower wages, and with rougher treatment than could whites. A Mississippi packing plant owner in the 1930s explains his preference for African-American workers for the efficiency it gave him in dealing with slackers and union agitators: "I take a club and beat the hell out of a couple of Negroes and conditions immediately settle back to normal."[82] Black women found paid employ easily

---

[78] Pete Daniel, *Shadow of Slavery: Peonage in the South, 1901–1969* (1990 [1972]), p. 26. Debt peonage must not be confounded with convict leasing, under which the state "rented out" criminals as laborers to farmers and corporations who worked them to death, often literally.

[79] Powdermaker, *After Freedom*, p. 88. For a fuller discussion of debt peonage, see Ransom and Sutch, *One Kind of Freedom*, chapter 8.

[80] W. E. B. Du Bois, *The Souls of Black Folk* (1990 [1903]), pp. 94–5. On the multiple mechanisms of "involuntary servitude" under Jim Crow, see Jonathan M. Wiener, "Class Structure and Economic Development in the American South, 1865–1955" (1979).

[81] Davis et al., *Deep South*, pp. 350–6, and Leon Litwack, *Trouble in Mind: Black Southerners in the Age of Jim Crow* (1998), pp. 136–7.

[82] Cited by McMillen, *Dark Journey*, p. 158.

enough in household service as cook, cleaner, laundress, and wet-nurse as all except the poorest white families retained domestics, but they did so for a pittance (as little as 25 cents a day for 14-hour work days, seven days a week, in early twentieth-century Mississippi) and at the cost of neglecting their own household given their strenuous schedules, not to mention the ever-present threat of sexual abuse by white men (who conveniently professed that no black female above the age of puberty was chaste).[83]

As for blacks in the skilled trades, they were gradually pushed out and down into unskilled labor while the tiny upper class of Negro professionals and entrepreneurs concentrated in cities were doomed to stagnation by their lack of access to credit, the crushing poverty of their black customer base, and the mounting refusal of whites to patronize them – when they did not object to their success and drive them out through official harassment, mob brutality, and targeted assault.[84] This limited but did not prevent "the growing differentiation of classes among Negroes, even in small communities," with the middle class of teachers, ministers, and a sprinkling of doctors and lawyers seeking to distance itself from the lower class, and especially its dissipated fraction involved in crime, by stressing family, moral discipline, and education.[85]

But Negro class formation did not dent the rigid framework of caste. Indeed, African Americans who had hoped that economic advancement and social uplift would gradually reduce the stigma of blackness, that the accumulation of wealth, the acquisition of education, and the mastery of manners would make their "skin lighter," discovered with dismay that, on the contrary, "evidence of blacks making good on that creed often provoked white resentment and violence rather than respect and acceptance."[86] This is because successful blacks presented a twofold menace for the structure of ethnoracial domination in the New South: on the material plane, they were potential competitors and threatened the monopoly of whites over desired material goods and positions; on the symbolic

---

[83] Hunter, *To "Joy My Freedom,"* and Rebecca Sharpless, *Cooking in Other Women's Kitchens: Domestic Workers in the South, 1865–1960* (2010).
[84] Dollard, *Caste and Class in a Southern Town*, p. 156; McMillen, *Dark Journey*, pp. 168–72, 180–5.
[85] W. E. B. Du Bois, "The Negroes of Farmville, Virginia" (1978 [1898]), and idem, "The Negroes of Dougherty County, Georgia" (1978 [1902]); Dollard, *Caste and Class*, pp. 83–91; Davis et al., *Deep South*, chapter 10.
[86] Litwack, *Trouble in Mind*, p. 151.

plane, they ruined the collective presumption of innate Negro inferiority and incapacity, which takes us to the next component of Jim Crow.

Social core: bifurcation and deference

The institutional epicenter of Jim Crow consisted in a set of *disjunctive relationships aimed at effecting the asymmetric separation of blacks and whites and at extracting deference* under what one might call the *principle of racial "less eligibility"*: that the lowest white should always stand above the highest Negro and thus receive his personal homage.[87] Accordingly, custom, the law, and violence were joined to sharply curtail social contacts between whites and blacks and to relegate the latter to separate and inferior residential districts (known as "darktowns"), public facilities and commercial establishments, waiting rooms and bathrooms, elevators and phone booths, and to the reserved "colored" section of trolleys and buses, saloons and movie houses, parks and beaches, hospitals and post offices, orphanages and retirement homes, even to separate jails, morgues, and cemeteries – Florida used a different set of gallows to execute white and black convicts sentenced to death.[88] Former slaves and their descendants were likewise prohibited from attending schools with whites (in some states, biracial education was made unconstitutional and, in Florida, the law mandated separate storage facilities for their textbooks)[89] and they resorted to creating their own churches when white churches insisted on granting them only second-class membership, if that. The commonly expressed justification for this meticulous institutional engineering was that, in the absence of social bifurcation, "the black race would contaminate and retard the white race" which, in the South, had reached a peak of civilization.[90]

---

[87] For variations on the many derivations of this central tenet of Southern racial rule, Dollard, *Caste and Class in a Southern Town*, chapter 8, "The Prestige Gain"; Powdermaker, *After Freedom*, pp. 23–42; Davis et al., *Deep South*, pp. 6 and 22; and Litwack, *Trouble in Mind*, pp. 181–3. Max Weber points out that "the sense of ethnic honor is a specific honor of the masses (*Massenehre*), for it is accessible to anybody who belongs to the subjectively believed community of descent" and that "the social honor of the 'poor whites' was dependent upon the social *déclassement* of the Negroes" (*Economy and Society*, p. 391).

[88] Litwack, *Trouble in Mind*, p. 236.

[89] Grossman, "A Chance to Make Good, 1900–1929," p. 362.

[90] Brundage, "Introduction," in Cole and Ring (eds.), *The Folly of Jim Crow*, p. 2.

Jim Crow as Caste Terrorism

In the first two decades of the twentieth century, the whole physical landscape of the region was thus modified by the erection of walls and partitions, the deployment of curtains and "whites only" (and "colored") signage in towns and cities, amplified by the spread of informal racial inscriptions (as with laundries that posted "No Negro Washing Taken"), and the construction of dual entrances to public buildings and commercial outlets. Dichotomizing racialized spaces increased social distance through physical disjunction and intensified the spatial isolation of African Americans. It also worked to "reestablish difference and hierarchy and to thwart black assertiveness" by scripting two fictional roles into the built environment: those of benevolent white masters and contented Negro servants.[91] Indeed, the signal exception to this rigid institutional separation concerned black servants, who were allowed to tread onto white spaces to deliver service as if they were living extensions – or pale social shadows – of their white patrons.

The law went into especially great detail in specifying the rules and roles of racial bifurcation in transport.[92] In Alabama, bus companies were required to have exclusive waiting rooms for whites and Negroes separated by "a partition constructed of metal, wood, strong cloth, or other material so as to obstruct vision between the sections." In Arkansas, railroads which failed to segregate were subject to a fine of $500 for each unsegregated train run. In Georgia, railroad employees who did not diligently act to eject a black passenger violating segregation instructions were guilty of a misdemeanor. In North Carolina, trolleys transporting whites only and blacks only had to bear illuminated signs reading "White" and "Colored" clearly visible from 300 feet after sunset. Deciding the passenger's race was up to the train conductor, and the company was protected from liability if he made "an honest mistake." But "if the conductor, through negligence, makes a mistake in taking a white passenger to be a Negro, the railroad company may be held liable for substantial damages, and in a proper case may be held liable for punitive damages."[93]

Institutional bifurcation was at once anchored in and amplified by the formalized asymmetry of a "racial etiquette" governing all

[91] Berrey, *The Jim Crow Routine*, pp. 21 and passim; Elizabeth Abel, *Signs of the Times: The Visual Politics of Jim Crow* (2010).
[92] Kennedy, *Jim Crow Guide*, pp. 183–5. For a full dissection of racial strictures on traveling and their pivotal role in the (re)production of Jim Crow, read Bay, *Traveling Black*.
[93] Kennedy, *Jim Crow Guide*, p. 184.

personal interactions, derived from the rules of engagement codified under slavery.[94] Crucially, blacks were *expected to display deference and submissiveness* at every turn in their encounters with whites on pain of being swiftly brought back in line by private reprisal or public sanction. Under the heading of the "Prestige Gain," anthropologist John Dollard encapsulates this expectation thus: whether rich or poor, "a member of the white caste has an automatic right to demand forms of behavior from Negroes which serve to increase his self-esteem" and produce "an illumination of the image of the self, an expansive feeling of being something special and valuable." Moreover, "this deference is demanded and not merely independently given," which means that it also "gives the gratification of mastering the other person."[95] Rules of reverent speech, attitude, and conduct must not only be observed; they must be observed with no apparent reservations: the Negro must show that "he accepts them as proper and right; he must conform willfully and cheerfully."[96] Such is the touchstone of racial domination as characterized in the prolegomena to this book (*infra*, pp. 26–7).

Deference is a crucial glue in a system of personalized domination; it drains dignity from the inferior to the superior party and it affirms the latter's legitimacy. Erving Goffman stresses that, when they take place in a vertical structure, deferential acts are so many outward tokens of regard for and allegiance to the superordinate; being "honorific and politely toned," they convey the ceremonial recognition of the hierarchy the latter embodies.[97] In the Jim Crow South, deference flowed exclusively from blacks to whites, regardless of class status, gender, and age, *in exchange for the provisional suspension of two modalities of violence*, the symbolic violence of public humiliation and the physical violence of aggression (and possibly death) of Negroes with which every single interracial interaction was pregnant, as indicated in figure 8.

Rules of face-to-face encounters converged to signify the inferiority and to diffuse the indignity of the descendants of slaves.[98] Whites were

---

[94] Bertram Wilbur Doyle, *The Etiquette of Race Relations in the South: A Study in Social Control* (1937). For an explication of the notion, see Jennifer Ritterhouse, "The Etiquette of Racial Relations in the Jim Crow South" (2007).
[95] Dollard, *Caste and Class in a Southern Town*, p. 174.
[96] Davis et al., *Deep South*, p. 23.
[97] Erving Goffman, "The Nature of Deference and Demeanor" (1959), pp. 473–502.
[98] They stipulated what Goffman calls "presentational rituals," that is, "acts through which the individual makes specific attestations to recipients concerning how he

Jim Crow as Caste Terrorism

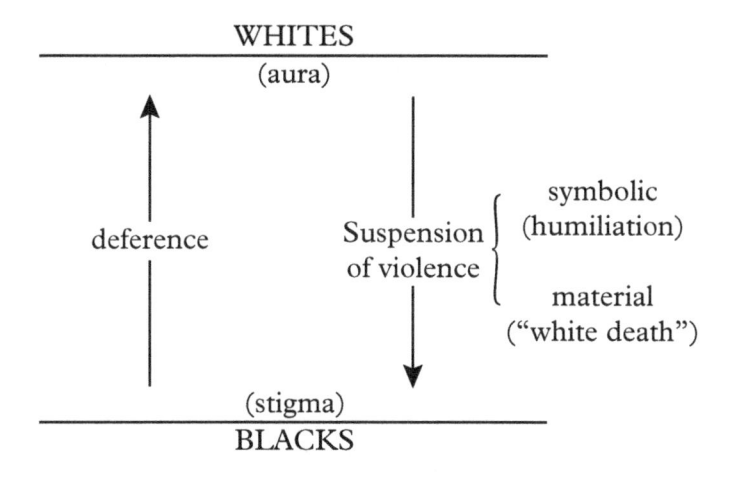

```
                    WHITES
                    (aura)
        ▲            │
        │            │          ⎧  symbolic
        │         Suspension    ⎨  (humiliation)
  deference       of violence   ⎩
        │            │             material
        │            │             ("white death")
        │            ▼
                   (stigma)
                   BLACKS
```

Figure 8 The economy of deference and violence.

to be addressed as "Ma'am" and "Sir" (or "captain" and "boss") but they never reciprocated these terms or any common courtesies toward African Americans, whom they called by their first names or hailed as "boy," "girl," and "auntie," regardless of age or context. White children learned from a young age that the term "lady" was to be used only in reference to white women and not Negro women. Taboos and sanctions regarding interracial address "appl[ied] with full force to telephone conversations" despite the practical difficulty of ascertaining the ethnicity of speakers, extended to newspaper reporting, and covered legal talk by counsel and judges in the courtroom, where black defendants were openly referred to as "nigras" (a cross between Negro and nigger).[99] In one Mississippi Delta town, the post office went to the trouble of erasing the mentions "Mr." and "Mrs." on letters mailed to colored residents. In another, white postal workers made a point of "always dropping the black people's mail on the floor instead of handing it to them."[100]

Blacks who insisted on being addressed as Mister or Miss risked ridicule, physical retaliation, banishment, or worse. In conversation with whites, they had to take off their hats, wear what Ralph Ellison

---

regards them and how he will treat them." Goffman, "The Nature of Deference and Demeanor," p. 485.

[99] Kennedy, *Jim Crow Guide: The Way It Was*, pp. 214–16.

[100] See, respectively, McMillen, *Dark Journey*, pp. 23–4, and Berrey, *The Jim Crow Routine*, p. 38.

called "the mask of meekness,"[101] and be extremely careful to never devalue, disparage, or laugh at their white interlocutors, comment on their physical appearance, or intimate that they were lying, acting on dishonorable intentions, or of an inferior class.[102] It was always safer to let the white person take the lead, drive the discussion, impose their views, and monopolize credit.

> **Taboo topics***
>
> Among the topics they did not like to discuss with Negroes were the following: American white women; the Ku Klux Klan; France, and how Negro soldiers fared while there; French women; [boxing world heavyweight champion] Jack Johnson; the entire Northern part of the United States; the Civil War; Abraham Lincoln; U.S. Grant; General Sherman; Catholics; the Pope; Jews; the Republican Party; slavery; social equality; Communism; the 13th and 14th amendments to the Constitution; or any topic calling for positive knowledge or manly self-assertion on the part of the Negro.
>
> * Topics to avoid in conversation with his white co-workers in an optical company in Memphis, from Richard Wright, "The Ethics of Living Jim Crow: An Autobiographical Sketch" (1937), pp. 29–30.

The astringent denial of black dignity translated into the *systematic refusal of reciprocity* in every domain of social intercourse, starting with circulation in physical space. African Americans had to swiftly step off the sidewalk to leave ample room for passing whites and take care to avoid bumping them or otherwise hampering their movement, on pain of being slapped, shoved into the street, assaulted, or arrested and jailed. This racially differentiated use of public space effectively "required blacks to actively participate in and physically acknowledge their subordinate status."[103] African-American southerners had to wait until all the white customers were served in stores and offices, and let whites cut ahead of them in lines as well as stand back

---

[101] Ralph Ellison, *The Collected Essays of Ralph Ellison* (2003), p. 110. Richard Wright elaborates: "I learned to lie, to steal, to dissemble. I learned to play that dual role which every Negro must play if he wants to eat and live" ("The Ethics of Living Jim Crow: An Autobiographical Sketch" [1937], pp. 27–8).
[102] Kennedy, *Jim Crow Guide*, pp. 216–17.
[103] Berrey, *The Jim Crow Routine*, p. 42.

and hold the door for them.[104] They were prohibited from trying on clothes, hats, or shoes; they were expected to step outside to consume food or drinks. They were required to approach white homes only from the back, even when the host was sitting on the front porch. So ingrained was the habit, and the belief that the Negro was a natural-born thief, that upon leaving their house white Mississippians locked the back door but left the front door open.[105]

Established mores similarly prohibited black motorists from holding the right of way or overtaking vehicles driven by whites, or from parking on the town's main streets. A minor car accident with a white motorist could prove fatal if the latter reacted with irrepressible ire: after a white lawyer driving 50 miles an hour caused a collision with a black driver at an intersection in Indianola, Mississippi, "a white bystander urged him to 'just kill the nigger' since he couldn't collect any money for damages."[106] It was dangerous for African Americans to own expensive automobiles or even buggies, which were perceived by whites as evidence of "impudence" liable to trigger violent reactions. Indeed, any outward mark of Negro affluence, success, and pride, indicative of the possible desire to be treated with respect by whites, such as dressing up and coming to town for shopping on a weekday, could result in vigorous reprimand and immediate police arrest, but also in vicious beatings and outright assassination with routine impunity for the white perpetrators. In some rural counties, merely driving an automobile could result in violent reprisal, as when whites in a small Georgia town forced a black farmer and his daughter to get out of their vehicle, doused the latter with kerosene and set it aflame, railing "From now on, you niggers walk into town, or use that old mule if you want to stay in this city."[107]

The taboo over titles extended to shaking hands and eating, drinking, or smoking together, indeed to any and all forms of intercourse that might imply social equality between the "races," viewed as gateways to the odium of sexual congress.[108] Anthropologist

---

[104] Davis et al., *Deep South*, p. 23.
[105] Powdermaker, *After Freedom*, pp. 47–8.
[106] Ibid., p. 49.
[107] Litwack, *Trouble in Mind*, p. 335.
[108] This class of action pertains to what Goffman calls "avoidance rituals": "Those forms of deference which lead the actor to keep at a distance from the recipient and not violate what Simmel has called the 'ideal sphere' that lies around the recipient." Goffman, "The Nature of Deference and Demeanor," p. 62.

Maurice Bloch reports that, "in all societies, sharing food is a way of establishing closeness while, conversely, the refusal to share is one of the clearest marks of distance and enmity."[109] Accordingly, in the eyes of Southern whites, mingling at meals implied an intimacy that threatened to breach the impermeable boundary between the gloried white "us" and the sullied black "them." Indeed, "bound up with notions of racial purity, this taboo against interracial dining mattered almost as much to most white Southerners as the taboo – and the longstanding laws – against interracial sex."[110]

This principle of the *generalized denial of equality and reciprocity* applied to the most anodyne parlor activities, such as playing cards, dice, dominoes, checkers, or pool together, which the state of Alabama banned even in private settings.[111] Blacks were prohibited from engaging in sporting competitions with whites, lest they match or best them, and so they were forced to develop their own separate athletic leagues, such as the seven Negro baseball leagues launched starting in the 1920s, which anchored a thriving economy of sporting entertainment aimed at urban black consumers, complete with their own "world series" and segregated hall of fame.[112] When black boxing champion "Papa" Jack Johnson knocked out Jim Jeffries, who had been drafted as the "Great White Hope" to regain the world heavyweight title on behalf of his race, in the "Fight of the Century" in Reno on the Fourth of July, 1910, dozens of riots broke out throughout the South and beyond as clusters of angry whites attacked African Americans on the streets in reprisal for this unspeakable affront to white masculinity. The film of the bout was banned from circulation lest it excite the impudent pride of blacks for whom Johnson was a larger-than-life race savior.[113]

Racial etiquette was tricky and risky as it was conjugated locally, which means that it varied imperceptibly across activities, across

---

[109] "The reason is that the sharing of food is, and is always seen to be, in some way or other, the sharing of that which will cause, or at least maintain, a common substance among those who commune together." Maurice Bloch, "Commensality and Poisoning" (1999), p. 133. Note that restrictions on commensality are typical of caste orders, as stressed by Veena Das, "Caste" (2001), p. 1529.

[110] Ritterhouse, "Daily Life in the Jim Crow South, 1900–1945."

[111] Kennedy, *Jim Crow Guide*, p. 202.

[112] Neil Lanctot, *Negro League Baseball: The Rise and Ruin of a Black Institution* (2004).

[113] Johnson had won the world title two years earlier in a fight with Canadian boxer Tommy Burns held in Sydney, Australia. Staging such an interracial bout for the honorific title of most manly man walking the planet was unthinkable in the United States. Randy Roberts, *Papa Jack: Jack Johnson and the Era of White Hopes* (1985).

Jim Crow as Caste Terrorism

towns and regions, as well as between "white quality" and "white trash." It took cognitive alertness and social skill to minimize trouble and danger arising from unwittingly violating an unwritten rule. "So much was left to custom [that] particularity seemed to be the only universal rule."[114] Thus African Americans coming into a new place would take the trouble to ask black residents as to the local standards of racial decorum so that they could adjust to white expectations of interdictions and displays of subservience. As for travel across the Southern states, middle-class African Americans who owned automobiles relied on *The Negro Motorist's Green Book*, a guidebook published from 1936 to 1966 which listed businesses, from lodging and restaurants to gas stations and stores, where blacks were served and could avoid inconvenience, rejection, humiliation, and violence triggered by unknowingly entering into forbidden white territory.[115]

But the chief obsession of whites concerned intimate congress across the color line as the region's distinctive civic culture "cast issues of politics and economics in terms of sexual danger," making "anti-miscegenation statutes and the racial identity laws that supported them the legal core of Jim Crow, the center from which a multitude of prohibitions and regulations radiated outward."[116] Fueled by white fixation on racial purity (defined by lineal descent excluding blacks and other dishonored categories), the legal ban on intermarriage occupied the highest rank in the long list of taboos bearing on sexual conduct across the caste line. Occasions for interracial congress were zealously surveilled and any infringement by black men, real or imagined, was savagely repressed, whereas tolerance and discretion applied to white men involved in sexual activity or concubinage with black women. Indeed, many prominent Southern whites, "including judges, governors, wealthy planters, made little or no secret of the fact that they had a negro family as a well as a white family,"[117] which was

---

[114] McMillen, *Dark Journey*, p. 11. For illustrations from New Orleans in the 1960s, see the memoir of Adolph Reed, *The South: Jim Crow and Its Afterlives*, pp. 13, 19–20, 37, 45, 47–8.

[115] Candacy A. Taylor, *Overground Railroad: The Green Book and the Roots of Black Travel in America* (2020). The *Green Book* was recently republished in simile format to popular acclaim, following the box-office success of the movie by the same title directed by Peter Farrelly.

[116] Dailey, *The Age of Jim Crow*, pp. xvi and xxix. For a fuller argument, read Jane Dailey, *White Fright: The Sexual Panic at the Heart of America's Racist History* (2020).

[117] Ray Stannard Baker, *Following the Color Line: American Negro Citizenship in the Progressive Era* (1964 [1908]), p. 165. See also Martha Hodes, *White Women, Black*

acceptable so long as such relations were not formally acknowledged, not cast in the language of sentiment, and the children born from them not incorporated into white society.

Indeed, there was a fundamental asymmetry in the economy of sexual exchanges south of the Mason-Dixon line: by virtue of their dominant caste position, white men had access to two categories of women, white and black, whereas black men and white women were restricted to their own castes in sexual choices. This allowed for the idealization of the Southern white woman as pure and asexual while the Negro woman was portrayed as hypersexual, debauched, and permanently available, falling "into the category of the unprotected woman."[118] Thus white men could have Negro girls, whether prostitutes, servants, or girls picked up on the streets, but under no circumstance could Negro men – whom whites saw as virtual rapists on the prowl – have white women, even prostitutes. Such a relation was regarded as more offensive even than incest and the black man involved in it essentially risked his life.[119]

The hysterical dread of "racial degeneracy" believed to ensue from mixing and justified by the self-evident and self-evidently abhorrent query, "Would you want your sister to marry a nigger?",[120] climaxed in periodic explosions of beatings, whippings, mob violence, torture, and rioting against black men who failed to "stay in their place" in the sexual order. In the last two decades of the nineteenth century, some 2,060 African Americans were lynched, one-third of them after being accused of sexual assault or mere improprieties toward white women. These caste murders were but the tip of an immense iceberg of ever-shifting real or imagined racial transgressions liable to be punished by humiliation and violent reprisal (as we shall see later in this chapter).[121]

Men: Illicit Sex in the Nineteenth-Century South (1997), and Randall Kennedy, *Interracial Intimacies: Sex, Marriage, Identity, and Adoption* (2012), chapter 2.

[118] "The Negro man is debarred from violent expressions or threats in defending his wife, sister or daughter, whereas within the white caste women are almost universally attended by energetic protectors." Dollard, *Caste and Class in a Southern Town*, p. 145. This sexual jeopardy was denounced with particular virulence by Du Bois, who wrote that he was prepared to forgive the white South for slavery, for fighting for secession, and for its "race pride," but not for "its wanton and continued and persistent insulting of the black womanhood which it sought and it seeks to prostitute to its lust." W. E. B. Du Bois, *Darkwater* (1921), p. 172.

[119] Davis et al., *Deep South*, p. 24.

[120] Dollard, *Caste and Class in a Southern Town*, p. 62.

[121] Joel Williamson, *A Rage for Order: Black–White Relations in the American South*

Jim Crow as Caste Terrorism

Anchoring and extending the exchange of deference for the suspension of violence was the *remanence of paternalism* from the days of slavery.[122] Especially in rural areas, whites saw themselves as benevolent patrons duty-bound to "take care of their Negroes." They idealized the old-timey "darkie," forever content and submissive, and took credit for providing protection and succor to a helpless inferior. Their brutality notwithstanding, planters were prompt to take credit for extending assistance to their tenants and croppers in the form of food, medical care, and protection from white violence and criminal justice entanglement. Black farmers routinely gave ritualized expressions of gratitude that no urban black would grant, but neither would ever be *publicly* treated as equal in dignity by whites, no matter how well-meaning. Hortense Powdermaker puts it well: "The emotions that accompany white attitudes toward the Negro run a gamut including affection, kindliness, pity, indulgence, fear, hostility. The one thing no white man will overtly give a Negro is respect."[123]

Institutional disjunction enforcing social distance and black isolation, the rigid "racial etiquette" of face-to-face interaction mandating deference, and asymmetric prohibitions of intimacy: these mechanisms converged to skew all social relations between whites and blacks in such a way as to forbid reciprocity between them, to interdict black dignity, and to *generalize social verticality in both the material and symbolic orders*. Such steep verticality, in turn, practically supplied "a continual demonstration that the Negro is inferior to the white man and 'recognizes' his inferiority," which "serves not only to flatter the ego of the white man, but also to keep the Negro from real participation" in the broader society.[124] Two key institutions from which blacks were violently barred, electoral politics and criminal justice, form the third, superstructural component that operated to

---

Since Emancipation (1986), p. 292. But see the dissenting view of Lisa Lindquist Dorr, *White Women, Rape, and the Power of Race in Virginia, 1900–1960* (2004), who stresses the gap between collective representation and practice in the handling of black-on-white rape and the internal divisions of whites along class and gender lines.

[122] On the paternalistic cast of American slavery, see Peter Kolchin, *American Slavery: 1619–1877* (2003), pp. 111–32; Eugene D. Genovese and Elizabeth Fox-Genovese, *Fatal Self-Deception: Slaveholding Paternalism in the Old South* (2010). This is also dissected by Schultz, *The Rural Face of White Supremacy*, chapters 1 and 6.

[123] Powdermaker, *After Freedom*, p. 42.

[124] Myrdal, *An American Dilemma*, p. 612.

bolster the economic infrastructure and sociosymbolic structure of Jim Crow.

Superstructural lock: political and judicial exclusion

To contest their economic abuse as sharecroppers, institutional seclusion, and personal mistreatment at the hands of random whites in everyday encounters, including the constant threat of violence, the first logical remedy for blacks would have been to put political pressure on the authorities to curtail or prohibit such practices. But, while on paper they were endowed with the right to vote by virtue of the 15th amendment to the federal constitution passed in 1870, in reality African Americans were methodically banished from the ballot box across the South. An assortment of arcane registration rules, residency requirements, poll taxes, literacy tests, "grandfather clauses," disqualifying criminal offenses, and the sheer chicanery and coercion of local officials effectively made them *zombie citizens* stripped of political capacity.[125] Any challenge to these restrictions was itself quashed by redoubled intimidation and unrestrained aggression, for it was "part of the Negro's caste 'place' that he does not vote and does not complain about being unable to do so."[126]

Denying political equality was construed by whites as essential to thwarting "social equality" and thence to safeguarding their putative racial purity and caste superiority by preventing "the un-American and inhuman leprosy" of intimate unions with "the somber hued, black-skinned, thick-lipped, bull-necked, brutal-hearted African."[127] The linked *triadic repudiation of political, social, and sexual horizontality* was in turn mandated by the alleged biological and moral inferiority of the Negro. The latter were amply documented by new ethnological and medical research, which portrayed the "Ethiopians" as biological

---

[125] V. O. Key, *Southern Politics in State and Nation* (1983 [1949]); C. Vann Woodward, *The Origins of the New South, 1877–1913* (1972), pp. 321–49; Myrdal, *An American Dilemma*, chapter 22; and Litwack, *Trouble in Mind*, pp. 218–99. The efforts of black and white progressives to release strictures on black political citizenship during the half-century after 1910 are captured by Kimberley Johnson, *Reforming Jim Crow: Southern Politics and State in the Age Before Brown* (2010), chapter 8.

[126] Dollard, *Caste and Class in a Southern Town*, p. 212.

[127] Georgia representative Seaborn Rodenberry, arguing in favor of a constitutional amendment barring marriage between whites and blacks, cited by Kennedy, *Interracial Intimacies*, p. 85.

Jim Crow as Caste Terrorism

threats, vectors of insanity, tuberculosis, and venereal infection, and fated to revert to savagery by the removal of the positive restraints of slavery.[128]

Round election time, candidates and the press inflamed racial passions by lamenting rising incidents of African-American "impudence" and "outrages" allegedly committed far and wide by libidinous blacks on the prowl for white females. Voting season called on whites to defend the "home front" through scurrilous "nigger baiting" suggesting a direct link between politics and sexual mixing, voting and rape, black access to the polls and the looming irruption of the Negro beast into the bedroom, sanctuary of the virtue of white women.[129] Hysterical public expressions of Negrophobia were de rigueur and fueled the collective racial animus subtending the entire social and symbolic edifice of Jim Crow. In the rural Mississippi of the 1930s, "one of the quickest ways for a politician to get notoriety was to kill a Negro; such an act would speed him on the way to getting office" by broadcasting the vigor of his personal commitment to caste supremacy.[130]

When informal pressure and violence proved insufficient to suppress the African-American clamor to partake in elections, the former confederate states turned to legal machinations to nullify the voting rights of their Negro citizens. Here, as on many other fronts, Mississippi provided a model. Using force and fraud, discrimination in registration and intimidation, the authorities of the Magnolia state cut the number of black voters from 96 percent of the voting eligible colored population in 1868 to a paltry 6 percent by 1892 (it was only 7 percent as late as 1964), compared to 70 percent for whites. In the capitol city of Jackson, white terror was such that only 1 of 270 registered African Americans dared to cast a ballot in 1875.[131] But this was still not deemed sufficient: the specter of "Negro domination" at the polls motivated the organization of a special state constitutional convention designed to circumvent the federal constitution in 1890.

The meticulosity of the legal work conducted "for no other purpose than to eliminate the nigger from politics; not the 'ignorant and vicious' as some of those apologists would have you believe, but the

---

[128] Stein, "'Nature Is the Author of Such Restrictions'."
[129] Edward L. Ayers, *Vengeance and Justice: Crime and Punishment in the Nineteenth-Century American South* (1984), pp. 237–44; Litwack, *Trouble in Mind*, p. 221, and Gilmore, *Gender and Jim Crow*, esp. chapter 4.
[130] Dollard, *Caste and Class in a Southern Town*, pp. 216–17.
[131] McMillen, *Dark Journey*, p. 39.

nigger," to quote the blunt words of Governor Vardaman (who viewed the Negro as "a lazy, lying lustful animal" akin to a hog), is instructive. The new requirements to exercise the franchise included being registered four months in advance, being a resident for two years in the state and a full year in the election district (likely to disqualify a "migratory race"), to have paid all taxes as well as a $2.00 annual poll tax (a high bar for poor sharecroppers), and to have committed none of a list of criminal offenses which included arson, bigamy, fraud, and petty theft, but not murder, rape, or grand theft, on the belief that the "furtive offenses of a patient, docile people" would specifically bar blacks. If needed, the vague last requirement, to read any section of the state constitution and "give a reasonable interpretation thereof," enabled local officials to admit illiterate whites while barring black applicants. All in all, "the new constitution dealt a crushing blow to black morale, but its suffrage measure had little practical impact on a people already largely hounded from politics."[132]

The other Southern states soon followed suit, altering their constitutions to institute "white primaries" and to multiply formal devices to block African Americans from the booth. New property, educational, and "character" requirements were generalized, whose application could be modulated by county registrars to ensure smooth Negro exclusion. In a one-party political system characterized by near-permanent electoral tenure, rampant corruption, and illegality at the polls (where the ballot was neither uniform nor secret), "the preferred method of denying their constitutional rights to blacks" consisted in playing on the decentralized architecture of the national bureaucratic field "to vest discretion in local officials and trust them to preserve white supremacy."[133]

The stratagems were endless: blacks seeking to vote could be handed tricky registration blanks to fill out with no assistance, ensuring that some error would be made that served as basis for denial; they could be told that registration cards had "run out," instructed again and again to "come another day," or flat out ignored. Their registration forms could get thrown into the wastebasket right in front of them, "lost" after submission, or their names mysteriously failed to appear on the voting rolls even after being duly registered.

---

[132] Ibid., p. 48.
[133] Michael J. Klarman, *From Jim Crow to Civil Rights: The Supreme Court and the Struggle for Racial Equality* (2006), p. 33. The standard work on the topic remains J. Morgan Kousser, *The Shaping of Southern Politics: Suffrage Restriction and the Establishment of the One-Party South, 1880–1910* (1974).

Jim Crow as Caste Terrorism

Registrars skipped the education test for white applicants but routinely disqualified African Americans for "mispronouncing a single word. Even professors at Tuskegee and other Negro universities have been disenfranchised by failing to pass these tests."[134] New rules could always be made up on the spot to reject black applicants, as when a county required that two duly registered white voters countersign their registration.[135] And if the accumulation of formal devices was not enough to deny blacks the suffrage, "another barrage of informal devices" came swiftly into play, ranging "from the insults and threats presented to the prospective Negro voter as he enters the polling place to the violence administered to his person and property by the Klan."[136] To complete the picture, in most localities, a few "good Negroes" (also known as "white folk's niggers" due to their humble and loyal demeanor) were permitted to vote to perfect the façade of democratic access.

The second possible shield against economic and social brutality is the judicial institution, which could have enforced basic rights, limited abuses, and deterred violence against blacks by sanctioning whites resorting to it. But, in the Jim Crow South, African Americans were founded to "look upon law and justice, not as protecting safeguards but as sources of humiliation and oppression."[137] For the local police, courts, and corrections, staffed exclusively by whites beholden to the civil religion of racial supremacy, effectively *made caste an extension of the law*. In this "strange atmosphere of consistent illegality," African Americans were routinely "arrested and sentenced for all kinds of actual or alleged breaks of the caste rules, sometimes even for incidents where it is clear that their only offense was to resist a white person's aggression."[138]

Policemen diligently repressed even minor transgressions of the racial etiquette of subservience, defended private white interests against Negroes on principle, and fostered the diffusion of racial punishment by buttressing the intimidation and violence wielded by planters, employers, and vigilantes. Their role as supercilious

---

[134] Myrdal, *An American Dilemma*, p. 484.

[135] William Henry Chafe et al. (eds.), *Remembering Jim Crow: African Americans Tell About Life in the Segregated South* (2013), p. 279.

[136] Myrdal, *An American Dilemma*, p. 489.

[137] Du Bois, *The Souls of Black Folk*, p. 176.

[138] Myrdal, *An American Dilemma*, p. 536. On the police, courts, and prisons as apparatuses of caste enforcement, see Amy Louise Wood and Natalie J. Ring (eds.), *Crime and Punishment in the Jim Crow South* (2019).

"watchdog against 'social equality'"[139] was further extended by the bus operators, gas meter readers, postal workers, tax collectors, and all manner of petty bureaucrats on the lookout for signs of black insubordination. In the eyes of patrolmen, untrained and issued from the poorest segment of white society, every Negro man was a born criminal and every Negro woman an instinctive prostitute; due to their putative debased nature, blacks understood only the language of force and were in need of strict controls. As a result, police brutality was the normal *modus operandi*; beatings were routine, with or without arrest, as were shootouts and reciprocal killings among white police and blacks presented by the authorities as "bad niggers."[140]

Southern courts operated in avowed violation of basic principles of procedural transparency and fairness, not to mention minimal standards of social dignity, and routinely trampled upon the rights of African Americans, with the acquiescence of the US Supreme Court, which repeatedly refused to intervene to correct the blatant racial bias in judicial proceedings in the South. Overall, black citizens "enjoyed relatively less procedural fairness than did slaves" after 1890.[141] The courts failed to enforce a range of criminal statutes when blacks were the victims (of murder, theft, or bigamy, for instance) but diligently pursued charges when their offenses harmed whites.[142] Flimsy or trumped-up evidence was routinely introduced to indict and convict African-American defendants; confessions obtained through beatings and torture were accepted into the record as was testimony from whites boasting of engaging in "nigger hunts"; overt expressions of partiality and prejudice among jurors were commonplace.

Judges denied motions to change venue even when the defendants had to be whisked into "mob-proof jails" in nearby counties for their safety and when their courtrooms were invaded by vociferous white

---

[139] Myrdal, *An American Dilemma*, p. 537. For a development and documentation of this point, read Brandon T. Jett, *Race, Crime, and Policing in the Jim Crow South: African Americans and Law Enforcement in Birmingham, Memphis, and New Orleans, 1920–1945* (2021).

[140] Gail Williams O'Brien, *The Color of the Law: Race, Violence, and Justice in the Post-World War II South* (1999), chapter 5. Conversely, black oral folklore and literature celebrated that figure as the heroic incarnation of resistance to white encroachment. Lawrence W. Levine, *Black Culture and Black Consciousness: Afro-American Folk Thought from Slavery to Freedom* (1978), pp. 407–20; Jerry H. Bryant, "Born in a Mighty Bad Land": The Violent Man in African American Folklore and Fiction* (2003).

[141] McMillen, *Dark Journey*, p. 202.

[142] Christopher Muller, "Freedom and Convict Leasing in the Postbellum South" (2018), pp. 376–7.

crowds. White attorneys endured death threats and drastic ostracization if they took black clients while black lawyers could hardly step forward to defend them since their race would be openly held against their client (in some states, they were not allowed to appear in court, period). As a result, countless defendants were tried and convicted without the benefit of an attorney well into the 1940s. Judges meted out swift and extreme punishment, barely respecting formalities – murder trials in Mississippi were commonly expedited in a half-day – to ensure a speedy guilty outcome liable to prevent angry white hordes from invading the courtroom to seize the defendant and members of his family: "In the case of threatened lynching, the court makes no pretense at justice; the Negro must be condemned, and usually condemned to death, before the crowd gets him."[143]

Black lawyers were scarce (there were none outside of major cities), largely self-taught, their clientele impecunious, and they faced insurmountable obstacles ranging "from petty harassment to total exclusion," including retaliatory disbarment proceedings if they performed their part to the dissatisfaction of the court.[144] In some counties, they were prohibited from entering the courtroom or being sworn in; in others, they had to argue their case from the gallery and were treated with open disdain by white judges and white witnesses, some of whom refused to answer their questions and insulted them on the stand during cross-examination. Racial disparities in sentencing were beyond astronomical: it was common knowledge in Georgia, for instance, that "many more black men spent years for stealing a farm animal than white men did for murdering blacks."[145] What is more, the court took effective jurisdiction only over more serious offenses committed by blacks against whites. Low-level infractions were generally left to be handled privately by planters and bosses in logging camps, where the lash was still in use.

A form of punishment has left an indelible mark on the history and iconography of the Jim Crow South: convict leasing followed by roadside chain gangs.[146] Ruined by the Civil War, their infrastructure

---

[143] Myrdal, *American Dilemma*, p. 553. "Rumors of mob action frequently plagued judicial proceedings" so that court justice "bordered on lynch law" and the "trial served merely to validate pretrial accusations" (McMillen, *Dark Journey*, p. 209).
[144] Litwack, *Trouble in Mind*, p. 250; Ayers, *Vengeance and Justice*, p. 76; Klarman, *From Jim Crow to Civil Rights*, pp. 156–8.
[145] Litwack, *Trouble in Mind*, p. 252.
[146] Contractual penal servitude, under which the state sells the labor power of convicts to private operators, was invented by New York state in the 1820s and adopted

in shambles, Southern states sought to avoid the cost of building and running prisons by leasing convicts to planters and companies in sectors such as railways, timber, and mining as well as for the production of cotton, sugar and tobacco.[147] Planters and companies paid the state a monthly fee per inmate ($3 in Georgia and $1.10 in Mississippi in the 1890s), shouldered the costs of their supervision, feeding, and upkeep, and put them to work under abject conditions that caused astronomical levels of attrition. In Mississippi in the 1880s, the annual mortality rate for convicts ranged from 6 to 16 percent and blacks suffered rates eight times those of whites, who were rarely taken outside prison walls. The result was that "not a single lease convict ever lived long enough to serve a sentence of ten years or more."[148] Women convicts were, moreover, subjected to rampant sexual abuse by overseers and other convicts. Children as young as eight were leased out because taxpayers refused to waste money on young blacks whom they regarded as incorrigible criminals; in the Magnolia state at century's end, one lease convict in four was a teenager or a child.[149] Convicts were beaten savagely and tortured for minor infractions, as well as routinely whipped, a punishment overseers regarded as especially apposite for blacks.

> **The murderous brutality of convict leasing***
>
> Hamilton's convicts worked at jobs that free labor did not like to do, in places [like mines and swamps] where free labor sometimes feared to go. Employers preferred them over Asians ("too fragile"), Irish ("too belligerent") and local blacks ("too slow"). . . . The men were chained for days in knee-deep pools of muck, "their thirst driving them to drink the water in which they were compelled to deposit their excrement." . . . The prisoners ate and slept on bare ground,

by nearly all Northern states during the following decade. Rebecca McLennan, *The Crisis of Imprisonment: Protest, Politics, and the Making of the American Penal State, 1776–1941* (2008), chapter 2.

[147] W. E. B. Du Bois, "The Spawn of Slavery: The Convict Lease System in the South" (2005 [1901]); Alex Lichtenstein, *Twice the Work of Free Labor: The Political Economy of Convict Labor in the New South* (1996); Ayers, *Vengeance and Justice*, chapter 6.

[148] David M. Oshinsky, *Worse than Slavery: Parchman Farm and the Ordeal of Jim Crow Justice* (1997), p. 46. See also the state-by-state tally in Matthew J. Mancini, *One Dies, Get Another: Convict Leasing in the American South, 1866–1928* (1996).

[149] Oshinsky, *Worse than Slavery*, p. 50.

> without blankets or mattresses, and often without clothes. They were punished for "slow hoeing" (ten lashes), "sorry planting" (five lashes), and "being light with cotton" (five lashes). Some who tried to escape were whipped "till the blood ran down their legs"; others had a metal spur riveted to their feet. Convicts dropped from exhaustion, pneumonia, malaria, frostbite, consumption, sunstroke, dysentery, gunshot wounds, and "shackle poisoning" (the constant rubbing of chains and leg irons against bare flesh)....
>
> On many railroads, convicts were moved from job to job in a rolling iron cage, which also provided their lodging at the site. The cage – eight feet wide, fifteen feet long, and eight feet high – housed upwards of twenty men. It was similar to "those used for circus animals," wrote a prison official, except it "did not have the privacy which would be given to a respectable lion, tiger, or bear."
>
> Prisoners were beaten for breaking the rules, for falling behind in their work, or sometimes for the pleasure of guards. In the 1870s, neighboring farmers complained that the groans and screams of "the convicts at night [are] often so absolutely heart-rending as to prevent sleeping." Camp officials responded by gagging the prisoner to muffle their cries.
>
> * David M. Oshinsky, *Worse than Slavery: Parchman Farm and the Ordeal of Jim Crow Justice* (1997), pp. 44–5, 61.

In Georgia as in other states, moreover, "the transition from penitentiary confinement to convict leasing coincided with a shift in the composition of its inmates" from white to black such that African Americans were leased at a rate 12 times that of whites. Punishment through convict leasing for property crime was deployed differentially across counties in proportion to the capacity of African Americans to gain some measure of socioeconomic independence by acquiring land or migrating to cities. This suggests that the policy was mobilized to keep blacks in their appointed social place and to stabilize the economic infrastructure of the caste regime.[150] From its inception in Mississippi in the 1860s to its extinction in Alabama in the late 1920s, convict leasing produced hefty profits for the states – Tennessee even sold the convicts' urine to local tanneries and their unclaimed corpses to the Nashville medical school – the companies who used them, and

---

[150] Muller, "Freedom and Convict Leasing in the Postbellum South," p. 369.

for labor agents who subleased them, as well as sheriffs who received a fee for each Negro they arrested on petty charges to turn into a lease convict. It partook of an interwoven *grid of forced labor* that included sharecropping, peonage and the monopolistic company store. It also served to "undermine legal equality, harden racial stereotypes, spur industrial development, intimidate free workers, and breed open contempt for the law."[151]

Four principles governed the functioning of criminal supervision and sanction. The first is the *structural meshing and functional surrogacy* of informal (customary, everyday) and formal (legal, bureaucratic) means of subordination of blacks: mob violence and judicial rule, far from being antithetical, worked in tandem. Second, the enforcement of caste rule, including the use of force, was *entrusted to every white Southerner through a tacit delegation* that turned the latter into de facto agents of the racial state. "Vigilance was backed up by the authority of white citizens to accuse, judge, and punish racial transgressions outside the court."[152] Third, black recalcitrance, resistance, and challenge to subordination were met with the *swift escalation* of legal and extralegal force.[153] "Violence, terror, and intimidation" were pervasive, and their confluence created "a psychic coercion that exists nearly everywhere in the South. A Negro can seldom claim the protection of the police and the courts if a white man knocks him down, or if a mob burns his house or inflicts bodily injuries on him or on members of his family. If he defends himself against a minor violence, he may expect a major violence. If he once 'gets it wrong', he may expect the loss of his job or other economic injury, and constant insult and loss of whatever legal rights he may have had."[154]

The fourth pivot of criminal justice in the Jim Crow South was *indifference and inaction toward crime among African Americans*. Whites regarded blacks as congenitally impulsive and violent, believing that they "take to crime as fish to water."[155] They cast little value on their life and honor. As a result, crimes amongst blacks were routinely ignored by the authorities, including assault, prostitution, and the rape of black women, fueling inordinate rates of violence in the

---

[151] Oshinsky, *Worse than Slavery*, p. 56. This is a more general observation: throughout the South, "whites destroyed blacks' faith in the law" (Ayers, *Vengeance and Justice*, p. 234).
[152] Berrey, *The Jim Crow Routine*, p. 104.
[153] Myrdal, *An American Dilemma*, pp. 485–6 and 489–90.
[154] Ibid., p. 485.
[155] Berrey, *The Jim Crow Routine*, p. 77.

Jim Crow as Caste Terrorism

African-American community. Caste thoroughly infected the hierarchy of offenses and decisively inflected their corresponding punishment: "If a nigger kills a white man, that's murder. If a white man kills a nigger, that's justifiable homicide. If a nigger kills a nigger, that's one less nigger."[156] Judicial adjudication and sentences striking black defendants were, moreover, modulated based on "whose nigger" they were, that is, on the status and interest of the white planter to whom they were attached by economic dependency and social fealty. Planters often intervened in favor of their cropper or farm hand as they were "loath to lose a good hand to prison."[157] But protection by a white patron was always precarious and only reinforced dependency and vulnerability.

Political exclusion and judicial excision have to be grasped together analytically, for they worked jointly to safeguard economic exploitation and marginalization and to bolster social separation and facilitate deference extraction. They also supported one another: electoral disfranchisement served to exclude blacks from juries and amputated their share of school funding and other public services. Conversely, judicial exclusion meant that blacks could not resort to the courts to enforce their paper right to vote and to obtain protection from routine white violence at the polls.[158]

The omnipresent specter of "white death"

As a regime of domination, Jim Crow is *extreme in three distinct yet cumulative senses*. First, it imposes *radical verticality* across the sweep of institutional sectors and stamps all spheres of social life with the principle of "less racial eligibility," leaving virtually no breathing room and not a shred of public dignity to the subordinate category, treated as a homogeneous and homogeneously ignoble compact. Accordingly, it also denies the latter the *institutional autonomy* which the ghetto would provide to Southern blacks who escaped through migration into the Fordist metropolis of the industrial North after

---

[156] Ayers, *Vengeance and Justice*, p. 231.
[157] McMillen, *Dark Journey*, p. 205.
[158] This suggests the need for more studies of *county and state* courts in the postbellum South, which have been neglected due to the bias of legal scholarship in favor of the Supreme Court, as shown by Klarman's influential *From Jim Crow to Civil Rights*. For a view of the lower and higher courts in Mississippi in the 1940s, see Davis et al., *Deep South*, pp. 510–23.

World War I and, secondarily, in the slowly expanding cities of the south after World War II.[159] This lack of autonomy made it difficult and slow to accumulate the minimal economic, social, and cultural capital liable to fuel collective mobilization and open civic contestation of white rule. This is not to gainsay the efforts of Southern blacks to build and sustain communal organizations; it is to stress the latter's thinness and brittleness as well as their susceptibility to brutal white penetration.[160] Lastly, and most significantly, Jim Crow is extreme in the generalized deployment of potential and actual *violence as means of ethnoracial deterrence and enforcement* on every front, economic, sociosymbolic, and political-judicial.

Violence plays a dynamic twofold role in any regime of racial rule: by exerting constraint and inflicting injury upon the body of the subordinate, it is *itself* a form of racial domination; but it is also an instrumentality deployed to uphold *other* elementary forms of racial domination, be they denigration, discrimination, segregation, or seclusion. In the case of the postbellum South, violence was pivotal in bolstering the three building blocks of Jim Crow: it enabled the transmutation of sharecropping into debt peonage and tenancy into crop liens (exploitation); it upheld the institutional bifurcation and isolation of blacks in social and physical space, and it primed the pump of deference (subordination); finally, it enforced political and judicial disenfranchisement (exclusion). Last but not least, violence functioned as a communicative device broadcasting white might and signifying black vulnerability.

This violence assumed three main forms, random and routine intimidation and assault in everyday life, hunting and lynching, and rioting, which converged to flood black lives with suffusive fear and the corrosive trauma of white aggression anticipated, threatened, avoided, or suffered.[161] For every racial menace and onslaught rever-

---

[159] Loïc Wacquant, *The Two Faces of the Ghetto* (2025), chapter 2.

[160] Chafe et al., *Remembering Jim Crow*; Leslie Brown, *Upbuilding Black Durham: Gender, Class, and Black Community Development in the Jim Crow South* (2008); Woodruff, *American Congo*. On the "feudalization of black life" in the half-century after abolition, see Joel Williamson, *The Crucible of Race: Black–White Relations in the American South Since Emancipation* (1984), pp. 52–61.

[161] Chafe et al., *Remembering Jim Crow*, chapter 1, "Bitter Truths." This is a central theme in Litwack's *Trouble in Mind*, esp. chapter 6. It was stressed earlier by Myrdal, *An American Dilemma*, chapter 27; Dollard, *Caste and Class in a Southern Town*, chapter 15, "White Caste Aggression"; Williamson, *A Rage for Order*, chapter 4: "In Violence Veritas"; and McMillen, *Dark Journey*, "The Instrument in Reserve," pp. 28–32 and chapter 7.

Jim Crow as Caste Terrorism

berated across the African-American community as it entered into its internal narrative channels and sedimented in its collective memory. As the novelist and Mississippi native Richard Wright remarked in his autobiography *Black Boy*, "the things that influenced my conduct as a Negro did not have to happen to me directly; I needed but to hear of them to feel their full effects in the deepest layers of my consciousness. Indeed, the white brutality that I had not seen was a more effective control of my behavior than that which I knew."[162] The sheer frequency, diversity, and unpredictability of white violence made it a particularly efficient tool of racial dissuasion and discipline. It was also a form of domination *sui generis*, laden with symbolic meaning, as when black cadavers were torn, burnt, riddled with bullets and otherwise desecrated and left hanging from trees at crossroads to broadcast their *abjection*.

I indicated in the preceding sections how individual menace, beatings, police arrests, and vigilante attacks worked to keep sharecroppers under the thumb of rural landlords, to impose institutional bifurcation, to secure spatial division, and to extract deferential submission out of reticent blacks in ordinary encounters. Rules of racial interaction were subtended by custom, law, and force, the latter of which whites felt was indispensable because they believed that the animal nature of Negroes was such that they only responded to violence. It was also a matter of internal caste obligation: "If a Negro curses a white, the white may knock the Negro down; and failure to do so may even be considered as a failure in his duty as a white." Or he may later gather a group to visit the Negro's home to punish him, say, administer a whipping and force him into exile by putting him on a train.[163] Dollard gives many examples of situations showing that "the demand for submission and adulation" by whites was "secured by force if it [was] not willingly given."[164] Minor violations of caste etiquette, such as failing to take one's hat off in the presence of a white person, were interpreted as symptomatic of the desire of African Americans to claim equal status and, by implication, to compete in the spheres of the economy, sex, and prestige and for this reason they had to be punctiliously repressed.

Lynching is intimately associated with Jim Crow in its academic and public image alike. But, as a form of "community justice"

---

[162] Wright, *Black Boy*, p. 172.
[163] Davis et al., *Deep South*, pp. 45–6.
[164] Dollard, *Caste and Class in a Southern Town*, pp. 175 and 179.

deviating from the legal formalities of court proceedings, it was not unique to that region of United States, nor was it directed exclusively at blacks. Rather, it was practiced across the country's regions, if concentrated on the Western frontier, and it struck mainly whites until the 1880s.[165] It is then that it abruptly "blackened" as it turned into a Southern instrument of caste power, material and symbolic, to prevent the former slaves from claiming their economic, civil, and political rights. Thus 90 percent of the lynchings recorded between 1882 and 1968 in the Deep South involved African-American victims, as opposed to 5 percent in the mountain states of the West and California.[166] Another common misperception is that lynching was mainly a response to sexual violations by black men. In fact, fully one-fourth of the 4,715 lynchings recorded between 1881 and 1946 were reactions to breaches of racial etiquette (sometimes as benign as insulting a white person), the same proportion as for rape and attempted rape.[167] The collective sense among whites that the victim had become "uppity" or impudent was enough to trigger a death sentence on the slightest pretext. And they knew that they could punish him with total impunity: in the period 1915–32, "of the tens of thousands of lynchers and onlookers, the latter not guiltless, only 49 were indicted and four have been sentenced."[168]

Yet *completed lynchings* were only the tip of the iceberg of *attempted and threatened* lynchings – Raper estimates them at one-third in the 1920s – and they sat on top of an even larger volume of executions and harsh judicial sentences meted out in haste as a means of preventing lynchings, in addition to "semi-official shootings."[169] Thousands were lynched but thousands more "were quietly murdered in isolated counties and dumped into rivers and creeks" without public notice and legal consequence.[170] And thousands more still were subjected to variegated violences short of killing, including beating, tarring

---

[165] Michael James Pfeifer, *Rough Justice: Lynching and American Society, 1874–1947* (2004).

[166] Orlando Patterson, *Rituals of Blood: Consequences of Slavery in Two American Centuries* (1998), p. 176.

[167] Ritterhouse, *Growing Up Jim Crow*, p. 36. A subtle account of the relation between caste etiquette and lynching is William J. Harris, "Etiquette, Lynching, and Racial Boundaries in Southern History: A Mississippi Example" (1995).

[168] Arthur F. Raper, *The Tragedy of Lynching* (2017 [1933]), p. 26.

[169] Ibid., pp. 15–32. A detailed case study of an averted lynching leading to a white-on-black pogrom and black counter-mobilization in Columbia, Tennessee, in 1946 is O'Brien, *The Color of the Law*.

[170] Litwack, "Jim Crow Blues," p. 11.

Jim Crow as Caste Terrorism

and feathering, and whipping. Dollard recounts the ordeal of a black man in rural Mississippi, well-known in the community for having a facial twitch, who was mistaken to have winked at a white woman (who knew well about his twitch). The latter's husband led a mob in front of the jail where the local police had locked the accused for his own protection. A mock trial was held on the street, which "gave the Negro the alternative of death by lynching, a long prison sentence, or a whipping," stipulated as 150 lashes. The accused chose the third option; he was taken to the edge of town, his hands and feet bound, and savagely whipped. A "friend at court," namely, the black man's white employer, intervened to make sure he would not get *murdered after* receiving his lashing. After which, the victim fled to the big city because it was unsafe for him to stay in a town where he could still get lynched at any time. This episode combines a false accusation, the threat of death by lynching, and gruesome lashing followed by exile, but it would show nowhere in the formal accounting of Jim Crow violence.[171]

More frequent still than lynchings were the "nigger hunts" during which dozens and sometimes hundreds of whites, heavily armed and often inebriated, driven by bloodhounds, would chase through the countryside after a Negro suspected of a crime. Manhunts, which could last a day and a night or longer, deserve their own rubric under the chapter on ethnoracial violence because they typically degenerated into "indiscriminate violence against innocent blacks who found themselves in the paths of posses. Posses resorted to intimidation, and often torture, to compel blacks to divulge the whereabouts or escape route of fleeing suspects. They shot down innocent blacks on the most flimsy pretexts" and left a trail of desolation, despair, and dread in their wake.[172] The manhunt also embodied the racial skew built in law enforcement as it rested "on the assumptions of the unlimited rights of white men and the absence of any rights on the part of an accused Negro. Simply by being accused of some crime, the latter – so the man-hunters feel – has forfeited every claim upon society."[173]

---

[171] Dollard, *Caste and Class in a Southern Town*, pp. 336–9.

[172] William Fitzhugh Brundage, *Lynching in the New South: Georgia and Virginia, 1880–1930* (1993), p. 35.

[173] Raper, *The Tragedy of Lynching*, p. 9. A gripping case study showing how manhunts and threats of lynching worked symbiotically with formal court proceedings that made a mockery of the judicial process is Melanie S. Morrison, *Murder on Shades Mountain: The Legal Lynching of Willie Peterson and the Struggle for Justice in Jim Crow Birmingham* (2018).

The posses that carried out manhunts enjoyed popular support and even the blessing of local authority, for they acted forcefully, not just to protect law-abiding citizens from crime, but also to uphold racial standards of conduct and subordination. They acted as *de facto* deputies of the Southern racial state. Such events created panic among the black community, as reprisals were typically directed, not just at the black "culprit" of a racial transgression but, if he escaped, against his family, by raping his wife, shooting his children, and looting and burning down his farm, and also against his neighbors. Whites could also recruit a "bad nigger" in the local community to kill that violator for a fistful of dollars.

Related in form to the manhunt were the targeted activities of white vigilante outfits that proliferated in the postbellum South, the most notorious and organized of which was the Ku Klux Klan (KKK) – two others were the paramilitary White League and the Knights of the White Camelia. In its first incarnation, spanning the decade after the Civil War, the KKK sought to combat the "evils" of Reconstruction and what it denounced as the "Africanization" of Southern society via the "mongrelization" of its population.[174] Its members fancied themselves as agents of law and order, needed to stem the rising tide of Negro crime, enforce the Black Codes, and suppress African-American as well as Republican political participation. The secret organization was forced to dissolve by the federal government in 1871.

The second Klan, initially launched as a commercial enterprise in 1915 and growing fraternal affiliates across the country, had "One hundred percent Americanism" as its founding creed, which entailed reclaiming the "white man's country" and restoring rigid patriarchy.[175] Riding and marching in armed throngs dressed in their white robes and hoods and planting their trademark burning crosses (regalia and ritual inspired by the pro-South and Negrophobe movie by D. W. Griffith, *Birth of a Nation*), KKK members aimed their threats and aggression, not only at African Americans, but also at Jews, Catholic, immigrants, and women who deviated from established gender norms. In the South, they believed themselves to be the frontline combatants in a race war which they waged by intimidation, assault, robbery, whippings, shootings, abduction, rape, torture, assassination, and the

---

[174] Elaine Frantz Parsons, *Ku-Klux: The Birth of the Klan during Reconstruction* (2015).
[175] MacLean, *Behind the Mask of Chivalry*; Feimster, *Southern Horrors*.

Jim Crow as Caste Terrorism

sacking and burning of black farms, earning their rightful place in the pantheon of American domestic terrorism.[176]

Racial violence in the postbellum South could also escalate to assume the collective form of the riot or, to be more precise, the *white-on-black pogrom* recalibrating the parameters of tolerable Negro behavior by targeting the group as such. Thus, in the early twentieth century, the Jim Crow regime was bolstered by a string of white pogroms that shook up coalescing African-American districts in Wilmington (North Carolina) in 1898, New Orleans in 1900, Atlanta in 1906, East St. Louis in 1917, Charleston (South Carolina), Knoxville (Tennessee), and Elaine (Arkansas) in 1919, Ocoee (Florida) in 1920 as well as a host of smaller towns in the Southern backcountry.[177] These attacks purported to suppress "the seeming idleness, criminality, physicality and super-sexuality" of black men as well as their desire to vote, to advance economically, and to push back at the boundaries of white domination. Racial rioting demonstrated "the capacity [of whites] to punish blacks almost at will, in any area, and as severely as they wanted"[178] if they dared challenge their social and symbolic position as perpetual *humiliores*.

The most destructive of these collective attacks was the 1921 pogrom targeting the Greenwood district of Tulsa, Oklahoma, known as the "Black Wall Street," which killed possibly hundreds of black residents – the exact death toll remains unknown and disputed to this day – injured nearly a thousand, and turned 35 prosperous city blocks into ashes, destroying some 1,300 homes and wiping out hundreds of businesses in less than 24 hours.[179] The trigger for this "race war"

---

[176] R. Blakesly Gilpin, "American Racial Terrorism from Brown to Booth to Birmingham" (2015).

[177] A rare black-on-white riot was the mutiny of Houston in 1917 caused by a police assault on African-American soldiers, in which members of the all-black 24th infantry regiment retaliated in a raid killing 11 civilians and five policemen. The perpetrators were court-martialed; 19 were sentenced to death and 41 to life imprisonment.

[178] Williamson, *A Rage for Order*, p. 148.

[179] Even though this explosion of ethnic violence, also known as the "Tulsa race war" and the "Black Wall Street massacre," has been painstakingly investigated, including by the 2001 Oklahoma Commission to Study the Tulsa Race Riot of 1921 sponsored by the state legislature, many of the basic facts about it remain in doubt or in dispute. For instance, the number of confirmed deaths is 39 but the total killed is estimated at between 75 and 300. See Alfred L. Brophy, *Reconstructing the Dreamland: The Tulsa Riot of 1921: Race, Reparations, and Reconciliation* (2003), and, for comparison, Lee E. Williams, *Anatomy of Four Race Riots: Racial Conflict in Knoxville, Elaine (Arkansas), Tulsa, and Chicago, 1919–1921* (2008).

was the attempted lynching of a black teenage delivery boy accused of sexual impropriety toward a white elevator girl, which armed black residents had intervened to stop. Hordes of whites then responded with rampaging violence aided and armed by the local police and national guardsmen. City authorities actively incited the killing, looting, and burning by deputizing white citizens and handing out badges and guns, as well as detaining some 6,000 black residents afterwards. But the structural forces behind the attack were resentment at the economic affluence of black Tulsans, the desire to seize valuable commercial land by industrial and railroad interests, and the will to put proud and prosperous African Africans back in their proper place of subservience.[180] *Riot as collective punishment* inflicted material destruction and physical pain; it also communicated a loud and urgent message: no matter how successful blacks were, they would remain an inferior caste whose conditional rights and prerogatives could be abridged at any time and even annihilated in an instant.

But most distinctive to Jim Crow was the flowering of *public torture lynching* as civic spectacle and racial sacrifice elaborated to affirm the unifying power of whiteness and project the despoliation of unruly black bodies.[181] To be sure, these racially festive lynchings – if one may be permitted this shocking expression – involving antemortem torture and postmortem desecration before an enthusiastic crowd, represented a minority of just under 10 percent of all reported lynchings.[182] But their material and symbolic impact was wholly disproportionate to their frequency because of the message of absolute ethnoracial power they sent, the sentiment of horror they generated, and the publicity they received through oral lore as well as their elaboration in white commercial culture in the form of newspaper stories, photographs, physical mementos, and postcards. Moreover, the staging of mock "people's trials" leading to ritualized caste killings turned pivots of *collective racial effervescence* affirming white supremacy was unique to the South, and to the more extreme regional forms of Jim

---

[180] Chris M. Messer, "The Tulsa Race Riot of 1921: Toward an Integrative Theory of Collective Violence" (2011).

[181] I borrow this expression from Garland David, "Penal Excess and Surplus Meaning: Public Torture Lynchings in Twentieth-Century America" (2005).

[182] Based on a study of 3,767 completed lynchings, Beck and Steward find that 7.7 percent of victims were physically tortured prior to death and 8.2 percent had their bodies desecrated. E. M. Beck and Stewart E. Tolnay. "Torture and Desecration in the American South, an Exclamation Point on White Supremacy, 1877–1950" (2019).

Jim Crow as Caste Terrorism

Crow rule.[183] These staged exhibitions of "community justice" riding on shared symbolism and emotions followed a formulaic script.[184] The black accused was snatched from jail or court (often with the complicity of the local sheriff), summarily identified and brutalized by his alleged white victims, forced to confess in an informal mock trial, and then transported with fanfare to a location chosen for its religious and political significance: a churchyard, an oak tree near the center of town, a bridge, or a crossroad, all symbols of transition. The ceremonial killing was scheduled days or weeks in advance to allow for newspaper publicity and the chartering of special excursion trains packed with excited crowds; companies released their employees so they could attend the festivities; whites driving over long distance jammed the roads to the announced murder site. Eager crowds could surpass ten thousands. On the appointed day, the spectators, comprising a broad cross-section of the local white population, including families with children in their Sunday best eager to picnic, were regaled for hours by the sadistic mutilation (involving a mix of skinning, cutting, soaking in kerosene, scorching with red hot irons, dismemberment, castration and even the force-feeding of genitals), slow burning, and eventual killing by hanging, goring, or shooting of the "bad niggah." At death, onlookers jumped into a frenzied scrum for prized souvenirs such as body parts of the sacrificed (a finger, a toe, teeth, crushed bones, a slice of cooked liver or heart) and picture card photographs produced on site by portable printing plants. The butchered and burnt body of the victim was then typically left to dangle from its rope for weeks as a gory visual advertisement for the awesome power of race justice while newspapers waxed eloquent about the carnival atmosphere of these "Negro barbeques."

---

[183] Brundage documents that torture and mutilating (though not perforation by gunfire) were reserved for black victims of lynching. Brundage, *Lynching in the New South*, p. 92.

[184] In piecing together this account, I draw on Orlando Patterson's stunning analysis of "Feast of Blood" in his book *Rituals of Blood*, as well as on Williamson, *A Rage for Order*, pp. 120–6; Philip Dray, *At the Hands of Persons Unknown: The Lynching of Black America* (2007); Grace Elizabeth Hale, *Making Whiteness: The Culture of Segregation in the South, 1890–1940* (2010), chapter 5, "Deadly Amusements"; Amy Louise Wood, *Lynching and Spectacle: Witnessing Racial Violence in America, 1890–1940* (2011); and Terry Anne Scott, *Lynching and Leisure: Race and the Transformation of Mob Violence in Texas* (2022). For visual accounts, see James Allen, *Without Sanctuary: Lynching Photography in America* (2000), and Dora Apel and Shawn Michelle Smith, *Lynching Photographs* (2007).

These festivals of caste rage were community events giving a lead role to lower-class "peckerwoods" but attended by "white quality," long tacitly supported by the churches, and overtly encouraged by the forces of order and by immunity from the authorities. Indeed, sheriffs, judges, and local police routinely appear in the photographs of lynchings that were popular as postcards and trade cards in the early twentieth century to commemorate the happening,[185] and no one would dare testify against the participants in any case. There was a ready-made phrase for coroners to inscribe these murders into the historical course of Southern racial normality: the victim had died "at the hands of persons unknown."[186] But they were not just ghastly warnings to all "uppity niggers" and white "nigger lovers" who would read and hear about them later through their endlessly reiterated social and commercialized telling. They were, according to Orlando Patterson, religiously inspired "sacrificial rituals of aversion" performed on the altar of the civil religion of race, which purified and sanctified the collective body of whiteness by expelling the polluted bodies of individual blacks who had refused their appointed place as deferential inferiors.[187]

Ultimately, the edifice of Jim Crow, with its core of systematic social separation governed by the principle of "no social equality" (subordination) resting on an economic infrastructure anchored by debt-driven sharecropping (exploitation) and stabilized by a superstructure of conjoint political and judicial disenfranchisement (exclusion), owed its solidity to the constant physical intimidation and stupendous volumes of violence it unleashed onto those who did not punctiliously conform to its dictates. John Dollard sums up the effect of this diffuse violence thus: "Every Negro in the South knows that he is under a kind of sentence of death; he does not know when his turn will come, but it may also be at any time. This tends to intimidate the Negro man into submission."[188] For African Americans, every encounter with Southern whites during this era was loaded with the possibility of unprovoked aggression and public repression; every setting and situation was colored, not just by overt contempt, but by

---

[185] Litwack, *Trouble in Mind*, p. 296, and Allen, *Without Sanctuary*. These photos, not for the faint of heart, can be viewed on the website: http://withoutsanctuary.org.

[186] Dray, *At the Hands of Persons Unknown*. This was the generic formula invoked after ordinary lynchings and other collective killings of Negroes, for instance, during manhunts.

[187] Patterson, *Rituals of Blood*, p. 218.

[188] Dollard, *Caste and Class in a Southern Town*, p. 359.

the looming specter of heinous assault and worse if they deviated from white expectations and demands for exhibitions of servility.[189] Something as banal as crossing into the *terra prohibita* of white space in a commercial establishment could trigger severe judicial repression or even murder: "If a Negro went into a white restaurant in our town and sat at a table and ordered a meal, our citizens would want to lynch him, or he would be arrested and a heavy fine imposed upon him."[190] That approving 1910 statement by a Florida newspaper editor sums up the smooth melting of legal and illegal violence in the enforcement of the Southern racial order. It also indicates how Jim Crow rule delegated to every white citizen the effective right to deploy violence as they saw fit in the service of upholding caste rule.

Proof that it never achieved legitimacy in the eyes of those it subdued, no other peace-time segregationist regime in modern history – not South Africa from the birth of the Republic in 1910 to the advent of apartheid in 1948, not Nazi Germany from the first anti-Jewish laws of 1933 to the entry into a war of conquest in 1939, not India from independence to the present toward the Dalits, not Tokugawa Japan from 1603 to 1867 toward its Buraku outcaste – relied so much on raw physical constraint and murderous brutality as America's second "peculiar institution."[191] Forced dispossession, constant intimidation, sudden expulsion, random assault and assassination by individuals and vigilante outfits acting with impunity, the unlawful application of legal force, public torture, lynching and pogroms: whites were bent on keeping their "darkies" down by all means necessary and to extort their assent if not consent to white supremacy. No wonder so many African Americans deemed free life in the New South "worser" than the days of slavery.[192]

---

[189] For black women, the specter of sexual assault by whites (as well as blacks) loomed even larger than that of lynching for men, as shown by McGuire, *At the Dark End of the Street*.
[190] Cited by Ritterhouse, *Growing Up Jim Crow*, p. 43.
[191] The raw materials for a reasoned comparison can be found in George M. Fredrickson, *White Supremacy: A Comparative Study of American and South African History* (1981); John W. Cell, *The Highest Stage of White Supremacy: The Origins of Segregation in South Africa and the American South* (1982); John Higginson, *Collective Violence and the Agrarian Origins of South African Apartheid, 1900–1948* (2014); Michael Burleigh and Wolfgang Wipperman, *The Racial State: Germany 1933–1945* (1991); Emanuel Marx, *State Violence in Nazi Germany: From Kristallnacht to Barbarossa* (2019); Mikiso Hane, *Peasants, Rebels, Women, and Outcastes* (1982); and Jean-François Sabouret, *L'Autre Japon, les Burakumin* (1983).
[192] Litwack, *Trouble in Mind*, p. 49; McMillen, *Dark Journey*, pp. 124–5.

Jim Crow as caste terrorism: virtues of conceptual clarity

Now we can assemble the economic infrastructure, the sociosymbolic structure, and the civic superstructure of Jim Crow into a single diagram in which these three elements are "glued" together by the different forms of violence, ranging from the use of illegal private force obeying "race custom" on the plantation and the streets to the deployment of legal public force guided by "Negro law" in the courts (see figure 9). This conception is well-defined, bounded, and

"Negro law" in the courts

– execution
– chain gang   **legal/public**
– convict labor
– incarceration
– fines and fees

– public torture
– lynching

– expulsion and banishment
– manhunts
– vigilante raids
– lynching, rape
– riot

           extralegal/
– lashing   **private**
– assault
– intimidation
– humiliation

"race custom" on the streets & plantation

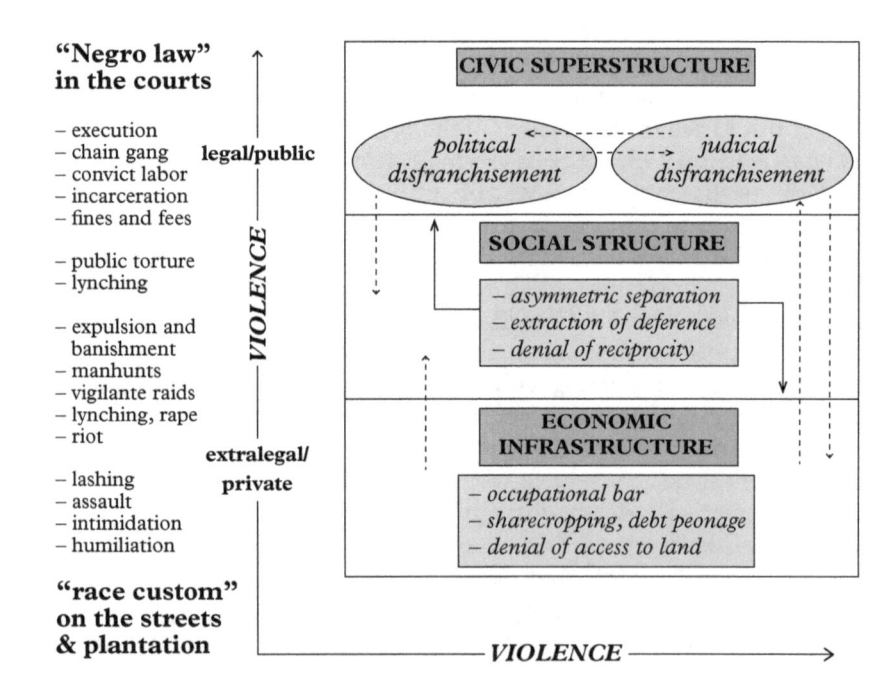

VIOLENCE

CIVIC SUPERSTRUCTURE
- *political disfranchisement* ↔ *judicial disfranchisement*

SOCIAL STRUCTURE
- *asymmetric separation*
- *extraction of deference*
- *denial of reciprocity*

ECONOMIC INFRASTRUCTURE
- *occupational bar*
- *sharecropping, debt peonage*
- *denial of access to land*

———— VIOLENCE ————→

Figure 9 The building blocks of Jim Crow as caste terrorism.

differentiated. It suggests that Jim Crow was a lot more, and a lot more ferocious, than "legally sanctioned and enforced segregation"[193] and it fruitfully replaces some vague notion of "racism," even of the structural variety.

---

[193] Chafe et al., *Remembering Jim Crow*, p. 13.

Jim Crow as Caste Terrorism

Putting these different elements together in a clear-cut and articulated model, I propose that we think of Jim Crow as a *regime of caste terrorism* because the ever-looming threat of "white death" twisted every interaction, permeated every institution, and penetrated deep into black subjectivity.[194] And it braced the dark armor protecting the other components of the system from challenge as well as tied them into an impervious organizational block as indicated by figure 9. Terror made agrarian superexploitation possible; it subtended the extraction of deference in face-to-face encounters; and it protected political and judicial exclusion. I do not use the term *caste terrorism* for rhetorical effect, for the shock value of the term, to sound "radical" by seeming to indict this nexus of institutions of white rule – I cautioned in the first chapter against falling into the logic of the trial, which inevitably skews inquiry, fuels emotions to the detriment of analysis, and defeats scientific clarity. I mean it as a technical characterization of what constitutes the distinctive cement of that regime of extreme racial domination. Both terms, caste and terrorism, are therefore in need of conceptual specification.

As for caste, I draw in equal measure on the classic works of the American "caste and class school" by W. Lloyd Warner and his followers (John Dollard, Hortense Powdermaker, Allison Davis, Burleigh and Mary Gardner, and St. Clair Drake), who conducted ethnographies of the Deep South in the interwar decades, and on the cross-cultural elaboration of Gerald Berreman aiming to extend the concept beyond the domain of Indian anthropology. In his 1936 article "American Caste and Class," Warner characterizes a caste division as one in which "privileges, duties, obligations, opportunities, etc., are unequally distributed" among hierarchical categories between which marriage is restricted and "where there is no opportunity for members of the lower groups to rise into the upper groups or of the members of the upper ones to fall into the lower ones."[195] He insists that class and

---

[194] "White death" is the expression used by one of Richard Wright's novelistic characters to refer to unpredictable death at the hands of a cluster of whites, "the threat which hung over every male black in the South" (*Black Boy*, p. 172). For another poignant literary expression of the specter of white violence, read Langston Hughes, *Home* (1934).

[195] W. Lloyd Warner, "American Caste and Class" (1936), p. 234. In *Yankee City* (1963, one-volume abridged edition, pp. 412–24, citation p. 417), Warner and his co-authors present a finely differentiated picture of American ethnic groups according to five somatic types and six cultural types and construct a scale of "group subordination" leading them to introduce the notion of "semi-caste" (applying to Asians and Pacific islanders) and "color caste" (blacks of American, Puerto Rican, and African

caste are orthogonal and antinomic principles of social organization: the class order permits and encourages mobility, upward and downward, along a triadic vertical layering (lower, middle, upper) while the caste order stipulates rigidity and the impossibility of moving across categories (black and white). Writing a short decade after Warner, Gunnar Myrdal similarly argued for the analytic superiority of the concept of caste over race in *An American Dilemma* (1944), on the epistemological ground that castes are self-evidently social constructions whereas race trades on a correspondence, explicit or implicit, between culture and nature. To use race as an analytic construct is effectively to endorse the racialist belief in biologized difference if not to validate white supremacy.[196]

Scanning comparative studies of stratification based on inherited inequality in five societies (India, Rwanda, north Pakistan, Japan, and the United States), Berreman spotlights two cross-cutting dimensions of group formation: the mode of recruitment (given at birth or achieved in life) and whether membership establishes a hierarchy or not. This yields four principles of social organization: kinship (ascribed, unranked), territorial community (achieved, unranked), class (achieved, ranked), and caste (ascribed, ranked).[197] In addition, Berreman dispels the static and quietist vision of caste by showing that "caste relations in India are just as much characterized by dissent, resentment, guilt, and conflict as are race relations in the United States." He shows that both formations contradict the democratic principles professed by their respective nation (there is "an Indian dilemma" à la Myrdal no less than an American one); and that

---

parentage) occupying the lowest position in the "total configuration of American society." For a contemporaneous critique of the caste and class school from a neo-Marxist perspective, read Oliver C. Cox, *Caste, Class, and Race: A Study in Social Dynamics* (1948), in which Cox maintains that "the race problem is an aspect of modern political-class antagonism" and caste exists only in Brahmanic India.

[196] The term race is "inappropriate in a scientific inquiry, since it has biological and genetic connotations which are incorrect in this context and which are particularly dangerous as they run parallel to widely spread false racial beliefs" (Myrdal, *An American Dilemma*, volume 2, p. 667).

[197] Gerald Berreman, "The Structure and Function of Caste Systems" (1966), pp. 304–7. See also idem, "Caste in India and the United States" (1960), and "Caste as Social Process" (1967). This is close to Béteille's minimalist definition of the caste among the Tamil of India as "a named group of persons characterised by endogamy, hereditary membership, and a specific style of life which sometimes includes the pursuit by tradition of a particular occupation and is usually associated with a more or less distinct ritual status in a hierarchical system." André Béteille, *Caste, Class and Power: Changing Patterns of Stratification in a Tanjore Village* (1965), p. 46.

both yield, to varying degrees, "self-conscious, bounded, corporate groups" that act as such in the political sphere.[198] Related works by anthropologists of Southeast Asia assembled by Edmund Leach in an influential book confirms these observations and stress the "exceptional social rigidity" and the absence of statutory mobility as key features of caste regimes.[199]

I build on Warner and Berreman to flesh out a thicker, and thus historically more restrictive, notion of caste that enables us to distinguish it from ranked but fluid and flexible forms of ascribed ethnicity – that is, a constellation located at the bottom end of the diagonal of racialization (see figure 3, *supra*, p. 87).[200] I propose that a caste regime is constituted by (i) a rank-ordering of (ii) birth-ascribed, descent-based groupings that are (iii) endogamous, in which (iv) membership is permanent and transmissible, and (v) whose hierarchical separation is justified by a collective belief in purity or congenital superiority. This definition is congruent with Max Weber's proposal that "[t]he caste is, indeed, the normal form in which ethnic communities that believe in blood relationship and exclude exogamous marriage and social intercourse usually associate with one another." The author of *Wirtschaft und Gesellschaft* continues: "Ethnic coexistence, based on mutual repulsion and disdain, allows each ethnic community to consider its own honor as the highest one; the caste structure brings about a social subordination and an acknowledgement of 'more honor' in favor of the privileged caste."[201]

By that specification, the social structure of the postbellum South fully qualifies as a caste regime – indeed, I would argue that, with suitable adaptations, this notion of caste continues to apply to this day in the United States and is analytically superior to the commonsensical notion of "race" when it comes to specifying the position of African Americans in social and symbolic space.[202] In retrieving

---

[198] Berreman, "The Structure and Function of Caste Systems," pp. 296 and 301.

[199] Edmund R. Leach (ed.), *Aspects of Caste in South India, Ceylon and North-West Pakistan* (1960).

[200] The range of ethnic modalities is scanned by Rogers Brubaker, "Ethnicity, Race, and Nationalism" (2009).

[201] Weber, *Economy and Society*, vol. 2, pp. 933 and 934.

[202] The popular book by Wilkerson makes a germane case from a narrative angle, but her notion of caste is conceptually confused: she sees it as operating *in addition to, and not in lieu of, race*. She also portrays Hitler's Germany as a caste society when the Nazis' goal was, not to rule over Jews, but to extirpate them entirely from their *Lebensraum* through deportation or extermination. Isabel Wilkerson, *Caste: The Origins of Our Discontents* (2020).

and specifying the concept of caste, moreover, I am joining back with none other than Du Bois who spoke of a "work caste" for slaves and a "caste of color" for free Negroes during and after slavery; he also used the opposition between "caste of condition" under bondage and a "caste of race" under Jim Crow. In a little-known but pivotal 1906 text on "The Negro Question in the United States," written at the behest of Max Weber for a German social science annual, he labels "slavery based on race and color" as "the worst of caste differences." In one of his early speeches explicating the goals of the Niagara movement, the precursor to the NAACP, Du Bois calls for the "abolition of all caste distinctions based simply on race and color."[203]

I now turn to the second term of the construct "caste terrorism." In the analytic sense, terrorism is the *strategic threat or use of spectacular public violence to convey a political message*. It entails dramatic and surprise attacks, often staged against innocent or representative victims, designed to amplify that message and to sow fear among a target population so as to achieve effects disproportionate to the means invested and the risks taken. I adapt here the definition elaborated by political scientist Martha Crenshaw, who was a pioneer in the comparative and historical study of terrorism, writing long before the current wave of global Islamic terrorism made it a topic of pressing policy and scholarly concern – her first book investigated the "revolutionary terrorism" of the FLN during the Algerian war of independence.[204]

Crenshaw stresses that, whether it is wielded in the context of violent resistance to a state or in the service of state interests, "terrorist violence communicates a political message; its ends go beyond damaging an enemy's material resources. The victims or objects of terrorist attack have little intrinsic value to the terrorist group but *represent a larger human audience whose reaction the terrorists seek*."[205] In the case of Jim Crow, the audience included both blacks and whites as it fortified at once their intraracial unity and their interracial enmity. Taking

---

[203] Du Bois, *Black Reconstruction*, pp. 30, 146; idem, "Die Negerfrage in den Vereinigten Staaten (The Negro Question in the United States)" (2006 [1906]); Philip S. Foner (ed.), *W. E. B. Du Bois Speaks: Speeches and Addresses, 1890–1919* (1970), p. 47.

[204] Martha Crenshaw, *Revolutionary Terrorism: The FLN in Algeria, 1954–1962* (1978), and Martha Crenshaw (ed.), *Terrorism in Context* (1995). For a broad review of core theories and issues in this sprawling and fast-growing area of research, see John Horgan and Kurt Braddock (eds.), *Terrorism Studies: A Reader* (2012). For a neo-Foucauldian dissection of terrorism that disputes the notion's "semantic consistency" and "normative certainty," read Verena Erlenbusch-Anderson, *Genealogies of Terrorism: Revolution, State Violence, Empire* (2018).

[205] Martha Crenshaw, "The Causes of Terrorism" (1981), p. 379, my italics.

the symbolic dimension seriously, the delivery of terroristic violence acts in the manner of an endlessly reiterated *rite of institution* in that it traces, dramatizes, and hardens the boundary between the agent and the target, or, more precisely, between the two groups to which they belong.[206]

> **Terroristic violence and the "mist of anxiety"***
>
> What matters is the fear of extralegal violence, not knowing when or how the danger may appear, not being able to organize oneself with reference to it, uncertainty, and the mist of anxiety raised under such conditions. This threat is all the more pervasive and insidious the higher the class position of the Negro, since the higher positions tend to draw more hostile affect. The Northerner, of course, has a somewhat similar experience, especially if he is a researcher on the "nigger question." He too feels an eerie sense of threat when he crosses the caste barrier in any way, such as by signs of courtesy toward Negroes, or when he is seen riding in a car with a Negro where it is not clear that his mission is a professional one.
>
> * John Dollard, *Caste and Class in a Southern Town* (1937), p. 361.

Summarizing current research in social and legal studies, LaFree and Ackerman provide another fruitful characterization of terrorism as "the threatened or actual use of illegal force directed against civilian targets by nonstate actors in order to attain a political goal through fear, coercion, or intimidation."[207] Except that, to cover the American South, we must relax the restriction of force to nonstate actor, since Jim Crow fused state and nonstate violence, and thereby admit the blurring of the line between legal and illegal force. We must also discard the notion that "terrorism feeds on the ability of groups to portray the government and their agents as illegitimate," for, when white Southerners took the mandate of the region's racial state into

---

[206] "To speak of a rite of institution is to suggest that any rite tends to consecrate or legitimate an arbitrary boundary, that is, to cause it to be misrecognized as arbitrary and recognized as legitimate, natural." Pierre Bourdieu, "Les rites comme actes d'institution" (1982b), p. 58.

[207] Gary LaFree and Gary Ackerman, "The Empirical Study of Terrorism: Social and Legal Research" (2009), p. 347.

their own hands, they did it not to contest that state's authority but to remedy its perceived inefficiency by acting as its diligent de facto deputies. Indeed, it is this *generalized deputization of white citizens to act as diligent overseers and violent enforcers of caste rule* that best characterizes the specificity of Jim Crow.

Caste terrorism resided in the myriad acts of surveillance, intimidation, threat, and assault, climaxing with public torture lynchings that both bound whites together into an effervescent collective unified by the pornographic display of its racial superiority and sent a paralyzing message of dissuasion to blacks should they violate the requirement of *reverent outward acquiescence* to their ethnic overlords.[208] *In nuce*, the crux of Jim Crow domination resides in the simple, stark alternative it imposed on every single African American living in the South during that somber half-century: offer deference or suffer white death, figurative or literal.

To conclude, why take the trouble to put in the onerous mental work to replace a folk concept with an analytic one? The answer lies in the *scientific profits* this produces: conceptual construction, clarification, and consolidation give us the leverage to formulate, reframe, and then answer questions with increased rigor and precision. The proposed ideal-typical model of Jim Crow as caste terrorism summed up by figure 9 provides a clear and solid baseline for producing, organizing, and reading data differently as well as for theoretical elaboration and historical comparison.

Theoretical elaboration: by specifying and then disaggregating the phenomenon, an analytic concept makes it possible to disclose the recurrent linkages and trace the functional loops between its constituents and to investigate the social causes and consequences of their extant (dis)articulation. For instance, the model of Jim Crow proposed here suggests that we study jointly racial exclusion from politics and criminal justice and think of them as germane institutions of civic honor, the opposite of race as social dishonor; spotlight a direct connection between the conception of race as (hypo) descent, the obsession with blood purity, and the virulence of boundary enforcement; elaborate the social foundations and workings of the

---

[208] For Durkheim, "collective effervescence" arises from the close physical assembly and intensified exchanges between people gathered "to commune in the same idea and the same sentiment." It has for effect to recharge and give collective representations – in this case, the shared belief in the purity and eminence of the ruling race – their "maximal intensity." Émile Durkheim, *Les Formes élémentaires de la vie religieuse. Le système totémique en Australie* (1995a [1912]), p. 493.

Jim Crow as Caste Terrorism

two major variants of Jim Crow emerging across monographs, racial despotism and racial paternalism; grasp together state and nonstate violence in the creation and perpetuation of ethnoracial hierarchy; and that we consider racial etiquette and formal segregation as alternative modalities of the regulation of ethnoracial relations, the one dominant in the countryside and the other in the city, thus grounding race-making firmly in social morphology.[209] Lastly, by showing its structural-functional coherence, the model of Jim Crow as caste terrorism helps us enrich the comparative analysis of the triadic logics of exit (migration, internal and external), voice (protest, individual and collective), and loyalty (within and across ethnic groups, family, and locality), suggesting that exit and voice can be responses, not just to the decline of organizations, but also to their flourishing when these organizations are socially injurious.[210]

Next, the robust analytic concept of caste terrorism elaborated in this chapter makes it possible to *compare and contrast the many Jim Crow regimes deployed within the postbellum South* across time and space along each of the four analytic dimensions it specifies and their elements. For instance, it can help us track the differential mix of ethnoracial violence in different states or in urban and rural counties in the same state, or in the same region across the decades, and systematically link this mix to changes in, say, agricultural production, migration patterns, or political struggles over the franchise. It enables us to enter into the specificities of a given empirical site and social constellation, say Jim Crow in Hancock county, Georgia, or Baltimore, Maryland, in the 1940s, without getting lost in its particularities and thus to generalize both within and across cases instead of falling into the methodological trap of idiography.[211]

The analytic construct of Jim Crow further gives us a checklist to track and link the four major forces that combined to erode the

---

[209] Ritterhouse points in this direction in "The Etiquette of Racial Relations in the Jim Crow South" (2007), p. 33. What is missing is the specification of what features of urbanism exactly undermine racial etiquette aside from anonymity and to disentangle these from cohort effects, as the growth of Southern cities in the 1880s coincided with the coming of age of the first generation of African Americans born after abolition. It also spawned a growing class division between town and country, as documented by Du Bois, "The Negroes of Farmville, Virginia," and Fon Louise Gordon, *Caste and Class: The Black Experience in Arkansas, 1880–1920* (2007).

[210] I am referring here to the classic analysis of Albert Hirschman, *Exit, Voice, and Loyalty: Responses to Decline in Firms, Organizations, and States* (1970).

[211] Compare Mark Schultz, *The Rural Face of White Supremacy*, with David Taft Terry, *The Struggle and the Urban South*.

reproduction of the regime over time by weakening each of its core components: agricultural mechanization and rural outmigration sapped its economic foundations; urbanization and evolving conceptions of personhood rendered the extraction of deference deeply problematic; civic mobilization fueled by rising education and spreading democratic ideals, along with federal state intervention, broke down barriers to the ballot box and the courthouse; and the generalized pacification of social space in capitalist societies after World War II rendered the levels and forms of violence that had sustained caste rule universally shocking and indefensible – even in the eyes of Southern whites.[212]

Specifying the four building blocks of Jim Crow as it operated in the postbellum South demonstrates that it never existed in the North (where the preeminent mode of ethnoracial control was the *urban ghetto* during the era of Fordist industrialism, a very different institutional contraption, as we shall see in the next chapter);[213] that it collapsed during the postwar decades under the weight of its structural contradictions and political liabilities; and the analytical inanity of tagging the contemporary criminal justice system as "the New Jim Crow" (a point that will be elaborated in chapter 4). It also indicates that the path toward a fuller understanding of Jim Crow as a regime of ethnoracial domination will require the active collaboration of history and sociology, as recommended over a century ago by Émile Durkheim and three decades ago by Pierre Bourdieu, so that we may meld analysis and depiction, explanation and interpretation, topology and genealogy, structure and event, rigorous theory-building and rich narrative.[214]

---

[212] The televised spectacle of overt violence wielded against peaceful blacks engaging in nonviolent demonstration was a major factor in raising civic support, especially among the Northern population, for ending legalized segregation and voting exclusion. The murder of Emmett Till and the trial of his killers marked an inflection point in public indignation at rampaging white violence in the South, as shown by Berrey, *The Jim Crow Routine*, pp. 113–20, and Timothy B. Tyson, *The Blood of Emmett Till* (2017).

[213] A usage that flirts with analogy but turns out to be rhetorical is Purnell et al., *The Strange Careers of the Jim Crow North: Segregation and Struggle Outside of the South* (2019). Even more problematic is the retroprojection of Jim Crow as a tag to designate the treatment of free blacks in Northern states prior to the Civil War by Richard Archer, *Jim Crow North: The Struggle for Equal Rights in Antebellum New England* (2017).

[214] Émile Durkheim, "Débat sur l'explication en histoire et en sociologie" (1975 [1908]); Philip Abrams, *Historical sociology* (1982); Pierre Bourdieu and Roger Chartier, *Le Sociologue et l'historien* (2010 [1988]).

Jim Crow as Caste Terrorism

Last, and most fruitfully still, an analytic concept enables us to *replace Jim Crow into the fuller universe of regimes of ethnoracial domination*, past and present, colonial, and metropolitan, global North and global South, so that we may at once better identify its specificities and enroll them to formulate a general theory of race as naturalizing classification and stratification, and of the place of violence, material and symbolic, in their historical (re)production. It invites comparison with other caste systems, such as the Indian and the Japanese; with other regimes of terroristic violence, such as the Nazi and the Soviet; with other systems of deference extraction, as with absolutist courts and imperial territories.[215] Viewing Jim Crow as caste terrorism invites us, that is, to see "Southern history as US history" and US history as world history,[216] so that we may finally grasp it, not as a sociological aberration produced by redoubled American *exceptionalism*, class and racial, but as the normal creature of American *extremism*.

---

[215] Susan Bayly, *Caste, Society and Politics in India from the Eighteenth Century to the Modern Age* (2001); Timothy Amos, *Caste in Early Modern Japan: Danzaemon and the Edo Outcaste Order* (2019); Eric A. Johnson, *Nazi Terror: The Gestapo, Jews, and Ordinary Germans* (2000); James Harris (ed.), *The Anatomy of Terror: Political Violence Under Stalin* (2013); Norbert Elias, *The Court Society* (1983 [1969]); and Susan M. Deeds, *Defiance and Deference in Mexico's Colonial North: Indians Under Spanish Rule in Nueva Vizcaya* (2010).

[216] I borrow this expression from the classic article by economic historian Laura F. Edwards, "Southern History as US History" (2009), to which I add global history. A call to put an end to "a distinctive southern history and historiography," separate from the broad currents of national history, is Lassiter and Crespino (ed.), *The Myth of Southern Exceptionalism*: "The notion of the exceptional South has served as a myth, one that has persistently distorted our understanding of American history" (p. 7).

4

Deadly Symbiosis: When Ghetto and Prison Meet and Mesh

You know they got me trapped in this prison of seclusion
Happiness, living on tha street is a delusion
Even a smooth criminal one day must get caught
Shot up or shot down with tha bullet that he bought
Nine millimiter kicking, thinkin' about what tha street do to me
'Cause they never talk peace in tha black community
All we know is violence, do that job in silence
Walk tha city streets like a rat pack of tyrants
Too many brothers daily headin' for tha big penn
Niggas comin' out worse off than when they went in.

Tupac Shakur, "Trapped" (Death Row Records, 1991)

Since the onset of the new century, a chorus of activist, scholarly, and policy voices has gradually risen to call for "criminal justice reform" aiming to stem, stop, or turn back America's frenetic drive to hyperincarceration that quintupled the population held behind bars in the three decades after 1973, making the United States world leader in criminal confinement.[1] Of the many facets of this gargantuan penal

---

[1] See the precise panorama drawn by Katherine Beckett, "The Politics, Promise, and Peril of Criminal Justice Reform in the Context of Mass Incarceration" (2018), and the perceptive reflections of Marie Gottschalk, *Caught: The Prison State and the Lockdown of American Politics* (2015), chapter 12. The year 1973 marks the low point of incarceration in postwar US history after a slow decline during the 1960s despite a sharp rise in crime. From that inflection point, penal confinement rose exponentially, doubling every decade to reach its peak in 2008 at 2.4 million behind bars, corresponding to 760 inmates per 100,000, between 6 and 12 times the rate of European

state, none has received more academic and public attention than *racial disparities in imprisonment*, to the point where one might be led to believe that incarceration is, intentionally or not, targeted on blacks as such, irrespective of class and place, and that ethnoracial bias in policing, the courts, and corrections is rampant and even surging.

This view is recorded by the shift in the titles of two books by one of the nation's leading students of penality, the legal scholar Michael Tonry. In 1995, his path-setting tome *Malign Neglect* was subtitled *Race, Crime and Punishment in America*. By 2011, the racial *j'accuse* was more direct in his book revisiting the same nexus, entitled *Punishing Race: A Continuing American Dilemma* – echoing Gunnar Myrdal's landmark study on the black question in the United States at the mid-twentieth-century point.[2] Is this to say that, in the interim, penalization expanded to encompass all African Americans regardless of their economic, social, and cultural capital? One could be excused to think so given the many influential books that have ridden on a direct link between race and hyperincarceration, including Bruce Western's *Punishment and Inequality* (2006), Becky Pettit's *Invisible Men: Mass Incarceration and the Myth of Black Progress* (2012), and Heather Schoenfeld, *Building the Prison State: Race and the Politics of Mass Incarceration* (2018).[3] Scholarship on the question is remarkably one-sided: a search on "punishment" and "disparity" on Google Scholar yields a meager 1,170 hits for *class* disparity and a whopping 18,200 for *racial* disparity.[4]

---

countries. This count does not include 81,000 juveniles in custody, 33,000 irregular migrants in immigration detention centers, and persons held overnight in police lockups, estimated at 40,000 in 2008 (equal to two-thirds of the total carceral population of France).

[2] Michael Tonry, *Malign Neglect: Race, Crime, and Punishment in America* (1995), and idem, *Punishing Race: A Continuing American Dilemma* (2011); Gunnar Myrdal, *An American Dilemma: The Negro Problem and Democracy* (1944, reprint 1962).

[3] Bruce Western, *Punishment and Inequality* (2006); Becky Pettit, *Invisible Men: Mass Incarceration and the Myth of Black Progress* (2012); Heather Schoenfeld, *Building the Prison State: Race and the Politics of Mass Incarceration* (2018).

[4] For panoramic coverage, see Katherine Beckett and Megan Ming Francis, "The Origins of Mass Incarceration: The Racial Politics of Crime and Punishment in the Post-Civil Rights Era" (2020), and Elizabeth Hinton and DeAnza Cook, "The Mass Criminalization of Black Americans: A Historical Overview" (2021). No equivalent overview of class and punishment exists.

"Racial disproportionality" in incarceration in the United States

Three brute facts stand out and give a measure of the grotesquely disproportionate impact of hyperincarceration on African Americans. First, the ethnic composition of the inmate population of the United States was *inverted* in the half-century following World War II, going from about 70 percent (Anglo) white in 1950 to 70 percent black and Latino by 2000. Next, although the difference between arrest rates for whites and blacks was stable between 1976 and 1992, with the percentage black oscillating between 29 percent and 33 percent of all arrestees for property crimes and between 44 and 47 percent for violent offenses, the white–black incarceration gap grew substantially at the close of the century, jumping from 1 to 6 in 1985 to 1 to 8 only a decade later (1).

This disparity is even more pronounced in terms of the retrospective incidence of incarceration. In 2001, 2.6 percent of all white males had served time in prison compared to 16.6 percent of black males, a difference of 14 percentage points compared to a difference of 7 percentage points in 1974 (when the white and black rates were 1.4 percent and 8.7 percent respectively) (2). This trend is all the more striking for occurring during a period when significant numbers of African Americans entered into and rose through the ranks of the police, the courts, and the corrections administration and when the more overt forms of racial discrimination that were commonplace in them into the 1970s were greatly reduced, if not stamped out.

Lastly, the lifelong cumulative probability of "doing time" in a state or federal penitentiary based on the imprisonment rates of the early 1990s was 4 percent for whites, 16 percent for Latinos and a staggering 29 percent for blacks (3). Given the class gradient of incarceration, this figure suggests that *a large majority of African Americans of (sub-)proletarian status are facing a prison term* of one or several years (and in many cases several terms) at some point in their adult life, with all the family, occupational, and legal disruptions this entails. Indeed, a black male without a high-school education born in the late 1960s had a 59 percent chance of serving time by the close of the century, compared to a 11 percent chance for a white high-school dropout and 5 percent for a black male with some college (4).

1. Michael Tonry, *Malign Neglect: Race, Crime, and Punishment in America* (1995), p. 64; Christopher Muller and Alexander F. Roehrkasse, "Racial and Class Inequality in US Incarceration in the Early Twenty-First Century" (2022).
2. Thomas P. Bonczar, *Prevalence of Imprisonment in the U.S. Population, 1974–2001* (2003).
3. Thomas Bonczar and Allen Beck, *Lifetime Likelihood of Going to State or Federal Prison* (1997).
4. Bruce Western, *Punishment and Inequality in America* (2006), p. 27.

Reframing black hyperincarceration

But no tome on race and punishment has garnered more public attention, reached a broader audience, and had a bigger practical influence than Michelle Alexander's blockbuster, *The New Jim Crow: Mass Incarceration in the Age of Color Blindness* (2010). The book deserves full credit for diffusing knowledge about, and energizing militancy against, the racialized expansion of the penal state.[5] The trouble is with the flawed thesis it advocates. Synthesizing research on the impact of criminal surveillance and sanctions on African Americans (without always giving proper acknowledgment to the works she recapitulates or borrows from),[6] the civil rights attorney asserts that the justice system has effectively resuscitated Jim Crow, turning the prison into a blunt instrument of "racial caste control" through the medium of the War on drugs.

The problem is that "Jim Crow" is never defined conceptually or characterized empirically; instead, the expression is deployed *metaphorically* by rhetorical invocations of the US South in the early twentieth century. Likewise with "caste," which Alexander uses "the way it is used in common parlance to denote a stigmatized racial group locked into an inferior position by law and custom,"[7] disregarding the

---

[5] Michelle Alexander, *The New Jim Crow: Mass Incarceration in the Age of Color Blindness* (2010). Militant spinoffs of the book include Daniel Hunter, *Building a Movement to End the New Jim Crow: An Organizing Guide* (2015), and Veterans and Hope, *The New Jim Crow Study Guide and Call to Action* (2016). The book has been assigned to entire college cohorts at elite universities and infamously banned by some prison authorities.

[6] This starts with the book's title and central thesis, which were formulated in 1999 by Ira Glasser, the executive director of the American Civil Liberties Union (ACLU), in a paper entitled "American Drug Laws: The New Jim Crow," widely read in legal circles. This article is not mentioned in *The New Jim Crow*.

[7] "Mass incarceration is, metaphorically, the new Jim Crow"; a system "not unlike Jim Crow"; a design "analogous to Jim Crow." Alexander, *The New Jim Crow*, p. 11,

fact that all members of a lower caste are trapped in a subordinate location regardless of socioeconomic standing, which, we are going to see, is emphatically not the case for African Americans when it comes to incarceration. As for the so-called War on drugs, it did prime the pump of penalization and dramatically expand the poor black population caught in the judicial net, but it fails to account for the brunt of the stunning growth of the prison population, half of which is composed of violent offenders, with some 200,000 serving life sentences around 2010, more than the total prison population in 1973.

Jim Crow, caste: as used by Alexander, these terms overlook, for the first, the all-encompassing mesh, suffusive rigidity, and unspeakable horrors of Jim Crow documented in the preceding chapter and, for the second, the steep class gradient that affects the operations of the police, courts, jail, probation, and prison, such that the population corralled behind bars, *black, white, and Latino,* is composed nearly *exclusively of (sub)proletarian men* mired in economic precarity, cultural destitution, and social marginality. A few indicators: in 2016, 85 percent of state prisoners had only a high-school education or less, as against a mere 3 percent a college degree (compared to 42 percent nationwide). A paltry 14 percent were married versus 50 percent for the general population. One in five convicts had lived in public housing (which accounts for less than 1 percent of all housing) and nearly half reported growing up in a single-parent household; 42 percent had parents or guardians who received welfare; and an astounding 17 percent had lived in a foster home, agency or institution, eight times the national rate. To top it all, some 59 percent had family members who had been incarcerated, including 21 percent a father only and 37 percent a sibling.[8] In short, there are virtually no middle-class prisoners in America (as in other advanced societies): the *penitentiary is a reservation for the precariat, regardless of color.* It follows

---

56, 12. The book is also filled with hyperbole tailored to arouse the reader's indignation. One typical example: "Today a criminal freed from prison has scarcely more rights and arguably less respect than a freed slave or a black person living 'free' in Mississippi at the height of Jim Crow" (*The New Jim Crow*, p. 13). Let us mention just two new rights: the right not to be (re)enslaved and sold as chattel and the right not to be lynched with impunity for "disrespecting" a white person. For a methodical dismantling of Alexander's thesis, read James Forman, Jr., "Racial Critiques of Mass Incarceration: Beyond the New Jim Crow" (2012).

[8] Lauren G. Beatty and Tracy L. Snell, *Profile of Prison Inmates, 2016* (2021). The judicial profile of state inmates is also telling: 13 percent are incarcerated for public disorder, 15 percent for drug offenses, 16 percent for property offenses, and a whopping 56 percent for violent crimes.

that, when they come out, former inmates find themselves caught in a dizzying tailspin of deep poverty, abiding social isolation, persistent joblessness, rampant violence, and chronic pain and addiction often leading to recidivism and a return to prison.[9]

But there is more: as incarceration ballooned around century's turn, the probability of imprisonment for black middle-class men (with some college) *decreased* by 27 percent, dropping from 2.9 percent to 2.1 percent between 1990 and 2008 while the same probability for black lower-class men (with less than high school) *doubled* from 19.6 percent to 37.2 percent.[10] The result is that the *class disparity* in incarceration among black men jumped from 1 to 6.7 in 1990 to 1 to 17.7 just 20 years later, while the *racial disparity* between whites and African Americans slumped from 1 to 7.5 in 1990 to 1 to 6.3 in 2008.[11]

This class bifurcation refutes the thesis that the prison has established a caste order. It would be a strange caste regime indeed that lets escape the middle- and upper-class members of the subaltern group while subjugating nearly as many members of the dominant group as it does of the outcaste population in raw numbers: in 2008, the country's prisons held 591,000 blacks but also 528,000 whites; among women, the count for the white inmates (51,000) surpassed that for their black counterparts (29,000). Extending beyond prison gates, 56 percent of the adult population placed under probation (a full 4.2 million) was white and only 29 percent black. Similarly, 41 percent of the 821,000 parolees were Euro-Americans as against 38 percent African Americans. As we saw in the previous chapter, Jim Crow did not spare any blacks, no matter their class, and, needless to say, it did not subjugate any whites. Furthermore, successful blacks were the preferential targets of routine caste violence in the postbellum South, which is the pattern exactly opposite to penal sanction in the age of hyperincarceration: educated black Americans have paradoxically "benefited" from the expansion of the penal state by seeing their incarceration rate go down.

---

[9] Bruce Western, *Homeward: Life in the Year After Prison* (2018).
[10] Pettit, *Invisible Men: Mass Incarceration and the Myth of Black Progress*, table 1.2, p. 15. Remarkably, Pettit does not comment on this stunning class divergence because it does not fit the predominant narrative of racial inequality in incarceration she wishes to support.
[11] Ibid., p. 15. See also Christopher Muller and Alexander F. Roehrkasse, "Racial and Class Inequality in US Incarceration in the Early Twenty-First Century" (2022).

From mass incarceration to hyperincarceration

The notion of mass incarceration was first applied, in Anglophone scholarship, to the internment of Japanese Americans during World War II pursuant to the belief that they posed a national security threat due to their presumed double allegiance (1). The adjective "mass" was apposite then insofar as the 125,000 corralled in some 75 concentration camps constituted the near-totality of the target population. The term resurged a decade later to characterize the runaway growth of the country's carceral population yielding astronomical rates of penal confinement by historical and comparative standards. In a landmark essay opening a 2001 special issue of the new journal *Punishment and Society* devoted to "Mass imprisonment: causes and consequences," the world's leading student of penality David Garland put the expression on the academic map and it quickly became the conventional designation in research, policy, and advocacy (2).

There are three problems with the concept of "mass incarceration." First, a condition concerning *three-fourths of one percent* of the US population hardly qualifies as a mass phenomenon. About 4 percent of Americans suffer from acute alcohol dependency; yet there is no general scholarly or policy alarm about "mass alcoholism" in the country. Also, the vast majority of criminals, the presumed target population, have not been captured and corralled. Second, mass suggests that the phenomenon is *indiscriminate*, affecting large swaths of the citizenry (as with mass media, mass culture, mass unemployment, etc.), implying that the penal net has been flung far and wide across social and physical space. But the ravenous expansion of the police, courts, jail, and prisons during the four decades following the ghetto uprisings of the 1960s has been finely targeted, first by class, second by that disguised brand of ethnicity called race, and third by place. This cumulative targeting has led to the *hyper*incarceration of one particular category, *lower-class black men trapped in the crumbling ghetto*, while leaving the rest of society – including, most remarkably, middle-class and upper-class blacks – practically untouched.

Third, and more important still, this *triple selectivity is a constitutive property of the phenomenon*: had the penal state been rolled out indiscriminately through policies resulting in the capture of vast numbers of whites and well-to-do citizens, capsizing their families and decimating their neighborhoods as it has for inner-city African Americans, its growth would have been speedily derailed and eventually stopped by political counter-action. "Mass" incarceration is socially tolerable and therefore workable as public policy only *so long as it does not reach the masses*: it is a figure of speech, which hides the multiple filters that operate to point the penal dagger.

1. Roger Daniels, *Prisoners Without Trial: Japanese Americans in World War II* (1993).
2. David Garland (ed.). *Mass Imprisonment: Social Causes and Consequences* (2001).

The New Jim Crow is a stunning rhetorical success built on analytical quicksand, historical approximation, and empirical obfuscation, with cherry-picked facts and anecdotes too often taking the place of systematic data mining.[12] Nonetheless, it is useful for our purposes because it spotlights five common mistakes in the scholarly and policy debate on race and punishment: (1) the scotomizing of the ghetto as a distinct historical stage and contraption of ethnoracial domination; (2) the elision of class and space via the unthinking conflation of the hyperghetto, as the core geographic target of penalization, with African Americans or with "communities of color" *in globo*; (3) the singular attribution of "mass incarceration" to the so-called War on drugs when narcotics offenders composed only 20 percent of the stock of prisoners (26 percent of black prisoners) at the peak of incarceration; (4) the elision of the millions of poor whites who cycle in and out of the criminal adjudication apparatus: in 2001, more white males (1.98 million) had ever served time in a penitentiary than black males (1.94 million)[13]; (5) the false equation of punishment with prison when the most prevalent criminal sanction by far is probation: in 2000, there were three times as many probationers

---

[12] There are four main reasons for the success of *The New Jim Crow*. The first is the simplicity of its thesis, involving the singular cause of "colorblind racism," encapsulated by its catchy title, which resonates with the common sense of activists and gives it the imprimatur of "scholarship." The second is its timing, coming out during the hopeful heydays of the first Obama presidency. The third is its evangelical tone tapping the deep well of racial guilt among white readers and class guilt among black readers. The fourth is that it gives a "pass" to the African-American bourgeoisie for its active support for superpunitive justice policies and thus an opportunity to redeem itself by reengaging the struggle for full citizenship for the lower class, a third Reconstruction centered on the penal state.

[13] Thomas P. Bonczar, *Prevalence of Imprisonment in the U.S. Population, 1974–2001* (2003).

Racial Domination

(3.8 million) as prisoners (1.3 million); for blacks alone, the figures were 604,000 prisoners for 1.4 million probationers.

This chapter focuses on the first two mistakes and correlatively tackles the third. It draws on the characterization of *seclusion* as the fourth elementary form of racial domination sketched in chapter 2 (see *supra*, pp. 137–9): the forcible relegation of a dishonored category to an exclusive zone of social and physical space such that this category develops parallel institutions within it. It argues that the conjoint explosion and accelerating racialization of incarceration in the United States after the acme of the Civil Rights Movement is not the product of a *return* to a prior regime of ethnoracial domination, least of all Jim Crow as specified in the preceding chapter. It is the result, rather, of the *collapse of the ghetto* as instrument of ethnoracial closure in the metropolis; its replacement by a *dual sociospatial formation* composed, on the one hand, of the hyperghetto for the black precariat and, on the other, of segregated or mixed black middle-class districts emerging in the inner or outer ring of the metropolis;[14] and the subsequent *institutional interlock* between the barren hyperghetto and the voracious carceral apparatus.

I implement the analytical principles enunciated in chapter 1 as regards the need to historicize, the imperative of disaggregation, and the rejection of the logic of the trial exemplified by the knee-jerk moral denunciation of the "New Jim Crow." Rather than bemoan "structural racism" in criminal adjudication, as has become *de rigueur* among scholars, activists, and legal professionals,[15] I put forth two interconnected theses. The first is a *historical thesis*, replacing the carceral institution in the full arc of ethnoracial division and domination in the United States since the country's colonial origins. The second is an *institutional thesis*, explaining the astounding upsurge in black incarceration over the second half of the twentieth century as a result of the obsolescence of the ghetto as device for caste control. This collapse created a need for a substitute contraption for keeping African Americans lacking skills and credentials "in their place," that is, in a subordinate and confined position in physical, social, and symbolic space.

---

[14] Loïc Wacquant, "Revisiting Territories of Relegation: Class, Ethnicity and the State in the Making of Advanced Marginality" (2015).
[15] Julian M. Rucker and Jennifer A. Richeson, "Toward an Understanding of Structural Racism: Implications for Criminal Justice" (2021); Hedwig Lee, "How Does Structural Racism Operate (in) the Contemporary US Criminal Justice System?" (2024). See my critique of this approach *supra*, pp. 188–97.

This functional imperative did not impose itself mechanically by dint of some structural magic. Rather, it met the wish of established city dwellers, working and middle class, *white and black*, to keep dispossessed and dishonored populations at a distance and to contain the spillover of the social and moral disorders gripping the postindustrial "inner city." These disorders were incarnated by the loathsome and fearsome figure of the "underclass," which emerged in the late 1970s and invaded the public sphere to inspire the joined policies of welfare contraction for the women of the hyperghetto (and their children) and penal expansion for their men (husbands, brothers, sons, and fathers), as both were marginalized by the correlative revamping of the labor market, the neoliberal state, and the dual metropolis.[16]

I further demonstrate that, in the post-Civil Rights era, the remnants of the dark ghetto and the fast-expanding penal apparatus have become tightly linked by a triple relationship of functional equivalency, structural homology, and cultural fusion. This relationship has spawned a *carceral continuum* that ensnares a supernumerary population of younger black men, who either reject or are rejected by the deregulated low-wage labor market, in a never-ending circulus between the two institutions.[17] These men are widely perceived by urban residents and city officials alike as a *public menace* and a *social burden* that requires stringent action on the part of government, extreme caution on the part of employers, and tenacious diffidence when it comes to landlords, which cannot but further weaken their social moorings and ability to "go legit."

This carceral mesh was solidified by two sets of concurrent and interrelated changes that took place in the long shadow of the ghetto uprisings of the 1960s. At the one end, sweeping economic and political forces have reshaped the structure, texture, and function of the urban Black Belt of mid-century to *make the ghetto more like a prison.* Here, I draw on the agonistic theory of race-making and the imperative of analytic disaggregation to specify the constituent components of the ghetto as a form of sociospatial *seclusion* and to show how these came unglued in the 1960s to spawn a new social formation, the *hyperghetto*, doubly segregated by race and class, devoid of an

---

[16] Loïc Wacquant, *The Invention of the "Underclass": A Study in the Politics of Knowledge* (2022), pp. 133–6, and idem, *Punishing the Poor: The Neoliberal Government of Social Insecurity* (2009), especially chapters 2 and 3, and pp. 304–14.

[17] This perverse and self-sustaining circulus is deftly illustrated with ethnographic and biographical materials by Reuben Jonathan Miller, *Halfway Home: Race, Punishment, and the Afterlife of Mass Incarceration* (2021).

economic role, and therefore trapping the most marginalized segments of the black urban proletariat which are the priority clientele of the penal state.[18]

At the other end, the "inmate society" that inhabited the penitentiary system of the country during the postwar decades broke down in ways that *made the prison more like a ghetto*. Not only did the ethnic mix of the carceral population turn over completely in a half-century, going from 70 percent white at the end of World War II to 70 percent black and Latino in 2000; racial identity also supplanted criminal identity as the dominant principle of vision and division behind bars, and the stratification of inmates changed accordingly, with ethnically based gangs taking over the regulation of space, social relations, and the contraband economy.[19] This created a toxic brew of conflict and violence causing prison authorities to escalate discipline, segmentation, and austerity, including the racial compartmentalization of carceral facilities and activities as means of institutional management, in routine violation of the US Supreme Court decision *Johnson v. California* (2005) narrowing the grounds for permissible segregation behind bars.[20]

The resulting *symbiosis between hyperghetto and prison* not only enforces and perpetuates the socioeconomic marginality and symbolic taint of the urban black precariat, feeding the runaway growth of the penal system that has become a major component of the neoliberal state. It also plays a pivotal role in the remaking of "race" and the redefinition of citizenship via the production of a racialized public culture of vilification of criminals. *Penal stigma has thus become stitched onto the double stigma of race and poverty*, suffusing the symbolic opposition between a (black) dangerous and undeserving "underclass," characterized by cultural deviation and antisocial behaviors, on the one side, and a meritorious and anxious (white and black) middle class, fearful of street criminals and scornful of the dissolute ways of welfare recipients, on the other.[21]

---

[18] Loïc Wacquant, *Urban Outcasts: A Comparative Sociology of Advanced Marginality* (2008), chapters 2–4, and idem, *The Two Faces of the Ghetto* (2025), chapters 6–8, for an extended contrast between ghetto and hyperghetto.

[19] Patrick Lopez-Aguado, *Stick Together and Come Back Home: Racial Sorting and the Spillover of Carceral Identity* (2018).

[20] Chad R. Trulson et al., "Racial Desegregation in Prisons" (2008).

[21] The scorn and fear of the black bourgeoisie for the black precariat is amply documented in James Forman, *Locking Up Our Own: Crime and Punishment in Black America* (2017). In Washington, DC, the African-American middle class, and espe-

Deadly Symbiosis

A fuller analysis, extending beyond the black hyperghetto, reveals that the increasing use of incarceration to shore up the bottom end of caste division in American society partakes of a broader "upsizing" of the penal sector of the state which, together with the drastic "downsizing" of its social sector, aims at imposing desocialized wage labor as a norm of citizenship for the deskilled fractions of the postindustrial working class.[22] This emerging government of poverty wedding the invisible hand of the deregulated labor market to the iron fist of an intrusive and omnipresent punitive apparatus is anchored, not by a "prison industrial complex," as with the demonic myth diffused by radical opponents to "mass incarceration,"[23] but by a *carceral-assistential mesh* mating workfare and prisonfare which carries out its mission to surveil, train, and neutralize the populations recalcitrant or superfluous to the new economic and ethnoracial regime according to a gendered division of labor, the men being handled by its penal wing while (their) women and children are managed by a revamped welfare-workfare scheme designed to buttress casual employment. It is this shift from the social to the penal treatment of urban marginality and its correlates at the foot of the class and caste structure, subsequent to the unraveling of the Fordist-Keynesian social compact, that has brought the prison back to the societal center, counter to the optimistic forecasts of its impending demise by analysts of the criminal justice scene in the early 1970s.[24]

To recognize that the hypertrophic growth of the penal institution is one component of a more comprehensive restructuring of the American state to impress the requirements of neoliberalism is not to negate or even minimize the special office of race in its advent.[25] If the

---

cially community leaders, viewed lower-class residents involved in crime as "the enemy within," "walking powder kegs," and "malicious members of our own race" (pp. 32, 63, 195). There is a long history of overt denigration of what Du Bois called "the criminal element" in black society and culture that is usually kept under the rug in accounts focusing on the black/white divide.

[22] Wacquant, *Punishing the Poor*, especially pp. 304–14.

[23] Angela Y. Davis, *The Prison Industrial Complex* (2001); Critical Resistance, *Abolition Now! Ten Years of Strategy and Struggle Against the Prison Industrial Complex* (2008); and Julia Sudbury (ed.), *Global Lockdown: Race, Gender, and the Prison-Industrial Complex* (2014).

[24] Calvert R. Dodge (ed.), *A Nation Without Prisons: Alternatives to Incarceration* (1975); Thomas Mathiesen, *The Politics of Abolition Revisited* (2014); Tommie Shelby, *The Idea of Prison Abolition* (2022).

[25] Loïc Wacquant, "Three Steps toward the Historical Anthropology of Actually Existing Neoliberalism" (2012).

prison offered itself as a viable vehicle of resolving the "black question" after the implosion of the dark ghetto – that is, for reformulating it in a way that both *invisibilized it and reactivated it* under new disguises: street crime, welfare dependency, and the "underclass" – it is surely because America is the one society that has pushed the market logic of commodification of social relations and state devolution the furthest.[26] But, conversely, if the US far outstrips all advanced nations in the international trend toward the penalization of social insecurity, it is because, just as the dismantling of welfare programs was accelerated by the conflation of blackness and undeservingness in national culture and politics,[27] the "great confinement" of the rejects of market society – the poor, the mentally ill, the homeless, the jobless and the useless – can be painted as a welcome "crackdown" on *them*, those dark-skinned criminals issued from a pariah group still considered alien to the national body. Thus, just as the color line inherited from the era of Southern slavery and Jim Crow subjugation directly determined the misshapen figure of America's "semi-welfare state" in the formative period of the New Deal,[28] the handling of the "underclass" question by the carceral institution at the close of the twentieth century is key to fashioning the visage of the neoliberal state in the twenty-first.

Four peculiar institutions

To ascertain the pivotal position that the penal apparatus has come to assume within the system of instruments of (re)production of ethnoracial hierarchy in the post-Civil Rights era, it is indispensable to adopt a historical perspective of the *longue durée* so as to situate the prison in the full lineage of institutions which, at each epoch, have carried out the *work of race-making* by drawing and enforcing the caste line that cleaves the national society asunder. These institutions produce stratification out of classification and racialize in the sense of

---

[26] Gøsta Esping-Andersen, *The Three Worlds of Welfare Capitalism* (1987); Joel Handler, *Down from Bureaucracy: The Ambiguity of Privatization and Empowerment* (1996); Jonas Pontusson, *Inequality and Prosperity: Social Europe vs. Liberal America* (2005).

[27] Martin Gilens, *Why Americans Hate Welfare: Race, Media, and the Politics of Anti-Poverty Policy* (1999); Michael B. Katz, *The Undeserving Poor: America's Enduring Confrontation with Poverty* (2013).

[28] Robert Lieberman, *Shifting the Color Line: Race and the American Welfare State* (1998); Ira Katznelson, *When Affirmative Action Was White* (2005).

naturalizing, homogenizing, and hierarchizing the populations they process.

Two features of America's *racial exceptionalism* must be spotlighted at the outset. First, the United States is the only nation in the world to define as "black" all persons with *any* known African *ancestry*, creating a rigid black/white division between two mutually exclusive "communities" in spite of widespread mixing across time evidenced by the wide range of hues among the African-American population.[29] Thus it is commonly estimated that three-fourths of persons deemed black have white ancestors and one-third Native American ancestors – W. E. B. Du Bois famously had French, Dutch, and Haitian ascendants; Martin Luther King had Irish and Amerindian blood; and Walter White was one sixty-fourth Negro and yet the leader of the NAACP. Next, the "one-drop rule" and the principle of strict hypodescent (pursuant to which the offspring of mixed unions are assigned to the category deemed inferior, here blacks, irrespective of phenotype, upbringing, and other social properties) are applied solely to African Americans, making them the only US ethnic group that cannot merge into white society through intermarriage. As we saw in the previous chapter, this highly peculiar conception of blackness arose in the American South to bolster the institution of slavery and was later deepened by Jim Crow rule in the post-abolition South.

Put succinctly, the task of *defining, confining, and controlling African Americans* in the United States has been successively shouldered by four "peculiar institutions" that have married all five of the elementary forms of racial domination – stigma, discrimination, segregation, seclusion, and violence: slavery, the Jim Crow regime of caste terrorism, the urban ghetto, and the novel organizational compound formed by the interlock between the vestiges of the imploding ghetto and the expanding carceral net, as set out in table 1.

The first three of these institutions, chattel slavery until the Civil War, Jim Crow operative in the agrarian South from the end of Reconstruction to the acme of the Civil Rights Revolution, and the ghetto arising in the twentieth-century Northern industrial city, have, each in its own manner, served two joined yet discordant purposes: to recruit, organize, and *extract labor* out of African Americans, on the one hand; and to demarcate and *seclude them* so

---

[29] Joel Williamson, *New People: Miscegenation and Mulattoes in the United States* (1980); F. James Davis, *Who Is Black?: One Nation's Definition* (1991); and Frank W. Sweet, *Legal History of the Color Line: The Rise and Triumph of the One-Drop Rule* (2005).

Table 1
The four "peculiar institutions" and their basis

Peculiar institution	Form of labor	Core of economy	Dominant social type
SLAVERY (1619–1865)	fixed unfree labor	plantation	slave
JIM CROW (South, 1877–1965)	free fixed labor	agrarian and extractive	sharecropper
GHETTO (North, 1917–1968)	free mobile labor	industrial manufacturing	factory worker
HYPERGHETTO + PRISON (1973–)	fixed surplus labor	postindustrial services	welfare recipient and criminal

that they would not "contaminate" the surrounding white society that viewed them as irrevocably inferior and vile because devoid of ethnic honor.

These two goals of *labor extraction and social ostracization* of a stigmatized category are in tension with one another inasmuch as to utilize the labor power of a group inevitably entails bringing it into regular intercourse and thereby invites the blurring or transgression of the boundary separating "us" from "them." Conversely, to immure a group in a separate physical and sociosymbolic space makes it more difficult to draw out and deploy its labor power in the most efficient way. When the tension between these two purposes, exploitation and ostracization, mounts to the point where it threatens to undermine either of them, its excess is drained, so to speak, and the institution restabilized, by resort to *physical violence*: the customary use of the lash and ferocious suppression of slave insurrections on the plantation, terroristic vigilantism and ritualized lynching in the postbellum South, and periodic bombings of Negro homes and pogroms against ghetto residents (such as the six-day riot that shook up Chicago in 1919) ensured that blacks kept to their appointed place in symbolic, social, and physical space in each epoch.[30]

---

[30] Thus the central place of violence in the black American collective experience and imagination, from Nat Turner, Frederick Douglass and Martin Delany to Ralph Ellison, Bayard Rustin, and Malcolm X. See Lawrence W. Levine, *Black Culture and Black Consciousness* (1977), and Ronald T. Takaki, *Violence in the Black Imagination* (1993).

Deadly Symbiosis

But the built-in instabilities of unfree labor and the inherent anomaly of caste partition in a formally democratic and highly individualistic society all but guaranteed that each "peculiar institution" would in time be undermined by the weight of its internal contradictions as well as by mounting black resistance and external opposition, to be replaced by its successor regime.[31] At each new stage, however, the apparatus of ethnoracial domination would become less total and less capable of encompassing all segments and all dimensions of the social life of the pariah group. As African Americans differentiated along class lines and acceded to full formal citizenship during the Second Reconstruction of the 1960s, the institutional complex charged with keeping them "separate and unequal" grew more differentiated and diffuse, allowing a growing middle and upper class of professionals, salary earners, professors, and high civil servants to *partially* compensate for the negative symbolic capital of blackness by their high-status cultural capital and proximity to centers of political power,[32] while lower-class blacks remained burdened by the triple stigma of "race," poverty, and putative immorality (as regards work and crime in particular).

> Keep the Negro in his place amongst his people, and he is healthy and loyal. Remove him, or allow him his newly discovered importance to remove him from his proper environment, and the Negro becomes a nuisance. He develops into an overbearing, inflated, irascible individual, overburdening his brain to such an extent about social equality that he becomes dangerous to all with whom he comes in contact.
>
> *The Property Owners' Journal*, cited in Chicago Commission on Race Relations, *The Negro in Chicago* (1920), p. 122.

---

[31] The "inherent instability of the slave relation" is demonstrated by Orlando Patterson in *Slavery and Social Death: A Comparative Study* (2018 [1982], p. 336), and that of bonded labor by Peter Kolchin in *Unfree Labor: American Slavery and Russian Serfdom* (1987, p. 359). The congenital incompatibility of caste separation and democracy is the fulcrum of Myrdal's influential analysis of the "American dilemma" of race.

[32] The social structure and cultural texture of this growing black bourgeoisie are dissected at three historical stages by E. Franklin Frazier, *Black Bourgeoisie* (1997 [1957]); Bart Landry, *The New Black Middle Class* (1987); Mary Pattillo, *Black Picket Fences: Privilege and Peril among the Black Middle Class* (2001); and Karyn R. Lacy, *Blue-Chip Black: Race, Class, and Status in the New Black Middle Class* (2007). A revealing first-hand account of life among the established segment of the black upper class is Margo Jefferson, *Negroland: A Memoir* (1915).

This historical schema should not be read as an ineluctable forward march toward ethnoracial equality so much as a transformation of the modalities and mechanisms of racial domination propelled by a combination of internal contradictions, black accommodation and resistance, and external cultural, political, and legal pressures. Each new phase of subjugation has entailed advances as well as setbacks.[33] Nonetheless, their sequence has marked a stepwise *"civilizing" of racial rule* (in Norbert Elias's sense of the term),[34] manifested most strikingly, in the contemporary period, by generalized public intolerance for overt prejudice, for visible discrimination, and for targeted ethnoracial violence. None of which puts an end to racial domination, but all of which contribute to expanding the possibilities for thwarting its mechanisms. It is fashionable nowadays, and it sounds suitably radical and *au courant*, to reject "narratives of racial progress" as illusory.[35] But the task of social science is not to fashion or rebut such grand narratives loaded with moral baggage; it is to establish the changing social conditions under which racialized exploitation, subordination, and exclusion occurs, and with what results in the different institutional sectors and tiers of social space. In so doing, social science can point paths toward remedial and transformative action.[36]

What is most striking over the span of the past century is the accelerating class differentiation of African Americans in social and physical space, in spite of relentless white pressure to homogenize them, making it possible for the *black bourgeoisie to escape the clutches of the fourth peculiar institution*, except when its class status gets blurred or erased (for instance, during a police stop while driving or in a "white space" where racial membership floods the scene).[37] This is evi-

---

[33] For an analysis of this stepwise pattern, see Philip A. Klinkner and Rogers M. Smith, *The Unsteady March: The Rise and Decline of Racial Equality in America* (1999), and, for an update, the germane diagnostic of Desmond S. King and Rogers M. Smith, *Still a House Divided: Race and Politics in Obama's America* (2011).

[34] For Elias, the "civilizing process" entails the growing role of social constraint toward self-constraint, the domestication of affect, the elaboration of courteous conduct and civility, and rising intolerance toward violence. Norbert Elias, *On Civilization, Power, and Knowledge: Selected Writings* (1998), chapters 1–3.

[35] Victor Erik Ray et al., "Critical Race Theory, Afro-Pessimism, and Racial Progress Narratives" (2018). See also my critique of Afropessimism, *supra*, pp. 91–9.

[36] I return to this question in the conclusion to the book, in which I retrace three paths to racial justice (*infra*, pp. 363–70).

[37] Elijah Anderson, *Black in White Space: The Enduring Impact of Color in Everyday Life* (2022).

denced, on the one side, by its *growing* geographic distance from the barren territory of the hyperghetto and, on the other, by the *decrease* in the probability of incarceration for college-educated blacks during the very period when the ghetto imploded and the prison population ballooned.[38]

It is further backed up by the fact that, after the acme of the Civil Rights Movement that mandated ethnic unity, the "silent majority" of the established African-American working and middle classes turned on what W. E. B. Du Bois castigated as "a distinct criminal class among the blacks," and supported the stringent policing and severe judicial policies that propelled hyperincarceration. "The black middle class renounced racial ties and denounced previously held progressive beliefs because they felt under assault by the urban black poor, who, they maintained, rejected the middle-class values of individual responsibility and respectability. This threat and its concomitant fear and anger caused the black silent majority to seek out technologies of control."[39] So much to say that the voracious penal state in revanchist America is at once a *race-making and a class-splitting institution*. Only by holding these two principles of classification and stratification together, class in the material order, ethnicity in the symbolic order, can we hope to grasp – and eventually thwart – the mechanisms perpetuating the fourth peculiar institution and its malignant ramifications.

1. Slavery turns racial (1619–1865)

From the first years of the colony to the Civil War, slavery was the institution that determined the collective identity and individual life chances of Americans of African parentage. Orlando Patterson has rightly insisted that slavery is essentially "a relation of domination and not a category of legal thought," and, moreover, a relation unusual for the inordinate volumes of material and symbolic violence it entails.[40] In the Americas (as opposed to, say, in the Islamic world, where it served no productive purpose), this violence was channeled to fulfill a definite economic end: to appease the insatiable appetite of the plantation for raw labor. The forcible importation of Africans

---

[38] Loïc Wacquant, "Class, Race and Hyperincarceration in Revanchist America" (2010b).
[39] Michael Javen Fortner, *Black Silent Majority: The Rockefeller Drug Laws and the Politics of Punishment* (2015), p. 153.
[40] Patterson, *Slavery and Social Death*, pp. 334 and passim.

and West Indians, and the rearing of their descendants under bondage (the country's enslaved population tripled to reach four million in the half-century after the slave trade was cut off in 1808), supplied the unfree and fixed workforce needed to produce the great staples that were the backbone of North America's preindustrial economy, tobacco, rice, sugar, and cotton. The dominant black social type of that era was the slave, but this was not a foregone conclusion of colonization.

In the early colonial period, indentured servitude was economically more advantageous than slavery and European transplants from England made up the brunt of the coerced labor force. Most English servants willingly sold themselves to work for terms of five or seven years in exchange for free transportation across the Atlantic and the promise of land upon release; others landed in America for being sentenced for crimes or kidnapped. They lived harshly and died early due to contagious diseases and their brutal work regimen; they could be sold, bartered and inherited during the length of their contract. By the second half of the seventeenth century, however, the growth of the tobacco trade, the need to encourage further voluntary immigration (which had decreased sharply due to the economic upturn in England), the increase in life expectancy of the slaves, and the powerlessness of African captives compared to European migrants and Amerindians combined to make slaves from Africa a better economic investment and thus the preferred source of labor.[41]

Yet, in early colonial Virginia, slaves and servants were subject to the same harsh labor conditions; they shared living arrangements; male slaves consorted with female servants and they sometimes absconded together; and color consciousness was muted at best. Moreover, among free persons, the key divide of both the classification and the stratification order was not race but class based on landed property and labor status. For two generations English settlers and freed Africans interacted on a plane of relative equality, showing that "the process of black debasement and degradation was not linear and preordained."[42]

This changed dramatically around the time of Bacon's Rebellion in 1676, which fueled the land-owning Virginians' fear of a class alliance

---

[41] David W. Galenson, *White Servitude in Colonial America: An Economic Analysis* (1982), and Kenneth Morgan, *Slavery and Servitude in North America, 1607–1800* (2000).

[42] Timothy Hall Breen and Stephen Innes, *"Myne Owne Ground": Race and Freedom on Virginia's Eastern Shore, 1640–1676* (1980), pp. 5 and 112–13.

Deadly Symbiosis

between European servants and African slaves that could topple the fragile social order.[43] So the settlers took to creating a legal and social wedge between these two categories, improving the lot of the former and worsening the lot of the latter. They tightened the codification of slavery, making it a lifetime and inheritable status; they stipulated that the offspring of the sexual union of a free male with a slave female would take on after their mother and thus be consigned to bondage. The result was that the vile condition of slavery became uniquely associated with blacks and their unfree descendants: *slavery had been racialized*.[44] Then the booming slave trade across the Atlantic became the main source of labor for the colonies. By the eighteenth century, the life expectancy of slaves had risen substantially so that they became a self-perpetuating workforce.[45]

During the colonial era, slavery was adapted to the specific conditions of the British colonies. Historian Peter Kolchin teases out four distinctive characteristics of the institution American-style whose combination makes it stand out in the broader panorama of human bondage: (1) slaves worked and lived in small holdings amidst a predominantly white population with whom they had frequent contact; (2) the vast majority of whites were not slave-owners but farmers, artisans, or laborers; (3) slave-owners were not absentee but resident landlords who personally ruled over their plantation, knew their slaves by name, and developed a paternalistic relation with them that somewhat softened the brutality of bondage; (4) by the American Revolution, four slaves out of every five were born in the colony – this "creolization" of slavery is virtually unique in the history of bondage.[46] This means that whites at large were familiar with enslaved persons of color and grew to symbolically associate blackness with bondage: racial stratification fostered the diffusion of racial classification.

---

[43] Edmund S. Morgan, *American Slavery, American Freedom: The Ordeal of Colonial Virginia* (1975).

[44] "The original decision to create what amounted to a racially derived status probably arose less from a consciousness of racial privilege than from palpable self-interest on the part of the members of a dominant class who had been fortunate enough to acquire slaves to supplement or replace their fluctuating force of indentured servants." George M. Fredrickson, *White Supremacy: A Comparative Study of American and South African History* (1981), p. 80.

[45] This is in sharp contrast with slavery in South America and the Caribbean; see, in particular, Orlando Patterson, *The Sociology of Slavery* (2022 [1967]).

[46] Kolchin, *American Slavery, 1619–1877*, pp. 40–9; Patterson, *Slavery and Social Death*, pp. 165–7.

The revolutionary period marked a rupture in the history of race and American slavery. For the first time, the institution came under fire with the spread of Enlightenment ideals stressing the malleability of human nature and the doctrine of "natural rights," freedom, and equality.[47] This critique was amplified by the Quakers, who thought human bondage immoral, and by the Christian evangelicals, for whom every person had the capacity to triumph over sin and the degradation of blacks was not innate but due to enslavement. Even some Southern planters came to the view that human bondage was economically inefficient as well as debasing for whites.[48] The French and the Haitian revolutions further strengthened the case of the abolitionists. The revolutionary war and rhetoric contributed to weakening an institution that directly violated the ideals of liberty and justice. In the North, slavery was marginal and moribund and so it was gradually abolished. In the South, on the contrary, it was strengthened by the Constitution, which recognized the rights of slave-owners to reclaim fugitives and counted "persons held to service or labour" (the euphemism for slaves) as three-fifths of a person for purposes of electoral apportionment, solidifying the national power of Southern politicians. All in all, "slavery was as important to the making of the Constitution as the Constitution was to the survival of slavery."[49]

After the Revolution, human bondage was abolished along the Eastern seaboard and prohibited north and west of the Ohio River, but it spread and solidified throughout the South, as the economic value of slaves rose in concert with the increase in the demand for cotton, the invention of the cotton gin, and the scarcity of labor in the new territories of the Southwest. Once it generalized, slavery transformed all of society, culture, and politics in its image, fostering the concentration of economic and state power in the hands of a small slaveholder class tied to lower-class whites by patronage relations and to their slaves by a paternalistic code and elaborate rituals of submission that enforced the latter's lack of cultural autonomy and sense of inferiority.[50] As for free blacks North and South, they

---

[47] David Brion Davis, *Inhuman Bondage: The Rise and Fall of Slavery in the New World* (2006), chapter 6; Seymour Drescher and Stanley L. Engerman (eds.), *A Historical Guide to World Slavery* (1998).

[48] Kolchin, *American Slavery, 1619–1877*, pp. 65–70.

[49] David Waldstreicher, *Slavery's Constitution: From Revolution to Ratification* (2010), p. 17.

[50] Williamson, *The New People*, (1986), pp. 15–27; Eugene D. Genovese, *Roll, Jordan, Roll: The World the Slaves Made* (1976), pp. 3–7, 70–5, and 797–8.

carried the stain of slavery and were viewed as vile and inferior. "Wherever they lived, [they] faced hardship, persecution, and physical insecurity."[51]

Whereas in the early decades of the colony the status of slave and servant were virtually indistinguishable – the terms were even used interchangeably – by the nineteenth century the dichotomous opposition between bondspeople and freepeople had been fully racialized. The militant defense of slavery after it came under attack generated an elaborate ideology justifying the subhuman condition imposed upon blacks by their inferior biological makeup, exemplified by the animalistic traits, in turn childish and bestial, attributed to the archetypal figure of Sambo. In the 1830s, the advocates of human bondage argued that the Negro was not only unfit for freedom but ideally suited for slavery; they could reach contentment only under the guidance of a benevolent master: "As long as the control of the master was firm and assured, the slave would be happy, loyal, and affectionate; but remove or weaken the authority of the master, and he would revert to type as a bloodthirsty savage."[52] In the ensuing decade, the "American school of ethnology" elaborated the first scientific defense of American slavery by popularizing the notion that blacks were physiologically different, biologically impaired, and morally deficient, a different species of *genus homo*. Josiah Nott, who presented himself as a specialist in "Niggerology" based on his experience as a physician, sought to counter the abolitionists and justified white repugnance to intermarriage by proposing that racial hybrids were less fertile than Negros and fated to go extinct in three generations.[53]

In the decades leading to the Civil War, the specter of insurrection and of the abolition of bondage resulted in increased hostility toward manumission, miscegenation, and "passing" by free Negroes, as well as in the generalization of a rigid twofold racial schema, based on the mythology that God had created blacks to be slaves and that one drop of "Negro blood" made one a Negro.[54] Slavery as a system of unfree labor thus spawned a suffusive racial culture which, in turn, remade bondage into something it was not at its outset: a color-coded

---

[51] Kolchin, *American Slavery, 1619–1877*, p. 84.
[52] George M. Fredrickson, *The Black Image in the White Mind: The Debate on Afro-American Character and Destiny, 1817–1914* (1971), p. 54.
[53] Ibid., pp. 76–82.
[54] Davis, *Who Is Black?*, pp. 41–2. See also the discussion *supra*, pp. 226–9.

institution of ethnoracial division.⁵⁵ Classification and stratification had been decisively aligned under the aegis of race.

2. Jim Crow terrorism (South, 1877–1965)

As we saw in chapter 3, emancipation posed a double and deadly menace to Southern society. The overthrow of bondage made slaves formally free laborers, which would eliminate the cheap and abundant workforce required to run the plantation economy, and even generate potential rivals as independent farmers. As for African-American access to civil and political rights, it promised to erode the color line initially drawn to bulwark slavery but since entrenched in both the South and the North of the country. More pressing still, it threatened to bring about the horror of "racial amalgamation" and thus despoil whites of their sense of ethnic purity and honor.⁵⁶

On the morrow of abolition, the Dixie ruling class promulgated the Black Codes to resolve the first problem by establishing "forced labor and police laws to get the freedman back to the fields under control."⁵⁷ These rules abridged the rights of African Americans to own or lease land, secure property, engage in business, and move across counties. Black men were required to carry proof of yearly employment on pain of being arrested for the crime of vagrancy and pressed into convict labor for white planters and industrialists. Black children were similarly forced into bonded labor disguised as apprenticeship. In short, the codes effectively "replace[d] slavery by customary serfdom and caste."⁵⁸

---

⁵⁵ The interaction of slavery and race, and how each transformed the other across the three broad "generations" of slaves during the seventeenth and eighteenth centuries – the "charter generations," the "plantation generations," and the "revolutionary generations" – is richly depicted by Ira Berlin in *Many Thousands Gone: The First Two Centuries of Slavery in North America* (1998).

⁵⁶ "The demand for submission and adulation from the Negroes . . . is rationalized in the case of Americans by the belief in the superiority of the white race, a superiority innate and not based on culture . . . Appeal is often made to instincts of racial purity to explain this passion for mastery [of the white race] . . . If the race struggle is not acute, deference flows smoothly from the lower to the higher caste . . . White people become aggressive as soon as Negro submission is withheld, and many stories are told of the 'what I did with that "uppity" nigger' type." John Dollard, *Caste and Class in a Southern Town* (1937), pp. 175, 176, 177.

⁵⁷ C. Vann Woodward, *American Counterpoint: Slavery and Racism in the North–South Dialogue* (1971), pp. 250–1.

⁵⁸ W. E. B. Du Bois, *Black Reconstruction in America, 1860–1889* (2017 [1935]), p. 224.

Deadly Symbiosis

In a second phase, through the 1890s, the white lower classes, pressed by the dislocations wrought by declining farm prices, demographic pressure, and capitalist industrialization, joined with the plantation elite to demand the political disenfranchisement and systematic exclusion of the former slaves from all major institutions:[59] the Jim Crow regime of agrarian superexploitation, ethnoracial bifurcation and extraction of deference, judicial and political exclusion, and terroristic subordination dissected in chapter 3 was born, which would hold African Americans in its brutal grip for some seven decades in the Southern states. This regime was abetted by the US Supreme Court, which validated the constitutionality of segregationist policies with its 1896 *Plessy v. Ferguson* decision, and supported by the federal government, which acted as a powerful engine for the national diffusion and legitimation of differentialist and exclusionary racial practices during the half-century preceding the Civil Rights Act of 1964: every major federal institution, from the US civil service and public employment exchanges to public housing and the armed forces, engaged in systematic discrimination against blacks.[60]

Under this regime, backed by custom, elaborate legal statutes, and ubiquitous violence, legal and extra-legal, African Americans were generally prevented from acquiring land and locked into sharecropping and tenancy arrangements via indebtedness that fixed black labor on white farms (often the same land on which they or their forebears had toiled as slaves), perpetuating the hegemony of the region's agrarian upper class and the work discipline of the antebellum plantation, even as the organizational unit moved from the gang to the patriarchal family. The minority of blacks who owned farms typically tilled small estates of bad land; theirs were minor operations lacking in capital and credit.[61] Those who were economically successful owed their good fortune, not just to diligent exertion, but also to publicly assuming their subservient position in the local caste society. One prosperous black farmer attributed his achievement to "hard work, slow saving, and staying in my place, acting humble, that's how I did it."[62]

---

[59] William Julius Wilson, *The Declining Significance of Race: Blacks and Changing American Institutions* (1980 [1978]), pp. 57–61.

[60] Desmond S. King, *Separate and Unequal: Black Americans and the U.S. Federal Government* (1995).

[61] W. E. B. Du Bois, *The Negro Landholder of Georgia* (1901).

[62] Hortense Powdermaker, *After Freedom: A Cultural Study of the Deep South* (1993 [1939]), p. 106.

As for sharecroppers, we saw in chapter 3 that they were kept in near-perpetual poverty and economic dependency by a vicious cycle of debt owed to their landlords: after harvest, "the tenant is given no sales receipt for his cotton, nor any itemized statement of his furnishings and advances, but is merely told that he has come out even, that some small amount is due him, or that he is in debt to the landlord."[63] The sharecropper who was cheated had no resort except to migrate to another plantation in hopes for a better owner. If he protested the settlement, he would be brutalized, chased out of the county, or murdered with virtual impunity. The central black figure of this regime of ruthless racial domination, then, was the sharecropper and his family, which toiled as a unit on the former plantation to eke out a living as a subservient peasantry living under the permanent specter of white violence. The economic opportunities of African Americans were severely truncated, not just in the cotton fields, but also in the emerging mining and industrial towns of the uplands where their employment was typically limited to the most hazardous and degrading jobs.[64]

The second "peculiar institution" sharply curtailed social contacts between whites and blacks by relegating the latter to separate residential districts and to the reserved "colored" section of commercial establishments and public facilities, saloons and movie houses, parks and beaches, trolleys and buses, waiting rooms and bathrooms.[65] Any and all forms of intercourse that might imply equality and reciprocity between the "races" and, worse yet, provide an occasion for sexual congress between black men and white women were rigorously forbidden. Blacks were expected to follow an unspoken but suffusive "racial etiquette" that dictated submissive behaviors honoring whites in every interaction: they were expected to address whites formally, to give them the right of way on the sidewalk and the road, to open doors for them, to greet them with meekness, to wait to be served in stores until after whites had been served, to enter their houses only from the back, and so on.[66] Failing to abide by these rules exposed African Americans to mockery, insult, police arrest, assault, or worse.

---

[63] Ibid., p. 84.
[64] William Powell Jones, *The Tribe of Black Ulysses: African American Lumber Workers in the Jim Crow South* (2005).
[65] Dollard, *Caste and Class in a Southern Town*, p. 62.
[66] For a fuller treatment of racial etiquette, see Jennifer Lynn Ritterhouse, "The Etiquette of Racial Relations in the Jim Crow South" (2007), and the discussion in chapter 3, *supra*, pp. 239–48.

Deadly Symbiosis

At the very top of the "rank order of discrimination" in the minds of whites was the bar against interracial marriage and sexual intercourse involving white women, ahead of everyday racial etiquette, segregation in public facilities, political disenfranchisement, judicial exclusion, and economic discrimination.[67] (Notably, the rank-order for blacks was just about the other way around, prioritizing economic opportunity and caring least about interracial sex.) Indeed, the idealized image of the purity of the white woman was zealously promoted by Southern whites and violently defended from any and all infringements, real or imagined, by black men portrayed as roving beasts lusting for white female flesh.[68] The latter were the urgent targets, not just of police attention and judicial diligence, but also of vicious assaults, beatings, whippings, ritualized torture, and ceremonial lynchings (discussed in chapter 3, *supra*, pp. 258–67). This is because, ultimately, "caste is based on marital prohibition and on exclusion from sexual contact of the lower-caste men."[69] This taboo was thus the lynchpin of the ethnoracial order of the South and terroristic violence its anchor. This explains why the murders and lynchings committed to punish blacks accused of sexual improprieties toward white women were met with the indulgence of the courts, and their perpetrators rarely prosecuted to conviction, for, as a Mississippi gentleman put it, "race is greater than law now and then, and protection of women transcends all law, human and divine."[70]

As for the police and the courts, far from protecting the formal rights of blacks, they were deployed to enforce "Negro law" and keep African Americans subordinate and acquiescent. In an effort to speed up judicial processing, guarantee convictions, and cow the local black community, the Southern police often tortured black defendants and witnesses, while judges, prosecutors, and juries looked the other way.[71] Blacks were also methodically banished from the ballot box

---

[67] Gunnar Myrdal, *An American Dilemma: The Negro Problem and Modern Democracy* (1944), pp. 60–1. Myrdal notes that this order flowed from the white doctrine of antiamalgamation which was national in scope but more rigidly supported in the South (pp. 57–9).
[68] Jane Dailey, *White Fright: The Sexual Panic at the Heart of America's Racist History* (2020), chapter 2.
[69] Dollard, *Caste and Class in a Southern Town*, p. 171.
[70] Cited by Neil R. McMillen, *Dark Journey: Black Mississippians in the Age of Jim Crow* (1990), p. 240.
[71] Silvan Niedermeier, *The Color of the Third Degree: Racism, Police Torture, and Civil Rights in the American South, 1930–1955* (2019). See also Amy Louise Wood and Natalie J. Ring (eds.), *Crime and Punishment in the Jim Crow South* (2019).

thanks to rules expressly designed to weed them out from the rolls, such as literacy tests, poll taxes, the requirement that their grandfather had voted, and disqualifying criminal offenses.[72] Again, when blacks dared protest their economic subordination, social ostracization, judicial exclusion, and political disfranchisement, they were met with escalating violence that assumed four main forms: individual aggression, pogroms, manhunts and lynchings whose threat was ubiquitous. Jim Crow was, in a literal sense, a *regime of social and state terror*.

One key institution of Jim Crow domination I did not discuss in chapter 3 is education. From the moment of abolition, African Americans demonstrated an unquenchable thirst for, and fervid commitment to, education, which they viewed as the gateway to social elevation and civic participation. The problem is, in the postbellum South, they faced a separate and grotesquely unequal school system. Schools for blacks were not only totally segregated; they were systematically under-staffed (exclusively by black teachers, whose average preparation in 1920 was the seventh grade), under-equipped, and under-funded, so that in some states their budget depended critically on donations from white Northern philanthropists.[73] Indeed, Du Bois computed that black taxpayers in the former slave states were subsidizing the very white schools from which their children were excluded.[74] For lack of public facilities in Mississippi in 1940, half of black children attended schools in tenant cabins, stores, churches, and in buildings deemed "unfit for cotton storage"; two in three facilities had no running water and nine in ten no outhouse.[75]

School attendance laws were not enforced in black establishments and the pressing need for child labor on the farm resulted in persistently high rates of truancy and illiteracy which perpetuated economic dependency, since illiterate sharecroppers were unable to decipher their accounts and calculate whether their landlords were cheating them. Moreover, education for blacks stressed craft and vocational training, so that children were pushed onto "industrial" tracks that prepared them for menial jobs in keeping with their lower-caste status. The greatest obstacle to improving African-American schools throughout the South was "the white fear of the revolutionary social

---

[72] McMillen, *Dark Journey*, chapter 2.
[73] James D. Anderson, *The Education of Blacks in the South, 1860–1935* (1988).
[74] W. E. B. Du Bois (ed.), *The Negro Common School: Report of a Social Study made under the Direction of Atlanta University* (1903), p. 91.
[75] McMillen, *Dark Journey*, pp. 84–5.

and economic implications of educating a subservient workforce" as well as the fear that "[education] would increase the Negro's desire for 'social equality' ... and the ultimate amalgamation of the two races."[76] Here we see how educational exclusion served to maintain black subordination in both the symbolic order of classification and the material order of stratification.

3. The ghetto (North, 1917–1968)

The very ferocity of Jim Crow on both the labor extraction and the social ostracization fronts sowed the seeds of its eventual ruin, for blacks fled the South by the millions as soon as the opportunity came. Three forces combined to rouse them to desert Dixie and rally to the surging metropolitan centers of the Midwest and Northeast in the half-century following the outbreak of World War I. The first was the economic crisis of cotton agriculture caused by the boll weevil and later by mechanization, as well as arrested urbanization in the South due to the industrial underdevelopment of the region. The second was the booming demand for unskilled and semi-skilled labor in the steel mills, packinghouses, factories, and railroads of the North, as the war cut off immigration from Europe, white workers got drafted to the front, and employers sent their recruiting agents scurrying through the South to entice African Americans to come toil for them.[77]

But economic push and pull factors merely set conditions of possibility: the trigger of the Great Migration that transformed the black community from a landless peasantry into an industrial proletariat, and with it the visage of American society *in toto*,[78] was the irrepressible will to escape the indignities of caste and its attendant material degradation, symbolic denigration, truncated life horizon, and

---

[76] The quotes are, respectively, McMillen, *Dark Journey*, p. 90, and Powdermaker, *After Freedom*, p. 299. As Dollard notes, white reasoning was "why spend money for Negro education if it tends, as most suspect, to unfit them for their caste and class roles." John Dollard, *Caste and Class in a Southern Town*, p. 194.

[77] Neil Fligstein, *Going North: Migration of Blacks and Whites from the South, 1900–1950* (1981), and Christopher Muller, "Exclusion and Exploitation: The Incarceration of Black Americans from Slavery to the Present" (2021).

[78] Carole Marks, *Farewell, We're Good and Gone: The Great Black Migration* (1989); Kimberley Louise Phillips, *Alabama North: African-American Migrants, Community, and Working-Class Activism in Cleveland, 1915–45* (1999). An insightful comparison of the springs, pathways, and impacts of the black and white migrations on the national society, culture, and politics is James N. Gregory, *The Southern Diaspora: How the Great Migrations of Black and White Southerners Transformed America* (2005).

Racial Domination

suffusive violence – the outmigration of blacks was heaviest in those counties of the Deep South where lynchings were most frequent.[79] These indignities were made all the more intolerable by the ongoing incorporation of "white ethnics" into national institutions and by the paradoxical role that the US played on the world stage as champion of those very freedoms which it denied Negros at home. The trek up to Chicago, Detroit, Philadelphia, Pittsburgh, and New York was thus undertaken by Southern blacks not just to "better their condition" but also to board the "train of freedom" (to recall the title of a well-known poem by Langston Hughes) on a journey filled with biblical imagery and political import: it was a race-conscious gesture of collective defiance and self-affirmation.[80]

Yankee life in the big city did offer salutary relief from the harsh grip of Southern caste domination and significantly expand the life chances of the former sharecroppers and domestics, but it did not turn out to be the "promised land" of racial equality, economic security, and full citizenship for which migrants yearned. For, in the Northern metropolis, African Americans came upon yet another device designed to allow white society to exploit their labor power while keeping them confined to a separate *Lebensraum*: the ghetto. As the Negro population rose, so did the animosity of urban whites toward a category they viewed as "physically and mentally unfit," "unsanitary," "entirely irresponsible and vicious," and therefore "undesirable as neighbors," in the terms reported to the 1920 Chicago Commission on Race Relations.[81]

"Primary beliefs" about the Negro at the dawn of Chicago's ghetto*

Mentality. The chief of these [beliefs] is that the mind of the Negro is distinctly and distinctively inferior to that of the white race, and so are all resulting functionings of his mind. The view is held by some

---

[79] Stewart E. Tolnay and E. M. Beck, *A Festival of Violence: An Analysis of Southern Lynchings, 1882–1930* (1995).

[80] James R. Grossman, *Land of Hope: Chicago, Black Southerners, and the Great Migration* (1989), esp. pp. 16–37, and Steward E. Tolnay, "The African American 'Great Migration' and Beyond" (2003).

[81] Cited in Allan H. Spear, *Black Chicago: The Making of a Negro Ghetto, 1890–1920* (1967), p. 22.

to be due to a difference in species, by others to more recent emergence from primitive life, and to others to backwardness in ascending the scale of civilization. For this reason it is variously assumed as a corollary that the mind of the Negro cannot be improved above a given level or above a given age; that his education should be adapted to his capacities, that is, he should mainly be taught to use his hands. . . .

Morality. Another of the primary beliefs is that Negroes are not yet capable of exercising the social restraints which are common to the more civilized white persons. Sometimes it is said that they are unmoral rather than immoral. This view, while charitably explaining supposed innate defects of character, places them outside the circle of the normal members of society. . . .

Criminality. The assumption back of most discussions of Negro crime is that there is a constitutional character weakness in Negroes and a consequent predisposition to sexual crimes, petty stealing, and crimes of violence. Sexual crimes are alleged and frequently urged in justification of lynching. Popular judgment takes stealing lightly, because Negroes evidence a marked immaturity and childishness in it. It is supposed that they appropriate little things and do not commit larger thefts. Crimes of violence are thought to be characteristic of Negroes because crimes involving deliberation and planning require more brains than Negroes possess . . .

Physical unattractiveness. Objections to contact are often attributed to physical laws which, it is said, make the sight or other sensory impression of the Negro unbearably repulsive . . .

Emotionality. This is commonly regarded as explaining features of conduct in Negroes, some of which are beautiful in their expression while others are ugly and dangerous. The supposed Negro gift of song is thus an accepted attribute of his emotional nature. So with his religious inclination. This same emotionalism is believed to lead him to drink and is frequently made to account for "his quick, uncalculated crimes of violence." . . .

It may help to comprehend the range of conclusions found in the literature on the subject of Negro traits to note the array of descriptive adjectives employed, thus: sensual, lazy, unobservant, shiftless, unresentful, emotional, shallow, patient, amiable, gregarious, expressive, appropriative, childish, religious, unmoral, immoral, ignorant, mentally inferior, criminal, excitable, imitative, repulsive, poetic, irresponsible, filthy, unintellectual, bumptious, overassertive, superficial, indecent, dependent, untruthful, musical, ungrateful, loyal, sporty,

> provincial, anthropomorphic, savage, brutish, happy-go-lucky, careless, plastic, docile, apish, inferior, cheerful.
>
> * Chicago Commission on Race Relations, *The Negro in Chicago: A Study of Race Relations and a Race Riot* (1920), pp. 438–42 and 449.

Patterns of ethnoracial discrimination and segregation that had hitherto been inconsistent and informal hardened in housing, schools, and public accommodations such as parks, playgrounds, bathing beaches, and swimming pools – which were particular points of tension as they involved close proximity of near-naked bodies, and thus raised the specter of sexual mingling. They were extended to the polity, where the promotion of a small cadre of black politicians handpicked by party leaders served to rein in the community's votes to the benefit of the white-controlled city machine.[82] They were systematized in the economy, where a "job ceiling" set conjointly by white employers and unions kept African Americans trapped in the lower reaches of the occupational structure, disproportionately concentrated in semi-skilled, manual, and servant work that made them especially vulnerable to business downturns.[83] And, when they tried to breach the color line in physical space by attempting to settle outside of their reserved perimeter in violation of restrictive covenants, blacks were assaulted on the streets by white "athletic clubs" and their houses firebombed by so-called "neighborhood improvement societies." They had no choice but to take refuge in the secluded territory of the Black Belt and to build within it a self-sustaining nexus of institutions that would both shield them from white rule and procure the needs of the castaway community: a "Black Metropolis" made for blacks and by blacks, lodged "in the womb of the white," yet hermetically sealed from it.[84]

The emergence of the dark ghetto in the 1910s was *crescive*, meaning, it grew gradually *from below* from the strategies of uncoordinated agents without a set plan other than the white thrust to create social and physical distance from a stigmatized category. Its consolidation around the 1940s was *enacted*: it was planned and implemented from

---

[82] Ira Katznelson, *Black Men, White Cities: Race, Politics and Migration in the United States, 1900–30, and Britain, 1948–68* (1976), pp. 83–5.

[83] St. Clair Drake and Horace R. Cayton, *Black Metropolis: A Study of Negro Life in a Northern City* (1993 [1945]), pp. 223–35; Wilson, *The Declining Significance of Race*, pp. 71–6.

[84] Drake and Cayton, *Black Metropolis*, p. 80.

above by the state in ways that were both intended and unintended. Thus the New Deal helped this parallel city coalesce by (1) further stimulating outmigration from the South via agricultural programs that excluded black farmers and farm laborers; (2) extending public aid to jobless African Americans living in the Northern metropolis (half of Chicago's Negro families were on relief in 1940); (3) building up its physical infrastructure through public works and amassing social housing in the segregated urban core, while refusing to insure loans to blacks seeking residence in white neighborhoods. After World War II, federal housing, lending, and transportation policies further conspired to keep African Americans firmly hemmed inside the expanding perimeter of the ghetto.[85]

This "black city within the white," as black scholars from Du Bois and Frazier to Oliver Cox and Kenneth Clark consistently characterized the ghetto,[86] discharged the same two basic functions that slavery and the Jim Crow regime had performed earlier, namely, to harness the labor of African Americans while cloistering their tainted bodies, and thereby avert both the specter of "social equality" and the odium of "miscegenation" that would inevitably result in the loss of white ethnic honor. But the ghetto differed from the two preceding peculiar institutions in that, by granting blacks a separate space of their own and a measure of organizational autonomy,[87] it enabled them to fully develop their own social and symbolic forms and thereby accumulate the group capacities needed to escalate the fight against continued caste subordination.

For the ghetto in its full-fledged form is a *double-edged sociospatial formation*: it operates as an instrument of *closure* from the standpoint of the dominant group; yet it also offers the subordinate category *protection* and a platform for succor and solidarity in the very movement whereby it sequesters it. Thus the urbanization of the descendants of slaves accelerated the merging of mulattoes and Negros into a single

---

[85] Harvard Sitkoff, *A New Deal for Blacks: The Emergence of Civil Rights as a National Issue: The Depression Decade* (1978); Arnold R. Hirsch, *Making the Second Ghetto: Race and Housing in Chicago 1940–1960* (2009 [1984]); Thomas J. Sugrue, *The Origins of the Urban Crisis: Race and Inequality in Postwar Detroit* (2005 [1996]); and Richard Rothstein, *The Color of Law: A Forgotten History of How Our Government Segregated America* (2017).

[86] Loïc Wacquant, "'A Black City Within the White': Revisiting America's Dark Ghetto" (1998b).

[87] Christopher Robert Reed, *The Rise of Chicago's Black Metropolis, 1920–1929* (2011), chapter 5.

overarching African-American identity.[88] It supplied the impetus for the gestation and growth of the gamut of organizations that took up the struggle for racial equality on the national stage, from the gradualist Urban League and National Association for the Advancement of Colored People to the militant Brotherhood of Sleeping Car Porters to the secessionist Universal Negro Improvement Association of Marcus Garvey.[89] In terms of the agonistic theory of group-making, *the ghetto boosted the "groupness" of African Americans*, giving them greater cultural unity and political cohesion even as it deepened their class division. It helped them become an officially recognized "instituted group."

Specifying the workings of the ghetto as mechanism of ethnoracial closure and control makes readily visible its *structural and functional kinship with the prison*: the ghetto is a manner of "ethnoracial prison" in that it encloses a stigmatized population which evolves within it its distinctive organizations and culture, while the prison functions as a "judicial ghetto" relegating individuals disgraced by criminal conviction to a secluded space harboring the parallel social relations and distinctive cultural norms that make up the "society of captives" described by carceral sociology. This kinship helps explain why, when the ghetto crashed in the 1960s under the press of economic restructuring that rendered African-American labor expendable and mass protest that finally won blacks the vote, the carceral institution offered itself as a substitute apparatus for enforcing the shifting color line and containing the segments of the black community devoid of economic utility and political pull. The coupling of the transformed core of the urban Black Belt, or hyperghetto, and the fast-expanding carceral archipelago that *together compose America's fourth "peculiar institution"* was fortified by two concurrent series of changes that tended to "prisonize" the ghetto and to "ghettoize" the prison. The next two sections examine each of these trends in turn.

---

[88] Williamson, *New People*, chapter 4.
[89] See Touré F. Reed, *Not Alms but Opportunity: The Urban League and the Politics of Racial Uplift, 1910–1950* (2008); Patricia Sullivan, *Lift Every Voice: The NAACP and the Making of the Civil Rights Movement* (2009); and E. David Cronon, *Black Moses: The Story of Marcus Garvey and the Universal Negro Improvement Association* (1960).

Deadly Symbiosis

How the ghetto became more like a prison

The *fin-de-siècle* hyperghetto presents four main characteristics that differentiate it sharply from the communal ghetto of the Fordist-Keynesian era and converge to render its social structure and cultural texture more akin to those of the prison: the overlaying of class segregation on top of racial segregation spawning extreme social monotony; the loss of an economic function of labor extraction; the substitution of state institutions of social control for communal institutions; and the decay of its "buffering function" leading to the depacification of everyday life. I consider each in turn by drawing a schematic contrast between the mid-century Bronzeville depicted by St. Clair Drake and Horace Cayton in *Black Metropolis* (1945) and the South Side of Chicago as I dissected it one half-century later based on fieldwork, official statistics, and survey data.

1. Class segregation overlays racial segregation

The dark ghetto of mid-century held within itself the full complement of black classes, for the simple reason that the black bourgeoisie was barred from escaping its cramped and compact perimeter while a majority of adults were gainfully employed in the gamut of occupations, with a strong concentration in blue-collar jobs for men and domestic work for women. True, from the 1920s onward, Chicago's South Side featured clearly demarcated subdivisions stratified by class, with the small elite of black doctors, lawyers, teachers, and businessmen residing in the stabler and more desirable neighborhoods adjacent to white districts at the southern end, while the families of laborers and domestic workers massed themselves in areas of blight, crime, and dissolution towards the northern end.[90]

But the social distance between the classes was limited by physical propinquity and by extensive family ties. Moreover, the black bourgeoisie's economic standing and fate rested on supplying goods and services to its lower-class brethren who could or would not obtain them from white institutions. It grew alongside black working-class consolidation in social and physical space. And all "brown" residents of the city were united in their common rejection of caste subordination and abiding concern to "advance the race," despite internecine

---

[90] E. Franklin Frazier, *The Negro Family in Chicago* (1932).

divisions and the mutual panning of "big Negroes" and "riff-raff."[91] As a result, the postwar ghetto was *integrated both socially and structurally* – even the "shadies" who earned their living from such illicit trades as the numbers game, liquor sale, prostitution, and other *risqué* recreation were entwined with the different classes.

Fast-forward to the *fin-de-siècle*: the black bourgeoisie still lived under strict segregation and its life chances continued to be curtailed by its geographic and symbolic contiguity with the African-American (sub)proletariat.[92] All the same, it had gained considerable physical distance from the heart of the ghetto by establishing satellite black neighborhoods at its periphery inside the city and in the suburbs.[93] Its economic basis had shifted from the direct servicing of the black community to the state, with employment in public bureaucracies accounting for most of the growth of professional, managerial, and technical positions held by African Americans over the preceding 30 years. The genealogical ties of the black bourgeoisie to the black poor also grew more remote and less dense.

What is more, the historic center of Bronzeville, encompassing the districts of Grand Boulevard, Oakland, and Washington Park, experienced massive depopulation and deproletarianization.[94] The adult population of 160,000 in 1950 was halved by 1980, when only one in four residents held a job compared to over one-half 30 years earlier. In 1950, the core of the South Side was home to some 42,400 operative laborers and craftsmen (one adult in four); by 1980 that figure had plunged to 6,300 (one adult in 16). The number of clerical and sales staff similarly plummeted from 5,300 to 2,200. This skewed occupational structure is not surprising considering that only

---

[91] Drake and Cayton, *Black Metropolis*, pp. 716–28.

[92] Pattillo, *Black Picket Fences*; Bart Landry and Kris Marsh, "The Evolution of the New Black Middle Class" (2011); Marcus Anthony Hunter and Zandria F. Robinson, "The Sociology of Urban Black America" (2016).

[93] It is not so much that the black middle class *moved out* of the "inner city," as argued by Wilson in *The Truly Disadvantaged* (1987). Rather, it *grew* outside of the historic core of the ghetto after its heyday. For the black bourgeoisie was minuscule at the mid-century point, and as early as the 1930s it had already established outposts beyond the perimeter of Bronzeville, as Drake and Cayton point out in *Black Metropolis*, p. 384. For a fuller discussion of the geographical dimension of class differentiation among African Americans, see Patrick Sharkey, "Spatial Segmentation and the Black Middle Class" (2014).

[94] The figures in this paragraph are computed from data compiled in Chicago Fact Book Consortium, *Local Community Fact Book 1950: Chicago Metropolitan Area* (1955), and idem, *Local Community Fact Book 1980: Chicago Metropolitan Area* (1984).

3 percent of adults in Bronzeville had a college degree. Lastly, three out of every four households were headed by a woman and six in ten received welfare support, while the official poverty rate hovered near the 50 percent mark.

This drastic lowering and homogenization of the class structure of the hyperghetto makes it akin to the monotonous class recruitment of the carceral institution, dominated as the latter is by the most precarious fractions of the urban proletariat of the unemployed, the casually employed, and the uneducated. Fully 36 percent of the half-million detainees housed by jails in the country in 1991 were jobless at the time of their arrest and another 15 percent worked only part-time or irregularly. One-half had not finished high school and two-thirds earned less than a thousand dollars a month that year; in addition, every other inmate had been raised in a home receiving welfare and a paltry 16 percent were married.[95] Residents of the hyperghetto and clients of the carceral institution thus present germane profiles in economic marginality and social disaffiliation.

2. Loss of a positive economic function

The transformed class structure of the hyperghetto is a direct product of its evolving position in the new urban political economy ushered by post-Fordism and neoliberal state policies. We have seen that, from the Great Migration of the interwar years to the 1960s, the dark ghetto served a positive economic function as reservoir of cheap and pliable labor for the city's factories. During that period, it was "directly exploited by outside economic interests, and it provide[d] a dumping ground for the human residuals created by economic change. These economic conditions [we]re stabilized by transfer payments that preserve[d] the ghetto in a poverty that recreate[d] itself from generation to generation," ensuring the ready availability of a low-cost workforce.[96] By the 1970s, this was no longer true as the engine of the metropolitan economy passed from manufacturing to business and knowledge-based services, and factories relocated from the central city to the mushrooming industrial parks of the suburbs and exurbs, as well as to anti-union states in the South and foreign countries of the newly industrializing global South.

---

[95] Caroline Wolf Harlow, *Profile of Jail Inmates 1996* (1998).
[96] Daniel R. Fusfeld and Timothy Bates, *The Political Economy of the Ghetto* (1984), p. 236.

Between 1954 and 1982, the number of manufacturing establishments in the Windy City dove from 10,288 to 5,203, while the number of production workers sank from nearly half a million to a mere 172,000. The demand for black labor plummeted accordingly, rocking the entire black class structure, given that half of all employed African Americans in Chicago were blue-collar wage earners at the close of World War II. Just as mechanization had enabled Southern agriculture to dispense with black labor two generations earlier, "automation and suburban relocation created a crisis of tragic dimension for unskilled black workers" in the North, as "for the first time in American history, the African American was no longer needed in the economic system" of the metropolis.[97]

The effects of technological upgrading and postindustrialization were intensified by (1) unflinching residential segregation, (2) the bankruptcy of public schools, and (3) the renewal of working-class immigration from Latin America and Asia to consign the vast majority of uneducated blacks to economic redundancy. At best, the hyperghetto now serves the *negative economic function of storage of a surplus population* devoid of market utility, in which respect it also resembles the prison which, *pace* the advocates of the left-demonology of the prison-industrial complex, is an economic sinkhole.

3. Substitution of state institutions of social control for communal institutions

The organizations that formed the framework of everyday life and anchored the social strategies of reproduction of urban blacks in the 1950s were group-based and group-specific establishments created and run by African Americans. The black press, churches, lodges and fraternal orders, social clubs and political (sub)machine knit together a dense array of resources and sociability that supported their quest for ethnic pride and group uplift. To its 200,000 members, the 500 religious outfits that dotted the South Side were not only places of worship and entertainment, but also a potent vehicle for individual and collective mobility within the specific order of the ghetto that cut across class lines and strengthened ingrown social

---

[97] Jeff Rifkin, *The End of Work. The Decline of the Global Labor Force and the Dawn of the Post-Market Era* (1995), p. 79. See also Sugrue, *The Origins of the Urban Crisis*, pp. 125–52; William Julius Wilson, *When Work Disappears: The World of the New Urban Poor* (1996); and Philip Moss and Chris Tilly, *Stories Employers Tell: Race, Skill, and Hiring in America* (2001).

control, even as black proletarians grumbled in endless "protest against the alleged cupidity and hypocrisy of church functionaries and devotees."[98]

In the economic realm, too, African Americans could seek or sustain the illusion of autonomy and advancement. Now, Negro entreprise was small-scale and commercially weak, the three most numerous types of black-owned firms being beauty parlors, grocery stores, and barber shops. But the popular "doctrine of the 'Double-Duty Dollar'," according to which buying from black concerns would "advance the race," promised a path to economic independence from whites, and the "numbers game" seemed to prove that one could indeed erect a self-sustaining economy within Black Metropolis.[99] With some 500 stations employing 5,000 and paying yearly wages in excess of a million dollars for three daily drawings, the "policy racket" was at once big business, a fixture of group fellowship, and a popular cult. Protected by crisscrossing ties and kickbacks to court officials, the police, and politicians, the "policy kings" were regarded as "Race Leaders, patrons of charity, and pioneers in the establishment of legitimate business."[100]

By the 1980s, the organizational ecology of the ghetto had been radically altered by the generalized devolution of public institutions and commercial establishments in the urban core as well as by the cumulative demise of black concerns caused by the confluence of market withdrawal, state retrenchment, and depopulation. The physical infrastructure and business base of the South Side had been decimated, with thousands of boarded-up stores and abandoned buildings rotting away along deserted boulevards strewn with debris and garbage. Arguably the most potent component of the communal ghetto, the church, lost its capacity to energize and organize social life on the South Side. Storefront operations closed in the hundreds and the congregations that endured either battled for sheer survival or battled local residents. In the early 1990s, on 63rd Street near Stony Island Avenue, the Apostolic Church of God, lavishly financed and patronized by an expatriate black bourgeoisie, was engaged in a trench war with the surrounding poor population which viewed it as an invader, so that the church had to fence itself up and hire a

---

[98] Drake and Cayton, *Black Metropolis*, pp. 710–11, 650.
[99] Ibid., pp. 430–1, 438–9.
[100] Ibid., p. 486; also Ivan Light, "Numbers Gambling among Blacks: A Financial Institution" (1977).

phalanx of security guards to enable its members to come into the neighborhood and attend its three services on Sunday.[101] Similarly, the black press had grown outside of the ghetto but virtually disappeared within it as a vector of public opinion: there were five black weeklies in Bronzeville when World War II broke out; 40 years later, the *Chicago Defender* alone remained in existence and then, only as a pale shadow of its former glorious self – it was sparsely distributed even at the heart of the South Side, whereas an estimated 100,000 read it and everyone discussed it fervently in the 1940s.[102]

The vacuum created by the crumbling of the ghetto's indigenous organizations has been filled by *state bureaucracies of social control*, themselves largely staffed by the new black middle class of mid-level public employees whose expansion hinges, not on its capacity to service its ethnic community, but on its willingness to assume the vexing role of *custodian* of the black urban precariat on behalf of white society. By the 1980s, the institutions that set the tone of daily life and determined the fate of most residents on Chicago's hyperghetto were (1) astringent and humiliating welfare programs, bolstered and replaced by "workfare" after 1996, designed to restrict access to the public aid rolls and push recipients into the low-wage labor market;[103] (2) decrepit public housing that subjected its tenants and the surrounding population to extraordinary levels of criminal insecurity, infrastructural blight, and official scorn (its management was so derelict that the Chicago Housing Authority was put under federal receivership in 1987); (3) permanently failing public health and public schools operating with resources, standards, and results worthy of countries of the global South; and (4), last but not least, the police, the courts, and these ground-level extensions of the penal apparatus that are probation officers, parole agents, and "snitches" recruited by the thousands by law enforcement agencies, often under threat

---

[101] On Christmas night in 1988, I attended mass at a Baptist church near the Robert Taylor Homes, the single largest concentration of public housing in Chicago (and, for that matter, in the United States) with a population of some 15,000. Participation was so sparse (about 60 people) that members of the audience had to join the choir impromptu to allow it to wade through its piteous repertoire. The atmosphere upon leaving the cavernous building was one of disaffection and depression. A few months later, the ramshackle structure was boarded up and, by the following Christmas, it had been razed and its lot left vacant.

[102] In the 1990s, the *Chicago Defender*'s role as "race paper" was taken up by *The Call*, the official organ of the Nation of Islam, but the latter's circulation was a fraction of its predecessor's and its impact incomparably smaller.

[103] Sharon Hays, *Flat Broke with Children: Women in the Age of Welfare Reform* (2004).

Deadly Symbiosis

of criminal prosecution, to extend the mesh of state surveillance and capture deep into the hyperghetto.[104]

4. Loss of "buffering function" and the depacification of everyday life

Along with its economic function of labor pool and the extensive organizational nexus it supported, the ghetto lost its capacity to buffer its residents from external forces. It is no longer Janus-faced, offering a sheltered space for collective sustenance and self-affirmation in the face of hostility and exclusion, as in the heyday of the Fordist-Keynesian social compact. Rather, it has devolved into a one-dimensional machinery for naked relegation, a human warehouse wherein are discarded those segments of urban society deemed disreputable, derelict, and dangerous. And, with the conjoint contraction of the wage-labor market and the welfare state in the context of unflinching segregation, it has become saturated with economic, social, and physical insecurity.[105]

Pandemic levels of crime have further depressed the local economy and ruptured the social fabric. Assaults and gunfire have become

[104] Jerome G. Miller, *Search and Destroy: African-American Males in the Criminal Justice System* (1997), pp. 102–3. For detailed accounts of the gross and systematic dysfunctioning of these institutions and their impact on residents of Chicago's hyperghetto, see Chicago Tribune, *The Worst Schools in America* (1992), on public education; Laurie Kay Abraham, *Mama Might Be Better Off Dead: The Failure of Health Care in Urban America* (1993), on public health; Sudhir Venkatesh, *American Project: The Rise and Fall of a Modern Ghetto* (2000) on public housing; William Ayers, *A Kind and Just Parent: The Children of Juvenile Court* (1997), on juvenile justice; and, on the police, John Conroy, *Unspeakable Acts, Ordinary People: The Dynamics of Torture* (2000), and Amnesty International, *Summary of Amnesty International's Concerns on Police Abuse in Chicago* (1999), including reports of more than a decade of rampant torture at Area 2 station on the South Side, involving mock executions, "Palestinian hangings," electric shocks with cattle prods, burnings with radiators and asphyxiation with plastic bags, in addition to the usual pattern of brutality, unjustified shootings and cover-ups, and the detention and interrogation of children in custody. For a chilling account from the standpoint of the victims of this institutionalized police lawlessness, read Laurence Ralph, *The Torture Letters: Reckoning with Police Violence* (2020).

[105] Douglas Massey and Nancy Denton, *American Apartheid: Segregation and the Making of the Underclass* (1993); Lauren J. Krivo and Ruth D. Peterson, "Extremely Disadvantaged Neighborhoods and Urban Crime" (1996); Jeffrey D. Morenoff and Robert J. Sampson, "Violent Crime and the Spatial Dynamics of Neighborhood Transition: Chicago, 1970–1990" (1997); Matthew R. Lee, "Concentrated Poverty, Race, and Homicide" (2000); John Hagedorn and Brigid Rauch, "Housing, Gangs, and Homicide: What We Can Learn from Chicago" (2007).

habitual, with homicide rates topping 100 for 100,000 at the core of the South Side in 1990, nearly ten times the national rate at its peak. The depacification of everyday life, shrinking of networks, and informalization of survival strategies have combined to give social relations in the hyperghetto a distinct carceral cast:[106] fear and danger pervade public space. Interpersonal relations are riven with suspicion and distrust, feeding mutual avoidance and retraction into one's private defended space. Resort to violence is the prevalent means for upholding respect, regulating encounters, and controlling territory; and relations with official authorities are suffused with animosity and diffidence – patterns familiar to students of social order in the contemporary American prison.[107]

Two examples illustrate well this increasing conformance of the hyperghetto to the carceral model. The first is the *"prisonization" of public housing*, as well as retirement homes, single-room occupancy hostels, homeless shelters, and other establishments for collective living intended for the precariat, which have come to look and feel just like houses of detention.[108] "Projects" have been fenced up, their perimeter placed under beefed-up security patrols and authoritarian controls, including identification-card checks, signing in, electronic monitoring, police infiltration, "random searches, segregation, curfews, and resident counts – all familiar procedures of efficient prison management."[109]

In the 1990s, the Chicago Housing Authority deployed its own police force and even sought to institute its own "misdemeanor court" to try misbehaving tenants on the premises. Residents of the Robert Taylor Homes, at the epicenter of the South Side, were subjected to video surveillance and required to bear special ID cards as well as pass

---

[106] Alex Kotlowitz, *There Are No Children Here: The Story of Two Boys Growing Up in the Other America* (1991); LeAlan Jones and Lloyd Newman, *Our America: Life and Death on the South Side of Chicago* (1997); Loïc Wacquant, "Inside the Zone: The Social Art of the Hustler in the Black American Ghetto" (1998a [1992]).

[107] For instance, Leo Carroll, *Hacks, Blacks, and Cons* (1974); James B. Jacobs, *Stateville: The Penitentiary in Mass Society* (1977); John Irwin, *Prisons in Turmoil* (1980).

[108] See the account of Naomi Gerstel et al., "The Therapeutic Incarceration of the Homeless" (1996) on homeless shelters and the vivid description of Chicago's "SRO Death Row" by Eric Klinenberg, "Denaturalizing Disaster: A Social Autopsy of the 1995 Chicago Heat Wave" (1999), pp. 269–72. Parallels between prison culture and the management of the Armory, New York's biggest homeless shelter, are suggested by Gwendolyn Dordick, *Something Left to Lose: Personal Relations and Survival Among New York's Homeless* (1997), pp. 126–49.

[109] Miller, *Search and Destroy*, p. 101.

through metal detectors, undergo pat-down searches, and report all visitors to a housing officer in the lobby.[110] In 1994, the CHA launched massive paramilitary raids under the code name "Operation Clean Sweep," involving predawn surprise searches of buildings leading to mass arrests and evictions in violation of basic constitutional rights quite similar to the periodic "shakedowns" intended to rid prison wards of shanks, drugs, and other contraband. As one elderly resident of a District of Columbia project being put under such quasi-penal supervision observed: "It's as though the children in here are being prepared for incarceration, so when they put them in a real lockdown situation, they'll be used to being hemmed in."[111]

Public schools in the hyperghetto similarly deteriorated to the point where they operated in the manner of *institutions of confinement* whose primary mission was not to educate but to ensure "custody and control" – to borrow the motto of many departments of corrections. Like the prison system, their recruitment was severely skewed along class and ethnoracial lines: at century's close, 75 percent of the pupils of Chicago's establishments came from families living under the official poverty line and nine of every ten were black or Hispanic. Like inmates, these children were herded into decaying and overcrowded facilities built like bunkers, where undertrained and underpaid teachers, hampered by a shocking penury of equipment and supplies – many schools had no photocopying machines, library, science laboratory, or even functioning bathrooms, and used textbooks that were 20-year-old rejects from suburban schools – strove to regulate conduct so as to maintain order and minimize violent incidents. The physical plant of most establishments resembled fortresses, complete with concertina wire on outside fences, bricked up windows, heavy locks on iron doors, metal detectors at the gates and hallways patrolled by armed guards conducting spot checks and body searches between buildings.

Over the years, essential educational programs were cut to divert funds for more weapons scanners, cameras, emergency telephones, sign-in desks, and security personnel whose duty was to repel unwanted intruders from the outside and hem students inside the

---

[110] Venkatesh, *American Project*, pp. 123–30.
[111] Cited by Miller, *Search and Destroy*, p. 101. On the dubious legality of military-style police raids on Chicago's housing projects and their imitation by other cities, see David E. B. Smith, "Clean Sweep or Witch Hunt: Constitutional Issues in Chicago's Public Housing Sweeps" (1993).

school's walls.[112] Indeed, it appears that the main purpose of these schools was simply to "neutralize" youth considered unworthy and unruly by holding them under lock for the day so that, at minimum, they do not engage in street crime. Certainly, it is hard to maintain that educating them was a priority when half of the city's high schools place in the bottom one percent of establishments nationwide on the American College Test and two-thirds of hyperghetto students failed to complete their cursus while those who do graduate read on average at 8th grade level.[113] At any rate, the carceral atmosphere of schools and the constant presence of armed guards in uniform in the lobbies, corridors, cafeteria, and playground of their establishment habituates the children of the hyperghetto to the demeanor, tactics, and interactive style of the correctional officers many of them are bound to encounter shortly after their school days are over.

How the prison became more like a ghetto

The three decades following the climax of the Civil Rights Movement not only witnessed a sea change in the function, structure, and texture of the dark ghetto in the postindustrial metropolis – in effect, its mutation into the hyperghetto. The racial and class backlash that reconfigured the city also ushered a sweeping transformation in the purpose and social organization of the carceral institution. Summarily put, the "Big House" that embodied the correctional ideal of melioristic treatment and community reintegration of inmates[114] gave way to a

---

[112] In 1992, the Division of School Safety of the New York City Board of Education had a budget of $73 million, a fleet of 90 vehicles, and over 3,200 uniformed security officers, which made it the ninth largest police force in the country, just ahead of that of Miami (John Devine, *Maximum Security: The Culture of Violence in Inner-City Schools* [1996], pp. 76–7). In 1968, this division did not exist. John Devine notes that lower-tier principals had as one of their major concerns the management of this "paramilitary force [which] has taken on an independent existence with its own organization and procedures, language, rules, equipment, dressing rooms, uniforms, vans, and lines of authority" (ibid., pp. 80–2).

[113] Chicago Tribune, *The Worst Schools in America*, pp. 12–13.

[114] One must be careful not to romanticize the carceral past: even in the heyday of rehabilitation (corresponding to the full maturation of the Fordist economy and Keynesian state), the prison did not much rehabilitate, owing to the abiding "priority given to institutional order, discipline, and security" (Edgardo Rotman, "The Failure of Reform: United States, 1865–1965" [1995], p. 195). But the ideal of treatment, the intervention of therapeutic professionals, and the deployment of rehabilitative routines did improve conditions of detention and reduce arbitrariness, cruelty, and

Deadly Symbiosis

race-divided and violence-ridden "warehouse" geared solely to neutralizing social rejects by sequestering them physically from society – in the way that a classical ghetto wards off the threat of defilement posed by the presence of a dishonored category by encaging it within its walls, but in an ambience resonant with the fragmentation, dread, and despair of the post-Fordist hyperghetto.

With the explosive growth of the incarcerated population leading to rampant overcrowding, the steep rise in the number of inmates serving long sentences, the spread of ethnically based gangs, the flood of drug offenders and especially of young offenders deeply rooted in the informal economy and oppositional culture of the street, the "inmate society" depicted in the classic prison research of the postwar decades foundered, as John Irwin observes in his 1990 preface to his classic book *The Felon*: "There is no longer a single, overarching convict culture or social organization, as there tended to be twenty years ago when *The Felon* was written. Most prisoners restrict their association to a few other prisoners and withdraw from prison public life. A minority associates with gangs, gamble, buy and sell contraband commodities, and engage in prison homosexual behavior. If they do so, however, they must act 'tough' and be willing to live by the new code, that is, be ready to meet threats of violence with violence."[115]

It is not easy to characterize the changes which remade the American prison in the image of the ghetto in the three decades following the turnaround of incarceration trends circa 1973. This is difficult, not only because of the "astonishing diversity" of establishments and regimens across levels of the carceral system and the different states,[116] but also because we have remarkably little on-the-ground data on social and cultural life inside the penitentiary after the demise of the Fordist-Keynesian regime. Sociologists have deserted the institution – with a firm push from corrections administrations that have grown increasingly closed and secretive – just as it was ascending to the front line of the instruments for the regulation of poverty and race.[117]

---

lawlessness behind bars. What is more, extensive "programming" helped achieve internal stability and instilled a forward-looking outlook among inmates.

[115] John Irwin, *The Felon* (1990 [1970]), p. vi.

[116] Norval Morris, "The Contemporary Prison, 1965–Present" (1995), p. 228. The persistence of these variations is documented by Christopher Wildeman et al., "Conditions of Confinement in American Prisons and Jails" (2018).

[117] Loïc Wacquant, "The Eclipse of Prison Ethnography in the Age of Mass Incarceration" (2002). This is in contrast with the persistence and profusion of

With the partial exception of women's facilities,[118] field studies based on direct observation have virtually disappeared, as research on American imprisonment shifted from close-up accounts of the internal order of the prison, its hierarchies, values, and mores, to distant analyses of incarceration rates, the dynamics and cost-effectiveness of penal management, sentencing, and fear of crime based primarily on official statistics, administrative reports, litigation findings, and large-scale surveys.[119] Nonetheless, one can provisionally single out six tendencies that have fortified the structural and functional meshing of the denuded hyperghetto and the hypertrophied prison archipelago in the large (post)industrial states that put the United States on the path to hyperincarceration.[120]

1. The racial division of everything

The relatively stable set of positions and expectations defined primarily in terms of criminal statuses and prison conduct that used to organize the inmate world has been replaced by a chaotic and conflictual setting wherein "racial division has primacy over all particular identities and influences all aspects of life."[121] The ward, tier, cell, and bed-bunk to which one is assigned; access to food, telephone,

---

fieldwork on carceral worlds in other advanced societies, as documented by Deborah H. Drake et al. (eds.), *The Palgrave Handbook of Prison Ethnography* (2015).

[118] Barbara Owen, *In the Mix: Struggle and Survival in a Women's Prison* (1996); Sandra Enos, *Mothering from the Inside: Parenting in a Women's Prison* (2001); Lynne Haney, *Offending Women: Power, Punishment, and the Regulation of Desire* (2010). For a panoramic review of the ebbs and flows of field studies of the carceral world, see Manuela Cunha, "The Ethnography of Prisons and Penal Confinement" (2014).

[119] See Jonathan Simon, "The 'Society of Captives' in the Era of Hyper-Incarceration" (2000). Note the parallel with social research on the ghetto: the field studies of the 1960s, focusing on ghetto *institutions* seen at ground level from the insider's point of view, disappeared by the 1970s to be replaced a decade later by survey-based research on the "underclass," i.e., *population aggregates* constructed from afar and from above via the manipulation of quantitative indicators.

[120] A different take, speculating on the further impact of age, crowding, offense type, and managerial style on the informal organization of convicts is Derek A. Kreager and Candace Kruttschnitt, "Inmate Society in the Era of Mass Incarceration" (2018).

[121] Irwin, *The Felon*, p. v; also Leo Carroll, "Race, Ethnicity, and the Social Order of the Prison" (1982); Robert Johnson, *Hard Time: Understanding and Reforming the Prison* (1996); Victor Hassine, *Life Without Parole: Living in Prison Today* (1999), pp. 71–8; Philip Goodman, "'It's just Black, White, or Hispanic': An Observational Study of Racializing Moves in California's Segregated Prison Reception Centers" (2008). The racialization of everything in prison is an extension of the same in jail: see Michael Walker, *Indefinite: Doing Time in Jail* (2022).

television, visitation, and in-house programs; one's associations and protections, which in turn determine the probability of being the victim or perpetrator of violence: all are set by one's ethnic community of provenance. Elective loyalty to inmates as a generic class, with the possibility of remaining non-aligned, has been superseded by forced and exclusive loyalty to one's "race" defined in rigid, caste-like manner, with no in-between and no position of neutrality – just as within the urban ghetto. And the central axis of stratification inside the "pen" has shifted from the vertical cleavage *between prisoners and guards*, marked by the proscription to "talk to a screw," "rat on a con," and exploit other inmates, to horizontal cleavages *among inmates* between blacks, Latinos, and whites (with Asians most often assimilated to whites and Middle Easterners given a choice of voluntary affiliation).[122]

In Gresham Sykes's classic account of *The Society of Captives*, the "argot roles" that compose the social structure and cultural fabric of the prison are all *specific to the carceral cosmos*:[123] "rats" and "center men" are defined as such because they betray the core value of solidarity among prisoners by violating the ban on communication with custodians; "merchants" peddle goods in the illicit economy of the establishment while "gorillas" prey on weak inmates to acquire cigarettes, food, clothing, and deference; similarly, "wolfs," "punks," and "fags" are descriptors of sexual scripts adopted behind bars. Finally, "ball busters" and "real men" are categories defined by the type of intercourse they maintain with guards: defiant and hopeless, the former give "screws" a hard time while the latter "pull their own time" without displaying either subservience or aggression. In John Irwin's portrait of the social organization of convicts in California prisons in the 1960s, the inmate subculture is not a response to prison deprivation but an import from the street.[124] Yet it is the criminal identities of "thief," "convict," and "square" that nonetheless predominate behind bars. In the warehouse prison of century's end, by contrast, racial affiliation has become what Everett Hughes calls the "master status trait" that submerges all other markers and governs

---

[122] This does not obviate the persistence of the role of the "old head" in the microcosm of the prison ward or cell block, as documented by Derek A. Kreager et al., "Where 'Old Heads' Prevail: Inmate Hierarchy in a Men's Prison Unit" (2017).
[123] Gresham Sykes, *The Society of Captives: A Study in a Maximum Security Prison* (1958).
[124] Irwin, *The Felon*.

all relations and spaces, from the cells and the hallways to the dining hall, the commissary, and the yard.[125]

To be sure, American prisons, both North and South, have long been segregated along ethnoracial lines, down to the two-men cell. But these lines used to *crosscut and stabilize* penitentiary demarcations as the social worlds of black and white inmates ran parallel to each other in "separate but equal" fashion, so to speak.[126] In the aftermath of the black mobilization of the 1960s and the rapid "darkening" of the imprisoned population, racial cleavages have grown to *undercut and supplant* carceral ones. And the perennial pattern of separation and avoidance that characterized race relations in the postwar years has been amplified by open hostility and aggression, particularly through the agency of gangs.

2. The "code of the street" overwhelms the "convict code"

Along with ethnoracial division, the predatory culture of the street, centered on hypermasculinist notions of honor, toughness, and coolness has entered into and transfigured the social structure and culture of jails and prisons. The "convict code," rooted in solidarity among inmates and antagonism towards guards, has in effect been swamped by the "code of the street," with its ardent imperative of individual "respect" secured through the militant display and actualization of readiness to mete out physical violence.[127]

Accordingly, "the old 'hero' of the prison world – the 'right guy' – has been replaced by outlaws and gang members. These two types have raised toughness and mercilessness to the top of prisoners' value systems."[128] Ethnically based street gangs and "supergangs," such as the Disciples, El Rukn, Vice Lords, and Latin Kings in Illinois, the Mexican Mafia, Black Guerrilla Family, and Aryan Brotherhood in California, and the Ñetas in New York, have taken over the illicit economy of the prison and destabilized the entire social system of inmates, forcing the latter to shift from "doing your own time" to "doing

---

[125] Everett C. Hughes, "Dilemmas and Contradictions of Status" (1984 [1945]). For a contemporaneous account, see John Irwin, *The Warehouse Prison: Disposal of the New Dangerous Class* (2004).
[126] James B. Jacobs, "Race Relations and the Prisoner Subculture" (1983), pp. 75–6.
[127] Gresham Sykes and Sheldon Messinger, "The Inmate Social System" (1960), pp. 6–10; Elijah Anderson, *Code of the Street: Decency, Violence, and the Moral Life of the Inner City* (1999).
[128] Irwin, *The Felon*, p. vii.

gang time." They have even precipitated a thorough restructuring of the administration of large-scale prison systems, from Illinois to California to Texas.[129] What matters here is not just that "prison gangs govern the American penal system," to cite the subtitle of David Skarbeck's stunning book, *The Social Order of the Underworld*, but that these gangs are structured and structuring along racial lines.[130]

Together with the compositional changes of the prison's clientele, the rising tide of drugs circulating *sub rosa*, and the consolidation of racially based gangs, the eclipse of the old inmate structure of power has resulted in increased levels of interpersonal and group brutality. So that "what was once a repressive but comparatively safe 'Big House' is now often an unstable and violent social jungle" in which social intercourse is infected with the same disruption, aggression, and unpredictability as in the hyperghetto.[131] Late-century prisoners "complain about the increased fragmentation and disorganization that they experience. Life in prison is no longer organized but instead is viewed as capricious and dangerous."[132] Those who return behind bars after spending extended periods outside invariably find that they do not recognize "the joint" and that they can no longer get along with their fellow inmates due to the prevailing anomie.[133]

The demise of the convict code*

The activities of these violent groups who, in the pursuit of loot, sex, and revenge, will attack any outsider have *completely unraveled any remnants of the old codes of honor* and tip networks that

---

[129] Jacobs, *Stateville*, pp. 137–74; Irwin, *Prisons in Turmoil*, pp. 186–92; George M. Camp, *Prison Gangs: Their Extent, Nature, and Impact on Prisons* (1985); Steve J. Martin and Sheldon Ekland-Olson, *Texas Prisons: The Walls Came Tumbling Down* (1987). A quarter-century later, the main anchor of urban gangs has migrated from the street to the jail and prison: Scott H. Decker and David C. Pyrooz, "The Real Gangbanging is in Prison" (2015).

[130] David Skarbek, *The Social Order of the Underworld: How Prison Gangs Govern the American Penal System* (2014).

[131] Johnson, *Hard Time*, p. 133.

[132] Geoffrey Hunt et al., "Changes in Prison Culture: Prison Gangs and the Case of the 'Pepsi Generation'" (1993).

[133] See, for instance, inmate Hassine's first-hand account of the conflict between "new inmates versus old heads" in the ghettoized "prison subcultures" marked by "their disrespect for authority, drug addition, illiteracy, and welfare mentality," in short, "all the evils of the decaying American inner city" (Hassine, *Life Without Parole*, pp. 41–2).

> formerly helped to maintain order. In a limited, closed space, such as a prison, threats or attacks like those posed by these groups cannot be ignored. Prisoners must be ready to protect themselves or get out of the way. Those who have chosen to continue to circulate in public, with few exceptions, have formed or joined a clique or gang for their own protection. Consequently, violence-oriented groups dominate many, if not most, large men's prisons.
>
> * John Irwin, *Prisons in Turmoil* (1980), p. 192, emphasis added.

When my best friend and chief informant from Chicago's South Side Ashante was sent to serve a six-year sentence in a low-security facility in downstate Illinois after having "stayed clean" on the outside for a decade following a stint of eight years at Stateville penitentiary, he promptly requested a transfer to a maximum-security prison: he was dismayed by the arrogance and unruliness of "young punks" from the streets of Chicago who ignored the old convict code, disrespected inmates with extensive prison seniority, and sought confrontation at every turn. Ashante knew well that, by moving to Stateville or Pontiac, he would endure a much more restrictive regimen in a more dreary physical setting with access to fewer if any programs, but he believed that a more predictable environment ruled by the norms of the "inmate society" of old made for a less risky sojourn.[134] The increased social entropy and commotion that characterizes prison life at century's close explains that "it is not uncommon to find 10 per cent of the population of large prisons in protective custody."[135] It accounts also for the proliferation of "supermax" penitentiaries across the country as authorities strive to restore order by relegating "the worst of the worst" inmates in special facilities where they are kept in near-total lockdown under detention regimes so austere that they are indistinguishable from torture in light of international human rights covenants.[136]

---

[134] The same reasoning applies in big-city jails, which have become so disrupted, violent, and punitive that many detainees hasten to plead guilty in order to be "sent to state" right away: "Better do a year in state [prison] than three months in this hell of a jail" is how several detainees at L.A.'s Men's Central Jail put it to me in summer of 1998.

[135] Morris, "The Contemporary Prison, 1965–present," p. 248.

[136] Roy D. King, "The Rise and Rise of Supermax: An American Solution in Search of a Problem?" (1999). For an in-depth study of this carceral institution and its extreme

Deadly Symbiosis

3. Purging the undesirables

The "Big House" of the postwar decades was animated by a consequentialist theory of punishment that, at least in theory, sought to resocialize inmates so as to lower the probability of re-offense once they returned to society, of which they were expected to become law-abiding if not productive members. Following the official repudiation of the philosophy of rehabilitation in the 1970s,[137] today's prison has for sole de facto purpose to effect retribution and to *incapacitate* offenders – and individuals thought to be likely to violate the law, such as parolees – both *materially*, by removing them physically into an institutional enclave, and *symbolically*, by drawing a hard and fast line between convicted criminals and law-abiding citizens.[138] In other words, penal expurgation operates both in the order of classification and stratification.

The "law-and-order" paradigm that gradually achieved undivided hegemony in crime and justice policy over the closing three decades of the twentieth century jettisons any notion of prevention and proportionality in favor of direct appeals to popular resentment through measures that dramatize the fear and loathing of crime viewed as the abhorrent conduct of terminally defective or deviant individuals.[139] "Such appeals to resentment", writes the Cambridge legal philosopher Andrew von Hirsch, "reflect an ideology of purging 'undesirables' from the body politic" in which incarceration is essentially a means for social and moral excommunication.[140] That makes the mission of the late-century prison identical to that of the classical ghetto, whose *raison d'être* was precisely to quarantine a polluting population from the urban body.

---

yet banalized regimen, read Keramet Reiter, *23/7: Pelican Bay Prison and the Rise of Long-Term Solitary Confinement* (2016).

[137] Francis A. Allen, *The Decline of the Rehabilitative Ideal* (1981).

[138] On the philosophy, practice, and contradictions of penal neutralization, see Franklin E. Zimring and Gordon Hawkins, *Incapacitation: Penal Confinement and the Restraint of Crime* (1995).

[139] "Three Strikes and You're Out," which mandates the lifelong incarceration of offenders in response to double recidivism, epitomizes this approach to "vengeance as public policy" (David Shichor and Dale K. Sechrest (eds.), *Three Strikes and You're Out: Vengeance as Public Policy* [1996]) in its disregard for proportionality and penological efficacy, as well as in its unabashed use of a catchy baseball metaphor that likens crime fighting to a kind of sport.

[140] Andrew von Hirsch, "Penal Theories" (1999), p. 676.

When the prison is used as an implement for social and cultural purging, like the ghetto, it no longer points beyond itself; it turns into a self-contained contraption which fulfills its function, and thus justifies itself, by its mere existence. And its inhabitants learn to live in the here-and-now, bathed in the concentrate of violence and hopelessness brewing within the walls. In his autobiographical description of the changing social structure and culture of a maximum-security facility in Pennsylvania over the previous 16 years, inmate Victor Hassine captures well the devolution of the Big House, pointing to eventual reentry into society, into a Warehouse leading nowhere but to a wall of despair: "Through this gradual process of deterioration, Graterford the prison became Graterford the ghetto, a place where men forgot about courts of law or the difference between right and wrong because they were too busy thinking about living, dying, or worse. Reform, rehabilitation, and redemption do not exist in a ghetto. There is only survival of the fittest. Crime, punishment, and accountability are of little significance when men are living in a lawless society where their actions are restrained only by the presence of concrete and steel walls. Where a prison in any real or abstract sense might promote the greater good, once it becomes a ghetto it can do nothing but promise violent upheaval."[141]

4. The proto-racialization of judicial stigma

The contemporary prison can be further likened to the ghetto in that, in the revanchist penal climate of the closing decades of the twentieth century, the stigma of penal conviction has been prolonged, diffused, and reframed in ways that assimilate it to an ethnoracial stigma attached *ad aeternum* to the body of its bearer. In other liberal-democratic societies, the status dishonor and civic disabilities of being a prisoner are temporary and limited: they affect offenders while they are being processed by the criminal justice system and typically wear off upon coming out of prison or shortly thereafter. To ensure this, laws and administrative rules set strict conditions and limits to the use and diffusion of criminal justice information, which are typically accessible only to judicial authorities.

Not so in the United States, where, on the contrary, (1) convicts are subjected to ever-longer and broader post-detention forms of social control and symbolic branding that durably set them apart from the

---

[141] Hassine, *Life Without Parole*.

rest of the population; (2) the arrest and prosecution records of individual inmates are readily available and actively disseminated by the authorities as well as private firms specialized in background checks;[142] (3) a naturalizing discourse suffused with genetic phraseology and animalistic imagery has swamped public representations of crime in the media, politics, and significant segments of scholarship.[143] In the 2010s, to reduce barriers to prisoner reentry, some states changed laws and administrative rules to allow for the expungement or sealing of criminal records for a limited class of convicts. But the process proves complicated, inconsistent, and inefficient, and it reaches a very small number of former prisoners.[144]

In 2000, all but two states required *postprison supervision* of offenders and 80 percent of all persons released from state penitentiaries were freed under conditional or community release; the average term spent on parole also increased steadily over the previous two decades to surpass 23 months in 1996 – nearly equal to the average prison term served of 25 months.[145] At the same time, parole services have become entirely focused on the administrative enforcement of safety and security, to the near-total neglect of job training, housing assistance, and substance abuse treatment, even though official records indicate that over three-fourths of state inmates suffer from narcotics or alcohol dependency. With fully 54 percent of offenders failing to complete their term of parole in 1997 (compared to 27 percent in 1984), and parole violators making up one-third of all persons admitted in state penitentiaries every year (two-thirds in California), *parole has become an appendage of the prison* which operates mainly to extend the social and symbolic incapacities of incarceration beyond its walls.[146] With the advent of the internet, corrections administrations

---

[142] On the extension of penal sanction beyond prison walls through the diffusion and remanence of individualized arrest, prosecution, and incarceration information, see James B. Jacobs, *The Eternal Criminal Record* (2015), and Sarah Esther Lageson, *Digital Punishment: Privacy, Stigma, and the Harms of Data-Driven Criminal Justice* (2020).
[143] Nicole Rafter, *The Criminal Brain: Understanding Biological Theories of Crime* (2008).
[144] Brian M. Murray, "A New Era for Expungement Law Reform: Recent Developments at the State and Federal Level" (2016).
[145] Joan Petersilia, "Parole and Prisoner Reentry in the United States" (1999).
[146] On the correlative transformation of the identity and practices of parole agents, see Mona Lynch, "Waste Managers? The New Penology, Crime Fighting, and Parole Agent Identity" (1998), and Robert Werth, "The Construction and Stewardship of Responsible Yet Precarious Subjects: Punitive Ideology, Rehabilitation, and 'Tough Love' Among Parole Personnel" (2013).

in many states, among them Illinois, Florida, and Texas, rushed to put their entire inmate databases online, further stretching the perimeter of penal infamy by making it possible for anyone to delve into the court and corrections records of inmates via the World Wide Web, and for employers and landlords to discriminate more broadly against ex-convicts in complete legality.

Florida convicts online

In 2000, the "Corrections Offender Network" rubric of the Florida prison administration allowed one to run searches by name, race, sex, identifiers (Social Security, passport or alien number, driver's license) and offense category. It provided not only the usual personal data (name and aliases, birth date, hair and eye color, height and weight, "scars, marks, and tattoos" with their exact description and location) and criminal justice information (current offense date, offense type, sentence date, case number and prison sentence length, plus an abbreviated incarceration history), but also a full-size color picture and the date of release as well as the current address for former inmates out on parole. This site received some 300,000 visits during its first year of operation.

This general movement toward longer and more encompassing post-detention measures of criminal justice supervision finds an extreme instantiation in the management of sex offenders under the regime of "Megan's Laws" voted in 1996 by federal and state governments in a stampede to appease displaced popular ire over child abuse. These laws mandate that authorities not only keep a registry of all (ex-)sex offenders in their jurisdiction, for periods extending up to life, but also notify the public of their whereabouts via mailings, posters, media announcements, CD-roms and public websites containing the files of ex-offenders coded by geographic area,[147] thus making permanent and highly visible the blemish attached to their conviction. In Louisiana, for instance, the (ex-)sex offender himself must notify in writing his landlord, neighbors, and the director of the

---

[147] Robert J. Martin, "Pursuing Public Protection through Mandatory Community Notification of Convicted Sex Offenders: The Trials and Tribulations of Megan's Law" (1996). For a fuller discussion, see Wacquant, *Punishing the Poor*, chapter 7.

local school and municipal parks of his penal status; he must also post warnings of his presence in a community newspaper within 30 days of his arrival. The law further authorizes "all forms of public notification," including posters, handbills, and bumper stickers – a judge can even request that the offender wear "a distinctive garb" that will readily identify him as a sex offender, in the manner of the yellow star or hat donned by Jews in the principalities of medieval Europe and in Hitler's Germany.[148]

In the second half of the 2000s, states from coast to coast promulgated measures generically known as "Jessica's Law." California's version, passed in 2006 and approved by referendum, has for name the Sexual Predator Punishment and Control Act. It increased penalties for sex offenses, eliminated good time credits, excluded probation, and lengthened parole for certain crimes, as well as imposed lifelong GPS monitoring of high-risk sex convicts. The latter were also prohibited from residing within 2,000 feet from schools, buses, and libraries or any place where children gather, which, in some counties, effectively forbid them from living in most cities.[149]

The resurgence and popularity of genetic pseudo-explanations of crime is another indicator of the bent towards the compulsory *racialization of criminals*, whose counterpart is the elective *ethnicization of crime victims*, who have been fabricated into a quasi-ethnic group,[150] complete with its distinctive idiom, insignia, pageantry, and official organizations that mobilize to demand "affirmative action" from the state on behalf of their members. One illustration from among a myriad: the compendium on crime edited by James Q. Wilson and Joan Petersilia, in which "twenty-eight leading experts look at the most pressing problem of our time" (according to the

---

[148] Scott A. Cooper, "Community Notification and Verification Practices in Three States" (1998).

[149] Bruce Zucker, "Jessica's Law Residency Restrictions in California: The Current State of the Law" (2014).

[150] Joel Best, "Victimization and the Victim Industry" (1997). The rise of the crime victims' movement in the United States has been accompanied by a flood of publications, from legal arguments and personal accounts to practical guides and social science studies. A panorama is Jeanna M. Mastrocinque, "An Overview of the Victims' Rights Movement: Historical, Legislative, and Research Developments" (2010). An unforeseen affluent to this movement has been the feminist mobilization against domestic violence and rape: see Marie Gottschalk, *The Prison and the Gallows: The Politics of Mass Incarceration in America* (2006), chapters 4 and 5, and Aya Gruber, *The Feminist War on Crime: The Unexpected Role of Women's Liberation in Mass Incarceration* (2021).

book's front cover blurb), opens with two long chapters that review "Criminogenic Traits" and "Biomedical Factors in Crime."[151] For Richard Herrnstein, a renowned Harvard psychologist and coauthor, with ultraright-wing ideologue Charles Murray, of the infamous treatise in scholarly racism, *The Bell Curve*, serious crimes are not culturally or historically defined but *male in se*, "crimes that are wrongs in themselves."[152] Now, "it would be an overstatement to say 'once a criminal always a criminal', but it would be closer to the truth than to deny the evidence of a unifying and long-enduring pattern of encounters with the law for most serious offenders." This pattern cannot be explained by "accidents, situations, and social forces," as these only "modulate the criminogenic factors" of low intelligence, antisocial personality, and male chromosomes.

The genetic roots of crime, Herrnstein continues, are further confirmed by the fact that offenders are "disproportionately nonectomorphic mesomorphs" (chunky and muscular with large bones), and sport "lower heart rates," "lower nervous system responsiveness to sudden stimuli," and "atypical patterns [of] brain waves." The Harvard psychologist regrets that research has turned up "only weak association between male hormones and criminal behavior or antisociality," but he promptly consoles himself by asserting that the Y chromosome elevates criminal behavior in "supermales" and "increases the risk of criminal incarceration by a factor of about ten" – based on the fact that the proportion of XYY male prisoners is ten times that in the general population.[153] Interestingly enough, Herrnstein does not discuss ethnoracial differences in criminality and, in his conclusion, he even disingenuously disavows – on feigned epistemological grounds – any effort to "frame questions about behavior in terms of causes" (although he has repeatedly turned correlation into causation in this very chapter). But it requires little effort to infer from his argumentation that, "just as night follows day," as he puts it, the hyperincarceration of blacks must be caused in part by their innate criminal propensity, given what he calls "a

---

[151] Richard Herrnstein, "Criminogenic Traits" (1995); Patricia A. Brennan et al. "Biomedical Factors in Crime" (1995). For a comprehensive recapitulation and meticulous dismantling of the resurgent genetic theorizing about crime in American criminology, read Julien Larrègue, *Héréditaire. L'éternel retour des théories biologiques du crime* (2020).

[152] Herrnstein, "Criminogenic Traits," pp. 40, 41, 62, 56–7, 58.

[153] Not a single source is cited for this rather stunning statistic, despite superabundant notes and references throughout the chapter.

Deadly Symbiosis

scientific consensus that criminal and antisocial behavior can have genetic roots."[154]

5. Bifurcated socioracial patterning of carceral recruitment and authority

The voracious prison and the naked hyperghetto not only display a similarly skewed recruitment and composition in terms of class and caste. The former also duplicates the authority structure characteristic of the latter in that it places a population of poor blacks under the direct supervision of whites – albeit, in this case, lower-class whites.

In the communal ghetto of the immediate postwar, black residents toiled under the rule of white landlords, white employers, white unions, white social workers, and white policemen.[155] Likewise, at century's end, the convicts of New York City, Philadelphia, Baltimore, Cleveland, Detroit, and Chicago, who are overwhelmingly African American, serve their sentence in establishments staffed by officers who are overwhelmingly white, as shown in figure 10. In Illinois, for instance, two-thirds of the state's 41,000 inmates are blacks who serve time under the watch of an 8,400 uniformed force that is 84 percent white.

While undergoing training as a prison guard for the state of New York, reporter Ted Conover was struck by the stark color contrast stamping his new occupation in the infamous penitentiary of Sing Sing: "Reflecting the demographic makeup of the state's small towns, the officer corps is overwhelmingly white. As inmates are overwhelmingly minority, the racial hierarchy at most facilities resembles that of South Africa under apartheid."[156] With the proliferation of detention facilities in rural areas, perversely, the economic stability and social welfare of lower-class whites from the declining hinterland has come to hinge on the continued socioeconomic marginality and penal

---

[154] Herrnstein, "Criminogenic Traits," pp. 62, 58. This is reaffirmed in the companion article by Brennan et al., who sum up their findings thus: "Criminal behavior in parents increases the likelihood of nonviolent crime in the offspring. This relationship is due, in part, to genetic transmission of criminogenic characteristics. This genetic effect is stronger for females and is especially important for recidivistic crime" (Brennan et al., "Biomedical Factors in Crime," pp. 87–8).

[155] Kenneth C. Clark, *Dark Ghetto: Dilemmas of Social Power* (1965).

[156] Ted Conover, *Newjack: Guarding Sing Sing* (2000), p. 26.

Racial Domination

State	Guards	Prisoners
New York	10.5	54.3
Pennsylvania	8.3	56.5
Maryland	8.7	77.2
Ohio	21.3	53.8
Michigan	14.3	55.7
Illinois	13.2	65.1

per cent African American (1997)

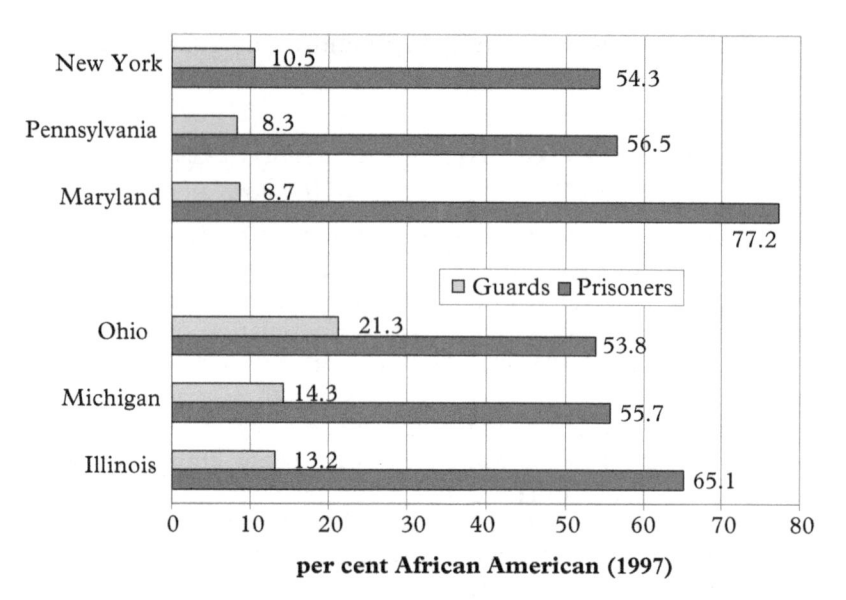

Source: Camille Graham Camp and George M. Camp (eds.), *The Corrections Yearbook 1998* (1998), pp. 13 and 130.

Figure 10 Black prisoners guarded by white correctional officers.

restraint of ever-larger numbers of subproletarian blacks from the urban core.[157]

6. Churning in and out of the (hyper)ghetto

The prison of the early twenty-first century further resembles the (hyper)ghetto for the simple reason that an overwhelming majority of its occupants originate from the racialized core of the country's major cities and return there upon release, only to be soon caught again in the police dragnet to be sent away for another, longer sojourn behind bars in a self-perpetuating cycle of escalating socioeconomic marginality and legal disability.

---

[157] By tracking the proliferation of penitentiaries in the American hinterland, John Eason has shown that "the prison functions as a state-sponsored public works program for disadvantaged rural communities" ("Prisons as Panacea or Pariah? The Countervailing Consequences of the Prison Boom on the Political Economy of Rural Towns" [2017], p. 7).

Interestingly, the phenomenon was first diagnosed and documented by inmates themselves. In the late 1980s, prison activist and scholar Eddie Ellis coordinated a geographic count of convicts in the New York state prison system and discovered that three of every four inmates serving a long sentence in it came from only *seven black and Latino neighborhoods* of New York City who also happened to be the poorest areas of the metropolis, including Harlem, the South Bronx, East New York, and Brownsville.[158] Every year these segregated and dispossessed districts furnished a fresh contingent of 25,000-odd inmates while 23,000 ex-convicts were discharged, most of them on parole, right back into these devastated areas. A conservative estimate, given a statewide felony recidivism rate of 47 percent, is that within a year, some 10,000 of them found their way back "upstate" and under lock and key. The fact that 46 percent of the inmates of New York state prisons issued from neighborhoods served by the 16 worst public schools of the city ensured that their clientele would be duly replenished for decades to come.

This is not a New York peculiarity. In 2001, Illinois prisons discharged 18,377 inmates, 85 percent of them black, and 53 percent of whom returned to Chicago. Of those returning to the Windy City, fully one-third landed in only six of the 77 community areas making up the metropolis. Two of those areas correspond to Chicago's historic ghetto of the South Side and three to its counterpart of the West Side (the seventh is a predominantly Puerto Rican neighborhood of concentrated poverty adjacent to the West Side).[159] All six are among the most segregated and poorest districts of the city, marred with high rates of crime, drug selling, housing dilapidation, family dissolution, infant mortality, school failure, and a shocking paucity of state services and commercial outlets. In every major postindustrial city, *prisoners churn in and out of the same dispossessed and disparaged districts,* and their level of spatial clustering has barely budged over the past two decades, even as cities lost population, concentrations

---

[158] Edwin Ellis, *The Non-Traditional Approach to Criminal Justice and Social Justice* (1993). It is revealing that these data should come from a survey of the geographic provenance of prisoners carried out by inmates themselves: they sensed at ground level what Ellis calls the "relation of symbiosis" emerging between the hyperghetto and the carceral system, even as government officials were oblivious to it. Policy think tanks such as the Urban Institute would catch up with this reality a full decade later and academic researchers two decades later.

[159] Nancy G. LaVigne et al., *A Portrait of Prisoner Reentry in Illinois* (2003), pp. 50–63.

of public housing got demolished, and poverty diffused to the suburbs.[160]

The extraordinary clustering of incarceration by place matters because it explains how the imprisonment rate of middle-class blacks could decrease at the same time as the rate for lower-class blacks boomed. This *class selectivity inside of race* is achieved by the police and judicial *targeting of the vestiges of the dark ghetto and assorted poor and segregated areas* in the dual city. Thus, in Chicago, the high-incarceration areas map perfectly onto the perimeter of the city's hyperghetto: the historic core of the South Side and West Side were by far the two zones with the highest number of convicts per resident, and the ranking of the city's 77 community areas based on that indicator proves highly stable over time for the period 1990–2005.[161] These neighborhoods were targeted, not because they are black, but because they are poor, dilapidated, and stigmatized, suffering as they do from decades of high crime, economic involution, and social disinvestment. They are seen as urban sores that fester and threaten the health of the city, the redoubt of the racialized "underclass" which needs to be brought under stern tutelage by forceful action. As a result, their residents are easy prey for tactics of hardline policing and punitive prosecution leading to mass arrests and expedited sentencing.

The hyperghetto is the dream territory for aggressive law enforcement skirting the bounds of legality: crime on its street is prevalent and visible; the residents are vulnerable because so many are on probation or parole and already have a criminal record;[162] they also do not possess the economic and cultural capital needed to post bail and

---

[160] Todd Clear, *Imprisoning Communities: How Mass Incarceration Makes Disadvantaged Communities Worse* (2007); David S. Kirk, "Where the Other One Percent Live: An Examination of Changes in the Spatial Concentration of the Formerly Incarcerated" (2019). See also the innovative work of Jessica T. Simes, *Punishing Places: The Geography of Mass Imprisonment* (2021), which confirms the high spatial concentration of incarceration for the entire state of Massachusetts and its clustering in areas of intense socioeconomic disadvantage in both urban and rural areas (increasing with the share of black residents even after controlling for arrest and crime rates).

[161] Robert J. Sampson and Charles Loeffler, "Punishment's Place: The Local Concentration of Mass Incarceration" (2010), pp. 24–5.

[162] Those who are on felony probation are also typically subjected to "four-way search clauses," meaning that the police can search their person, their belongings, their car and their residence without warrant or motive. This makes it easier to detect the possession of drugs, weapons, and stolen merchandise but also to catch more mundane violations of probation or parole such as a sharing a room or riding in a car with a person who is also under community supervision.

litigate their case. Moreover, their precarious life circumstances make it impossible for them to delay the resolution of their judicial matter – for instance, they could lose their low-wage jobs if they stay locked up in jail or keep absenting themselves to attend court hearings. The result is that people in the hyperghetto are easy to charge (if only for "violating" their probation or parole), and they will take an early "deal" from the district attorney and plead guilty to reduced charges to get out of jail post haste, setting themselves up for the next round of arrest and prosecution.[163]

Adopting the same belligerent penal strategy in middle-class neighborhoods, *black or white*, would be inefficient and indeed self-defeating: crime there is subterranean and occurs behind closed doors; the residents know their rights and will battle for them; they have civic connections and political pull; they can hire private attorneys who will slow down the legal process and appear in court on their behalf, thereby sparing them the loss of time and dignity. After arrest, they will generally be released from jail (if they have been locked up at all) on their own recognizance (due to having solid "ties to the community") or on bail, and so they are prepared to multiply preliminary hearings and to force the case to trial if it is to their advantage.

To carry out mass arrests and assembly-line charging of middle-class defendants would waste scarce police resources and tie up prosecutors for naught, throwing a huge monkey wrench into the wheels of the court. This is why, as they migrated into segregated or ethnically mixed middle-class districts away from the hyperghetto, *middle-class blacks gained the physical and social distance necessary to escape hyper-penalization.* As a result, they saw their probability of going to prison decrease during the period of accelerated growth of the penal state, even as they continued to be overpoliced relative to whites.[164] This spatial targeting of the hyperghetto also helps explains how racial disparities in arrest, charging, prosecution, and sentencing

---

[163] After arraignment in county criminal court, prosecutors like to figuratively "dangle the jailhouse keys" in front of defendants eager to end remand detention and get home to "sleep in their own bed," as court lingo has it. In the urban counties of California, felony offenders who plead guilty (or no contest) are typically released on probation for three to five years with "years hanging over their head," meaning that violating their probation will automatically translate into a prison sanction.

[164] This did not, however, protect middle-class blacks from arbitrary police stops when walking or driving outside of their neighborhood. See Joe Soss and Vesla Weaver, "Police Are Our Government: Politics and the Policing of Race-Class Subjugated Communities" (2017).

increased during the same decades when the criminal legal bureaucracy became more racially diverse and when overt forms of judicial discrimination were reduced if not eliminated.

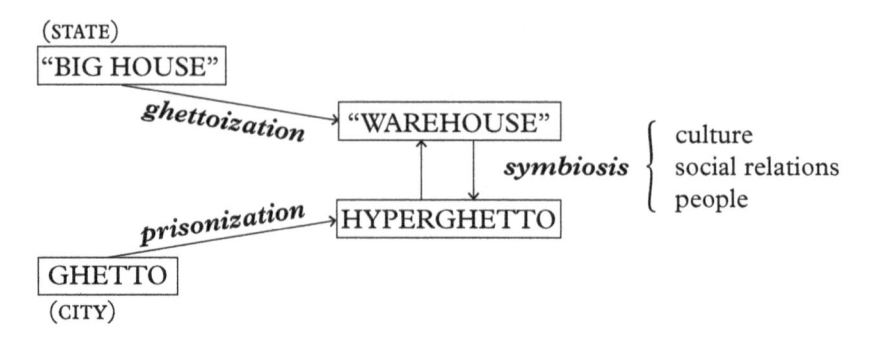

```
(STATE)
[ "BIG HOUSE" ]
        ghettoization → [ "WAREHOUSE" ]          ⎰ culture
                              ↕ symbiosis        ⎱ social relations
        prisonization → [ HYPERGHETTO ]            people
[ GHETTO ]
(CITY)
```

Figure 11 The symbiosis between hyperghetto and warehouse prison.

Figure 11 deconstructs the story of race and hyperincarceration, commonly but wrongly attributed to the War on drugs ushering in the return of Jim Crow, into its constituent parts, pursuant to the mandate to disaggregate racial domination: the ghettoization of the rehabilitative Big House into the neutralizing Warehouse as an agency of the state; the prisonization of the communal ghetto into the class-homogeneous and institutionally denuded hyperghetto in the postindustrial city; and the resulting relationship of mutual imbrication between the barren hyperghetto and the bulimic carceral machinery, cemented by the intense traffic of people, social relations, and cultural constructs between the two, giving way to the fourth peculiar institution.

How prison is remaking "race" and reshaping citizenship

The convergent changes that have "prisonized" the ghetto and "ghettoized" the prison in the aftermath of the Civil Rights Revolution suggest that the stupendous and mounting over-representation of lower-class African Americans behind bars during the four decades following the race riots of the 1960s does not stem simply from the discriminatory deployment of specific criminal policies such as drug interdiction, as proposed by Michael Tonry; from the combination of the collapse of urban labor markets, the diffusion of law-and-order politics in a competitive two-party system, and democratic localism as Bruce Western, Katherine Beckett, and Vanessa Barker would have it; from the sheer destabilizing effects of the increased penetration of inner-city neighborhoods by the penal state, as Todd Clear argues; or from the canonization of the right to protection from lawless racial violence in the immediate postwar period, as Naomi Murakawa contends.[165] Not that these factors are not pertinent, for clearly they are involved in the hyperincarceration of lower-class African Americans. Indeed, they are not mutually exclusive and can be added to one another to expand explanation.

But this enumeration fails to capture the precise nature and the full magnitude of the transformations that have interlocked the naked hyperghetto and the voracious prison via a relation of *functional equivalency* – they serve one and the same purpose, the coercive confinement of a deprived and defamed population – and *structural homology* – they comprise and comfort the same type of diffident social relations and racialized authority patterns – to *form a single institutional mesh* suited to fulfilling anew the mission historically imparted to America's "peculiar institutions."

Only with a decisive historic twist: for the first time in the long history of African-American subjugation, the prison is both a *race-making and a class-splitting institution*. It primarily corrals, not blacks as a dishonored ethnic category, but *(sub)proletarian* blacks trapped in the remnants of the communal ghetto, letting a growing number of middle-class blacks seep through its net – even as they continued to sport rates of incarceration similar to those of lower-class whites by century's end. Indeed, the black bourgeoisie and the established black working class that managed to escape from the historic ghetto as it crumbled have long actively, if ambivalently, supported the aggressive rolling out of the police, jail, and penitentiary to contain the street dangers and disorders created by the heinous "underclass" that threatened their social tranquility, material well-being, and moral standing.[166]

---

[165] Tonry, *Malign Neglect* (1995); Katherine Beckett, *Making Crime Pay: Law and Order in Contemporary American Politics* (1999); Vanessa Barker, *The Politics of Imprisonment: How the Democratic Process Shapes the Way America Punishes Offenders* (2009); Bruce Western, *Punishment and Inequality in America* (2006); Clear, *Imprisoning Communities*; Naomi Murakawa, *The First Civil Right: How Liberals Built Prison America* (2014).

[166] Barker, *The Politics of Imprisonment*, pp. 146–52; Fortner, *Black Silent Majority*; Forman, *Locking Up Our Own*; Wacquant, *The Invention of the "Underclass."* Elijah

The thesis of the structural-functional coupling of the remnants of the ghetto with the carceral archipelago is supported by *the timing of racial transition*: with a lag of about a dozen years, the "blackening" of the carceral population followed closely on the heels of the ghetto riots that stamped the demise of the Black Belt as a viable instrument of caste containment in the urban-industrial setting, just as, a century earlier, the sudden penal repression of African Americans had helped to shore up "the walls of white supremacy as the South moved from an era of racial bondage to one of racial caste."[167] It is also verified by the *geographic patterning* of racial disproportionality and its evolution: outside of the South – which for historical reasons disclosed in chapter 3 requires a separate analysis – the black–white gap in incarceration was especially pronounced and increased fastest in those formerly industrial states of the Midwest and Northeast that are the historic cradle of the Northern ghetto.[168]

The intertwining of the remnants of the urban Black Belt and the fast-expanding carceral apparatus is further evidenced, and in turn powerfully abetted, by the *fusion of ghetto and prison culture*, as vividly expressed in the lyrics of "gangsta rap" singers and hip-hop artists, in graffiti and tattooing,[169] and in the dissemination, to the urban core and beyond, of language, dress, and interaction patterns innovated inside of jails and penitentiaries. The fusion of street and prison has even spawned a new social type playing a key role in masculine socialization among the black precariat of the hyperghetto, the "prisonized old head":[170] an older man with extensive experience of, and knowledge about, the carceral world who tutors younger men in the ways of the criminal justice apparatus, leading them to learn and embrace the cultural scripts, mores, and routines prevalent within penal institutions.

Anderson provides a rich account of this internecine class conflict between "decent" and "street" families within the hyperghetto in *Code of the Street*.

[167] David M. Oshinsky, *Worse Than Slavery: Parchman Farm and the Ordeal of Jim Crow Justice* (1996), p. 57.

[168] Marc Mauer, "Racial Disparities in Prison Getting Worse in the 1990s" (1997).

[169] See, respectively, Brian Cross, *It's Not About a Salary: Rap, Race, and Resistance in Los Angeles* (1993), and Susan A. Phillips, *Wallbangin': Graffiti and Gangs in L.A.* (1999), pp. 152–67.

[170] Forrest Stuart and Reuben Jonathan Miller, "The Prisonized Old Head: Intergenerational Socialization and the Fusion of Ghetto and Prison Culture" (2017). See also Lopez-Aguado on what he aptly labels "the spillover of carceral identity" in *Stick Together and Come Back Home*.

Deadly Symbiosis

The advent of spatially concentrated hyperincarceration for lower-class blacks has in effect rendered moot the classic dispute, among scholars of punishment, between the *deprivation thesis*, formulated by Gresham Sykes, for whom the social structure and cultural mores of inmates are an endogenous adaptation to the "pains of imprisonment," and the *importation thesis*, proposed in response by John Irwin and Donald Cressey, according to which prison roles and values are brought in from street culture.[171] This alternative has been transcended by the fusion of street and carceral social relations and culture, with the resulting mix being *re-exported* to the hyperghetto and diffused throughout society via the commercial circuits catering to the teenage consumer market, professional sports, and even the mainstream media. Witness the widespread adolescent fashion of baggy pants worn with the crotch down to mid-thigh and the resurgent popularity of body art featuring prison themes and icons – often unbeknownst to those who wear them – not to mention the peaking popularity of the prison as a theme of music and YouTube videos, movies, and television series such as *Oz* and *Orange Is the New Black*.[172]

I indicated earlier that slavery, Jim Crow terrorism, and the ghetto are *race-making institutions*, which is to say that they do not simply *process* an ethnoracial division that would exist outside of and independently from them, suspended in some kind of historical ether. Rather, each *produces* (or co-produces) this division (anew) out of inherited demarcations and disparities of group power and inscribes it at every epoch in a distinctive constellation of material and symbolic forms, ranging from legal codes to collective expectations to subjective dispositions.[173] And all have consistently racialized the arbitrary boundary setting African Americans apart from all others in the United States by actively denying its cultural origin in history, ascribing it instead to the fictitious necessity of biology, and by erasing differences within the black population so as to treat it as a homogeneous and unchanging compact.

The highly particular conception of "race" as blackness that America has invented, virtually unique in the world for its rigidity,

---

[171] Sykes, *The Inmate Society*, chapter 4; John Irwin and Donald R. Cressey, "Thieves, Convicts and the Inmate Culture" (1962).

[172] Dawn K. Cecil, *Prison Life in Popular Culture: From the Big House to Orange Is the New Black* (2015).

[173] To be more precise, each institution (re)inscribes race as a naturalizing principle of social vision and division in the structure of social space and in the depths of habitus, as indicated by figure 7 in chapter 2 (*supra*, p. 200).

salience, and consequentiality, is a direct outcome of the momentous collision between slavery and democracy as modes of organization of work and politics *after* bondage had been established as the principal form of labor conscription and control in a underpopulated colony home to a precapitalist system of production.[174] As shown in the previous chapter, the Jim Crow regime reworked the racialized boundary between slave and freeperson into a rigid caste separation between "whites" and "coloreds" – comprising all persons of known African ancestry, no matter how distant and minimal – that infected every crevice of the postbellum social system in the South. The ghetto, in turn, imprinted this dichotomy onto the spatial makeup and institutional architecture of the industrial metropolis in the age of Fordism. So much so that, in the wake of the "race riots" of the 1960s, which in truth were uprisings against intertwined caste and class subordination, "urban" and black became near-synonymous in policy-making as well as everyday parlance – and even in large sectors of social science. And the "crisis" of the city came to stand in for the enduring contradiction between the individualistic, mobile, and competitive tenor of American life, on the one hand, and the continued fixation and seclusion of African Americans within it, on the other.[175]

As a new century dawned, it befell the fourth "peculiar institution" born of the *interlocking* of the hyperghetto and the carceral archipelago to remold the social meaning and significance of "race" in accordance with the dictates of the deregulated economy and the neoliberal state. Now, the penal apparatus has long served as accessory to ethnoracial domination by helping to stabilize a regime under attack or bridge the hiatus between successive regimes. Thus the Black Codes of Reconstruction were key to keeping African-American labor in place following the demise of slavery, while the criminalization of civil rights protests in the South in the 1950s aimed to retard the agony of Jim Crow.[176] But the role of the carceral institution at the

---

[174] Barbara Jean Fields, "Race and Ideology in American History" (1982).

[175] Wacquant, *Invention of the "Underclass,"* pp. 22–6. Two empirical indicators of the continued seclusion of blacks in American social space are their persistently and inordinately high rates of residential segregation and marital endogamy.

[176] On the omnipresent role of the police in upholding the caste order, see Amy Louise Wood and Natalie J. Ring (eds.), *Crime and Punishment in the Jim Crow South* (2019), and Brandon T. Jett, *Race, Crime, and Policing in the Jim Crow South: African Americans and Law Enforcement in Birmingham, Memphis, and New Orleans, 1920–1945* (2021).

Deadly Symbiosis

peak of incarceration in 2008 was different in that, for the first time in US history, it had arguably been elevated to the rank of main machine for race-making as it actively reinforced the conflation of black people of all walks of life with the "criminal element" in their midst – intensifying the "homogenizing" effect of race discussed in chapter 1 (*supra*, pp. 91–2).

Among the manifold effects of the wedding of hyperghetto and prison into an extended carceral mesh, perhaps the most consequential is the practical revivification and official *solidification of the century-old association of blackness with criminality* and devious violence.[177] Along with the return of Lombroso-style mythologies about criminal atavism and the wide diffusion of bestial metaphors in the journalistic and political field (where mentions of "superpredators," "wolf-packs," "animals," and the like were commonplace at century's close), the extreme overincarceration of blacks supplied a powerful common-sense warrant for "using color as a proxy for dangerousness."[178] Indeed, the courts have consistently authorized the police to employ race as "a negative signal of increased risk of criminality" and legal scholars have rushed to endorse it as "a rational adaptation to the demographics of crime," made salient and verified, as it were, by the blackening of the prison population, even though such practice entails major inconsistencies from the standpoint of constitutional law.[179] Throughout the urban criminal justice chain, the formula "Young + Black + Male" is openly equated with "probable cause" justifying the arrest, questioning, bodily search, and detention of millions of African-American males every year.[180]

In the era of racially and spatially targeted "law-and-order" policies and their sociological pendant, racially and economically skewed hyperincarceration, the reigning public image of the criminal is not just that of "a *monstruum* – a being whose features are inherently different from ours,"[181] but that of a *black* monster, as young African-American men from the "inner city" came to personify the explosive

---

[177] The consolidation of this vision conflating black and criminal in the late nineteenth century is examined in the essential book by Khalil Gibran Muhammad, *The Condemnation of Blackness: Race, Crime, and the Making of Modern Urban America* (2010).

[178] Randall Kennedy, "Race, Law, and Suspicion: Using Color as a Proxy for Dangerousness" (1997), p. 136.

[179] Ibid., pp. 143, 146.

[180] Elizabeth A. Gaynes, "Young + Black + Male: Probable Cause" (1993).

[181] Dario Melossi, "Changing Representations of the Criminal" (2000), p. 311.

mix of moral degeneracy and mayhem.[182] The conflation of masculine blackness with street crime in collective representation and government policy (the other side of this equation being the conflation of feminine blackness with welfare) thus re-activated "race" by giving a legitimate outlet to the expression of anti-black animus in the form of the public vituperation of criminals and convicts. As writer John Edgar Wideman points out, "It's respectable to tar and feather criminals, to advocate locking them up and throwing away the key. It's not racist to be against crime, even though the archetypal criminal in the media and the public imagination almost always wears 'Willie' Horton's face. Gradually, 'urban' and 'ghetto' have become code words for terrible places where only blacks reside. Prison is rapidly being re-lexified in the same segregated fashion." Indeed, when "to be a man of color of a certain economic class and milieu is equivalent in the public eye to being a criminal," being processed by the penal system is tantamount to being made black, and "doing time" behind bars is at the same time "marking race."[183]

A second major effect of the penalization of the "race question" via the hypertrophic expansion of the prison system has been to thoroughly *depoliticize* it well into the 2010s. For reframing the problems posed by the persistence of ethnoracial division and friction in the wake of the ghetto's demise as issues of law enforcement automatically delegitimizes any attempt at collective resistance and redress. For years, established organizations of civic voice for African Americans and the black political elite would not confront head on the run-up of hyperincarceration in their community for fear that this would validate the very conflation of blackness and crime in public perception that was at the very root of the phenomenon. Worse, they came out in support of the aggressive policing and harsh judicial measures that fed disproportionate lower-class black imprisonment.

In his ground-breaking book, *Locking Up Our Own*, legal scholar James Forman shows how the African-American middle class turned on the hyperghetto precariat, whom they saw as "black-faced traitors"

---

[182] Thus the commercial success, based on prurient fascination, of the autobiographical account of the well-named Los Angeles gang member Monster Kody. Sanyika Shakur, *Monster: The Autobiography of an L.A. Gang Member* (1993).

[183] John Edgar Wideman, "Doing Time, Marking Race" (1995), pp. 504, 505. Gowan reports that white ex-convicts forced to settle in inner-city St. Louis to be close to parole agencies upon being released from Missouri prisons complained that the criminal justice system is "turning them into blacks." Teresa Gowan, "Excavating Globalization from Street Level: Homeless Men Recycle their Pasts" (2000).

and "the enemy within" for their criminal behavior.[184] In the name of preserving the gains of the Civil Rights Movement, chief among them public safety, they supported tough-on-crime measures as regards drugs, gun control, stop-and-search, and criminal sentencing. To be sure, black officials at the local level did not *just* champion expanded and diligent law enforcement; they also clamored for more jobs, better schooling, and expanded housing.[185] And white demand for the sweeping expansion of the penal state in response to the rise of economic insecurity, the burst of ethnic anxiety, and the looming specter of the "underclass" would have likely sufficed to produce the explosion of incarceration centered on the "inner city."

Yet it remains that the class abyss that had opened among the African-American population propelled penalization from within. Indeed, support for diligent and astringent law enforcement was reinforced by the fact, noted long ago by W. E. B. Du Bois, that the tenuous position of the black bourgeoisie in the socioracial hierarchy rests critically on its ability to distance itself from its unruly lower-class brethren: to offset the symbolic disability of blackness, middle-class African Americans must forcefully communicate to whites that they have "absolutely no sympathy and no known connections with any black man who has committed a crime."[186]

Even riots, the last weapon of protest left to an urban precariat spurned by a political field thoroughly dominated by the white suburban electorate and corporations, have been rendered purposeless by mass penal confinement. It is commonly believed that "race riots" in the United States crested in the 1960s and then vanished, save for anomalous outbursts such as in Miami in 1980 and Los Angeles in 1992. In reality, the ghetto uprisings of 1963–8 were succeeded by a rolling *wave of upheavals inside of prisons*, from Attica and Soledad to facilities throughout Michigan, Tennessee, Oklahoma, Illinois, West Virginia, and Pennsylvania, among others.[187] But, by moving from

---

[184] Forman, *Locking Up Our Own*, pp. 29, 32. For further analyses of the role of blacks in pushing for punitive state action, see Randall Kennedy, *Race, Crime, and the Law* (1997), and Fortner, *Black Silent Majority*, especially chapter 4, "Crime, Class, and Conflict in the Ghetto."

[185] Forman, *Locking Up Our Own*, p. 12.

[186] Du Bois, cited in Scott Christianson, *With Liberty for Some: Five Hundred Years of Imprisonment in America* (1998), p. 228.

[187] Morris, "The Contemporary Prison, 1965–Present," pp. 248–9; Bert Useem and Peter Kimball, *States of Siege: U.S. Prison Riots, 1971–1986* (1989). For a deep dive into the most iconic carceral riot in US history, read Heather Ann Thompson, *Blood in the Water: The Attica Prison Uprising of 1971 and Its Legacy* (2017); for a dissection of the

the open stage of the streets to the closed perimeter of penitentiary, these outbursts differed from their predecessors of the 1960s in three important ways. First, ghetto riots were highly visible and, through the media, interpellated the highest authorities in the land. Carceral riots, on the contrary, were never conspicuous to start with – unless they caused many deaths and major destruction, as with Attica in 1971 and the New Mexico state prison uprising and massacre of 1980. Moreover, they rapidly grew less and less perceptible to the point of virtually *disappearing* from the public scene.

Next, revolts inside prisons have received *administrative* responses from within the correctional bureaucracy in lieu of political responses from without, and these responses have only compounded the problem: the approach of the state to inmate belligerence in the 1950s was to "intensify the therapeutic thrust in prisons"; 30 years later, it was to intensify the drive to "classify, separate, and isolate," to toughen discipline, routinize the use of "lockdown," and to multiply "special housing units" and "supermax" facilities.[188] A third difference between the uproarious ghetto uprisings of decades past and the diffuse, muffled, carceral riots that replaced them is that the latter typically pit, not blacks against whites, but *one subordinate ethnic group against another*, such as African Americans versus Mexican Americans (or Sureños versus Norteños within the latter category), thereby further diminishing the likelihood that they will receive a broad sociopolitical interpretation connecting them to the transformed ethnoracial order on the outside.[189] By entombing poor blacks in the concrete walls of the prison, then, the penal state effectively smothered and silenced subproletarian revolt.

By assuming a central role in the neoliberal government of race and urban marginality, at the crossroads of the deregulated low-wage labor market, a revamped "welfare-workfare" apparatus designed to impress casual employment, and the vestiges of the ghetto, the

---

most deadly carceral riot, Mark Colvin, *The Penitentiary in Crisis: From Accommodation to Riot in New Mexico* (1992).

[188] See, respectively, Rotman, "The Failure of Reform: United States, 1865–1965," and Irwin, *Prisons in Turmoil*, p. 228.

[189] This is not to say, of course, that all prison upheavals are caused by racial conflict. The typical carceral riot involves a range and mix of grievances, from routine guard abuse, inadequate food and medical care to arbitrary and repressive management to idleness and lack of rehabilitative programs. But ethnoracial divisions and tensions are always a propitious backdrop, if not a major causal factor, of violent incidents, real or perceived, inside of houses of detention.

Deadly Symbiosis

overgrown carceral web of the United States has become a major engine of symbolic production in its own right.[190] It is not only the preeminent institution for signifying and enforcing blackness, much as slavery was during the first three centuries of US history. Just as bondage effected the "social death" of imported African captives and their descendants on American soil, *hyperincarceration also induces the civic death* of those it ensnares by "extruding" them from the social compact: they are "insiders who have fallen" and suffer "generalized dishonor."[191] Despite recent reforms rolling back restrictions instituted around century's turn, American inmates are the continuing target of a threefold movement of exclusionary closure[192]:

1. Prisoners are denied access to valued *cultural capital*: just as university credentials are becoming a prerequisite for employment in the (semi-)protected sector of the labor market, inmates have been expelled from higher education by being made ineligible for Pell Grants, starting with drug offenders in 1988, continuing with convicts sentenced to death or lifelong imprisonment without the possibility of parole in 1992, and ending with all remaining state and federal prisoners in 1994. This expulsion was voted by Congress for the sole purpose of accentuating the symbolic divide between criminals and "law-abiding citizens" in spite of overwhelming evidence that prison educational programs drastically cut recidivism as well as helped maintain carceral order.[193]
2. Prisoners are systematically excluded from *social redistribution* and public aid in an age when work insecurity makes access to such programs more vital than ever for those dwelling in the lower regions of social space. Laws deny welfare payments, veterans' benefits, and food stamps to anyone in detention for more

---

[190] The argument that follows is influenced by Garland's neo-Durkheimian explication of "penality as a set of signifying practices" that "help produce subjectivities, forms of authority and social relations" at large. David Garland, "Punishment and Culture: The Symbolic Dimension of Criminal Justice" (1991). See also the subtle demonstration of Philip Smith, *Punishment and Culture* (2008), especially chapter 7.

[191] On the logic of intrusive and extrusive social death, see Patterson, *Slavery and Social Death*, pp. 38–45; on "generalized dishonor" as one of three constituents of slavery along with total coercion and natal alienation, pp. 2–8 and 13.

[192] A fuller listing and discussion of the myriad disabilities attached to a prison conviction is David S. Kirk and Sara Wakefield, "Collateral Consequences of Punishment: A Critical Review and Path Forward" (2018).

[193] Joshua Page, "Eliminating the Enemy: The Import of Denying Prisoners Access to Higher Education in Clinton's America" (2004).

than 60 days. The Work Opportunity and Personal Responsibility Act of 1996 known as "welfare reform" further banishes most ex-convicts from Medicaid, public housing, Section 8 vouchers, and related forms of assistance. In spring of 1998, President Clinton denounced as intolerable "fraud and abuse" perpetrated against "working families" who "play by the rules" the fact that some prisoners (or their households) continued to get public payments due to lax bureaucratic enforcement of these prohibitions. And he proudly launched "unprecedented federal, state, and local cooperation as well as new, innovative incentive programs" using the latest "high-tech tools to weed out any inmate" who still received benefits, including the disbursement of bounties to counties who promptly turned in identifying information on their jail detainees to the Social Security administration.

3. Convicts are banned from *political participation* via "criminal disenfranchisement" practiced on a scale and with a vigor unimagined in any other country. As of 2000, all but four members of the Union denied the vote to mentally competent adults residing in detention facilities; 39 states forbade convicts placed on probation from exercising their political rights and 32 states also interdicted parolees. In 14 states, ex-felons were barred from voting even when they were no longer under criminal justice supervision – *for life* in ten of these states. The result is that nearly 4 million Americans had temporarily or permanently lost the ability to cast a ballot, including 1.47 million who were not behind bars and another 1.39 million who had served their sentence in full.[194] A mere quarter of a century after acceding to full voting rights, one black man in seven nationwide was banned from the electoral booth through penal disenfranchisement and seven states permanently denied the vote to more than one-fourth of their black male residents.

Through this *triple exclusion*, the prison, and the criminal legal apparatus more broadly, contribute to the ongoing *reconstruction of the "imagined community" of Americans* around the polar opposition

---

[194] Jamie Fellner and Marc Mauer, *Losing the Vote: The Impact of Felony Disenfranchisement in the United States* (1998); Jeff Manza and Christopher Uggen, *Locked Out: Felon Disenfranchisement and American Democracy* (2008); Amy E. Lerman and Vesla M. Weaver, *Arresting Citizenship: The Democratic Consequences of American Crime Control* (2014). For an update that examines the voting impact of the full range of contacts with the penal state, see Ariel R. White, "Political Participation amid Mass Incarceration" (2022).

between praiseworthy "working families" – implicitly white, suburban, and deserving – and the despicable "underclass" of criminals, loafers, and leeches, a two-headed antisocial hydra personified by the dissolute teenage "welfare mother" on the female side and the dangerous street "gangbanger" on the male side – by definition darkskinned, urban, and undeserving.[195] The former are exalted as the living incarnation of genuine American values: self-control, deferred gratification, subservience of life to labor, and reverence for the law. The latter is vituperated as the loathsome embodiment of their abject desecration, the "dark side" of the "American dream" of affluence and opportunity for all believed to flow from morality anchored in work and family. And the line that divides them is increasingly being drawn, materially and symbolically, by the jail and the prison and their tentacles, probation, parole, court-mandated programming, and surveillance fostered by the digital diffusion of criminal records.[196]

On the other side of that line lies an institutional setting unlike any other. Building on his celebrated analyses of the economy of ancient Greece, classical historian Moses Finley has introduced a fruitful distinction between "societies with slaves" and "genuine slave societies."[197] In the former, slavery is but one of several modes of labor control and the division between slave and free is neither impermeable nor axial to the entire social order. In the latter, enslaved labor is epicentral to both economic production and class structure, and the slave–master relation provides the pattern after which other social relations are built or distorted, such that no corner of culture, society, and self is left untouched by it. The astronomical overrepresentation of poor blacks in houses of penal confinement and the increasingly tight meshing of the denuded hyperghetto with the carceral archipelago suggests that, owing to America's adoption of hyperincarceration as a queer social policy designed to discipline the dispossessed and contain the dishonored, (sub)proletarian African Americans now dwell, not in a society with prisons as their white compatriots do, but in *the first genuine prison society* in history.

---

[195] Wacquant, *The Invention of the "Underclass,"* pp. 132–40.
[196] Michelle S. Phelps, "The Paradox of Probation: Community Supervision in the Age of Mass Incarceration" (2013); James Kilgore, "Progress or More of the Same? Electronic Monitoring and Parole in the Age of Mass Incarceration" (2013); Sarah Esther Lageson, "Criminal Record Stigma and Surveillance in the Digital Age" (2022).
[197] Moses Finley, "Slavery" (1968).

History, penality, and place

What are the lessons of the rise of the fourth peculiar institution geared to subordinating African Americans for the agonistic theory of racial domination? I will single out three, concerning the need for historical casting, the centrality of the penal state, and the role of space and place in race-making. The first is that it is indispensable to *historicize and disaggregate the mechanisms* of domination over the long run to weigh their legacies inscribed in bodies (say, fear of the police percolating across generations) and in things (say, segregated urban poverty). In addition to grasping institutions as sedimentations of action through time, it is also crucial to avoid the *fallacy of continuity*, which assumes a seamless sequence of apparatuses whereby each one smoothly gives way to the next to fulfill an unchanging function. For the racialization of slavery and the transition across phases of racial domination involved rupture, opportunity, and invention.

When slavery was established in the early colonies, it was a means of recruiting and managing labor akin to serfdom and a novel institution in need of codification, for it did not exist in England. A series of nested decisions had to be made, among them whether bondage applied for a set number of years or *durante vita*; whether the status would be inheritable and through what filiation; and what rights and obligations the slaves and the masters would have. There never emerged a single body of "slave law" applying uniformly across jurisdictions.[198] More decisively still, the merging of bondage and ethnoracial division was not inexorable for the latter did not precede or cause the former: "In the 17th century New World colonies, as the English were institutionalizing a form of slavery for which they had no precedents, they were also constructing the ideological components of race. This historical linkage gave rise to a new form of servitude known as *racial slavery*."[199] Had the British not established naval superiority in the 1670s and the material condition of the English working class not improved then, the transatlantic slave trade would not have boomed and indentured servants would have remained the more profitable and thus the main source of labor in the colonies, changing the historical path of state, social space, and subjectivity.

Jim Crow terrorism was not the ineluctable outcome of abolition but the contingent result of patterned struggles aiming to redraw

---

[198] Rosemary Brana Shute, "United States Law" (1998), pp. 255–7.
[199] Audrey Smedley, "Race and Racism" (1998), p. 322.

Deadly Symbiosis

social and symbolic space in the post-Civil War South. In the aftermath of abolition, the former slaves seized on and actualized new historical possibilities in both family, religion, work, unionism, and politics. The outcome of the "three-cornered battle" between planters, ex-slaves, and poor whites was not preordained.[200] Moreover, Reconstruction under federal authorities could have been extended and entrenched, creating a different racial playing field. The 15 years it lasted were indeed, in the words of historian Eric Foner, an "unfinished revolution."[201]

Likewise, the rise of the ghetto in the 1920s was not a mechanical correlate of regional migration and urbanization but the outcome of violent struggles waged in and over physical space as the medium and anchor of group-making.[202] Its implosion was ineluctable by the 1960s given the macrostructural shift from industry to services that made it redundant and surging black mobilization against caste rule in the city.[203] But the subsequent turn to the penalization of urban marginality translating into racialized hyperincarceration was not a foregone conclusion. Indeed, the United States was a global pioneer in correctional rehabilitation into the mid-1970s. Politicized prisoners like Eldridge Cleaver and George Jackson were then literary celebrities; the prisoners' rights movement was pushing federal courts to intervene and regulate medieval carceral conditions; prison reform was undertaken and widely debated from New Jersey to Illinois to California; and the confined population was decreasing slowly in spite of the rise in crime.[204] In 1973, when the prison population hit its low point in a half-century, no one, politician, state official, or scholar, imagined that the country was about to enter into a half-century of carceral hyperinflation.

---

[200] W. E. B. Du Bois, *Black Reconstruction, 1860–1880* (2017 [1935]), p. 673. A vivid account of black community life and institutions in the postbellum South is Daniel B. Thorp, *Facing Freedom: An African American Community in Virginia from Reconstruction to Jim Crow* (2017).
[201] Eric Foner, *Reconstruction: America's Unfinished Revolution, 1863–1877* (1988).
[202] Cameron McWhirter, *Red Summer: The Summer of 1919 and the Awakening of Black America* (2011); Wacquant, *The Two Faces of the Ghetto*, chapter 1.
[203] William Julius Wilson, *The Truly Disadvantaged: The Inner City, the Underclass and Public Policy* (1987); Peter B. Levy, *The Great Uprising: Race Riots in Urban America during the 1960s* (2018).
[204] James B. Jacobs, "The Prisoners' Rights Movement and Its Impacts, 1960–80" (1980); Ronald Berkman, *Opening the Gates: The Rise of the Prisoners' Movement* (1979); Eric Cummins, *The Rise and Fall of California's Radical Prison Movement* (1994).

Racial Domination

The second lesson is that the *penal wing of the state plays a crucial role in race-making* and this is true not only in postindustrial America but in every advanced society. Students of "race and ethnicity" are gravely derelict in their duties when they leave that institution out of their purview.[205] Maghrebis, Manouches and West Africans in France, Caribbeans and Pakistanis in England, Romas and Turks in Germany, Romanians and Albanians in Italy, Surinamese and Moroccans in the Netherlands, Palestinians in Israel, Aboriginals in Australia and Maoris in New Zealand: everywhere marginalized populations branded by ethnoracial stigma are massively overpoliced and overincarcerated at rates that generally *surpass* the overincarceration of blacks in the United States. In 1997, the ratio between the proportion of foreigners behind bars and their weight in the country's population was 11.2 in Spain, 10.5 in Italy, 7.4 in the Netherlands, 4.6 in France and 4.3 in Sweden, as against 3.9 for black Americans (a ratio that has fallen to 2.9 in 2020).[206] Everywhere these populations are perceived as particularly prone to criminal activity, hence their tenuous civic status, and their disproportionate imprisonment serves as *prima facie* evidence that they indeed are, setting up a racial self-fulfilling prophecy whereby the dominant public image of the category is fashioned out from the cardboard cutout of its law-breaking members. *Group-making thus occurs under color of criminality and in the long shadow of the prison.* Race and penality fuse to draw a bright boundary around a dark population.

The police, the criminal court, and the prison matter to racial domination because the state is the fount of public honor and thus dishonor. In Bourdieu's explication, it carries out "positive acts of 'institution' which consists, for instance, in designating someone as

---

[205] *Ethnic & Racial Studies* has published all of seven articles with the word "prison," "jail," or "incarceration" in their title in 46 years. *Sociology of Race and Ethnicity* has likewise featured five short articles on policing and zero on the jail, courts, penitentiary and their extensions since its launch in 2015, and none discusses how policing remakes race. An extensive panorama of work in the mold of "racial formation theory" covering a bibliography of 174 titles includes all of six references on punishment, none of which are discussed in the text (Aliya Saperstein et al., "Racial Formation in Perspective: Connecting Individuals, Institutions, and Power Relations" [2013]). Put differently, there are lots of studies of race done by scholars of punishment but virtually no studies of punishment done by scholars of race.

[206] Loïc Wacquant, "Penalization, Depoliticization, and Racialization: On the Overincarceration of Immigrants in the European Union" (2006), p. 86. Moreover, these ratios are raw underestimates: they do not take into account the second generation of immigrants and "people of color" who are nationals.

having the dignity to occupy a position," but also "negative acts of institution (we should rather say destitution or degradation) which consists in stripping someone of the dignity that had been granted them."[207] The infliction of a criminal justice sanction is one such "negative act" which signifies demerit and strikes the condemned with temporary or permanent exclusion from the civic community. Like race, judicial sanction is a form of *negative symbolic capital guaranteed by the state*. It thus creates an organic association between punishment, danger, pollution, and race, a taint that even the most accomplished member of the ethnically subaltern cannot quite rub off.

This brings us to third lesson of the rise of the fourth peculiar institution for the sociology of race-making and group-making more generally, which concerns the *role of place*. Here again, scholars of "race and ethnicity" have been timid at best in their engagement with this question, limiting their consideration of the spatial genesis and functioning of racial division to the routine study of residential segregation, political geography, and neighborhood effects, focusing on how race shapes space but overlooking how socially appropriated and symbolically marked space shapes race.[208] This lack of interest is all the more surprising considering that the foundational student of the intersection of place-making and race-making is none other than Du Bois, whose *Philadelphia Negro*, published two decades before the Chicago School launched its manifesto for urban sociology, documents how securing the territory of the Seventh ward impacted the institutions and collective psychology of the coalescing black community, and thence black–white relations in the city.[209]

In the collective imaginary of the dual metropolis in the neoliberal era, white and black, the desolate hyperghetto emerges as the physical materialization and fearsome haunt of the heinous "underclass" – a district of danger, dread, and dissolution, an affront to the cherished

---

[207] Pierre Bourdieu, *Sociologie générale*, vol. 1. *Cours au Collège de France, 1981–1983* (2015), p. 34.

[208] A rare intervention in this direction is Jennifer LaFleur, "The Race that Space Makes: The Power of Place in the Colonial Formation of Social Categorizations" (2021), who writes: "The dominant view among social scientists is that space takes the position of a dependent variable whose constitution is predicted on a series of independent variables, including race. An intellectual commitment to questioning the ontological status of race requires, however, a purposeful flip in the typical causal assumptions about the relationship between race and space" (p. 512).

[209] W. E. B. Du Bois, *The Philadelphia Negro: A Social Study* (2010 [1899]). For an extended interpretation of that dynamic, read Marcus Anthony Hunter, *Black Citymakers: How* The Philadelphia Negro *Changed Urban America* (2013).

values said to hold the nation together and to nourish its promise: work, family, and individual responsibility.[210] All African Americans, regardless of social status, walk in its sulfurous shadow and are suspected of suffering from its ills, for a *negative place makes for a negative race*. Territorial stigma inflects and intensifies ethnoracial stigma to create a toxic symbolic brew.

But there is more: the *state secretes and polices race through space* – I use the verb "to police" here in the twofold sense of regulation and law enforcement. On both sides of the Atlantic, the material and symbolic violence of the police, courts, jail, and prison is aimed as a matter of course at the dispossessed and dishonored populations located in the nether region of social and physical space. The hyperghetto in the US and the defamed districts of dispossession in Western Europe, the *banlieues* of France, *sink estates* of Great Britain, *Problemquartier* of Germany, and *quartieri degradati* of Italy, are the staging grounds where the trialectic of symbolic, social, and physical space gets rearticulated to remake and reinscribe race in bodies, in the form of cognitive categories and moral emotions, and material realities, as places to avoid and people to loathe.

---

[210] Wacquant, *The Invention of the "Underclass*,*"* pp. 133–9, in particular the academic coining of the "underclass area," pp. 54–5.

Coda

From Racial Domination to Racial Justice

"There is in the minds of most educated people, especially in the social sciences, a dichotomy that seems to me to be quite disastrous: the dichotomy between *scholarship* and *commitment* – between those who dedicate themselves to scientific work, which is done according to scholarly methods for the benefit of other scholars, and those who commit themselves and take their knowledge outside. The opposition is artificial and, in fact, one must be an autonomous scholar who works according to the rules of scholarship to be able to produce a committed knowledge, that is, a *scholarship with commitment*."
Pierre Bourdieu, "Pour un savoir engagé" (2001)

"Race" is not an "essentially contested concept," as famously defined by the Scottish philosopher Walter Bryce Gallie more than a half-century ago,[1] so much as a *confused and confusing category* – in the original etymological sense of instrument of public accusation (*kategorein*). Displacing it from its reflexively doxic position in contemporary social analysis cannot but help the historical sciences in their quest to illuminate the vexed nature, recurrent forms, and varied mechanisms of *ethnoracial domination* as the exploitation, subordination, and exclusion of naturalized human groupings, and thence to forge robust tools for fighting its concrete manifestations. This is a delicate and paradoxical operation: surgically removing the category from our theoretical toolkit while keeping the phenomenon in focus

[1] Walter Bryce Gallie, "Essentially Contested Concepts" (1955). For an argumentation to the contrary, read the pointed paper by Magali Bessone, "Race as Essentially Contested Concept" (2023).

as one variant, and a particularly abrasive one, of an agonistic sociology of group-making grounded in the dialectic of classification and stratification.

This is the agenda pursued by the present book, which has sketched a neo-Bourdieusian theory of ethnoracial domination as a layered and architectured phenomenon composed of *varied combinations of elementary forms*: categorization (comprising classification, prejudice, bias, and stigma), discrimination (differential treatment and disparate impact), segregation (in social and physical space), seclusion (covering the ghetto, camp, and reservation), and violence (in its consumptive and instrumental varieties). Each of these forms is in turn subtended by multiple mechanisms, themselves racial and non-racial, and linked together they form different regimes of racial domination. The intellectual and political line I have followed to get there may be summed up thus: we must *disaggregate* racial domination on paper in order to increase our capacity to *dismantle* it in reality, piece by piece. For that, we need to rebalance the relationship between the analytics and the politics of race and grant the former more autonomy from the latter than it has received to date. This is not a tactical retreat into the ivory tower of academe but a graduated engagement, composed of *two moments, the scientific and the politic*. In Pierre Bourdieu's expression of *scholarship with commitment*, scholarship writes its tune and follows its own drummer before joining the civic band to march the streets.

Being a committed scholar of ethnoracial domination, an explosive topic if there ever was one, entails affirming the imperative of epistemological rupture and vigilance à la Bachelard. Thus, when developing a concept, we must aim for semantic clarity and axiological neutrality, logical consistency and type specificity, and heuristic productivity both empirical and theoretical, and this applies to the analytic of race as to any category.[2] Correspondingly, we must strive to avoid conceptual under-specification, conflation, and overreach of the kind that besets the notions of structural racism and racial capitalism. For this, it is vital that we separate out – however difficult that might turn out to be – our political and moral from our analytic impulses when we execute our distinctive mission of sociological production.

---

[2] For a fuller argument on how to craft solid concepts, see Loïc Wacquant, *The Invention of the "Underclass": A Study in the Politics of Knowledge* (2022), pp. 172–8, and idem, *The Two Faces of the Ghetto* (2025), prologue.

Coda

Varieties of racial domination

Disaggregating opens the way for recognizing structural variability and functional versatility. Here we can learn from the lively debates on the "varieties of capitalism" triggered by the germinal work of John Hall and David Soskice, based on the thesis that the capitalist economy is not coordinated and governed everywhere in the same way,[3] and recognize the *varieties of modes of racial domination* in different societies and epochs, anchored by different combinations of naturalizing classification and stratification. The fruitfulness of this approach is demonstrated by Orlando Patterson in his little-known yet fundamental essay on "Four Modes of Ethno-Somatic Stratification," showing how the same root population, the descendants of Africans, were differentially incorporated in the United States (binary mobilization), Latin America (hegemonic whitening), the Caribbean (pluralistic under-development) and northern Europe (proletarian incorporation), "each mode refer[ring] to a unique configuration of ethno-racial ideology, ethno-demographic mix, ethno-class stratification, and level of societal racialization."[4] But how do we prevent or tame the potential proliferation of types that has beset the literature on varieties of capitalism?

Inspired by the distinction that Moses Finley establishes between "genuine slave societies," in which slavery is epicentral to the economy, social structure, and polity, and "societies with slaves," in which human bondage exists but is marginal to the institutional order,[5] I submit that we gain from making a germane distinction between "genuine race-divided societies" and "societies with race." This allows us to differentiate regimes of racial domination along key dimensions rather than lumping them together under an overcapacious and vague notion of "racialized social system" defined as "societies in

---

[3] The classic statement is the opening chapter of Peter Hall and David Soskice (eds.), *Varieties of Capitalism: The Institutional Foundations of Comparative Advantage* (2001); for an extension of the framework beyond core Western nations, see Magnus Feldmann, "Global Varieties of Capitalism" (2019); a cogent critique of the framework is Dorothee Bohle and Béla Greskovits, "Varieties of Capitalism and Capitalism '*Tout Court*'" (2009).

[4] Orlando Patterson, "Four Modes of Ethno-Somatic Stratification: The Experience of Blacks in Europe and the Americas" (2005), p. 67.

[5] Moses Finley, "Slavery" (1968). For historical instantiations of these two types within the same polity, look no further than the South and North of the United States around the time of the American Revolution, as portrayed by Peter Kolchin, *American Slavery, 1619–1877* (2003), chapter 3.

which economic, political, social, and ideological levels are partially structured by the placement of actors in racial categories."[6]

In genuine *race-divided societies*, ethnoracial partitioning is paramount to the symbolic order; it underpins the economy, cleaves social space, fashions state structure and functioning, stamps physical space in its image, and seeps deep into subjectivity to craft a racial habitus – that is, a set of racialized and racializing dispositions.[7] Boundaries between categories are bright, rigid, and impermeable. The bureaucratic field recognizes and enforces those boundaries and deploys the gamut of public policies accordingly so as to impart race with force and materiality. Racial division suffuses everyday, commercial, and civic culture, and shapes intimate relations. The architecture of institutions routinely deepens and perpetuates the disparities between the different categories, thus increasing and entrenching groupness. In such societies, race is not just a mental category but produces full-fledged, *instituted ethnoracial groups* (in the language adopted in figure 7, *supra*, p. 200), capable of acting as such on the historical stage. A social formation that comes close to this ideal type in history is South Africa under apartheid where no corner of the society escaped race effects and where the imposition of racial order was overt, blunt, and systematic.[8]

By contrast, in *societies with race*, ethnoracial division is present but muted and ancillary to the symbolic order; economic functioning does not depend on it; nation-making is not driven by the foundational or continued exclusion of racialized populations. These populations are present and may be marginalized, discriminated against, and disparaged, even subjected to violence, but the fundamental cleavage of social space is not racial; it rests on class, citizenship, region, religion, or some other principle of vision and division. The ethnic poles of aura and stigma are attenuated if not extinguished. Naturalizing categorization may operate in everyday life but it is superficial and inconsistent; it may flare up in the political field, yet the latter does not turn on cultivating and exploiting ethnic fissures. The boundaries between categories are fuzzy and situational, and they allow for

---

[6] Eduardo Bonilla-Silva, "Rethinking Racism: Toward a Structural Interpretation" (1997), p. 469.

[7] These include, but are not limited to, what historian George Frederickson calls "overtly racist regimes" (*A Short History of Racism* [2002], pp. 1–2). For reasons that should by now be clear to the reader, I prefer to avoid this accusatory formulation.

[8] Gay Seidman, "Is South Africa Different? Sociological Comparisons and Theoretical Contributions from the Land of Apartheid" (1999).

mobility, mixing, and passing. Race may grow to be salient without for that being consequential, or it is consequential in one sector of social life (say, the labor market) but not in another (say, marital options). In short, ethnoracial membership is not what Everett C. Hughes calls a "master status trait" determining individual and collective life chances and identity by swamping other social attributes.[9] As a result, collectivity formation based on race remains suspended between a "group on paper" and a "practical group." Efforts to mobilize along ethnoracial lines are weak and diffuse, attempts to gain official recognition absent or unsuccessful. Contemporary Norway hews close to this type, notwithstanding the long-standing marginalization of the Sámi and the recent growth and differential treatment of a distinct population of non-Western immigrants and refugees.[10]

Instead of treating capitalism and race as two cohesive and unchanging entities that are necessarily intermeshed, then, we are better served by considering them as points along *two continua that are analytically decoupled.* The varieties of capitalism can be reconceptualized along the axis of *commodification* (of land, labor, money, and core public goods). The varieties of regimes of ethnoracial domination can be reconceptualized along the axis of *racialization* (the extent to which classification and stratification are naturalized). Particular historical social formations can then be plotted in the bidimensional space formed by varieties of capitalism and varieties of racial rule as indicated in figure 12. In the contemporary era, the United States and South Africa are two societies characterized by a high degrees of both commodification and racialization; Norway stands in the opposite corner, with high regulation of the economy and high ethnic cohesion. Canada falls into the high racialization–low commodification quadrant while Argentina belongs to the high commodification–low racialization box. A given country can also travel along each of these dimensions, for instance, by implementing policies of economic deregulation (neoliberalism) or fostering ethnic recognition, affirmative action, and reparations (multiculturalism).

Exponents of racial capitalism keep us locked in the top right quadrant, assuming that all capitalistic societies are fully racialized and all fully racialized societies are capitalistic, missing out on all the variants

---

[9] Everett C. Hughes, "Dilemmas and Contradictions of Status" (1984 [1945]).
[10] Arnfinn H. Midtbøen, "The Making and Unmaking of Ethnic Boundaries in the Public Sphere: The Case of Norway" (2018). See also Tobias Hübinette et al. (eds.), *Race in Sweden: Racism and Antiracism in the World's First "Colourblind" Nation* (2023).

that are historically and politically relevant. A social science committed to the civic good must be able to acknowledge and capture these variations so as to identify the best practicable levers of action to reduce the societal distortions and social harm that capitalism and racial domination cause when they join in the particular manner that they do.

```
              – COMMODIFICATION +

              Canada          │          USA
                              │
          +                   │
  RACIALIZATION               │
          – – – – – – – – – – ┼ – – – – – – – – – –
                              │
          –                   │
                              │
              Norway          │        Argentina
```

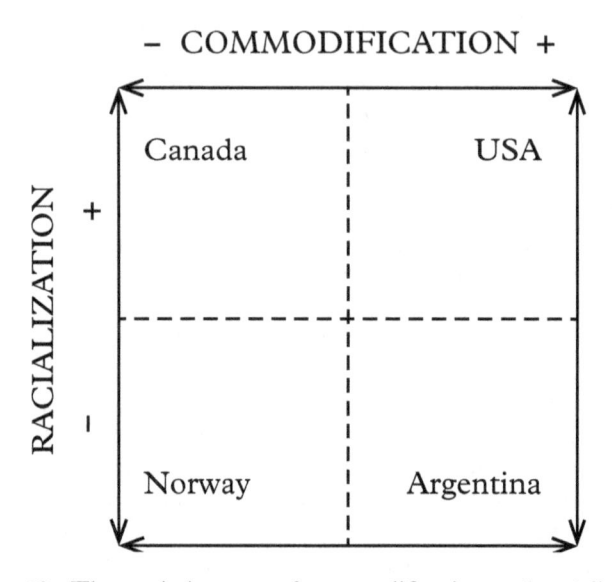

Figure 12 The analytic space of commodification and racialization.

At this juncture, it is inevitable that some readers will regress into the logic of the trial and protest indignantly that this conceptual distinction "minimizes" what they would characterize wholesale as "racism" in the latter type of society. But, as I argued in chapter 1 (*supra*, pp. 72–8), it is vital to clearly distinguish analytic from moral and political judgment if we are to advance a robust theory of racial domination that recognizes its varieties. To not condemn is not to condone; it is to insist that the task of social science is neither to inculpate nor to disculpate whole societies but to parse their order and scrutinize their trajectory. To reiterate: race-divided society and society with race are *two ideal types in the Weberian sense*, ideal in the sense of *ideational* (not perfect, best, supreme), situated at the opposite ends of a continuum in which we can provisionally slot different societies or, as the case may be, the same society at different times. An ideal type is not an end but a means; not a description of reality but a tool with which to describe reality; not synthetic but analytic. It is neither true nor false, only theoretically and empirically heuristic or not. In this case, we can add: politically heuristic or not.

The key features that help us locate a social formation along the continuum running from genuine race-divided society and society with race include (1) the demographic weight of the racialized population; (2) its salience in public space and the visibility of ethnic markers; (3) its concentration in social and physical space (including endogamy, school segregation and residential segregation); (4) its role and integration in the national economy; (5) the civic ideology and political culture; (6) the structure and policies of the state, including the official recognition and enumeration of racialized populations. All of these features are determined by the history of group formation and division, with slavery, colonization, and migration playing major roles, but roles they may change in the course of time.

Absent a Finley-type distinction between genuine race-divided societies and societies with race for comparative analysis across the globe and the centuries, we risk throwing pell-mell into the same basket of "racism" social formations whose structural makeup and historical trajectory are vastly different – feudal Japan, colonial Angola, and present-day Hungary – simply because some variant of "race and racism" is operative in all of them. This distinction can help us formulate a series of novel comparative historical questions: what determines the rise of the one type as against the ascent of the other? Are there generic precursors to each of the two types? What mechanisms reproduce and secure each in its distinctive configuration? Can race-divided societies evolve into societies with race and through what route, or are they doomed to forever replicate their ignoble past, as Afropessimism would have it?[11] Can societies with race devolve into race-divided societies as naturalized ethnicity remakes their social organization, culture, and politics? How does the state routinely operate to either bolster or weaken the office of race in a given society? What are the conditions of formation of a racial habitus in each of them and how do they differ? How do you deracialize symbolic space, social space, and physical space, the three constituents of any social formation and anchors of group-making?[12] Obviously, it is

---

[11] A counter to this vision is Tianna S. Paschel, *Becoming Black Political Subjects: Movements and Ethno-Racial Rights in Colombia and Brazil* (2016), which shows how domestically feeble black activists can, with the strategic support of transnational organizations, obtain tangible measures by the state to acknowledge and reduce ethnoracial inequality.

[12] Loïc Wacquant, *Bourdieu in the City: Challenging Urban Theory* (2023a), pp. 6–11.

no happenstance if many of the race-divided societies of the Western world are the lineal descendants of its empires. The colonial domain is the crucible of racial virulence across institutions – this is why its study is essential to the agonistic sociology of race-making. But not all settler colonies spawned full-blown race-divided societies in their metropole, to wit Portugal, France, and the Netherlands. What accounts for this structural decentering of race as a social principle of vision and division and what forces pull it to the center?

Two contrastive ideal types for one analytical agenda. *The current politics of race demands that we reject that distinction. The analytics of race commands us to affirm it.* This is where advocacy and scholarship must find a compromise without invalidating their distinctive mission, or part ways as the case may be when the pressure of activism and political struggle require blanket concepts and accusatory rhetoric.[13] It is my hope that this book has demonstrated to its readers that a compromise is possible and that scholarship makes its greatest contribution to the struggle for racial justice when it follows its own rules and criteria, no holds barred. I will ask them to ponder these words from W. E. B. Du Bois: "In the discussion of great social problems it is extremely difficult for those who are themselves actors in the drama to avoid the attitude of partisans and advocates. And yet I take it that the examination of the most serious of the race problems of America is not in the nature of a debate but rather a joint endeavor to seek the truth beneath a mass of assertion and opinion, of passion and distress. And I trust that whatever disagreements may arise between those who view the situation from opposite sides of the color line will be rather in the nature of additional information than of contradiction."[14]

Three paths to racial justice

Justice is a protean and polyvalent concept amenable to multiple readings going back 25 centuries to Plato's *Republic* and Aristotle's

---

[13] Social scientists do not help the social movements they wish to serve when they engage in an *academic race to radicalism* in which one must imperatively argue to the Left of the next person in order to burnish one's political credentials. While they play out well on campus, especially with the younger generations, such moves can cloud analytical judgment and thence reduce the real-life purchase of the knowledge produced.

[14] W. E. B. Du Bois, "The Relation of the Negroes to the Whites in the South" (1978 [1901]), p. 253.

Coda

Nicomachean Ethics. Indeed, there are nearly as many conceptions of it as there are strands in political philosophy.[15] To avoid falling into these inextricable scholastic debates, I cursorily define social justice as an *institutional arrangement that ensures the fair allocation of fundamental rights and resources* such that members of different groupings can live with dignity and actualize their full potential. Racial justice is a derivation of social justice which is itself a derivation of justice: it is justice achieved by a racialized group, practical or instituted.[16]

In normatively democratic society, *racial domination is a practical, ongoing negation of social justice*. Its three facets – exploitation, subordination, and exclusion based on categorical membership – are so many affronts to individual and group fairness and obstacles to self-realization. The five elementary forms of ethnoracial domination undermine justice in the realm of cognition, personal interaction and organizational processing, distribution in social and physical space, institutional access, and physical integrity, respectively. Thus the widespread diffusion of demeaning and aversive representations of members of a racialized category – the Sinti in twentieth-century Austria, Zimbabwean immigrants in post-apartheid South Africa, or the First Nations, Inuit and Métis in contemporary Canada[17] – violates the right to personal self-worth and collective dignity. Discriminatory

---

[15] Kymlicka lists no fewer than eight lineages: utilitarianism, liberal egalitarianism, libertarianism, Marxism, communitarianism, citizenship theory, multiculturalism, and feminism. Will Kymlicka, *Contemporary Political Philosophy: An Introduction* (2002). For a panorama of classical and contemporary views, see Michael Sandel (ed.), *Justice: A Reader* (2007). I thank Magali Bessone and Philippe van Parijs for guiding me through the thicket of theories of justice.
[16] I draw in equal parts on John Rawls's notion of justice as fairness (*A Theory of Justice* [1999 (1971)]); Armatya Sen's capability theory (*The Idea of Justice* [2010]), and Iris Marion Young's critique of distributive justice and schema of the "five faces of oppression" (*Justice and the Politics of Difference* [1990], chapter 2). Three provocative revisions of Rawls's theory to cover ethnoracial justice specifically are Tommie Shelby, *Dark Ghettos: Injustice, Dissent, and Reform* (2016), chapter 1; Charles W. Mills, "Racial Justice" (2018), and Magali Bessone, "À quelles conditions une théorie de la justice raciale est-elle pensable? Adopter, abandonner ou adapter le cadre rawlsien" (2022). See also the exchange between Mills and Shelby in the inaugural issue of *Critical Philosophy of Race* (2013), and the older but still stimulative arguments of Bernard R. Boxill, *Blacks and Social Justice* (1992). For contrast, see the notion of racial justice under the heading of "racial democracy" drawing on John Dewey proposed by Mustafa Emirbayer and Matthew Desmond in *The Racial Order* (2015), pp. 301–13.
[17] Sybil Milton, "Sinti and Roma in Twentieth-Century Austria and Germany" (2000); Godwin Dube, "Levels of Othering: The Case of Zimbabwean Migrants in South Africa" (2017); Cherie D. Werhun and April J. Penner, "The Effects of Stereotyping and Implicit Theory: On Benevolent Prejudice toward Aboriginal Canadians" (2010).

treatment by the police, which is well documented against persons of North and Sub-Saharan African origins in France, where it is designated by the folk expression "*contrôle au faciès*" (literally "face-based check"), while officially denied, is a particularly severe violation of ethnoracial justice since that arm of the state is supposed to embody republican neutrality and enforce civic equality.[18]

The forcible enclosure of Palestinians in barren "ethnic neighborhoods" in Israeli cities, refugee camps in the occupied territories, and the gigantic open-air prison that is the Gaza strip is a signal denial of ethnoracial justice on the segregation and seclusion fronts. Sweeping violence by both the Israeli state and Israeli settlers deployed to enforce this geographical confinement and social subordination is a further infringement on legal fairness as well as communal integrity.[19] It follows that *diminishing the scope and intensity of each elementary form of domination* as well as loosening their linkages enhance the prospect for, and the realization of, ethnoracial justice.

The diagram of the two-dimensional space of ethnicity offers further guidance for thinking about the struggle for ethnoracial justice as taking three possible paths, starting from caste as the position of maximum racialization in terms of both symbolic rigidity, stigmatic burden, and material disparity (figure 13). The first route travels upward along the vertical axis on the right-hand side of the diagram (the side of racialized ethnicity) in the *material order of distribution*. It consists in policies of redistribution or *equalization*, whereby inequalities between ethnoracial categories are gradually reduced and eventually annulled, even as the categorical distinction between them remains clear-cut and salient. Some view the reduction of material disparities as the precondition for acceding to collective dignity and full participation in the civic compact. This route is represented in paradigmatic form by policies of "affirmative action," such as those pursued by India for the "scheduled classes," Brazil for the trio *preto, pardo,* and *indigena*, and the United States for "underrepresented minorities."[20] These policies

---

[18] Fabien Jobard et al., "Mesurer les discriminations selon l'apparence. Une analyse des contrôles d'identité à Paris" (2012).

[19] Silvia Pasquetti, *Refugees Together and Citizens Apart: Control, Emotions, and Politics at the Palestinian Margins* (2023); Neve Gordon, *Israel's Occupation* (2008); Nir Gazit, "State-Sponsored Vigilantism: Jewish Settlers' Violence in the Occupied Palestinian Territories" (2015); Jean-Pierre Filiu, *Histoire de Gaza* (2012).

[20] Sunita Parikh, *The Politics of Preference: Democratic Institutions and Affirmative Action in the United States and India* (1997); João Feres Júnior et al., *Ação afirmativa. Conceito, história e debates* (2018); David Lehmann, *The Prism of Race: The Politics and Ideology of Affirmative Action in Brazil* (2018). For a deft dissection of the logics of affirmative action as the "decoupling of race and class," see Daniel Sabbagh, "The Paradox of

aim at closing the gap between the target group and the dominant group by granting preferential access to education, employment, and business opportunities. They *reduce consequentiality but reinforce salience* and entrench officially defined categorical boundaries by attaching enhanced material rewards to membership.[21]

```
ORDINARY              SYMBOLIC/RECOGNITION        RACIALIZED
ETHNICITY                  [salience]             ETHNICITY
```

destigmatization ②

deracialization ③

① *equalization*

MATERIAL/DISTRIBUTION [consequentiality]

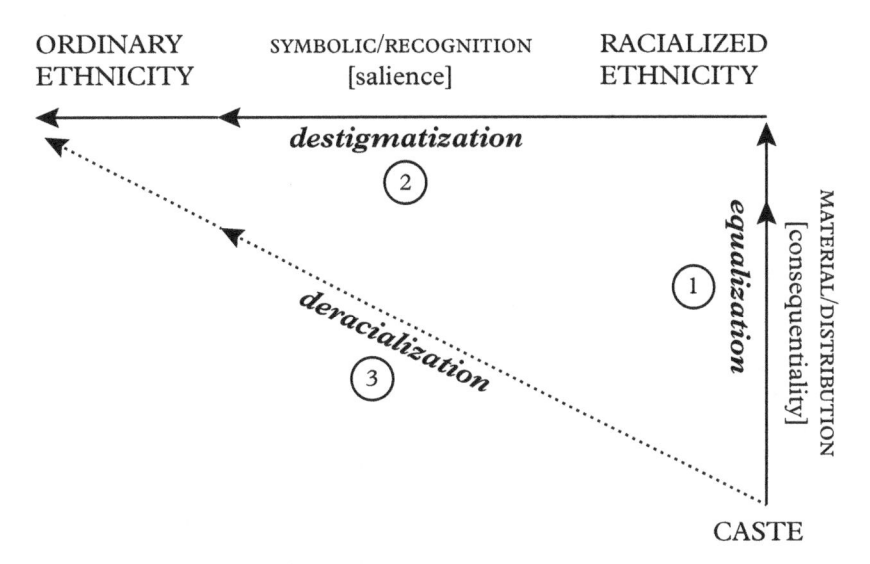

CASTE

Figure 13 Three paths to racial justice.

The second route takes us along the horizontal axis going leftward, from racialized to ordinary ethnicity, from stigma to aura; it consists in rendering ethnoracial division more fluid and less injurious in the *symbolic order of recognition*. It entails, in particular, the *destigmatization* of the subordinate category such that it may be granted a greater and eventually an equal share of honor.[22] This is pursued by such policies as educational campaigns and the official proclamation of a day, week, or month dedicated to showcasing and celebrating the culture,

---

Decategorization: Deinstitutionalizing Race through Race-Based Affirmative Action in the United States" (2011).

[21] Stanley R. Bailey et al., "How States Make Race: New Evidence from Brazil" (2018).

[22] See the work of Michèle Lamont, summed up in "Addressing Recognition Gaps: Destigmatization and the Reduction of Inequality" (2018), and the studies of Brazil, Canada, Israel, France, South Africa, Sweden and the United States gathered in Michèle Lamont and Nissim Mizrachi (eds.), *Responses to Stigmatization in Comparative Perspective* (2013).

Racial Domination

history, and achievements of otherwise demeaned ethnic categories, as when the Laosian state sponsors the annual festival celebrating the culture of Khmou, the country's largest minority, repressed by the previous regime, as part of the adoption of a new official grammar of ethnicity.[23] It is also exemplified by state measures aiming to institutionalize and support ethnic differences, as with the Soviet Union nationalities policy which sponsored languages and trained national elites in thousands of scattered territories as a means of binding them to the union.[24]

This is the path taken by advocates of the Roma at the European level, who have sought to decrease the taint of membership as a condition for collective identification and mobilization to fight discrimination, segregation, ghettoization, and violence. International Romani Day was established in 1990 on April 8 yearly by the World Romani Congress of the International Romani Union (founded in 1971). Small crowds attend the march in major cities across Europe on that day, mostly in Eastern and Central Europe. In response, the European Union has instituted cultural events and sponsored educational programs aimed at fighting anti-Roma prejudice and broadcasting Romani cultural accomplishments. Over the past decade, it has sought to move along the structural inequality axis as well by fostering the "social inclusion" of the Roma in their respective nation-states, but its efforts have been hampered by the timidity of its acknowledgment of the denigration of *romipen* (Romaness) which activists see as a "precondition for inclusion."[25]

The strategy of destigmatization fights racial domination in the Weberian order of status, the subjective perception of dignity by outsiders, by lessening the negative charge of symbolic capital. It takes the outward form of respect and social esteem and translates into an expanded feeling of self-worth. By stressing and valorizing categorical membership, it also shines a light on disparities in the Weberian order

---

[23] Pierre Petit, "Ethnic Performance and the State in Laos: The Boun Greh Annual Festival of the Khmou" (2013).

[24] Yuri Slezkine, "The USSR as a Communal Apartment, Or How a Socialist State Promoted Ethnic Particularism" (1994), and Terry Martin, *The Affirmative Action Empire: Nations and Nationalism in the Soviet Union, 1923–1939* (2001).

[25] "The EU has begun to devote more attention to the socio-economic integration of Roma, particularly in the fields of employment and education, which fits with its preferred politics of redistribution approach. However, this ignores the prejudice which Roma endure because of their ethnic identity, the fact that they are seen and treated in categorical terms" (Aidan McGarry, "The Dilemma of the European Union's Roma Policy" [2012], p. 133).

Coda

of class, the material distribution of economic, cultural, and social capital, and thus can help promote strategies of equalization.[26] There is a *synergy between the symbolic-cognitive and the material-institutional dimensions of racial justice*, but it can be positive, as when increased recognition and redistribution reinforce each other, or negative, as when the deterioration of the life chances of a group fuels prejudice against it by seeming to validate it, or when the perceptual devaluation of a group invites mistreatment and exclusion.[27]

This leads us to the third path to racial justice, which is the more challenging route politically and institutionally: it consists in traveling leftward along the diagonal of racialization, from the bottom-right to the top-left of the diagram, effecting simultaneously the reduction of ethnoracial inequality and the erosion of ethnoracial categorization. The two modalities of existence of race – classification and stratification – are intimately linked and so must be their transformation. Bourdieu explicates: "Like the stigma attached to a skin color or an ethnic or religious membership, [symbolic capital] is made by the gaze, but to change the gaze, it would be necessary at least – although this would not be sufficient, given the hysteresis of habitus – to change the social conditions of which the gaze is the product, that is, the structure of the distribution of capital."[28]

This is the route of outright *deracialization* whereby ethnicity becomes not just less consequential but also less salient, where membership becomes labile and optional, and eventually attenuated to the point of vanishing. It is the route of the Burakumin in Japan after the Dōwa policy designed to foster assimilation in the last three decades of the twentieth century: affirmative action on the housing and education front reduced the material penalty of membership but it also effaced identification with the category, leading to mass passing or merging into the national body of the "Yamato race," much to the chagrin of the Buraku Liberation League which was pushing

---

[26] The dialectic of the material and the symbolic, class and status, salience and consequentiality, mirrors the dialectic of redistribution and recognition at the center of the theory of justice elaborated by Nancy Fraser, "From Redistribution to Recognition? Dilemmas of Justice in a 'Postsocialist' Age" (1999). I see this *ex post facto* coincidence as validating my conception of the first two paths to racial justice.

[27] Both causal loops were at work in entrenching the predicament of the Algerian workers trapped in the shantytowns of the Parisian periphery in the 1950s, as shown by Abdelmalek Sayad, *Un Nanterre algérien, terre de bidonvilles* (1995), and discussed *supra*, pp. 141–2.

[28] Pierre Bourdieu, *Sociologie générale*, vol. 2. *Cours au Collège de France, 1983–1986* (2016), p. 1175.

for ethnic boosting.²⁹ In its most accomplished incarnation, logically, *ethnoracial justice extinguishes itself* because it effaces both the symbolic and the material foundations of ethnicity.

The path of deracialization is emphatically not a move toward "color-blind racism" because it entails *both* the attenuation of the salience of ethnoracial divides *and* the diminution leading to the eventual elimination of material penalties for categorical membership. It is a logical albeit not always a historical possibility – or, to put it differently, it is in many cases socially arduous and existentially improbable. This is because populations that have experienced deep racialization and fought ethnic disparagement and oppression long and hard, some of them for centuries, are fated to develop strong collective identities based on the honor acquired in that very fight and the solidarity it generates.³⁰ It is also because the experience of shared suffering binds members of the subordinate category to one another like no other force.³¹ When it is extreme and suffusive, unless there is a path for mass "passing" as with the Burakumin, racial domination fosters high groupness and groupness in turn fosters irrevocable attachment to one's collective.

This is the *historical irony and crux of symbolic domination*: the dominated comes to identify with and even defend the categorical boundary initially imposed upon them by the dominant. They become viscerally wedded to it, wedded from within, because they have somatized that very relation of domination in the form of categories of collective self-perception – there is no suggestion here that this attachment is not genuine, even though it is *arbitrary* in the sense that it could have been otherwise. Pierre Bourdieu speaks of "the logic of a domination exerted in the name of a symbolic principle known and recognized by the dominant as well as by the dominated, a language (or an accent), a lifestyle (or a way of thinking, speaking, or acting), and, more gener-

---

²⁹ John H. Davis Jr., "Blurring the Boundaries of the Buraku(min)" (2000); Noah McCormack, "Affirmative Action Policies under the Postwar Japanese Constitution: On the Effects of the Dōwa Special Measures Policy" (2018).

³⁰ Read the provocative philosophical rumination on dignity as the collective reaffirmation of blacks in the face of white domination by Norman Ajari, *La Dignité ou la mort. Éthique et politique de la race* (2019).

³¹ It is one of the insights of Émile Durkheim in *Les Formes élémentaires de la vie religieuse* (1995a [1912]) that shared suffering creates vigorous social bonds and identities. This is abundantly demonstrated for Jews by Esther Benbassa, *Suffering as Identity: The Jewish Paradigm* (2010); and for black Americans by Robin D. G. Kelley and Earl Lewis (eds.), *To Make Our World Anew: A History of African Americans* (2000), and Tommie Shelby, *We Who Are Dark: The Philosophical Foundations of Black Solidarity* (2005).

Coda

ally, a distinctive property, emblem or stigma, of which the most efficient symbolically is that perfectly arbitrary and non-predictive bodily property, skin color."[32]

It is the same submission to the arbitrariness of the history of ethnoracial domination that makes it impossible for intellectual approaches such as racial formation, color-blind racism, Critical Race Theory, intersectionality, Du Boisian sociology, and post/decolonial thought to envisage the erasure of ethnoracial identities *simpliciter* inasmuch as they are committed to a *racial ontology* as opposed to a *racialized historicity*.[33] They cannot envisage and therefore theorize a world without ethnoracial division. Indeed, they see the very discussion of that hypothetical state as a dangerous denial of the *ubiquity and eternity of "race."*[34] This is the epistemic crossroads where proclaimed constructivism crashes into remanent essentialism.

How do groups travel along the two axes of the triangle of ethnoracial domination? The answer is in the agonistic theory of group-making: *through historical struggles* waged in the symbolic order of classification and in the material order of stratification. The first entails challenging, changing, and possibly eroding the valence and salience of ethnoracial taxonomies in everyday life, in fields of cultural production, and in the state. The second involves reducing their consequentiality by redistributing economic and political resources so as to close ethnoracial gaps in the material order and thus challenge the effective ordering of groups. The key point here is that ethnoracial categories do not exist as groups prior to the struggle, but rather are *forged as such in the battle over recognition and distribution*:

---

[32] Pierre Bourdieu, *La Domination masculine* (1998), pp. 7–8.

[33] See the demonstration of the impossibility of deracialization for critical race theory by Daniel Sabbagh, "De la déracialisation en Amérique. Apports et limites de la Critical Race Theory" (2021). As for Du Bois on the eternity of ethnoracial formation, read his early essay on "The Conservation of Races" (1996 [1897]). His *oeuvre* is immense and sprawling so one can find in his writings support for the opposite position, for instance in his discussion of whiteness as a modern realization in his 1910 piece on "The Souls of White Folks" (reprinted in *Darkwater* [1920]). But, on my reading, Du Bois is a racial *conditionalist* and not a racial *constructivist*.

[34] The impossibility, nay, the very unthinkability of full deracialization is well expressed by W. J. T. Mitchell his 2010 W. E. B. Du Bois lecture, published as *Seeing Through Race* (2012), in which he writes: "A 'color-blind' post-racial world is neither achievable nor desirable. Against popular claims that race is an outmoded construct that distracts from more important issues," Mitchell contends that "race remains essential to our understanding of social reality. Race is not simply something to be seen but is among the fundamental media through which we experience human otherness. Race also makes racism visible and is thus our best weapon against it."

Racial Domination

"It is in the struggles that make the history of the social world that the categories of perception of the social world are constructed and, by the same token, the groups constructed after these categories."[35] It is my hope that the conceptual instruments fashioned and the theoretical propositions advanced in the present book can contribute, however modestly and obliquely, to advancing those struggles.

Historicity of racial domination

Disrupting the drive to inculpate in retrospect, we must grant full historicity to social formations, in the sense that societies are not necessarily and forever *prisoners* of their own history. A nation born of a settler colony, drenched in racial violence and scorn, grounded in group spoliation and marginalization, cannot erase its brutal past, but it can implement significant social, political, and cultural transformations, driven from below by activist mobilization or from above by intellectuals, politicians, and the state, that erode current ethnoracial difference and inequalities. Here again, the triangle of racial domination is useful to streamline possible remedies. Official apologies, truth and reconciliation commissions, the creation of dedicated memorials and museums, and the revision and teaching of the history of racial domination work in the symbolic order of recognition (along the horizontal axis). Affirmative action, compensation, restitution, and reparations operate in the material realm of distribution (along the vertical axis).

These are some of the imperfect yet necessary tools available to begin the arduous collective work of acknowledging the past to change the present and open the spectrum of possibilities for the future.[36] The panoply of measures recently adopted by the Canadian

---

[35] Pierre Bourdieu, "Décrire et prescrire" (1985), p. 195.

[36] The historical drivers and vexed political, institutional, and moral dilemmas of reparations blues are laid bare by John Torpey, *Making Whole What Has Been Smashed: On Reparations Politics* (2006). For case studies, see David Lyons and Michael K. Brown, *Redress for Historical Injustices in the United States: On Reparations for Slavery, Jim Crow, and Their Legacies* (2007); Federico Lenzerini (ed.), *Reparations for Indigenous Peoples: International and Comparative Perspectives* (2008); Magali Bessone, *Faire justice de l'irréparable. Esclavage colonial et responsabilité contemporaine* (2020); and Jaqueline Bhabha et al., *Time for Reparations: A Global Perspective* (2021). For a panorama of reconciliation, see Richard A. Wilson, *The Politics of Truth and Reconciliation in South Africa: Legitimizing the Post-Apartheid State* (2001); Catherine Lu, *Justice and Reconciliation in World Politics* (2017); and Jelke Boesten, *Performances of Injustice: The Politics of Truth, Justice and Reconciliation in Kenya* (2018).

Coda

government, including its public apology to the country's indigenous people, its payment of limited reparations for the cultural genocide perpetrated by the residential schools for Amerindians, and its official anti-racism strategy guiding the gamut of public policies are baby steps in that direction. But, unless they translate into a significant reallocation of resources and a major boost to the life chances of the historically racialized group, these measures, whether judicial, legislative, or executive, can just as well remain empty gestures, diversionary tactics, or cosmetic acts to give a sheen to official multiculturalism.[37]

Much as demands to "defund" the police and "abolish" the prison in the United States may end up making modest but realistic reforms of the penal state more difficult (if only by diverting limited activist energy), leaving millions of defendants and convicts in the lurch, there is every reason to believe that the push for reparations will everywhere yield moral rather than material recompense for past racial atrocities, or involve sums, endowments (such as "baby bonds"), or programs (facilitating access to housing or education) unlikely to make a palpable difference for the majority of the category wronged.[38] It is also guaranteed, not just to revive raw prejudice, but also to feed *racial resentment*, grounded in aggrieved appeals to fairness and deservingness on the part of the class-subordinate members of the dominant ethnic group (generic "poor whites"). Ethnoracial resentment is the most powerful collective emotion fueling the ascent of right-wing national-populism across advanced societies as the latter promises to restore a bygone era of doxic national closure and ethnic domination.[39] Rising academic and civic interest notwithstanding, advocates of racial justice must thus prepare for *reparation blues*.

---

[37] Bonnie McElhinny, "Reparations and Racism, Discourse and Diversity: Neoliberal Multiculturalism and Canadian Age of Apologies" (2016).

[38] In the United States, material reparations for the enslavement of African Americans alone (not counting Jim Crow and ghetto exactions) would run into the hundreds of trillions of dollars according to conservative computations. Simply closing the wealth gap between whites and blacks would come to a staggering $12 trillion, twice the annual budget of the federal government and equivalent to nearly $1 million for each eligible African-American household (according to William A. Darity, Jr. and A. Kirsten Mullen, *From Here to Equality: Reparations for Black Americans in the Twenty-First Century* [2022]). There is no viable political path toward distributing even 1 percent of that sum on a nationwide basis.

[39] Reinhard Olschanski, *Ressentiment. Über die Vergiftung des europäischen Geistes* (2015); Éric Fassin, *Populisme. Le grand ressentiment* (2017); Arlie Russell Hochschild, *Strangers in their Own Land: Anger and Mourning on the American Right* (2018); Darren W. Davis and David C. Wilson, *Racial Resentment in the Political Mind* (2021).

Moreover, the quest for racial justice cannot rely solely on racial springs and criteria, because, as a result of ethnoracial domination itself, subordinate ethnic groups typically sport a class structure gravely skewed toward the bottom. This means that *racial justice is unattainable without the simultaneous or prior realization of social justice*, that is, a transformation of the class structure and dynamics entailing (i) the reduction of the span of inequality or the socioeconomic distance between the top and bottom rungs; (ii) the elevation of the bottom rungs above a minimum standard permitting full and dignified participation in society; (iii) the abridgement of the prerogatives of capital in all of its forms (economic, cultural, social, and symbolic) in the workings of instruments of social reproduction such as the school, labor market, and laws of inheritance; and (iv) the universal distribution of core public goods such as safety, education, welfare, medical care, housing, and a healthy environment.[40] In societies around the globe, many of the deepest disparities between dominant and subordinate groups in the ethnoracial order are produced by non-racial mechanisms, in particular by the logic of *cumulative disadvantage* that perpetuate the penalties of class, citizenship, and place across institutions, along the life course, and across the generations.[41]

One concrete recommendation: a tangible and urgent measure advancing ethnoracial justice, and one that could be implemented promptly through deliberate legal and bureaucratic overhaul, is to put an end to the targeted, humiliating, and brutal policing of racialized populations in public space. The Black Lives Matter movement sprung in response to the repeated killings of unsuspecting and defenseless African-American men by excessive or abusive law enforcement, followed, more often than not, by judicial leniency. This movement has resonated across borders and oceans because the discriminatory scrutiny, arbitrary arrests, and intensive harassment of urban residents by the police based on ethnic phenotype, place, and perceived legal status is generalized and well documented across advanced societies, including Britain, France, Germany, Italy, Spain,

---

[40] This implies a repudiation of policies fostering "equal opportunity" which only change at the margins the distribution of a small minority of people into social positions when the problem is the structural arrangement of these positions, independently from the allocation mechanisms.

[41] For a discussion of this dynamic in the case of criminal punishment, see Megan C. Kurlychek and Brian D. Johnson, "Cumulative Disadvantage in the American Criminal Justice System" (2019).

Coda

Scandinavia, Canada, and Australia.[42] This is especially the case in neighborhoods of relegation where poor young men from stigmatized categories are subjected to the "slow violence" of intensified and rough policing translating into feelings of humiliation, resentment, and rage as well as into injury, death, and episodic rioting.[43] Racially biased law enforcement generates an atmosphere of trepidation, fosters a sentiment of injustice and delegitimizes public institutions among the target populations, and creates a bellicose disposition, a

---

[42] See, respectively, for Britain, Ben Bowling and Coretta Phillips, "Disproportionate and Discriminatory: Reviewing the Evidence on Police Stop and Search" (2007), and Shaka Yesufu, "Discriminatory Use of Police Stop-and-Search Powers in London, UK" (2013); for France, Fabien Jobard et al., "Mesurer les discriminations selon l'apparence. Une analyse des contrôles d'identité à Paris" (2012), and Emmanuel Blanchard, "Contrôle au faciès. Une cérémonie de dégradation" (2014); for Germany, Bernd Belina, "Der Alltag der Anderen: Racial Profiling in Deutschland?" (2016), and Özden Dumanli, "The Relationship Between the Police and Third-Generation Turkish Immigrants in Germany" (2021); for Italy, Fabio Quassoli and Adriana Carbonaro, "'Cattivi con i clandestini': controllo ed esclusione dei migranti nell'Italia contemporanea" (2013), and Giulia Fabini, *Polizia e migranti in città. Negoziare il confine nei contesti locali* (2023); for Spain, José García Añón et al., *Identificación policial por perfil étnico en España* (2013), and Lorea Arenas García and Elisa García España, "Police Stop and Search in Spain: An Overview of Its Use, Impacts and Challenges" (2022); for Scandinavia, Ragnhild Sollund, "Racialisation in Police Stop and Search Practice: The Norwegian Case" (2006), and Randi Solhjell et al., "'We Are Seen as a Threat': Police Stops of Young Ethnic Minorities in the Nordic Countries" (2019); for Canada, Scot Wortley and Akwasi Owusu-Bempah, "The Usual Suspects: Police Stop and Search Practices in Canada" (2011); idem, "Race, Police Stops, and Perceptions of Anti-Black Police Discrimination in Toronto, Canada over a Quarter Century" (2022); and Anne-Marie Livingstone et al., "Le profilage racial à Montréal, effets des politiques et des pratiques organisationnelles" (2020); and, for Australia, Chris Cunneen, *Conflict, Politics and Crime: Aboriginal Communities and the Police* (2020).

[43] Rory Kramer and Brianna Remster, "The Slow Violence of Contemporary Policing" (2022). Historically, ethnoracial riots and uprisings in the metropolis have been triggered by an accumulation of incidents between the police and the residents of poor segregated districts on both sides of the Atlantic (in Los Angeles in 1994, Cincinnati in 2001, the Parisian periphery in 2005 and 2003, Copenhagen in 2007, London in 2011, Stockholm in 2013, Ferguson in 2014, Baltimore in 2015, etc., for the more spectacular ones). Two close-up studies of the ferment for those riots are Manuel Boucher, *Casquettes contre képis. Enquête sur la police de rue et l'usage de la force dans les quartiers populaires* (2013), and Simon Balto, *Occupied Territory: Policing Black Chicago from Red Summer to Black Power* (2019). A political-economic interpretation that stresses class and state at the cost of underestimating the racial dimension is Margit Mayer et al. (eds.), *Urban Uprisings. Challenging Neoliberal Urbanism in Europe* (2016). A more balanced account is Mustafa Dikeç, *Urban Rage: The Revolt of the Excluded* (2017).

siege mentality, and a feeling of impunity among the forces of order.[44]

And for good reason: residents of the nether regions of social and physical space are effectively stripped down by unfair police treatment to the status of *zombie citizens* or denizens whose fundamental rights are abridged as a matter of course and for whom the *police is the frowning visage of the state*, a state that is there not to protect but to exclude them.[45] This is a civic and political flashpoint in both genuine race-divided societies, in which police violence is routinely lethal, and societies with race, in which police violence is muffled, that public authorities would be well advised to tamp down as it is slow-burning and self-perpetuating. Moreover, as suggested in the conclusion of chapter 4 on the fusion of penality and place, denigrated ethnicity and stigmatized neighborhood have become so intricately interwoven in the era of advanced marginality that it is impossible to separate them in the etiology of the mutual scorn and hostility that binds the police and young men from districts of defamation.[46]

At this point, many readers will object that my framework does not make room for the lived experience and knowledges of the dominated. This is to confound the phenomenology and the sociology of racial domination. If we are serious about reducing the social damage and human wreckage of ethnoracial rule, *epistemological populism is not an option*. We need to know, with the provisional certainty that social science provides, how the machinery of domination operates in reality, not in the "good sense" of its victims, to use the formulation of Antonio Gramsci.[47] Audre Lorde's oft-cited phrase "the master's

---

[44] For three national variants of this police vision, see François Bonnet and Clotilde Caillault, "The Invader, the Enemy Within and They-Who-Must-Not-Be-Named: How Police Talk about Minorities in Italy, the Netherlands and France" (2015).

[45] See, in the case of the United States, Joe Soss and Vesla Weaver, "Police Are Our Government: Politics, Political Science, and the Policing of Race-Class Subjugated Communities" (2017), and Monica C. Bell, "Police Reform and the Dismantling of Legal Estrangement" (2017).

[46] Boucher, *Casquettes contre képis*; Guillaume Roux and Sébastian Roché, "Police et phénomènes identitaires dans les banlieues: entre ethnicité et territoire. Une étude par focus groups" (2016); and Guillaume Roux, "Expliquer le rejet de la police en banlieue: discriminations, 'ciblage des quartiers' et racialisation. Un état de l'art" (2017).

[47] How could the American slave, deprived of literacy, beaten down, and tied to the narrow horizon of the plantation, grasp the logics of slavery, its economic, legal, and financial organization, its ties of the imperial expansion of the United States, Atlantic commodity markets, and global capitalism, as disclosed by Walter Johnson's *River of Dark Dreams: Slavery and Empire in the Cotton Kingdom* (2013)? Does the "subjugated knowledge" produced by inmates in a concentration camp give them purchase on the

tools will never dismantle the master's house" may be morally pleasing and politically uplifting as it celebrates the cunning and capacities of the subaltern. But it is demonstrably false. One example: the fight against legal racial segregation in the United States, culminating in the 1954 *Brown v. Board of Education* decision by the US Supreme Court, used the law to fight the law.[48] One can – and should – use science, a flawed product of Western modernity, involved in the invention of the most virulent variant of "race," to illumine and to help undermine racial domination.

Only social science can capture the hidden and counterintuitive mechanisms that (re)produce domination. One illustration is the sociology of residential segregation which allows us to identify the many forces that conspire to produce the spatial seclusion of racialized populations, most of which are not accessible to the consciousness of the segregated: ostracism and violence by neighbors, racial steering and rental discrimination by real estate agencies, mortgage exclusion by banks, biased housing rules and policies by government, but also invisible non-racial factors such as class composition; the propensity of states to distribute and disperse social housing, provide public transport, and homogenize the quality of life in different areas; and, to top it all, "social structural sorting" based on neighborhood proximity and familiarity and ethnically segmented networks of information and advice on housing.[49] Realizing that segregation flows from many sources reveals that it can be maintained *in the absence* of prejudice and discrimination in the housing market and that the segregated routinely and unwittingly contribute to its perpetuation. Their "good sense" is of little use to establish those empirical facts.

This is emphatically not to mean that the experience, consciousness, and knowledge of the subaltern do not matter and should be evacuated outright, as absolutist objectivism à la Durkheim would stipulate. On the contrary, they are part and parcel of the full reality

---

architecture and functions of the Nazi policy of forced labor, organized displacement, and extermination, or is the social historian better situated to grasp and disclose them (Nikolaus Wachsmann, *KL: A History of the Nazi Concentration Camps* [2015])?

[48] For a full account of the role of federal law in taking down the segregative structures of the Jim Crow South, see Michael J. Klarman, *From Jim Crow to Civil Rights: The Supreme Court and the Struggle for Racial Equality* (2004). For an analysis of how the law has shaped generations of affirmative action programs, see Daniel Sabbagh, *Les Paradoxes de la discrimination positive aux États-Unis* (2003).

[49] Maria Krysan and Kyle Crowder, *Cycle of Segregation: Social Processes and Residential Stratification* (2017).

that social science must capture – as indicated in my discussion of the mandate to "demarcate and repatriate" (*supra*, pp. 78–80). Only folk knowledge cannot serve as the *epistemic basis* of the model that sociology constructs, if only because domination operates in good measure "behind the back" of agents, through invisible and impersonal mechanisms that are not accessible to ordinary perception in everyday intercourse and must be excavated by means of analytic constructs.[50]

For those scholars, generally in the humanities, who see the reliance on scientific reason, method, and observation as culpable capitulation to a Western modernity responsible for the global racial predicament in the first place,[51] I would ask: in the battle to explain, erode, and ultimately undo ethnoracial domination piece by piece, are we *better off with or without social science*? Should we rely for guidance on the practical knowledge infusing its subjective and local experience or on the analytical and empirical knowledge of its objective determinants *and* of their felt effects in the everyday life of the racialized? Does the phenomenology of ethnoracial oppression suffice to give us a theoretical and practical grasp of it, or should we develop a sociology that encompasses this phenomenology as the "objectivity of the second order," but also embeds it in the "objectivity of the first order" as proposed in my agonistic model of racial rule as a violent form of group-making? *Responsum est in quaestione.*

---

[50] A good example of the wedding of the objectivist (top-down) and subjectivist (bottom-up) approach rooted in the epistemological priority of the analytic moment is Orlando Patterson's *The Sociology of Slavery* (2022 [1967]), which grounds the experience, personality, social institutions, and tactics of resistance of the slaves in the history and economic structure of Jamaican slavery, and not the other way around: "An examination of the lives of the slaves must begin with an understanding of the socio-economic order of their master since, within this wider framework the slaves were merely one element, albeit the most important, in the total structure and functioning of the slave system" (p. 15).

[51] See the critique of my analytical model from the standpoint of postcolonial theory by María do Mar Castro Varela, "Unruhe bewahren. Eine unordentliche Antwort auf Loïc Wacquants Plädoyer für eine Diskurskorrektur" (2023), and my response in the same issue of the *Berliner Journal für Soziologie*: "Ein Plädoyer für eine genetische Soziologie ethnorassischer Herrschaft. Eine Antwort auf meine deutschen Kritikerinnen" (2023b).

Acknowledgments

Over too many years to count, I have presented chunks and variants of the core arguments of this book in academic and activist venues in a half-dozen countries at the behest of colleagues in disciplines spanning the social sciences. I would like to thank them collectively without the usual enumeration that scholars deploy as an index of their social and symbolic capital in the profession. I worked on this book without the benefit of any generous grant or fancy sabbatical, and without an army of research assistants the old-fashioned way, tracking down and grappling with texts and ideas as they coalesced. I want to acknowledge the stimulation of working in the best sociology department on Planet Earth, bar none, owing to its unparalleled intellectual firepower, openness and diversity, and first-rate doctoral apprentices. Tamar Young earned special appreciation for enabling me to concentrate on reading and writing free of the usual teaching and office troubles beyond the classroom for the past year.

Lately, a wide circle of colleagues, students, and friends, from across disciplines, generations, and oceans, took from their precious time to read and react to various versions of chapters and sections of this book as well as to share their expertise on specific topics. I apologize in advance to those I must surely be forgetting. I am grateful for the critiques, queries, and suggestions of Aja Antoine, Magali Bessone, Jérôme Bourdieu, Robert Braun, Rogers Brubaker, Gwénaële Calvès, Jenae Carpenter, Andy Clarno, Matt Desmond, Frank Dikötter, Mustafa Emirbayer, Jason Ferguson, Ricarda Hammer, Douglas Hartmann, Anna Kamanzi, Glenn Loury, Aliza Luft, Marcello Maneri, Ellis Monk, Ann Morning, Silvia Pasquetti, Orlando Patterson, Khoi Quach, Daniel Sabbagh, Jean-Baptiste

Schaub, Silvia Sebastiani, David Showalter, Susan Thomson, Philippe van Parijs, Andreas Wimmer, and Michael Zanger-Tischler. I also learned much from the questions and objections raised by participants to the Science-Po workshop on discrimination in Paris in June of 2022 where I presented a skeletal version of the final theoretical framework.

Chapter 3 calls for separate acknowledgments because it required highly specific knowledge beyond my initial purview. It could not have been envisaged, let alone written, if not for the intellectual generosity of colleague historians who provided an irreverent outsider to their field with general guidance and bibliographic pointers that helped me pick my own way through the thick forest of the historiography of the "Jim Crow South" (whatever that may mean to them): Stephen Berrey at Michigan, Jane Dailey and Adam Green at Chicago, Glenda Gilmore at Yale, Evelyn Higginbotham at Harvard, Waldo Martin at Berkeley, and Jennifer Ritterhouse at George Mason University. In addition, Stephen Berrey, Fitzhugh Bundage, Robin Kelley, and Touré Reed subjected the full chapter to close scrutiny. None of them should be held responsible for my errors of fact and interpretation. I am also grateful for the reactions and suggestions of the participants to the Workshop on Culture and History at Harvard University where a rudimentary variant of the chapter was presented in Spring 2017 and where I benefited from the pressing queries of Orlando Patterson and his students.

Finally, I owe a singular intellectual and personal debt to Chris Muller and Victor Lund Shammas for reading and commenting in detail on the entire book in multiple drafts as I was writing them. They continually pressed me to keep rolling and to make my arguments clearer and tighter, and, if the latter are still errant and unconvincing, it is entirely my fault. The constant presence of Sophie was likewise essential even as she kept her comments on the book strictly to herself.

References

Abega, Sévérin Cécile and Patrice Bigombe Logo (eds.). 2006. *La Marginalisation des Pygmées d'Afrique Centrale*. Paris: Éditions Maisonneuve-Larose.
Abel, Elizabeth. 2010. *Signs of the Times: The Visual Politics of Jim Crow*. Berkeley, CA: University of California Press.
Abraham, Laurie Kay. 1993. *Mama Might Be Better Off Dead: The Failure of Health Care in Urban America*. Chicago, IL: University of Chicago Press.
Abrams, Philip. 1982. *Historical Sociology*. Ithaca, NY: Cornell University Press.
Abu-Laban, Yasmeen and Abigail B. Bakan. 2019. *Israel, Palestine and the Politics of Race: Exploring Identity and Power in a Global Context*. London: Bloomsbury.
Abu-Lughod, Janet L. 1980. *Rabat: Urban Apartheid in Morocco*. Princeton, NJ: Princeton University Press.
Adi, Hakim. 2023. *Many Struggles: New Histories of African and Caribbean People in Britain*. London: Pluto.
Agee, James. 2013 [1936]. *Cotton Tenants: Three Families*. Brooklyn, NY: Melville House.
Agier, Michel (ed.). 2014. *Un Monde de camps*. Paris: La Découverte.
Ajari, Norman. 2019. *La Dignité ou la mort. Éthique et politique de la race*. Paris: La Découverte.
Alba, Richard D. 1990. *Ethnic Identity: The Transformation of White America*. New Haven, CT: Yale University Press.
Alexander, Michelle. 2010. *The New Jim Crow: Mass Incarceration in the Age of Colorblindness*. New York: New Press.
Allen, Francis A. 1981. *The Decline of the Rehabilitative Ideal*. New Haven, CT: Yale University Press.
Allen, James. 2000. *Without Sanctuary: Lynching Photography in America*. Santa Fe, NM: Twin Palms.

Allport, Gordon. 1954. *The Nature of Prejudice.* Reading, MA: Addison-Wesley.
Amnesty International. 1999. *Summary of Amnesty International's Concerns on Police Abuse in Chicago.* London: Amnesty International, AMR/51/168/99.
Amos, Timothy. 2019. *Caste in Early Modern Japan: Danzaemon and the Edo Outcaste Order.* New York: Routledge.
Amselle, Jean-Loup. 2011. *L'Ethnicisation de la France.* Paris: Éditions Lignes.
Andersen, Chris. 2014. *Métis: Race, Recognition, and the Struggle for Indigenous Peoplehood.* Vancouver: University of British Columbia Press.
Anderson, Elijah. 1999. *Code of the Street: Decency, Violence, and the Moral Life of the Inner City.* New York: Knopf.
Anderson, Elijah. 2022. *Black in White Space: The Enduring Impact of Color in Everyday Life.* Chicago, IL: University of Chicago Press.
Anderson, James D. 1988. *The Education of Blacks in the South, 1860–1935.* Chapel Hill, NC: University of North Carolina Press.
Andersson, Mette and Johan Fredrik Rye. 2023. "Gray Racialization of White Immigrants: The Polish Worker in Norway." *Nordic Journal of Migration Research* 13, no. 2: 1–17.
Añón, José García, Ben Bradford, José Antonio García Sáez, Andrés Gascón Cuenca, and Antoni Llorente Ferreres. 2013. *Identificación policial por perfil étnico en España. Informe sobre experiencias y actitudes en relación con las actuaciones policiales.* Valencia: Editorial Tirant lo Blanch.
Apel, Dora and Shawn Michelle Smith. 2007. *Lynching Photographs.* Berkeley, CA: University of California Press.
Archer Mann, Susan. 1990. *Agrarian Capitalism in Theory and Practice.* Chapel Hill, NC: University of North Carolina Press.
Archer, Richard. 2017. *Jim Crow North: The Struggle for Equal Rights in Antebellum New England.* New York: Oxford University Press.
Arnesen, Eric (ed.). 2003. *Black Protest and the Great Migration: A Brief History with Documents.* Boston, MA: Bedford.
Aurillac, Michel. 1987. *L'Afrique à coeur. La coopération, un message d'avenir.* Paris: Berger Levrault.
Austin, Gareth. 2000. "Markets, Democracy and African Economic Growth: Liberalism and Afro-Pessimism Reconsidered." *The Round Table* 89, no. 357: 543–55.
Ayers, Edward L. 1984. *Vengeance and Justice: Crime and Punishment in the Nineteenth-Century American South.* New York: Oxford University Press.
Ayers, William. 1997. *A Kind and Just Parent: The Children of Juvenile Court.* Boston, MA: Beacon Press.
Azuma, Eiichiro. 2019. *In Search of Our Frontier: Japanese America and Settler Colonialism in the Construction of Japan's Borderless Empire.* Berkeley, CA: University of California Press.
Bachelard, Gaston. 1938. *La Formation de l'esprit scientifique. Contribution à une psychanalyse de la connaissance objective.* Paris: Vrin.

References

Bachelard, Gaston. 1940. *La Philosophie du non*. Paris: PUF.
Bachelard, Gaston. 1980. *Épistémologie*. Paris: PUF.
Bachman, Ronet. 1992. *Death and Violence on the Reservation: Homicide, Family Violence, and Suicide in American Indian Populations*. Santa Barbara, CA: ABC-Clio.
Bahuchet, Serge. 1991. "Les Pygmées d'aujourd'hui en Afrique centrale." *Journal des Africanistes* 61, no. 1: 5–35.
Bailey, Stanley R. 2008. "Unmixing for Race Making in Brazil." *American Journal of Sociology* 114, no. 3: 577–614.
Bailey, Stanley R., Fabrício M. Fiahlo, and Mara Loveman. 2018. "How States Make Race: New Evidence from Brazil." *Sociological Science* 5: 722–51.
Bailey, Zinzi D., Justin M. Feldman, and Mary T. Bassett. 2021. "How Structural Racism Works – Racist Policies as a Root Cause of US Racial Health Inequities." *New England Journal of Medicine* 384, no. 8: 768–73.
Baisley, Elizabeth. 2014. "Genocide and Constructions of Hutu and Tutsi in Radio Propaganda." *Race & Class* 55, no. 3: 38–59.
Baker, Ray Stannard 1964 [1908]. *Following the Color Line: American Negro Citizenship in the Progressive Era*. New York: Harper & Row.
Baldwin, Davarian L. 2007. *Chicago's New Negroes: Modernity, the Great Migration. and Black Urban Life*. Chapel Hill, NC: University of North Carolina Press.
Balto, Simon. 2019. *Occupied Territory: Policing Black Chicago from Red Summer to Black Power*. Chapel Hill, NC: University of North Carolina Press.
Banaji, Mahzarin R. and Anthony G. Greenwald. 2013. *Blindspot: Hidden Biases of Good People*. New York: Bantam.
Bancel, Nicolas, Thomas David, and Dominic Thomas (eds.). 2014. *L'Invention de la race. Des représentations scientifiques aux exhibitions populaires*. Paris: La Découverte.
Banton, Michael. 1979. "Analytical and Folk Concepts of Race and Ethnicity." *Ethnic & Racial Studies* 2, no. 2: 127–38.
Banton, Michael. 1987. *Racial Theories*. Cambridge: Cambridge University Press.
Banuazizi, Ali and Myron Weiner (eds.). 1998. *The State, Religion, and Ethnic Politics: Afghanistan, Iran, and Pakistan*. Syracuse, NY: Syracuse University Press.
Baranowski, Shelley. 2011. *Nazi Empire: German Colonialism and Imperialism from Bismarck to Hitler*. Cambridge: Cambridge University Press.
Barker, Vanessa. 2009. *The Politics of Imprisonment: How the Democratic Process Shapes the Way American Punishes Offenders*. New York: Oxford University Press.
Başkan, Birol. 2014. *From Religious Empires to Secular States: State Secularization in Turkey, Iran, and Russia*. London: Routledge.

Bay, Mia. 2021. *Traveling Black: A Story of Race and Resistance*. Cambridge, MA: Harvard University Press.

Bayly, Susan. 2001. *Caste, Society and Politics in India from the Eighteenth Century to the Modern Age*. Cambridge: Cambridge University Press.

Beatty, Lauren G. and Tracy L. Snell. 2021. *Profile of Prison Inmates, 2016*. Washington, DC: Bureau of Justice Statistics.

Beauchemin, Cris, Christelle Hamel, and Patrick Simon. 2016. *Trajectoires et origines. Enquête sur la diversité des populations en France*. Paris: INED Éditions.

Beaud, Stéphane and Gérard Noiriel. 2021. *Race et sciences sociales. Essai sur les usages publics d'une catégorie*. Marseilles: Agone.

Beaud, Stéphane and Michel Pialoux. 1999. *Retour sur la classe ouvrière. Enquête aux usines Peugeot de Sochaux-Montbéliard*. Paris: Fayard.

Beck, E. M. and Stewart E. Tolnay. 2019. "Torture and Desecration in the American South, an Exclamation Point on White Supremacy, 1877–1950." *Social Currents* 6, no. 4: 319–42.

Beckett, Katherine. 1999. *Making Crime Pay: Law and Order in Contemporary American Politics*. New York: Oxford University Press.

Beckett, Katherine. 2018. "The Politics, Promise, and Peril of Criminal Justice Reform in the Context of Mass Incarceration." *Annual Review of Criminology* 1: 235–59.

Beckett, Katherine and Megan Ming Francis. 2020. "The Origins of Mass Incarceration: The Racial Politics of Crime and Punishment in the Post-Civil Rights Era." *Annual Review of Law and Social Science* 16: 433–52.

Beeby, James and Donald G. Nieman. 2002. "The Rise of Jim Crow, 1880–1920." Pp. 336–47 in *A Companion to the American South*. Edited by John B. Boles. Malden, MA: Blackwell.

Belina, Bernd. 2016. "Der Alltag der Anderen: Racial Profiling in Deutschland?" Pp. 125–46 in *Sicherer Alltag. Politiken und Mechanismen der Zicherheitskonstruction im Alltag*. Edited by Bernd Dollinger and Henning Schmidt-Semisch. Wiesbaden: Springer.

Bell, Derrick. 1992. *Faces at the Bottom of the Well: The Permanence of Racism*. New York: Basic, new edition 2018.

Bell, Monica C. 2017. "Police Reform and the Dismantling of Legal Estrangement." *The Yale Law Journal* 126: 2054–150.

Bell-Fialkoff, Andrew. 1993. "A Brief History of Ethnic Cleansing." *Foreign Affairs* 72, no. 3: 110–21.

Benbassa, Esther. 2010. *Suffering as Identity: The Jewish Paradigm*. London: Verso.

Benner, Laurence A. 2010. "The California Public Defender: Its Origins, Evolution and Decline." *California Legal History* 5: 173–216.

Benot, Yves. 1994. *Massacres coloniaux, 1944–1950. La IVe République et la mise au pas des colonies françaises*. Paris: La Découverte.

Bensa, Alban. 1988. "Colonialisme, racisme et ethnologie en Nouvelle-Calédonie." *Ethnologie française* 18, no. 2: 188–97.

References

Bentouhami, Hourya. 2015. *Races, cultures, identités. Une approche féministe et postcoloniale*. Paris: PUF.
Bereni, Laure. 2023. *Le Management de la vertu. La diversité en entreprise à New York et à Paris*. Paris: Presses de Science-Po.
Berkman, Ronald. 1979. *Opening the Gates: The Rise of the Prisoners' Movement*. Lexington, MA: Lexington Books.
Berlin, Ira. 1998. *Many Thousands Gone: The First Two Centuries of Slavery in North America*. Cambridge, MA: Harvard University Press.
Bernardot, Marc. 2008. *Loger les immigrés. La SONACOTRA 1956–2006*. Paris: Le Croquant.
Berreman, Gerald D. 1960. "Caste in India and the United States." *American Journal of Sociology* 66, no. 2: 120–7.
Berreman, Gerald D. 1966. "The Structure and Function of Caste Systems." Pp. 277–307 in *Japan's Invisible Race: Caste in Culture and Personality*. Edited by George De Vos and Hiroshi Wagatsuma. Berkeley, CA: University of California Press.
Berreman, Gerald D. 1967. "Caste as Social Process." *Southwestern Journal of Anthropology* 23, no. 4: 351–70.
Berreman, Gerald D. 1972. "Race, Caste, and Other Invidious Distinctions in Social Stratification." *Race* 23, no 4: 385–414.
Berrey, Stephen A. 2015. *The Jim Crow Routine: Everyday Performances of Race, Civil Rights, and Segregation in Mississippi*. Chapel Hill, NC: University of North Carolina Press.
Bessone, Magali. 2013. *Sans distinction de race? Une analyse critique du concept de race et de ses effets pratiques*. Paris: Vrin.
Bessone, Magali. 2017. "Quel genre de groupe sont les races? Naturalisme, constructivisme et justice sociale." *Raisons politiques* 66: 121–42.
Bessone, Magali. 2020. *Faire justice de l'irréparable. Esclavage colonial et responsabilité contemporaine*. Paris: Vrin.
Bessone, Magali. 2022. "À quelles conditions une théorie de la justice raciale est-elle pensable? Adopter, abandonner ou adapter le cadre rawlsien." *Revue Philosophique de Louvain* 119, no. 4: 561–84.
Bessone, Magali. 2023. "Race as Essentially Contested Concept." Paper presented at the Berlin Freie Universität Workshop on "Race in a European Context," February 8.
Bessone, Magali and Matthieu Renault. 2021. *W. E. B. Du Bois: Double conscience et condition raciale*. Paris: Amsterdam.
Bessone, Magali and Daniel Sabbagh (eds.). 2015. *Race, racisme, discriminations. Anthologie de textes fondamentaux*. Paris: Hermann.
Bessone, Magali and Philippe Uirfalino. 2017. "Entités collectives et groupes nominaux." *Raisons politiques* 66: 5–11.
Best, Joel. 1997. "Victimization and the Victim Industry." *Society* 34, no. 4: 9–17.
Béteille, André. 1965. *Caste, Class and Power: Changing Patterns of Stratification in a Tanjore Village*. Berkeley, CA: University of California Press.

Béteille, André. 1990. "Race, Caste and Gender." *Man* (N.S.) 25, no. 3: 489–504.
Bethencourt, Francisco. 2013. *Racisms: From the Crusades to the Twentieth Century*. Princeton, NJ: Princeton University Press.
Bhabha, Jaqueline, Margareta Matache, and Caroline M. Elkin. 2021. *Time for Reparations: A Global Perspective*. Philadelphia, PA: University of Pennsylvania Press.
Bijl, Paul. 2012. "Colonial Memory and Forgetting in the Netherlands and Indonesia." *Journal of Genocide Research* 14, no. 3/4: 441–61.
Bilge, Sirma. 2020. "The Fungibility of Intersectionality: An Afropessimist Reading." *Ethnic & Racial Studies* 43, no. 13: 2298–326.
Blackhawk, Ned. 2006. *Violence over the Land: Indians and Empires in the Early American West*. Cambridge, MA: Harvard University Press.
Blackmon, Douglas A. 2008. *Slavery by Another Name: The Re-Enslavement of Black Americans from the Civil War to World War II*. New York: Anchor.
Blanchard, Emmanuel. 2014. "Contrôle au faciès. Une cérémonie de dégradation." *Plein droit* 103: 11–15.
Blanton, Hart and James Jaccard. 2008. "Unconscious Racism: A Concept in Pursuit of a Measure." *Annual Review of Sociology* 34: 277–97.
Blassingame, John W. 1979. *The Slave Community: Plantation Life in the Ante-Bellum South*. New York: Oxford University Press.
Bloch, Maurice. 1999. "Commensality and Poisoning." *Social Research* 66, no. 1: 133–49.
Bloxham, Donald. 2003. "The Armenian Genocide of 1915–1916: Cumulative Radicalization and the Development of a Destruction Policy" *Past & Present* 181: 141–91.
Blum, Lawrence. 2002. *"I'm Not a Racist, But ...": The Moral Quandary of Race*. Ithaca, NY: Cornell University Press.
Bobo, Lawrence D. 2011. "Somewhere between Jim Crow and Post-Racialism: Reflections on the Racial Divide in America Today." *Daedalus: Journal of the American Academy of Arts and Sciences* 140, no. 2: 11–36.
Boesten, Jelke. 2018. *Performances of Injustice: The Politics of Truth, Justice and Reconciliation in Kenya*. Cambridge: Cambridge University Press.
Bohle, Dorothee and Béla Greskovits. 2009. "Varieties of Capitalism and Capitalism 'Tout court'." *European Journal of Sociology/Archives Européennes de Sociologie* 50, no. 3: 355–86.
Bonczar, Thomas P. 2003. *Prevalence of Imprisonment in the U.S. Population, 1974–2001*. Washington, DC: Bureau of Justice Statistics.
Bonczar, Thomas P. and Allen Beck. 1997. *Lifetime Likelihood of Going to State or Federal Prison*. Washington, DC: Bureau of Justice Statistics.
Bonilla-Silva, Eduardo. 1997. "Rethinking Racism: Toward a Structural Interpretation." *American Sociological Review* 62, no. 3: 465–80.
Bonilla-Silva, Eduardo. 2015a. "The Structure of Racism in Color-Blind, 'Post-Racial' America." *American Behavioral Scientist* 59, no. 11: 1358–76.
Bonilla-Silva, Eduardo. 2015b. "More than Prejudice: Restatement,

References

Reflections, and New Directions in Critical Race Theory." *Sociology of Race and Ethnicity* 1, no. 1: 73–87.

Bonilla-Silva, Eduardo. 2021 [2008]. *Racism without Racists: Color-Blind Racism and the Persistence of Racial Inequality in the United States*. Lanham, MD: Rowman & Littlefield.

Bonilla-Silva, Eduardo. 2021. "What Makes Systemic Racism Systemic?" *Sociological Inquiry* 91, no. 3: 513–33.

Bonnet, François and Clotilde Caillault. 2015. "The Invader, the Enemy Within and They-Who-Must-Not-Be-Named: How Police Talk about Minorities in Italy, the Netherlands and France." *Ethnic & Racial Studies* 38, no. 7: 1185–201.

Bontems, Vincent. 2010. *Bachelard*. Paris: Les Belles Lettres.

Boucher, Manuel. 2013. *Casquettes contre képis. Enquête sur la police de rue et l'usage de la force dans les quartiers populaires*, Paris: L'Harmattan.

Bourdieu, Pierre. 1958. *Sociologie de l'Algérie*. Paris: PUF, revised edition 1980.

Bourdieu, Pierre. 1968a. *Le Métier de sociologue*. Paris: EHESS.

Bourdieu, Pierre. 1968b. "Structuralism and Theory of Sociological Knowledge." *Social Research* 35, no. 4: 681–706.

Bourdieu, Pierre. 1977. "Sur le pouvoir symbolique." *Annales. Économies, sociétés, civilisations* 32, no. 3: 405–11.

Bourdieu, Pierre. 1979. *La Distinction. Critique social du jugement*. Paris: Minuit.

Bourdieu, Pierre. 1980a. *Le Sens pratique*. Paris: Minuit.

Bourdieu, Pierre. 1980b. *Questions de sociologie*. Paris: Minuit.

Bourdieu, Pierre. 1980c. "Le mort saisit le vif. Les relations entre l'histoire incorporée et l'histoire réifiée." *Actes de la recherche en sciences sociales* 32: 3–14.

Bourdieu, Pierre. 1980d. "L'identité et la représentation. Éléments pour une réflexion critique sur l'idée de région." *Actes de la recherche en sciences sociales* 35: 63–72.

Bourdieu, Pierre. 1981. "Décrire et prescrire. Les conditions de possibilité et les limites de l'efficacité politique." *Actes de la recherche en sciences sociales* 38: 69–73.

Bourdieu, Pierre. 1982a. *Leçon sur la leçon*. Paris: Minuit.

Bourdieu, Pierre. 1982b. "Les rites comme actes d'institution." *Actes de la recherche en sciences sociales* 43: 58–63.

Bourdieu, Pierre. 1984a. "Espace social et genèse des 'classes'." *Actes de la recherche en sciences sociales* 52: 3–14.

Bourdieu, Pierre. 1984b. "La délégation et le fétichisme politique." *Actes de la recherche en sciences sociales* 52/53: 49–55.

Bourdieu, Pierre. 1987. *Choses dites*. Paris: Minuit.

Bourdieu, Pierre. 1989a [1987]. "Social Space and Symbolic Power." *Sociological Theory* 7, no. 1: 14–25.

Bourdieu, Pierre. 1989b. *La Noblesse d'État. Grandes Écoles et esprits de corps*. Paris: Minuit.

Bourdieu, Pierre. 1991. "The Peculiar History of Scientific Reason." *Sociological Forum* 6, no. 1: 3–26.
Bourdieu, Pierre. 1993a. "Esprits d'État. Genèse et structure du champ bureaucratique." *Actes de la recherche en sciences sociales* 96: 49–62.
Bourdieu, Pierre. 1993b. "À propos de la famille comme catégorie réalisée." *Actes de la recherche en sciences sociales* 100: 32–6.
Bourdieu, Pierre. 1994. *Raisons pratiques. Sur la théorie de l'action*. Paris: Seuil.
Bourdieu, Pierre. 1997. *Méditations pascaliennes*. Paris: Seuil.
Bourdieu, Pierre. 1998. *La Domination masculine*. Paris: Seuil.
Bourdieu, Pierre. 2000 [1982, 1991]. *Langage et pouvoir symbolique*. Paris: Seuil/Points.
Bourdieu, Pierre. 2001a. *Science de la science et réflexivité*. Paris: Raisons d'agir Éditions.
Bourdieu, Pierre. 2001b. "Pour un savoir engagé." Pp. 33–41 in *Contre-feux 2. Pour un mouvement social européenn*. Paris: Raisons d'agir Éditions.
Bourdieu, Pierre. 2002. *Interventions, 1961–2001. Science sociale et action politique*. Marseilles: Agone.
Bourdieu, Pierre. 2011 [2000]. "With Weber, Against Weber." Pp. 111–24 in *The Legacy of Pierre Bourdieu*. Edited by Simon Susen and Bryan Turner. Cambridge: Anthem.
Bourdieu, Pierre. 2012. *Sur l'État. Cours au Collège de France, 1989–1992*. Paris: Seuil and Raisons d'agir Éditions.
Bourdieu, Pierre. 2015. *Sociologie générale*, vol. 1. *Cours au Collège de France, 1981–1983*. Paris: Seuil and Raisons d'agir Éditions.
Bourdieu, Pierre. 2016. *Sociologie générale*, vol. 2. *Cours au Collège de France, 1983–1986*. Paris: Seuil and Raisons d'agir Éditions.
Bourdieu, Pierre. 2023. *Impérialismes. Circulation internationale des idées et luttes pour l'universel*. Paris: Raisons d'agir Éditions.
Bourdieu, Pierre and Roger Chartier. 2010 [1988]. *Le Sociologue et l'historien*. Marseilles: Agone.
Bourdieu, Pierre and Loïc Wacquant. 1999 [1998]. "The Cunning of Imperialist Reason." *Theory, Culture & Society* 6, no. 1: 41–58.
Bourdieu, Pierre, Jean-Claude Chamboredon and Jean-Claude Passeron. 1968. *Le Métier de sociologue. Préalables épistémologiques*. Paris: EHESS.
Bourgois, Philippe. 1989. *Ethnicity at Work: Divided Labor on a Central American Banana Plantation*. Baltimore, MD: Johns Hopkins University Press.
Bowen, John Richard. 1996. "The Myth of Global Ethnic Conflict." *Journal of Democracy* 7, no. 4: 3–14.
Bowker, Geoffrey C. and Susan Leigh Star. 1999. "The Case of Race Classification and Reclassification under Apartheid." Pp. 195–225 in *Sorting Things Out: Classification and Its Consequences*. Cambridge, MA: MIT Press.

References

Bowling, Ben and Coretta Phillips. 2007. "Disproportionate and Discriminatory: Reviewing the Evidence on Police Stop and Search." *The Modern Law Review* 70, no. 6: 936–61.

Boxill, Bernard R. 1992. *Blacks and Social Justice*. Lanham, MD: Rowman & Littlefield.

Brahim, Rachida. 2021. *La Race tue deux fois. Une histoire des crimes racistes en France, 1970–2000*. Paris: Syllepse.

Brattain, Michelle. 2005. "Miscegenation and Competing Definitions of Race in Twentieth-Century Louisiana." *The Journal of Southern History* 71, no. 3: 621–58.

Braun, Robert. 2019. *Protectors of Pluralism: Religious Minorities and the Protection of Jews in the Low Countries during the Holocaust*. New York: Cambridge University Press.

Breen, Timothy Hall and Stephen Innes. 1980. *"Myne Owne Ground": Race and Freedom on Virginia's Eastern Shore, 1640–1676*. New York: Oxford University Press.

Brennan, P. A., S. A. Mednick, and J. Volavka. 1995. "Biomedical Factors in Crime." Pp. 65–90 in *Crime*. Edited by James Q. Wilson and Joan Petersilia. San Francisco, CA: ICS Press.

Brinbaum, Yaël and Annick Kieffer. 2009. "Les scolarités des enfants d'immigrés de la sixième au baccalauréat. Différenciation et polarisation des parcours." *Population* 64, no. 3: 507–54.

Broch-Due, Vigdis. 2004. *Violence and Belonging: The Quest for Identity in Post-Colonial Africa*. London: Routledge.

Brodkin, Karen. 1998. *How Jews Became White Folks and What That Says about Race in America*. New Brunswick, NJ: Rutgers University Press.

Brophy, Alfred L. 2003. *Reconstructing the Dreamland: The Tulsa Riot of 1921: Race, Reparations, and Reconciliation*. New York: Oxford University Press.

Brown, Julian. 2016. *The Road to Soweto: Resistance and the Uprising of 16 June 1976*. London: Boydell & Brewer.

Brown, Leslie. 2008. *Upbuilding Black Durham: Gender, Class, and Black Community Development in the Jim Crow South*. Durham, NC: Duke University Press.

Brown, Nikki and Barry M. Stentiford (eds.). 2008. *The Jim Crow Encyclopedia*, 2 volumes. Santa Barbara, CA: ABC-Clio.

Brubaker, Rogers. 1995. "Aftermaths of Empire and the Unmixing of Peoples: Historical and Comparative Perspectives." *Ethnic & Racial Studies* 18, no. 2: 189–218.

Brubaker, Rogers. 2002. "Ethnicity Without Groups." *Archives européennes de sociologie/European Journal of Sociology* 43, no. 2: 163–89.

Brubaker, Rogers. 2004. *Ethnicity Without Groups*. Cambridge, MA: Harvard University Press.

Brubaker, Rogers. 2009. "Ethnicity, Race, and Nationalism." *Annual Review of Sociology* 35: 21–42.

Brubaker, Rogers. 2015. *Grounds for Difference*. Cambridge, MA: Harvard University Press.

Brubaker, Rogers and David D. Laitin. 1998. "Ethnic and Nationalist Violence." *Annual Review of Sociology* 24: 423–52.

Brubaker, Rogers, Mara Loveman, and Peter Stamatov. 2004. "Ethnicity as Cognition." *Theory & Society* 33, no. 1: 31–64.

Brubaker, Rogers, Margit Feischmidt, Jon Fox, and Liana Grancea. 2006. *Nationalist Politics and Everyday Ethnicity in a Transylvanian Town*. Princeton, NJ: Princeton University Press.

Bruenig, Matt. 2020. "The Racial Wealth Gap Is About the Upper Classes. The top decile disparities drive almost the entire racial wealth gap." People's Policy Project, www.peoplespolicyproject.org, accessed on 29 June 2022.

Brun, Solène and Claire Cosquer. 2022. *Sociologie de la race*. Paris: Armand Colin.

Brundage, William Fitzhugh. 1993. *Lynching in the New South: Georgia and Virginia, 1880–1930*. Urbana, IL: University of Illinois Press.

Brundage, William Fitzhugh. 1997. "American Slavery: A Look Back at *The Peculiar Institution*." *The Journal of Blacks in Higher Education* 15: 118–20.

Bryant, Jerry H. 2003. *"Born in a Mighty Bad Land": The Violent Man in African American Folklore and Fiction*. Bloomington, IN: Indiana University Press.

Buggs, Shantel Gabrieal, Cassi Pittman Claytor, San Juanita García, Onoso Imoagene, Verna Keith, Hadi Khoshneviss, Catherine Lee, Sarah Mayorga-Gallo, Victor E. Ray, and Wendy D. Roth. 2020. "Systemic Anti-Black Racism Must Be Dismantled: Statement by the American Sociological Association Section on Racial and Ethnic Minorities." *Sociology of Race and Ethnicity* 6, no. 3: 289–91.

Burbank, Jane and Frederick Cooper. 2011. *Empires in World History: Power and the Politics of Difference*. Princeton, NJ: Princeton University Press.

Burch, Traci. 2015. "Skin Color and the Criminal Justice System: Beyond Black–White Disparities in Sentencing." *Journal of Empirical Legal Studies* 12, no. 3: 395–420.

Burden-Stelly, Charisse. 2020. "Modern US Racial Capitalism." *Monthly Review* 72, no. 3: 8–20.

Burger, Thomas. 1976. *Max Weber's Theory of Concept Formation*. Durham, NC: Duke University Press.

Burleigh, Michael and Wolfgang Wipperman, 1991. *The Racial State: Germany 1933–1945*. Cambridge: Cambridge University Press.

Calvès, Gwénaële. 2013. "La discrimination, une expérience impossible." *Revue française de science politique* 63, no. 6: 1208–11.

Calvès, Gwénaële. 2022. *La Laïcité*. Paris: La Découverte.

Calvès, Gwénaële and Diane Roman. 2016. "La discrimination à raison de la précarité sociale: progrès ou confusion?" *Revue de droit du travail* 9: 526–31.

References

Cammillieri-Subrenat, Anne. 2002. "L'incitation à la haine et la Constitution." *Revue internationale de droit comparé* 54, no. 2: 513–48.
Camp, Camille Graham and George M. Camp (eds.). 1998. *The Corrections Yearbook 1998*. Middletown, CT: Criminal Justice Institute.
Camp, George M. 1985. *Prison Gangs: Their Extent, Nature, and Impact on Prisons*. Washington, DC: US Department of Justice, Office of Legal Policy, Federal Justice Research Program.
Canguilhem, Georges. 1968. *Études d'histoire et de philosophie des sciences*. Paris: Vrin.
Carbado, Devon W. and Daria Roithmayr. 2014. "Critical Race Theory Meets Social Science." *Annual Review of Law and Social Science* 10: 149–67.
Carmichael, Stokely and Charles V. Hamilton. 1967. *Black Power: The Politics of Liberation*. New York: Vintage, new edition 1992.
Carroll, Leo. 1974. *Hacks, Blacks, and Cons: Race Relations in a Maximum Security Prison*. Lexington, MA: Lexington Books.
Carroll, Leo. 1982. "Race, Ethnicity, and the Social Order of the Prison." Pp.181–201 in *The Pains of Imprisonment*. Edited by Robert Johnson and Hans Toch. Beverly Hills, CA: Sage.
Castel, Robert. 2007. *La Discrimination négative. Citoyens ou indigènes?*. Paris: Seuil.
Castro Varela, María do Mar. 2023. "Unruhe bewahren. Eine unordentliche Antwort auf Loïc Wacquants Plädoyer." *Berliner Journal für Soziologie* 33, no. 1–2: 43–55.
Cecil, Dawn K. 2015. *Prison Life in Popular Culture: From the Big House to Orange is the New Black*. Boulder, CO: Lynne Rienner Publishers.
Çelik, Zeynep. 1997. *Urban Forms and Colonial Confrontation: Algiers under French Rule*. Berkeley, CA: University of California Press.
Cell, John W. 1982. *The Highest Stage of White Supremacy: The Origins of Segregation in South Africa and the American South*. Cambridge: Cambridge University Press.
Chafe, William Henry, Raymond Gavins, and Robert Korstad (eds.). 2013. *Remembering Jim Crow: African Americans Tell About Life in the Segregated South*. New York: New Press.
Chandra, Kanchan. 2006. "What Is Ethnic Identity and Does It Matter?" *Annual Review of Political Science* 9: 397–424.
Chapoutot, Johann. 2014. *La Loi du sang. Penser et agir en nazi*. Paris: Gallimard.
Chatterjee, Anasua. 2017. *Margins of Citizenship: Muslim Experiences in Urban India*. New York: Routledge.
Chicago Commission on Race Relations. 1920. *The Negro in Chicago: A Study of Race Relations and a Race Riot*. Chicago, IL: University of Chicago Press.
Chicago Fact Book Consortium. 1955. *Local Community Fact Book 1950: Chicago Metropolitan Area*. Chicago, IL: Chicago Review Press.

Chicago Fact Book Consortium. 1984. *Local Community Fact Book 1980: Chicago Metropolitan Area*. Chicago, IL: Chicago Review Press.

Chicago Tribune. 1992. *The Worst Schools in America*. Chicago, IL: Chicago Review Press.

Christian, Michelle, Louise Seamster, and Victor Ray. 2019. "New Directions in Critical Race Theory and Sociology: Racism, White Supremacy, and Resistance." *American Behavioral Scientist* 63, no. 13: 1731–40.

Christianson, Scott. 1998. *With Liberty for Some: Five Hundred Years of Imprisonment in America*. Boston, MA: Northeastern University Press.

Christopher, A. J. 2001. *The Atlas of Changing South Africa*. New York: Routledge.

Clammer, John. 1985. "Ethnicity and the Classification of Social Differences in Plural Societies: A Perspective from Singapore." *Journal of Asian and African Studies* 20, no. 3/4: 141–55.

Clark, Kenneth C. 1965. *Dark Ghetto: Dilemmas of Social Power*. Amherst, MA: University of Massachusetts Press.

Clarno, Andy. 2017. *Neoliberal Apartheid: Palestine/Israel and South Africa after 1994*. Chicago, IL: University of Chicago Press.

Clear, Todd. 2007. *Imprisoning Communities: How Mass Incarceration Makes Disadvantaged Communities Worse*. New York: Oxford University Press.

Cobb, James. 2022. *C. Vann Woodward: America's Historian*. Chapel Hill, NC: University of North Carolina Press, reprint 1989.

Cohen, Stanley. 2001. *States of Denial: Knowing about Atrocities and Suffering*. Cambridge: Polity.

Cohen, William B. 1980. *The French Encounter with Africans: White Response to Blacks, 1530–1880*. Bloomington, IN: Indiana University Press, new edition 2003.

Cole, Stefanie and Natalie J. Ring (eds.). *The Folly of Jim Crow: Rethinking the Segregated South*. Arlington, TX: Texas A&M University Press.

Collins, Bennett, Meghan C. Laws, and Richard Ntakirutimana. 2021. "Becoming 'Historically Marginalized Peoples': Examining Twa Perceptions of Boundary Shifting and Re-Categorization in Post-Genocide Rwanda." *Ethnic & Racial Studies* 44, no. 4: 576–94.

Collins, Patricia Hill. 2015. "Intersectionality's Definitional Dilemmas." *Annual Review of Sociology* 43: 1–20.

Collins, Patricia Hill and Silma Bilge. 2020. *Intersectionality*, 2nd edition. Cambridge: Polity.

Collins, Randall. 1979. *The Credential Society: A Historical Sociology of Education and Stratification*. New York: Oxford University Press, new edition 2019.

Collins, Randall. 2008. *Violence: A Micro-Sociological Theory*. Princeton, NJ: Princeton University Press.

Colvin, Mark. 1992. *The Penitentiary in Crisis: From Accommodation to Riot in New Mexico*. Albany, NY: SUNY Press.

References

Conover, Ted. 2000. *Newjack: Guarding Sing Sing*. New York: Random House.
Conroy, John. 2000. *Unspeakable Acts, Ordinary People: The Dynamics of Torture*. Berkeley, CA: University of California Press.
Conte, Edouard and Cornelia Essner. 1995. *La Quête de la race. Une anthropologie du Nazisme*. Paris: Hachette.
Conzen, Kathleen Neils, David A. Gerber, Ewa Morawska, George E. Pozzetta, and Rudolph J. Vecoli. 1998. "The Invention of Ethnicity in the United States." Pp. 22–9 in *Major Problems in American Immigration and Ethnic History*. Edited by Jon Gjerde. Boston, MA: Houghton Mifflin.
Cooper, Anna Julia. 2006 [1925]. *Slavery and the French and Haitian Revolutionists*. Edited by Frances R. Keller. Lexington, MD: Rowman & Littlefield.
Cooper, Frederick. 2014. *Citizenship between Empire and Nation: Remaking France and French Africa, 1945–1960*. Princeton, NJ: Princeton University Press.
Cooper, Frederick and Ann Laura Stoler (eds.). 1997. *Tensions of Empire: Colonial Cultures in a Bourgeois World*. Berkeley, CA: University of California Press.
Cooper, Scott A. 1998. "Community Notification and Verification Practices in Three States." Pp. 103–6 in *National Conference on Sex Offender Registries*. Washington, DC: Bureau of Justice Statistics.
Cope, R. Douglas. 1994. *The Limits of Racial Domination: Plebeian Society in Colonial Mexico City, 1660–1772*. Madison, WI: University of Wisconsin Press.
Cornell, Stephen. 1990. *The Return of the Native: American Indian Political Resurgence*. New York: Oxford University Press.
Cornell, Stephen and Douglas Hartmann. 2004. "Conceptual Confusion and Divides: Race, Ethnicity, and the Study of Immigration." Pp. 23–41 in *Not Just Black and White: Historical and Contemporary Perspectives on Immigration, Race, and Ethnicity in the United States*. Edited by Nancy Foner and George M. Fredrickson. New York: Russell Sage Foundation.
Cornell, Stephen and Douglas Hartmann. 2006. *Ethnicity and Race: Making Identities in a Changing World*. Newbury Park, CA: Sage Publications.
Cox, Oliver C. 1948. *Caste, Class, and Race: A Study in Social Dynamics*. New York: Monthly Review Press.
Crenshaw, Martha. 1978. *Revolutionary Terrorism: The FLN in Algeria, 1954–1962*. Stanford, CA: Hoover Institution.
Crenshaw, Martha. 1981. "The Causes of Terrorism." *Comparative Politics* 13, no. 4: 379–99.
Crenshaw, Martha (ed.). 1995. *Terrorism in Context*. University Park, PA: Pennsylvania State University Press.
Crespino, Joseph. 2009. *In Search of Another Country: Mississippi and the*

Conservative Counterrevolution. Princeton, NJ: Princeton University Press.

Crețan, Remus, Petr Kupka, Ryan Powell, and Václav Walach. 2022. "Everyday Roma Stigmatization: Racialized Urban Encounters, Collective Histories and Fragmented Habitus." *International Journal of Urban and Regional Research* 46, no. 1: 82–100.

Critical Resistance. 2008. *Abolition Now! Ten Years of Strategy and Struggle Against the Prison Industrial Complex*. Oakland, CA: AK Press.

Cronon, E. David. 1960. *Black Moses: The Story of Marcus Garvey and the Universal Negro Improvement Association*. Madison, WI: University of Wisconsin Press.

Cross, Brian. 1993. *It's Not About a Salary: Rap, Race, and Resistance in Los Angeles*. New York: Verso.

Cummins, Eric. 1994. *The Rise and Fall of California's Radical Prison Movement*. Stanford, CA: Stanford University Press.

Cuñha, Manuela. 2014. "The Ethnography of Prisons and Penal Confinement." *Annual Review of Anthropology* 43: 217–33.

Cunneen, Chris. 2020. *Conflict, Politics and Crime: Aboriginal Communities and the Police*. London: Routledge.

Cunningham, Vincent. 2020. "The Argument of 'Afropessimism'." *The New Yorker*, 20 July.

Da Rocha Valente, Rubia and Brian J. L. Berry. 2020. "Residential Segregation by Skin Color: Brazil Revisited." *Latin American Research Review* 55, no. 2: 207–26.

DaCosta, Kimberly McClain. 2007. *Making Multiracials: State, Family, and Market in the Redrawing of the Color Line*. Stanford, CA: Stanford University Press.

DaCosta, Kimberly A. 2020. "Multiracial Categorization, Identity, and Policy in (Mixed) Racial Formations." *Annual Review of Sociology* 46: 335–53.

Dailey, Jane (ed.). 2009. *The Age of Jim Crow: A Norton Casebook in History*. New York: Norton.

Dailey, Jane. 2020. *White Fright: The Sexual Panic at the Heart of America's Racist History*. New York: Basic Books.

Dailey, Jane, Glenda Elizabeth Gilmore, and Bryant Simon (eds.). 2000. *Jumpin' Jim Crow: Southern Politics from Civil War to Civil Rights*. Princeton, NJ: Princeton University Press.

Daniel, Pete. 1990 [1972]. *Shadow of Slavery: Peonage in the South, 1901–1969*. Urbana, IL: University of Illinois Press.

Daniels, Roger. 1993. *Prisoners Without Trial: Japanese Americans in World War II*. New York: Hill & Wang.

Dantzler, Prentiss, Elizabeth Korver-Glenn, and Junia Howell. 2022. "Introduction: What Does Racial Capitalism Have to Do with Cities and Communities?" *City & Community* 21, no. 3: 163–72.

References

Darity, William A. Jr. and A. Kirsten Mullen. 2022. *From Here to Equality: Reparations for Black Americans in the Twenty-First Century*. Chapel Hill, NC: University of North Carolina Press.

Das, Veena. 2001. "Caste." Pp. 1529–32 in *International Encyclopedia of the Social and Behavioral Sciences*. Edited by Neil J. Smelser and Paul B. Baltes. Amsterdam: Elsevier.

Davenport, Lauren. 2020. "The Fluidity of Racial Classifications." *Annual Review of Political Science* 23: 221–40.

Davidson, Naomi. 2017. *Only Muslim: Embodying Islam in Twentieth-Century France*. Ithaca, NY: Cornell University Press.

Davis, Allison, Burleigh B. Gardner, and Mary R. Gardner. 1941, 2009. *Deep South: A Social Anthropological Study of Caste and Class*. Charleston, SC: University of South Carolina Press.

Davis, Angela J. 2007. *Arbitrary Justice: The Power of the American Prosecutor*. New York: Oxford University Press.

Davis, Angela Y. 2001. *The Prison Industrial Complex*. Oakland: AK Press.

Davis, Darren W. and David C. Wilson. 2021. *Racial Resentment in the Political Mind*. Chicago: University of Chicago Press.

Davis, David Brion. 2006. *Inhuman Bondage: The Rise and Fall of Slavery in the New World*. New York: Oxford University Press.

Davis, F. James. 1991. *Who Is Black? One Nation's Definition*. University Park, PA: Penn State University Press.

Davis Jr, John H. 2000. "Blurring the Boundaries of the Buraku(min)." Pp. 110–22 in *Globalization and Social Change in Contemporary Japan*. Edited by J.S. Eades, Tom Gill, and Harumi Befu. Melbourne: Transpacific Press.

Davis, Kathy. 2008. "Intersectionality as Buzzword: A Sociology of Science Perspective on What Makes a Feminist Theory Successful." *Feminist Theory* 9, no. 1: 67–85.

de la Fuente, Alejandro and Ariela J. Gross. 2020. *Becoming Free, Becoming Black: Race, Freedom, and Law in Cuba, Virginia, and Louisiana*. New York: Cambridge University Press.

De Zwart, Frank and Caelesta Poppelaars. 2007. "Redistribution and Ethnic Diversity in the Netherlands: Accommodation, Denial and Replacement." *Acta Sociologica* 50, no. 4: 387–99.

Dean, Lorraine T. and Roland J. Thorpe, Jr. 2021. "What Structural Racism Is (or Is Not) and How to Measure It: Clarity for Public Health and Medical Researchers." *American Journal of Epidemiology* 191, no. 9: 1521–6.

Decker, Scott H. and David C. Pyrooz. 2015. "The Real Gangbanging is in Prison." Pp. 143–62 in *The Oxford Handbook of Prisons and Imprisonment*. Edited by John Wooldredge and Paula Smith. New York: Oxford University Press.

Deeds, Susan M. 2010. *Defiance and Deference in Mexico's Colonial North:*

Indians Under Spanish Rule in Nueva Vizcaya. Austin, TX: University of Texas Press.

Degler, Carl N. 1971. *Neither Black nor White: Slavery and Race Relations in Brazil and the United States.* Madison, WI: University of Wisconsin Press, reprint 1986.

Delgado, Richard and Jean Stefancic. 2023. *Critical Race Theory: An Introduction.* New York: New York University Press.

Delon, Margot. 2019. "Des 'Blancs honoraires'? Les trajectoires sociales des Portugais et de leurs descendants en France." *Actes de la recherche en sciences sociales* 228: 4–28.

Denord, François. 2020. "Domination." Pp. 225–52 in *Dictionnaire International Pierre Bourdieu.* Edited by Gisèle Sapiro. Paris: Éditions du CNRS.

Desmond, Matthew and Mustafa Emirbayer. 2009a. "What Is Racial Domination?" *Du Bois Review: Social Science Research on Race* 6, no. 2: 335–55.

Desmond, Matthew and Mustafa Emirbayer. 2009b. *Racial Domination, Racial Progress: The Sociology of Race in America.* New York: McGraw-Hill.

Devine, John. 1996. *Maximum Security: The Culture of Violence in Inner-City Schools.* Chicago, IL: University of Chicago Press.

Dias, Amanda S. A. 2013. *Aux Marges de la ville et de l'État. Camps palestiniens au Liban et favelas cariocas.* Paris: Karthala.

Dikeç, Mustafa. 2017. *Urban Rage: The Revolt of the Excluded.* New Haven, CT: Yale University Press.

Diken, Bülent and Carsten B. Laustsen. 2005. *The Culture of Exception: Sociology Facing the Camp.* New York: Routledge.

Dikötter, Frank. 1992. *The Discourse of Race in Modern China.* New York: Oxford University Press, second edition 2015.

Dikötter, Frank (ed.). 1997. *The Construction of Racial Identities in China and Japan: Historical and Contemporary Perspectives.* Honolulu, HA: University of Hawaii Press.

Dikötter, Frank. 2001. "Race in China." Pp. 495–510 in *Companion to Racial and Ethnic Studies.* Edited by John Solomos and David Theo Goldberg. Cambridge, MA: Blackwell.

Dikötter, Frank. 2008. "The Racialization of the Globe: An Interactive Interpretation." *Ethnic & Racial Studies* 31, no. 8: 1478–96.

Dixon, Angela R. and Edward E. Telles. 2017. "Skin Color and Colorism: Global Research, Concepts, and Measurement." *Annual Review of Sociology* 43: 405–24.

Dobbin, Frank and Alexandra Kalev. 2022. *Getting to Diversity: What Works and What Doesn't.* Cambridge, MA: Harvard University Press.

Dodge, Calvert R. (ed.). 1975. *A Nation Without Prisons: Alternatives to Incarceration.* Lexington, MA: Lexington Books.

Doering, Jan and Efe Peker. 2022. "How Muslims Respond to Secularist

References

Restrictions: Reactive Ethnicity, Adjustment, and Acceptance." *Ethnic & Racial Studies* 45, no. 15: 2956–77.
Dollard, John. 1937. *Caste and Class in a Southern Town*. Madison, WI: University of Wisconsin Press, reprint 1988.
Domínguez, Virginia R. 1993. *White by Definition: Social Classification in Creole Louisiana*. New Brunswick, NJ: Rutgers University Press.
Dordick, Gwendolyn. 1997. *Something Left to Lose: Personal Relations and Survival Among New York's Homeless*. Philadelphia, PA: Temple University Press.
Dorlin, Elsa. 2006. *La Matrice de la race. Généalogie sexuelle et coloniale de la nation française*. Paris: La Découverte.
Doron, Claude-Olivier. 2016. *L'Homme altéré. Races et dégénérescence (XVIIe–XIXe siècles)*. Paris: Champ Vallon.
Dorr, Lisa Lindquist. 2004. *White Women, Rape, and the Power of Race in Virginia, 1900–1960*. Chapel Hill, NC: University of North Carolina Press.
Douds, Kiara Wyndham and Michael Hout. 2020. "Microaggressions in the United States." *Sociological Science* 7: 528–43.
Douglas, Mary. 1956. *Purity and Danger: An Analysis of Concept of Pollution and Taboo*. London: Routledge, new edition 2002.
Douglas, Raymond M. 2002. "Anglo-Saxons and Attacotti: The Racialization of Irishness in Britain between the World Wars." *Ethnic & Racial Studies* 25, no. 1: 40–63.
Douglass, Patrice, Selamawit D. Terrefe, and Frank B. Wilderson, III. 2018. "Afro-Pessimism." *Oxford Bibliographies*, DOI: 10.1093/obo/9780190280024-0056.
Dovidio, John F., Peter Glick, and Laurie A. Rudman (eds.). 2008. *On the Nature of Prejudice: Fifty Years after Allport*. Cambridge, MA: Wiley.
Dower, John. 1987. *War without Mercy: Race and Power in the Pacific War*. New York: Pantheon.
Doyle, Bertram Wilbur. 1937. *The Etiquette of Race Relations in the South: A Study in Social Control*. Chicago, IL: University of Chicago Press.
Doytcheva, Milena. 2007. *Une Discrimination positive à la française? Ethnicité et territoire dans les politiques de la ville*. Paris: La Découverte.
Drake, Deborah H., Rod Earle, and Jennifer Sloan (eds.). 2015. *The Palgrave Handbook of Prison Ethnography*. Basingstoke: Palgrave Macmillan.
Drake, St. Clair and Horace R. Cayton. 1993 [1945]. *Black Metropolis: A Study of Negro Life in a Northern City*. Chicago, IL: University of Chicago Press. expanded edition 1993.
Dray, Philip. 2007. *At the Hands of Persons Unknown: The Lynching of Black America*. New York: Modern Library.
Drescher, Seymour and Stanley L. Engerman (eds.). 1998. *A Historical Guide to World Slavery*. New York: Oxford University Press.
Du Bois, William E. B. 1898. "The Study of the Negro Problems." *The Annals of the American Academy of Political and Social Science* 11, no. 1: 1–23.

Du Bois, William E. B. 1901. *The Negro Landholder of Georgia*. Washington, DC: Bulletin of the US Department of Labor.

Du Bois, William E. B. (ed.). 1903. *The Negro Common School: Report of a Social Study made under the Direction of Atlanta University*. Atlanta, GA: Atlanta University Press.

Du Bois, William E. B. 1920. *Darkwater*. New York: Harcourt Brace.

Du Bois, William E. B. 1978 [1898]. "The Negroes of Farmville, Virginia." Pp. 165–95 in *W. E. B. Du Bois on Sociology and the Black Community*. Edited by Dan S. Green and Edwin Driver. Chicago, IL: University of Chicago Press.

Du Bois, William E. B. 1978 [1901]. "The Relation of the Negroes to the Whites in the South." Pp. 253–70 in *W. E. B. Du Bois on Sociology and the Black Community*. Edited by Dan S. Green and Edwin Driver. Chicago, IL: University of Chicago Press.

Du Bois, William E. B. 1978 [1902]. "The Negroes of Dougherty County, Georgia." Pp. 154–65 in *W. E. B. Du Bois on Sociology and the Black Community*. Edited by Dan S. Green and Edwin Driver. Chicago, IL: University of Chicago Press.

Du Bois, William E. B. 1990 [1903]. *The Souls of Black Folk*. New York: Vintage/The Library of America.

Du Bois, William E. B. 1996 [1897]. "The Conservation of Races." Pp. 38–47 in *The Oxford W. E. B. Du Bois Reader*. Edited by Eric J. Sundquist. New York: Oxford University Press.

Du Bois, William E. B. 2005 [1901]. "The Spawn of Slavery: The Convict Lease System in the South." In *Race, Crime, and Justice: A Reader*. Edited by Shaun Gabbidon and Helen Taylor Greene. London: Routledge.

Du Bois, William E. B. 2006 [1906]. "Die Negerfrage in den Vereinigten Staaten (The Negro Question in the United States)." *CR: The New Centennial Review* 6, no. 3: 241–90.

Du Bois, William E. B. 2010 [1899]. *The Philadelphia Negro: A Social Study*. Philadelphia, PA: University of Pennsylvania Press.

Du Bois, William E. B. 2017 [1935]. *Black Reconstruction, 1860–1880*. New York: Routledge.

Dube, Godwin. 2017. "Levels of Othering: The Case of Zimbabwean Migrants in South Africa." *Nationalism and Ethnic Politics* 23, no. 4: 391–412.

Dubet, François, Olivier Cousin, Éric Macé, and Sandrine Rui. 2013. *"Pourquoi moi?" L'expérience des discriminations*. Paris: Seuil.

Dubow, Saul. 1995. *Scientific Racism in Modern South Africa*. Cambridge: Cambridge University Press.

Dumanli, Özden. 2021. "The Relationship Between the Police and Third-Generation Turkish Immigrants in Germany." *Turkish Journal of Diaspora Studies* 1, no. 2: 37–55.

Duneier, Mitchell. 2016. *Ghetto: The Invention of a Place, the History of an Idea*. New York: Farrar, Straus and Giroux.

References

Durkheim, Émile. 1975 [1908]. "Débat sur l'explication en histoire et en sociologie." Pp. 199–217 in *Textes*. Volume 1, *Éléments de théorie sociale*. Paris: Minuit.
Durkheim, Émile. 1995a [1912]. *Les Formes élémentaires de la vie religieuse. Le système totémique en Australie*. Paris: PUF.
Durkheim, Émile. 1995b [1893]. *De la division du travail social*. Paris: PUF.
Durkheim, Émile and Marcel Mauss. 2017 [1903]. *De quelques formes primitives de classification*. Paris: PUF.
DuRocher, Kristina. 2011. *Raising Racists: The Socialization of White Children in the Jim Crow South*. Lexington, KY: University Press of Kentucky.
Duus, Peter. 1998. *The Abacus and the Sword: The Japanese Penetration of Korea, 1895–1910*. Berkeley, CA: University of California Press.
Dwyer, Philip. 2017. "Violence and Its Histories: Meanings, Methods, Problems." *History & Theory* 56, no. 4: 7–22.
Dwyer, Philip. 2022. *Violence: A Very Short Introduction*. Oxford: Oxford University Press.
Dwyer, Philip and Amanda Nettelbeck (eds.). 2017. *Violence, Colonialism and Empire in the Modern World*. London: Palgrave Macmillan.
Eason, John M. 2017. "Prisons as Panacea or Pariah? The Countervailing Consequences of the Prison Boom on the Political Economy of Rural Towns." *Social Sciences* 6, no. 1: 1–23.
Edwards, Laura F. 2009. "Southern History as US History." *The Journal of Southern History* 75, no. 3: 533–64.
Einaudi, Jean-Luc. 1994. "Octobre 1961, un massacre au coeur de Paris." *Hommes & Migrations* 1175, no. 1: 35–40.
Eisenstein, James, Roy B. Flemming, and Peter F. Nardulli. 1988. *The Contours of Justice: Communities and their Courts*. Boston, MA: Little, Brown.
Eitle, David. 2009. "Dimensions of Racial Segregation, Hypersegregation, and Black Homicide Rates." *Journal of Criminal Justice* 37, no. 1: 28–36.
Elder-Vass, Dave. 2010. *The Causal Power of Social Structures: Emergence, Structure and Agency*. Cambridge: Cambridge University Press.
Elias, Norbert. 1983 [1969]. *The Court Society*. New York: Pantheon.
Elias, Norbert. 1998. *On Civilization, Power, and Knowledge: Selected Writings*. Chicago, IL: University of Chicago Press.
Elkins, Caroline. 2022. *Legacy of Violence: A History of the British Empire*. New York: Random.
Ellis, Edwin. 1993. *The Non-Traditional Approach to Criminal Justice and Social Justice*, mimeograph. Harlem, NY: Community Justice Center.
Ellis, Edwin. 1998. "An Interview with Eddie Ellis." *Humanity and Society* 22, no. 1: 98–111.
Ellison, Ralph. 2003. *The Collected Essays of Ralph Ellison*. Edited by John Callahan. New York: Modern Library Classics.
Emirbayer, Mustafa and Matthew Desmond. 2015. *The Racial Order*. Chicago, IL: University of Chicago Press.

Enos, Sandra. 2001. *Mothering from the Inside: Parenting in a Women's Prison.* Binghamton, NY: SUNY Press.

Ergin, Murat. 2014. "The Racialization of Kurdish Identity in Turkey." *Ethnic & Racial Studies* 37, no. 2: 322–41.

Éribon, Didier. 1986. *Michel Foucault.* Paris: Plon.

Erichsen, Casper and David Olusoga. 2010. *The Kaiser's Holocaust: Germany's Forgotten Genocide and the Colonial Roots of Nazism.* London: Faber & Faber.

Erlenbusch-Anderson, Verena. 2018. *Genealogies of Terrorism: Revolution, State Violence, Empire.* New York: Columbia University Press.

Erlenbusch-Anderson, Verena. 2022. "Historicizing White Supremacist Terrorism with Ida B. Wells." *Political Theory* 50, no. 2: 275–304.

Escafré-Dublet, Angéline, Virginie Guiraudon, and Julien Talpin. 2023. "Fighting Discrimination in a Hostile Political Environment: The Case of 'Colour-Blind' France." *Ethnic & Racial Studies* 46, no. 4: 667–85.

Esping-Andersen, Gøsta. 1987. *The Three Worlds of Welfare Capitalism.* Princeton, NJ: Princeton University Press.

Essner, Cornelia. 1995. "Qui sera 'juif'? La classification 'raciale' nazie des 'lois de Nuremberg' à la 'conférence de Wannsee'." *Genèses* 21: 4–28.

Evans, Ivan. 1997. *Bureaucracy and Race: Native Administration in South Africa.* Berkeley, CA: University of California Press.

Fabini, Giulia. 2023. *Polizia e migranti in città. Negoziare il confine nei contesti locali.* Rome: Carocci.

Falola, Toyin. 2009. *Colonialism and Violence in Nigeria.* Bloomington, IN: Indiana University Press.

Fanon, Frantz. 2011 [1956]. "Racisme et culture." Pp. 326–44 in *Œuvres.* Paris: La Découverte.

Fantasia, Rick. 1989. *Cultures of Solidarity: Consciousness, Action, and Contemporary American Workers.* Berkeley, CA: University of California Press.

Fasseur, Cees. 1994. "Cornerstone and Stumbling Block: Racial Classification and the Late Colonial State in Indonesia." Pp. 31–56 in *The Late Colonial State in Indonesia: Political and Economic Foundations of the Netherlands Indies, 1880–1942.* Edited by Robert Bridson Cribb. Amsterdam: Cellar Book.

Fassin, Didier. 2002. "L'invention française de la discrimination." *Revue française de science politique* 52, no. 4: 403–23.

Fassin, Éric. 2017. *Populisme. Le grand ressentiment.* Paris: Éditions Textuel.

Fassin, Éric and Didier Fassin (eds.). 2006. *De la question sociale à la question raciale. Représenter la société française.* Paris: La Découverte

Feagin, Joe R. 2020. *The White Racial Frame: Centuries of Racial Framing and Counter-Framing.* New York: Routledge.

Feeley, Malcolm M. 1983. *Court Reform on Trial: Why Simple Solutions Fail.* New York: Basic Books. Reprint Quid Pro Books, 2013.

References

Feimster, Crystal N. 2009. *Southern Horrors: Women and the Politics of Rape and Lynching*. Cambridge, MA: Harvard University Press.

Feldman, Glenn. 2004. *The Disfranchisement Myth: Poor Whites and Suffrage Restriction in Alabama*. Athens, GA: University of Georgia Press.

Feldmann, Magnus. 2019. "Global Varieties of Capitalism." *World Politics* 71, no. 1: 162–96.

Fellner, Jamie and Marc Mauer. 1998. *Losing the Vote: The Impact of Felony Disenfranchisement in the United States*. Washington, DC: The Sentencing Project and Human Rights Watch.

Feres Júnior, João, Luiz Augusto Campos, Verônica Toste Daflon, and Anna Carolina Venturini. 2018. *Ação afirmativa. Conceito, história e debates*. Rio de Janeiro: Editora da Universidade do Estado do Rio de Janeiro.

Fibbi, Rosita, Arnfinn H. Midtbøen, and Patrick Simon. 2021. *Migration and Discrimination*. Berlin: Springer.

Fields, Barbara J. 1982. "Race and Ideology in American History." Pp. 143–77 in *Region, Race, and Reconstruction: Essays in the Honor of C. Vann Woodward*. Edited by J. Morgan Kousser and James M. McPherson. New York: Oxford University Press.

Fields, Barbara J. 1990. "Slavery, Race and Ideology in the United States of America." *New Left Review* 181, no. 1: 95–118.

Fields, Karen E. and Barbara J. Fields. 2014. *Racecraft: The Soul of Inequality in American Life*. London: Verso.

Filiu, Jean-Pierre. 2012. *Histoire de Gaza*. Paris: Fayard.

Finley, Moses. 1968. "Slavery." Pp. 307–13 in *International Encyclopedia of the Social Sciences*. Edited by David L. Sills and Robert K. Merton. New York: Macmillan and the Free Press.

Fischer-Tiné, Harald and Susanne Gehrmann (eds.). 2008. *Empires and Boundaries: Race, Class, and Gender in Colonial Settings*. New York: Routledge.

Fleming, Crystal Marie. 2017. *Resurrecting Slavery: Racial Legacies and White Supremacy in France*. Philadelphia, PA: Temple University Press.

Fligstein, Neil. 1981. *Going North: Migration of Blacks and Whites from the South, 1900–1950*. New York: Academic Press.

Fligstein, Neil. 2021. *The Banks Did It: An Anatomy of the Financial Crisis*. Cambridge, MA: Harvard University Press.

Flynn, Charles L. Jr. 1999. *White Land, Black Labor: Caste and Class in Late Nineteenth-century Georgia*. Baton Rouge, LA: Louisiana State University Press.

Flynt, Wayne. 2004. *Dixie's Forgotten People: The South's Poor Whites*. Bloomington, IN: Indiana University Press.

Foley, Neil. 1998. *The White Scourge: Mexicans, Blacks, and Poor Whites in Texas Cotton Culture*. Berkeley, CA: University of California Press.

Foner, Eric. 1988. *Reconstruction: America's Unfinished Revolution, 1863–1877*. New York: Harper & Row.

Foner, Philip S. (ed.). 1970. *W. E. B. Du Bois Speaks: Speeches and Addresses, 1890–1919*. New York: Pathfinder Press.

Forman, James Jr. 2012. "Racial Critiques of Mass Incarceration: Beyond the New Jim Crow." *New York University Law Review* 87: 101–46.

Forman, James Jr. 2017. *Locking Up Our Own: Crime and Punishment in Black America*. New York: Farrar, Straus and Giroux.

Fortner, Michael Javen. 2015. *Black Silent Majority: The Rockefeller Drug Laws and the Politics of Punishment*. Cambridge, MA: Harvard University Press.

Foucault, Michel. 1975. *Surveiller et punir. Naissance de la prison*. Paris: Gallimard.

Foucault, Michel. 1976. *Histoire de la* sexualité. Vol. 1. *La volonté de savoir*. Paris: Gallimard.

Foucault, Michel. 1980. *Power/Knowledge: Selected Interviews and Other Writings, 1972–1977*. New York: Pantheon.

Foucault, Michel. 1994a. *Dits et écrits*, 4 volumes. Paris: Gallimard.

Foucault, Michel. 1994b [1982]. "Technologies du soi," in *Dits et écrits*, volume 4. Paris: Gallimard.

Foucault, Michel. 1997. *Ethics: Subjectivity and Truth. Essential Works of Michel Foucault, 1954–1984*. Vol. 1. New York: New Press.

Fourcaut, Annie. 1986. *Bobigny, banlieue rouge*. Paris: Éditions de l'Atelier.

Fournier, Lauren. 2021. *Autotheory as Feminist Practice in Art, Writing, and Criticism*. Cambridge, MA: MIT Press.

Frantz, Klaus. [1993] 1999. *Indian Reservations in the United States: Territory, Sovereignty, and Socioeconomic Change*. Chicago, IL: University of Chicago Press.

Fraser, Nancy. 1999. "From Redistribution to Recognition? Dilemmas of Justice in a 'Postsocialist' Age." *New Left Review* 212: 68–149.

Frazier, E. Franklin. 1932. *The Negro Family in Chicago*. Chicago, IL: University of Chicago Press.

Frazier, E. Franklin. 1997 [1957]. *Black Bourgeoisie*. New York: Simon and Schuster.

Fredrickson, George M. 1971. *The Black Image in the White Mind: The Debate on Afro-American Character and Destiny, 1817–1914*. Hanover, NH: Wesleyan University Press, expanded edition 1987.

Fredrickson, George M. 1981. *White Supremacy: A Comparative Study of American and South African History*. New York: Oxford University Press.

Fredrickson, George M. 1996. *Black Liberation: A Comparative History of Black Ideologies in the United States and South Africa*. New York: Oxford University Press.

Fredrickson, George M. 2002. *Racism: A Short History*. Princeton, NJ: Princeton University Press.

Fredrickson, George M. 2005. "Mulattoes and Métis. Attitudes Toward Miscegenation in the United States and France since the Seventeenth Century." *International Social Science Journal* 57, no. 183: 103–12.

References

Frémeaux, Jacques. 2010. *De quoi fut fait l'empire. Les guerres coloniales au XIXe siècle*. Paris: Éditions du CNRS.

French, Jan Hoffman. 2009. *Legalizing identities: Becoming Black or Indian in Brazil's Northeast*. Chapel Hill, NC: University of North Carolina Press.

Furber, David. 2004. "Near as Far in the Colonies: The Nazi Occupation of Poland." *The International History Review* 26, no. 3: 541–79.

Fusfeld, Daniel R. and Timothy Bates. 1984. *The Political Economy of the Ghetto*. Carbondale, IL: Southern Illinois University Press.

Galenson, David W. 1982. *White Servitude in Colonial America: An Economic Analysis*. New York: Cambridge University Press.

Gallie, Walter Bryce. 1955. "Essentially Contested Concepts." *Proceedings of the Aristotelian Society* 56: 167–98.

Galonnier, Juliette. 2015. "The Enclave, the Citadel and the Ghetto: The Threefold Segregation of Upper-Class Muslims in India." *International Journal of Urban and Regional Research* 39, no. 1: 92–111.

Gandhi, Leela. 2019. *Postcolonial Theory: A Critical Introduction*. New York: Columbia University Press.

Gans, Herbert J. 1979. "Symbolic Ethnicity: The Future of Ethnic Groups and Cultures in America." *Ethnic & Racial Studies* 2, no. 1: 1–20.

García, Lorea Arenas and Elisa García España. 2022. "Police Stop and Search in Spain: An Overview of Its Use, Impacts and Challenges." *InDret* 3: 233–57.

Garland, David. 1991. "Punishment and Culture: The Symbolic Dimension of Criminal Justice." *Studies in Law, Politics, and Society* 11: 191–222.

Garland, David (ed.). 2001. *Mass Imprisonment: Social Causes and Consequences*. Newbury Park, CA: Sage.

Garland, David. 2005. "Penal Excess and Surplus Meaning: Public Torture Lynchings in Twentieth-Century America." *Law & Society Review* 39, no. 4: 793–834.

Gavins, Raymond. 2004. "Literature on Jim Crow." *OAH Magazine of History* 18, no. 2: 13–16.

Gaynes, Elizabeth A. 1993. "Young + Black + Male: Probable Cause." *Fordham Urban Law Journal* 20, no 3: 612–40.

Gazit, Nir. 2015. "State-Sponsored Vigilantism: Jewish Settlers' Violence in the Occupied Palestinian Territories." *Sociology* 49, no. 3: 438–54.

Gee, Gilbert C. and Chandra L. Ford. 2011. "Structural Racism and Health Inequities: Old Issues, New Directions." *Du Bois Review: Social Science Research on Race* 8, no. 1: 115–32.

Gellman, Eric S. 2012. *Death Blow to Jim Crow: The National Negro Congress and the Rise of Militant Civil Rights*. Chapel Hill, NC: University of North Carolina Press.

Genovese, Eugene D. 1976. *Roll, Jordan, Roll: The World the Slaves Made*. New York: Vintage.

Genovese, Eugene D. and Elizabeth Fox-Genovese. 2010. *Fatal Self-Deception: Slaveholding Paternalism in the Old South*. New York: Cambridge University Press.

Gerlach, Christian. 2010. *Extremely Violent Societies*. New York: Cambridge University Press.

Gerstel, Naomi, Cynthia J. Bogard, Jeff McConnell, and Michael Schwartz. 1996. "The Therapeutic Incarceration of the Homeless." *Social Service Review* 70, no. 4: 543–72.

Ghiles-Meilhac, Samuel. 2016. "Qui parle pour les Noirs de France?." la viedesidees.fr, 12 October.

Ghodsee, Kristen. 2009. *Muslim Lives in Eastern Europe: Gender, Ethnicity, and the Transformation of Islam in Postsocialist Bulgaria*. Princeton, NJ: Princeton University Press.

Ghosh, Durba. 2017. *Gentlemanly Terrorists: Political Violence and the Colonial State in India, 1919–1947*. Cambridge: Cambridge University Press.

Gilbert, Alan. 2012. "On the Absence of Ghettos in Latin American Cities." Pp. 191–224 in *The Ghetto: Contemporary Global Issues and Controversies*. Edited by Ray Hutchinson and Bruce D. Haynes. Boulder, CO: Westview.

Gilens, Martin. 1999. *Why Americans Hate Welfare: Race, Media, and the Politics of Anti-Poverty Policy*. Chicago, IL: University of Chicago Press.

Gilmore, Glenda Elizabeth. 1996. *Gender and Jim Crow: Women and the Politics of White Supremacy in North Carolina, 1896–1920*. Chapel Hill, NC: University of North Carolina Press.

Gilmore, Ruth Wilson. 2021. "Geographies of Racial Capitalism." Antipode Foundation Film, https://www.youtube.com/watch?v=2CS627aKrJI.

Gilmore, Ruth Wilson. 2022. *Abolition Geography: Essays Towards Liberation*. London: Verso.

Gilpin, R. Blakesly. 2015. "American Racial Terrorism from Brown to Booth to Birmingham." Pp. 143–55 in *The Routledge History of Terrorism*. Edited by Randall D. Law. New York: Routledge.

Giraud, Michel. 1980. "Races, classes et colonialisme à la Martinique." *L'Homme et la société* 55: 199–214.

Gjerde, Jon. 1998. "The Invention of Ethnicity in the United States." Pp. 22–9 in *Major Problems in American Immigration and Ethnic History*. Edited by Jon Gjerde. Boston, MA: Houghton Mifflin.

Glasser, Ira. 1999. "American Drug Laws: The New Jim Crow." *Albany Law Review* 63, no. 3: 703–24.

Glassman, Jonathon. 2011. *War of Words, War of Stones: Racial Thought and Violence in Colonial Zanzibar*. Bloomington, IN: Indiana University Press.

Glenn, Evelyn Nakano. 2004. *Unequal Freedom: How Race and Gender Shaped American Citizenship and Labor*. Cambridge, MA: Harvard University Press.

Glenn, Evelyn Nakano (ed.). 2009. *Shades of Difference: Why Skin Color Matters*. Stanford, CA: Stanford University Press.

References

Go, Julian. 2018. "Postcolonial Possibilities for the Sociology of Race." *Sociology of Race and Ethnicity* 4, no. 4: 439–51.

Go, Julian. 2021. "Three Tensions in the Theory of Racial Capitalism." *Sociological Theory* 39, no. 1: 38–47.

Go, Julian. 2023. *Policing Empires: Militarization, Race, and the Imperial Boomerang in Britain and the US*. New York: Oxford University Press.

Goertz, Gary. 2020. *Social Science Concepts and Measurement*. Princeton, NJ: Princeton University Press.

Goffman, Erving. 1959. "The Nature of Deference and Demeanor." *American Anthropologist* 58, no. 3: 473–502.

Goffman, Erving. 1963. *Stigma: Notes on the Management of Spoiled Identity*. New York: Touchstone.

Golash-Boza, Tanya Marie. 2011. *Yo Soy Negro: Blackness in Peru*. Gainesville, FL: University Press of Florida.

Golash-Boza, Tanya. 2016. "A Critical and Comprehensive Sociological Theory of Race and Racism." *Sociology of Race and Ethnicity* 2, no. 2: 129–41.

Gold, Steven J. 2004. "From Jim Crow to Racial Hegemony: Evolving Explanations of Racial Hierarchy." *Ethnic & Racial Studies* 27, no. 6: 951–68.

Goldberg, David Theo. 2002. *The Racial State*. Malden, MA: Blackwell.

Goldfield, David. 1991. *Black, White, and Southern: Race Relations and Southern Culture, 1940 to the Present*. Baton Rouge, LA: Louisiana State University Press.

Goldstein, Donna. 2003. *Laughter Out of Place: Race, Class, Violence, and Sexuality in a Rio Shantytown*. Berkeley, CA: University of California Press.

Gone, Joseph P., William E. Hartmann, Andrew Pomerville, Dennis C. Wendt, Sarah H. Klem, and Rachel L. Burrage. 2919. "The Impact of Historical Trauma on Health Outcomes for Indigenous Populations in the USA and Canada: A Systematic Review." *American Psychologist* 74, no. 1: 20–35.

Goodman, Philip. 2008. "'It's just Black, White, or Hispanic': An Observational Study of Racializing Moves in California's Segregated Prison Reception Centers." *Law & Society Review* 42, no. 4: 735–70.

Gordon, Fon Louise. 2007 *Caste and Class: The Black Experience in Arkansas, 1880–1920*. Athens, GA: University of Georgia Press.

Gordon, Neve. 2008. *Israel's Occupation*. Berkeley, CA: University of California Press.

Gottreich, Emily. 2007. *The Mellah of Marrakesh: Jewish and Muslim Space in Morocco's Red City*. Bloomington, IN: Indiana University Press.

Gottschalk, Marie. 2015. *Caught: The Prison State and the Lockdown of American Politics*. Princeton, NJ: Princeton University Press.

Gottschalk, Marie. 2006. *The Prison and the Gallows: The Politics of Mass Incarceration in America*. Cambridge: Cambridge University Press.

Gould, Stephen Jay. 1981. *The Mismeasure of Man*. New York: Norton.
Gowan, Teresa. 2000. "Excavating Globalization from Street Level: Homeless Men Recycle Their Pasts." Pp. 74–105 in *Global Ethnography: Forces, Connections, and Imaginations*. Edited by Michael Burawoy. Berkeley, CA: University of California Press.
Graeber, David. 2011. *Debt: The First Five Thousand Years*. New York: Melville House.
Green, Adam. 2007. *Selling the Race: Culture, Community, and Black Chicago, 1940–1955*. Chicago, IL: University of Chicago Press.
Greenberg, Stanley. 1980. *Race and Class in Capitalist Development: Comparative Perspectives*. New Haven, CT: Yale University Press.
Greenwald, Anthony G. and Mahzarin R. Banaji. 2017. "The Implicit Revolution: Reconceiving the Relation between Conscious and Unconscious." *American Psychologist* 72, no. 9: 861–71.
Gregory, James N. 2005. *The Southern Diaspora: How the Great Migrations of Black and White Southerners Transformed America*. Chapel Hill, NC: University of North Carolina Press.
Gross, Ariela. 2008. *What Blood Won't Tell: A History of Race on Trial in America*. Cambridge, MA: Harvard University Press.
Grossman, James R. 1989. *Land of Hope: Chicago, Black Southerners, and the Great Migration*. Chicago, IL: University of Chicago Press.
Grossman, James R. 2000. "A Chance to Make Good, 1900–1929." Pp. 345–408 in *To Make the World Anew: A History of African Americans*. Edited by Robin D. G. Kelley and Earl Lewis. New York: Oxford University Press.
Gruber, Aya. 2021. *The Feminist War on Crime: The Unexpected Role of Women's Liberation in Mass Incarceration*. Berkeley, CA: University of California Press.
Guglielmo, Thomas Angelo. 2000. *White on Arrival: Italians, Race, Color, and Power in Chicago, 1890–1945*. New York: Oxford University Press.
Guillaumin, Colette. 2017 [1972]. *L'Idéologie du racisme. Genèse et langage actuel*. Paris: Mouton.
Guillory, Monique. 1999. *Some Enchanted Evening on the Auction Block: The Cultural Legacy of the New Orleans Quadroon Balls*. New York: NYU Press.
Hacking, Ian. 1985. "Making Up People." Pp. 160–71 in *Reconstructing Individualism*. Edited by T. L. Heller. Stanford, CA: Stanford University Press.
Hacking, Ian. 1999. *The Social Construction of What?* Cambridge, MA: Harvard University Press.
Hacking, Ian. 2005. "Why Race Still Matters." *Daedalus: Journal of the American Academy of Arts and Sciences* 134, no. 1: 102–16.
Haddad, Marine. 2018. "Des minorités pas comme les autres? Le vécu des discriminations et du racisme des ultramarins en métropole." *Revue française de sociologie* 59, no. 4: 649–76.
Hagedorn, John and Brigid Rauch. 2007. "Housing, Gangs, and Homicide:

References

What We Can Learn from Chicago." *Urban Affairs Review* 42, no. 4: 435–56.

Hagood, Margaret Jarman. 1930. *Mothers of the South: Portraiture of the White Tenant Farm Woman*. Chapel Hill, NC: University of North Carolina Press.

Hahn, Steven. 2005. *A Nation Under Our Feet: Black Political Struggles in the Rural South from Slavery to the Great Migration*. Cambridge, MA: Harvard University Press.

Hale, Grace Elizabeth. 2010. *Making Whiteness: The Culture of Segregation in the South, 1890–1940*. New York: Vintage.

Haley, Sarah. 2016. *No Mercy Here: Gender, Punishment, and the Making of Jim Crow Modernity*. Chapel Hill, NC: University of North Carolina Press.

Hall, Bruce S. 2011. *A History of Race in Muslim West Africa, 1600–1960*. Cambridge: Cambridge University Press.

Hall, Bruce S. 2019. "Race." Pp. 177–200 in *A Cultural History of Western Empires in the Modern Age*. Edited by Patricia M. E. Lorcin. London: Bloomsbury Academic.

Hall, Bruce S. 2020. "Reading Race in Africa and the Middle East." *Antropologia* 7, no. 1: 33–44.

Hall, Peter and David Soskice (eds.). 2001. *Varieties of Capitalism. The Institutional Foundations of Comparative Advantage*. Oxford: Oxford University Press.

Hall, Stuart. 2017. *The Fateful Triangle: Race, Ethnicity, Nation*. Cambridge, MA: Harvard University Press.

Hanchard, Michael G. 2018. *The Spectre of Race: How Discrimination Haunts Western Democracy*. Princeton, NJ: Princeton University Press.

Handler, Joel. 1997. *Down with Bureaucracy: The Ambiguity of Privatization and Empowerment*. Princeton, NJ: Princeton University Press.

Hane, Mikiso. 1982. *Peasants, Rebels, Women, and Outcastes*. New York: Pantheon.

Haney, Lynne. 2010. *Offending Women: Power, Punishment, and the Regulation of Desire*. Berkeley, CA: University of California Press.

Hannaford, Ivan. 1996. *Race: The History of an Idea in the West*. Baltimore, MD: Johns Hopkins University Press.

Hardimon, Michael. 2017. *Rethinking Race: A Case for Deflationary Realism*. Cambridge, MA: Harvard University Press.

Harlow, Caroline Wolf. 1998. *Profile of Jail Inmates 1996*. Washington, DC: Bureau of Justice Statistics.

Harris, James (ed.). 2013. *The Anatomy of Terror: Political Violence Under Stalin*. New York: Oxford University Press.

Harris, J. William. 1995. "Etiquette, Lynching, and Racial Boundaries in Southern History: A Mississippi Example." *The American Historical Review* 100, no. 2: 387–410.

Harris, Marvin. 1980. *Patterns of Race in the Americas*. New York: Norton.

Harvey, David. 1973. *Social Justice and the City*. Baltimore, MD: Johns Hopkins University Press.
Hassine, Victor. 1999. *Life Without Parole: Living in Prison Today*, 2nd edition. Los Angeles: Roxbury.
Hatch, Anthony Ryan. 2022. "The Data Will Not Save Us: Afropessimism and Racial Antimatter in the COVID-19 Pandemic." *Big Data & Society* 9, no. 1: https://doi.org/10.1177/20539517211067948.
Hattam, Victoria. 2007. *In the Shadow of Race. Jews, Latinos, and Immigration Politics in the United States*. Chicago, IL: University of Chicago Press.
Hawkins, Mike. 1997. *Social Darwinism in European and American Thought, 1860–1945*. Cambridge: Cambridge University Press.
Hawley, Amos A. 1950. *Human Ecology: A Theory of Community Structure*. Glencoe, IL: Free Press.
Hays, Sharon. 2004. *Flat Broke with Children: Women in the Age of Welfare Reform*. New York: Oxford University Press.
Hedström, Peter and Peter Bearman (eds.). 2009. *The Oxford Handbook of Analytical Sociology*. New York: Oxford University Press.
Heilbron, Johan. 1995. *The Rise of Social Theory*. Minneapolis, MN: University of Minnesota Press.
Hellman, Deborah. 2008. *When Is Discrimination Wrong?* Cambridge, MA: Harvard University Press.
Heng, Geraldine. 2018. *The Invention of Race in the European Middle Ages*. New York: Cambridge University Press.
Herbelin Catherine. 2016. *Architectures du Vietnam colonial*. Paris: CTHS Éditions.
Herpin, Nicolas. 2006. *Le Pouvoir des grands. De l'influence de la taille des hommes sur leur statut*. Paris: La Découverte.
Herrnstein, Richard. 1995. "Criminogenic Traits." Pp. 39–64 in *Crime*. Edited by James Q. Wilson and Joan Petersilia. San Franciso, CA: ICS Press.
Hervik, Peter (ed.). 2019. *Racialization, Racism, and Anti-Racism in the Nordic Countries*. London: Palgrave Macmillan.
Hibou, Béatrice. 2011. *Anatomie politique de la domination*. Paris: La Découverte.
Hicken, Margaret T., Lewis Miles, Solome Haile, and Michael Esposito. 2021. "Linking History to Contemporary State-Sanctioned Slow Violence through Cultural and Structural Racism." *The Annals of the American Academy of Political and Social Science* 694, no. 1: 48–58.
Higginbotham, Evelyn Brooks. 1994. *Righteous Discontent: The Women's Movement in the Black Baptist Church, 1880–1920*. Cambridge, MA: Harvard University Press.
Higginson, John. 2014. *Collective Violence and the Agrarian Origins of South African Apartheid, 1900–1948*. New York: Cambridge University Press.
Hinton, Elizabeth and DeAnza Cook. 2012. "The Mass Criminalization of

References

Black Americans: A Historical Overview." *Annual Review of Criminology* 4: 261–86.
Hirsch, Andrew von. 1999. "Penal Theories." Pp. 659–83 in *The Handbook of Crime and Punishment*. Edited by Michael Tonry. Oxford: Oxford University Press.
Hirsch, Arnold R. 2009 [1984]. *Making the Second Ghetto: Race and Housing in Chicago 1940–1960*. Chicago, IL: University of Chicago Press.
Hirsch, Arnold R. and Joseph Logsdon (eds.). 1992. *Creole New Orleans: Race and Americanization*. Baton Rouge, LA: Louisiana State University Press.
Hirschman, Albert O. 1970. *Exit, Voice, and Loyalty: Responses to Decline in Firms, Organizations, and States*. Cambridge, MA: Harvard University Press.
Hobbs, Allyson. 2014. *A Chosen Exile: A History of Racial Passing in American Life*. Cambridge, MA: Harvard University Press.
Hochschild, Adam. 1998. *King Leopold's Ghost: A Story of Greed, Terror, and Heroism in Colonial Africa*. New York: Picador.
Hochschild, Arlie Russell. 2018. *Strangers in their Own Land: Anger and Mourning on the American Right*. New York: New Press.
Hochschild, Jennifer L. and Vesla Weaver. 2007a. "Policies of Racial Classification and the Politics of Racial Inequality." Pp. 159–82 in *Remaking America: Democracy and Public Policy in an Age of Inequality*. Edited by Joe Soss, Jacob S. Hacker, and Suzanne Mettler. New York: Russell Sage Foundation.
Hochschild, Jennifer L. and Vesla Weaver. 2007b. "The Skin Color Paradox and the American Racial Order." *Social Forces* 86, no. 2: 643–70.
Hochschild, Jennifer L., Vesla M. Weaver, and Traci R. Burch. 2012. *Creating a New Racial Order: How Immigration, Multiracialism, Genomics, and the Young Can Remake Race in America*. Princeton, NJ: Princeton University Press.
Hodes, Martha. 1997. *White Women, Black Men: Illicit Sex in the Nineteenth-Century South*. New Haven, CT: Yale University Press.
Hoetink, Harry. 1985. "'Race' and Color in the Caribbean." Pp. 55–84 in *Caribbean Contours*. Edited by Sidney Mintz and Sally Price. Baltimore, MD: Johns Hopkins University Press.
Hollinger, David A. 2003. "Amalgamation and Hypodescent: The Question of Ethnoracial Mixture in the History of the United States." *The American Historical Review* 108, no. 5: 1363–90.
Holloway, Jonathan Scott. 2013. *Jim Crow Wisdom: Memory and Identity in Black America since 1940*. Chapel Hill, NC: University of North Carolina Press.
Horgan, John and Kurt Braddock (eds.). 2012. *Terrorism Studies: A Reader*. London: Routledge.
Horwitz, Gordon. 2008. *Ghettostadt: Łódź and the Making of a Nazi City*. Cambridge, MA: Harvard University Press.

Houben, Vincent J. H. 2008. "Boundaries of Race: Representations of Indisch in Colonial Indonesia Revisited." Pp. 66–85 in *Empires and Boundaries: Race, Class, and Gender in Colonial Settings*. Edited by Harald Fischer-Tiné and Susanne Gehrmann. London: Routledge.

Hu, Cathy. 2022. *The Struggle to Define Justice: Community Organizing in the Criminal Courts*, MA thesis, Department of Sociology, University of California Berkeley.

Hübinette, Tobias, Catrin Lundström, and Peter Wikström (eds.). 2023. *Race in Sweden: Racism and Antiracism in the World's First "Colourblind" Nation*. London: Routledge.

Hudson, Nicholas. 1996. "From 'Nation' to 'Race': The Origin of Racial Classification in Eighteenth-Century Thought." *Eighteenth-Century Studies* 29, no. 3: 247–64.

Hughes, Everett C. 1984 [1945]. "Dilemmas and Contradictions of Status." Pp. 141–52 in *The Sociological Eye*. Edited by David Riesman and Howard S. Becker. New Brunswick, NJ: Transaction.

Hughes, Langston. 1934. *Home*. Reprinted in *The Ways of White Folks*. New York: Vintage, 1990.

Hunt, Geoffrey, Stephanie Riegel, Tomas Morales, and Dan Waldorf. 1993. "Changes in Prison Culture: Prison Gangs and the Case of the 'Pepsi Generation'." *Social Problems* 40, no. 3: 398–409.

Hunt, Nancy Rose. 2015. *A Nervous State: Violence, Remedies, and Reverie in Colonial Congo*. Durham, NC: Duke University Press.

Hunter, Daniel. 2015. *Building a Movement to End the New Jim Crow: An Organizing Guide*. New York: Hyrax Publishing.

Hunter, Marcus Anthony. 2013. *Black Citymakers: How* The Philadelphia Negro *Changed Urban America*. New York: Oxford University Press.

Hunter, Marcus Anthony and Zandria F. Robinson. 2016. "The Sociology of Urban Black America." *Annual Review of Sociology* 42: 385–405.

Hunter, Tera W. 1997. *To "Joy My Freedom": Southern Black Women's Lives and Labors after the Civil War*. Cambridge, MA: Harvard University Press.

Husak, Douglas. 2023. "Six Questions about Overcriminalization." *Annual Review of Criminology* 6: 265–84.

Hutchinson, Harry William. 1957. *Village and Plantation Life in Northeastern Brazil*. Seattle, WA: University of Washington Press.

Ichou, Mathieu. 2018. *Les Enfants d'immigrés à l'école. Inégalités scolaires du primaire à l'enseignement supérieur*. Paris: PUF.

Ignatiev, Noel. 1994. *How the Irish Became White*. Cambridge, MA: Harvard University Press.

Ingrao, Christian. 2016. *La Promesse de l'Est. Espérance nazie et génocide, 1939–1943*. Paris: Seuil.

Ireland, Patrick. 2008. "Comparing Responses to Ethnic Segregation in Urban Europe." *Urban Studies* 45, no. 7: 1333–58.

References

Irwin, John. 1980. *Prisons in Turmoil*. Boston: Little, Brown.
Irwin, John. 1990 [1970]. *The Felon*. Berkeley, CA: University of California Press.
Irwin, John. 2004. *The Warehouse Prison: Disposal of the New Dangerous Class*. Los Angeles, CA: Roxbury.
Irwin, John and Donald R. Cressey. 1962. "Thieves, Convicts and the Inmate Culture." *Social Problems* 10, no. 2: 142–55.
Isaac, Benjamin. 2013. *The Invention of Racism in Classical Antiquity*. Princeton, NJ: Princeton University Press.
Isenberg, Nancy. 2016. *White Trash: The 400-Year Untold History of Class in America*. New York: Penguin.
Ismard, Paulin (ed.). 2021. *Les Mondes de l'esclavage. Une histoire comparée*. Paris: Seuil.
Issar, Siddhant. 2021. "Listening to Black Lives Matter: Racial Capitalism and the Critique of Neoliberalism." *Contemporary Political Theory* 20, no. 1: 48–71.
Itzigsohn, José and Karida L. Brown. 2020. *The Sociology of WEB Du Bois*. New York: New York University Press.
Jacobs, James B. 1977. *Stateville: The Penitentiary in Mass Society*. Chicago, IL: University of Chicago Press.
Jacobs, James B. 1980. "The Prisoners' Rights Movement and Its Impacts, 1960–80." *Crime and Justice* 2: 429–70.
Jacobs, James B. 1983. "Race Relations and the Prisoner Subculture." Pp. 61–79 in *New Perspectives on Prisons and Imprisonment*. Ithaca, NY: Cornell University Press.
Jacobs, James B. 2015. *The Eternal Criminal Record*. Cambridge, MA: Harvard University Press.
Jacobson, Matthew Frye. 1998. *Whiteness of a Different Color: European Immigrants and the Alchemy of Race*. Cambridge, MA: Harvard University Press.
Jaffrelot, Christophe and Laurent Gayer (eds.). 2012. *Muslims in Indian Cities: Trajectories of Marginalisation*. New York: Columbia University Press.
Jaffrelot, Christophe, Sharik Laliwala, and Sophie Renaut. 2020. "Les paradoxes de la ghettoïsation en Inde. Le cas de Juhapura." *Critique* 872/873: 48–63.
James, C. L. R. 1963. *The Black Jacobins: Toussaint L'Ouverture and the San Domingo Revolution*. New York: Random House, new edition Vintage, 1989.
Janken, Kenneth Robert. 2003. *White: The Biography of Walter White, Mr. NAACP*. New York: The New Press.
Jefferson, Margo. 1915. *Negroland: A Memoir*. New York: Vintage.
Jett, Brandon T. 2021. *Race, Crime, and Policing in the Jim Crow South: African Americans and Law Enforcement in Birmingham, Memphis, and New Orleans, 1920–1945*. Baton Rouge, LA: Louisiana State University Press.

Jobard, Fabien, René Lévy, John Lamberth, and Sophie Névanen. 2012. "Mesurer les discriminations selon l'apparence. Une analyse des contrôles d'identité à Paris." *Population* 67, no. 3: 423–51.

Johnson, Brian D. and Pilar Larroulet. 2019. "The 'Distance Traveled': Investigating the Downstream Consequences of Charge Reductions for Disparities in Incarceration." *Justice Quarterly* 36, no. 7, 1229–57.

Johnson, Cedric. 2023. *After Black Lives Matter*. London: Verso.

Johnson, Charles S. 1934. *Shadow of the Plantation*. New York: Routledge.

Johnson, Eric A. 2000. *Nazi Terror: The Gestapo, Jews, and Ordinary Germans*. New York: Basic Books.

Johnson, Kimberley. 2010. *Reforming Jim Crow: Southern Politics and State in the Age Before Brown*. New York: Oxford University Press.

Johnson, Michael P. and James L. Roark. 1984. *Black Masters: A Free Family of Color in the Old South*. New York: W.W. Norton.

Johnson, Paul. 1987. *A History of the Jews*. New York: Harper.

Johnson, Robert. 1996. *Hard Time: Understanding and Reforming the Prison*, 2nd edition. Belmont, CA: Wadsworth Publishing.

Johnson, Walter. 2013. *River of Dark Dreams: Slavery and Empire in the Cotton Kingdom*. Cambridge, MA: Harvard University Press.

Johnson, Walter with Robin D.G. Kelley (eds.). 2018. *Race, Capitalism, Justice*. Cambridge, MA: MIT Press.

Jones, Jacqueline. 1985. *Labor of Love, Labor of Sorrow: Black Women, Work, and the Family, from Slavery to the Present*. New York: Basic Books, new edition 2010.

Jones, LeAlan and Lloyd Newman. 1997. *Our America: Life and Death on the South Side of Chicago*. New York: Washington Square Press.

Jones, William Powell. 2005. *The Tribe of Black Ulysses: African American Lumber Workers in the Jim Crow South*. Urbana, IL: University of Illinois Press.

Jordan, Winthrop D. 1968. *White over Black: American Attitudes toward the Negro, 1550–1812*. Chapel Hill, NC: University of North Carolina Press, new edition 2012.

Jung, Moon-Kie and João H. Costa Vargas (eds.). 2021. *Antiblackness*. Durham, NC: Duke University Press.

Kagabo, José and Vincent Mudandagizi. 1974. "Complainte des gens de l'argile. Les Twa du Rwanda." *Cahiers d'études africaines* 53: 75–87.

Kahn, Jonathan. 2017. *Race on the Brain: What Implicit Bias Gets Wrong about the Struggle for Racial Justice*. New York: Columbia University Press.

Kalyvas, Stathis N. 2003. "The Ontology of 'Political Violence': Action and Identity in Civil Wars." *Perspectives on Politics* 1, no. 3: 475–94.

Kaplan, Gregory B. 2012. "The Inception of *limpieza de sangre* (Purity of Blood) and its Impact in Medieval and Golden Age Spain." Pp. 19–41 in *Marginal Voices: Studies in Converso Literature of Medieval and Golden Age Spain*. Edited by Amy I. Aronson-Friedman and Gregory B. Kaplan. London: Brill.

References

Karklins, Rasma. 1986. *Ethnic Relations in the USSR: The Perspective from Below*. Boston: Allen & Unwin.

Karstedt, Susanne. 2013. "Contextualizing Mass Atrocity Crimes: Moving Toward a Relational Approach." *Annual Review of Law and Social Science* 9: 383–404.

Katz, Michael B. 2013. *The Undeserving Poor: America's Enduring Confrontation with Poverty*. New York: Basic Books.

Katzew, Ilona and Susan Deans-Smith (eds.). *Race and Classification: The Case of Mexican America*. Stanford, CA: Stanford University Press.

Katznelson, Ira. 1976. *Black Men, White Cities: Race, Politics and Migration in the United States, 1900–30, and Britain, 1948–68*. Chicago, IL: University of Chicago Press.

Katznelson, Ira. 2005. *When Affirmative Action Was White: An Untold History of Racial Inequality in Twentieth-Century America*. New York: Norton.

Keane, John. 1996. *Reflections on Violence*. London: Verso.

Kelley, Blair and Claudrena Harold. 2020. "The Historiography of the Black South from Reconstruction to Jim Crow." Pp. 245–73 in *Reinterpreting Southern Histories: Essays in Historiography*. Edited by Craig Thompson Friend and Lorri Glover. Baton Rouge, LA: Louisiana State University Press.

Kelley, Robin D. G. 1994. *Race Rebels: Culture, Politics, and the Black Working Class*. New York: Free Press.

Kelley, Robin D. G. 2000. "Preface." Pp. xi–xxvi in Cedric Robinson, *Black Marxism: The Making of the Black Radical Tradition*. Chapel Hill, NC: University of North Carolina Press.

Kelley, Robin D. G. 2015 [1990]. *Hammer and Hoe: Alabama Communists during the Great Depression*. Chapel Hill, NC: University of North Carolina Press.

Kelley, Robin D. G. 2017. "What Did Cedric Robinson Mean by Racial Capitalism?" *Boston Review* 12.

Kelley, Robin D. G. and Earl Lewis (eds.). 2000. *To Make Our World Anew: A History of African Americans*. New York: Oxford University Press.

Kendi, Ibram X. 2022. "The Double Terror of Being Black in America." *The Atlantic*, 20 May.

Kennedy, Randall. 1997. "Race, Law, and Suspicion: Using Color as a Proxy for Dangerousness." Pp. 136–67 in *Race, Crime and the Law*. New York: Pantheon.

Kennedy, Randall. 2012. *Interracial Intimacies: Sex, Marriage, Identity, and Adoption*. New York: Vintage.

Kennedy, Stetson. 1990 [1959]. *Jim Crow Guide: The Way It Was*. Boca Raton, FL: Florida Atlantic University Press.

Kertzer, David and Dominique Arel (eds.). 2002. *Census and Identity: The Politics of Race, Ethnicity, and Language in National Censuses*. Cambridge: Cambridge University Press.

Key, V. O. 1983 [1949]. *Southern Politics in State and Nation*. New York: Knopf.

Kiernan, Ben. 2007. *Blood and Soil: A World History of Genocide and Extermination from Sparta to Darfur*. New Haven, CT: Yale University Press.

Kilgore, James. 2013. "Progress or More of the Same? Electronic Monitoring and Parole in the Age of Mass Incarceration." *Critical Criminology* 21: 123–39.

Kim, Nadia Y. 2008. *Imperial Citizens: Koreans and Race from Seoul to LA*. Stanford, CA: Stanford University Press.

King, Anthony D. 1976. *Colonial Urban Development: Culture, Social Power and Environment*. London: Routledge, reprint 2017.

King, Desmond S. 1995. *Separate and Unequal: Black Americans and the U.S. Federal Government*. New York: Oxford University Press.

King, Desmond S. 2002. *Making Americans: Immigration, Race, and the Origins of the Diverse Democracy*. Cambridge, MA: Harvard University Press.

King, Desmond S. and Rogers M. Smith. 2011. *Still a House Divided: Race and Politics in Obama's America*. Princeton, NJ: Princeton University Press.

King, Roy D. 1999. "The Rise and Rise of Supermax: An American Solution in Search of a Problem?" *Punishment & Society* 1, no. 2: 163–86.

King, Ryan D. and Michael T. Light. 2019. "Have Racial and Ethnic Disparities in Sentencing Declined?" *Crime and Justice* 48, no. 1: 365–437.

Kirk, David S. 2019. "Where the Other 1 Percent Live: An Examination of Changes in the Spatial Concentration of the Formerly Incarcerated." *RSF: The Russell Sage Foundation Journal of the Social Sciences* 5, no. 1: 255–74.

Kirk, David S. and Sara Wakefield. 2018. "Collateral Consequences of Punishment: A Critical Review and Path Forward." *Annual Review of Criminology* 1: 171–94.

Kirkness, Paul and Andreas Tijé-Dra (eds.). 2017. *Negative Neighbourhood Reputation and Place Attachment: The Production and Contestation of Territorial Stigma*. London: Routledge.

Kirmayer, Laurence J. 1994. "Suicide among Canadian Aboriginal Peoples." *Transcultural Psychiatric Research Review* 31, no. 1: 3–58.

Kirschenman, Joleen and Kathryn M. Neckerman. 1991. "'We'd Love to Hire Them, but . . .': The Meaning of Race for Employers." Pp. 203–34 in *The Urban Underclass*. Edited by Paul Peterson and Christopher Jencks. Washington, DC: Brookings Institution.

Klarman, Michael J. 2006. *From Jim Crow to Civil Rights: The Supreme Court and the Struggle for Racial Equality*. New York: Oxford University Press.

Klinenberg, Eric. 1999. "Denaturalizing Disaster: A Social Autopsy of the 1995 Chicago Heat Wave." *Theory & Society* 28, no. 2: 239–95.

References

Klinkner, Philip A. and Rogers M. Smith. 1999. *The Unsteady March: The Rise and Decline of Racial Equality in America*. Chicago, IL: University of Chicago Press.

Klose, Fabian. 2013. *Human Rights in the Shadow of Colonial Violence: The Wars of Independence in Kenya and Algeria*. University Park, PA: University of Pennsylvania Press.

Knowles, Louis L. and Kenneth Prewitt (eds.). *Institutional Racism in America*. Englewood Cliffs, NJ: Prentice Hall.

Koger, Larry. 1985. *Black Slaveowners: Free Black Slave Masters in South Carolina, 1790–1860*. Jefferson, NC: McFarland & Company.

Kohler-Hausmann, Issa. 2018. *Misdemeanorland: Criminal Courts and Social Control in an Age of Broken Windows Policing*. Princeton, NJ: Princeton University Press.

Kohler-Hausmann, Issa. 2022. "Don't Call It a Comeback: The Criminological and Sociological Study of Subfelonies." *Annual Review of Criminology* 5: 229–53.

Kolchin, Peter. 1990. *Unfree Labor: American Slavery and Russian Serfdom*. Cambridge, MA: Harvard University Press.

Kolchin, Peter. 2003. *American Slavery: 1619–1877*. New York: Hill and Wang.

Korn, Alina. 2008. "The Ghettoization of the Palestinians." Pp. 116–30 in *Thinking Palestine*. Edited by Ronit Lentin. London: Zed Books.

Kotlowitz, Alex. 1991. *There Are No Children Here: The Story of Two Boys Growing Up in the Other America*. New York: Anchor.

Kousser, J. Morgan. 1974. *The Shaping of Southern Politics: Suffrage Restriction and the Establishment of the One-Party South, 1880–1910*. New Haven, CT: Yale University Press.

Kovel, Joel. 1984. *White Racism: A Psychohistory*. New York: Columbia University Press.

Kramer, Rory and Brianna Remster. 2022. "The Slow Violence of Contemporary Policing." *Annual Review of Criminology* 5: 43–66.

Kreager, Derek A. and Candace Kruttschnitt. 2018. "Inmate Society in the Era of Mass Incarceration." *Annual Review of Criminology* 1: 261–83.

Kreager, Derek A., Jacob T. N. Young, Dana L. Haynie, Martin Bouchard, David R. Schaefer, and Gary Zajac. 2017. "Where 'Old Heads' Prevail: Inmate Hierarchy in a Men's Prison Unit." *American Sociological Review* 82, no. 4: 685–718.

Krivo, Lauren J. and Ruth D. Peterson. 1996. "Extremely Disadvantaged Neighborhoods and Urban Crime." *Social Forces* 75, no. 2: 619–48.

Krysan, Maria and Kyle Crowder. 2017. *Cycle of Segregation: Social Processes and Residential Stratification*. New York: Russell Sage Foundation.

Kuhn, Thomas S. 1970 [1962]. *The Structure of Scientific Revolutions*. Chicago, IL: University of Chicago Press.

Kuper, Leo. 1968. "Segregation." Pp. 144–50 in *International Encyclopedia of* the *Social Sciences*. Edited by David L. Sills and Robert K. Merton. New York: Macmillan and the Free Press.

Kurlychek, Megan C. and Brian D. Johnson. 2019. "Cumulative Disadvantage in the American Criminal Justice System." *Annual Review of Criminology* 2: 291–319.

Kymlicka, Will. 2002. *Contemporary Political Philosophy: An Introduction*. Oxford: Oxford University Press.

La Vigne, Nancy G., Cynthia A. Mamalian with Jeremy Travis and Christy Visher. 2003. *A Portrait of Prisoner Reentry in Illinois*. Washington, DC: Urban Institute.

Lacy, Karyn R. 2007. *Blue-Chip Black: Race, Class, and Status in the New Black Middle Class*. Berkeley, CA: University of California Press.

Ladányi, János. 1993. "Patterns of Residential Segregation and the Gypsy Minority in Budapest." *International Journal of Urban and Regional Research* 17, no. 1: 30–41.

Ladányi, János and Iván Szelényi. 2001. "The Social Construction of Roma Ethnicity in Bulgaria, Romania, and Hungary During Market Transition." *Review of Sociology* 7, no. 2: 79–89.

Ladányi, János and Iván Szelényi. 2006. *Patterns of Exclusion: Constructing Gypsy Ethnicity and the Making of an Underclass in Transitional Societies of Europe*. New York: Columbia University Press.

LaFleur, Jennifer. 2021. "The Race That Space Makes: The Power of Place in the Colonial Formation of Social Categorizations." *Sociology of Race and Ethnicity* 7, no. 4: 512–26.

LaFree, Gary and Gary Ackerman. 2009. "The Empirical Study of Terrorism: Social and Legal Research," *Annual Review of Law and Social Science* 5: 347–74.

Lageson, Sarah Esther. 2020. *Digital Punishment: Privacy, Stigma, and the Harms of Data-Driven Criminal Justice*. New York: Oxford University Press.

Lageson, Sarah Esther. 2022. "Criminal Record Stigma and Surveillance in the Digital Age." *Annual Review of Criminology* 5: 67–90.

Lahmon, W. T. Jr. 2003. *Jump Jim Crow: Lost Plays, Lyrics, and Street Prose of the First Atlantic Popular Culture*. Cambridge, MA: Harvard University Press.

Lamont, Michèle. 2018. "Addressing Cognition Gaps: Destigmatization and the Reduction of Inequality." *American Sociological Review* 83, no. 3: 419–44.

Lamont, Michèle and Nissim Mizrachi (eds.). 2013. *Responses to Stigmatization in Comparative Perspective*. London: Routledge.

Lancaster, Guy. 2014. *Racial Cleansing in Arkansas, 1883–1924: Politics, Land, Labor, and Criminality*. Lexington, MD: Lexington Books.

Lanctot, Neil. 2004. *Negro League Baseball: The Rise and Ruin of a Black Institution*. Philadelphia, PA: University of Pennsylvania Press.

References

Landry, Bart. 1987. *The New Black Middle Class*. Berkeley, CA: University of California Press.
Landry, Bart and Kris Marsh. 2011. "The Evolution of the New Black Middle Class." *Annual Review of Sociology* 37: 373–94.
Lardinois, Roland. 1985. "Les luttes de classement en Inde." *Actes de la recherche en sciences sociales* 59: 78–83.
Larrègue, Julien. 2020. *Héréditaire. L'éternel retour des théories biologiques du crime*. Paris: Seuil.
Lassiter, Matthew D. and Joseph Crespino (eds.). 2009. *The Myth of Southern Exceptionalism*. New York: Oxford University Press.
Lawrence, Bonita. 2003. "Gender, Race, and the Regulation of Native Identity in Canada and the United States: An Overview." *Hypatia* 18, no. 2: 3–31.
Le Bras, Gabriel (ed.). 2009. *Retour de la race. Contre les statistiques ethniques*. Paris: Éditions de l'Aube.
Le Bart, Christian. 2020. *Petite sociologie des Gilets jaunes. La contestation en mode post-institutionnel*. Rennes: Presses Universitaires de Rennes.
Le Cour Grandmaison, Olivier. 2005. *Coloniser, exterminer. Sur la guerre et l'État colonial*. Paris: Fayard.
Lê, Jérôme, Patrick Simon, and Baptiste Coulmont. 2022. "La diversité des origines et la mixité des unions progressent au fil des générations." *Insee Première* no. 1910.
Leach, Edmund R. (ed.). 1960. *Aspects of Caste in South India, Ceylon and North-West Pakistan*. Cambridge: Cambridge University Press, reprint 1971.
Lebron, Christopher J. 2017. *The Making of Black Lives Matter: A Brief History of an Idea*. New York: Oxford University Press.
Lecourt, Dominique. 1969. *L'Épistémologie historique de Gaston Bachelard*. Paris: Vrin.
Lecourt, Dominique. 2018 [1975]. *Marxism and Epistemology: Bachelard, Canguilhem, Foucault*. London: Verso.
Lee, Hedwig. 2024. "How Does Structural Racism Operate (in) the Contemporary US Criminal Justice System." *Annual Review of Criminology* 7: https://doi.org/10.1146/annurev-criminol-022422-015019.
Lee, Matthew R. 2000. "Concentrated Poverty, Race, and Homicide." *The Sociological Quarterly* 41, no. 2: 189–206.
Legassick, Martin and David Hemson. 1976. "Foreign Investment and Reproduction of Racial Capitalism in South Africa." London: Anti-Apartheid Movement, discussion paper no. 2.
Lehmann, David. 2018. *The Prism of Race: The Politics and Ideology of Affirmative Action in Brazil*. Ann Arbor, MI: University of Michigan Press.
Leicht, Kevin T. 2008. "Broken Down by Race and Gender? Sociological Explanations of New Sources of Earnings Inequality." *Annual Review of Sociology* 34: 237–55.

Lelyveld, Joseph. 1985. *Move Your Shadow: South Africa, Black and White.* New York: Crown.
Lenzerini, Federico (ed.). 2008. *Reparations for Indigenous Peoples: International and Comparative Perspectives.* New York: Oxford University Press.
Leovy, Jill. 2015. *Ghettoside: A True Story of Murder in America.* New York: Spiegel and Grau.
Lerman, Amy E. and Vesla M. Weaver. 2014. *Arresting Citizenship: The Democratic Consequences of American Crime Control.* Chicago, IL: University of Chicago Press.
Leroy, Justin and Destin Jenkins. (eds.). 2021. *Histories of Racial Capitalism.* New York: Columbia University Press.
Levenson, Zachary and Marcel Paret. 2022. "The Three Dialectics of Racial Capitalism: From South Africa to the US and Back Again." *Du Bois Review: Social Science Research on Race*: doi: 10.1017/S1742058X22000212.
Levine, Kay L. and Ronald F. Wright. 2012. "Prosecution in 3-D." *Journal of Criminal Law and Criminology* 102: 1119–80.
Levine, Lawrence W. 1977. *Black Culture and Black Consciousness: Afro-American Folk Thought from Slavery to Freedom.* New York: Oxford University Press.
Levy, Peter B. *The Great Uprising: Race Riots in Urban America during the 1960s.* New York: Cambridge University Press.
Lewis, Bernard. 1990. *Race and Slavery in the Middle East: An Historical Enquiry.* Oxford: Oxford University Press.
Lewis, Catherine and J. Richard Lewis (eds.). 2009. *Jim Crow America: A Documentary History.* Fayetteville, AR: University of Arkansas Press.
Li, Zhigang and Fulong Wu. 2008. "Tenure-Based Residential Segregation in Post-Reform Chinese Cities: A Case Study of Shanghai." *Transactions of the Institute of British Geographers* 33, no. 3: 404–19.
Liauzu, Claude. 2004. *Colonisation. Droit d'inventaire.* Paris: Armand Colin.
Lichtenstein, Alex. 1996. *Twice the Work of Free Labor: The Political Economy of Convict Labor in the New South.* New York: Verso.
Lie, John. 2004. *Modern Peoplehood.* Cambridge, MA: Harvard University Press.
Lie, John. 2008. *Zainichi (Koreans in Japan): Diasporic Nationalism and Postcolonial Identity.* Berkeley, CA: University of California Press.
Lie, John, 2009. *Multiethnic Japan.* Cambridge, MA: Harvard University Press.
Lieberman, Evan S. and Prerna Singh. 2012. "The Institutional Origins of Ethnic Violence." *Comparative Politics* 45, no. 1: 1–24.
Lieberman, Robert. 1998. *Shifting the Color Line: Race and the American Welfare State.* Cambridge, MA: Harvard University Press.
Light, Ivan. 1977. "Numbers Gambling among Blacks: A Financial Institution." *American Sociological Review* 42, no. 6: 892–904.

References

Link, Bruce G. and Jo C. Phelan. 2001. "Conceptualizing Stigma." *Annual Review of Sociology* 27: 363–85.

Lippard, Cameron, D., J. Scott Carter, and David G. Embrick (eds.). 2020. *Protecting Whiteness: Whitelash and the Rejection of Racial Equality*. Seattle, WA: University of Washington Press.

Litwack, Leon. 1998. *Trouble in Mind: Black Southerners in the Age of Jim Crow*. New York: Knopf.

Litwack, Leon. 2004. "Jim Crow Blues." *OAH Magazine of History* 18, no. 2: 7–11.

Livingstone, Anne-Marie, Marie Meudec, and Rhita Harim. 2020. "Le profilage racial à Montréal, effets des politiques et des pratiques organisationnelles." *Nouvelles pratiques sociales* 31, no. 2: 126–44.

Logan, John R. and Harvey L. Molotch. 2007 [1987]. *Urban Fortunes: The Political Economy of Place*. Berkeley, CA: University of California Press.

Londoño, Ernesto. 2023. "How 'Defund the Police' Failed." *New York Times Magazine*, June 16.

Lopez, Yoann. 2010. *Les Questions noires en France. Revendications collectives contre perceptions individuelles*. PhD dissertation in Sociology, University of Bordeaux 2.

Lopez-Aguado, Patrick. 2018. *Stick Together and Come Back Home: Racial Sorting and the Spillover of Carceral Identity*. Berkeley, CA: University of California Press.

Lorcin, Patricia M. E. 1995. *Imperial Identities: Stereotyping, Prejudice and Race in Colonial Algeria*. London: I.B. Tauris.

Lorde, Audre. 1984. "The Master's Tools Will Never Dismantle the Master's House." In *Sister Outsider: Essays and Speeches*. New York: The Crossing Press.

Loury, Glenn C. 2021 [2002]. *The Anatomy of Racial Inequality*. Cambridge, MA: Harvard University Press.

Loveman, Mara. 2014. *National Colors: Racial Classification and the State in Latin America*. New York: Oxford University Press.

Lowery, Malinda Maynor. 2010. *Lumbee Indians in the Jim Crow South: Race, Identity, and the Making of a Nation*. Chapel Hill, NC: University of North Carolina Press.

Lu, Catherine. 2017. *Justice and Reconciliation in World Politics*. Cambridge: Cambridge University Press.

Lucas, Samuel R. 2009. *Theorizing Discrimination in an Era of Contested Prejudice: Discrimination in the United States*, vol. 1. Philadelphia, PA: Temple University Press.

Lucas, Samuel R. 2013. *Just Who Loses? Discrimination in the United States*, vol. 2. Philadelphia, PA: Temple University Press.

Luft, Aliza. 2015. "Toward a Dynamic Theory of Action at the Micro Level of Genocide: Killing, Desistance, and Saving in 1994 Rwanda." *Sociological Theory* 33, no. 2: 148–72.

Luft, Aliza and Susan Thomson. 2021. "Race, Nation, and Resistance to State Symbolic Power in Rwanda Since the 1994 Genocide." *Political Power & Social Theory* 38: 105–34.

Lum, Kathryn Gin. 2022. *Heathen: Religion and Race in American History*. Cambridge, MA: Harvard University Press.

Luttikhuis, Bart and A. Dirk Moses (eds.). 2018. *Colonial Counterinsurgency and Mass Violence: The Dutch Empire in Indonesia*. London: Routledge.

Lynch, Mona. 1998. "Waste Managers? The New Penology, Crime Fighting, and Parole Agent Identity." *Law & Society Review* 32, no. 4: 839–70.

Lyons, David and Michael K. Brown. 2007. *Redress for Historical Injustices in the United States: On Reparations for Slavery, Jim Crow, and Their Legacies*. Durham, NC: Duke University Press.

MacLean, Nancy. 1994. *Behind the Mask of Chivalry: The Making of the Second Ku Klux Klan*. New York: Oxford University Press.

Madley, Benjamin. 2005. "From Africa to Auschwitz: How German South West Africa Incubated Ideas and Methods Adopted and Developed by the Nazis in Eastern Europe." *European History Quarterly* 35, no. 3: 429–64.

Maghbouleh, Neda, Ariela Schachter, and René D. Flores. 2022. "Middle Eastern and North African Americans May not be Perceived, nor Perceive Themselves, to be White." *Proceedings of the National Academy of Sciences* 119, no. 7: e2117940119.

Magubane, Zine. 2004. *Bringing the Empire Home: Race, Class, and Gender in Britain and Colonial South Africa*. Chicago, IL: University of Chicago Press.

Malaquias, Assis. 2007. *Rebels and Robbers: Violence in Post-Colonial Angola*. Uppsala: Nordiska Afrikainstitutet.

Malmberg, Bo, Eva K. Andersson, Michael M. Nielsen, and Karen Haandrikman. 2018. "Residential Segregation of European and Non-European Migrants in Sweden: 1990–2012." *European Journal of Population* 34, no. 2: 169–93.

Mamdani, Mahmood. 2001. *When Victims Become Killers: Colonialism, Nativism, and the Genocide in Rwanda*. Princeton, NJ: Princeton University Press.

Mamdani, Mahmood. 2020. *Neither Settler nor Native: The Making and Unmaking of Permanent Minorities*. Cambridge, MA: Harvard University Press.

Mancini, Matthew J. 1996. *One Dies, Get Another: Convict Leasing in the American South, 1866–1928*. Columbia, SC: University of South Carolina Press.

Mann, Michael. 2005. *The Dark Side of Democracy: Explaining Ethnic Cleansing*. New York: Cambridge University Press.

Manza, Jeff and Christopher Uggen. 2008. *Locked Out: Felon Disenfranchisement and American Democracy*. New York: Oxford University Press.

References

Marks, Carole. 1989. *Farewell, We're Good and Gone: The Great Black Migration*. Bloomington, IN: Indiana University Press.

Martin, Robert J. 1996. "Pursuing Public Protection through Mandatory Community Notification of Convicted Sex Offenders: The Trials and Tribulations of Megan's Law." *The Boston Public Interest Law Journal* 26: 26–56.

Martin, Steve J. and Sheldon Ekland-Olson. 1987. *Texas Prisons: The Walls Came Tumbling Down*. Austin, TX: Texas Monthly Press.

Martin, Terry. 2001. *The Affirmative Action Empire: Nations and Nationalism in the Soviet Union, 1923–1939*. Ithaca, NY: Cornell University Press.

Marx, Antony W. 1998. *Making Race and Nation: A Comparison of the United States, South Africa, and Brazil*. New York: Cambridge University Press.

Marx, Emanuel. 2019. *State Violence in Nazi Germany: From Kristallnacht to Barbarossa*. London: Routledge.

Masclet, Olivier. 2017. *Sociologie de la diversité et des discriminations*. Paris: Armand Colin.

Massey, Douglas S. 2012. "Reflections on the Dimensions of Segregation." *Social Forces* 91, no. 1: 39–43.

Massey, Douglas and Nancy Denton. 1993. *American Apartheid: Segregation and the Making of the Underclass*. Cambridge, MA: Harvard University Press.

Mastrocinque, Jeanna M. 2010. "An Overview of the Victims' Rights Movement: Historical, Legislative, and Research Developments." *Sociology Compass* 4, no. 2: 95–110.

Mathiesen, Thomas. 2014. *The Politics of Abolition Revisited*. London: Routledge.

Matsinhe, David M. 2011a. *Apartheid Vertigo: The Rise in Discrimination against Africans in South Africa*. Ashbury: Ashgate.

Matsinhe, David M. 2011b. "Africa's Fear of Itself: The Ideology of *Makwerekwere* in South Africa." *Third World Quarterly* 32, no. 2: 295–313.

Mauer, Marc. 1997. "Racial Disparities in Prison Getting Worse in the 1990s." *Overcrowded Times* 8, no. 1: 8–13.

Mayer, Margit, Catharina Thörn, and Håkan Thörn (eds.). 2016. *Urban Uprisings. Challenging Neoliberal Urbanism in Europe*. London: Palgrave Macmillan.

Maylam, Paul. 1995. "Explaining the Apartheid City: 20 Years of South African Urban Historiography." *Journal of Southern African Studies* 21, no. 1: 19–38.

Mazower, Mark. 2009. *Hitler's Empire: How the Nazis Ruled Europe*. New York: Penguin.

McCormack, Noah. 2018. "Affirmative Action Policies under the Postwar Japanese Constitution: On the Effects of the Dōwa Special Measures Policy." *Asia-Pacific Journal: Japan Focus* 16, no. 5: 1–23.

McCorquodale, John. 1986. "The Legal Classification of Race in Australia." *Aboriginal History* 10, no. 1–2: 7–24.

McElhinny, Bonnie. 2016. "Reparations and Racism, Discourse and Diversity: Neoliberal Multiculturalism and the Canadian Age of Apologies." *Language & Communication* 51: 50–68.

McGarry, Aidan. 2012. "The Dilemma of the European Union's Roma Policy." *Critical Social Policy* 32, no. 1: 126–36.

McGuire, Danielle. 2010. *At the Dark End of the Street: Black Women, Rape, and Resistance*. New York: Vintage.

McLennan, Rebecca M. 2008. *The Crisis of Imprisonment: Protest, Politics, and the Making of the American Penal State, 1776–1941*. New York: Cambridge University Press.

McMillen, Neil R. 1990. *Dark Journey: Black Mississippians in the Age of Jim Crow*. Urbana, IL: University of Illinois Press.

McRae, Elizabeth Gillespie. 2018. *Mothers of Massive Resistance: White Women and the Politics of White Supremacy*. New York: Oxford University Press.

McWhirter, Cameron. 2011. *Red Summer: The Summer of 1919 and the Awakening of Black America*. New York: Henry Holt.

Medina, José. 2012. *The Epistemology of Resistance: Gender and Racial Oppression, Epistemic Injustice, and Resistant Imaginations*. New York: Oxford University Press.

Meghji, Ali. 2021. "Just What Is Critical Race Theory, and What Is It Doing in British Sociology? From 'Britcrit' to the Racialized Social System Approach." *The British Journal of Sociology* 72, no. 2: 347–59.

Meghji, Ali. 2022. *The Racialized Social System: Critical Race Theory as Social Theory*. Cambridge: Polity.

Meierhenrich, Jens (ed.). 2014. *Genocide: A Reader*. New York: Oxford University Press.

Melossi Dario. 2000. "Changing Representations of the Criminal." *British Journal of Criminology* 40, no. 2: 296–320.

Menjívar, Cecilia. 2021. "The Racialization of 'Illegality'." *Daedalus: Journal of the American Academy of Arts and Sciences* 150, no. 2: 91–105.

Menjívar, Cecilia. 2023. "State Categories, Bureaucracies of Displacement, and Possibilities from the Margins." *American Sociological Review* 88, no. 1: 1–23.

Merle, Isabelle. 2020. *Expériences coloniales. La Nouvelle-Calédonie, 1853–1920*. Paris: Belin.

Merton, Robert K. 1948. "Discrimination and the American Creed." Pp. 99–126 in *Discrimination and National Welfare*. Edited by Robert M. MacIver. New York: Harper.

Merton, Robert K. 1987. "Three Fragments from a Sociologist's Notebooks: Establishing the Phenomenon, Specified Ignorance and Strategic Research Materials." *Annual Review of Sociology* 13: 1–28.

Messer, Chris M. 2011. "The Tulsa Race Riot of 1921: Toward an Integrative

References

Theory of Collective Violence." *Journal of Social History* 44, no. 4: 1217–32.

Metcalf, Thomas R. 2013. "Colonial Cities." Pp. 753–69 in *The Oxford Handbook of Cities in World History*. Edited by Peter Clark. New York: Oxford University Press.

Michelot, Isabelle. 2007. "Du Neg nwe au Beke Goyave, le langage de la couleur de la peau en Martinique." *Publifarum* 7: 53.

Midtbøen, Arnfinn H. 2018. "The Making and Unmaking of Ethnic Boundaries in the Public Sphere: The Case of Norway." *Ethnicities* 18, no. 3: 344–62.

Miles, Robert. 2003. *Racism*. London: Tavistock.

Miletsky, Zebulon Vance. 2022. *Before Busing: A History of Boston's Long Black Freedom Struggle*. Chapel Hill, NC: University of North Carolina Press.

Miller, Jerome G. 1997. *Search and Destroy: African-American Males in the Criminal Justice System*. Cambridge: Cambridge University Press.

Miller, Reuben Jonathan. 2021. *Halfway Home: Race, Punishment, and the Afterlife of Mass Incarceration*. Boston, MA: Little, Brown.

Mills, C-Wright. 1940. "Situated Actions and Vocabularies of Motive." *American Sociological Review* 5, no. 6: 904–13.

Mills, Charles W. 2014 [1997]. *The Racial Contract*, 2nd anniversary edition. London: Cornell University Press.

Mills, Charles W. 2018. "Racial justice." *Aristotelian Society Supplementary Volume* 92, no. 1: 69–89.

Milton, Sybil. 2000. "Sinti and Roma in Twentieth-Century Austria and Germany." *German Studies Review* 23, no. 2: 317–31.

Minca, Claudio. 2005. "The Return of the Camp." *Progress in Human Geography* 29, no. 4: 405–12.

Minow, Martha. 2022. "Equality vs. Equity." *American Journal of Law and Equality* 1, no. 1: 167–93.

Mitchell, Ojmarrh. 2005. "A Meta-Analysis of Race and Sentencing Research: Explaining the Inconsistencies." *Journal of Quantitative Criminology* 21: 439–66.

Mitchell, W. J. T. 2012. *Seeing Through Race*. Cambridge, MA: Harvard University Press.

Mommsen, Hans. 1997. Cumulative Radicalisation and Progressive Self-Destruction as Structural Determinants of the Nazi Dictatorship." Pp. 75–87 in *Stalinism and Nazism: Dictatorships in Comparison*. Edited by Ian Kershaw and Moishe Lewin. Cambridge: Cambridge University Press.

Monk Jr., Ellis P. 2014. "Skin Tone Stratification among Black Americans, 2001–2003." *Social Forces* 92, no. 4: 1313–37.

Monk Jr., Ellis P. 2015. "The Cost of Color: Skin Color, Discrimination, and Health among African-Americans." *American Journal of Sociology* 121, no. 2: 396–444.

Monk Jr., Ellis P. 2016. "The Consequences of 'Race and Color' in Brazil." *Social Problems* 63, no. 3: 413–30.

Monk Jr., Ellis P. 2019. "The Color of Punishment: African Americans, Skin Tone, and the Criminal Justice System." *Ethnic & Racial Studies* 42, no. 10: 1593–612.

Monk Jr., Ellis P. 2021. "The Unceasing Significance of Colorism: Skin Tone Stratification in the United States." *Daedalus: Journal of the American Academy of Arts and Sciences* 150, no. 2: 76–90.

Monk Jr., Ellis P. 2022. "Inequality without Groups: Contemporary Theories of Categories, Intersectional Typicality, and the Disaggregation of Difference." *Sociological Theory* 40, no. 1: 3–27.

Monk Jr., Ellis P., Michael H. Esposito, and Hedwig Lee. 2021. "Beholding Inequality: Race, Gender, and Returns to Physical Attractiveness in the United States." *American Journal of Sociology* 127, no. 1: 194–241.

Montejano, David. 1994. *Anglos and Mexicans in the Making of Texas, 1836–1986*. Austin, TX: University of Texas Press.

Moodley, Kogila and Heribert Adam. 2000. "Race and Nation in Post-Apartheid South Africa." *Current Sociology* 48, no. 3: 51–69.

Moore, Robert I. 1987. *The Formation of a Persecuting Society: Authority and Deviance in Western Europe 950–1250*. Cambridge, MA: Blackwell.

Mora, G. Cristina. 2014. *Making Hispanics: How Activists, Bureaucrats, and Media Constructed a New American*. Chicago, IL: University of Chicago Press.

Morenoff, Jeffrey D. and Robert J. Sampson. 1997. "Violent Crime and the Spatial Dynamics of Neighborhood Transition: Chicago, 1970–1990." *Social Forces* 76, no. 1: 31–64.

Morgan, Edmund S. 1975. *American Slavery, American Freedom: The Ordeal of Colonial Virginia*. New York: Norton.

Morgan, Kenneth. 2000. *Slavery and Servitude in North America, 1607–1800*. Edinburgh: Edinburgh University Press.

Morning, Ann. 2008. "Ethnic Classification in Global Perspective: A Cross-National Survey of the 2000 Census Round." *Population Research and Policy Review* 27: 239–72.

Morning, Ann and Marcello Maneri. 2022. *An Ugly Word: Rethinking Race in Italy and the United States*. New York: Russell Sage Foundation.

Morris, Aldon D. 1986. *The Origins of the Civil Rights Movement: Black Communities Organizing for Change*. New York: Free Press.

Morris, Norval. 1995. "The Contemporary Prison, 1965–Present." Pp. 226–59 in *The Oxford History of the Prison*. Edited by Norval Morris and David Rothman. New York: Oxford University Press.

Morrison, Melanie S. 2018. *Murder on Shades Mountain: The Legal Lynching of Willie Peterson and the Struggle for Justice in Jim Crow Birmingham*. Durham, NC: Duke University Press.

Moss, Kirby. 2010. *The Color of Class: Poor Whites and the Paradox of Privilege*. Philadelphia, PA: University of Pennsylvania Press.

References

Moss, Philip and Chris Tilly. 2001. *Stories Employers Tell: Race, Skill, and Hiring in America*. New York: Russell Sage Foundation.
Muhammad, Khalil Gibran. 2010. *The Condemnation of Blackness: Race, Crime, and the Making of Modern Urban America*. Cambridge, MA: Harvard University Press.
Mullaney, Thomas. 2011. *Coming to Terms with the Nation: Ethnic Classification in Modern China*. Berkeley, CA: University of California Press.
Muller, Christopher. 2018. "Freedom and Convict Leasing in the Postbellum South." *American Journal of Sociology* 124, no. 2: 367–405.
Muller, Christopher. 2021. "Exclusion and Exploitation: The Incarceration of Black Americans from Slavery to the Present." *Science* 374, no. 6565: 282–6.
Muller, Christopher and Alexander F. Roehrkasse. 2022. "Racial and Class Inequality in US Incarceration in the Early Twenty-First Century." *Social Forces* 101, no. 2: 803–28.
Muller, Christopher and Daniel Schrage. 2021. "The Political Economy of Incarceration in the Cotton South, 1910–1925." *American Journal of Sociology* 127, no. 3: 828–66.
Mullings, Leith. 2005. "Interrogating Racism: Toward an Antiracist Anthropology." *Annual Review of Anthropology* 34: 667–93.
Munro, John. 2017. *The Anticolonial Front: The African American Freedom Struggle and Global Decolonisation, 1945–1960*. Cambridge: Cambridge University Press.
Murakawa, Naomi. 2014. *The First Civil Right: How Liberals Built Prison America*. New York: Oxford University Press.
Murch, Donna. 2022. *Assata Taught Me: State Violence, Racial Capitalism, and the Movement for Black Lives*. Chicago, IL: Haymarket Books.
Murray, Brian M. 2016. "A New Era for Expungement Law Reform: Recent Developments at the State and Federal Levels." *Harvard Law and Policy Review* 10: 361–84.
Muschalek, Marie. 2019. *Violence as Usual: Policing and the Colonial State in German Southwest Africa*. Ithaca, NY: Cornell University Press.
Musterd, Sako. 2005. "Social and Ethnic Segregation in Europe: Levels, Causes, and Effects." *Journal of Urban Affairs* 27, no. 3: 331–48.
Myers, Ella. 2019. "Beyond the Psychological Wage: Du Bois on White Dominion." *Political Theory* 47, no. 1: 6–31.
Myrdal, Gunnar. 1944. *An American Dilemma: The Negro Problem and Modern Democracy*, 2 vols. New York: Harper, reprint 1962.
Naepels, Michel. 2013. *Conjurer la guerre. Violence et pouvoir à Houaïlou (Nouvelle-Calédonie)*. Paris: Éditions de l'EHESS.
Nagel, Joane. 1996. *American Indian Ethnic Renewal: Red Power and the Resurgence of Identity and Culture*. New York: Oxford University Press.
Nagel, Joane. 2003. *Race, Ethnicity, and Sexuality: Intimate Intersections, Forbidden Frontiers*. New York: Oxford University Press.
Nasiali, Minayo. 2016. *Native to the Republic: Empire, Social Citizenship,*

and *Everyday Life in Marseille since 1945*. Ithaca, NY: Cornell University Press.

National Academy of Science. 2022. *Structural Racism and Rigorous Models of Social Inequity: Proceedings of a Workshop*. Washington, DC: NAS Press.

Ndiaye, Pap. 2009. *La Condition noire. Essai sur une minorité française*. Paris: Calmann-Lévy.

Niedermeier, Silvan. 2019. *The Color of the Third Degree: Racism, Police Torture, and Civil Rights in the American South, 1930–1955*. Chapel Hill, NC: University of North Carolina Press.

Nightingale, Carl H. 2012. *Segregation: A Global History of Divided Cities*. Chicago, IL: University of Chicago Press.

Nilsen, Alf Gunvald and Srila Roy (eds.). 2015. *New Subaltern Politics: Reconceptualizing Hegemony and Resistance in Contemporary India*. Oxford: Oxford University Press.

Nirenberg, David. 2015. *Communities of Violence: Persecution of Minorities in the Middle Ages*. Princeton, NJ: Princeton University Press.

Nobles, Melissa. 2000. *Shades of Citizenship: Race and the Census in Modern Politics*. Stanford, CA: Stanford University Press.

Noiriel, Gérard. 1988. *Le Creuset français. Histoire de l'immigration, XIXe–XXe siècles*. Paris: Seuil. (English translation: *The French Melting Pot: Immigration, Citizenship, and National Identity*, University of Minnesota Press, 1996).

Norwood, Kimberly Jade (ed.). 2013. *Color Matters: Skin Tone Bias and the Myth of a Postracial America*. New York: Routledge.

Oberti, Marco and Edmond Préteceille. 2016. *La Ségrégation urbaine*. Paris: La Découverte.

O'Brien, Gail Williams. 1999. *The Color of the Law: Race, Violence, and Justice in the Post-World War II South*. Chapel Hill, NC: University of North Carolina Press.

Ohlmeyer, Jane. 2016. "Conquest, Civilization, Colonization: Ireland, 1540–1660." Pp. 21–47 in *The Princeton History of Modern Ireland*. Edited by Richard Bourke and Ian McBride. Princeton, NJ: Princeton University Press.

Olschanski, Reinhard. 2015. *Ressentiment. Über die Vergiftung des europäischen Geistes*. Berlin: Wilhelm Fink Verlag.

Omi, Michael and Howard Winant. 2015. *Racial Formation in the United States*, 3rd edition. New York: Routledge.

Onwudiwe, Ebere and Minabere Ibelema (eds.). 2003. *Afro-Optimism: Perspectives on Africa's Advances*. New York: Praeger.

Oshinsky, David M. 1996. *Worse Than Slavery: Parchman Farm and the Ordeal of Jim Crow Justice*. New York: Free Press.

Owen, Barbara. 1996. *In the Mix: Struggle and Survival in a Women's Prison*. Binghamton, NY: SUNY Press.

Pagden, Anthony. 2001. *Peoples and Empires: A Short History of European*

References

Migration, Exploration, and Conquest, from Greece to the Present. New York: Modern Library.

Pagden, Anthony. 2015. *The Burdens of Empire: 1539 to the Present.* Cambridge: Cambridge University Press.

Page, Joshua. 2004. "Eliminating the Enemy: The Import of Denying Prisoners Access to Higher Education in Clinton's America." *Punishment & Society* 6, no. 4: 357–78.

Pager, Devah and Hana Shepperd. 2008. "The Sociology of Discrimination: Racial Discrimination in Employment, Housing, Credit, and Consumer Markets." *Annual Review of Sociology* 34: 181–209.

Pan Ké Shon, Jean-Louis. 2009. "Ségrégation ethnique et ségrégation sociale en quartiers sensibles. L'apport des mobilités résidentielles." *Revue française de sociologie* 50, no. 3: 451–87.

Pan Ké Shon, Jean-Louis and Gregory Verdugo. 2014. "Ségrégation et incorporation des immigrés en France. Ampleur et intensité entre 1968 et 2007." *Revue française de sociologie* 55, no. 2: 245–83.

Pandey, Gyanendra. 2013. *A History of Prejudice: Race, Caste, and Difference in India and the United States.* New York: Cambridge University Press.

Pappe, Ilan. 2006. *The Ethnic Cleansing of Palestine.* Oxford: Oneworld.

Paret, Marcel. 2022. *Fractured Militancy: Precarious Resistance in South Africa after Racial Inclusion.* Ithaca, NY: Cornell University Press.

Parikh, Sunita. 1997. *The Politics of Preference: Democratic Institutions and Affirmative Action in the United States and India.* Ann Arbor, MI: University of Michigan Press.

Park, Linette. 2020. "Afropessimism and Futures of . . . A Conversation with Frank Wilderson." *The Black Scholar* 50, no. 3: 29–41.

Park, Robert and Ernest Burgess. 1925. *The City.* Chicago, IL: University of Chicago Press.

Parsons, Elaine Frantz. 2015. *Ku-Klux: The Birth of the Klan during Reconstruction.* Chapel Hill, NC: University of North Carolina Press.

Parvez, Z. Fareen. 2017. *Politicizing Islam: The Islamic Revival in France and India.* New York: Oxford University Press.

Paschel, Tianna S. 2016. *Becoming Black Political Subjects: Movements and Ethno-racial Rights in Colombia and Brazil.* Princeton, NJ: Princeton University Press.

Pasquetti, Silvia. 2019. "Experiences of Urban Militarism: Spatial Stigma, Ruins and Everyday Life." *International Journal of Urban and Regional Research* 43, no. 5: 848–69.

Pasquetti, Silvia. 2023. *Refugees Together and Citizens Apart: Control, Emotions, and Politics at the Palestinian Margins.* New York: Oxford University Press.

Patterson, Orlando. 1997. *The Ordeal of Integration: Progress and Resentment in America's "Racial" Crisis.* New York: Civitas Books.

Patterson, Orlando. 1998. *Rituals of Blood: Consequences of Slavery in Two American Centuries.* New York: Civitas Books.

Patterson, Orlando. 2005. "Four Modes of Ethno-Somatic Stratification: The Experience of Blacks in Europe and the Americas." Pp. 67–122 in *Ethnicity, Social Mobility, and Public Policy: Comparing the USA and UK*. Edited by Glenn C. Loury, Tariq Modood, and Steven M. Teles. Cambridge: Cambridge University Press.

Patterson, Orlando. 2018 [1982]. *Slavery and Social Death: A Comparative Study*. Cambridge, MA: Harvard University Press.

Patterson, Orlando. 2019. "The Denial of Slavery in Contemporary American Sociology." *Theory & Society* 48, no. 6: 903–14.

Patterson, Orlando. 2022 [1967]. *The Sociology of Slavery: Black Society in Jamaica 1655–1838*. Cambridge: Polity.

Pattillo, Mary. 1999. *Black Picket Fences: Privilege and Peril among the Black Middle Class*. Chicago, IL: University of Chicago Press.

Peach, Ceri. 1996. "Does Britain Have Ghettos?" *Transactions of the Institute of British Geographers* 21, no. 1: 216–35.

Peiretti-Courtis, Delphine. 2022. *Corps noirs et médecins blancs. La fabrique du préjugé racial, XIXe–XXe siècles*. Paris: La Découverte.

Pendas, Devin O. 2017. "Racial States in Comparative Perspective." Pp. 116–44 in *Beyond the Racial State: Rethinking Nazi Germany*. Edited by Devin O. Pendas, Mark Roseman, and Richard F. Wetzell. Cambridge: Cambridge University Press.

Pendas, Devin O., Mark Roseman, and Richard F. Wetzell (eds.). 2017. *Beyond the Racial State: Rethinking Nazi Germany*. Cambridge: Cambridge University Press.

Pérez, Raúl. 2022. *The Souls of White Jokes: How Racist Humor Fuels White Supremacy*. Stanford, CA: Stanford University Press.

Peristiany, John George and Julian Pitt-Rivers (eds.). 1992. *Honor and Grace in Anthropology*. Cambridge: Cambridge University Press.

Peteet, Julie. 2005. *Landscape of Hope and Despair: Palestinian Refugee Camps*. University Park, PA: University of Pennsylvania Press.

Petersen, Roger Dale. 2002. *Understanding Ethnic Violence: Fear, Hatred, and Resentment in Twentieth-Century Eastern Europe*. Cambridge: Cambridge University Press.

Petersilia, Joan. 1999. "Parole and Prisoner Reentry in the United States." Pp. 479–529 in *Prisons*. Edited by Michael Tonry and Joan Petersilia. Chicago, IL: University of Chicago Press.

Petit, Pascale, Mathieu Bunel, Emilia Ene, and Yannick L'Horty. 2016. "Effets de quartier, effet de département. Discrimination liée au lieu de résidence et accès à l'emploi." *Revue économique* 67, no. 3: 525–50.

Petit, Pierre. 2013. "Ethnic Performance and the State in Laos: The Boun Greh Annual Festival of the Khmou." *Asian Studies Review* 37, no. 4: 471–90.

Pettit, Becky. 2012. *Invisible Men: Mass Incarceration and the Myth of Black Progress*. New York: Russell Sage Foundation.

References

Pfeifer, Michael James. 2004. *Rough Justice: Lynching and American Society, 1874–1947*. Urbana, IL: University of Illinois Press.

Phelps, Michelle S. 2013. "The Paradox of Probation: Community Supervision in the Age of Mass Incarceration." *Law & Policy* 35, no. 1/2: 51–80.

Phelps, Michelle S. 2020. "Mass Probation from Micro to Macro: Tracing the Expansion and Consequences of Community Supervision." *Annual Review of Criminology* 3: 261–79.

Phillips, Kimberley Louise. 1999. *Alabama North: African-American Migrants, Community, and Working-Class Activism in Cleveland, 1915–45*. Urbana, IL: University of Illinois Press.

Phillips, Susan A. 1999. *Wallbangin': Graffiti and Gangs in L.A.* Chicago, IL: University of Chicago Press.

Picker, Giovanni. 2017. *Racial Cities: Governance and the Segregation of Romani People in Urban Europe*. London: Routledge.

Piketty, Thomas. 2022. *Mesurer le racisme, vaincre la discrimination*. Paris: Seuil.

Pontusson, Jonas. 2005. *Inequality and Prosperity: Social Europe vs. Liberal America*. Ithaca, NY: Cornell University Press.

Posel, Deborah. 2001. "Race as Common Sense: Racial Classification in Twentieth-Century South Africa." *African Studies Review* 44, no. 2: 87–114.

Postero, Nancy Grey. 2007. *Now We Are Citizens: Indigenous Politics in Postmulticultural Bolivia*. Stanford, CA: Stanford University Press.

Poupeau, Franck. 2020. "Lutte(s)." Pp. 525–7 in *Dictionnaire International Pierre Bourdieu*. Edited by Gisèle Sapiro. Paris: Éditions du CNRS.

Powdermaker, Hortense. 1993 [1939]. *After Freedom: A Cultural Study of the Deep South*. Madison, WI: University of Wisconsin Press.

Powell, Eve Troutt. 2003. *A Different Shade of Colonialism: Egypt, Great Britain, and the Mastery of the Sudan*. Berkeley, CA: University of California Press.

Powell, Ryan and John Lever. 2017. "Europe's Perennial 'Outsiders': A Processual Approach to Roma Stigmatization and Ghettoization." *Current Sociology* 65, no. 5: 680–99.

Prewitt, Kenneth. 2005. "Racial Classification in America: Where Do We Go from Here?" *Daedalus: Journal of the American Academy of Arts and Sciences* 134: 5–17.

Prowse, Gwen, Vesla M. Weaver, and Tracey L. Meares. 2020. "The State from Below: Distorted Responsiveness in Policed Communities." *Urban Affairs Review* 56, no. 5: 1423–71.

Purnell, Bryan and Jeanne Theoharis, with Komozi Woodward (eds.). 2019. *The Strange Careers of the Jim Crow North: Segregation and Struggle Outside of the South*. Binghamton, NY: SUNY Press.

Quassoli, Fabio and Adriana Carbonaro. 2013. "'Cattivi con i clandestini': controllo ed esclusione dei migranti nell'Italia contemporanea." *Rassegna italiana di sociologia* 14, no. 3: 401–22.

Quijano, Aníbal. 2007. "Coloniality and Modernity/Rationality." *Cultural Studies* 21, no. 2–3: 168–78.

Quillian, Lincoln. 2006. "New Approaches to Understanding Racial Prejudice and Discrimination." *Annual Review of Sociology* 32: 299–328.

Quisumbing King, Katrina. 2022. "The Global Color Line and White Supremacy: W. E. B. Du Bois as a Grand Theorist of Race." In *The Oxford Handbook of W. E. B. Du Bois*. Edited by Aldon Morris et al. Oxford: Oxford University Press.

Rabinowitz, Howard N. 1988. "More than the Woodward Thesis: Assessing the Strange Career of Jim Crow." *The Journal of American History* 75, no. 3: 842–56.

Rafter, Nicole. 2008. *The Criminal Brain: Understanding Biological Theories of Crime*. New York: NYU Press.

Ralph, Laurence. 2020. *The Torture Letters: Reckoning with Police Violence*. Chicago, IL: University of Chicago Press.

Ralph, Michael and Maya Singhal. 2019. "Racial Capitalism." *Theory & Society* 48, no. 6: 851–81.

Ransom, Roger L. and Richard Sutch. 2001. *One Kind of Freedom: The Economic Consequences of Emancipation*, 2nd edition. New York: Cambridge University Press.

Raper, Arthur F. 2017 [1933]. *The Tragedy of Lynching*. Chapel Hill, NC: University of North Carolina Press.

Rawls, John. 1999 [1971]. *A Theory of Justice*. Cambridge, MA: Harvard University Press.

Ray, Victor Erik, Antonia Randolph, Megan Underhill, and David Luke. 2017. "Critical Race Theory, Afro-Pessimism, and Racial Progress Narratives." *Sociology of Race and Ethnicity* 3, no. 2: 147–58.

Razack, Saleem and Thirusha Naidu. 2022. "Honouring the Multitudes: Removing Structural Racism in Medical Education." *The Lancet* 400, no. 10368: 2021–3.

Reed, Adolph L. Jr. 2022. *The South: Jim Crow and Its Afterlives*. London: Verso.

Reed, Christopher Robert. 2011. *The Rise of Chicago's Black Metropolis, 1920–1929*. Urbana, IL: University of Illinois Press.

Reed, John Shelton. 1986. *The Enduring South: Subcultural Persistence in Mass Society*. Chapel Hill, NC: University of North Carolina Press.

Reed, Touré F. 2008. *Not Alms but Opportunity: The Urban League and the Politics of Racial Uplift, 1910–1950*. Chapel Hill, NC: University of North Carolina Press.

Régent, Frédéric. 2007. *La France et ses esclaves*. Paris: Grasset.

Reid Andrews, George. 2016. *Afro-Latin America: Black Lives, 1600–2000*. Cambridge, MA: Harvard University Press.

Reiter, Keramet. 2016. *23/7: Pelican Bay Prison and the Rise of Long-Term Solitary Confinement*. New Haven, CT: Yale University Press.

References

Reskin, Barbara. 2012. "The Race Discrimination System." *Annual Review of Sociology* 38: 17–35.
Rheinberger, Hans-Jörg. 2010. *On Historicizing Epistemology*. Stanford, CA: Stanford University Press.
Rieff, David. 1998. "In Defense of Afro-pessimism." *World Policy Journal* 15, no. 4: 10–22.
Rifkin, Jeff. 1995. *The End of Work. The Decline of the Global Labor Force and the Dawn of the Post-Market Era*. New York: Tarcher and Putnam.
Ringer, Fritz K. 1997. *Max Weber's Methodology: The Unification of the Cultural and Social Sciences*. Cambridge, MA: Harvard University Press.
Ritterhouse, Jennifer Lynn. 2006. *Growing Up Jim Crow: How Black and White Southern Children Learned Race*. Chapel Hill, NC: University of North Carolina Press.
Ritterhouse, Jennifer Lynn. 2007. "The Etiquette of Racial Relations in the Jim Crow South." Pp. 20–44 in *Manners and Southern History*. Edited by Ted Ownby. Jackson, MS: University Press of Mississippi.
Ritterhouse, Jennifer Lynn. 2018. "Daily Life in the Jim Crow South, 1900–1945." *Oxford Research Encyclopedias, American History*, online at: https://doi.org/10.1093/acrefore/9780199329175.013.329.
Roberts, Alaina. 2023. *I've Been Here All the While: Black Freedom on Native Land*. Philadelphia, PA: University of Pennsylvania Press.
Roberts, Dorothy. 2011. *Fatal Invention: How Science, Politics, and Big Business Re-Create Race in the Twenty-First Century*. New York: New Press.
Roberts, Randy. 1985. *Papa Jack: Jack Johnson and the Era of White Hopes*. New York: Simon and Schuster.
Robinson, Cedric J. 2000 [1983]. *Black Marxism: The Making of the Black Radical Tradition*. Chapel Hill, NC: University of North Carolina Press.
Robinson, Cedric J. 2019. *On Racial Capitalism, Black Internationalism, and Cultures of Resistance*. Edited by H. L. T. Quan, foreword by Ruth Gilmore. London: Pluto.
Robinson, William I., Salvador Rangel, and Hilbourne A. Watson. 2022. "The Cult of Cedric Robinson's *Black Marxism*: A Proletarian Critique." *Midwestern Marx* (online), 3 October.
Rocha, Zarine L. and Brenda S. A. Yeoh. 2021. "Managing the Complexities of Race: Eurasians, Classification and Mixed Racial Identities in Singapore." *Journal of Ethnic and Migration Studies* 47, no. 4: 878–94.
Roemer, John E., Woojin Lee, and Karine Van der Straeten 2007. *Racism, Xenophobia, and Distribution: Multi-issue Politics in Advanced Democracies*. Cambridge, MA: Harvard University Press.
Romani, Rose (ed.). 1995. *The Nazi Genocide of the Sinti and Roma*. Berlin. Documentary and Cultural Centre of German Sinti and Roma.
Ross, Marlon Bryan. 2004. *Manning the Race: Reforming Black Men in the Jim Crow Era*. New York: NYU Press.
Roth, Cecil. 1930, 1975. *History of the Jews in Venice*. New York: Schocken.

Roth, Wendy D. 2005. "The End of the One-Drop Rule? Labeling of Multiracial Children in Black Intermarriages." *Sociological Forum* 20, no. 1: 35–67.

Roth, Wendy D. 2018. "Unsettled Identities amid Settled Classifications? Toward a Sociology of Racial Appraisals." *Ethnic & Racial Studies* 41, no. 6: 1093–112.

Rothstein, Richard. 2017. *The Color of Law: A Forgotten History of How Our Government Segregated America.* New York: Liveright Publishing.

Rotman, Edgardo. 1995. "The Failure of Reform: United States, 1865–1965." Pp. 169–97 in *The Oxford History of the Prison*. Edited by Norval Morris and David J. Rothman. New York: Oxford University Press.

Roux, Guillaume. 2017. "Expliquer le rejet de la police en banlieue: discriminations, 'ciblage des quartiers' et racialisation. Un état de l'art." *Droit et société* 97, no. 3: 555–68.

Roux, Guillaume and Sébastian Roché. 2016. "Police et phénomènes identitaires dans les banlieues: entre ethnicité et territoire. Une étude par focus groups." *Revue française de science politique* 66, no. 5: 729–50.

Rucker, Julian M. and Jennifer A. Richeson. 2021. "Toward an Understanding of Structural Racism: Implications for Criminal Justice." *Science* 374, no. 6565: 286–90.

Ruiz-Tagle, Javier. 2018. "Bringing Inequality Closer: A Comparative Look at Socially Diverse Neighbourhoods in Chicago and Santiago de Chile." Pp. 139–64 in *Divercities: Understanding Super-Diversity in Deprived and Mixed Neighbourhoods*. Edited by Stijn Oosterlynck and Gert Verschraegen. Bristol: Policy Press.

Saada, Emmanuelle. 2007. *Les Enfants de la colonie. Les métis de l'Empire français entre sujétion et citoyenneté*. Paris: La Découverte.

Sabbagh, Daniel. 2003. *Les Paradoxes de la discrimination positive aux États-Unis*. Paris: Economica.

Sabbagh, Daniel. 2011. "The Paradox of Decategorization: Deinstitutionalizing Race through Race-Based Affirmative Action in the United States." *Ethnic & Racial Studies* 34, no. 10: 1665–81.

Sabbagh, Daniel. 2021. "De la déracialisation en Amérique. Apports et limites de la Critical Race Theory." *Droit et société* 108: 287–301.

Sabbagh, Daniel. 2022. "Le 'racisme systémique': un conglomérat problématique." *Mouvements*, hors-série, 2: 56–74.

Sabbagh, Daniel. 2023. "De la race en sciences sociales (France, XXIe siècle). Éléments pour une synthèse comparative." *Politix* 35, no. 140: 125–88.

Sabouret, Jean-François. 1983. *L'Autre Japon, les Burakumin*. Paris: Maspéro.

Safi, Mirna. 2013. *Les Inégalités ethnoraciales*. Paris: La Découverte.

Sampson, Robert J. and Janet L. Lauritsen. 1997. "Racial and Ethnic Disparities in Crime and Criminal Justice in the United States." Pp. 311–74 in *Ethnicity, Crime, and Immigration: Comparative and Cross-*

References

National Perspectives. Edited by Michael Tonry. Chicago, IL: University of Chicago Press.

Sampson, Robert J. and Charles Loeffler. 2010. "Punishment's Place: The Local Concentration of Mass Incarceration." *Daedalus: Journal of the American Academy of Arts and Sciences* 139, no. 3: 20–31.

Sandel, Michael (ed.). 2007. *Justice: A Reader*. New York: Oxford University Press.

Saperstein, Aliya and Aaron Gullickson. 2013. "A 'Mulatto Escape Hatch' in the United States? Examining Evidence of Racial and Social Mobility during the Jim Crow Era." *Demography* 50, no. 5: 1921–42.

Saperstein, Aliya, Andrew M. Penner, and Ryan Light. 2013. "Racial Formation in Perspective: Connecting Individuals, Institutions, and Power Relations." *Annual Review of Sociology* 39: 359–78.

Saraçoğlu, Cenk. 2011. *Kurds of Modern Turkey: Migration, Neoliberalism and Exclusion in Turkish Society*. London: Tauris.

Sartre, Jean-Paul. 1946. *Réflexions sur la question juive*. Paris: Gallimard.

Saussol, Alain. 1981. *L'Héritage. Essai sur le problème foncier mélanésien en Nouvelle-Calédonie*. Paris: Société des océanistes.

Sayad, Abdelmalek, with the collaboration of Eliane Dupuy. 1995. *Un Nanterre algérien, terre de bidonvilles*. Paris: Editions Autrement.

Sayad, Abdelmalek. 2021. *Femmes en rupture de ban. Entretiens inédits avec deux Algériennes*. Paris: Raisons d'agir Éditions.

Schachter, Ariela, René D. Flores, and Neda Maghbouleh. 2021. "Ancestry, Color, or Culture? How Whites Racially Classify Others in the US." *American Journal of Sociology* 126, no. 5: 1220–63.

Schaub, Jean-Frédéric. 2015. *Pour une histoire politique de la race*. Paris: Seuil.

Schaub, Jean-Frédéric. 2018. "Temps et race." *Archives de Philosophie* 81, no. 3: 455–75.

Schaub, Jean-Frédéric and Silvia Sebastiani. 2021. *Race et histoire dans les sociétés occidentales (XVe–XVIIIe siècles)*. Paris: Albin Michel.

Scheper-Hughes, Nancy and Philippe Bourgois (eds.). 2004. *Violence in War and Peace: An Anthology*. Malden, MA: Blackwell.

Schilt, Kristen and Danya Lagos. 2017. "The Development of Transgender Studies in Sociology." *Annual Review of Sociology* 43: 425–43.

Schimmack, Ulrich. 2021. "The Implicit Association Test: A Method in Search of a Construct." *Perspectives on Psychological Science* 16, no. 2: 396–414.

Schoenfeld, Heather. 2018. *Building the Prison State: Race and the Politics of Mass Incarceration*. Chicago, IL: University of Chicago Press.

Schor, Paul. 2009. *Compter et classer. Histoire des recensements américains*. Paris: Éditions de l'EHESS.

Schultz, Mark. 2005. *The Rural Face of White Supremacy: Beyond Jim Crow*. Urbana, IL: University of Illinois Press.

Scott, Terry Anne, 2022. *Lynching and Leisure: Race and the Transformation of Mob Violence in Texas*. Little Rock, AK: University of Arkansas Press.

Seamster, Louise and Victor Ray. 2018. "Against Teleology in the Study of Race: Toward the Abolition of the Progress Paradigm." *Sociological Theory* 36, no. 4: 315–42.

Seidman, Gay. 1999. "Is South Africa Different? Sociological Comparisons and Theoretical Contributions from the Land of Apartheid." *Annual Review of Sociology* 25: 419–40.

Sen, Amartya. 2010. *The Idea of Justice*. Cambridge, MA: Belknap Press.

Sénac, Réjane 2012. *L'Invention de la diversité*. Paris: PUF.

Sewell, William H., Jr. 2005. *Logics of History: Social Theory and Social Transformation*. Chicago, IL: University of Chicago Press.

Sexton, Jared. 2016. "Afro-Pessimism: The Unclear Word." *Rhizomes: Cultural Studies in Emerging Knowledge* 29: 1–21.

Shaffer, Hannah. 2023. "Prosecutors, Race, and the Criminal Pipeline." *University of Chicago Law Review*: in press.

Shakur, Sanyika. 1993. *Monster: The Autobiography of an L.A. Gang Member*. New York: Atlantic Monthly Press.

Sharkey, Patrick. 2008. "The Intergenerational Transmission of Context." *American Journal of Sociology* 113, no. 4: 931–69.

Sharkey, Patrick. 2014. "Spatial Segmentation and the Black Middle Class." *American Journal of Sociology* 119, no. 4: 903–54.

Sharpless, Rebecca. 2010. *Cooking in Other Women's Kitchens: Domestic Workers in the South, 1865–1960*. Chapel Hill, NC: University of North Carolina Press.

Shelby, Tommie. 2005. *We Who Are Dark: The Philosophical Foundations of Black Solidarity*. Cambridge, MA: Harvard University Press.

Shelby, Tommie. 2014. "Racism, Moralism, and Social Criticism." *Du Bois Review: Social Science Research on Race* 11, no. 1: 57–74.

Shelby, Tommie. 2016. *Dark Ghettos: Injustice, Dissent, and Reform*. Cambridge, MA: Harvard University Press.

Shelby, Tommie. 2022. *The Idea of Prison Abolition*. Princeton, NJ: Princeton University Press.

Shepard, Todd. 2006. *The Invention of Decolonization: The Algerian War and the Remaking of France*. Ithaca, NY: Cornell University Press.

Shichor, David and Dale K. Sechrest (eds.). 1996. *Three Strikes and You're Out: Vengeance as Public Policy*. Thousand Oaks, CA: Sage Publications.

Shim, Ruth S. 2021. "Dismantling Structural Racism in Psychiatry: A Path to Mental Health Equity." *American Journal of Psychiatry* 178, no. 7: 592–8.

Shute, Rosemary Brana. 1998. "United States Law." Pp. 255–7 in *A Historical Guide to World Slavery*. Edited by Seymour Drescher and Stanley L. Engerman. New York: Oxford University Press.

Siddle, Richard M. 2012. *Race, Resistance and the Ainu of Japan*. New York: Routledge.

References

Silberman, Roxane and Irène Fournier. 2006. "Les secondes générations sur le marché du travail en France: une pénalité ethnique ancrée dans le temps. Contribution à la théorie de l'assimilation segmentée." *Revue française de sociologie* 47, no. 2: 243–92.

Silverstein, Paul A. 2018. *Postcolonial France: Race, Islam, and the Future of the Republic*. London: Pluto Press.

Simes, Jessica T. 2021. *Punishing Places: The Geography of Mass Imprisonment*. Berkeley, CA: University of California Press.

Simmons, LaKisha Michelle. 2015. *Crescent City Girls: The Lives of Young Black Women in Segregated New Orleans*. Chapel Hill, NC: University of North Carolina Press.

Simon, Jonathan. 2000. "The 'Society of Captives' in the Era of Hyper-Incarceration." *Theoretical Criminology* 4, no. 3: 285–308.

Simon, Patrick. 2017. "The Failure of the Importation of Ethno-Racial Statistics in Europe: Debates and Controversies." *Ethnic & Racial Studies* 40, no. 13: 2326–32.

Simon, Patrick, Victor Piché, and Amélie A. Gagnon (eds.). 2015. *Social Statistics and Ethnic Diversity: Cross-National Perspectives in Classifications and Identity Politics*. Berlin: Springer.

Sitkoff, Harvard. 1978. *A New Deal for Blacks: The Emergence of Civil Rights as a National Issue: The Depression Decade*. New York: Oxford University Press.

Skarbek, David. 2014. *The Social Order of the Underworld: How Prison Gangs Govern the American Penal System*. New York: Oxford University Press.

Slezkine, Yuri. 1994. "The USSR as a Communal Apartment, Or How a Socialist State Promoted Ethnic Particularism." *Slavic Review* 53, no. 2: 414–52.

Small, Mario Luis and Devah Pager. 2020. "Sociological Perspectives on Racial Discrimination." *Journal of Economic Perspectives* 34, no. 2: 49–67.

Smedley, Audrey. 1998. "Race and Racism." Pp. 321–6 in *A Historical Guide to World Slavery*. Edited by Seymour Drescher and Stanley L. Engerman. New York: Oxford University Press.

Smedley, Brian D. 2012. "The Lived Experience of Race and Its Health Consequences." *American Journal of Public Health* 102, no. 5: 933–5.

Smith, David E. B. 1993. "Clean Sweep or Witch Hunt: Constitutional Issues in Chicago's Public Housing Sweeps." *Chicago-Kent Law Review* 69: 505–48.

Smith, J. Douglas. 2002. *Managing White Supremacy: Race, Politics, and Citizenship in Jim Crow Virginia*. Chapel Hill, NC: University of North Carolina Press.

Smith, Justin E. H. 2015. *Nature, Human Nature, and Human Difference. Race in Early Modern Philosophy*. Princeton, NJ: Princeton University Press.

Smith, Lahra. 2013. *Making Citizens in Africa: Ethnicity, Gender, and National Identity in Ethiopia*. New York: Cambridge University Press.

Smith, Phillip. 2008. *Punishment and Culture*. Chicago, IL: University of Chicago Press.
Smith, Rogers M. 2003. *Stories of Peoplehood: The Politics and Morals of Political Membership*. New York: Cambridge University Press.
Smythe, Hugh H. 1948. "The Concept 'Jim Crow'." *Social Forces* 27, no. 1: 45–8.
Snowball, Lucy and Don Weatherburn. 2007. "Does Racial Bias in Sentencing Contribute to Indigenous Overrepresentation in Prison?" *Australian & New Zealand Journal of Criminology* 40, no. 3: 272–90.
Sofsky, Wolfgang. 1993. *Die Ordnung des Terrors. Das Konzentrationlager*. Berlin: Fischer Verlag.
Sokol, Jason. 2008. *There Goes My Everything: White Southerners in the Age of Civil Rights, 1945–1975*. New York: Vintage.
Solhjell, Randi, Elsa Saarikkomäki, Mie Birk Haller, David Wästerfors, and Torsten Kolind. 2019. "'We Are Seen as a Threat': Police Stops of Young Ethnic Minorities in the Nordic Countries." *Critical Criminology* 27, no. 4: 347–61.
Sollors, Werner. 2001. "Ethnicity and Race." Pp. 97–104 in *Companion to Racial and Ethnic Studies*. Edited by John Solomos and David Theo Goldberg. Cambridge, MA: Blackwell.
Sollund, Ragnhild. 2006. "Racialisation in Police Stop and Search Practice: The Norwegian Case." *Critical Criminology* 14, no. 3: 265–92.
Soss, Joe and Vesla Weaver. 2017. "Police Are Our Government: Politics and the Policing of Race-Class Subjugated Communities." *Annual Review of Political Science* 20: 565–91.
Spain, Daphne. 1992. *Gendered Spaces*. Chapel Hill, NC: University of North Carolina Press.
Spear, Allan H. 1967. *Black Chicago: The Making of a Negro Ghetto, 1890–1920*. Chicago, IL: University of Chicago Press.
Spohn, Cassia. 2000. "Thirty Years of Sentencing Reform: The Quest for a Racially Neutral Sentencing Process." *Criminal Justice* 3, no. 1: 427–501.
Spohn, Cassia. 2017. "Race and Sentencing Disparity." *Reforming Criminal Justice: A Report of the Academy for Justice on Bridging the Gap Between Scholarship and Reform* 4: 169–86.
Spohn, Cassia and Jerry Cederblom. 1991. "Race and Disparities in Sentencing: A Test of the Liberation Hypothesis." *Justice Quarterly* 8, no. 3: 305–27.
Stampp, Kenneth M. 1989 [1956]. *Peculiar Institution: Slavery in the Ante-Bellum South*. New York: Vintage.
Stauber, Roni and Raphael Vago (eds.). 2007. *The Roma, a Minority in Europe: Historical, Political and Social Perspectives*. Budapest: Central European University Press.
Stein, Melissa. 2012. "'Nature Is the Author of Such Restrictions': Science, Ethnological Medicine, and Jim Crow." Pp. 124–49 in *The Folly of Jim*

References

Crow: Rethinking the Segregated South. Edited by Stefanie Cole and Natalie J. Ring. Arlington, TX: Texas A&M University Press.

Steinmetz, George. 2008a. *The Devil's Handwriting: Precoloniality and the German Colonial State in Qingdao, Samoa, and Southwest Africa*. Chicago, IL: University of Chicago Press.

Steinmetz, George. 2008b. "The Colonial State as a Social Field: Ethnographic Capital and Native Policy in the German Overseas Empire before 1914." *American Sociological Review* 73, no. 4: 589–612.

Steinmetz, George (ed.). 2013. *Sociology and Empire: The Imperial Entanglements of a Discipline*. Durham, NC: Duke University Press.

Steinmetz, George. 2014. "The Sociology of Empires, Colonies, and Postcolonialism." *Annual Review of Sociology* 40: 77–103.

Steinmetz, George. 2016. "Social Fields, Subfields and Social Spaces at the Scale of Empires: Explaining the Colonial State and Colonial Sociology." *The Sociological Review* 64, no. 2: 98–123.

Stewart, Michael. 2013. "Roma and Gypsy 'Ethnicity' as a Subject of Anthropological Inquiry." *Annual Review of Anthropology* 42: 415–32.

Stoler, Ann. 1992. "Sexual Affronts and Racial Frontiers: European Identities and the Cultural Politics of Exclusions in Colonial Southeast Asia." *Comparative Studies in Society and History* 34, no. 3: 514–51.

Stoler, Ann Laura. 1997. "Racial Histories and Their Regimes of Truth." *Political Power and Social Theory* 11, no. 1: 183–206.

Stoler, Ann Laura. 2002. *Carnal Knowledge and Imperial Power: Race and the Intimate in Colonial Rule*. Berkeley, CA: University of California Press.

Stone, Dan. 2019. *Concentration Camps: A Very Short Introduction*. Oxford: Oxford University Press.

Strong, Pauline Turner. 2005. "Recent Ethnographic Research on North American Indigenous Peoples." *Annual Review of Anthropology* 34: 253–68.

Stuart, Forrest and Reuben Jonathan Miller. 2017. "The Prisonized Old Head: Intergenerational Socialization and the Fusion of Ghetto and Prison Culture." *Journal of Contemporary Ethnography* 46, no. 6: 673–98.

Sturkey, William. 2019. *Hattiesburg: An American City in Black and White*. Cambridge, MA: Harvard University Press.

Stuurman, Siep. 2000. "François Bernier and the Invention of Racial Classification." *History Workshop Journal* 50, no. 1: 1–21.

Stuurman, Siep. 2017. *The Invention of Humanity: Equality and Cultural Difference in World History*. Cambridge, MA: Harvard University Press.

Sudbury, Julia (ed.). 2014. *Global Lockdown: Race, Gender, and the Prison-Industrial Complex*. London: Routledge.

Sue, Christina and Tanya Golash-Boza. 2013. "'It Was Only a Joke': How Racial Humor Fuels Race-blind Ideologies in Mexico and Peru." *Ethnic & Racial Studies* 36, no. 10: 1577–94.

Sue, Derald Wing and Lisa Spanierman. 2020. *Microaggressions in Everyday Life*. New York: Wiley.

Sugrue, Tom. 2005 [1996]. *The Origins of the Urban Crisis: Race and Inequality in Postwar Detroit*. Princeton, NJ: Princeton University Press.
Sullivan, Patricia. 2009. *Lift Every Voice: The NAACP and the Making of the Civil Rights Movement*. New York: New Press.
Susewind, Raphael. 2017. "Muslims in Indian Cities: Degrees of Segregation and the Elusive Ghetto." *Environment and Planning A* 49, no. 6: 1286–307.
Sweet, Frank W. 2005. *Legal History of the Color Line: The Rise and Triumph of the One-Drop Rule*. Palm Coast, FL: Backintyme.
Sykes, Gresham. 1958. *The Society of Captives: A Study in a Maximum Security Prison*. Princeton, NJ: Princeton University Press.
Sykes, Gresham and Sheldon Messinger. 1960. "The Inmate Social System." Pp. 6–10 in *Theoretical Studies in the Social Organization of the Prison*. Edited by Richard Cloward et al. New York: Social Science Research Council.
Táíwò, Olúfẹ́mi O. 2022. *Elite Capture: How the Powerful Took over Identity Politics (and Everything Else)*. Chicago, IL: Haymarket Books.
Takaki, Ronald T. 1993. *Violence in the Black Imagination*. New York: Oxford University Press.
Tambiah, Stanley J. 1996. *Levelling Crowds: Ethnonationalist Conflicts and Collective Violence*. Berkeley, CA: University of California Press.
Tan, Eugene K. B. 2001. "From Sojourners to Citizens: Managing the Ethnic Chinese Minority in Indonesia and Malaysia." *Ethnic & Racial Studies* 24, no. 6: 949–78.
Tanovich, David M. 2004. "Moving Beyond Driving While Black: Race, Suspect Description and Selection." *Ottawa Law Review* 36: 315–48.
Taylor, Candacy A. 2020. *Overground Railroad: The Green Book and the Roots of Black Travel in America*. New York: Abrams.
Taylor, Christopher C. 2011. "Molders of Mud: Ethnogenesis and Rwanda's Twa." *Ethnos* 76, no. 2: 183–208.
Taylor, Keeanga-Yamahtta. 2016. *From #BlackLivesMatter to Black Liberation*. Chicago, IL: Haymarket Books.
Taylor, Keeanga-Yamahtta. 2019. *Race for Profit: How Banks and the Real Estate Industry Undermined Black Homeownership*. Chapel Hill, NC: University of North Carolina Press.
Telles, Edward E. 1992. "Residential Segregation by Skin Color in Brazil." *American Sociological Review* 57, no. 2: 186–97.
Telles, Edward E. 2004. *Race in Another America: The Significance of Skin Color in Brazil*. Princeton, NJ: Princeton University Press.
Telles, Edward. 2014. *Pigmentocracies: Ethnicity, Race, and Color in Latin America*. Chapel Hill, NC: University of North Carolina Press.
Telles, Edward and Tianna Paschel. 2014. "Who is Black, White, or Mixed Race? How Skin Color, Status, and Nation Shape Racial Classification in Latin America." *American Journal of Sociology* 120, no. 3: 864–907.
Telles, Edward E. and Christina A. Sue. 2009. "Race Mixture: Boundary

References

Crossing in Comparative Perspective." *Annual Review of Sociology* 35: 129–46.
Terry, David Taft. 2019. *The Struggle and the Urban South: Confronting Jim Crow in Baltimore before the Movement.* Athens, GA: University of Georgia Press.
Testart, Alain. 2018. *L'Institution de l'esclavage. Une approche mondiale.* Paris: Gallimard.
Thiara, Ravi K. 1999. "The African-Indian Antithesis? The 1949 Durban 'Riots' in South Africa." Pp. 161–84 in *Thinking Identities: Ethnicity, Racism and Culture*. Edited by Avtar Brah, Mary J. Hickman, and Máirtín Mac an Ghaill. London: Palgrave Macmillan.
Thomas, Charlotte. 2018. *Pogroms et ghetto. Les musulmans dans l'Inde contemporaine.* Paris: Karthala.
Thomas, Martin. 2012. *Violence and Colonial Order: Police, Workers and Protest in the European Colonial Empires, 1918–1940.* Cambridge: Cambridge University Press.
Thompson, Heather Ann. 2017. *Blood in the Water: The Attica Prison Uprising of 1971 and Its Legacy.* New York: Vintage.
Thomson, Susan M. 2009. "Ethnic Twa and Rwandan National Unity and Reconciliation Policy." *Peace Review* 21, no. 3: 313–20.
Thorp, Daniel B. 2017. *Facing Freedom: An African American Community in Virginia from Reconstruction to Jim Crow.* Charlottesville, VA: University of Virginia Press.
Tiles, Mary. 1984. *Bachelard: Science and Objectivity.* Cambridge: Cambridge University Press.
Tilly, Charles. 1992. *Coercion, Capital, and European States, AD 990–1992.* Cambridge, MA: Blackwell.
Tindall, George B. (ed.). 1966. *A Populist Reader: Selections from the Works of American Populist Leaders.* New York: Harper Torchbooks.
Tolnay, Stewart E. 1999. *The Bottom Rung: African American Family Life on Southern Farms.* Champaign, IL: University of Illinois Press.
Tolnay, Steward E. 2003. "The African American 'Great Migration' and Beyond." *Annual Review of Sociology* 29: 209–32.
Tolnay, Stewart E. and E. M. Beck. 1992. "Racial Violence and Black Migration in the American South, 1910 to 1930." *American Sociological Review* 57, no. 1: 103–16.
Tolnay, Stewart E. and E. M. Beck. 1995. *A Festival of Violence: An Analysis of Southern Lynchings, 1882–1930.* Urbana, IL: University of Illinois Press.
Tonry, Michael. 1995. *Malign Neglect: Race, Crime, and Punishment in America.* New York: Oxford University Press.
Tonry, Michael. 2011. *Punishing Race: A Continuing American Dilemma.* New York: Oxford University Press.
Torpey, John. 2006. *Making Whole What Has Been Smashed: On Reparations Politics.* Cambridge, MA: Harvard University Press.

Travis, Jeremy, Bruce Western, and Steve Redburn (eds.). 2014. *The Growth of Incarceration in the United States: Exploring Causes and Consequences.* Washington, DC: National Academy of Sciences.

Tribalat, Michèle. 2016. *Statistiques ethniques, une querelle bien française.* Paris: L'Artilleur.

Tripier, Maryse. 1991. *L'Immigration dans la classe ouvrière en France.* Paris: L'Harmattan.

Troesken, Werner. 2004. *Water, Race, and Disease.* Cambridge, MA: MIT Press.

Trounstine, Jessica. 2018. *Segregation by Design: Local Politics and Inequality in American Cities.* New York: Cambridge University Press.

Trulson, Chad R., James W. Marquart, Craig Hemmens, and Leo Carroll. 2008. "Racial Desegregation in Prisons." *The Prison Journal* 88, no. 2: 270–99.

Truong, Fabien. 2013. *Des Capuches et des hommes. Trajectoires de "jeunes de banlieue."* Paris: Buchet-Chastel.

Twine, France Winddance and Jonathan Warren (eds.). 2003. *Racing Research, Researching Race: Methodological Dilemmas in Critical Race Studies.* New York: NYU Press.

Tyson, Timothy B. 2017. *The Blood of Emmett Till.* New York: Simon and Schuster.

Ulmer, Jeffery T. 2019. "Criminal Courts as Inhabited Institutions: Making Sense of Difference and Similarity in Sentencing." *Crime and Justice* 48: 483–522.

Useem, Bert and Peter Kimball. 1989. *States of Siege: U.S. Prison Riots, 1971–1986.* New York: Oxford University Press.

Van den Berghe, Pierre L. 1967. *Race and Racism: A Comparative Perspective.* New York: Wiley.

Venkatesh, Suhdir. 2000. *American Project: The Rise and Fall of a Modern Ghetto.* Cambridge, MA: Harvard University Press.

Verdugo, Gregory. 2011. "Logement social et ségrégation résidentielle des immigrés en France, 1968–1999." *Population* 66, no. 1: 171–96.

Verghese, Ajay. 2016. *The Colonial Origins of Ethnic Violence in India.* Stanford, CA: Stanford University Press.

Veterans of Hope. 2016. *The New Jim Crow Study Guide and Call to Action.* Scotts Valley, CA: CreateSpace.

Vidal, Cécile, 2019. *Caribbean New Orleans: Empire, Race, and the Making of a Slave Society.* Chapel Hill, NC: University of North Carolina Press.

Volovitch-Tavares, Marie-Christine. 2016. *100 ans d'histoire des Portugais en France, 1916–2016.* Paris: Michel Lafon.

Wachsmann, Nikolaus. 2015. *KL: A History of the Nazi Concentration Camps.* London: Abacus.

Wacquant, Loïc. 1997. "For an Analytic of Racial Domination." *Political Power & Social Theory* 11, no. 1: 221–34.

References

Wacquant, Loïc. 1998a [1992]. "Inside the Zone: The Social Art of the Hustler in the Black American Ghetto." *Theory, Culture & Society* 15, no. 2: 1–36.
Wacquant, Loïc. 1998b. "'A Black City Within the White': Revisiting America's Dark Ghetto." *Black Renaissance* 2, no. 1: 141–51.
Wacquant, Loïc. 2000. "The New 'Peculiar Institution': On the Prison as Surrogate Ghetto." *Theoretical Criminology* 4, no. 3: 377–89.
Wacquant, Loïc. 2002. "The Curious Eclipse of Prison Ethnography in the Age of Mass Incarceration." *Ethnography* 3, no. 4: 371–97.
Wacquant, Loïc (ed.). 2005a. *Pierre Bourdieu and Democratic Politics: The Mystery of Ministry*. Cambridge: Polity Press.
Wacquant, Loïc. 2005b. "Race as Civic Felony." *International Social Science Journal* 57, no. 183: 127–42.
Wacquant, Loïc. 2006. "Penalization, Depoliticization, and Racialization: On the Overincarceration of Immigrants in the European Union." Pp. 83–100 in *Perspectives on Punishment: The Contours of Control*. Edited by Sarah Armstrong and Lesley McAra. Oxford: Clarendon Press.
Wacquant, Loïc. 2008. *Urban Outcasts: A Comparative Sociology of Advanced Marginality*. Cambridge: Polity.
Wacquant, Loïc. 2009. *Punishing the Poor: The Neoliberal Government of Social Insecurity*. Durham, NC: Duke University Press.
Wacquant, Loïc. 2010a. "Designing Urban Seclusion in the Twenty-First Century: The 2009 Roth-Symonds Lecture." *Perspecta* 43: 164–75.
Wacquant, Loïc. 2010b. "Class, Race and Hyperincarceration in Revanchist America." *Daedalus: Journal of the American Academy of Arts and Sciences* 139, no. 3: 74–90.
Wacquant, Loïc. 2010c. "Prison Reentry as Myth and Ceremony." *Dialectical Anthropology* 34, no. 4: 605–20.
Wacquant, Loïc. 2011. "A Janus-Faced Institution of Ethnoracial Closure: A Sociological Specification of the Ghetto." Pp. 1–31 *The Ghetto: Contemporary Global Issues and Controversies*. Edited in Ray Hutchison and Bruce Haynes. Boulder, CO: Westview.
Wacquant, Loïc. 2012. "Three Steps to a Historical Anthropology of Actually Existing Neoliberalism." *Social Anthropology/Anthropologie Sociale* 20, no. 1: 66–79.
Wacquant, Loïc. 2013. "Symbolic Power and Group-Making: On Pierre Bourdieu's Reframing of Class." *Journal of Classical Sociology* 13, no. 2: 274–91.
Wacquant, Loïc. 2015. "Revisiting Territories of Relegation: Class, Ethnicity and the State in the Making of Advanced Marginality." *Urban Studies Journal* 53, no. 6: 1077–88.
Wacquant, Loïc. 2018. "Four Transversal Principles for Putting Bourdieu to Work." *Anthropological Theory* 18, no. 1: 3–17.
Wacquant, Loïc. 2022. *The Invention of the "Underclass": A Study in the Politics of Knowledge*. Cambridge: Polity.

Wacquant, Loïc. 2023a. *Bourdieu in the City: Challenging Urban Theory*. Cambridge: Polity.

Wacquant, Loïc. 2023b, "Ein Plädoyer für eine genetische Soziologie ethnorassischer Herrschaft. Eine Antwort auf meine deutschen Kritikerinnen." *Berliner Journal für Soziologie* 33: 57–68.

Wacquant, Loïc. 2023c. "Carnal Concepts in Action." *Thesis Eleven*, https://doi.org/10.1177/07255136221149782.

Wacquant, Loïc. 2025. *The Two Faces of the Ghetto*. Cambridge: Polity Press.

Wacquant, Loïc, Tom Slater, and Virgílio Borges Pereira. 2014. "Territorial Stigmatization in Action." *Environment & Planning A* 46, no. 6: 1270–80.

Wade, Peter. 2004. "Images of Latin American *Mestizaje* and the Politics of Comparison." *Bulletin of Latin American Research* 23, no. 3: 355–66.

Wagatsuma, Hiroshi. 1967. "The Social Perception of Skin Color in Japan." *Daedalus: Journal of the American Academy of Arts and Sciences* 96, no 2: 407–43.

Wagatsuma, Hiroshi and George DeVos (eds.). 2021 [1966]. *Japan's Invisible Race: Caste in Culture and Personality*. Berkeley, CA: University of California Press.

Wagley, Charles. 1965 [1958]. "On the Concept of Social Race in the Americas." Pp. 531–45 in *Contemporary Cultures and Societies in Latin America*. Edited by Dwight B. Heath and Richard N. Adams. New York: Random House.

Walden, Donald Wayne. 2000. *The Southern Peasant: Poor Whites and the Yeoman Ideal*. Austin, TX: University of Texas.

Waldstreicher, David. 2010. *Slavery's Constitution: From Revolution to Ratification*. New York: Hill and Wang.

Walker, Anders. 2018. "New Takes on Jim Crow: A Review of Recent Scholarship." *Law and History Review* 36, no. 1: 173–9.

Walker, Michael L. 2022. *Indefinite: Doing Time in Jail*. New York: Oxford University Press.

Walter, Dierk. 2017 [2014]. *Colonial Violence: European Empires and the Use of Force*. New York: Oxford University Press.

Ward, Jason Morgan. 2011. *Defending White Democracy: The Making of a Segregationist Movement and the Remaking of Racial Politics, 1936–1965*. Chapel Hill, NC: University of North Carolina Press.

Warikoo, Natasha. 2019. *The Diversity Bargain and Other Dilemmas of Race, Admissions, and Meritocracy at Elite Universities*. Chicago, IL: University of Chicago Press.

Warner, W. Lloyd. 1936. "American Caste and Class." *American Journal of Sociology* 42, no. 2: 234–7.

Warner, W. Lloyd. 1963. *Yankee City*, abridged edition. New Haven, CT: Yale University Press.

Waters, Mary C. 1990. *Ethnic Options: Choosing Identities in America*. Berkeley, CA: University of California Press.

References

Waters, Mary C. 2009. *Black Identities: West Indian Immigrant Dreams and American Realities*. Cambridge, MA: Harvard University Press.

Weber, Eugen. 1976. *Peasants into Frenchmen: The Modernization of Rural France, 1870–1914*. Stanford, CA: Stanford University Press.

Weber, Max. 1949 [1904]. "'Objectivity' in Social Science and Social Policy." Pp. 50–112 in *The Methodology of the Social Sciences*. Edited by Edward A. Shils and H. A. Finch. New York: Free Press.

Weber, Max 1949 [1920]. *The Methodology of the Social Sciences*. Edited by Edward A. Shils and H. A. Finch. New York: Free Press.

Weber, Max. 1950 [1920]. *The City*. New York: Free Press.

Weber, Max. 1958 [1919]. "Science as a Vocation." *Daedalus: Journal of the American Academy of Arts and Sciences* 87, no. 1: 111–34.

Weber, Max. 1978 [1918–22]. *Economy and Society: An Outline of Interpretive Sociology*. Berkeley, CA: University of California Press, 2 vols.

Weber, Max. 1992 [1965]. *Essais sur la théorie de la science*. Paris: Plon.

Weber, Max. 2020. *La Domination*. Translation by Isabelle Kalinowski, introduction by Yves Sintomer. Paris: La Découverte.

Weddington, George. 2019 "Political Ontology and Race Research: A Response to 'Critical Race Theory, Afro-Pessimism, and Racial Progress Narratives'." *Sociology of Race and Ethnicity* 5, no. 2: 278–88.

Weise, Julie M. 2015. *Corazón de Dixie: Mexicanos in the US South since 1910*. Chapel Hill, NC: University of North Carolina Press.

Welch, Cheryl B. 2003. "Colonial Violence and the Rhetoric of Evasion: Tocqueville on Algeria." *Political Theory* 31, no. 2: 235–64.

Welch, Rhiannon Noel. 2016. *Vital Subjects: Race and Biopolitics in Italy*. Liverpool: Liverpool University Press.

Werhun, Cherie D. and April J. Penner. 2010. "The Effects of Stereotyping and Implicit Theory: On Benevolent Prejudice toward Aboriginal Canadians." *Journal of Applied Social Psychology* 40, no. 4: 899–916.

Werth, Robert. 2013. "The Construction and Stewardship of Responsible Yet Precarious Subjects: Punitive Ideology, Rehabilitation, and 'Tough Love' Among Parole Personnel." *Punishment & Society* 15, no. 3: 219–46.

Western, Bruce. 2006. *Punishment and Inequality in America*. New York: Russell Sage Foundation.

Western, Bruce. 2018. *Homeward: Life in the Year After Prison*. New York: Russell Sage Foundation.

Western, John. 1997 [1981]. *Outcast Cape Town*. Berkeley, CA: University of California Press.

Whalen, Eamon. 2022. "The Police are Defunding Minneapolis: Two Years since George Floyd was Murdered, the Minneapolis Police Department is a Fiscal Disaster," *Mother Jones*, August 30.

White House. 2023. Advancing equity and racial justice through the federal government. *The White House*. https://www.whitehouse.gov/equity/

White, Ariel R. 2022. "Political Participation amid Mass Incarceration." *Annual Review of Political Science* 25: 111–30.

White, Deborah Gray. 1999. *Too Heavy a Load: Black Women in Defense of Themselves, 1894–1994*. New York: Norton.

White, Walter. 2002 [1929]. *Rope and Faggot: A Biography of Judge Lynch*. Notre Dame, IN: University of Notre Dame Pess.

Whitman, James Q. 2017. *Hitler's American Model: The United States and the Making of Nazi Race Law*. Princeton, NJ: Princeton University Press.

Wideman, John Edgar. 1995. "Doing Time, Marking Race." *The Nation* 261: 503–5.

Wiener, Jonathan M. 1979. "Class Stucture and Economic Development in the American South, 1865–1955." *The American Historical Review* 84, no. 4: 970–92.

Wihtol de Wenden, Catherine and Rémy Leveau. 2001. *La Beurgeoisie. Les trois âges de la vie associative issue de l'immigration*. Paris: CNRS Éditions.

Wildeman, Christopher, Maria D. Fitzpatrick, and Alyssa W. Goldman. 2018. "Conditions of Confinement in American Prisons and Jails." *Annual Review of Law and Social Science* 14: 29–47.

Wilderson, Frank B., III. 2020. *Afropessimism*. New York: Liveright Publishing.

Wilkerson, Isabel. 2020. *Caste: The Origins of Our Discontents*. New York: Random House.

Wilkinson, Aaron B. 2020. *Blurring the Lines of Race and Freedom: Mulattoes and Mixed Bloods in English Colonial America*. Chapel Hill, NC: University of North Carolina Press.

Williams, Lee E. 2008. *Anatomy of Four Race Riots: Racial Conflict in Knoxville, Elaine (Arkansas), Tulsa, and Chicago, 1919–1921*. Jackson, MI: University Press of Mississippi.

Williams, Vernon J. 2006. *The Social Sciences and Theories of Race*. Urbana, IL: University of Illinois Press.

Williamson, Joel. 1980. *New People: Miscegenation and Mulattoes in the United States*. New York: Free Press.

Williamson, Joel. 1984. *The Crucible of Race: Black–White Relations in the American South Since Emancipation*. New York: Oxford University Press.

Williamson, Joel. 1986. *A Rage for Order: Black–White Relations in the American South Since Emancipation*. New York: Oxford University Press.

Wilson, Kathleen (ed.). 2004. *A New Imperial History: Culture, Identity, and Modernity in Britain and the Empire, 1660–1840*. Cambridge: Cambridge University Press.

Wilson, Richard A. 2001. *The Politics of Truth and Reconciliation in South Africa: Legitimizing the Post-Apartheid State*. Cambridge: Cambridge University Press.

Wilson, William Julius. 1976. "Class Conflict and Jim Crow Segregation in the Postbellum South." *Pacific Sociological Review* 19, no. 4: 431–46.

References

Wilson, William Julius. 1980 [1978]. *The Declining Significance of Race: Blacks and American Institutions*, 2nd edition. Chicago, IL: University of Chicago Press.
Wilson, William Julius. 1987. *The Truly Disadvantaged: The Inner City, the Underclass and Public Policy*. Chicago, IL: University of Chicago Press.
Wilson, William Julius. 1996. *When Work Disappears: The World of the New Urban Poor*. New York: Knopf.
Wimmer, Andreas. 2008. "Elementary Strategies of Ethnic Boundary Making." *Ethnic & Racial Studies* 31, no. 6: 1025–55.
Wimmer, Andreas. 2012. *Waves of War: Nationalism, State Formation, and Ethnic Exclusion in the Modern World*. New York: Cambridge University Press.
Wimmer, Andreas. 2013. *Ethnic Boundary Making: Institutions, Power, Networks*. New York: Oxford University Press.
Wimmer, Andreas. 2015. "Race-Centrism: A Critique and Research Agenda." *Ethnic & Racial Studies* 38, no. 13: 2186–205.
Wimmer, Andreas and Nina Glick Schiller. 2002. "Methodological Nationalism and Beyond: Nation-State Building, Migration and the Social Sciences." *Global Networks* 2, no. 4: 301–34.
Winant, Howard. 2001. *The World is a Ghetto: Race and Democracy Since World War II*. New York: Basic Books.
Winant, Howard. 2015. "Race, Ethnicity and Social Science." *Ethnic & Racial Studies* 38, no. 13: 2176–85.
Winant, Howard. 2016. "Is there a Racial Order? Comments on Emirbayer and Desmond." *Ethnic & Racial Studies* 39, no. 13: 2285–92.
Wolfe, Patrick. 2002. "Race and Racialisation: Some Thoughts." *Postcolonial Studies: Culture, Politics, Economy* 5, no. 1: 51–62.
Wolfe, Patrick. 2006. "Settler Colonialism and the Elimination of the Native." *Journal of Genocide Research* 8, no. 4: 387–409.
Wolfe, Patrick. 2016. *Traces of History: Elementary Structures of Race*. London: Verso.
Wood, Amy Louise. 2011. *Lynching and Spectacle: Witnessing Racial Violence in America, 1890–1940*. Chapel Hill, NC: University of North Carolina Press.
Wood, Amy Louise and Natalie J. Ring (eds.). 2019. *Crime and Punishment in the Jim Crow South*. Urbana, IL: University of Illinois Press.
Woodruff, Nan Elizabeth. 2009. *American Congo: The African American Freedom Struggle in the Delta*. Cambridge, MA: Harvard University Press.
Woodward, C. Vann. 2001 [1957]. *The Strange Career of Jim Crow*, fifth edition. New York: Oxford University Press.
Woodward, C. Vann. 1971. *American Counterpoint: Slavery and Racism in the North–South Dialogue*. Boston, MA: Little, Brown.
Woodward, C. Vann. 1972. *The Origins of the New South, 1877–1913*. Baton Rouge, LA: Louisiana State University.

Woodward, C. Vann. 1988. "*Strange Career* Critics: Long May They Persevere." *The Journal of American History* 75, no. 3: 857–68.

Worden, Nigel. 2011. *The Making of Modern South Africa: Conquest, Apartheid, Democracy*. Malden, MA: Wiley.

Wormser, Richard. 2003. *The Rise and Fall of Jim Crow*. New York: Saint-Martin's Griffin.

Wortley, Scot and Akwasi Owusu-Bempah. 2011. "The Usual Suspects: Police Stop and Search Practices in Canada." *Policing & Society* 21: 395–407.

Wortley, Scot and Akwasi Owusu-Bempah. 2022. "Race, Police Stops, and Perceptions of Anti-Black Police Discrimination in Toronto, Canada over a Quarter Century." *Policing: An International Journal* 45, no. 4: 570–85.

Wright, Gavin. 2006. *Slavery and American Economic Development*. Baton Rouge, LA: Louisiana State University Press.

Wright, George C. 2004. *Life Behind a Veil: Blacks in Louisville, Kentucky, 1865–1930*. Baton Rouge, LA: Louisiana State University Press.

Wright, Gwendolyn. 1991. *The Politics of Design in French Colonial Urbanism*. Chicago, IL: University of Chicago Press.

Wright, Richard. 1937. "The Ethics of Living Jim Crow: An Autobiographical Sketch." In *American Stuff: An Anthology of Prose and Verse by Members of the Federal Writers' Projects*. New York: Viking Press.

Wright, Richard. 2020 [1945]. *Black Boy*, 75th anniversary edition. New York: Harper.

Wynter, Sylvia. 1996. "1492: A New Worldview." Pp. 5–57 in *Race, Discourse and the Origin of the Americas: A New World View*. Edited by Vera Lawrence Hyatt and Rex Nettleford. Washington, DC: Smithsonian Institution Press.

Yang, Anand A. 2021. *Empire of Convicts: Indian Penal Labor in Colonial Southeast Asia*. Berkeley, CA: University of California Press.

Yesufu, Shaka. 2013. "Discriminatory Use of Police Stop-and-Search Powers in London, UK." *International Journal of Police Science and Management* 15, no. 4: 281–93.

Young, Crawford. 1994. *The African Colonial State in Comparative Perspective*. New Haven, CT: Yale University Press.

Young, Iris Marion. 1990. *Justice and the Politics of Difference*. Princeton, NJ: Princeton University Press.

Zack, Naomi (ed.). 2016. *The Oxford Handbook of Philosophy and Race*. New York: Oxford University Press.

Zamora, Sylvia. 2022. *Racial Baggage: Mexican Immigrants and Race Across the Border*. Stanford, CA: Stanford University Press.

Zander, Ulrike. 2013. "La hiérarchie 'socio-raciale' en Martinique. Entre persistances postcoloniales et évolution vers un désir de vivre ensemble." *Revue Asylon(s)* 11.

References

Zang, Xiaowei. 2015. *Ethnicity in China: A Critical Introduction*. Cambridge: Polity.

Zimmerer, Jürgen. 2005. "The Birth of the Ostland Out of the Spirit of Colonialism: A Postcolonial Perspective on the Nazi Policy of Conquest and Extermination." *Patterns of Prejudice* 39, no. 2: 197–219.

Zimring, Franklin E. and Gordon Hawkins. 1995. *Incapacitation: Penal Confinement and the Restraint of Crime*. New York: Oxford University Press.

Zinoman, Peter B. 1996. *The Colonial Bastille: A Social History of Imprisonment in Colonial Viet Nam, 1862–1940*. Berkeley, CA: University of California Press.

Zucker, Bruce. 2014. "Jessica's Law Residency Restrictions in California: The Current State of the Law." *Golden Gate University Law Review* 44: 101–16.

Index of names

Page numbers in **bold** refer to figures in the text

A
Alexander, Michelle 42, 211, 281–2
Allport, Gordon 120
Aristotle 162
Ashante, former prisoner 325
Atuahene, Bernadette 73n70
Aurillac, Michel 91

B
Bachelard, Gaston 1
  and epistemological obstacles xii, 6–7, 78
  and epistemological rupture 34, 86, 356
  and epistemological vigilance 7–8, 34
  and historical epistemology xii, 4, 5–8
Bailey, Zinzi 185
Banton, Michael 49n7
Barker, Vanessa 339
Beckett, Katherine 339
Bernier, François 53n20
Berreman, Gerald 269, 270, 271
Bessone, Magali 208, 209
Béteille, André 223n35
Bloch, Maurice 244

Blum, Lawrence 175
Blumenbach, Johann Friedrich 53
Bonilla-Silva, Eduardo 77, 181–2, 183–4
Bourdieu, Pierre 5, 32, 352–3, 367
  and capital 12n38, 13–14, 106n171, 202, 367
  and citizenship 25, 198
  and classification 4, 13, 14–15, 24, 107, 119
  and region as principle of classification 198, 199n250
  and cognition 4, 12, 20–2
  and demarcation 35–6, 78, 79
  and denegated ethnicity 78, 79, 80
  and dispositions 12, 22, 199
  and France 24, 25
  and genetic structuralism 3, 12, 14, 217
  and group-making 12–14
    agonistic theory of 3, 13, 38, 207, 310, 370
    and race-making 198–201, 202
  and habitus 12, 14, 22, 107
  and Jim Crow 217, 276
  and perception 13, 14, 15, 79, 80n92

Index of names

and positions in social space/
structure 12, 13, 22, 24, 79
and race-making 107, 198–201, 202
and racial domination 2–3, 18, 20–3, 26
  and social order 21, 22, 23, 25
  and symbolic domination 20–2, 369
and racism 23–5, 74
and repatriation 35–6, 80
and scholarship 74, 77, 355, 356
and scorn 24, 199n250
and social principle of vision and division xii, 25, 27
and space, public 4, 12–16
and space, social 4, 12–16, 24, 119, 120, 196
and stratification xii, 14, 15, 119, 367
and symbolic power 13, 87, 217
  and symbolic order xii, 14, 202
  and symbolic power theory 4, 12–16, 119, 120, 196
and symbolic violence xii, 2–3, 21–2
and Weber 20, 22
Brubaker, Rogers 32
  and groupism 75, 207
  and race-making 197, 198, 201, 204, 207
Buffon, Georges-Louis 53
Bundy, Clive 104n166
Burch, Traci 195–6
Byers, J. Willington 230

C

Calhoun, John C. 41
Canguilhem, Georges 5, 6, 78
Carmichael, Stokely and Hamilton, Charles V. 175
Casas, Bartolomé de la 51
Clear, Todd 339
Cleaver, Eldridge 351
Clinton, Bill 348
Cohen, William 51

Cole, Stefanie and Ring, Natalie J., *Folly of Jim Crow* 214
Collins, Randall 146
Columbus, Christopher 51
Conover, Ted 333
Cooper, Anna Julia 57–8
Cooper, Frederick and Stoler, Ann Laura 58
Cornell, Stephen and Hartmann, Douglas **82**, 83
Cox, Oliver Cromwell 168
Crenshaw, Martha 272–3
Cunningham, Vincent 96
Cuvier, Georges 53

D

DaCosta, Kimberly 32
Dailey, Jane 212
Davis, F. James 96
Degler, Carl 67
Desmond, Matthew and Emirbayer, Mustafa 16, 32
  Emirbayer and Desmond 83–4, 198n248
Dollard, John 240, 305n76
  and violence 259, 261, 266, 273
Douglas, Mary 145
Drake, St Clair and Cayton, Horace 68, 311
Du Bois, W. E. B. xi, xiii, 73, 291, 353, 362
  and class 295, 345
  and Jim Crow 217, 236, 246n118, 272, 304
  and racial capitalism 168, 217, 304
Durkheim, Émile 28, 44, 276, 375
  and denegated ethnicity 78

E

Elias, Norbert 294
Ellis, Eddie 335
Ellison, Ralph 241–2
Emirbayer, Mustafa and Desmond, Matthew 83–4, 198n248
  Desmond and Emirbayer 16, 32

Index of names

F
Fanon, Frantz 179
Faulkner, William 227
Finley, Moses 349, 357
Foner, Eric 351
Forman, James 344
Foucault, Michel 5, 18–20, 26, 39, 78
Frederickson, George 38

G
Gallie, Walter Bryce 355
Gans, Herbert 88
Garland, David 284
Gilbert, Alan 139
Gínes de Sepúlveda, Juan 51
Gobineau, Joseph-Arthur 48, 54
God 231, 299
Goffman, Erving 121–2, 123, 209, 240
Golash-Boza, Tanya 74
  with Christina Sue 129
Goldberg, David Theo 151
Goldstein, Donna 129
Gramsci, Antonio 374

H
Hacking, Ian 15n45
Hall, Bruce 59
Hall, John and Soskice, David 357
Hall, Stuart 81
Hanchard, Michael 29
Hassine, Victor 328
Hemson, David 161
Herrnstein, Richard 332
Hollande, President 103n161
Hughes, Everett C, 359
Hughes, Langston 210, 306, 323
Hurston, Zora Neale 46

I
Irwin, John 321, 323, 325–6
  and Cressey 341

J
Jackson, George 351
James, C. L. R. 58

Johnson, "Papa" Jack 244
Jordan, Winthrop 51

K
Kant, Immanuel 22
Kendi, Ibram 185
Kennedy, Stetson 228
King, Desmond 82
King, Martin Luther 291
King, Ryan D. and Light, Michael T. 195
Kolchin, Peter 297
Koyrè, Alexandre 5, 78
Kuhn, Thomas 6

L
LaFree, Gary and Ackerman, Gary 273
Lamarck, Jean-Baptiste 53
Leach, Edmund R. 271
Lee, Hedwig 186, 190–1
Lee, Spike 184
Legassick, Martin 161
Leroy, Justin and Jenkins, Destin, *Histories of Racial Capitalism* 163–4, 165
Lie, John 32–3, 105n169
Linnaeus, Carolus 48, 53
Lorde, Audre 374–5
L'Ouverture, Toussant 58
Loveman, Mara 32
Lucas, Samuel 127
Luft, Aliza 150

M
McMillen, Neil 22n39
Mamdani, Mahmoud 58, 142
Mann, Michael 151
Marable, Manning 168
Marx, Karl 11, 85
  and capitalism 73–4
  and analytical concepts 78
Massey, Douglas 133, 134
Mauss, Marcel 112
Mazower, Mark 63

Index of names

Merton, Robert K. 123
Mills, Charles W. 80
Mitchell, Ojmarrh 195
Monk, Ellis 32, 97
Murakawa, Naomi 339
Murray, Charles 332
Myrdal, Gunnar 270, 279

N
Nott, Josiah 299

O
Omi, Michael and Winant, Howard 76–7, **82**, 82, 179, 180–1

P
Pagden, Anthony 53n20
Pandey, Gyanendra 29
Paschel, Tiana 109
Patterson, Orlando 59, 94–5, 167, 266, 295, 357, 376n49
Peiretti-Courtis, Delphine 48n4
Pendas, Devin 170
Pettit, Becky 279
Powdermaker, Hortense 247

R
Raper, Arthur F. 260
Reskin, Barbara 127–8
Rice, Thomas Dartmouth "Daddy" 210, 212
Ritterhouse, Jennifer 213
Robinson, Cedric 161–3
Rodney, Walter 168
Rucker, Julian M. and Richeson, Jennifer A. 189
Ruiz-Tagle, Javier 134

S
Saperstein, Aliya and Gullickson, Aaron 225–6
Sartre, Jean-Paul 79, 208
Sayad, Abdelmalek 141
Schaub, Jean-Frèdèric 29
  and Sebastiani 50

Schoenfeld, Heather 279
Shakur, Tupac 278
Skarbeck, David 325
Smythe, Hugh 215
Spohn, Cassia and Cederblom, Jerry 195
Stampp, Kenneth 41
Stoler, Ann Laura 55, 58
Sue, Christina and Golash-Boza, Tanya 129
Sykes, Gresham 323, 341

T
Taylor, Keeanga-Yamahtta 184
Thomas, Charlotte 139n139
Till, Emmett 276n212
Tonry, Michael 190–1, 279, 338

V
Van den Berghe, Pierre L. 155n133
Vardaman, Governor 250
von Hirsch, Andrew 327

W
Walter, Dierk 153
Warner, W. Lloyd 40, 269–70, 271
Watson, Tom 110
Weber, Max 24, 26, 39, 271, 366
  and Bourdieu 20, 22
  and class 10, 366
  and closure 4, 10, 88, 132
  and conduct 11, 17n52
  and demarcation 78, 79, 85
  and descent 8, 9, 207
  and groups 4, 8–12
    and group-making 9, 10, 207
    status groups theory xii, 9–10, 86–7
  and honor/dishonor 87, 207–8
  and ideal type xii, 4, 10–12, 89, 215, 360–1
  and power 17–18, 132
  and race as a subtype of ethnicity xii, 9–10
  and racialization 85, 86–7, 88–9

Index of names

Weber, Max (*cont.*)
  and scholarship 74, 78
  and social action 9, 17n54, 20
Wells, Ida B. 223n35
Western, Bruce 279, 339
White, Walter F. 67–8, 291
Wideman, John Edgar 344
Wilderson, Frank 92–3, 98
Wilkerson, Isabel 271n202
Williams, Eric 168

Wilson, James Q. and Petersilia, Joan 331
Wimmer, Andreas 16n48, 32, **82**, 84–5, 107n173, 197–8, 207
Winant, Howard 49n6, 72–3
  with Omi **82**, 82, 179, 180–1
Wittgenstein, Ludwig 33, 46, 185
Wolfe, Patrick 57, 142
Woodward, C. Vann 211
Wright, Richard 242, 259, 269n194

Index of notions

Page numbers in **bold** refer to figures in the text

A
abjection 76n80, 97, 150, 259
abolition of police 186
abolition of prisons 34, 186, 289
abolition of slavery 34, 186–7, 226, 298, 299
Aboriginal people, Australia 194n240
acceptability, social 116, 152, 173
action, collective 202, 206, 208
action, political 13n41
action, social 9, 17n54, 20, 188, 198
activism 106, 370, 372
    and group-making 108–9, 310
    and hyperincarceration 344, 345, 351
    and Jim Crow 275, 276
    and racial justice 163, 166, 175
    see also resistance to domination
activism, black 98
    see also Black Lives Matter movement; Civil Rights Movement
activism, justice 61, 189n230, 193n237
activist posing 34
addiction 283, 284, 307, 319, 321, 329, 347

address, modes (racial etiquette) of 241–2
Adi-Dravidas people 69
African American people 210–77
    and abjection 76n80, 97, 150, 259
    and activism 106, 310
    and Afropessimism 92–3, 94
    and caste 135, 137, 291, 342
    and class 157, 191–2, 283, 284, 285n12, 293, 294–5, 311
    and color of skin 68–70, 156–7
    and criminal justice 34n97, 191–2, 195–6, 197, 253, 345, 372–3
    and criminality 256–7, 307, 332–3, 343–5, 348, 349
    and culture 252n140, 341
    and discrimination 68–70, 125, 127, 129, 156, 303
    and education 23, 106, 157, 295, 304–5, 307, 345
    and employment opportunities 237, 253, 302, 311, 345
    fear of 296–7, 304–5
    free African Americans 298–9, 300
    and ghettos 284, 291, 309–10, 312, 333, 339, 344
    and God 231, 299

Index of notions

African American people (*cont.*)
  and honor/dishonor 292, 309
  and hyperghettos 134, 340
    and class 191, 311, 312, 336, 337, 339, 344–5
    and hyperincarceration 43, 183, 281–90, **334, 338**, 348
    lower-class/poor 282–3, 284, 336, 338–9, 341, 344, 346, 349
    middle-class/bourgeoisie 282–3, 284, 311, 336, 337, 339
    and class 282–3, 284, 295, 311, 336–9, 341, 344, 346, 349
  and hypodescent 61, 67, 96, 115, 152, 224, 291
  and identity 295, 310
  and incarceration 157, 280, 285, 286, 340
    and class 283, 284, 295
  and inequality 157, 225, 303, 304
  and institutions 291–3, 341
  and masculinity 343–4, 349, 373
  and prisons 333, 340, 346, 349
  and religion 48n5, 307
  and resistance to domination 99, 293, 294
    and Jim Crow 220–1, 222, 256, 272
  and seclusion/segregation 135, 137, 138, 242, 291
  and stigma/stigmatization 122–3, 293, 354
  and structural racism 125, 191, 195, 196, 197
  and violence 147, 218, 236, 258–9, 263, 307, 343
  and wealth gap 157, 190, 371n38
  see also ghettos; hyperghetto; Jim Crow; prison; slavery
African people 69–71, 364
Africanization 262
Afro-Brazilian people 119, 122
Afropessimism 36, 76n80, 91–9
  see also pessimism, racial
agency 202, 220, 222
of people and groups 3, 14, 15n47, 97, 162, 176, 220, 222, 324
  symbolic 14, 33, 206
aggression 128n49, 240, 266, 304
  micro-aggression 128n49
agonism 207
  agonistic theory of group-making 3, 13, 38, 310, 370
agriculture 296–7
  and Jim Crow 232–4, 269, 276, **292**, 305, 309
  see also farmers; plantations
Ahmedabad, India 139
Alabama 227, 239, 244
Alameda County, California 183
alchemy 12, 198
Algeria 23–4, 60
Algerian people 103n161, 133, 141–2, 153–4
Algerian War of Liberation 141
American Constitution 248, 298
  see also Supreme court, US
"American dream" 349
American North 276, 298, 305–10
American Revolution 298
American South 94
  and industrialization 305, 313
  and Jim Crow 224, 226–7, 231, 245, 250, 254, 273–4, 301
Amsterdam 133
analytics xii, 1–45, 74, 88, 356, 362
ancestry *see* classification; descent
anti-ghettos 104
  see also ghettos; hyperghettos
anti-miscegenation law 224, 245
antipathy, group 120
antisemitism 50, 55, 64–6, 79
  see also Jewish people
anxiety, mist of 273
apartheid 80, 133, 172–4, 267, 358
apologies (for past racial harm) 370, 371
  see also justice, racial
appearance, physical *see* phenotype
appraisal, racial 118–19

Index of notions

Arab people 60
Archimedean position ii, 61
architecture of ethnoracial domination 154–60
Argentina 359, **360**
argumentum ad populum 72
 see also fallacy
Arkansas 216, 227, 239, 263
arrests, mass 319, 336, 337
Aspen Institute 177–8
assault 148, **149**
 and caste 303, 308, 317–18
 and Jim Crow 218, 237, 267
 and Maghrebine people 102, 103
assimilation 66, 81, 83, 90, 105, 150, 169, 368
Attica penitentiary 346
attractiveness, physical 307
aura 36, 122, **241**, 358
 and diagonal of racialization 86, 87
 and horizontal racialization **85**, 365
 see also stigma/stigmatization
Australia 194n240, 373
authority, symbolic 31
automobile driving (under Jim Crow) 243, 245
autonomy 138, 257–8, 298, 309, 315, 356
 intellectual autonomy 74
 relative autonomy 7, 126
aversion/avoidance rituals 243–4, 266

B

Bachelard, Gaston
 and epistemological obstacles 188
 and epistemological rupture 7–8
 and epistemological vigilance 7, 34, 356
Bacon's Rebellion 296
bail 188n230, 336–7
Balkans 206
Bantu people 172, 173, 174
beatings 243, 252, 254, 255
belief, collective 9, 49, 87, 120, 271, 274n208

belief, in race
 and classification and stratification 75, 79
 and descent 8–9, 51, 83, 90
 and racism 48, 76, 83, 90, 91, 144, 196, 284
 and blackness 48n5, 52, 229, 243, 295, 306–8, 341–2
 and Jim Crow 229, 243, 270, 300, 341–2
 and white supremacy 270, 300
Béteille, André 62, 270n197
bias
 and categorization 120–1, 154, **155**
 and criminal justice 193, 195, 252, 279, 373
 and discrimination 128, 130
Big House (prison) 320, 325, 327, 328, 338
 see also penal state; prison; rehabilitation as penal philosophy
biology and nature 53, 170, 341
 and diagonal of racialization 88–9, 90
biopower 20
Birth of a Nation (Griffith) movie 262
Black Belt, urban 42, 287, 308, 310, 340
 see also ghettos; hyperghettos
Black Codes 232, 262, 300, 342
Black Death 50
Black Lives Matter movement 61, 99n152, 106, 163n155, 372
black people
 Caribbean 209, 224, 357
 French 204–5, 207
blackness 96–8, 227
 and belief 48n5, 52, 229, 243, 295, 306–8, 341–2
 and hypodescent 61, 67, 96, 115, 152, 224, 291
 and nesting/subsumption 97, 228
 see also one-drop rule; phenotype; skin color

453

Index of notions

blood purity 41, 50–1, 56, 63, 64, 76, 115–16, 170
   and Jim Crow 213, 245, 248, 274, 303
      and caste 90n118, 271, 300
      and one-drop rule 227, 229, 230
      and Nazi Germany 64, 170
   see also ancestry; descent; one-drop rule
body/embodiment 32, 198, 349
   see also dispositions; habitus
Bolivia 80
bombing 292
Boston Review 163
boundaries 26, 70, 75, 352, 358–9
   bright boundaries 352, 358
   and elementary forms of racial domination 113, 115, 120, 129, 158, 169, 170
      and ethnoracial categories 10, 67, 135–6, 140, 207, 208
      and seclusion 135–6, 140
      and violence 147, 152, 154
   flexible boundaries 139, 171, 180, 271
   impermeable boundaries 152, 244, 358
   porous boundaries 84, 120, 208
   rigid boundaries 70, 208, 358
   and Wimmer 16n48, 84–5, 107n173, 198n247
bourgeoisie, black *see* black people, middle-class/bourgeoisie
Brahmin people 69
Brazil 109, 116, 117, 119, 122, 135–6, 152, 365
Brazilian people 66–7
   Afro-Brazilian people 119, 122
Britain 297, 350, 372
   and Ireland/Irish people 52–3, 63, 148, 162, 169
Bronzeville, Chicago 311, 312–13, 316
Brown v. Board of Education 68, 375

"brutality," pole of (Jim Crow) 216
Budapest 135
buffering 226, 311, 317–20
Bulgaria 116, 158, 171
Buraku Liberation League 368
Burakumin people 119–20, 123, 137, 267, 368
bureaucratic field 27, 99, 108, 114, 116, 124, 155, 171, 205, 250, 358
businesses, black 300, 315

C

California 124, 331, 337n163
camps 3n4, 102, 137, 138n81, 140–2, 145, 202, 364, 375n46
Canada 202, 359, **360**, 363, 373
capital 13–14, 130, 199, 367
   cultural capital 93, 258, 293, 336, 347, 367
   economic capital 217, 258, 336, 367
   ethnographic capital 170
   social capital 160, 258, 367
   symbolic capital 87, 160, 217, 353;
      see also aura; honor/dishonor; prestige; stigma/stigmatization
   Bourdieu 12n38, 14, 106n171, 202, 367
      and groups/group-making 202, 205
      negative/positive 44, 122, 293, 353
      and racial justice 353, 367
capitalism 20, 73–4, 359
   capitalist society 17, 162
   and class 73–4, 166
   credential capitalism 165
   and dispossession 163, 164
   neoliberal capitalism 359
      and hyperghettos 288–90, 342, 353–4
      and hyperincarceration 165, 289
      and prisons 288–90, 342
      and "underclass" 287, 290, 353–4

Index of notions

racial capitalism 28n83, 37, 47, 113, 161–8, 187, 356, 359–60
  and Du Bois 168, 217, 304
  and religion 164, 167
  varieties of 357
carceral continuum 43, 287
carceral-assistential mesh 289
caste 210–77
  and African American people 135, 137, 291, 342
  and biology/nature 88–9, 90
  and blood purity 271, 300
  caste domination 42
  and class 269–71, 273, 333–4, 342, 373n42
  definition 269–70, 270n197, 271
  and diagonal of racialization 88–9, 90
  and ghettos 306, 332–3, 340
  and hyperincarceration 281–2, 283, 289, 332–3
  and India 62, 270
  and Japan 56, 57
  and Jim Crow 42, 264, 267, 269, 281–2, 300, 303, 342
    and criminal justice 251, 256, 257
    and deference **268**, 269, 274, 276, 300n56
    and hierarchy 269, 270, 271
    and law 251, 268
    and positions in social space/structure 246, 270n195, 301
    and rank 270, 271
    and white supremacy 270, 274
  and marriage 269, 271
  and membership 270, 271
  and origins of race 56, 57, 58
  and racial justice 364, **365**
  and segregation 132–3, 135
  and sexual intercourse/congress 246, 271, 303
  and slavery 272, 342
  and subordination 223, 271, 311–12
  and violence 264, 267, 272, 273–4, 342
  and assault 303, 308, 317–18
  and race riots 342, 373n42
  and ritualized caste murder 150, 152
  and white people 264, 266, 270, 340
caste system 23–4, 56, 62, 270, 277
  see also outcaste
caste terrorism 218, 221, 222–3, 268–77, 300–5, 341, 351–2
catastrophism 77, 104
categorical framework of racial classification, US 37n102
categories, ethnoracial 118, 146
  and classification struggles 107–8, 370
  and inequality/subordination 140, 194, 225
  and perception 21, 88, 113, 130, 369, 370
    and Bourdieu 13, 14, 15, 79, 80n92
  and classification 101, 102, 104
  and South Africa 80, 370
  and subordination 140, 194, 363
  see also boundaries; taxonomies
categories, naturalized 27, 358
categorization 89, 112, 113–23, 356, 367
  and architecture of ethnoracial domination 154, **155**
  and bias 120–1, 154, **155**
  and Bourdieu 12, 356
  and Brazil 116, 117, 119, 122
  and Burakumin people 119–20, 123
  and censuses 116–17, 118
  and class 114–15, 117, 159
  and classification 113–14, 119, 120, 139, 152, 154
    and region as principle of classification 116, 117
  and cognition xi, 113, 118–21, 130
  and descent 97, 115–16

Index of notions

categorization (*cont.*)
  and educational attainment 114–15, 120
  and group-making 118, 356
  and identity 117–18, 122, 171, 209
  and institutionalism 4, 110, 116, 118
  logics of 15, 71, 203
  and marriage/intermarriage 114–15, 171, 172
  and nationality 110, 117
  and officialization 116, 152n125, 202
  and phenotype 114, 115, 116, 119n19, 158
  and realization of categories 12, 80
  and religion 152, 201
  and Roma people 116, 119, 171
  and social, physical and public space 117, 120
  and South Africa 80, 116, 370
  and stigma/stigmatization 89, 120, 121–3, 154, 358
Catholicism 225, 226, 262
censuses, national 67n51, 116–17, 118
  US Census Bureau 108–9, 228
centrism 30, 71, 75, 166–7, 207
chain gangs (Jim Crow) 253–5
charisma 17
  see also aura
Charlestown, South Carolina 224
checkerboard of ethnoracial violence 148–50
Chicago 147, 306–8, 314–16
  and Bronzeville 311, 312–13, 316
  and hyperghettos 311, 335, 336
  and seclusion/segregation 134, 138
Chicago Commission on Race Relations 293, 306–8
Chicago Defender weekly 316, 316n102
Chicago Housing Authority 316, 318–19
Chicago School of urban sociology 131

child labor 233, 254, 300, 304
China 75–6, 131, 203
Chinese people 127
Christian people 49–50, 51, 298
  see also Catholicism; Protestantism, British
churches 50, 304, 314–16
  and Jim Crow 221, 225, 228, 238, 266
churning of black men into and out of prison 334–8
cities
  colonial 60, 131, 135
  industrial 41, 291, 342
  postindustrial 43, 287, 289, 320, 335, 338
  see also ghettos; hyperghettos
citizenship 39, 79, 124, 137, 293, 358, 372
  American citizenship 43, 285n12, 288, 289, 293, 306
  and Bourdieu, Pierre 25, 198
  and colonialism 58, 60
  and French people 60, 127
  reshaped by prison 338–49
  Western citizenship 54, 58
civil rights *see* rights
Civil Rights Movement 68, 131–2, 221, 223, 295, 320, 345
"civility," pole of (Jim Crow) 216
civilizing 294
class
  and African American people 157, 191–2, 283, 284, 285n12, 293, 294–5, 311
  and capitalism 73–4, 166
  and caste 269–70, 273, 333–4, 342
  and categorization 114–15, 117, 159
  and class consciousness 22, 79
  and classification/classification struggles 24, 110–11, 295
  and class-splitting institutions 42, 157, 295, 339

Index of notions

and criminal justice 191–2, 195, 196, 197, 336, 337, 353, 373n42, 375
and discrimination 125n40, 126, 159
and employment opportunities 237, 311, 312, 345
and France 24, 125n40, 126
and ghettos 135, 287–8, 310, 311, 332–3
and group-making 10, 199, 202, 207, 208–9
and hyperghettos 287–8, 311–13, 319, 333–6
and hyperincarceration 332–3, 349
and incarceration 104–5, 282–3, 284, 285, 287–8, 295, 313, 336, 339
and Jim Crow 42–3, 111, 227, 229, 237, 245, 269–70
and origins of race 51, 53, 61
and prisons 222n33, 283
and racial justice 372, 375
and racial mechanisms 61, 197, 372
and Roma people 158, 159
and segregation 131, 132, 135, 165, 311–13
and slavery 296, 349
and social, physical and public space 80, 273, 285, 294–5, 312, 358
and stratification 73–4, 295
and subjugation 283, 339
and Weber 10, 367
and white people 157, 219–20, 225, 227, 229, 285, 298, 301, 333–4, 339
see also individual classes; precariat, black; race-making; racism; racism, class; segregation; subalterns; "underclass"
classification 168–74
and apartheid 172–4
and architecture of ethnoracial domination 154, 155
and belief in race 75, 79
and Bourdieu 4, 13, 14–15, 24, 107, 119, 367
and class 24, 110–11, 295
classification systems 114, 116, 119, 134, 139, 152, 154, 206, 224
and diagonal of racialization 86–9, 90
and discrimination 24, 101–2, 119, 154
and doxa/doxic 118, 125
educational classification 24
gradational system of 67, 139
and group-making 82–3, 107, 119, 201, 202, 206–7
and habitus 88, 110, 155, 199, 201, 206
and honor 169, 206
logics of 107, 171, 174
and Martinique 114, 116
natural classification 113
and Nazi Germany 116, 170
and phenotype 62–8, 76, 114, 152, 173
and public perception **100**, 101, 102, 104
and racial justice 367, 370
and recursivity 15, 120, 206
and segregation 171, 172
and slavery 62, 114, 297
social classification (specificity of) 113
and social, physical and public space 14–15, 107, 119, 144, 174, 231
state classification 108–9, 168–74, 202, 206
and stratification 14–15, 86, 99–106, 119, 155, 206, 231, 295, 297, 357
and penal state 290–1, 327
and taxonomies 170–2, 206
and United States 37n102, 61–2, 71, 76–7, 118, 169, 357
see also descent, phenotype, region as principle of classification

Index of notions

classification struggles 106–11
  and Bourdieu 4, 13, 107
  and categorization 113–14, 120
  and class 110–11, 295
  and ethnoracial categories 107–8, 370
  and gender 107, 110
  and group-making 107, 204, 370
  and habitus 107, 198
  Martinique 114, 116
  and states 108–9, 202
  and symbolic struggle 106, 107, 122, 206
  and United States 108–9, 110–11
class-splitting *see* institutions
closure 88, 286, 309, 310, 347
  and Weber 4, 10, 88, 132
clustering 132, 133, 139, 158, 335–6; *see also* segregation
"code of the street" 324–6
coercion, psychic 18, 256
cognition 27, 36, 79–80, 107, 123, 197–9, 222, 245
  and Bourdieu 4, 12, 20–2
  and Brubaker 16n47, 197, 198
  and categorization xi, 113, 118–21, 130
  see also recognition; symbolic power
Colombia 109
colonialism 2, 141–4, 362, 370
  Britain 296–7, 350
    and Ireland/Irish people 52–3, 63, 148, 162, 169
  and economy 296, 342
  France 143–4, 362
    and Algerian people 23–4, 60, 103n161, 133, 141–2, 153–4
  Germany 63–6, 169–70
  and indigenous people 142–4, 153
  and origins of race 51–3, 56, 57–9, 60, 75, 91, 362
  and paternalism 23, 297
  and religion 57, 60, 154
  and seclusion/segregation 23–4, 135, 142–4
  and indentured servants 115, 296
  and slavery 55, 297, 350
  United States 81, 135, 143
  and violence 58, 153–4, 364
  Western 2, 51, 75, 153
color of skin 62–70, 75–6, 152
  and black people 68–70, 156–7
  and blackness 96–8, 227
  and consciousness 204, 296
  and doxa/doxic 67, 96
  and elementary forms of racial domination 114–15, 156
  light skin color 68–9, 97, 115, 125, 195–6, 228, 229
  United States 62, 97, 125, 156–7, 229
  see also phenotype
commodification 290, 359–60
common sense 36, 88, 168, 173, 343
  bureaucratic and everyday 74, 169
  journalistic and political 343
  scholarly 6, 39, 48–9, 78, 183; *see also* doxa/doxic
  Bachelard 4, 7, 86
  and science 48, 49
Communist Party, France 135
community, imagined 348–9
compensation
  symbolic 217, 293
  for racial harm 370, 371
compliance (as effect of domination) 17, 21, 26, 27
complicity (with domination) 22, 48, 72–3, 187
concentration camps 140, 284
concept
  analytic 7, 22, 29, 78, 214, 274–6, 277
  essentially contested 168
  folk 7, 39, 78, 81, 138, 212, 223, 274
conceptual lumping 44, 118, 357
conceptual relationship of ethnicity and race 36, 82–5
conceptual speculative bubbles 168

Index of notions

concubinage 225n41, 226, 245
conduct 20, 22, 319
   and discrimination 123, 129–30
   and incarceration 322, 327
   and Jim Crow 240, 245, 259, 262, 307
   and racism, structural 182, 194–5
   and Weber 11, 17n52
conflict, racial *see* pogrom, rioting
confusion, conceptual/mental xi, 48–9, 112, 176–7, 181, 214n11
congruence, degree of (of concepts) 117, 118
consciousness 22, 24, 75, 79, 204, 297, 373
   caste consciousness *see* caste
   class consciousness 22, 79
   color consciousness 204, 296
   Conseil Représentatif des Associations Noires (CRAN) 204–5
consequentiality 36, 99–106, 120, 152, 207, 359
   and racial justice 365, 368, 370
   see also salience
constructivism 15, 32, 37, 49, 205, 208, 369
contested versus doxic ethnoracial classifications 118–19
continuum of ethnicity *see* ethnicity
"convict code" 324–6
convict leasing 253–5, 256
corrections administrations 321, 329
"Corrections Offender Network," Florida 330
cotton industry 40n108, 233, 234, 298, 305
courts/courtrooms 103, 121, 132, 194n240
   and Jim Crow 27, 40, 218, 235, 252–3
   and penal state 43, 343
   and racism, structural 189n230, 192
   and records 330

see also criminal justice; Supreme Court, US
credentials 23, 24, 27, 165, 202, 347
creolization of slavery 297
criminal justice 188–97, 251–7
   and African American people 34n97, 191–2, 195–6, 197, 253, 345, 372–3
   and bail 189n230, 336–7
   and bias 193, 195, 252, 279, 373
   and caste 251, 256, 257
   and class 34n97, 191–2, 195, 196, 197, 336, 337, 353, 373n42, 375
   and criminal defense 192, 253
   and criminal records 194, 196, 329, 330, 349
   and criminality 252, 256–7
   and discrimination 195, 196
   and economy 235–6, 253–5, 256, 257, 342
   and fairness/unfairness 194, 252
   and guilty pleas 194, 196–7, 326n134
   and hyperghettos 192, 316–17, 336–7, 338, 343
   and hyperincarceration 41, 278, 283, 327, 328–33, 347
   and incarceration 189–90, 195, 278
   and inequality 189, 190, 191–2, 194n240, 252, 256
   and Jim Crow 251–7, **268**
   and judges 192, 241, 252–3, 266, 303
   and law/law enforcement 189–90, 196, 252, 268, 303
   and murder/homicide 185, 191, 253, 256
   and New Jim Crow 157, 276, 285–6
   and parole 283, 327, 331
   and penal state 328–9, 338
   and police/policing 192, 251–2, 336, 337, 372–3
   and probation 192, 193n237, 283, 285–6, 336n162, 348

Index of notions

criminal justice (*cont.*)
  and property crime/theft 255, 280
  and prosecutors 103, 192, 193–4, 337
  and punishment 148, 243, 253–4, 255, 257, 260, 261, **268**, 317n104
  and racial disparity 195–6, 253
  and recidivism/reoffending 283, 327n139, 329, 333n154, 335, 347
  and reform 38, 97n168, 105, 193, 278
  and staffing 192, 251, 332–3
  and stereotyping 252, 256
  and structural racism 38, 186, 188–97
  and United States 105, 188–97, 251–7, 278, 328–33, 337n163
  and victims of crime 191, 252, 265, 266
  and vigilante groups 189–90, 262
  and white people 243, 253, 256, 257, 261
  see also courts/courtrooms; hyperincarceration; incarceration; Jim Crow; penal state; prison; prisonization; racism, structural; sentencing; violence
criminality 331–3
  and black people 256–7, 307, 332–3, 343, 344–5, 348, 349
  as characteristic of Negroes 230, 243, 252, 307
  and criminal justice 252, 256–7
  fear of 237, 288, 322, 344
  and genetics 329, 331–3
  and hyperghettos **292**, 317–18, 336, 340, 344n182
  and masculinity 331–2, 344, 349
  and parole 327, 330, 336, 344n182
  and stigma/stigmatization 288, 293, 328, 352
  and surveillance 329–31, 349

Critical Race Theory (CRT) 179–80, 369
Croatian people 206
Crusades 50
culture 24, 159, **338**, 376
  and African American people 252n140, 341
  ethnic culture 159, 366
  folk culture/culture of the people 24, 252n140, 376
  ghetto/street culture 340, 341
  and history 88, 90
  and language 70, 116, 144, 171, 203, 366, 369
  prison culture 323, **338**, 340, 341
  and religion 24, 85, 88, 89

D

Dalit people 62, 187, 267
Darwinism, Social 54
death
  civic 347
  social 94, 347
  "white death" 257–67, 269
death sentences 253, 260
death ("white death") 257–67, 269
defense, criminal 192, 253
deference 27, 40, 122, 218, **241**, 243n108, 257, 259, 269, 276, 301
  and caste terrorism **268**, 269, 274, 276, 300n56
  and racial etiquette 217, 240–1, 247
  and segregation 238–9, 240–1
  and violence 247, 258
defiance 18, 306
degrouping 205–6
delegation/deputization (by the state) 199, 205, 256, 274
demarcation 35–6, 78–9, 85, 112, 376
  see also rupture, epistemological
democracy 270–1, 339, 341–2
demonization 57n30, 165, 289, 314
  see also "underclass"

Index of notions

denegated ethnicity 78–85, 88
  see also ethnicity
denigration 60, 69, 159, 160, 207
  and ghettos 103, 138, 305, 366
  and Jim Crow 221, 258
  symbolic denigration 89, 103n162
density, ethnic 103, 133
depoliticization 344–5, 352
deracialization 44, 83, 169
  and diagonal racialization 90, **365**
  and racial justice 361–2, **365**, 368
  see also justice, racial
descent 33, 81, 173, 291
  and belief in race 8–9, 51, 83, 90
  and categorization 97, 115–16
  and Jim Crow 224, 229, 245, 271, 274
  and Weber 8, 9, 207
  see also ancestry; blood purity; hyperdescent; hypodescent
desertion, ethnic 119
  see also passing
deserving/undeserving (category) 43, 288, 290, 348
destabilization of inner cities 324, 339
destigmatization 44, **365**, 366, 367
diagonal of racialization 36, 47, **87**, 89, 106, 271, 367
Dictionary of American English 210
difference 50, 162
  and diagonal of racialization 87, 91
  and hierarchy xii, 26, 239
  and inequality 35, 87, 370
  and Jim Crow 239, 270
  and phenotype 62, 65, 70, 83
dignity 95
  and ghettos 138, 139
  and Jim Crow 240–1, 242, 247, 252, 257
  and racial justice 353, 363, 364, 367
  and stigmatization 122, 208
  and symbolic capital 160, 367
  see also honor/dishonor, stigma
dirtiness 70, 102, 141, 182, 236

disadvantage, cumulative 128, 196, 372
disaggregative approach 47, 77, 112, 179, 191, 274, 287, 350, 356
  and Jim Crow 215, 286, 338
  see also analytics; architecture of ethnoracial domination
discernment 79
  see also cognition
discontinuity (epistemic, historical) 5, 6, 78, 186
discrimination 2, 101–3, 123–30, 294, 308
  and African American people 68–70, 125, 127, 129, 156, 303
  and architecture of ethnoracial domination 154, **155**
  and bias 128, 130
  and class 125, 126, 158, 159
  and classification 24, 101–2, 119, 154
  discrimination by place 125–6
  and disparity 126, 128
  disparate impact as facet of discrimination 113, 123, 124, 154, **155**, 356
  as an elementary form of racial domination 113, 123–30, 156, 356
  and France 102–3, 124, 125n40, 126, 130, 364
  horizontal discrimination 126–7
  and hostility 128n49, 129
  and Jim Crow 213, 215, 249, 301, 303
  and life chances 86, 97, 123
  micro-discrimination 128–9
  and nationality 123, 124
  negative discrimination 123–4
  phenomenology of discrimination 129–30
  and policing 102, 364
  positive discrimination 124
  and religion 120n25, 121, 123

Index of notions

discrimination (*cont.*)
  and segregation 128, 135, 154, 215, 303
  and space 125–6, 128, 154
  and structural racism 125, 196
  systemic discrimination 196
  über/meta discrimination 127
  and United States 124, 125, 127–8, 135, 156
disease, infectious 135, 230, 231
disenfranchisement
  criminal 348
  and Jim Crow 251, 258, 266, **268**, 301
  political and judicial 303, 348
disgrace, group 205–9, 210
  see also stigma
dishonor *see* capital; honor/dishonor; stigma/stigmatization
disjunction
  conceptual **82**, 82–3
  institutional 247
disparate impact (as facet of discrimination) 113, 123, 124, 154, **155**, 356
disparity, racial 337–8, 358
  and criminal justice 195–6, 253
  and discrimination 126, 128
  and incarceration 279, 283
dispersion (as opposite of segregation) 132, 136
displacements, epistemic 34
  see also obstacles, epistemological
dispositions, embedded 27, 179
  systems of 12, 22, 199, **200**, 205, 221
  see also cognition; habitus
dispossession 103n162, 148, 163, 164, 267, 353, 354
  see also marginality/marginalization; poverty
disproportionality, racial 279–80, 340
dissimilarity index 103, 133–4
distance 127, 239, 308, 337
  physical distance 134, 312

social distance 23, 134, 195, 247, 311
symbolic distance 127
see also segregation
District Attorneys/prosecutors 103, 192, 193–4, 337
diversity 118, 159, 180n209
  and diversity consultants 2, 187n226
Division of School Safety, New York 320n112
domination
  and agonistic theory 14
  analytic specification 16–29
  in Bourdieu, Pierre 20–3
  definition 26
  elementary forms of 27–8
  in Foucault, Michel 18–20
  neo-Bourdieusian theory of racial domination 2, 44, 45–6, 106, 198, 356
  pure types of 27
  three faces of 26
  in Weber 17–18
  see also racial domination
"Double-Duty Dollar" 315
Dōwa districts, Japan 119, 120, 368
doxa/doxic vii, 21, 37, 166, 167
  and classification 118, 125
  and color 67, 96
  and history 48, 67, 109, 118
  and Jim Crow 212–23, 227, 229
  and Omi and Winant 82, 180
Durban riots 147
Durkheim, Émile 79, 149, 274n208
Dutch East Indies 127

E
economy 79, 157
  and colonialism 296, 342
  and criminal justice
    and convict leasing 253–5, 256
    and industrialization/industrial development 254, 256, 342
    and labor, forced 235, 254, 256

Index of notions

and plantations 235–6, 254, 257
and economic capital 217, 258, 336, 367
and economic extraction 11, 26, 138, 273, 292, 305, 311
and exploitation 165–6, 313
and ghettos 276, 305–6, 313, 351
and hyperghettos 313–14, 315
and Jim Crow 218, 232–8, 255–6, 258, **268**, 269, 276, **292**, 305, 309
and plantations 232, 233, 234–6, **292**, 295–7, 300, 301
political economy 79, 159–60, 313
and prisons 288–90, 323, 342
and slavery 167, 292, 295–7, 300, 342, 350
and South Africa 160, 359
and states 159–60, 358, 361
and violence 160, 164, 292
see also capitalism; labor; racial capitalism
educational attainment *see* schools/schooling
educational opportunities *see* schools/schooling
elections 218, 249
see also voting rights
elementary forms of racial domination, five 27–8, 29, 37, 113–56, 363
and color of skin 114–15, 156
and emotionality 127, 130, 150, 207
and ghettoization 103–4, 137–9, 156, 158, 160
and institutions 156, 159
and penal state 157, 165, 187, 189
and prejudice 120, 123, 154, 156
and racial mechanisms 28, 29, 154, 159, 177, 185, 356
and Roma people 145, 157–9, 171
see also analytics; architecture of ethnoracial domination; categorization; classification; disaggregative approach; discrimination; seclusion; segregation; violence
eligibility, principle of less racial 40, 238, 257
elimination, ethnic 138n81, 143, 145, 152, 205–6, 249
elite
  black elites 228
  elitism 24
  nobility 51, 53
  urban elites 132
  white elites 157, 216, 227, 229
emotion 307
  fear as collective emotion 120, 150, 247
  resentment 237, 264, 270, 327, 373
  see also anxiety; fear; scorn
empire-building 59, 60, 63–6
employment opportunities 130, 174
  and black people 236–7, 302, 311, 345
  and class 237, 311, 312, 345
  and ghettos 308, 311, 312, 313, 314, 337
  and incarceration 283, 313, 337
  and Jim Crow 236–7, 256, **268**, 302, 304–5
encasement, material xii, 2–3, 27, 71
enclaves 133, 139, 327
  see also clustering; ghettos
England/English people 50, 52–3, 162, 169, 296, 350
  and Irish people 52–3, 169
Enlightenment 33, 35n98, 36n101, 298
entrepreneurs, symbolic 13, 108, 201
epistemology, historical xii, 4, 5–8
  see also analytics; Bachelard, Gaston; obstacles, epistemological; populism, epistemological; rupture, epistemological; vigilance, epistemological
equality
  of opportunity 372n39
  political equality 248

Index of notions

equality (*cont.*)
  social equality as refusal of
    interracial intimacy 54, 231,
    243, 244, 248, 252, 266, 293,
    305, 309
  see also inequality
equalization 44, 364, **365**, 367
equity 175n195, 177n201, 178,
  187n225
error, theoretical primacy of 6
essentialism 24, 49, 50, 56, 369
eternalization (as element of
  racialization) 91, 159
Ethnic & Racial Studies journal
  352n205
ethnic cleansing 65, 80, 145, 148, **149**,
  150, 151
ethnicity
  continuum of ethnicity ii, 36, 47,
    85, 122
  denegated ethnicity 78–85, 188
  disguised/veiled ethnicity ii, 221
  naturalized ethnicity 27, 39, 43, 85
  and race 9–10, 48–9, 197–8
    conceptual relationship of
      ethnicity and race 36, 82–5
    race as subtype of xii, 9, 33, 36, 81,
      88
  symbolic ethnicity 88
  thick/racialized ethnicity 36, 58, 71,
    152, 188
    and diagonal of racialization **85**,
      87, 88–90, 364, **365**
  thin/ordinary ethnicity 36, **85**, 88,
    171, 188, **365**
ethnicization 83, 85, 87, 331
ethnoracial domination *see*
  domination, racial
etiquette, racial 239–45, 247, 259,
  260, **268**, 269, 275, 302
eugenics 54, 76
Eurasian people 171, 204
Euro-American people 83, 84, 283
Eurocentric vision of history 56
Eurocentrism 56, 75

Europe 109, 137, 357, 366
European people 35, 182
European Union 2, 366
everyday life 128–30, 170–1, 311,
  317–20, 370
exceptionalism, racial 214n11, 277,
  291
exclusion 35, 42–3, 166, 184, 197
  and ethnic cleansing 65, 145, 151
  as face of domination 26–7, 29,
    140
  and incarceration 347–8, 353
  and Jim Crow 27, 38, 40, 248–57,
    258, 266, 269, 274, 301
  political and judicial exclusion
    248–57, 269
  and racial justice 363, 367
  and violence 145, 258, 266
exclusivism 94, 160
excommunication, moral 327
executions 260, **268**, 317n104
exploitation 292
  and domination, racial 23, 26–7,
    363
  and economy 165–6, 313
  as face of domination 26, 40, 218
  and ghettos 138, 313
  and Jim Crow 27, 40, 258, 266,
    269
  and seclusion 138, 142
  and violence 145, 153–4, 258, 266
  see also extraction, economic
expropriation 165
extermination 56, 57
  see also racial war, genocide
extraction, economic 11, 26, 138, 273,
  292, 305, 311
  see also exploitation
extremism, American 277

F
fairness/unfairness 124, 194, 252
  see also equality; equity
fallacy 182, 184, 185, 186, 209, 350
families 136, 199, 282, 311, 348, 349

Index of notions

farmers 53, 110–11, 162, 297
  and Jim Crow 236n78, 247, 255, 300, 301, 309
  see also agriculture; plantations; sharecropping
fear
  of black people 296–7, 304–5
  as collective emotion 120, 150, 247
  of criminality 237, 288, 322, 344
  of ghettos 103, 318
  of violence 41, 146, 258, 272, 273
feminism 93, 132, 209
fiction, sociological 187
field hands, hired 232, 235
flexibility (of ethnoracial categories) 66, 139, 171, 180, 225, 271
Florida 216, 227, 238, 263, 330
fluidity thesis 15–16
folk notions *see* concept, folk
Folly of Jim Crow (Cole and Ring) 214
Fordism 164, 202, 257, 276, 289, 342
"four-way search clauses" 336n162
France 50, 71, 117–18
  and Bourdieu 24, 25
  and class 24, 125n40, 126
  and colonialism 143–4, 362
    and Algerian people 23–4, 60, 103n161, 133, 141–2, 153–4
  and discrimination 102–3, 124, 125n40, 126, 130, 364
  and educational attainment 105, 126
  French law 125n40, 143
  and ghettoization 103–4, 158
  and immigration 25, 90, 102–4, 141–2
  and integration 103–4, 134
  and Islamic people 60, 124
  and Maghrebine people 102–3, 126, 130, 352
  and Moroccan people 133, 141–2
  and policing 102, 364
  and Portuguese people 90, 133
  and racial inequality 102, 103–4, 105

  and salience and consequentiality of ethnicity 101–4, 105
  and ethnic segregation 103–4, 133–4, 135, 136
  and Turkish people 103, 133–4
  and violence 103n161, 153–4
Frederickson, George 55
free people, black 296, 298–9
French people 60, 105, 127, 204–5
  black 127, 204–5
French Revolution 298

G

gallows 238
gangs **149**, 321, 324–6
  see also chain gangs, prison gangs
gender 31, 36, 71, 79, 80, 84, 124, 155, 157n138, 208–9
  and Bourdieu/neo-Bourdieusian theory 22n72, 198
  and classification struggles 107, 110
  and Jim Crow 218–19, 247n121, 262
  and labor, division of 132, 164, 289
genetics 170, 188, 270n196, 329, 331–3
genocide 53, 109, **149**, 150, 152
  see also ethnic cleansing
geography 35, 220n24, 340
Georgia, US 195, 216, 228, 234, 239, 243
  and criminal justice 195, 253, 254, 255
Germany 63–6, 169–70, 372
ghettoization 37, 103–4, 137–9, 156, 158, 188
  and France 103–4, 158
  of prisons 37, 43, 156, 320–38, 340
  and stigma/stigmatization 137–8, 328
ghettos 49n6, 305–20
  and American North 276, 305–10
  and Big House (state) 320, 325, 327, 328, 338
  and Black Belt states 287, 308

Index of notions

ghettos (*cont.*)
  and black people 284, 291, 306–10, 333, 344
  and caste 306, 332–3, 340
  and class 135, 287–8, 310, 311, 332–3
    and black people, middle-class/bourgeoisie 312, 339
  communal ghettos 313, 333, 338, 339
  and denigration 103, 138, 305, 366
  and dignity 138, 139
  and economy 276, **292**, 305–6, 313, 351
  and employment opportunities 308, 311, 312, 313, 314, 337
  and exploitation 138, 313
  fear of 103, 318
  and group-making 310, 351
  and identity 138–9, 310
  implosion of 42, 290, 351
  and incarceration 284, 286, 287–90, 310, 323, 336
  and industrialization/industrial development **292**, 305, 313, 314
  and inequality 138, 309, 310
  and institutions 37, 137–8, 139, 286, 291, **292**, 317
  and integration 132, 139, 312
  and Jim Crow 42–3, 276, 305–10
  and penal state 320, 325, 327, 328, 338
  and prisonization 43, 310, 311–20, 328
  and race-making 323, 341
  and rioting 101, 340, 345, 346
  and seclusion 137–40, 286, 287–8
  and segregation 132, 133, 135, 308
  and social, physical and public space 137, 308, 309, 351
  and solidarity 138, 309
  see also anti-ghettos; hyperghettos
global South 35, 154n132, 313
globalism, methodological 31

Google Books NGram viewer 211
Google Scholar 279
governmentality 20
Graterford prison 328
Great Migration 221, 305–6
Group Areas Act, South Africa 172, 173
groupism 74–5, 207
group-making xii, 33, 38, 197–209, 352, 359, 368–70
  and activism 9, 17n54, 108–9, 202, 206, 208, 310
  and Bourdieu 12–14
    agonistic theory of group-making 3, 13, 38, 207, 310, 370
    and race-making 198–201, 202
  and categorization 118, 356
  and class 10, 199, 202, 207, 208–9
  and classification and stratification 107, 119, **200**, 201, 202, 206–7, 370
  and region as principle of classification 197, 198, 199, 209
  and ghettos 310, 351
  and groupness 201, 204–5
  and habitus 198, 201, 206
  and inscription 199, **200**
  and institutionalization 118, 203, 205
  and labor of symbolic and material construction 199, **200**
  and membership 199, **200**, 201–2, 270
  and naming of groups 199, **200**
  and organization 199, **200**
  and racialization 88–9, 207
  and sedimentation 199, **200**
  and social groups 199, **200**, 201, 203–4, 208, 209
  and social, physical and public space 198, **200**, 201, 202, 202n263, 205–6, 208
  and South Africa 127, 358
  and states 199, **200**, 202–3, 361

Index of notions

and Weber 9, 10, 207
see also race-making
groupness 27, 201, 204–5, 310, 358, 368–9
groups on checkerboard of ethnoracial violence **149**
groups, social
  bystanders 144–5, 149–50
  perpetrator groups 144, 148–9, 150
  social fabrication of groups 199, **200**, 203
  violated/targeted groups 144, 148–9
  see also group-making
guilt, white 180n209, 226, 285n12
guilty pleas 194, 196–7, 326n134, 337

H

habits 86, 174
habitus 36, 37, 75, 186n221, 221
  and Bourdieu, Pierre 12, 14, 22, 107
  and classification 88, 107, 110, 155, 198, 199, 201, 206
  and group-making 198, 201, 206
  hysteresis of 16, 205–6, 367
  and "race-divided societies" and "societies with race" 358, 361
  racial habitus 358, 361
  see also Bourdieu, Pierre; classification; dispositions, systems of; physical space; social space
hair 53n20, 62, 67, 75, 86n109, 90, 115, 116 158, 173, 227
Haitian Revolution 298
Han people, China 75–6, 203
Harvard Implicit Association Test 121
hate crime 146
heredity *see* ancestry; descent
hermeneutics 5
heuristics 11, 168, 188, 192, 361
hibernophobia 63
hierarchization (as dimension of racialization) 24, 55, 91, 116, 291

hierarchy, ethnoracial xii, 291, 333
  and Jim Crow 239, 257, 269, 270, 275
  see also verticality
Hispanic people 108–9, 319
historical epistemology xii, 4, 5–8, 78
  see also Bachelard, Gaston; Bourdieu, Pierre; Canguilhem, Georges
historicist ontology 32, 206
historicity 88, 99, 369, 370–6
historicization 34–5, 48–55, 186, 350
history 12, 36, 350–1
  and culture 88, 90
  and doxa/doxic 48, 67, 109, 118
homicide *see* murder/homicide
homogeneity 75, 186, 207, 208, 257
homogenization 91, 159, 291, 313, 343
homosexuality 124, 262
honor/dishonor 159, 167, 347, 352–3
  and African American people 292, 309
  and aura 36, 86, 87, 122, 365
  and classification 169, 206
  codes of 325–6
  and Jim Crow 217, 230, 232, 233, 271, 274
  and racial justice 366, 368
  and states 169, 206
  and stigmatization 122, 366
  and symbolic capital 87, 353
  and Weber 87, 207–8
horizontality 126–7, 138, 147, 207, 248, 323
  and diagonal of racialization **87**, 87, 89, 365, 370
  see also verticality
hostility 191
  and discrimination 128n49, 129
  and ethnicity 50, 57, 69, 120
  and Jim Crow 227, 247, 273
  and segregation 132, 135, 141, 324

Index of notions

housing
  housing, social/public 136, 222, 282, 309, 316, 318–19, 375
  low-income households/ neighborhoods 134, 135, 136, 158, 313
  markets 126, 374
  middle-class housing 345
Houston, Texas 263n177
human nature 145–6
human rights 261, 326
humanity 48, 51, 95, 101
humiliation 240, **241**, 251, **268**
  see also deference; dishonor; scorn; stigma/stigmatization
humor, ethnic 129
Hungary/Hungarian people 158, 171, 204
  see also Roma people
hunts/manhunts 252, 261–2, 269, 304
Hutu people 69–70, 109, 150, 209
hyperdescent 115
hyperghettos 42–3, 287, 288–90, **292**, 311–20, 324, 337–8, 339, 342, 353–4
  and Chicago 311, 312–13, 314–16, 335, 336
  and class 287–8, 311–13, 319, 334–6
    and black, lower-class 191, 311, 312, 313, 336
    and black, middle-class 337, 339, 344–5
    and black precariat 286, 288, 316, 318, 340
    and "underclass" 42, 287, 336, 339, 353–4
  and criminal justice 192, 316–17, 319, 336, 336–8, 343
  and criminality **292**, 317–18, 336, 340, 344n182
  and culture, prison and ghetto/street 323, 324–6, 338, 340, 341
  and economy 287, 288–90, 311–12, 313–14, 315, 317, 339, 342, 353–4
  and educational attainment/ opportunities 313, 320, 335, 345
  and employment opportunities 311, 312, 313, 314, 337
  and everyday life 311, 317–20
  and incarceration 188, 286, 287–90, 313, 334–8, 339, 341, 349
  and institutions 42, 139, **292**, 311, 314–16, 339
  and law enforcement 148, 316, 336
  and marginality/marginalization 43, 287, 288, 289, 313, 333–4
  and masculinity 324, 340
  and parole 327, 330, 336, 344n182, 348
  and postindustrial cities 43, 287, 289, 320, 335, 338
  and poverty 313, 335–6
  and prisons 288–90, 310, 321, 323, 328, 335–6, **338**, 341, 342–4
  and segregation 131, 134, 288, 311–13, 314
  and social relations 310, 318, **338**
  and social/public housing 316, 318–19
  and surveillance 192, 281, 317, 318–19
  and violence 147–8, 318, 339
  and welfare 313, 316, 317
  and white people 333, 345
  see also penal state; prisonization
hyperincarceration 38, 41–3, 182–3, 281–90, 338–49, 348
  and activism 344, 345, 351
  and caste 281–2, 283, 289, 332–3
  and class 183, 287–8, 334–6, 349
    and blacks, lower-class/poor 282–3, 284, 295, 336, 338–9, 341, 344, 346, 349
    and blacks, middle-class/ bourgeoisie 282–3, 284, 295, 311, 336, 337, 339

Index of notions

and criminal justice 41, 278, 283, 327, 328–33, 347
and demonization 165, 289
and educational opportunities 335, 347
and hyperghettos 188, 287–8, 334–6, 339
and law enforcement 344, 345
and law-and-order policies 295, 327, 330, 331, 339, 343
and marginality/marginalization 346, 351
and neoliberal capitalism 165, 289
and parole 283, 327, 331
and probation 283, 336n162, 348
as queer social policy 349
and undesirables 306, 327
and welfare 289, 347–8
and white people 182–3, 283, **334, 338**
see also incarceration; penal state
hypermasculinity 324
hyperracialization 57
hypersegregation 156
hypnotic points 133, 134n68
hypodescent 61, 67, 96, 115, 152, 224, 291
see also descent, hyperdescent
hyporacialization 57
hysteresis 16, 205–6, 367
hysteria (racial) 226–7

I

ideal type
  and "genuine slave societies" versus "societies with slaves" 349
  and Jim Crow 40, 215, 274–6
  and "societies with race" versus "race-divided societies" 44, 357–8, 360–1, 362
  Weber 4, 10–12, 89, 215, 360–1
identity 2, 9, 152, 368
  African American identity 295, 310
  and categorization 117–18, 122, 171, 209

and choice 86, 87, 89
collective identity 62, 138–9, 295, 368–9
criminal identity 288, 323
and diagonal of racialization 86, 87, 89
ethnoracial identity 117
and ghettos 138–9, 310
and groups 9, 202, 368–9
and incarceration 288
and Jim Crow 227, 245, 288
presumed identity 9
and race-making 60, 180, 202
and region as principle of classification 198, 199
spoiled identity 122, 209
Illinois 330, **334**, 335
illiteracy 248, 304, 325n133, 374n46
immigration 2, 31, 133
  and France 25, 90, 102–4, 141–2
  and United States 81, 262, 296, 305, 314
  see also migration, internal
Immorality Amendment Act, South Africa 172
Imperialism/imperial 23, 57, 58, 60, 63–6, 152–4, 169–70, 203, 358, 374n46
importation thesis (of carceral culture) 341
incapacitation 327
incarceration 278–88, 290–311
  and addiction 283, 284, 321, 347
  and black people 157, 280, 283, 284, 285, 286, 295
  and class 104–5, 282–3, 284, 285, 287, 288, 295, 336, 339
  and criminal justice 189–90, 195, 278
  and drugs, War on 281, 282, 285, 338
  and educational attainment 104–5, 157, 280, 282, 283, 295, 313
  and employment opportunities 283, 313, 337

Index of notions

incarceration (*cont.*)
  and exclusion 347–8, 353
  and gangs 321, 324
  and ghettos 284, 286, 287–90, 310, 323, 336, 340
  and homogenization 291, 313
  and hyperghettos 286, 287–90, 313, 327, 334–8, 341, 349
  and isolation 283, 346
  and Jim Crow 281–3, 285
  and labor markets 287–8, 289
  and marginality/marginalization 282, 352
  and marriage/intermarriage 282, 313
  and men 280, 283, 284, 285, 287, 289
  and poverty 283, 289, 335–6
  and racial disparity 279, 283
  rates of 104–5, 190–1, 278n1, 280, 283, 285, 288, 352
  and recidivism/reoffending 283, 329
  and seclusion 286, 287–8
  and social, physical and public space 283, 286, 322, 346
  and stratification 288, 290–1, 323, 327
  and violence 283, 321, 324, 325, 339
  and white people 104–5, 280, 283, 285, 298, 333–4, 339
  see also hyperincarceration
incarceration, mass *see* hyperincarceration
India 62, 132–3, 139, 147, 267, 270, 365
Indian Appropriations Act 143
Indian people 147
Indian Removal Act 143
Indianola, Mississippi 234, 243
indigenous people 129, 142–4, 194n240, 316, 371
  and Canada 202, 371
  and colonialism 142–4, 153

indigenous rights 109
  and Native American people 142–3, 148, 201
  and violence 148, 153
Indisch people 204
individuals and violence **149**
Indochina 153–4
Indonesian people 127
industrialization/industrial development
  and American South 305, 313
  and criminal justice 254, 256
  and ghettos **292**, 305, 313, 314
  and Jim Crow 254, 256, 342
inequality 58–9, 128
  and black people 157, 225, 303, 304
  and classification and stratification 44, 169
  and criminal justice 189, 190, 191–2, 194n240, 252, 256
  and diagonal of racialization 87, 87–8
  and difference 35, 86, 370
  economic inequality 157, 166
  and France 102, 103–4, 105
  and ghettos 138, 309, 310
  and Jim Crow 213, 215, 225, 243, 252, 256, 302
    political 248–9, 257
    social 231, 243, 248–9, 257, 266, 309
  and life chances 44, 86
  material inequality 102
  naturalized inequality 58–9
  political inequality 248–9, 257
  and positions in social space/structure 35, 372n39
  and racial capitalism 164, 166
  and racial justice 44, 363–4, 367, 372
  and salience and consequentiality 102, 103–4
  social inequality 231, 243, 248, 257, 266, 303, 304, 309

Index of notions

and structural racism 178, 185, 189, 190, 191–2, 194n240
and United States 77, 104–5, 157, 169, 185
see also equality; equity
inequity 178
infant mortality 182
inferiority 66, 122n30
   and Jim Crow 217, 231, 247, 248, 292
   and slavery 52, 240
   see also honor/dishonor
inferiorization 75, 129, 144, 159, 162, 207
in-group alignment 209
inscription (of symbolic category) 199, **200**
institutional bifurcation 27, 40, 239–40, 258, 289
institutional mesh 339
institutionalization 94, 366
   and categorization 4, 110, 116, 118
   and group-making 118, 203, 205
institutions 41–3, 181, 290–311
   and African American people 291–3, 341
   and class 42, 157, 295, 339
   class-splitting institutions 42–3, 157, 295, 339
   communal institutions (of ghetto) 42, 139, 221, 311, 314–16
   and elementary forms of racial domination 156, 159
   and ghettos 137–8, 139, 286, 291, **292**, 311
   as Janus-faced institutions 37, 137, 317
   and hyperghettos 42, 139, **292**, 311, 314–16, 339
   and hyperincarceration 41–3, 295
   and Jim Crow 22, 221–2, 291, **292**
   parallel institutions 137–8, 154, 286
   peculiar institutions 41–3, 290–311, 339

and prisons/prisonization 157, 311, 338–9
race-making institutions 37, 151, 157
and seclusion 113, 137–8, 154, 291–2, 342
and slavery 291, **292**, 341, 350
and social control 311, 314–16
and social, physical and public space 292, 294, 358
and states 37, 151, 311, 314–16
and welfare **292**, 316
see also Jim Crow; penal state; prisonization
insurrection **149**, 226, 292, 299
see also riots
integration 159
   and France 103–4, 134
   and ghettos 132, 139, 312
   and segregation 132, 134, 203
interests, material 217
intermarriage patterns 131n57
intermediate ethnoracial category 115, 225
   see also color of skin; mulatto people
International Romani Day/Union 366
intersectionality 61, **82**, 83–4, 85
intimidation 113, 148
   and ghettos 147n109
   and Jim Crow 221, 248, 251, 256, 258, 261, 273
   and caste terrorism **268**, 274
   and plantations 234–5, 266
   and vigilante groups 262, 267
   and voting rights 249, 266
intuition, speculative depreciation of 6
Ireland/Irish people 52–3, 63, 148, 162, 169
Irish Republican Army (IRA) 148
Irish-American people 90
Islamic people 49–50, 139, 147, 206
   France 60, 124
isolation, social 133, 231, 239, 258, 283, 346

471

Index of notions

Israel 80, 206, 364
Italy 352, 372

J

Jackson, Mississippi 249
Janus-faced institutions, ghettos as 37, 137, 317
Japan 90
  and Burakumin people 119–20, 123, 137, 267, 368
  and caste 56, 57
  and categorization 119–20, 123
  Dōwa districts 119, 120, 368
  and extermination 56, 57
  and World War II 56–7, 150–1
Japanese American people 284
Japanese people 69
"Jessica's Law," California 331
Jewish people 49–50, 79, 147, 170
  and seclusion 137, 138
  United States 90, 262
Jim Crow 38–40, 210–77
  and activism 275, 276
  and agency 220, 222
  and Alabama 227, 239, 244
  and Arkansas 216, 227, 239, 263
  and asymmetric separation 238–48, **268**
  and belief in race 229, 243, 270, 300
  and blood purity 213, 224–30, 245, 248, 271, 274, 300, 303
  and Bourdieu 217, 276
  and caste 42, 269, 281–2, 303
    and blood purity 271, 300
    and criminal justice 251, 256, 257
    and deference **268**, 269, 274, 276, 300n56
    and hierarchy 269, 270, 271
    and law 251, 268
    and positions in social space/ structure 246, 270n195, 301
    and rank 270, 271
    and violence 264, 267, 342

  and white supremacy 270, 274
  and caste terrorism 111, 221, 222–3, 268–77
  and class 42–3, 111, 237, 245, 253, 269–70
  and white people 219, 220, 227, 229, 301
  and concubinage 225n41, 226, 245
  and corpses 255, 259
  and criminal justice 251–7, 268, 303
  and convict leasing 253–5, 256
  and courts/courtrooms 27, 40, 218, 235, 252–3
  and death sentences 253, 260
  and executions 260, **268**
  and Georgia 253, 254, 255
  and industrialization/industrial development 254, 256
  and inequality 252, 256
  and judges 241, 252–3, 266, 303
  and labor, forced 235, 254, 256
  and Mississippi 253, 254
  and mock trials 261, 264–6
  and murder 253, 256
  and New Jim Crow 157, 276, 285–6
  and plantations 235–6, 254, 257
  and police/policing 217, 251–2
  and punishment 253–4, 257, 261
  and stereotyping 252, 256
  and subordination 255, 256
  and trumped up charges 235, 252
  and victims of crime 252, 265, 266
  and violence 243, 251–5, 256, 258, 261, 264–6, 303
  and criminality of black people 230, 243, 252, 256–7, 307
  and deference 218, 238–48, 257, 259
  and caste terrorism **268**, 269, 274, 276, 300n56
  and racial etiquette 217, 240–1, 247

Index of notions

and segregation 238–9, 240–1
and violence 247, 258
and descent 224, 229, 245, 271, 274
and difference 239, 270
and dignity 240–1, 242, 247, 252, 257
and disaggregative approach 215, 286, 338
and doxa/doxic 212–23, 227, 229
and Du Bois 217, 236, 246n118, 272, 304
and economy 232–8, **268**
  and agriculture 232–4, 269, 276, **292**, 305, 309
  and convict leasing 253–5, 256
  and farmers 236n78, 247, 255, 300, 301, 309
  and Fordism 257, 276, 342
  and honor/dishonor 232, 233
  and industrialization/industrial development 254, 256, 342
  and mining industry 236, 254
  and peonage 218, 232–8, 258, **268**
  and plantations 232, 233, 234–6, **292**, 300
  and profitability 233–4, 255–6
  and railroad/railway companies 210–11, 254, 255, 264
  and sharecropping 218, 232–8, 258–9, 266, **268**, **292**, 301, 302, 304
and educational opportunities 217, 238, 304–5
and employment opportunities 236–7, 256, **268**, 302, 304–5
and exploitation 27, 40, 258, 266, 269
and Florida 216, 227, 238, 263
and gender 218–19, 247n121, 262
and Georgia 216, 228, 234, 239, 243, 253, 254, 255
and ghettos 42–3, 276, 305–10
and hierarchy 239, 257, 269, 270, 271, 275

and history 212–23, 274, 350–1
and honor/dishonor 217, 230, 271, 274
  and economy 232, 233
and hostility 227, 247, 273
and ideal type 12, 40, 215, 274–6
and identity 227, 245, 288
and incarceration 281–3, 285
and inequality 213, 215, 225
  and criminal justice 252, 256
  and political inequality 248–9, 257
  and racial etiquette 243, 302
  and social inequality 231, 243, 248–9, 257, 266, 309
and institutions 22, 221–2, 291, **292**
  and institutional bifurcation 27, 40, 239–40, 258, 289, 341
and labor 230, 232, 236, 237, 305, 342
  and child labor 233, 254, 300, 304
  and criminal justice 235, 254, 256
  and forced labor 235, 236, 254, 256, 291, 300, 342
  and land ownership 232, 255, 264, **268**, 300, 301
and law 227, 228, 238, 239, 304, 375, 378
  anti-miscegenation law 224, 245
  and caste 251, 268
  and law enforcement 235–6, 252, 261
  "Negro law" 268, 303
  Plessy v. Fergusson 212, 301
  and segregation 212, 213–14, 301
  and less racial eligibility 40, 238, 257
and Louisiana 224, 225
and lynching postcards 264, 266
and marriage/intermarriage 213, 225, 228, 245, 282, 291, 299, 303
  and caste 269, 271

Jim Crow (*cont.*)
  and marriage/intermarriage (*cont.*)
    and one-drop rule 156n135, 224, 225
  and men, black 228–9, 246
  and migration 221, 255, 262, 275, 276, 305–6
  and Mississippi 216, 222, 249–50, 304
    and criminal justice 253, 254
    and one-drop rule 227, 228–9, 231
    and racial etiquette 241, 243
    and sharecropping 234, 235
    and violence 235, 236, 249
  and mortality rates 230, 254
  and mulatto people 224–5, 226–7, 228–9, 230
  and Nazi Germany 39, 66, 138n81
  and nesting/subsumption 228, 229
  and newspapers 217, 241, 264, 265
  and North Carolina 216, 239, 263
  and "passing" 226, 227, 228
  and paternalism 216, 227, 236, 247, 275
  and patriarchy 218, 233, 262, 301
  and peonage 218, 232–8, 258, **268**
  and phenotype 224–7, 228, 229, 242
  and police/policing 217, 251–2
  and protection 236, 247, 256, 257
  and race relations 211, 216, 223
  and racial etiquette 239–45, **268**, 269, 275, 302
    and conduct 240, 245, 259, 262, 307
    and dignity 242, 247
    and motorists 243, 245
    and reciprocity 242–4, 247
    and social equality 243, 244
    and taboos 242, 243–4
    and violence 259, 260
  and racial mechanisms 214, 247
  and racial mixing 224–30, 291
  and railroad/railway companies 210–11, 239, 254, 255, 264
  and rank 270, 271
  and reciprocity 65, 242–4, 247, **268**, 302
  and Reconstruction 262, 293, 342, 351
    and Black Codes 232, 262, 300, 342
  and religion 221, 225, 226, 228, 230, 238, 265, 266, 314
  and resistance to domination 220–1, 222, 256, 272
  and respect 243, 247, 282n7
  and rights, civil 221, 223, 260, 300, 342
  and rights, political 260, 300, 342
  and rights, voting 218, 248–51, 257, 258, 303–4
  and rural/peri-urban areas 216, 221, 243, 247, 275
  and segregation 211
    and deference 238–9, 240–1, 247
    and discrimination 215, 303
    and educational opportunities 238, 304
    and hierarchy 239, 247, 275
    and humiliation 240, **241**
    and law 212, 213–14, 301
    and one-drop rule 227, 231
  and servants 224, 236–7, 239
  and sexual congress/marriage 228
    and concubinage 225n41, 226
    and infectious disease 230, 248
    and lynchings 246, 303
    and one-drop rule 224, 225, 225n41, 226
    and racial etiquette 243–4, 245–6, 302
    and violence 246, 303
  and slavery 40, 210, 218, 224–5, 226, 229, 342
  and "social equality" 231, 243, 244, 248, 252, 266, 293, 305, 309

Index of notions

and social, physical and public space 221, 231, 242, 258, 276, 351
and isolation 231, 239, 258
positions in 232, 237, 246, 263, 270n195, 271, 273, 301
and violence 258, 267
and solidarity 232, 235
and space, symbolic 231, 271, 351
and stigma/stigmatization 218, **241**
and structural racism 38, 39
and structure, social **268**, 271
and structure, symbolic/sociosymbolic 216–17, 248, 268, 271
and subordination 27, 38, 40, 214, 223
and criminal justice 255, 256
and violence 256, 258, 261, 266
and Supreme Court 212, 252, 301
and taboos 241, 245, 303
and racial etiquette 242, 243–4
and tenancies 233, 258, 301, 302
and Tennessee 255, 263
and terrorism 40–1, 218, 221, 223, 268–77, 300–5, 341, 351–2
Ku Klux Klan (KKK) 218, 232, 251, 262–3
and urban areas 216, 221, 258, 275, 305
and vagrancy 235, 300
and verticality 247, 257, 270
and vigilante groups 226, 262
and violence
and aggression 240, 266, 304
and assassination 243, 262
and assault 218, 237, 267
and beatings 243, 252, 254, 255
and executions 260, **268**
and fear of violence 258, 272, 273
and hunts/manhunts 252, 261–2, 269, 304
and lashings/whippings 234–5, 246, 253, 254, 255, 259, 261, 262, 303

and lynchings 150, 246, 253, 258, 259–61, 264–6, 303, 304, 306
and mock trials 261, 264–6
and murder/homicide 234, 253, 256, 257, 260, 303
and public/private violence 218, 234, 272
and rape 247n121, 249, 256, 260, **268**
and rioting 244, 245–6, 258, 263–4, **268**, 342, 373n42
and sexual abuse 237, 254, 260, **268**
and shootings 260, 261
and threat of violence 234, 236, 269, 272, 273
and torture 150, 246, 252, 254, 261, 262, 264–6, **268**, 303, 317n104
and "white death" 257–67, 269, 269n194
and violence, symbolic 221, 240, **241**, 259
and denigration 221, 258
and discrimination 213, 215, 249, 301, 303
and disenfranchisement 251, 258, 266, **268**, 301
and exclusion 27, 38, 40, 248–57, 258, 266, 269, 274, 301
and humiliation 240, **241**, 251, **268**
and inferiority 217, 231, 247, 248, 292
and oppression 211, 251
and ostracization 211, 253, 305
and subjugation 283, 290
and subservience 245, 251, 264, 301, 302
and Virginia 216, 224
and voting rights 248–51, 257, 258, 303–4
and disenfranchisement 251, 258, 266, **268**, 301

475

Index of notions

Jim Crow (*cont.*)
  and voting rights (*cont.*)
    registration of voting rights 249, 250–1, 303–4
  and "white death" 257–67, 269, 269n194
  and white patronage 225, 237, 247, 257
  and white supremacy 35, 212–14, 216, 221, 250, 300
    and caste 264, 270, 274
    and violence 258, 264, 267
  and whiteness 217, 227, 264, 266
  and women
    and black women 228, 236–7, 246, 254
    and sexual congress/marriage 224, 228, 246, 303
    Southern women 226, 246, 303
    and white women 224, 226, 246, 303
  see also caste; intimidation; "Jump Jim Crow" lyrics; one-drop rule; terrorism; violence; violence, symbolic; white people
Jim Crow, New 42–3, 157, 276, 285–6
Johnson v. California, US Supreme Court 288
journalism 68, 138–9, 343
judges 192, 241, 252–3, 266, 303
"Jump Jim Crow" lyrics 210, 212
justice, racial 44, 355–76
  and activism 163, 166, 175
  and caste 364, **365**
  and class 372, 375
  and classification and stratification 367, 370
  and color-blind racism 368
  and compensation 370, 371
  and consequentiality 365, 368, 370
  and deracialization 361–2, **365**, 368
  and destigmatization 45, **365**, 366, 367
  and diagonal racialization **365**, 367
  and dignity 353, 363, 364, 366
  and equalization 364, **365**
  and exclusion 363, 367
  and honor/dishonor 366, 368
  and inequality 44, 364, 367, 372
  and life chances 367, 371
  and recognition 359, 361, 366, 367, 370
  and reconciliation 109, 370
  and reparation 370, 371
  and salience 365, 368, 370
  and states 364, 365–6
  and symbolic capital 353, 367
  and United States 365, 371n38, 375
  see also deracialization
justice, social 363, 372

K

Kallas people 69
Kanak people 143–4
Kentucky 227
Khmer Rouge 152
Khmou people 366
killing, mass **149**, 185
kneecapping 148
Knights of the White Camelia 262
knowledge 19, 22, 44
  knowledge formation 5, 6, 8, 78
  see also analytics; Bachelard, Gaston; concept, analytic; concept, folk; epistemology; "lemming effect"
Korea 56
Ku Klux Klan (KKK) 218, 232, 251, 262–3
Kulak people 206
Kurdish people 90

L

labor 160, 295–6
  cheap labor 300, 311, 313
  and dirtiness 102, 182, 236
  division of 132, 164, 289
  forced/bonded labor 160, 295–6
  and hyperghettos 311, 313, 317

Index of notions

and Jim Crow 230, 232, 236, 237, 256, 291, 305, 342
 and child labor 233, 254, 300, 304
 and criminal justice 235, 254, 256
 labor extraction 291, 311
 see also convict leasing; economy; peonage
labor markets 126, 141, **292**, 300
 and hyperghettos 287, 317, 339
 and incarceration 287–8, 289
 see also employment opportunities
labor of symbolic and material construction 199, **200**
laïcité, French 124
land ownership 296
 and Jim Crow 232, 255, 264, **268**, 300, 301
language traditions 70, 116, 144, 171, 203, 366, 368
Laos 366
lashings/whippings 234–5, 246, 253, 254, 255, 259, 261, 262, 303
Latin America 139, 357
law 31, 173, 189–90, 348, 350
 French 125n40, 143
 and Jim Crow 227, 228, 236, 238, 239, 304, 375
  anti-miscegenation law 224, 245
  and caste 251, 268
  "Negro law" 268, 303
  and segregation 212, 213–14, 301
 law-and-order policies 327, 330, 331, 339, 343
 and South Africa 171, 172
law enforcement 373
 and hyperghettos 148, 316, 336
 and hyperincarceration 344, 345
 and Jim Crow 235–6, 252, 261
lawyers 253, 254
legitimacy 68, 106, 124, 150, 164, 240, 267
leisure activities/sport 174, 244, 341
"lemming effect" 167

life chances 4, 99, 306
 and discrimination 86, 97, 123
 and equality 44, 86
 and racial justice 367, 371
 see also inequality
life expectancy 296, 297
life sentences 282, 347
liminality, ontological 95, 209
"*limpieza de sangre*" 50
lockdowns (prison) 326, 346
logic of the trial 35, 72–8, 139, 145, 186, 269, 360
logics 73, 188, 275
 of categorization 15, 71, 203
 of classification 107, 171, 174
Louisiana 96, 224, 225, 329–31
lower-class/poor areas/people
 and criminality 289n21, 295
 and stigma/stigmatization 122, 288, 293
 subalterns 57, 94, 137, 147, 222n33, 283, 353, 375
 see also "underclass"
lower-class/poor blacks 42–3, 293, 295
 and criminal justice 34n97, 192, 196
 and hyperghettos 191, 311, 312, 336, 339
 and hyperincarceration 282–3, 284, 336, 338–9, 341, 344–5, 346, 349
 and prisonization 318, 340
 and prisons 333, 346, 349
lower-class/poor whites 282, 298
 and incarceration 285, 333–4, 339
 and Jim Crow 219, 220, 301
loyalty 275, 323
lynchings 68, 151, 152
 attempted lynchings 260–1
 and collective effervescence 274n206
 and Jim Crow 216, 218, 223, 246, 253, 258, 259–61, 304, 306
 and caste murder 150, 152, 246

Index of notions

lynchings (*cont.*)
  and Jim Crow (*cont.*)
    and postcards 264, 266
    public torture lynchings 150, 264–6
    and sexual congress/marriage 246, 303

M

Macon County, Georgia 234
macro-segregation 134, 135
Maghrebine people 102–3, 126, 130
Makwerekwere (South Africa) 70–1
Malay/Chinese opposition 21
manumission 95, 226, 299
marginality/marginalization 102, 140, 148, 159, 282, 359, 374
  and hyperghettos 43, 287, 288, 289, 313, 333–4
  and hyperincarceration 346, 351
  and incarceration 282, 352
  and stigma 125, 352, 374
marriage/intermarriage 131
  and categorization 114–15, 171, 172
  and incarceration 282, 313
  and Jim Crow 213, 225, 228, 245, 282, 291, 299, 303
    and caste 269, 271
    and one-drop rule 156n135, 224, 225
Martinique 114–15, 116
Maryland 227, **334**
masculinity 84
  and black people 343–4, 349, 373
  and criminality 331–2, 344, 349
  and hyperghettos 324, 340
Massachusetts 336n160
master status trait 323, 359
mechanisms, racial 294, 355, 372
  and class 61, 197, 372
  and elementary forms of racial domination 28, 29, 154, 159, 177, 185, 356
  micro-mechanisms 135

and segregation 135, 136, 158, 375
and social mechanisms 28, 39, 44, 177, 197, 214, 247
and structural racism 188, 189, 190, 196, 197
media, mainstream 341
medical research 48n4, 178, 248
"Megan's Laws" 330
melting, ethnic 63
membership, group 199, **200**, 201–2, 270, 271
men 54, 124, 280, 285, 343
  black men 228–9, 246, 283, 284, 285, 311, 334–8
  and incarceration 283, 284, 285, 287, 289
  and Jim Crow 228–9, 246
  white men 245–6, 253, 261, 280, 283, 285
  see also masculinity; white people
MENA (Middle East and North Africa) people 118–19
mestizaje 139
method of ideal type 8–12
  see also Weber, Max
method of residuals 126, 195
Métis people 202, 226
Mexico 129
Michigan **334**
micro-aggression 128n49
micro-discrimination 128–9
micro-mechanisms 135
micro-segregation 134
middle-class areas/people 98, 285n12, 344–5
  districts 42, 286, 337
  and ghettos 312, 339
  and hyperghettos 337, 344–5
  and hyperincarceration 282–3, 284, 311, 336, 337, 339
migrants, European 305
migrants, German 148
migration, internal 221, 255, 275, 276, 305–6, 309
  see also immigration

Index of notions

military, US 169
mining industry 236, 254, 302
minstrel shows 210
miscegenation 63, 299, 309
   and Jim Crow 224, 225, 226, 228, 245
misrecognition 21, 87, 273n206
Mississippi
   and Jim Crow 216, 222, 249–50, 304
   and criminal justice 253, 254
   and one-drop rule 227, 228–9, 231
   and racial etiquette 241, 243
   and sharecropping 234, 235
   and violence 235, 236, 249
Mixed Marriage Act, South Africa 172
mixing, racial 96, 104, 108, 114–16, 171, 202
   and Jim Crow 224–30, 291
   and mixed marriages 172, 173, 225
   see also caste; color of skin; marriage/intermarriage; miscegenation; one-drop rule
mobility, social 67, 98, 103–4, 114, 270, 314–15
mongrelization 262
   see also mixing, racial
morality 73, 172, 293, 301, 307
morbidity rates 230
Moroccan people 133, 141–2
mortality rates 182, 230, 254
motorists (Jim Crow rules) 243, 245
mulatto people 54, 114–15, 202, 224–5, 226–7, 228–9, 230
   see also miscegenation; mixing, racial
multiculturalism 109, 359, 371
multiplicity 29, 159
multiracial people 108, 156n135, 213, 227
   see also miscegenation; mixing, racial
murder/homicide **149**, 185, 318
   and caste 150, 152
   and criminal justice 191, 253, 256

   and Jim Crow 234, 253, 256, 257, 260, 303
   and mass murder **149**, 185
   and structural racism 185, 191
   see also lynchings; torture
Muslims *see* Islamic people

N

naming of groups 199, **200**
Nanterre shantytown, France 141–2
National Association of Short-Statured Persons (NOSSA) 124n37
National Liberation Front (FLN) 142
National Unity and Reconciliation (NURC) campaign 109–10
nationalism 31–2, 60, 197–8
nationality 81, 110, 117, 123, 124
nation-building 151
Native American people 142–3, 148, 201, 265, 291
Native Resettlement Act, South Africa 172
naturalization 91, 159, 188, 291, 355
   naturalized categories 27, 358
   naturalized ethnicity 27, 39, 43, 85
   naturalized inequality 58–9, 164
nature and biology 2, 21, 25, 36, 53, 83, 84, 88–9, 122, 230–1, 270
navy, British 350
Nazi Germany 63–6, 80, 182, 271n202
   and blood purity 64, 170
   and classification and stratification 116, 170
   and Jim Crow 39, 66, 138n81
   and violence 145, 267
   see also Third Reich
necklacing 148
"Negro law" 268, 303
Negro Motorist's Green Book 245
Negroes
   characteristics of 236, 250, 259, 293, 299, 306–8
   and criminality 230, 243, 252, 307

479

Index of notions

Negroes (*cont.*)
  characteristics (*cont.*)
    Mississippi 231, 243
    and one-drop rule 224, 226, 227, 229–31
Negrophobia 55, 249
neighborhoods *see* ghettos; hyperghettos; lower-class/poor areas/people; middle-class areas/people; segregation; stigma/stigmatization
neo-Bourdieusian theory of racial domination 2, 44, 45–6, 106, 198, 356
neoliberalism *see* capitalism
neo-slavery 40
nesting/subsumption (of concepts) 116, 350
  and blackness 97, 228
  and conceptual relationship of ethnicity and race **82**, 84–5
  and Jim Crow 228, 229
Netherlands 133, 203, 352, 362
networks, social 198, 233, 318, 325
  and racism, structural 174, 188
  and segregation 22, 27, 80, 128, 131, 134, 136, 375
New Caledonia 143–4
New Deal 290, 309
New Jim Crow 42–3, 157, 276, 285–6
New Mexico state prison 346
New Orleans 263
New York state **334**, 335
newspapers 217, 241, 264, 265, 331
Niagara movement 272
nobility 51, 53
nominalism, dynamic 15n45
North African people 102, 141
North Carolina 216, 239, 263
Norway 182n211, 359, **360**

O

Oakland, California 191–2
Obama presidency 76–7, 181, 285n12
obedience 17n52, 18, 19, 22
  see also domination
objectification 12, 23
objectivity 36, 75, 79, 201, 376
  see also demarcation; rupture, epistemological
objects, as perspective of ideas 6, 13, 20, 40, 79
obstacles, epistemological xii, 6–7, 78, 188
Occidentalism 55, 76, 166
occupation 174
octoroon people 225
officialization of ethnic categories 116, 152n125, 202
  see also classification
Ohio **334**
Oklahoma 263–4
"old heads" 323n122, 340
one-drop rule 156, 223–31, 291
  and blood purity 227, 229, 230
  and concubinage 225n41, 226
  Louisiana 224, 225
  and marriage/intermarriage 124, 156n135, 224, 225
  Mississippi 227, 228–9, 231
  and mulatto people 224–5, 226–7, 230
  and Negroes 224, 226, 227, 229–31
  and nesting/subsumption 228, 229
  and phenotype 224, 225–7
  and public health 230, 231
  and religion/churches 225, 226
  and segregation 227, 231
  and sexual intercourse/congress 224, 225, 225n41, 226
  and slavery 218, 229
  and white people 224, 225, 226
    and elite, white 227, 229
  see also ancestry; classification; descent
ontology 12, 32, 95, 199–201, 206, 209, 369
oppression 35, 56, 74, 117, 156, 208
  and color of skin 63, 97n148, 220

Index of notions

five faces of 26n79, 156n134
and Jim Crow 211, 251
paradox of 26n79, 105n169
order, symbolic
   and Bourdieu xii, 14, 202
   and classification 99, 202, 247, 295, 358, 366, 370
   see also symbolic power
organization 42, 64, 94, 101, 105, 106, 109, 116, 137–8, 176, 186, 197, 199, **200**, 205, 221, 258, 275, **292**, 309–10, 314–17, 320–1, 331
ostracization 138, 211, 253, 292, 305
outcaste 70n62, 115, 267, 283
out-group alignment 119, 209
overlapping/intersection (concepts, categories) **82**, 83–4, 85, 122, 151, 191

P

Pacific War, World War II 56–7
pacification/depacification 59, 276, 311, 318
pains of imprisonment 341
Palestinian people 80, 206, 364
"paradox of oppression" 26n79, 105n169
paranoia, ethnoracial 130, 227
parenthood, single 282, 349
Paris, France 135
parochialism, continental 56
   see also US-centrism, Occidentalism
parole 329
   and hyperghettos 327, 330, 336, 344n182, 348
   and hyperincarceration 283, 327, 331
"passing" 119, 158, 226, 227, 228, 299, 368
paternalism
   and colonialism 23, 297
   and Jim Crow 216, 227, 236, 247, 275
   and slavery 41–2, 297, 298

pathology 177n201, 230n56
patriarchy 92, 218, 233, 262, 301
patronage, white 225, 237, 247, 257, 298
patterning 211, 212, 332–4, 340
Pell Grants 347
penal reform 157, 328
penal state 42–3, 281, 285n12, 295, 350–4
   and classification and stratification 290–1, 327
   and courts/courtrooms 43, 343
   and elementary forms of racial domination 157, 165, 187, 189
   and ghettos 320, 325, 327, 328, 338
   and hyperghettos 288, 339
   and police/policing 148, 333, 336, 337
   and security 317, 320n112, 325–6, 329
   and hyperincarceration 283, 284–5, 289–90, 295, 337, 345, 346, 352
   see also hyperincarceration; incarceration; penalization/penal policy; prison; prisonization; sanctions, penal
penalization/penal policy 105, 279, 282, 285, 290, 337, 344, 345, 351
Pennsylvania **334**
peonage 218, 232–8, 258, **268**
peoplehood 24, 83
   see also group-making
People's Party, US 110
perception 21, 88, 113, 130, 368, 370
   Bourdieu 13, 14, 15, 79, 80n92
   and classification 101, 102, 104
   public **100**, 101, 102, 104
   see also categorization; cognition; phenomenology
persecution 29, 50, **149**, 299
Peru 129
Peruvian people 62

Index of notions

pervasiveness 39, 68, 152, 181, 256, 273
pessimism, racial 76, 361
  see also Afropessimism
phenomenology 79, 129, 220, 374, 376
  see also consciousness, perception
phenotype 36n101, 56, 62–8, 70, 80, 82–3, 90, 97
  and belief in race 76, 83
  and categorization 114, 115, 116, 119n19, 158
  and classification and stratification 62–8, 76, 114, 115, 116, 152, 173, 227, 228, 242
  and difference 62, 65, 70, 83
  and hair texture 53n20, 173
  and Jim Crow 224–7, 228, 229, 242
  and South Africa 70–1, 116, 152
  see also blackness; color of skin
philanthropy 175, 304
phobia 225
  see also hibernophobia; Negrophobia; xenophobia
physical space 16, 37, 43, 60, 61, 80, 91, 113, 117–18, 126, 127n48, 130–7, 158, 172, 174, 202, 205–7, 286, 294, 308, 351, 356, 358, 361
place 125–6, 350–4
  see also space, physical; space, social
plantations
  and Jim Crow 232, 233, 234–6, 254, 257, **292**, 301
  and slavery 292, 295–7, 300
  see also farmers; sharecropping
plea bargaining 194–5
Plessy v. Fergusson, US Supreme Court 212, 301
pogroms 68, 113, 139, 148, **149**, 151, 263, 267, 292, 304
police/policing
  and class 336, 337, 373n42
  and criminal justice 192, 251–2, 337, 372–3

and discrimination 102, 364
and hyperghettos 148, 333, 336, 337
and Jim Crow 217, 251–2
and policy-making 303, 342
and social and physical space 372–3, 374
and structural racism 186, 192
and violence 148, **149**, 252, 372–4
policies see law; penal policy; redistribution policies; social policy
policing, in-group 148
"policy kings" 315
Polish people 64–6, 182n211
politicians 109, 110, 298, 308
politics of race 3–4, 117
  versus analytics 3, 44, 74, 356, 362
pollution, racial 70, 145, 182n211, 208
  in Japan 56, 120
  in United States 43, 266, 327
  see also miscegenation; racial mixing; stigma/stigmatization
population numbers 134, 165, 314
Population Registration Act, South Africa 172, 173
populism 2, 24, 75, 78, 217
populism, epistemological 75, 78, 374
porosity of racial boundaries 158, 207
Portugal 50, 362
Portuguese people 90, 133
positions in social space/structure 26, 51, 74n73, 75, 91, 130, 147, 158, 176
  and Bourdieu, Pierre 12, 13, 22, 24, 79
  and caste 246, 270n195, 301
  and categorization, classification and stratification 107, 119, 120
  and class 273, 312
  and discrimination 128, 154
  and group-making **200**, 202n263, 208
  and incarceration 286, 322

Index of notions

and inequality 35, 372n39
and Jim Crow 232, 237, 246, 263, 270n195, 271, 273, 301
positivism 5, 6, 53n20
postindustrialism 292
  and postindustrial cities 43, 287, 289, 320, 335, 338
  and working class 289, 314
poverty 196, 234, 283, 289, 313, 335–6
power 3n4, 12–19, 88, 198, 217
  and Bourdieu xii, 4, 12–16, 87, 202, 217
  and Foucault 18–20
  and obedience 17n52, 18, 19, 22
  "power-knowledge" 19
  symbolic power 106, 108, 169
  see also domination, symbolic violence
precariat, black 42–3, 282, 344–5
  and hyperghettos 286, 288, 316, 318, 340
precarity 140, 282
predation, racial 72–3
prejudice 48n4, 252, 294, 367
  and elementary forms of racial domination 120, 123, 154, 156
press, black 221, 314, 316
prestige 122, 240, 259
  see also aura; capital
primordialism, race 36, 94
prison 41, 189–90, 322–4
  abolition of 34, 186, 289
  and black people 333, 340, 346, 349
  and class 222n33, 283, 333, 346, 349
  culture of prisons 323, **338**, 340, 341
  deprivation in prisons 323, 341
  and gangs 288, 321, 324–5
  ghettoization of 37, 43, 156, 320–38, 340
  and hyperghettos 288–90, 335, **338**, 342
  and institutions 157, 339

life in prison 323–6
  and lockdowns 326, 346
  "old heads" in 323n122, 340
  and penal sanctions 283, 285, 329, 337n163, 353
  prison economy 288–90, 323, 342
  prison revolts 345–6
  prison society 349
  prison terms 253, 280, 321, 329; *see also* sentencing
  and rehabilitation 320n114, 327, 328, 351
  and released prisoners 329–31, 334, 337
  and respect 324, 326
  and social structure 323, 324, 328
  and solidarity 323, 324
  and subjugation 283, 339
  "supermax" penitentiaries 326, 346
  "warehouse" prisons 321, 323, 328, **338**
  white prison guards 333–4
  women's prisons 322
  see also hyperincarceration; incarceration
Prison Industrial Complex 165, 314
prisoners
  black prisoners 333–4; *see also* hyperincarceration; incarceration; prison
  prisoner numbers *see* incarceration
  prisoners' rights movement 351
  released prisoners 329–31, 334, 337
"prisonfare" 289
prisonization 311–20
  and class 287–8, 318, 319, 333–6, 340
  and ghettos 43, 310, 311–20, 328
  and institutions 325–6, 338–9
  and public schools 314, 316, 319
  and security 317, 318–20, 325–6, 329
  and segregation 288, 311–13, 314
  and surveillance 192, 281, 317, 318–19

Index of notions

privileges, positive and negative 9, 87
probation 192, 193n237, 283, 285–6, 336n162, 348
problematics 7, 58, 123, 141, 206
production, cultural 98, 138–9, 208
   fields of 22, 99, 107–8
   and salience 99, 370
professional people, black 237, 253, 311
profitability 233–4, 255–6
property crime/theft 243, 250, 255, 280, 307
Property Owners' Journal 293
prosecutors/District Attorneys 103, 192, 193–4, 337
protection 236, 247, 256, 257, 309, 339
protection of women 303
Protestantism, British 52–3, 226
proto-racialization 328–33
public health 135, 230, 231, 316
public services 141, 172
punishment 232, 253–4, 257, 327
   see also death sentences; executions; lashings/whippings; lynchings; penal state; sentencing
purging of undesirables 327–8
purity 57, 90n118, 145, 152, 244, 271
   see also blood purity

Q

quadroons 96, 225, 227
Quakers 298
quarantine 132, 231, 327
queuing (racial) 242

R

race as subtype of ethnicity xii, 9, 33, 36, 81, 88
Race Classification Board, South Africa 173
race custom *see* etiquette, racial
race, origins of 49–55, 61–72
   and caste 56, 57, 58
   and class 51, 53, 61
   and colonialism 51–3, 56, 57–9, 60, 63–6, 75, 91, 362
   and religion 49–51, 52–3
   and race riots *see* rioting
   and scientific racism 53–5, 63, 298, 299
   and slavery 51–3, 59
   and Western racism 55, 56
race, real and nominal kinds 208
race relations 211, 216, 223, 270, 324
race, use of term 270n196
race-centrism 207
"race-divided societies" 44, 357–62, 374
   and social formation 358, 361
   see also "societies with race"
race-making 362
   and Bourdieu 107, 198–201, 202
   and Brubaker 197, 201, 204, 207
   and class 110–11, 199, 202, 203
   and classification and stratification 62, 82–3, 106–11, 199, **200**, 201, 202, 206–7
   and cognition 107, 197–9
   and ghettos 323, 341
   and historicization 34–5, 48–55
   and homogeneity 207, 208
   and identity 60, 180, 202
   and incarceration 339, 343, 352
   and indigenous people 109, 201, 202
   and institutions 37, 151, 157, 341, 341n173
   and politics of race 110–11, 117
   and racialization 106, 207
   and social and physical space 198, 201, 202, 207, 350–4
   and states 108–9, 151, 198, 199, **200**, 202–3, 352, 354
   and symbolic power 198, 202
   and United States 108–9, 110–11, 202
   see also group-making

Index of notions

racial capitalism 28n83, 37, 47, 113, 161–8, 187, 356, 359–60
  and Du Bois 168, 217, 304
racial domination
  definition 16–29
  foundations of 80n92
  neo-Bourdieusian theory of 2, 44, 45–6, 106, 198, 356
  triangle of racial domination 367–70
  types of 17, 20–3, 233, 240, 357–62, 368
  see also Bourdieu, Pierre; colonialism; criminal justice; disaggregative approach; elementary forms of racial domination, five; exclusion; exploitation; Foucault, Michel; ghettos; hyperghettos; hyperincarceration; incarceration; Jim Crow; justice, racial; logics; mechanisms; penal state; prisonization; Weber, Max
Racial Formation in the United States (Omi and Winant) 179, 180–1
racial formation theory 82–3
racial gap 194, 197, 370
racial progress, narratives of 92, 294
racial reason, cunning of 76
racial rule, geography of 35, 56–61
racial state 14, 108, 151, 169, 170, 172, 174, 213, 256, 262, 273–4
racialization
  and Argentina 359, **360**
  and aura 86, 87
  and biology and nature 88–9, 90
  and Canada 359, **360**
  and caste 88–9, 90
  and choice 86, 87, 89
  and classification and stratification 87, 90, 106
  and commodification 359, **360**
  diagonal of racialization 36, 86–91, 106, 364, **365**, 367, 370

  and difference 86, 91
  and "genuine race-divided societies" 359–60
  and group-making 88–9, 207
  and history and culture 88, 90
  and honor 86–7, 207
  horizontal racialization 85, **87**, 87, 89, 207, 365, 370
  and identity 86, 87, 89
  and inequality 86, 87–8
  and racial justice **365**, 367
  and "societies with race" 359–60
  and thick/racialized ethnicity 85, 86, 88–90, 364, **365**
  and thin/ordinary ethnicity 85, 88, **365**
  and United States 359, **360**
  vertical racialization 86, 87
  and Weber 85, 86–7, 88–9
  see also deracialization; hyperracialization; hyporacialization; proto-racialization
"Racialized Social System" (RSS) 181–4, 357
racism 23–5, 49, 72–5, 295–300, 322–4
  and class 24, 61, 183, 191–2, 195, 196, 197
  origins of the word 175, 176
  see also belief, in race; Bourdieu, Pierre; class; colonialism; hyperghettos; hyperincarceration; racism, structural; slavery
racism, class 24
  see also class
racism, colonial *see* colonialism
racism, color-blind 285n12, 368, 368
racism, individual 179
racism, institutional 175, 188–9
racism of intelligence 24
racism, scientific 53–5, 63, 298, 299
racism, state 25
  see also states

Index of notions

racism, structural 37–9, 44, 76, 174–97
  and bias 193, 195
  and black people 125, 191, 195, 196, 197
  and class 183, 191–2, 195, 196, 197
  and conduct 182, 194–5
  and criminal justice 38, 186, 188–97
    and courts/courtrooms 189n230, 192
    and criminal records 194, 196
    and guilty pleas 194, 196–7, 326n134
    and law 189–90, 195
    and murder/homicide 185, 191
    and police/policing 186, 192
    and probation 192, 193n237
    and prosecutors 192, 193–4
    and sentencing 192, 193, 194–7
  and discrimination 125, 196
  and inequality 178, 185
    and criminal justice 189, 190, 191–2, 194n240
  and Jim Crow 38, 39
  and networks, social 174, 188
  and racial gap 194, 197
  and racial mechanisms 188, 189, 190, 196, 197
  and racism, institutional 175, 188–9
  and racism, systemic 175, 179, 183
  and rhetoric 176, 179, 181, 188, 189
  and social and physical space 186, 192
  and United States 76–7, 181, 182–3, 185, 187n226, 188–97
  and white supremacy 182–4, 186
racism, systemic 175, 179, 181, 183–4, 187
racism, Western 55, 56
railroad/railway companies 210–11, 239, 254, 255, 264

rape 151, 247n121, 249, 256, 260, **268**, 331n150
rationalism, historical 4, 5, 20
reality, social 11, 44, 79, 80, **100**, 102, 104
  historical 11, 17
realization of categories 12, 80
  see also categorization
recidivism/reoffending 283, 327n139, 329, 333n154, 335, 347
reciprocity 40, 138
  and Jim Crow 65, 241, 242–4, 247, **268**, 302
recognition 21, 44, 80
  gradations of 86
  intersubjective recognition 80
  official recognition 118, 359, 361
  public recognition 124, 206, 209
  symbolic order of 366, 367, 370
reconciliation, racial 109, 370
Reconstruction 293, 342, 351
  and Black Codes 232, 262, 300, 342
recursivity (between classification and stratification) 15, 120, 206
Red Power group 201
redemption 92, 95, 328
redistribution policies 109, 347, 364, 367
red-lining 135, 180, 185
reform 38, 97n168, 105, 193, 278
  see also rights; welfare reform
reformism, radical 34
regimes of racial domination *see* colonialism; hyperghettos; hyperincarceration; Jim Crow; racial domination; slavery
region as principle of classification 33, 57, 154, 162, 358
  and Bourdieu, Pierre 198, 199n250
  and categorization and classification 107, 110, 116, 117
  and culture and history 36n101, 88–9

Index of notions

and group-making 197, 198, 199, 209
rehabilitation as penal philosophy 320n114, 327, 328, 351
release from prison 329–31, 334, 337
religion 28, 31, 367
   and black people 48n5, 307
   and capitalism 164, 167
   and categorization 152, 201
   and churches 221, 225, 228, 238, 266, 314–16
   and colonialism 57, 60, 154
   and culture 24, 85, 88, 89
   and discrimination 120n25, 121, 123
   and Jim Crow 221, 225, 226, 228, 230, 238, 265, 266, 314
   and origins of race 49–51, 52–3
   as paramount symbolic power 106, 108, 169
   as principle of vision and division 31, 33, 36n101, 38, 107, 116, 131, 197, 198, 358
   and slavery 52–3, 167, 299
   see also antisemitism; Catholicism; Christian people; Islamic people; Jewish people; Protestantism, British
Renaissance Europe 137, 160
reoffending *see* recidivism/reoffending
reparations (racial) 370, 371
repatriation 80, 204
   and demarcation 35–6, 78, 112, 376
   and denegated ethnicity 78, 79
Republicanism 262
resentment 127, 130, 150, 207, 237, 264, 270, 327, 373
Reservation and Separate Amenities Act, South Africa 172
reservations 137, 142–4, 148
residence, place of 128, 174
   see also segregation
resistance to domination 75, 90, 130, 206, 309, 344, 376n40

   and black people 99, 220–1, 222, 256, 272, 293, 294
   and violence 22, 272
   see also activism, agency
respect 206, 318, 367
   and Jim Crow 243, 247, 282n7
   and prisons 324, 326
restitution 370
retribution 327
revolutions, world-historical 54
rhetoric 176, 179, 181, 188, 189
rights
   civil rights
      Civil Rights Movement 43, 68, 131–2, 221, 223, 295, 320, 345
      civil rights reform 77, 181, 231n60
      and Jim Crow 218, 221, 223, 248–51, 257, 258, 260, 300, 303–4, 342
      and voting rights 218, 248–51, 257, 258, 303–4, 308, 348
   human rights 261, 326
   indigenous rights 109
   legal rights 256
   natural rights 54, 298
   political 260, 300, 34
   prisoners' rights 351
   Rights of Man 58
rioting 147, 152, 373
   and class 342, 373n42
   and ghettos 101, 340, 345, 346
   and Jim Crow 244, 245–6, 258, 263–4, **268**, 342, 373n42
   and prisons 245–6, 345
   see also Civil Rights Movement; pogrom; violence
rite of institution 273
Roma people 116, 119, 135, 145, 157–9, 171, 366
Romania 158, 171, 204
Rorschach test 116
rupture, epistemological 7–8, 34, 86, 356

Index of notions

rural/peri-urban areas 192, 333–4
and Jim Crow 216, 221, 243, 247, 275
Rwanda 69–70, 109–10, 150, 209

S

sacrality 149, 152
safety, public 345
salience (of classification, race) 36, 99–106, 120, 152, 207, 361
and racial justice 365, 368, 370
see also consequentiality
sanctions, penal 283, 285, 329, 337n163, 353
see also penalization; incarceration; policy, penal;
Santiago de Chile 134
Scandinavia 373
"School of ethnology," American 54, 299
schools/schooling 19, 107, 186
and African American people 23, 106, 157, 295, 304–5, 307, 345
and attendance laws 304
Canada (for native peoples)
and categorization and classification 114–15, 116, 120, 174, 202
and credentials 23, 24, 27, 165, 202, 347
Dōwa schools 120
educational attainment 106, 114–15, 120, 157, 295, 304–5, 313, 320
in France 105, 126
and incarceration 104–5, 157, 280, 282, 283, 295, 313
educational opportunities 23, 217, 238, 304–5, 307, 335, 345
and hyperincarceration 335, 347
and ghettos 313, 314, 316
and hyperghettos 313, 320, 335, 345
and prisonization 314, 316, 319
and Jim Crow 217, 238, 257, 304–5
public 35, 314, 316, 319–20, 335

and secondary education 280, 282, 313
and segregation 128, 131
white schools 304
science 31
and action/politics xiii, 74, 355
scientific autonomy viii, 7
scientific racism 53–5, 63, 298, 299
scientific reasoning 72, 376; see also analytics; Bachelard, Gaston; disaggregative approach; rationalism, historical
scorn 29, 120, 150, 207, 288, 316, 370, 374
and Bourdieu, Pierre 24, 199n250
and Twa people 69, 70n62
seclusion 137–44
and architecture of ethnoracial domination 154, **155**
and black people 137, 138, 242, 291
and camps 137, 140–2
and colonialism 142–4
as an elementary form of racial domination 113, 137–44, 356
and exploitation 138, 142
and ghettos 137–40, 286, 287–8
and incarceration 286, 287–8
and indigenous people 142–3, 148
and institutions 113, 137–8, 154, 291–2, 342
and Jewish people 137, 138
and reservations 137, 142–4, 148
and solidarity 138, 142
and space 137, 144
and United States 137, 142–3, 148
Second Reconstruction 293
security 243, 317, 318–20, 325–6, 329
sedimentation (of categories) 199, **200**
segregation 130–7, 324, 361
and caste 132–3, 135
and centrality 133
and class 131, 132, 135, 165, 311–13

Index of notions

and classification and stratification 171, 172
and clustering 132, 133
and colonialism 23–4, 135
and color 131, 135–6
color segregation 131, 135–6
and discrimination 128, 135, 154, 215, 303
and dispersion 132, 136
and dissimilarity index 103, 133–4
as an elementary form of racial domination 113, 120, 130–7, **155**, 156, 356
four-dimensional segregative profile 133
and France 103–4, 133–4, 135, 136
and ghettos 132, 133, 135, 308
and hostility 132, 135, 141, 324
and hyperghettos 131, 134, 288, 311–13, 314
hypersegregation 156
and hypnotic points 133, 134n68
and India 132–3, 139, 267
and integration 132, 134, 203
and Jim Crow 211, 212, 213–14, 215, 301, 303
  and deference 238–9, 240–1, 247
  and educational opportunities 238, 304
  and hierarchy 239, 247, 275
  and humiliation 240, **241**
  and one-drop rule 227, 231
longitudinal segregation 134
macro-segregation 134, 135
micro-segregation 134
and networks, social 22, 27, 80, 128, 131, 134, 136, 375
occupational segregation 120
and public transport 136, 239
and racial mechanisms 135, 136, 158, 375
and red-lining 135, 180, 185
residential segregation 131–7, 158, 171, 375

and Roma people 135, 158
and social structural sorting 136, 375
and social/public housing 136, 222, 375
and South Africa 133, 172, 267
and states 136–7, 171
and United States law 212, 213–14, 301, 375
and violence 135, 240, 267
semantics 188
sentencing
  and death sentences 253, 260
  and executions 260, **268**, 317n104
  and life sentences 282, 347
  and prison terms 253, 280, 321, 329
  and structural racism 192, 193, 194–7
separation, asymmetric 238–48, **268**
separation, hierarchical 271
see also penal policy; penalization
Serbia 206
serfdom 160, 350
"series," Sartrian 208
servants 160, 311
  and colonialism 115, 296
  indentured servants 52, 115, 160, 224, 296, 350
  and Jim Crow 224, 236–7, 239
  and slavery 52, 296–7, 299, 350
settlers
  English 52–3, 296–7
  French 23, 143
  Israeli 364
  see also capitalism; colonialism; racial capitalism
sex/sexual
  abuse 237, 254, 260, **268**, 307
  and caste 246, 271, 303
  intercourse/congress 296
  and Jim Crow 224, 225, 228, 246, 303
    and concubinage 225n41, 226
    and infectious disease 230, 248

Index of notions

sex/sexual (*cont.*)
   and Jim Crow (*cont.*)
      and racial etiquette 243–4, 245–6, 302
      and violence 246, 303
      and one-drop rule 224, 225, 225n41, 226
      offenders 330–1
      see also blood purity; marriage/intermarriage; miscegenation; mixing, racial
   Sexual Predator Punishment and Control Act ("Jessica's Law") 331
sharecropping 218, 232–8, **268, 292**, 301, 304
   and violence 234–5, 258, 259, 266, 302
shootings 260, 261
Sicily 50
Singapore 171
Sinti people 145, 363
skin color *see* color of skin
"slave societies" versus "societies with slaves" 167, 349, 357
slavery 2, 82, 295–300
   abolition of 34, 186–7, 226, 298, 299
   and Afropessimism 92, 94–6
   and caste 272, 342
   chattel slavery 122n30, 291
   and class 296, 349
   and classification and stratification 62, 114, 297
   and colonialism 55, 297, 350
   and economy 167, 292, 295–7, 300, 342, 350
   and England 52–3, 350
   and indentured servants 52, 296–7, 299, 350
   and inferiority 52, 240
   as an institution 291, **292**, 341, 350
   and Jim Crow 40, 210, 218, 224–5, 226, 229, 342
   slave law 350
   and life expectancy 296, 297
   and origins of race 51–3, 55, 59
   and ownership 297, 298
   and paternalism 41–2, 247, 297, 298
   racial slavery 350
   and redemption 92, 95
   and religion 52–3, 167, 299
   "slavery of debt" 236
   slaveholder class 95, 298
   "slaveness" 92, 94, 98
   and slaves as human beings 95, 101
   and social relations 95, 349
   and violence 95–6, 295
snitches 148, 174, 191
social compact, Fordist-Keynesian 289
social control 122, 311, 314–16, 328
social engineering 213
social formation 58, 136, 358, 361, 370
social movements 13, 108, 175, 362n13
   see also Civil Rights Movement
social ontology 12, 206
social order 21, 22, 23, 25
social policy 349
social principle of vision and division 44, 55, 106, 155, 341n173, 362
   and Bourdieu xii, 25, 27
social relations 18, 58, 66, 112, 182, 238–48, 341
   and hyperghettos 310, 318, **338**
   and slavery 95, 349
   see also etiquette, racial
Social Science Research Council (SSRC) 166
social sciences 72–5, 78, 92–3, 168, 212–23, 375–6
social space 24, 36, 44, 75, 80, 131n57, 132, 144, **155**, 158, 198, 199, 201, 202, 205, 294, 350, 361–2
   black social space 221, 231, 342n175

Index of notions

and classification struggles 107–8, 110, 115, 120
and pacification 276
and prisoners 347
and "race-divided societies" 358
and segregation 130–1
and "societies with race" 358
and symbolic power (Bourdieu) 4, 12–16, 22n71, 79, 106, 119
social structural sorting 136, 375
social structure
   and Jim Crow **268**, 271
   and prisons 323, 324, 328, 341
"societies with race" 44, 357, 358–60, 361
   see also "race-divided societies"
"societies with slaves" 349, 357
Sociology of Race and Ethnicity journal 352n205
solidarity 98, 129, 142
   black solidarity 98, 235
   and ghettos 138, 309
   and Jim Crow 232, 235
   and prisons 323, 324
   and seclusion 138, 142
   white solidarity 232
South Africa
   and apartheid 80, 133, 172–4, 267, 358
   and economy 160, 359
   and group-making 127, 358
   and phenotype 70–1, 116, 152
   and racial categorization 80, 116, 370
   and violence 147, 152, 267
South African people 70–1, 147, 172
South Carolina 96, 224–5, 263
Southern Populists 217
Southern United States *see* American South
Soviet Union 117, 148, 203, 206, 366
space, physical 60, 126, 127n48, 137–44, 192, 284, 292, 354, 373

and categorization 117, 120
and class 80, 294, 311, 358
and classification 144, 172–4, 206
and ghettos 43, 137, 308, 351
and group-making 202, 205, 207, 351
and incarceration 283, 286
and Jim Crow 242, 258, 267
and "race-divided societies" and "societies with race" 358, 361
and seclusion 137, 144
and segregation 16, 37, 113, 130–2, 155, 292, 308, 311
and states 202, 205, 353–4, 374
and violence 258, 267
   see also segregation; social space
space, public 125–6
and Bourdieu 4, 12–16
and categorization 117, 120
and class 80, 285, 294–5, 358
and classification 14–15, 144, 174, 231
and criminal justice 192, 254
and dispossession 103n162, 148, 353
and ghettos 137, 308, 309, 351
and group-making 198, 201, 202, 205–6
and incarceration 283, 286, 346
and institutions 292, 294, 358
and isolation 231, 239, 258, 283, 346
and Jim Crow 221, 231, 239, 242, 258, 267
and police/policing 372–3, 374
and structural racism 186, 192
and seclusion 137, 144
and segregation 130–1, 292, 308
and "societies with race" and "race-divided societies" 358, 361
and stratification 14, 15, 144, 231
   see also space, physical; space, social
space, social 36, 186, 350, 374
and black social space/subjectivity 221, 342n175, 347

Index of notions

space, social (*cont.*)
  and Bourdieu, Pierre 4, 12–16, 24, 119, 120, 196
  and categorization 107–8, 110, 115, 117, 118, 120
  and class 24, 80, 117, 294–5
  and classification and stratification 14–15, 107–8, 110, 144, 155, 174, 231
  and group-making 75, 198, 201, 202, 204, 205–6, 207
  and incarceration 284, 286, 347
  and institutions 292, 294, 341n273, 358
  and isolation 231, 258
  and Jim Crow 221, 231, 258, 276, 351
  and seclusion 137, 286
  and segregation 37, 130–1, 132, 144, **155**, 158, 292
  and "societies with race" and "race-divided societies" 44, 358, 361
  and states 118, 198, 354, 373
  see also physical space, social space, symbolic space
Spain 50, 147, 352, 372
spatialization 55, 56–61, 64, 112
sport/leisure activities 174, 244, 341
staffing 192, 251, 332–3
states
  and classification and stratification 108–9, 116–18, 168–74, 202, 206
  and economy 159–60, 358, 361
  and honor/dishonor 169, 206
  and institutions 37, 151, 311, 314–16
  and racial justice 364, 365–6
  role of 14, 37
  and segregation 136–7, 171
  and violence 80, 145, 148, **149**, 150–3, 160, 339, 354
  see also racial state, welfare state
status groups, theory of xii, 9–10, 86–7

stereotyping 51, 129, 144, 252, 256
stigma/stigmatization 121–3, 288, 328–33
  and African American people 122–3, 293, 354
  and categorization 89, 120, 121–3, 154, 358
  and criminality 288, 293, 328, 352
  and dignity 122, 208
  and ghettoization 137–8, 328
  and honor/dishonor 122, 366
  and Jim Crow 218, **241**
  and lower-class/poor people 122, 288, 293
  and marginality/marginalization 125, 352, 374
  and racial justice 45, **365**, 366, 367
  and Roma people 158, 159
  and social control 122, 328
  and territory 125, 159
  see also purity
stratification 99, 168–74, 357
  and apartheid 172, 173, 174
  and Bourdieu xii, 14, 15, 119, 367
  ethnosomatic stratification 62
  and group-making 199, **200**, 202, 206–7, 270
  and incarceration 288, 290–1, 323, 327
  and racialization 86, 90
  and social, physical and public space 14, 15, 144, 231
  and United States 37n102, 61–2
  see also classification
"structural" 176, 184
structural complexity 159
structural racism 38, 44, 47, 73n70, 105n169, 174–97
  and African Americans 125, 191, 195, 196, 197
  anthropomorphized 185
  and Bonilla-Silva, Eduardo 77, 181–4

Index of notions

and criminal justice 38, 186, 188–97
and Critical Race Theory (CRT) 179–80
and discrimination 125, 196
and individual racism 179
and inequality 178, 185, 189, 190, 191–2, 194n240
and institutional racism 175
and Jim Crow 38, 39
and logic of the trial 76–7, 186
as lumpy notion 37, 44
mystification of 174–88
popularity of 175, 177, 178
and Omi and Winant 76–7, 179–181
and racial mechanisms 188, 189, 190, 196, 197
and murder 185, 191
and police/policing 186, 192
and state policies 185
and public space 186, 192
and Racialized Social System (RSS) 181–4
and "structural classism" 184
and "structural sexism" 184
and United States 76–7, 181, 182–3, 185, 187n226, 188–97
and white supremacy 182–4, 186
structuralism, genetic 3, 12, 14, 217
structure
social structure **268**, 271, 323, 324, 328, 341
space, social symbolic/sociosymbolic structure 51, 60, 115, 216–17, 248, 268
struggle, material 106
see also classification struggles; symbolic struggles
subalterns 57, 94, 137, 147
and criminal justice 353, 375
and prisons 222n33, 283
subjectivity 13, 19, 31, 60, 75
and objectivity 75, 79, 201
see also consciousness; habitus; phenomenology

subordination 26–7, 31, 63–6, 140, 283, 286, 290, 294, 339
as "face of domination" 26
and caste 223, 271, 311–12
and ethnoracial categories 140, 194, 363
and Jim Crow 27, 38, 40, 214, 223, 256, 258, 261, 266
and criminal justice 255, 256
and violence 145, 256, 258, 261, 266
subpersons, racial (Charles W. Mills) 35, 64
subservience 40, 245, 251, 264, 301, 302, 349
subsidiarity of race 32
see also race as denegated ethnicity
subsumption/nesting (of concepts) 116, 350
and blackness 97, 228
and conceptual relationship of ethnicity and race **81**, 84–5
and Jim Crow 228, 229
suffusion thesis 15, 16
"supermax" penitentiaries 326, 346
"superpredators" 343
Supreme Court, US 143, 288
Brown v. Board of Education 68, 212, 375
and Jim Crow 212, 252, 301
Plessy v. Fergusson 212, 301
Surinamese people 133
surrationalisme 5
surveillance 102, 172, 276
and criminality 329–31, 349
and hyperghettos 192, 281, 317, 318–19
Sweden 352
symbiosis **338**
see also hyperghettos; incarceration; prison
symbolic power *see* power
symbolic space 80, 126, 130n56, 144, 202, 231, 271, 286, 292, 351
and Jim Crow 231, 271, 351
see also classification

Index of notions

symbolic struggles   15n45, 106, 107, 122
  see also classification struggles
System *S*   182

T
taboos   118, 129, 241, 243–4, 245, 303
  see also racial etiquette, purity
Tamil society   61, 69
tautology   182, 186
  see also fallacy
taxonomies   21, 22, 53, 76, 108, 115–16, 118
  and classification and stratification 170–2, 206
  and groups   206, 370
  see also categories, ethnoracial
television   214n10, 276n212, 323, 341
tenancies   233, 258, 301, 302
Tennessee   255, 263
territory   64, 125, 138, 142, 159
  see also place; physical space; social space
terrorism   40, 146, **149**
  and Jim Crow   40–1, 218, 221, 223, 268–77, 300–5, 341, 351–2
  see also caste terrorism; "white death"
terrorist groups   218, 232, 251, 262–3, 272
Texas   330
theft/property crime   243, 250, 255, 280, 307
theories of race   27, 29–30, 155n133
  see also "American school" of ethnology; Bourdieu, Pierre; Critical Race Theory (CRT); group-making; neo-Bourdieusian theory of racial domination; racial domination theory; racial formation theory; racialized social system; status groups, theory of; structural racism; Weber, Max
think tanks   175, 335n158

Third Reich   39, 170
  see also Nazi Germany
threat of violence   234, 236, 269, 272, 273
  see also intimidation
"Three Strikes and You're Out"   327
titles of courtesy   217, 243
  see also etiquette, racial
tolerance/intolerance   50, 52, 101, 103–4, 245
torture   326
  and Jim Crow   246, 252, 254, 261, 262, **268**, 303, 317n104
  public torture lynchings   150, 264–6
trade   52, 101, 138, 143, 296, 297, 350
transparency   252
transport, public   136, 239, 375
trauma   3n4, 109, 166, 258
travel   245
trials, mock   261, 264–6
truancy   304
Tudors   169
Tulsa, Oklahoma   263–4
Turkey   146
Turkish people   103, 133–4
Tutsi people   69–70, 109, 150, 209
Twa people   69–70

U
"underclass"   47, 61, 112, 166, 175n195, 188–9, 322n119, 345, 349
  and capitalism   166, 287, 290, 353–4
  and hyperghettos   42–3, 287–8, 336, 339, 353–4
  and incarceration   287, 288, 336, 339
undesirables   306, 327
unemployment   283
  see also employment opportunities; labor
United States   35, 61–72, 159, 188–97, 210–77, 278–354
  and Afropessimism   92–4, 96–8

Index of notions

American North 276, 298, 305–10
American South 94
   and industrialization 305, 313
   and Jim Crow 224, 226–7, 231, 245, 250, 254, 273–4, 301
   and Archimedean position ii, 61
   Black Belt states 42, 287, 308, 340
   and capitalism 165, 167, 289–90
   and Census Bureau 108–9, 228
   and class 110–11, 156–7
   and classification and stratification 37n102, 61–2, 71, 76–7, 108–9, 110–11, 118, 169, 357
   and colonialism 82, 135, 143
   and color of skin 62, 97, 125, 156–7, 229
   and discrimination 124, 125, 127–8, 135, 156
   and immigration 81–2, 262, 296, 305, 314
   and incarceration rates 278n1, 280
   and inequality 77, 104–5, 157, 169, 185
   and Jewish people 90, 262
   and law 212, 213–14, 301, 348, 375
   and racial justice 365, 371n38, 375
   and racialization 90, 359, **360**
   and seclusion 137, 142–3, 148
   and segregation 132, 134, 135, 156, 212, 213–14, 301, 375
   and structural racism 76–7, 181, 182–3, 185, 187n226, 188–97
   and Supreme Court 143, 288
      Brown v. Board of Education 68, 212, 375
      and Jim Crow 212, 252, 301
      Plessy v. Fergusson 212, 301
   and World War II 56–7, 150–1
   see also cities, industrial; cities, postindustrial; criminal justice; economy; ghettos; hyperghettos; hyperincarceration; incarceration; individual states; industrialization/industrial development; institutions; Jim Crow; penal state; plantations; slavery; violence
universities 2, 23, 99, 180n209, 251, 347
   see also credentials, schools
urban areas 193
   and black people 342, 344
   and Jim Crow 216, 221, 258, 275, 305
   see also ghettos; hyperghettos
Urban Institute 175n195, 177n201, 335n158
urbanization/urbanism 164, 275n209, 276, 305, 309–10, 351
US centrism 30

V

vagrancy 235, 300
Valladolid *disputatio* 51
variability, functional 37, 159
vengeance 327n139
Venice 138
verticality 86, 87, 247, 257, 270, 323
   see also horizontality
victims of crime 148, 191, 252, 265, 266, 331
vigilance, epistemological 7–8, 34
vigilante groups 189–90, 226, 262
violence 94
   and African American people 147, 218, 236, 258–9, 263, 307, 343
   and aggression 240, 266, 304
   antiblack violence 94
   and assassination 243, 262
   and assault 102, 103, 148, **149**, 218, 237, 267, 303, 308, 317–18
   and beatings 243, 252, 254, 255
   and caste 272, 273–4
      and assault 303, 308, 317–18
      and Jim Crow 264, 267, 342
      and race riots 342, 373n42
      and ritualized caste murder 150, 152
   and violence 264, 267

Index of notions

violence (*cont.*)
   and caste terrorism 40–1, 218, 221, 222–3, 268–77, 300–5, 341, 351–2
   and coercion 21, 150
   and colonialism 58, 153–4, 364
   and convict leasing 253–5, 256
   and criminal justice 354
      and executions 260, **268**, 317n104
      and Jim Crow 243, 251–7, 258, 260, 264–6, 303
      lashings/whippings 234–5, 246, 253, 254, 255, 259, 261, 262, 303
      and police/policing 148, **149**, 252, 372–4
      and torture 252, 254, 303
   cumulative radicalization of violence 152
   and deference 247, 258
   and economy 160, 164, 292
   as an elementary form of racial domination 113, 144–54, **155**, 156, 356
   escalation of violence 151–2
   and ethnic cleansing/genocide 80, 145, 148, **149**, 150, 151, 152
   and exclusion 145, 258, 266
   and executions 260, **268**
   and exploitation 145, 153–4, 258, 266, 269
   fear of 41, 146, 258, 272, 273
   and France 103n161, 153–4
   and gangs **149**, 325
   and hunts/manhunts 252, 261–2, 269, 304
   and hyperghettos 147–8, 318, 339
   and incarceration 283, 321, 324, 325, 339
   and India 147, 267
   and indigenous people 148, 153
   and institutions 256, 292, 294
   and insurrection **149**, 226, 292, 299
   and Jim Crow 39, 218, 234–8, 240–77, 300–5
   and rioting 244, 245–6, 258, 263–4, **268**, 342, 373n42
   and torture 150, 246, 252, 254, 261, 262, 264–6, **268**, 303, 317n104
   and lashings/whippings 234–5, 246, 253, 254, 255, 259, 261, 262, 303
   and mass killing **149**, 185
   material violence 221, 354
   and Mississippi 235, 236, 249
   and mock trials 261, 264–6
   and Nazi Germany 145, 267
   non-state violence 273, 275
   physical violence 240, 292, 324
   and lynching postcards 264, 266
   and public/private violence 218, 234, 272
   and racial etiquette 242, 243, 259, 260
   and rape 151, 247n121, 249, 256, 260, **268**, 331n150
   and religion 265, 266
   and resistance to domination 22, 272
   and segregation 135, 240, **241**, 267
   and sexual abuse 237, 254, 260, **268**
   and sexual intercourse/congress 246, 303
   and sharecropping 234–5, 258, 259, 266, 302
   and shootings 260, 261
   and slavery 95–6, 295
   and social and physical space 258, 267
   and South Africa 147, 152, 267
   and state/nonstate violence 273, 275
   and states 80, 103n161, 145, 148, **149**, 150–3, 160, 273–4, 275, 339, 354
   and subordination 145, 256, 258, 261, 266
   and threat of violence 234, 236, 269, 272, 273

Index of notions

and violated/targeted groups 144–5, 148–50
and voting rights 249, 251, 258
and "white death" 257–67, 269, 269n194
and white supremacy 258, 267
see also ghettos; hyperghettos; Jim Crow; lynchings; racial war; rioting; torture; symbolic violence
violence, symbolic 27, 36, 88, 106, 273, 295, 354
and Bourdieu xii, 2–3, 21–2, 80
and denigration 60, 69, 159, 160, 207, 221, 258
and ghettos 103, 138, 305, 366
symbolic denigration 89, 103n162
and discrimination 213, 215, 249, 301, 303
and disenfranchisement 251, 258, 266, **268**, 301, 303, 348
and exclusion 27, 38, 40, 248–57, 258, 266, 269, 274, 301
and humiliation 240, **241**, 251, **268**
and inferiority 52, 66, 122n30, 217, 231, 240, 247, 248, 292
and oppression 35, 56, 74, 117, 156, 208, 211, 251
and color of skin 63, 97n148, 2 20
and ostracization 138, 211, 253, 292, 305, 375
and slavery 52, 240
and subjugation 63–6, 140, 283, 290, 294, 339
and subservience 40, 245, 251, 264, 301, 302, 349
see also caste; deference; intimidation; Jim Crow
violence, terroristic *see* caste terrorism; terrorism
Virginia 216, 224, 296–7
visibility 122–3

vocational training 304
voting rights 248–51, 257, 258, 303–4, 308, 348

W

walls 132, 239, 244, 321, 328, 340, 346
Walter White paradox 67–8
war 59, 154
racial 56, **149**, 151
World War I 305
World War II 56–7, 148, 150–1, 284
War on drugs 281, 282, 285, 338
"warehouse" prison 321, 323, 328, **338**
wealth gap 157, 190, 371n38
welfare reform 348
welfare, social 282, 309
and hyperghettos 313, 316, 317
and hyperincarceration 289, 347–8
and institutions **292**, 316
and women 287, 289, 349
welfare states 136, 289–90
Western centrism 71
Whipping *see* lashings/whippings
"white death" 257–67, 269, 269n194
White League 262
white people 35, 63–6, 81, 212–23, 243
and belief in race 270, 300
and blood purity 225, 226, 227, 300
and caste 264, 266, 270, 274, 340
and class
  elite/upper class 157, 225, 227, 229
  lower class/poor 219–20, 285, 298, 301, 333–4, 339
and criminal justice 243, 253, 256, 257, 261
and hyperghettos 333, 345
and hyperincarceration 182–3, 283, **334**, **338**
illiterate white people 250

Index of notions

white people (*cont.*)
  and incarceration 104–5, 280, 283, 285, 298, 333–4, 339
  and sexual congress/marriage 224, 226, 228, 245–6, 303
  Southern white people 221, 226, 231n60, 233, 243, 245–6, 256, 266, 303
  and structural racism 182–4, 186
  and violence 258, 261, 264, 267
  and voting rights 250, 270
  white men 245–6, 253, 261, 280, 283, 285
  white women 226, 246, 303
  see also blood purity; etiquette, racial; Jim Crow; one-drop rule; white supremacy
"white primaries" 250
white supremacy 104–5
  and belief in race 270, 300
  and caste 264, 270, 340
  and Jim Crow 35, 212–14, 216, 221, 300
    and caste 264, 270, 274
    and violence 258, 264, 267
    and voting rights 250, 270
  and Southern whites 177n201, 221
  and structural racism 182–4, 186
"whitecappers" 232
whiteness 69, 76, 83n191, 104n166, 178, 369n33
  and Jim Crow 217, 227, 264, 266
women 209, 226, 254, 283, 303
  black women 228, 236–7, 246, 254, 283, 311, 349
  and employment opportunities 236–7, 311
  and sexual congress/marriage 224, 228, 246, 303
  Southern women 226, 246, 303
  and welfare 287, 289, 349
  white women 224, 226, 246, 283, 303
  women convicts 254
Woodward thesis 211
Work Opportunity and Personal Responsibility Act 347–8
workfare 289, 346
working class people 135, 202, 227, 339
  and English people 169, 350
  and postindustrialism 289, 314
  see also lower-class areas/people
World Romani Congress, International Romani Union 366
World War I 305
World War II 56–7, 148, 150–1, 284

X
xenophobia 25

Y
"Yellow Vests" 201
young people, black 343–4, 373
YouTube 341

Z
Zainichi people 90
Zimbabwean people 70–1
zombie citizens 248, 374